Music in American Education

MUSIC EDUCATION SOURCE BOOK
NUMBER TWO

A compendium of data, opinions
and recommendations ✛ ✛ ✛
compiled from the reports of
investigations, studies and
discussions conducted by the
Music in American Education
Committees of the MENC during the period 1951-54 ✛ ✛
with which is included selected
material from other sources

Edited by

HAZEL NOHAVEC MORGAN

Published by

MUSIC EDUCATORS NATIONAL CONFERENCE

64 East Jackson Blvd., Chicago 4, Illinois

Washington Office

N.E.A. Building, 1201 Sixteenth Street, N.W., Washington 6, D. C.

780.72 m97a
c.2

CONTENTS

SECTION ONE

Professional and Public Relations
of the Music Educator

SECTION TWO

Preschool and Kindergarten
Elementary, Rural

SECTION THREE

Junior and Senior High Schools

SECTION FOUR

Colleges and Universities

SECTION FIVE

General and Special Areas
in Music Education

APPENDIX

Editor's Foreword

MUSIC IN AMERICAN EDUCATION, successor and companion volume to the first *Music Education Source Book,* has come into existence as a result of two major forces:

—The urgency of continuing to meet the universal need of all music education for information and assistance,

—The united desires and efforts of thousands of professionally minded individuals who have given unstintingly of their time, experience, and best thinking so that music education, as a profession and an art, might better serve all the children of all the people.

The major portion of the content of this book is the cumulative result of work done by local, state, division, and national committee members over a period of three years. It should be noted that all parts of the United States of America have been represented in these composite contributions and that an attempt has been made to include outstanding aspects of music activities at all grade levels.

Only a very small amount of material from the first *Music Education Source Book* has been included in this volume. The bases for these inclusions were: (1) By request of the national committee chairman. (2) Where there was a lack of adequate current material.

Selected articles and addresses of universal interest have been included. The extreme length of certain reports made some deletions necessary due to page limitations. A few blocks of other material were omitted in order to minimize repetition caused by natural overlapping in report content submitted.

The reader will discover controversial ideas and emphatic statements from opposing viewpoints. He will find differences or disagreements which reflect varying practices in certain areas. Regrettably, he will find insufficient data in some instances or undue stress given to unique personal enthusiasms—perhaps to the exclusion of ideas held by others. However, this book is a great storehouse of information and record; it is a tribute to music as it functions in American education, and a monument to the devotion of all those whose contributions have made this volume possible.

The purpose of the book has been to provide guidance for those less experienced, inspiration for those striving to achieve, clarification for those in doubt, and stimulation for future progress. It should be an incentive for further investigation in order to substantiate, disprove, or to expand inconclusive data.

It has been an interesting, revealing, and rewarding experience to edit this book. I have striven humbly to merit the confidence of my colleagues in this editorial assignment and am grateful for the opportunity to be of service to the Music Educators National Conference.

HAZEL NOHAVEC MORGAN

MUSIC EDUCATORS SOURCE BOOK NO. 2

I**T IS FAMILIAR HISTORY** that the Music Educators National Conference made tremendous strides with professional activity in the forties. Two great membership-wide organization projects contributed to this progress: (1) The "Widening Horizons" and (2) the "Music Education Advancement" programs. Through them music education was jolted out of what had become a sort of smug complacency, at least in some areas of the country. This self-satisfied condition led into a routine, in many situations chiefly characterized by extreme emphasis on the development of highly skilled performing organizations, almost to the exclusion of other phases of music education and at the expense of large numbers of children in the schools. Through the above-named MENC programs of activity, music educators broadened their horizons, were made increasingly conscious of the importance of music for *all* the children in the school, and became more and more aware of the wealth of material and ideas available for general school music activities as well as for special performing groups. All of this development in the minds and experiences of music teachers came to a publication climax in the first *Music Education Source Book,* and in numerous special MENC publications such as "Music for Everybody," "Handbook for Teaching Piano Classes," "Handbook on 16mm. Films for Music Education," "Bibliography of Research Studies in Music Education," "Music Rooms and Equipment" (recently in its third and much enlarged edition). Numerous other bulletins and publications of various types were produced in this period or stemmed therefrom, including the "Teacher Aids" ("Information Leaflets") and other issues from the Music Education Research Council and from various MENC committees. Two examples of MENC publications which had their inception in this period were the guidance bulletin, "Your Future as a Teacher of Music in the Schools," and the new MENC periodical, *Journal of Research in Music Education,* now in its third volume.

Each decade brings its own developments and changes. It is characteristic of educators that they are seldom long at any one kind of activity without finding new ways for carrying it on, and new fields in which to use it. Our curiosity as music educators was intrigued by some of the things learned; interests had broadened and a desire created to apply that new knowledge to more areas of music education.

A 1950 survey of the MENC membership showed that there were two points on which most members agreed. *First,* it was evident that there was an aroused and interested membership, clamoring for more opportunities to participate in the professional work of the organization. And *second,* it was apparent that the changing times had developed music education to the point where many new, additional and different phases of music needed study by those who were engaged in the profession.

⌖

So it was that the *Music in American Education* program came into being, involving a tremendous number of active school and college music teachers. These people, working on state, division and national committees, studied almost every facet of this complex profession, comparing ideas from different parts of the country, evaluating what was found, and frequently recommending changes. They delved into a fascinating variety of areas; into the ordinary, everyday music education curricula in its relation to a new world, and into many fields entirely new to us. The objective behind the organization of this new set of committees was to bring into new and clear focus the ideas which had developed and progressed beyond earlier MENC programs; to allow many individuals to participate in bringing these ideas together so that each report would include as many different points of view as possible; to consider music education as a major vocation, with professional status in its activities, in its administration, and in the schooling and degrees of those engaged in it; to bring into focus the constantly increasing variety of resources available in the modern school to help the teacher; to make sure that with all our devoted interest in teaching music to all children in regular schoolrooms and in putting music into the community, we would not forget about the exceptional child and his needs—or about the needs of any others in American life who must be affected by music; finally, to look at all of music education in its relation to American life, from the work of the teacher of the small child on to graduate programs, adult education and community activities, and to provide a means of presenting this picture to our own profession and to the public.

From this vast activity on the part of many people comes this new Source Book. Coming in a new decade, it provides a new look at many of the same problems discussed in the first *Music Education Source Book*. The added and expanded content areas give evidence of the masterly way in which the many working committees investigated the entire field of music education.

✠

This new Source Book is not a record of the past. It is rather a picture, which, through the live, interested and selfless work of capable people is able both to reflect *today* in music education, and at the same time to give a look at *tomorrow*, where we are confident Music in American Education will be a vital, continuing influence and power in American life.

MARGUERITE V. HOOD

DEDICATION

THIS BOOK IS DEDICATED to the men and women whose faith in music as a factor in education has made it possible for the music education profession to reach its present status of dignity and importance among the professional areas of human service.

In a broad sense the dedication reaches back more than a century—perhaps to the time of Lowell Mason and those who were contemporary with him in promoting and activating the first practical programs of music instruction in the American schools. Certainly the dedication of this book must include in its citation the pioneers who in the late eighties and early nineteen hundreds laid the foundation for the Music Educators National Conference as we know it today.

From the same viewpoint, but moving our historical sights to a closer focus, this dedication can be properly directed to those music education leaders who took the initiative in broadening and extending the cooperative principles and practices of the organization to keep pace with the vastly increasing number of potential, active participants. These leaders were pioneers in the developments which began a quarter century or so ago and were the progenitors of the state-division-national plan of organization and member participation which is directly responsible for the production of this book.

It should be noted that the purposes served by such a book as this are only partly gauged by the contents as sources of information and inspiration to the thousands who use it for reference or study. Also must the measure of its value to the field take into account the opportunities and incentives for professional self-improvement afforded the many people who worked in and with the committees whose reports provided the core of the content. In these aspects, at least, *Music in American Education* and its predecessor, the first *Music Education Source Book*, are distinctive.

✠

Since this dedication virtually encompasses all of the members of the MENC, past and present, although primarily directed to the leaders and workers of recent years, a few general comments of historical significance may be pertinent, and in any event should be of interest to younger members.

The Music Educators National Conference has always been an association of co-workers. From its birth as the Music Supervisors National Conference, the word *conference* has had significance. The very first meeting at Keokuk in 1907, though not specifically designed for that purpose, was a "conference." Then—as now—school music teachers and supervisors found it stimulating and profitable to get together and talk shop. They liked to tell each other about their experiences and opinions, and to have their turns to demonstrate their points with pupil groups.

And so it was that the music teachers and supervisors at the Keokuk meeting formed an organization in order to provide for future and regular conferences of school music specialists. Many functions were added to the annual schedule of the organization from year to year, but the fundamental work of the membership has been through the conference, or intimate, type of activity—committee meetings, workshops, demonstrations, clinics, group meetings—and constantly more and more committee group work.

Since 1907, there always have been committees, most of them fruitful—at least for the committee members who benefited by their conferences through group meetings or through correspondence. In earlier years, because of lack of funds or good organization management, some of the beneficial values of the work of these committees failed to reach the members at large. Nevertheless, a great mass of the results of such group work has been made available to the constituency in published reports and in the Conference yearbooks (and in the books of proceedings which from 1910 to 1930 preceded the yearbooks), as well as in reports of the Research Council and of other groups.

It is probably true, however, that the tangible results as evidenced by publications were in some respects actually less vital than the effect of the cooperative work-study-argument processes on the existing and potential leadership of the organization.

And so the conference and co-worker spirit grew and flourished. *Music educators learned how to work together.* They had no professional or trade secrets; rather, they shared with each other their experiences, their good thinking, their ambitions, and even out of their differences they made progress.

Although the committee activities of the organization were in reality the heart and power of the organization from its inception, the early routines for committee assignments were more or less formal, sometimes perfunctory. Committees usually followed pre-established patterns and were productive or not, depending on the vision and energy of the chairmen and their committee constituents, and the current need for action in the areas represented by the committees.

Russell V. Morgan, who was elected president of the Music Educators National Conference in 1930 (the organization was then operating under the name Music Supervisors National Conference), sensed the need for some device that would retain and preserve and extend in usefulness the original *conference* principles. In 1907, every one of the sixty-eight members of the organization could be assigned to a committee post or to other responsibility. But what to do with over three thousand school music teachers—each a leader, at least in his own community?

Mr. Morgan had faith that committee or group work was vital to the continuing success of the organization, which represented the composite usefulness and power of the newly recognized profession of music education. It was Morgan who pioneered in the program which paved the way for the type of committee activity which produced this book.

In a letter written to a colleague in 1930 Mr. Morgan said, in effect, "Our [organization] resources have grown beyond the possibility of utilizing them unless there is expansion of the formal routines set up by precedents and constitutional provisions. . . . In such an organization as ours, each member has the same right to derive benefits and make contributions, if he so wishes, as was the case when there were less than one hundred members. Expansion of the committee, or small-group-conference idea, seems to be the solution. . . . But we should make no mistake. Committees for busywork only cannot justify the existence of the organization which tolerates them. . . . It is not important to have committees just because we always have had such committees, or because we must have a means of recognizing important persons. It is vital to our kind of organization to utilize in the most effective way possible the resources of our membership in order to accomplish the things we agree need to be done. . . . If these things are done through groups working together, it is good. Whether or not the achievements are complete does not matter if through group work our members have opportunity to think and work constructively. . . . The real results of committee work are only partly divulged in the reports read or printed (and every committee report deserves the light of a hearing at least). . . . The total power of our group is enhanced by the growth of the individuals who wholeheartedly or even casually take part in these cooperative assignments and projects, even though nothing ever appears in print to record their efforts and contributions."

And thus the first extensive development in organized MENC committee work on a large scale was initiated by Russell Morgan when he was president of the MENC (1930-1932). It was his ambition to extend participation in committee activities to include younger music educators who had not previously had opportunity to receive and gain the benefits such participation afforded. The number of committees was enlarged, chairmanships which previously had been held by veterans were in some instances transferred to less well-known members of the organization, and there was a much extended scope of activities both in connection with committee responsibilities for convention presentations and also in preparation of special reports. It was to Russell Morgan's credit that the first published compilation of MENC committee reports as such was printed in a pamphlet distributed at the 1932 convention in Cleveland. These reports were included in the 1932 MENC Yearbook.

The plan inaugurated by Mr. Morgan was continued in the next biennium by President Walter H. Butterfield, and in the 1934-1936 biennium President Herman F. Smith picked up and carried the democratic idea still further by making a national survey, enlisting the cooperation of hundreds of Conference members who were asked to recommend persons whom they knew to have special interests and qualifications for assignment to committee responsibilities.

Here then was the beginning of the development of the nationwide committee organization in which hundreds of MENC members have been privileged to take active parts. By 1940, with the rapid development of the state unit plan, there came the need for further integration and unification of organized committee effort beginning at the state level. In this period, when President Fowler Smith (1940-1942) inaugurated the Music Education in Wartime Program, much of the work of the organization was being done through committees and by mail. Wartime restrictions were in large part responsible for further extension of the MENC committee operations. In the fall of 1942, five hundred and thirty-one members of the MENC were appointed by President Lilla Belle Pitts (1942-1944) to the thirty-eight curriculum committees set up under the program of "Widening Horizons for Music Education." The reports of these committees were combined in a mimeographed volume published in 1944. That same year the work thus begun was taken up by six parallel sets of committees appointed by the presidents of the six MENC Divisions. The reports and recommendations submitted by these regional committees were integrated with the 1944 reports and published in a printed volume in 1946.

Meantime, another complement of committees, this time forty in number, was organized on a nationwide basis to draft the final reports, which supplied the bulk of material for the first Source Book. In all, some two thousand members and friends of the MENC served on or with the state, division, and national committees as members or consultants. For MENC Source Book Number One credit must be given in some degree to each of the two thousand members and friends of MENC.

The Music Education Advancement Program set up during the administration of President John C. Kendel (1944-1946) further extended the state-division-national committee organization plan. This program was continued during two bienniums, under the administrations of Luther A. Richman (1946-1948) and Charles M. Dennis (1948-1950), and laid the foundation for the Music in American Education committee organization inaugurated by President Marguerite V. Hood (1950-1952) and carried on by President Ralph E. Rush (1952-1954). Results of the work of the committees during this later period have been made available to the music education field through the *Music Educators Journal* and through various publications, chief of which of course is the volume in your hands.

Based on the experience directly growing out of the previous years in organized membership participation activities is the Music in American Life commission and committee organization plan inaugurated in 1954 by President Robert A. Choate (1954-1956). This further development in the utilization of membership participation directly stems from the motivating principles of conference activity briefly described here, and it can be expected to carry to still further desirable ends the group cooperation procedures which were begun by the MENC founders in Keokuk in 1907.

✠

It is believed that the names of all of the members of the state-division-national committee organization who shared in the preparation of the reports on which this volume is based are included in the listing in the appendix. If anyone is omitted, it is an inadvertence.

Without question, all the contributors, and the thousands of music educators, students, and friends of music education who find the volume useful will join heartily in this dedication, which is in reality to the abiding spirit of the MENC pioneers and their successors, whose faith, enthusiasm, and diligent work made it possible for the music education profession to carry on the type of activity exemplified in this book.

CLIFFORD V. BUTTELMAN

MUSIC IN AMERICAN EDUCATION

SECTION ONE

Professional and Public Relations
of the Music Educator

Music in General Education
Chairman: Lloyd V. Funchess, Baton Rouge, La.

✠

The Administration of Music Education
Coordinating chairman: Harold C. Youngberg, Oakland, Calif.

For Cities of 100,000 and Over
Kenneth Hjelmervik, chairman, Baltimore, Md.

For Smaller Cities
Frederic Fay Swift, chairman, Oneonta, N. Y.

✠

The Supervision of Music Education
Chairman: Lorrain E. Watters, Des Moines, Iowa

✠

Music Education and International Relations
Chairman: Lilla Belle Pitts, New York, N. Y.

CHAPTER I

MUSIC IN GENERAL EDUCATION

The Stake of Music in Education [1]

THE STAKE OF MUSIC in education can be analyzed from many viewpoints. The discussion here is limited to three aspects: (a) The artistic implications of music in education; (b) the general educative value of music in education; and (c) the place of music in education from a functional standpoint.

Artistic Implications. From the artistic standpoint, music, as it is taught in the schools of the United States, incorporates artistic values in its methods and techniques. Because of this the results of the teaching and guidance in the field of music show a technical proficiency unmatched by any other country in the world. For this we are grateful to you, the music educators, and to your great organization which has been so largely responsible for this whole development.

I earnestly encourage you to continue this endeavor for proficiency in music education. In this sense we want you to be a tightly compartmentalized part of education because only in this way can we hope to have a continuance of the great work you have started—the fine performance of these musical groups. To this end you must not only insist on your rights as *music educators*, but you must continue to emphasize also the necessity of certain areas of specialization within your ranks. Some of you will necessarily devote your energies to the business of increasing your stature as specialists in one of the several areas of your profession as conductors of bands, orchestras, or choirs. All of this is quite necessary to insure competence in these areas for your students. But I very strenuously urge you *not* to carry these ambitions of specialization beyond reasonable limits. The borders within your own field of specialization cannot be defined for you. We can only advise you.

If music is to be made a thing of beauty and a joy forever in the lives of all children, then the ideal of cooperation and of unity must direct the field of music education in America. Those of us in administration and in general education must be very sure that our music programs are controlled by persons who are dedicated to the stake of *music in education* and not to the individual *music specialist's stake in education*. Therefore, as you develop these fine bands and orchestras and choruses which we want so much, be sure that you always keep foremost in your mind the *importance* of maintaining the integrity of your total profession—music education— and the relative *unimportance* of over-emphasizing compartmentalization *within your own field*.

The General Educative Values of Music. All are aware these days of the growing necessity to make as complete as possible the education of our boys and girls. The responsibility is great to the millions of pupils in our elementary schools in developing, through well-planned experiences, their native love and interest in music. Then, as they grow toward maturity, they will gain in the ability to utilize these experiences in the enjoyment of creating and listening to good music.

You will agree that while children are in elementary school their education should be as effective as it is possible to make it. The man or woman who is in the field of music education and who does not have the needs of this large group of the school population in mind, is, in my opinion, not a true educator.

[1] From an address by Benjamin C. Willis, General Superintendent of Schools, Chicago, Illinois, given at the MENC Biennial Convention, Chicago, 1954.

Then there are the thousands and thousands of students whose formal education terminates in high school. They also need as complete an education as possible before embarking on their individual careers. Many of these high school students have never had an opportunity to participate in your bands, your orchestras and your choruses, and yet, all of you would agree that they are entitled to music as an essential part of their secondary school education. It would be a sad commentary on our position as educators if we failed to provide adequate music education for these young citizens. They are entitled to the immediate and future benefits which participation in musical activities provides.

Similarly, colleges and universities must be continually on the alert and must be evaluating their curricula to see that their graduates are properly equipped in all phases of education. The day for defending the place of music in our college curriculum is past. Something more than earning a living and specializing in professions is involved, for educators now recognize that it is necessary to provide for the college student a variety of rich musical experiences so that he may derive both immediate and future satisfaction from music.

Business and professional leaders are deeply interested in the training given students for their careers—in the pure sciences, the natural sciences, business education, and so on. However, there is a growing conviction that the liberal arts are basic and that by no means should they be neglected in the anxiety to turn out graduates who are qualified only in the techniques of their chosen occupations. Business, industry, and the professions need people who can think beyond the business office, the laboratory, the shop, and the sales meeting; people whose education is sufficiently balanced to meet the challenges of civic, social, and vocational life.

Music is a vital part of a balanced education. It has a very real stake in the education of our students—from elementary school through college.

Administrators need your help in this great task and responsibility. We need musicians who are educators. We need music educators who can tell us not only what is *good music* but what *music is good for*. Here is your real and live and challenging responsibility. You can reach only a small portion of this large aggregate of our school population to whom I refer through participation in your bands, orchestras, and choruses.

By all means continue your pursuits in this direction, but widen your concepts of your responsibility to the masses of our school population. Realize the educational value of music activities at every school level and strive earnestly to make them available for *all* pupils. You cannot do this alone but administrators cannot do it without you. Working together it can be accomplished.

The Functional Value of Music. Any subject has a functional value when it contributes to the general well-being of the individual and when it helps him to participate fully and more effectively in the life of the society in which he lives and works. Certainly music has functional value, and this is related to the important responsibility it has in education for citizenship.

Music education always has had an important place in the curriculum of democracies. Over two thousand years ago music was a part of the education of every Greek citizen. Those of us who believe that music has a stake in American education today have our convictions considerably strengthened when we read the sections of Plato's *Republic* (Books 2 and 3) in which he expresses this program of education: "Gymnastics for the body and *music for the soul*." Greek music, art, and poetry were bound up with civic life, closely allied to the religious festivals which were then the heart and soul of the nation. So today it does not seem too much of a boast to say that one of the most important contributions music education makes in *our* curriculum is one of *education for citizenship*.

2

Guiding Principles. There are specific contributions which music can make in educating for citizenship. Some guiding principles on which administrators and music educators can build a music education program which will contribute to the development of desirable citizenship traits are:

(1) Music offers an opportunity for self-expression through a group activity. Thus, it has a socializing value which is beneficial for the uninhibited students who learn the importance of working as part of a group. It is of unquestionable benefit and an indispensable experience for the more inhibited students who may, through this one avenue of participation in a school activity, learn the all-important principles of good citizenship—self-assurance, self-realization, personal security, and respect for the achievements of others. Certainly through encouraging individual initiative and group cooperation, music education is helping to develop good citizens.

(2) Music offers an opportunity to develop moral and spiritual values and to satisfy aesthetic needs. Young people are expressing, creating, or enjoying beauty when they are singing a song, playing a tune, or just listening. Likewise, music provides a wholesome means of enjoying leisure and can be a powerful influence for good. Youngsters participating in good music are not likely to be numbered among our juvenile delinquents. As music educators you have the privilege of helping these young people live well-adjusted lives and thus become better, happier citizens.

(3) Music provides a medium through which boys and girls can make direct contributions to their community during their school days and thus acquire a consciousness of the responsibility of the individual to the community. This is borne out by the fact that in most of the communities in the United States it is the school music groups—the bands, orchestras, and choruses in elementary schools, in high schools and in colleges—which furnish the focus for the music life of the community. These activities provide an outlet for self-expression and for belonging, which are two basic human needs, and at the same time build that spirit of cooperation upon which democracy depends for its very existence.

(4) Music offers a medium for understanding other people, their culture, and their problems. This is not to say that the mere singing and playing of music of various countries by our boys and girls makes them necessarily understand those countries. The people of some countries have been playing each other's music for centuries and at periodic intervals these peoples have been at war with each other. However, music is a universal tool of communication; it transcends the boundaries of nations; it promotes the brotherhood of man.

With good teaching, teaching with imagination the music of other countries in our classrooms, and through our classrooms reaching our homes and communities, we contribute enormously to the stature of our future citizens who want to live in a peaceful world with the citizens of other countries.

(5) Through music the student is led to a realization that the arts, of which music is one, have been of indisputable importance throughout all history. As a matter of fact, the arts are the permanent purveyors of history from one civilization to another. An understanding of the thoughts, ideals, and aspirations of preceding generations is needed to build a background for good citizenship.

At the risk of under-emphasizing many of the other important functions of music in the curriculum at all levels of education today, I believe I would put *education for citizenship* as its most important function. This concept is a very logical and necessary base from which many of the other values to be derived from music as a part of education, can follow. This is *music's most important stake in education*.

3

Music educators who are teaching music as a fundamental part of our American way of life and who are analyzing the challenge of music in education for citizenship are making notable and invaluable contributions to the all-round education of our boys and girls.

Educators of this type are needed and can be used in all levels of music education from preschool through college and the university. Such educators are not committed to a program of idealisms which claim that music does all things for all people. Instead, they do their utmost to help young people in the schools to become as literate as possible in the field of music. Well-balanced individuals—musicians and educators—have a keen realization that music is a means through which boys and girls can learn to play and work together; that it is a means through which better citizens can be developed; that music contributes to the richness of family life; that it offers many vocational opportunities for our young citizens. In the hands of these persons the stake of music in education, which is considerable, will be assured.

Music—A Vital Force in Education [1]

We who were pioneers in the work know the struggles we had and what difficulties have been overcome in bringing school music to a point of recognition by either the musicians or the educators. In the long pull of securing attention from school people, as being a factor in education and making our work really worth while as teachers of music, we older supervisors have borne the burden of the heat of the day in bringing the work from its humble beginnings to its present place in the sun.

Standards have been raised, work has improved, opportunities have multiplied, the field has been enlarged, recognition has come; and now to the younger, better educated, better equipped, better paid supervisors of today the door is wide open, the vista so alluring and so assured that we of yesterday wish we might begin all over again for the very joy of it.

The great war, whose shadow is still over us, settled a few things in the educational world, as in the commercial, financial, and other realms. It was not the over-scientific, over-specialized education of the military caste of the enemy that won the war . . . but the compelling *heart* power of the appeal from stricken countries . . . sentiment and sympathy, love and law, soul and spirit, took our whole people into it, like the wing sweep of an avenging angel, in righting a great world wrong. It was not our military prowess . . . nor yet our commercial instincts, but the keen sense of righteousness and honesty learned in our public schools.

And so it comes about . . . a swinging back of the pendulum from the over-emphasis placed upon industrial and vocational training, commercial and utilitarian courses, to a saner mixture of the cultural subjects that make for right understanding and right living, and sensible serving in the upbuilding of the community, the state, and the nation, to those things that bring a realization of the spirit of "All for Each and for All."

School music has more to offer in the service of this newly awakened sense of the need of closer relationship of all classes, more to offer to the newly organized centers of communal thought, more to give toward the rapid Americanization of our latecomers, more to give toward building and keeping a high morale, a better spirit of happiness and joy in life, than any other one branch of study in the curriculum.

Music has at least as much to offer in mental discipline, in stirring the powers of discrimination, coordination, selection, and judgment, as any other one subject—

---

[1] Response by Frances Elliott Clark to the address of welcome at the twelfth annual meeting of the Music Supervisors National Conference, St. Louis, Missouri, 1919. Reprinted from *Music Educators Journal*, April-May 1954.

and, next to reading, better stimulates the imagination. It correlates with other branches better than any other, save reading and writing, and even as a vocational subject it is second only to those of the most populous trades, while as a socializing function it has absolutely no peer.

The hour of *music as education* has struck. Not music for fun nor entertainment, nor as a pastime or accomplishment, nor yet as an art, standing alone— although at times it may be any or all of these—*but as one of the great vital forces of education.*

It only remains for the school music supervisors to rise to their new duties and opportunities to make school music in every city, village, and rural community the very heart of the school life, the focal point of all neighborhood activities, and a part of all civic work. It must be made a dynamic force in the life of every child everywhere, country as well as city, through being not a highbrow appendage, a beautiful but useless fringe on the garment, but a real servant of education.

The doors are open. Every great national musical or educational organization is behind the work of community music. High schools almost everywhere are giving credit for music courses, school orchestras multiply and will lead on directly to the municipal orchestra. Much hearing of the best music is raising the standards of taste and appreciation. The field is white for the harvest and the laborers all too few. . . .

We of yesteryear builded better than we knew. We have not toiled in vain. And so, as we call upon the younger music educators to take up the advanced work which we with prophetic eye see in the aurora of the new day, let us bid them Godspeed.

Moral and Spiritual Values in Music Education [1]

I

"If moral and spiritual values are to be found in music education, they must be found in the music educator."

It is true that the work of the artist is of the nature of revelation. What he reveals to his fellow men through his art may be truth so exalted that neither he nor any other man can verbalize it, much less incarnate it. The old adage, "Practice what you preach," is often construed to mean that we should not preach "more than we can practice." I disagree emphatically.

The prophet is a *speaker for* rather than a *speaker before.* But the prophet is a *speaker for* the divine. Therefore, the truth he proclaims is always beyond us. In the light of truth revealed or proclaimed we should have the moral courage and spiritual audacity to declare that we aim at standards of character, personality, and achievement, which we have not reached and may never reach.

Some years ago, prior to the recent successful conquest of Mt. Everest, an organization of mountain climbers was making a supreme effort finally to send two of their number to what has been called "the top of the world." The time came for the last assault. Upward into the cloud and mist these two brave men climbed. They were never seen again. No one knows whether they reached the top or not. But a great thing was said about them by their comrades. When they had descended from their tragically futile mission, they said, "When last we saw our friends, *they were headed* for the top and still climbing."

---

[1] From an address by Earl E. Harper, Dean, Department of Fine Arts, State University of Iowa, Iowa City, given at the MENC Biennial Convention, Chicago, 1954.

That man or woman who, through carelessness, indifference, self-indulgence, weakness, or perhaps cowardice, turns back from continuing effort to achieve his ideals actually joins the ranks of those who stand against what he believes.

The truth which preachers of religion proclaim will endure in spite of moral failure among those who preach. Nevertheless, when the proclamation of a spiritual ideal has been identified with a man whose lifework is religious ministry, if that man makes moral shipwreck of his own life, he becomes a traitor to truth.

It is presumable that educators are all united in agreement that moral and spiritual values are vitally important in the culture of individuals and the civilizations of nations.

Most of us are so convinced of the necessity of moral life and spiritual inspiration in human experience that if we should conclude that music education, or education in the Fine Arts generally, does not offer us a work which we can do and through which we can express, manifest, and measurably implement our ideals, then we will get out of it.

The first question we must ask ourselves concerning any cherished ideal is whether we believe in it to the point of complete personal dedication.

II

Moral and spiritual values are most important of all values in personal life, and in the corporate life of men and women banded together in a profession, a state, a nation, or a world order.

There is a distinction with a difference between moral and spiritual values. Moral values have to do with the rules and practices of daily life. Spiritual values have to do with the genesis of and authority for these rules.

Moral values issue in ethical codes. Spiritual values involve not only motivation to live by these codes, but they tap the mainsprings of dynamic power without which men cannot long endure the struggle to live ethically, righteously and justly, with major emphasis upon self-sacrifice to mankind.

Moral values may be validated dialectically by our study of history. Spiritual values are rooted and grounded in man's faith in a divine intelligence creatively responsible for and regnantly powerful in the universe.

A structured statement of moral values may be likened to an intelligently devised, ingeniously constructed, and marvelously complicated machine. Spiritual values represent the power which makes the machinery operate. An excellent framework of ethical standards expressed in a beautifully articulated code is possible without reference to religio-spiritual values.

The tide of human reverence and devotion to religious ideals ebbs and flows as time moves on. The present day is one of terrible concern about moral standards and almost desperate turning to spiritual ideals. Moral degradation comparable to that of Sodom of the Old Testament, the Roman Empire of the early Christian era, or of Central Europe in the interval between the first and second world wars, threatens us in the United States of America today. Faced with increasing moral bankruptcy in the areas of juvenile delinquency, crime in its many ugly aspects, national and political disharmony, and international tension, strain, and fear, men are anxiously asking whether divine help cannot be invoked to solve the problems which mortal intelligence faces with deepening hopelessness.

III

The most important thing in the life and work of a man or woman is his or her basic total philosophy of life.

No man or woman in any walk of life is engaged in work more naturally adapted to the realization, proclamation, and promotion of moral and spiritual values than are music educators.

First, there are great disciplinary values inherent in your relation as educators to the youth whom you teach. The conductor of a musical organization must carry out his work with an innate sense of command, and with acknowledgment on the part of the personnel involved that he has authority. This can and too often does breed a petty tyranny.

We should continuously remind ourselves that we live in an age of increasing leisure time. There are those who exclaim that this means correlatively advancing culture. The plain truth is that additional leisure in many instances means a new crime wave. What is important is the use which is made of this time. No more enjoyable, attractive, or worth-while engagement of time and attention of people, and especially youth, freed from labor has been discovered or can be imagined than music as a recreational experience.

Second, to the great extent that the vast literature of the art of music interprets reality in human life we are dealing with works of art which proclaim moral and spiritual values.

We do not need to use works of art to point morals. Through art life finds interpretation. And when works of art are presented in any media which thus interpret life, they preach their own sermons. Sometimes, perhaps, we are so charmed with the artistic masterpiece as entertainment that we fail to realize the profound truth involved.

In public concerts and in our recorded programs in music rooms we can and do bring to responsive audiences the sacred oratorios of Bach, Handel, and Haydn, the magnificent symphonic psalms of Honegger and Vaughan Williams, and the requiems and Masses of Brahms, Verdi, and César Franck. In our lounges, halls, and galleries we hang paintings and place sculptured figures which interpret man's desire and quest for spiritual enlightenment through the ages. Men and women of all faiths and no faith find in these common inspiration.

Third, of all the Fine Arts, music has been and continues to be the greatest instrument of man's quest for moral and spiritual values in life.

Evidence of the truth of this assertion is to be found in the fact that men, whatever may be their religious faith, spend from one-third to one-half of all the time they are engaged in corporate worship participating in or listening to singing and the playing of instruments. Added emphasis to this truth is the fact that an enormous portion of all the money men give to and spend on the religious quest through organized religion is spent in one way or another for music. The creation of a Commission on Church Music and Worship, or Worship and the Fine Arts by nearly every religious faith and denomination, and the establishment of a Department of Worship and the Arts as a major subdivision of the National Council of Churches of Christ in the United States of America give practical emphasis and bear eloquent testimonial to the importance of music in the realization, proclamation, and promotion of moral and religious values in human life.

Perhaps we cannot hope to add to the sum total of human wisdom concerning music as a bridge from the world of the sense to the world of the spirit, but we can remind ourselves of certain important facets of religious life and worship which are involved.

First, music is a marvelously effective means of spiritual impression. From the time "Jubal struck his chorded shell" and men, listening, felt that no less than a God must dwell in its hollow, this great art has somehow made men feel that their lives are more than mortal, that a divine spirit impinges upon them wherever they are and whatever they are doing.

7

Second, music, whether instrumental, in prelude, offertory, response, and postlude; or vocal, as a setting for anthem, hymn, chant, or introit, is an incomparable means of spiritual expression. Even the stranger in a worshiping congregation as he stands to sing a hymn engages actively and vocally in prayer, praise, meditation and exhortation.

Third, music as a universal language of the spirit brings men of all faiths into spiritual unity in a consummate realization that there are great universal fundamentals of faith which are common to all, whether they are Hebrews, Roman Catholics, Protestants, or followers of ethnic religions.

Music educators find a great avocational employment of their talents and techniques, fraught with a sense of dignified and helpful service, in the musical ministry of religion. And so important has this aspect of the ministry become that more and more opportunities open every day for a professional career in this artistic religious service.

Conclusion. I have asked you to consider the fact that if moral and spiritual values are to be found in music education they must be found in the music educator; that moral and spiritual values are ultimate values, transcendent, but permeative of the entire structure of life and education; and that in the art of music, educators have a matchless opportunity to lead those whom we educate into an experience of discipline, high moral purpose and conduct, and spiritual growth.

"Art in its nobler form is one of the great quickeners of moral endeavor. This power it holds in no small degree due to the fact that it contains a transcendent element. The artistic impulse is not content until it has created something more perfect than yet finds embodiment in our experience; it strives to suggest that 'eye hath not seen or ear heard.' Herein it is at one with the moral impulse, which is not satisfied to leave things as it finds them, but seeks to remould them into a more perfect order. Both the moral and artistic impulse are alike haunted by a vision of ideal perfection. Art, no less than reflection, may recall us to our better selves by suggesting in forms of beauty those ideals for which it is alike our duty and our joy to strive." [1]

Members of the music education profession, if you accept and discharge the *responsibilities* which rest upon you in your life and work, you will bring moral guidance to the people of our land which will impart happiness and stability into the social life of America, and measurably strengthen our democracy to meet the fierce frontal attacks and insidious undermining influences which threaten it. If you do this, you will deserve to be numbered with the prophets, priests, and seers as benefactors of the race.

But if you realize the *possibilities* of your work in revitalizing the spiritual life of mankind and in assisting man to tap the ultimate source of spiritual values and inspiration, you will deserve to be canonized with the saints.

General Education and the Music Teacher [2]

Few things are more difficult to evaluate than the trends in the life and institutions of one's own day. Yet for the educator, and particularly the teacher working in the area of the arts, it is of paramount importance that he clearly identify himself with the current of public thought and action.

Probably two of the most interesting trends in education at the beginning of the second half of the twentieth century are: *First,* the mounting numbers of children, young people, and adults interested in educational activities; and, *second,*

---

[1] Walter Goodnow Everett, *Moral Values.*

[2] From an address by Hobart H. Sommers, Assistant Superintendent of Schools, Chicago, Illinois, given at the MENC Southwestern Conference, Springfield, Missouri, 1953.

the increasing acceptance of the terms "general education" and "special education," together with the problems created by that acceptance. Regarding the first phenomenon of the rising numbers of breathing souls thirsting for knowledge in these United States, little needs to be said. The continuing high birth rate, pressing closely behind the wave of war babies about to engulf our high schools; the high employment figure that provides money enough to send all the children to high school even in these days of inflation; the newly developed interest in higher education stimulated by government subsidy of veteran education; the lengthening of our span of life by the great medical achievements of the past twenty years which gives us new leisure time for adult education—all are contributing factors to the steadily mounting percentage of our increasing population which is demanding the professional services of trained educators.

In the Harvard Report, "General Education in a Free Society," [1] general education was defined as education for an informed, responsible life in our society, as dealing with common standards and common purposes. Special education was described as looking more directly to worldly success by equipping people for certain specific tasks. To quote a sentence, "Taken as a whole, education seeks to do two things: Help young people to fulfill the unique, particular functions in life which it is in them to fulfill, and fit them so far as it can for those common spheres which, as citizens and heirs of a joint culture, they will share with others." The report was accepted quite universally and most of us agreed that in the secondary school the student would receive an education having two aspects, the general and the specialized. The nature and the proportion of the two and the relationship of the various subject areas to this philosophy have been a mounting concern.

The adjective "general" in educational use has all but displaced the older word "liberal." It is generally agreed that the first use of the term "general education" applied to the offerings above the level of the public high school, as early proponents believed that changes were needed in the college curriculum. General education was a reaction against overspecialization, against the imbalance between the pursuit of special interest and the attaining of a broader culture that an educated man was expected to possess. It was reaction, too, against the fragmentation of the curriculum which had developed through the acceptance of the right of the American student to make a selection of his college courses after exposure to a brief core curriculum.

Clarence H. Faust said: "General education has for its function to prepare young people to deal not with the special problems parceled out in our society to the members of the various occupations and professions, but with the problems which confront all members of our society alike; such problems as our domestic and foreign policies, our political leadership, our individual relations with the physical universe and our personal philosophies." [2] General education appears from this point of view to be the preparation of youth to deal with the personal and social problems with which all men in a democratic society are confronted.

Robert Havighurst of the University of Chicago, in the Fifty-First Yearbook of the National Society for the Study of Education (1953) had the following contribution to make: "Although the American educational scene gives the impression of great diversity . . . there is a wide area of basic agreement as to the proper aims of general education." These might be summed up as follows:

—To develop critical intelligence, capable of being applied in many fields.

—To develop and improve moral character.

—To develop and improve citizenship.

---

[1] The Harvard Committee, *General Education in a Free Society* (Cambridge, Mass.: Harvard University Press, 1945).

[2] Clarence H. Faust, *Ideas of Practical Education* (Chicago: University of Chicago Press, 1950).

9

—To create intellectual unity and communion of minds among as large a population as possible.

—To equalize opportunity as far as is possible through education for individual economic and social improvement.

In *Democratic Teaching in Secondary Schools*, Stiles and Dorsey say, "General Education does not seem to be concerned with the preparation for specific jobs, nor does it attempt to develop any particular work skill. It seeks to develop attitudes and habits of doing well whatever one attempts, of fair treatment of those with whom we work, and respect for those whose work differs from ours. General education strives to help students develop habits that apply to qualities such as promptness, attention to detail, care in handling materials, skill in human relationship, and willingness to work cooperatively for the good of the group.

In the fields of recreation, politics, community service, and social life, general education trains youth to make adjustments and progress toward goals that will be realized in later life. A partial adjustment is made in high school through participation in activities that contribute to these various fields. Information and firsthand experiences gained through general education concerning people and their relationships, economic, political, cultural and ethical, help youth to begin progress toward life goals." [1]

These last paragraphs could just as well have been written by a music educator on the subject of "The Purpose of Music Education in the Program of General Education," because a well-rounded program of music experiences planned for the elementary and the high school is in itself a general education program for all young people. There should be no straining to identify the music program with general education; their objectives are coordinate.

In November of 1953, *The Bulletin* of the National Association of Secondary-School Principals carried the fascinating title, "The Function of Music in the Secondary-School Curriculum." [2] The opening paragraphs on the general objectives of music education in the high school are worth repeating. The following are only selected quotations, but they serve to indicate the parallel purpose of general education and music education.

"Music is an important and contributing factor in the general objectives of the secondary school, as music education gives young people the opportunity to find a richer life through music. It emphasizes the value of human living. It assists in developing an integrated person. Music may be a hobby, a recreation, or a valuable educational experience.

"Music education offers activities which develop the social aspects of life. Group activities in music offer effective ways of developing cooperation, discipline, personal initiative, individual responsibility, and human relations. There are obvious socializing factors in these group activities inasmuch as the pupils work not only with their fellow students but also with the faculty of the school and the people in the community.

"Music education contributes to the health of the students and to the mental and emotional health which is known to respond to the stimulus of music. It exerts a refining influence on the emotions. Through the performance of music, there is developed the combination of mental and muscular control and coordination.

"Music education develops good work habits. It demands and encourages discipline, and develops wholesome ideals of conduct. Group performance encourages the merging of individual efforts with those of others; it develops proper respect

---

[1] Lindley J. Stiles and Mattie F. Dorsey, *Democratic Teaching in the Secondary Schools* (New York: J. B. Lippincott Company, 1950).

[2] Available in reprint from Music Educators National Conference. $1.00.

for the rights of others; it emphasizes human relations and collaboration, providing rich and significant experiences in which many share.

"Music education contributes to the development of citizenship by helping to produce an integrated personality; by teaching love of country, pride in its achievements, knowledge of its history, and a neighborly regard for the people of other lands through their music.

"Music education aims to contribute to recreation by providing a sense of relaxation and renewal in the activities of the music groups."

Three out of four types of extra-curricular activities suggested by E. G. Williamson, Dean of Students at the University of Minnesota, as having usefulness in general education, have counterpoints in a good music program.

(1) Community and school programs in the arts, music, and dramatics may add to the student's aesthetic maturity.

(2) Participation in and observation of school activities and contests may maintain morale through relaxation and enjoyment.

(3) Active membership in one or more of the varied clubs and organizations may bring maturity of interpersonal relationship through group enterprises.

Here again the music program in the schools can qualify under the yardstick of general education. School and community programs in the arts and music form the backbone of the American high school public presentations to their immediate communities. As these programs develop the student's aesthetic maturity, maintain his morale, and give maturity to his understanding of group activities, they should be considered as activities in the general education program and not of specialized nature.

The greatest problems of our time are the right use of leisure, the performance of the duties of citizenship, and the establishment of a community in this country and the world. General education, as a good definition, would then be anything received in school which helps to solve any one of these three great problems of the time. There is justification for appraising the contributions to education of out-of-class experiences as well as those which take place in the formal classroom. The high school boy in the band or orchestra may get more general education in his music activities than through his contact with the specialized fields of Spanish and geometry. The premise that some kinds of learning, especially in the area of human relationships and relative values, take place in the direct experiences of human beings rather than in abstract and artificial situations should be accepted readily. The basis for education must be experience. The public, long accustomed to the bookish presentations of the academic world, has been slow to recognize this fact.

All personal philosophies of music education should be examined in order to discover whether you are a teacher of music subjects or whether, in addition to your instruction in special areas, you also make your contribution to general education. Ask yourself these ten questions:

(1) Do you believe that a good music program in the elementary and high school is one that all should enjoy and all should have an opportunity to join? Do you think your music program should be a part of the lives of all of the students in the school, or are you looking only for the talented and good students who may be interested and "do well" in your subject? Are you looking for your program to add to the life of all of the pupils, or are you interested in teaching music as a satisfaction to your own desires?

(2) Do you believe that attitudes and good human relations can be fostered through a music program? Jacques Barzam in *Teacher in America* says that it is impossible to teach responsibility and democracy. His view is that these qualities are attitudes which must be slowly developed. Do you believe that the music teacher,

the band director, and the orchestra conductor have the best opportunity of any educator to develop these attitudes? Do you make your own opportunities?

(3) Have you learned that children are often influenced more by the pressures around them than by the subjects on their daily program? Have you made a study of music education in relation to sociometry, the measurement of attitudes of social acceptance or rejection through expressed preferences among members of a social grouping?

(4) Does your philosophy of teaching produce activities which are stimulating both mentally and physically?

(5) Do you believe that through music you are teaching a real appreciation of the heritage of civilization? Have you consciously prepared yourself to teach good citizenship through music? Does your program contribute to the building of character; provide an outlet for adolescent energy; give parents a guide for a normal development of the means for the expression of emotion?

(6) Can you relate and integrate your music program with the rest of the curriculum or do you see just yourself in everything?

(7) Have you undertaken the challenge to help your chief administrator and the sub-administrators to understand that the music program is a part of general education?

(8) On the other hand, are music teachers sympathetic and helpful with the aims and objectives of other members of the faculty or secretly disdainful of their activities?

(9) Have you so much faith in your program that you like to have the school revolve around your activities?

(10) Have you developed a set of values and learned in the promotion of your program when it is a good time to stop?

What is the point of our interest in the coordinate objectives of general education and the music teacher? Bertrand Russell, in his book, *The Impact of Science on Society*, said, "There are certain things that our age needs. . . . It needs compassion and a wish that mankind should be happy; it needs the desire for knowledge and the determination to eschew pleasant myths; it needs above all courageous hope and the impulse to creativeness." A candidate for a high office in our government said recently, "The challenge of our faith and our time is the insensate worship of matter organized in a vast international conspiracy. But the goal of life is more than material advance; it is now and through all eternity the triumph of spirit over matter."

Music education must contribute to the great need for a positive philosophy that will change the weakness of our fears and suspicions into the strength of faith. Walter Reuther, president of the CIO, stated, "In this period of fear and uncertainty in the world when freedom is being challenged by the forces of Communist tyranny, we need more than technical competence—we need a philosophy that anchors us firmly to basic human and democratic values. A general education is necessary to give us an understanding of the total world environment in which we live and in which we must work out the question of democratic survival." It is only as our cultural life and our industrial and business life can be intermingled so that there will be no business without culture and no culture without vocation that the schools can educate men for a free society.

American culture is a practical manifestation of democratic living. It is not learning alone nor the love of knowledge for its sake alone, but a compound of practical traditions and a reverence for traditions of curiosity and zeal; it is an awareness of the problems of the atomic age and the consciousness of the obligation of the individual to the whole human race. American education has about reached a position where it is ready to admit that it must do more than teach subjects; it must develop a philosophy of living.

In its critical period of decision as to the future direction of educational thinking, the music educator has an enviable responsibility. With the realization of the force and possibilities of music education in both the general and special fields can come a quickening of the American spirit, a deepening of emotion and sentiment, a mounting sense of seriousness, and a national integrity which is something new on the American scene. Through music education can come an understanding of the true relationship between the realistic success of American material achievements and the corresponding possibilities of our unlimited future.

The Place of the General Educator in Facilitating an Expanding Music Program [1]

School administrators and general educators have a definite responsibility in helping a program of music education to expand. More than any art, music is the technique of bringing absolute beauty in its greatest intensity and charm. Music is a potent shaper of the quality of life and of personality. Every school administrator should be cognizant of these important generalizations. Unless school administrators know the price and value of music in a school curriculum they will miss an important value in the life of children in their schools. Those who know the power of the resonance and the melody of the voice, raise their level of intellect and enhance their lives.

General educators can expand and better promote music education if they provide music experiences as an essential part of life—never apart from it. Otherwise, schools tend to satisfy cheap emotional cravings and promote trivia which lead to nothing.

Happy are children who sing and play because music vivifies human behavior. This psychological attribute should be a cue to all educators to provide music atmosphere to all children in all grades for all schools. Many of us have seen lethargic children in classrooms respond when a song is sung or a tune played. We find an impressive set of human impulses to sing, to participate and even to whistle a tune. These reactions lead to interest and joy in learning. School administrators should capitalize on these emotional tones and sensitize all teachers to these psychological advantages which music produces.

School administrators can expand music education by providing opportunities for expression. Music festivals, operettas, and concerts create a distinct public approval and satisfaction. These should be encouraged and extended in scope. Parents, especially, appreciate school music performances.

A Chicago high school principal in his annual report to the State Superintendent of Instruction said: "The choral pupils not only learn to harmonize, to acquire good tone quality, to learn rhythm and the various musical forms, they also learn that the elements of discipline, attention, punctuality, team work, and cooperation are most important. They acquire good morale and inspiration by joining in the enjoyment of choral compositions."

Today, much is said about human relations. Here is another opportunity to promote music because it is one of the most significant unifying forces of all nations. It is a great experience of intercommunication among all persons. In this way music enhances emotionalizing influences and very definitely helps in building social vision in people.

---

[1] From an address by Thaddeus J. Lubera, Assistant Superintendent of Schools, Chicago, Illinois, given at the MENC Biennial Convention, Chicago, 1954.

The generalists in American education can better facilitate music education if in their program of teaching they intensify emotional attitudes toward things that are wholesome and create aversion to those which are cheap and vulgar. A basic responsibility of American education is the maintenance of high standards in music education. School administrators everywhere will help to extend a program of music if they will see beauty in music as a thing of worth in the service of good, and things of worth they will never see dragged in the mire. Perhaps this calls for a professional transformation of education in its purposes and its processes.

It may be the fullest potentialities of music education will never be realized unless boards of education and the public in general lend greater financial support for the fine arts—particularly music. Those who say that we can dispense with music because it's expensive, travel with "dim lights." Perhaps they are intellectually desiccated. They see only flowing configuration of figures and never realize that music produces a symphony of life filled with color, depth, and intensity of pleasure.

Music as an Art in General Education [1]

Interest in the objectives of general education has placed all subjects under the microscope where much of what is observed is not reassuring to those who wish their field to be functional. The music educator and the school administrator need to look at music education in a new light.

In an effort to educate the rising generation to carry on the life of the race, a careful system of grading and age classification and a rather clear-cut division of subject matter, have been established. There has been a trend in the past twenty years to break down the walls between subjects, and to establish larger areas within which the child finds educational activities and experiences.

On the basis of such broad divisions, consideration should be given to what the youth must learn in order that the life of the race be continued and the quality of its civilization improved.

To speak and write intelligently, to read with comprehension, to handle number concepts; these are basic—hence the "3 R's."

Music and art, too, have provided communication since the early days of the race. Bards sang heroic sagas and artists drew or painted on cave walls. The medieval troubador was the gossip columnist of his day; he also carried the culture of one locality to another in his rondels. During our era, music has served as a means of communicating those emotions too deep for speech, too lofty for prose.

The sense of well-being that accompanies and follows the act of singing is well recognized. The release of personal tensions through music in this world of suspicion and apprehensiveness is of increasing importance.

Music offers a form of expression used and understood for thousands of years by humanity in every clime and of whatever color; the *common touch* in its best sense; the live essence of every people, which can be savored by any who take the small pains necessary to learn the techniques. The musician should be the most tolerant of persons—ready for naturalization as a citizen of the world. With music educators there is but one aristocracy—that of talent. Music written by men and women of all nations is heard and performed with no thought of their religious and political beliefs or the color of their skins. Music, as a field of interest, shared by our colleagues in all countries, constitutes an area of common understanding.

A basic objective in the preparation of the rising generation is an awareness of a cultural heritage—the buildings, objects, writings, philosophies, paintings, and music, which, because of artistry, skill, spiritual discernment, or unique relationship

---

[1] By Charles M. Dennis, Director of Music, San Francisco Public Schools. Reprinted from *California Journal of Secondary Education*, November 1952.

to a period, have come to be venerated or at least generally admired. They serve as models of, or guideposts to, what the race recognizes as good. During certain periods they may lose caste, but sooner or later their inherent value is again perceived. To be in ignorance of the great products of our culture is to remain a savage.

The worship of applied science such as has characterized the past half century has resulted in a belittling of cultural pursuits except in a form one can sell. But the false gods are never eternal, and the artist in man which requires him to do as beautifully as he can whatever is before him to do will not be downed.

General education is concerned with the improvement of the self in all phases of education. The term "frill" has been overworked by shortsighted critics. Here is a definition of frills and essentials worth repeating:

Frills—Those subjects in school curricula that yield nothing useful or cultural above the sixth grade except to specialized students.

Essentials—Subjects and activities that quicken the subjective self, develop personality and character, and prepare for enriched and useful life.

Few school subjects prepare so well for constructive use of leisure time as does music. It can range from playing cello in a string quartet to escaping into a dream world of beautiful sound patterns, depending on the ability and need of the individual. Music can ameliorate the harshness of life and minister to the depressed and insecure. It can enrich the personality and increase individual happiness. It can contribute to personal fulfillment and self-realization. It can train for accuracy and integrity. It is true that while music educators have recognized these values, they have commonly been thought of as by-products to be absorbed through contact with music and not as end results. They have not been emphasized, projected, and accepted as objectives by teacher and pupil. The school administrator is partly responsible for this. When the music education program is considered only as a medium for public relations, an accessory to the athletic program, or an agency for entertaining the student body, there is little likelihood that it ever will achieve its educational potential. Whether or not the music student develops integrity, courage, tolerance, democratic living, a world outlook, or discernment of spiritual values becomes of little importance while excellence of performance remains the ultimate goal.

There are encouraging signs of dissatisfaction with such a philosophy among music educators. If and when new goals such as have been indicated here attract teachers and administrators in sufficient numbers, the secondary schools may be expected to follow what has happened to music in elementary education during the past fifty years. There is little reason to anticipate that our ensembles will suffer, either in numbers or quality. Whatever may be lost in proficiency will be compensated for by an expansion in the number of students enjoying musical experiences adapted to their abilities and a resulting community attitude based on the fact that a majority of its members have retained something very worth while which they discovered in school. Where can be found a better measure of the value of a school curriculum than the quality of citizenship which it produces in the community which it serves?

The Function of Music in General Education [1]

Philosophy of Music in General Education

(1) The function of music in general education should be not only to provide opportunity for the gifted child to experience and perform music at the level of

---

[1] From the report submitted by Rogers Whitmore, Columbia, Missouri, Southwestern Division Chairman, Music in American Education Committee on Music in General Education, and Harold E. George, Merriam, Kansas, Acting Chairman.

his capabilities, but should also provide for the enrichment and development of the personalities of all students through their heritage as citizens of America and the world. Music is needed to contribute to the rounding out of the whole child as a process of his natural development and should be a part of his daily experience.

(2) There is some phase of music in which every child can succeed. Equipment and opportunity for him to feel success must be provided. The child needs to be given confidence in every possible music activity.

Relationship of the Music Program
to the Whole School Program

(1) Music should be a part of the whole curriculum. While those engaged in teaching this phase of our education program must realize that they have problems and responsibilities that are peculiar to the field of music, they also must accept the fact that if music is to fill its proper place in the life of the student, school and community, it must be considered as a part of a composite and complex system dealing with all phases of the life of an individual and the society in which he lives.

(2) The music teacher should be close in his relationship with the administrator and others in the school.

(3) The music program will not be any better than the administrator desires it to be.

Problems That Exist in the Field of
Music in General Education

It is hoped that the following listing of problems will help to center attention and result in constructive thinking.

(1) How can all children be reached by music?

(2) How can those who do not voluntarily elect music be interested?

(3) How can provision be made for all levels of ability in music activities?

(4) How can select groups be maintained and simultaneously provide opportunities for all who wish to participate in music activities?

(5) Good music foundations frequently are not given in the elementary grades. How can this situation be improved?

(6) The pressure of performance programs is very great. How can this aspect of music education be handled to allow for adequate class work?

(7) The division between vocal and instrumental music activities in the schools has improved greatly. What can be done to expedite and enhance unification and cooperative understanding?

(8) Music people often do not take time to participate in faculty meetings and general educational affairs, probably due to overload. What can be done to impress the importance of this association upon music educators?

(9) Adequate materials and time for planning are necessary for efficient music work. How can information about proper teaching load be given to general administrators?

(10) Some school music people have a "conservatory philosophy" for music which makes it difficult for them to get along with fellow educators. How can a functioning philosophy be established?

(11) How can a more adequate training program for potential school music teachers be maintained in order that music teachers will better adjust themselves to the entire school program?

16

The Duality of Music [1]

General education has been defined as an effort to prepare youth to deal intelligently with personal and social problems common to all men in a democratic society. It is the unifying element in a culture—utilitarian only in the sense that it prepares, not for making a living but for living rationally today.

Music has an important place in general education because, as one of the arts, it clarifies and enriches our emotional life, satisfies our need for beauty and, through its communicative power, promotes understanding and good will. There are, of course, other cogent reasons for its importance, but those cited are sufficient to justify its essential role in a program of general education.

In planning such a program, the duality of music often is overlooked. Music is both a public and a private art or, as Filson Young puts it, "There are two souls of music; one universal and impalpable, the other individual and intimate." These intimate values of music for the self equal its universal values for society. Sometimes the message of music is best heard in private. There is no qualitative difference between the solitary enjoyment of music and group enjoyment of it. By stressing the social or group values of music, there is a tendency to forget that education is for *self* as well as for *society* and that there are private, individual values in music that are unique, which deserve to be fully understood and utilized. Education should promote these unique personal values as well as the more obvious social ones.

Another aspect of music's duality is its use for both aesthetic and recreational or utilitarian purposes. Although both these uses are equally valid, music educators often overstress the latter use. Art should not only be recreation; it also should be a *re-creation* of the individual, and it can be when its true meaning is understood and communicated to others.

It is the task of music educators to discern and to utilize these dual aspects of music. The student's ability should be developed to make and enjoy music *alone* as well as in a group, and to recognize that music is not only for pleasure but also for the enrichment of the human spirit.

---

[1] By Howard A. Murphy, Professor of Music Education, Teachers College, Columbia University, New York, New York.

CHAPTER II

ADMINISTRATION OF A MUSIC EDUCATION PROGRAM

THE RESULT OF MUCH investigation in the area of administration and supervision as it functions in a music department is available in two bulletins: *The Function of Music in the Secondary-School Curriculum* (published by MENC in cooperation with the National Association of Secondary-School Principals, 1952), and *Music Supervision and Administration in the Schools* (compiled by the Music Education Research Council of the MENC).

Because this detailed material is already in printed form, this chapter will report on two types of situations dealing largely with administration but with many implications for supervision.

I

In Cities With Less Than One Hundred Thousand Population [1]

The administrative assignments of the music director in small cities are important responsibilities. In every school system some *one* individual should be assigned the administrative responsibilities. His title may be head of the department, department coordinator, chairman of the music education program, etc. This person should work with the other school administrators in preparing such items as courses of study, schedules, in-service training, salaries of the music staff, accrediting of music courses, budgets and financing, philosophy of music teaching, public relations, etc. He should be consulted in the construction of music rooms and in the purchase of supplies and equipment to be used in the music education program, and work with the superintendent of schools and others in providing an efficient program in education through music. Time should be allowed for this administrative work. Because the majority of these administrative responsibilities are widespread, it is recommended that teacher-training institutions preparing music teachers should offer courses covering them.

The administration of music in small cities may be divided into five areas. The one in charge of administering the music education program will be referred to hereafter as coordinator.

(1) **Duties Within the Department.** The coordinator should arrange for and conduct meetings of classroom and music teachers, and should guide the selection of materials and techniques so that the work of one grade will integrate with the total program of music education.

Working with other music teachers as well as school administrators and classroom teachers, the coordinator should aid in determining standards of performance; should assist with making class schedules which allow for a minimum amount of time to be devoted to music instruction each week in each grade, and frequency of visitations by music specialists; arrange for appointment and selection of music personnel; arrange accreditation for the various music organizations in the school system; and administer the program of music testing within his school.

Permanent records in music might be maintained in his office as well as a central music library.

---

[1] From the report submitted by Frederic Fay Swift, Oneonta, New York. National Chairman, Music in American Education Committee on The Administration of Music Education in Cities with Less Than One Hundred Thousand Population.

(2) **Financial.** The coordinator should be in charge of preparing a budget covering all phases of music education, present this budget to his school administrator, and administer such funds as are approved for the music activities.

Requisitions, bids for instruments and other equipment, repairs and upkeep of instruments, including piano tuning, instructional supplies, etc., should be arranged for by the coordinator and proper records kept. Music education expenses are usually a part of the general school education budget.

It is suggested that the school have an adequate amount of money appropriated each year on a per-pupil basis and that the musical needs of all the children in the school be considered in the expenditures of these funds.

(3) **Duties Outside of the Department.** As community music activities take time and effort away from the school program, the coordinator should be guided by the over-all school policy.

Community music activities should be supported, when proper to do so, by all members of the music staff, and school music teachers should work with the professional musicians within the community. The coordinator, by serving as a member of various civic music groups, can aid in guiding community music activities. Adult education classes may be scheduled in the school or in cooperation with a neighborhood college.

(4) **Promotional.** The coordinator should be responsible for news releases pertaining to the music department and see to it that music activities within his school are given suitable publicity. Programs where parents will be able to see the actual program of music education in action should be arranged, as well as concerts, festivals, etc. Requests for concerts, parades, broadcasts, and TV appearances should be scheduled through the coordinator's office. The coordinator should cooperate with other administrative officers of the school in arranging a yearly calendar of events.

Music and athletics have been recognized as splendid media for public relations in any community. The program of public relations should be planned rather than entered into as requests are received.

(5) **General Education.** The coordinator, music staff, and school administrator should be in agreement on their philosophy of general education. Such a philosophy will allow for the growth and development of music within the school and the community; for children to learn through musical experiences in singing, playing, creative music, listening experiences, and in learning facts about music; that each child be encouraged to develop his musical interests, abilities, and skills as far as his own desires and capabilities allow; that the music program should provide for all of the children but also for the gifted child. The coordinator should guide the philosophy of the music department along proper lines in which he truly believes.

The administrative duties of the one in charge of music in cities under 100,000 population will include and will overlap to some extent those indicated for large cities, but naturally will include some of the more detailed activities of the small town music teacher.

II

The Administration of Music Education in Cities of More Than One Hundred Thousand [1]

In a large city, the very size of the staff of certificated music teachers employed demands that the responsibility for the organization of administration and super-

---

[1] From the report submitted by Harold C. Youngberg, Oakland, California, National Chairman, Music in American Education Committee on The Administration of Music Education in Cities of More Than One Hundred Thousand.

vision of a music program be vested in one individual. Since this person may delegate the duties and functions of supervision in the general music, vocal, and instrumental areas to assistants, he becomes the chief administrative officer who also serves, to a greater or lesser degree, as a supervisor. There is no fine line of demarcation between the functions of administration and supervision, as the two tend to overlap in most school situations. The larger the school system, the more likely is the chief music officer to spend the greater part of his time in the administration and direction of the music program. He may be designated as the head music supervisor, the coordinator, the chief music consultant, the chairman of the department or, in many cases, the director of music education. The last title is comprehensive and explanatory as it indicates that responsibility in several areas of the music instructional program will be delegated to supervisors or consultants while he guides and directs the over-all program.

The work of this administrative director includes an almost unlimited list of duties which largely classify themselves in the areas of selection, assignment and professional development of teacher personnel, the organization of the program at various grade levels, the development of curriculum, inter-administrative relationships, research, preparation of financial budgets, promotion and public relations, testing and evaluation, keeping of necessary records, and development of departmental philosophy. Much of this is done democratically with the assistance of several or all members of the supervisory and teaching staff.

The director should not act in an autocratic manner if he desires to win and maintain the loyalty and respect of the members of the department. High professional relations with colleagues should be maintained as well as an awareness of their problems. It is necessary constantly to keep abreast of the best practices and thinking in other educational areas. The director of music in a large city needs to be a musician and an educator, as well as a link between school and community in the interpretation of the music program to the public.

PERSONNEL

Selection of Staff. (Since the success of the music program in any school system is largely dependent on the quality of its personnel, the utmost care should be exercised in the selection of the teaching staff.) The schools may be inadequately housed and equipped but still carry on with a reasonable amount of success if there are master teachers at work.

(The selection of teachers is usually done by a personnel department. A few cities use the examination method for the selection of qualified candidates, but in most cases the music director makes recommendations to the personnel department and the superintendent in charge of the particular level for which the candidate is being chosen. Certainly, the candidate must be qualified in character, personality, musicianship, teaching skill, musical and educational preparation, and ability and desire to work unselfishly with children and colleagues.

Whatever method the large school system uses in the selection of music teachers, *the final responsibility for approval should rest with the music administrator* who can best evaluate the musical qualifications and preparation needed for successful teaching in the specific area under consideration.)

Assignment and Teaching Load. The success of the teacher will depend largely on the teaching situation and specific preparation for the position to be filled.

The teacher's classroom teaching load and program should be considered from the following standpoints:

(1) *Time for Planning.* Every teacher needs time for preparation or conference, particularly at the secondary level.

20

(2) *Comparable Load With Other Teachers.* It is generally understood that the music teacher may occasionally carry larger classes than the academic teacher for the sake of group success. Equivalent credit should be given for time involved in the preparation and presentation of public performances. Additional instructional personnel should be provided when the time comes to relieve the problem of over-enrollment in classes. A growing music department should not be penalized for lack of teacher time. Classes which are small due to specialized student needs should not be subject to rigid pupil-teacher ratio, but should be averaged or balanced with the larger enrollment in other classes.

(3) *Evaluation.* If there is doubt as to the success of a teacher in any given teaching situation, the administrator, after a conference with the teacher and principal, may recommend the transfer of the teacher to another school. The super-intendent or principal may call upon the supervisor or administrator for an evaluation of the teacher's work, but the responsibility for retention or release of the teacher should rest eventually with the superintendent.

Staff Development. It is the prime responsibility of music administration to unify, inspire, and develop good professional relations within the music staff. A staff working with a singleness of purpose is in a position to make itself felt in the community.

Administration is also responsible for musical and professional growth among teachers. Many methods are used, such as:

(1) *Workshops.* May be operated during or after school hours, Saturdays, or during the summer.

(2) *Teachers Meetings.* May be regularly scheduled or called as needed. Should be preceded by agendas and followed by summaries.

(3) *Classroom Demonstrations and Discussions.* Demonstrations may be given by successful teachers or by supervisors.

(4) *Technique and Method Classes.* Often given for academic credit and/or for salary increment credit if they meet over a considerable period of time. They may include techniques for piano, instruments and voice, conducting, organization of classroom work, or methods of teaching.

(5) *Bulletins.* These should deal with musical growth problems, be clearly written, and to the point.

(6) *Teacher-Supervisor-Administrator Planning.* For the sake of good democratic practices and *esprit de corps* within the staff, a good deal of growth is accomplished through joint planning, especially when such planning is translated into resultant action.

ORGANIZATION

The Elementary School (Kindergarten through sixth grade). It is assumed that music is considered as a subject of its own, as well as a vitalizing force in the several other educational areas. How best to present this program of music is a responsibility of music administration together with the cooperation of general administration. The music program should have emphasis placed on singing, listening, rhythmic, instrumental, music reading, and playing activities. Some of these may be emphasized more than others, but a balance is desirable. Many large cities tend to the self-contained classroom with guidance and direction from a few supervisors, consultants, or resource and helping teachers. Others use a combination of a small supervisory personnel working with helping or consultant teachers within buildings. Still others tend to a system of semi-departmentalization with classroom teachers who are specifically trained in music, art, science, physical education, etc.

During this current period of teacher shortages when personnel departments cannot be too selective as to the qualifications of the teachers they employ, it would seem that help of consultant, resource, or supervisory staff would be more essential than ever before, especially at the elementary level. Even with the best in-service aid, the classroom teacher, except in unusual instances, cannot provide opportunity for the full realization of individual musical needs.

With the trend toward the principal being the supervisor of his school, the role of the supervising consultant becomes more, rather than less, important. The principal cannot be expected to be totally qualified in all instructional fields and dependence upon the aid of specialists, particularly in music, is natural.

The Junior High School (Grades seven through nine). Music is normally presented by a special teacher in all general music, vocal, and instrumental areas in these grades. The offerings throughout the larger cities vary greatly, but a recent survey showed an overwhelming opinion favoring some type of general music in the seventh and eighth grades, bearing either full or half academic credit.[1] For the junior high school student, this may be the first opportunity to study under the guidance of a fully trained music teacher, and the door may be opened for a full realization of the inspiring influence of music. All types of instrumental and vocal participation should be available.

The attention should be centered on helping the adolescent child to secure a broad education through vocal or instrumental music, preferably both. Music should be scheduled continuously, even if less often than daily, through the seventh and eighth grades.

Senior High School (Grades nine or ten through twelve). With very few exceptions, music in the large city senior high school is offered on an elective basis. The offering needs to be wide enough to meet individual needs and desires. Some time during this period the average student, as well as the talented one, should be scheduled for music. Provision should be made for participation in glee clubs, choirs, orchestras and/or bands, as well as in theory, voice culture, music literature and history, and in some cases, dance band.

It is recommended that a minimum of seven periods be scheduled in the school day. Some large schools which are operating on a six-period day include a pre-period so that at least one musical organization can be scheduled before school without conflict. In this way, many students can participate daily in two musical activities if they so desire. It is recommended that all music groups and classes be scheduled on a five-day-per-week basis and granted equivalent credit with academic classes.

Most large senior high schools make it possible for students studying with private teachers to take examinations set up by the music administrator for at least partial school credit. It is required generally that such a student be a *bona fide* member of a school musical organization.

Junior College (Grades thirteen and fourteen). Many large and some of the smaller cities are continuing public education through the fourteenth grade by way of a junior college organization. It is part of the responsibility of music administration to see that a representative offering of music subjects is available to all junior college students and that a fine arts requirement, including some music, is in effect.

CONTINUITY BETWEEN ADMINISTRATIVE LEVELS

Because of the high mortality rate of music students between elementary school and junior high school, and between junior high school and senior high school, the administrative officer should develop ways and means to assure continuity of participation on the part of a large majority of the students. Several methods are in use in large cities to circumvent this.

---

[1] Research questionnaire by E. Lawrence Barr, Kalamazoo, Michigan, National Chairman, Music in American Education Committee on Music for Secondary Schools.

(1) Visits by the junior high school special music teachers to the feeding elementary schools, and similar visits by senior high school music teachers to the junior high schools to acquaint them with the musical opportunities in the school of the next level.

(2) Assembly programs presented in a lower school by musical organizations from the school of the next level.

(3) Coordination of enrollment blanks may be used whereby the music teacher in the junior high school, for example, may acquaint the senior high school teacher with the incoming class, giving the musical experience and ability of each student. The junior high school counselor who plans the program of entering senior high school students would receive copies of these blanks and subsequently attempt to schedule interested and talented students for music.

(4) Conferences with counselors may be called by the music administrator to acquaint these people with the advantages of musical participation from one school level to another. The administrator should prepare a master list of music classes for the counselors and principals to assist them in scheduling ongoing students into music.

MATERIALS AND SUPPLY SERVICES

It is the responsibility of the music administrator to provide various teaching materials in sufficient quantity to carry on a balanced program of music instruction.

Textbooks. Textbooks and other instructional materials are generally selected and approved by the administrator after careful consultation with the teaching staff. The purchasing is then done by the school purchasing department from requisitions prepared by the administrator or by other authorized staff members.

Small Supplies. Items of small supplies and equipment which are in constant demand in the classroom should be stored at one central point where they are available for efficient distribution. There should be a circulated list of such items so that some of these may be ordered by principals on semester or annual requisition basis.

Audio-Visual Materials. Audio and visual materials are generally distributed through the audio-visual department. The administrator sees that teachers have catalogs of the aids pertinent to music teaching and makes suggestions to the audio-visual department in regard to new materials in the field. These may be secured on loan and previewed by a committee of teachers who recommend the useful items for purchase.

Central Libraries. Many large cities use the central music library system for the distribution of supplementary choral and octavo music, orchestra, band, and small ensemble music. This is an efficient practice. The central library is most efficiently conducted when it is operated by a full- or part-time librarian who keeps the library in order, checks music in and out on request, mends and repairs damaged music, and orders replacement of missing parts or copies. Only such music as is in more than occasional demand should be kept in this library; otherwise, it may be stored in an accessible place in a warehouse or distribution center of the school system. For the most efficient use of the library, teachers should be provided with an up-to-date catalog of all available music, and they should be permitted to browse through the library in order to make intelligent decisions regarding choice of teaching materials. The use of a central library should not preclude the possibility of maintaining a library of music in each school.

RESEARCH AND RECORDS

Research. The music administrator, in order to keep the music department at its highest state of efficiency, should be constantly engaged in research and experimentation, and when significant results are obtained, these should be made available to all persons interested. This activity should involve many members of the staff.

In addition to the research which is purely educational, the administrator should study the problems of housing, equipment, supplies, repair, and maintenance as a long-term program of planning. Basically, all study and research should be carried on for the purpose of improvement of the department. Any results of such study are significant only if they are translated into action.

Records. Records of student progress are generally kept within the school itself, but many other records need to be kept by the administrator. These may include such items as a perpetual inventory of equipment, records of repair, and participation and growth of the department.

CURRICULUM DEVELOPMENT

Changing educational philosophy and trends make it necessary for the music curriculum to be under constant examination and that ways and means be set up for its revision and improvement. The administrator needs to be aware of these trends and interpret them to his staff. The development of the curriculum should then be the joint responsibility of director, supervisors, and teachers. It should include the music activities that are to be carried on, together with clearly defined objectives of the total program. The director guides the curriculum practices and affords frequent opportunities to evaluate the results.

It must be noted that the music curriculum will not be the same in all large schools. There should be freedom of action to apply the curriculum according to student background and preparation, according to economic advantages and disadvantages of the various communities within the city, and according to the weaknesses and strengths of the individual teachers.

BUDGET MAKING

Some states have specifications upon which budgets must be set up by law. In others, no pattern is set and yet a budget must be constructed which can be clearly interpreted. All boards of education are limited in the amount of money available for operation, and all departments must be considered in the distribution of this money. Therefore, there must be consideration of the immediate needs for the year, as well as a long-range plan of expenditure.

Budget Subdivisions. The following subdivisions usually are considered in budgets of large cities.

Instructional Salaries. This is the largest cost in the operation of a music program, and is usually the responsibility of general administration. Salaries of music teachers in large cities are a part of a general school salary schedule.

Textbooks, Instructional Methods, etc. Basically adopted or state-printed textbooks are normally provided from other funds than the music budget. Music administration is responsible for determining the variety and quantity of books to be provided.

Instrumental methods books, supplementary instrumental music, choral octavo music, community song books, etc., will be provided normally from the music budget, and provision must be made for inclusion of such items.

Supplies. Music is in this item in some cities, but in others it refers to the smaller items of equipment which do not come under capital outlay. Usually included are: strings, ligatures, reeds, staff liners, drum pads, small percussion articles, music paper, phonograph recordings, printed forms, repair materials, etc.

Basic Equipment.[1] This covers music equipment for new buildings and the replacement of major items.

---

[1] See Appendix, p. 307.

(1) *Pianos.* Basic sets of specifications should be made in order that pianos of consistently even quality are purchased.

(2) *Band and Orchestra Instruments.*

—Basic specifications should be set up for purposes of bidding. Some school systems request first-line instruments for the secondary schools and second-line instruments for the elementary schools.

—A basic instrumentation should be determined for schools at the various levels, and the equipment budget planned over a period of years so that the desired instrumentation eventually can be reached.

—Where new schools are being added to the present existing number of schools, it is advisable to include funds as a part of the total school cost to cover the complete basic instrumentation list as part of the instructional equipment.

—It is advisable to set up a plan for depreciation of equipment over a given number of years so that some budget for instruments purchased may be applied to replacement. Because of rising cost of repair, worn-out instruments should be discarded or disposed of according to board of education regulations.

(3) *Phonographs, Radios, Tape Recorders, Television Sets, etc.* These should be purchased on a rigid specification basis. These standards could be set up by the administrator in consultation with the audio-visual department. Standardization will result in faster and less expensive repair.

(4) *Orchestra and Chorus Risers, Music Stands, Instrument Storage Racks, etc.* These may be purchased or built in the school shops. Such items as portable risers may be stored at a central place where they are available on call from the various schools.

(5) *Repair and Maintenance.* This item deserves careful thought if equipment is to be kept in readiness for use. Means should be developed to have repairs done efficiently and quickly so that instruments are not out of use for long periods of time.

—Piano tuning should be done regularly with a minimum of two tunings per year, additional tuning as needed. Piano tuning may be awarded on bids but some large school systems employ one or more full-time tuners who not only tune, but repair and rebuild pianos.

—Band and orchestra instrument repair may be handled from rental funds. In states where no rental fee can be collected according to law, the repairing must be paid from budget funds. Some schools have regularly employed repairmen who work on a specified salary while others use reputable music stores on a job basis. Both methods have advantages and disadvantages. Permanently employed men may find they cannot keep up with the work at peak seasons and may not be equally capable of repairing all varieties of instruments. The farming-out of work, on the other hand, may mean greater expense as well as the necessity of inspection both before and after repair. The major repairs should be done in the summer when all damaged instruments can be assembled in a central place, and the music repairmen place bids.

(6) *Miscellaneous Expenses.* There are many financial items which cannot be categorized in the previous headings. Festival expenses, such as rental of organs and pianos, the hiring of accompanists, special stage and lighting effects, transportation, printing of programs, etc., are examples of such miscellaneous expenditures. It is advisable to include funds in the budget request to cover such situations.

PROMOTIONAL ACTIVITIES AND PUBLIC RELATIONS

Music administration must assume not only its responsibility for part of the total education of the child, but it also must interpret the music program to the citizens of the community. Since no subject in the curriculum lends itself better to public display than music, care must be exerted to see that all performance is of the best possible quality. By the same token, administration must see to it that music is not taught purely for performance sake at the expense of a well-rounded program where every student is able to participate at his own level.

There are many methods of acquainting the public with the objectives, aims, and results of the music program.

Support of Other Community Groups. A vital interest and participation on the part of the administrator in acceptable artistic activities of the community will lead to much support of the school music program.

Publicity. Legitimate means of publicity can help keep the public informed of the departmental activities. Such publicity should be with the approval of the superintendent of schools or such persons as he may delegate to screen and edit information to be made widely available. The administrator should maintain friendly relations with all community agencies which are in a position to publicly promote the school music activities.

Departmental Information to Parents. Keeping parents informed as to the curricular offerings is one of the best methods of promotion. This may be done by leaflet, brochure, mimeographed information, etc. In large cities this needs to be approved by the school administration.

Cooperation with Churches. Much care should be exercised in deciding when school organizations are to appear before church groups and in what capacity. Most schools have a code or an understanding regarding such relations.

Relations with Civic and Community Organizations. The feeling is widespread that school organizations should participate only in such events as are civic, patriotic, or of an educational nature, and that the sponsoring groups are noncommercial, noncompetitive, nonpolitical, and nonsectarian.

Concerts and Festivals. Such activities should be the outgrowth of regular planned classroom work and should represent the best possible quality of performance. Where there are many schools in the system, the administrator should clear dates for individual school concerts to avoid conflicts. City-wide festivals should be planned and organized by the music director and his staff in cooperation with the principals and any other administrators concerned. This affords fine interdepartmental and interadministrational relations.

Relations with the Musicians Union. Administration generally subscribes to the code of ethics adopted by the American Federation of Musicians, the Music Educators National Conference, and the American Association of School Administrators.[1] The music administrator should support actively these friendly relations with the musicians in the professional field.

Relations with the Commercial Trade. The music administrator acts to protect the commercial music distributor by preventing the duplication of copyrighted materials and discourages members of his staff from unethically recommending any specific merchandising establishment for the purchase of musical materials. This must be watched diligently in large cities where music merchandising is highly competitive.

The administrator must establish a policy for discouraging the unethical practice whereby school employees accept rebates or commissions from commercial concerns resulting from sales of instruments or materials to schools or students. It is recommended that a code similar to that covering relations with the Musicians

---

[1] See "Code of Ethics" in Appendix, p. 316.

26

Union be drawn up by the MENC in conjunction with the musical industries and distributors to eliminate this practice entirely.

Attitude Toward Private Instruction. Private teaching contributes greatly to the success of the school music program. The school music staff should maintain friendly working relations with private teachers and private study should be encouraged.

It is generally agreed that the school music staff should not recommend specific private instructors to students. Some large cities distribute a list of accredited or acceptable private teachers from which students may make their own selections.

INTERADMINISTRATIONAL RELATIONSHIPS

Relations with Other Departments. There has been too much of a tendency on the part of the music department to operate independently from other areas of the curriculum. Since music contributes only in part to the development of the child, the musician must work cooperatively with the teachers and administrators in other fields, being constantly alert to the best efforts and thinking contributed by these people. If this is not the case, music again will be put into the light of a frill and an appendage to the educational system.

Democratic Planning. The music administrator cannot afford to work independently from his staff. If a growing and harmonious atmosphere is to prevail, there needs to be democratic and cooperative planning in all projects which concern the whole department. Only if the staff is constantly conscious of this inclusion in departmental planning will there be an active situation where real leadership can be developed. It is the duty of the administrator to develop such leadership among his staff members, and it can be done by delegating responsibility when agreed-upon principles are to be put into action. Only by close cooperation of all people involved can a practical and workable philosophy for the music program in large cities be developed, and only then can music take its rightful place among the other areas of learning.

Selected Bibliography—Music Administration

GENERAL EDUCATION

Anderson, Vernon, Grim, P. R., and Gruhn, Wm. T. *Principles and Practices of Secondary Education.* New York: The Ronald Press, 1951. Chapters VI and XVII.

Campbell, C. M. *Practical Applications of Democratic Administration.* New York: Harper and Brothers, 1953.

Douglas, Harl. *Modern Administration of Secondary Schools.* Boston: Ginn and Company, 1954.

————. *Secondary Education.* New York: The Ronald Press, 1952. Chapters II, VIII, XXII.

Edmonson, J. B., Roemer, J., and Bacon, F. *The Administration of the Modern Secondary School* (4th ed.). New York: The Macmillan Company, 1953. Chapters I, II, III, XIX, and XXIII.

French, Will, Hull, J. D., and Dodds, B. L. *American High School Administration: Policies and Procedures.* New York: Rinehart & Company, Inc., 1951. Chapters XV, XVI, XXIV, and XXVI.

Hagman, Harlan L. *The Administration of American Public Schools.* New York: McGraw-Hill Book Company, Inc., 1951. Chapters I to VI, XII, XX, and XXI.

Lawson, Douglas E. *School Administration: Procedures and Policies.* New York: Odyssey Press, 1953. Chapters I, III, V, and VI.

Reavis, Wm. C., Pierce, P., Stulken, E., and Smith, B. *Administering the Elementary School.* New York: Prentice-Hall, Inc., 1953. Chapters VII, VIII, XI, and XII.

Yauch, Wilbur. *Improving Human Relations in School Administration.* New York: Harper and Brothers, 1949.

Yeager, William A. *Administration and the Pupil.* New York: Harper and Brothers, 1949.

MUSIC EDUCATION

Brooks, Marian B. and Brown, Harry. *Music Education and the Elementary School.* New York: American Book Company, 1946. Chapters VI, VII, XVI, and XVII.

Davis, Ennis. *More Than a Pitchpipe.* Boston: C. C. Birchard & Company, 1941. Chapters V and VI.

Dykema, Peter and Gehrkens, Karl. *The Teaching and Administration of High School Music.* Boston: C. C. Birchard & Company, 1941. Chapter XXX and Appendix.

Hindsley, Mark. *School Band and Orchestra Administration.* New York: Boosey & Hawkes, Inc., 1940.

Jones, Llewellyn Bruce. *Building the Instrumental Music Department.* New York: Carl Fischer, Inc., 1949.

Jones, Vincent. *Music Education in the College.* Boston: C. C. Birchard & Company, 1949. Chapter VII.
Mathews, Paul Wentworth. *You Can Teach Music.* New York: E. P. Dutton & Co., Inc., 1953. Chapters X and XI.
Morgan, Russell V. *Music: A Living Power in Education.* New York: Silver Burdett Company, 1953. Chapter IX.
Mursell, James. *Education for Musical Growth*, Part Three. New York: Ginn and Company, 1948.
————. *Music in American Schools.* New York: Silver Burdett Company, 1953. Chapters I, II, and V.
Myers, Louise Kifer. *Teaching Children Music in the Elementary School.* New York: Prentice-Hall, Inc., 1952. Chapters IX and XII.
Normann, Theodore. *Instrumental Music in the Public Schools.* Bryn Mawr, Pa.: Theodore Presser Company, 1939. Chapters III, IV, and V.
Wilson, Harry Robert. *Music in the High School.* New York: Silver Burdett Company, 1941. Part III.

MENC PUBLICATIONS

Business Handbook of Music Education. Distributed without charge by the Music Industry Council through MENC.
Function of Music in the Secondary-School Curriculum, The. Published in cooperation with the National Association of Secondary-School Principals. 1952. $1.00.
Music Buildings, Rooms, and Equipment. 1955.
Music Education Source Book. Edited by Hazel Nohavec Morgan. 1947. 4th Printing, 1951. $3.50.
Music Educators Journal, the official magazine of MENC.
Music for Everybody. Deals with school-community music relations and activities. 1950. $1.00.
Music in the Elementary School. Especially pertinent are the articles "The Elementary School Principal and His Music Program," by Marion Flagg; "Elementary School Curriculum" (reprinted from *Music Education Source Book*, pp. 4-8) ; "What Should Be Expected from the Classroom Teacher," by Karl D. Ernst; "Outline of a Program for Music Education," prepared by Music Education Research Council, William R. Sur, chairman. 1951. 50¢.
Music Supervision and Administration in the Schools. 1949. 50¢.
Musical Development of the Classroom Teacher. An enlightening presentation of the various forms and types of in-service aids in music being used throughout the country with concrete examples given in each case. 1951. 50¢

CHAPTER III

THE SUPERVISION OF MUSIC EDUCATION[1]

THE DIFFERENCES in the actual duties of supervisors are directly related to the size of the city or school system. In the small community with one or but a few elementary schools, the music supervisor does all the teaching of music and is, in reality, more a traveling teacher than a supervisor. In medium-sized cities, the teaching services of the music supervisor are spread more thinly, and it becomes necessary for classroom teachers to be instructed to carry on the music lessons through teachers' meetings, demonstration teaching, song outlines, and manuals or courses of study to be used as guides. The music supervisor continues to teach on a traveling schedule.

In the cities, the music supervisor is called upon to give expert advice to the administration in such matters as teacher selection and teacher evaluation, purchase of pianos, phonographs, and music books. In larger communities it is natural that the supervisor becomes responsible for certain matters pertaining to administration.

The changes which brought more administrative responsibilities for the music supervisor have created a need for specialization, not only for music teachers but for the music supervisors themselves. Today, there are supervisors for special phases of music and, in many cases, supervisors of music at the elementary level and at the secondary level. In some large cities, the supervision of bands and orchestras is so extensive as to be separated.

The growth and improvement of symphony orchestras, symphonic bands, and a cappella choruses in high schools, and the heavy enrollment in these groups, has created such teaching responsibilities that high school teachers are no longer free to travel to other schools to combine part-time supervision with teaching. At the present time, therefore, there are many kinds of music teaching positions and a variety of supervisory assignments.

The duties, authority, and responsibility of each type of position are determined by the school administration and, for the most part, the differences are still determined by the size of the school system rather than by any difference in the general philosophy of education, and of supervision in particular. Any discussion of the supervision of music must take into account the variety of music teaching or supervision assignments.

Types of Positions in Music Supervision

The Director of Music Education. This type of position is found in cities of approximately 60,000 and extends to the largest cities. The position generally involves no teaching assignments but has rather numerous administrative duties. This person is responsible for music education, in general, throughout the city. His duties include music instruction, teacher recruitment and selection, teacher assignments, heading the music courses of study, textbook selection, teacher-training in service, public relations, preparation of budgets, purchase of equipment, and technical adviser in all matters pertaining to music.

---

[1] From the report submitted by Lorrain E. Watters, Des Moines, Iowa, National Chairman, Music in American Education Committee on The Supervision of Music Education.

Attention of the reader is directed to Music Education Research Council Bulletin No. 18, *Music Supervision and Administration in the Schools*, Music Educators National Conference, 1949.

There are variations in different cities in the degree of responsibility a director may have in any of the above activities. For example in some cities directors have little or no authority in teacher selection, in book selection, or for giving advice in planning buildings. There is much evidence, however, that school superintendents are more than willing to widen the scope of the position when the person has demonstrated an ability to give dependable professional service.

The Director of Instrumental Music (Assistant Director or Supervisor of Instrumental Music). In large cities there is frequently a director (or supervisor) of instrumental music who is an instrumentalist and an experienced teacher of bands, orchestras, or instruments. The duties generally include responsibility for the instrumental music instruction and serving as advisor to the director in any of the duties listed under that position. Except in very large cities, such a position generally involves more time spent in classrooms in connection with actual instruction.

The Director of Vocal Music (Assistant Director or Supervisor of Vocal Music). In cities there may also be a director (or supervisor) of vocal music who, like the director or supervisor of instrumental music, spends the greater part of his or her time in the classrooms but assists the director in any of the duties listed under that position.

The Supervisor of Elementary Music. In cities there is frequently a supervisor charged with responsibility for the music in the elementary schools who assists the director as requested in any of his duties, but who spends most of his time in the school classrooms. Such positions rarely carry much administrative responsibility or authority. Unfortunately, such supervisors may have as many as thirty or forty elementary schools to visit, with the result that visits to the same teacher are infrequent.

In the larger cities it is generally necessary to employ a staff of several traveling supervisors of elementary schools, each of whom is assigned a number of buildings to visit at regular intervals to direct and assist the classroom teachers to teach their own grade music.

In smaller towns there may be only one person teaching music in the high school and supervising in the grades. Some high schools have their own teachers of band and orchestra, with other teachers in charge of choral music. Music in large junior high schools may be taught by full-time music teachers, or in smaller schools by the high school teachers part-time, or by the teachers who also teach music in elementary grades.

In towns having several elementary schools, a supervisor of elementary music may be found dividing her time between buildings, but probably more a traveling music teacher than supervisor.

Many states have state supervisors whose duties are largely administrative, advisory, and promotional, but who are giving more and more attention to in-service training for teachers in the field. A significant trend is found in the increase of the number of music supervisors at the county level.

Many colleges and universities, which give conscientious attention to the training of music teachers, maintain critic teachers who direct the "practice teaching" of student teachers. Strictly speaking, the work of the critic teacher, though related to the in-service training duties of supervisors in the field, is not properly considered supervision, as interpreted in this discussion.

Need for Supervision—Primary Grades

Many school systems, even in this day of teacher shortages, list the ability to teach music among requirements of primary teachers before employment.

Most authorities in music education agree that practically all primary teachers can teach their own music, with the benefit of occasional supervisory help and some reasonable provision for in-service training. There are very few primary teachers who are tone deaf, or who cannot carry a tune and by themselves learn to sing the simple primary songs. Those few who cannot carry a tune may exchange classes and teaching service with another primary teacher in the same building. It should be mentioned that modern school music song series have made available recordings of the children's songs, which are a remarkable teaching aid to primary teachers of limited singing ability.

It is being demonstrated constantly that primary teachers can teach their classroom music satisfactorily and prefer to do their own music teaching, once they have been encouraged by music supervisors and given confidence through in-service training in their ability to do so.

The attitude and understanding of the building principal toward the singing program is of tremendous importance since it is the responsibility of the principal to see that music, as well as the other desirable classroom experiences, is being given attention in each class. Most experienced principals, as well as music educators, know that almost all children can be helped to sing on the tune with their class if some intelligent effort is made on the part of the teacher to help those pupils who appear to be less alert or experienced in responding to melody and rhythm.

If the classroom teachers are expected to teach their own music, there is great need for a music specialist to direct in-service training and to help each teacher improve her own ability to teach music. It has been demonstrated that the great majority of primary teachers can teach music effectively, provided the right type of supervisory help is available. This is *not* the case in the intermediate grades.

Need for Supervision—Intermediate Grades

At the intermediate grade level even an average standard of classroom music often seems to be too difficult for most classroom teachers, and practically impossible for them without adequate supervisory help. The college preparation of intermediate classroom teachers is insufficient in music, owing to the wide range of subject requirements. Minimum requirements for one to teach music in an intermediate grade are as follows:

(1) Ability to sing (carry the tune) of the songs of the grade. Ability to sing naturally means ability to sing with a pleasing tone quality, with reasonably good vocal habits and correct diction in order to provide good teaching examples for children to imitate and follow.

(2) Ability to read music of the grade in order to learn the songs and to be able to present them to children.

(3) Some knowledge of, and ability to interpret, notation regarding rhythm, keys, chromatics, and note values, at least not inferior to that of the more musical children of the grade.

(4) Some ability to play piano accompaniments and to play songflutes and the autoharp is highly desirable, probably necessary.

(5) Some background of information about music literature, composers, the contributions of various peoples, and practical understanding of the social significance of music.

(6) Knowledge of the different musical instruments, at least not inferior to that of the pupils of the grade.

(7) Ability to carry a simple harmony part. Practically all children are potentially able to sense and enjoy part-singing or simple harmony. Two-part singing

is generally very successful in fifth grade, and many fourth grades sing two-part songs when the teacher is capable of making the most of children's natural, but latent, ability. Few, if any, teachers can develop the harmonic feeling of children unless they themselves have enough ear training to be able to hear and carry the simple second part.

Simple three-part singing in the sixth grade is recognized nationally as reasonable, attainable, and an important classroom experience. Teachers who can present and develop two-part harmony rarely find much difficulty with three-part harmony, so far as their own hearing ability is concerned; but a teacher who cannot give the children leadership in two-part music is hopelessly unable to cope with even the simplest three-part chords.

Radio, television, and widespread use of recordings in homes give modern children a great deal of information, background, and interest in music. Normal children of the intermediate grades, many of whom are already learning to play piano and the instruments of the band and orchestra, will quickly surpass the intermediate classroom teacher who has not had college courses or music instruction *unless the school system provides a competent person to help these teachers grow in music through a simple nontechnical in-service training program.*

Administrators in many school systems who are aware of the natural possibilities of children to learn music readily, and of their dependence upon competent teaching, have adopted a plan of limited departmentalization in intermediate grades which provides music instruction by specially trained teachers at no added instructional expense. Classes pass to the music room on schedule with the music teacher carrying the full pupil hour load.

This plan of providing talented and trained teachers for music in these grades, obviously administratively practical, can be accomplished at no extra expense, reduces need for traveling teachers, and even makes possible a decrease in the overhead of the supervisory staff.

Several successful plans in current operation have the advantage of better music instruction and less added instructional costs, for example:

(1) Music teachers give full time to grades IV, V, and VI in elementary schools with enrollments of over 200.

(2) Assign the music teacher to intermediate grades in two smaller elementary schools on alternating days with the art teacher.

(3) Music teachers give full time to the intermediate grades, with either teaching or supervisory responsibility for music in the primary grades of the same building.

(4) Music teachers teach music in the intermediate grades with other part-time teaching assignments, either in academic subjects in the building or in music in a neighboring junior high school.

(5) Require classroom teachers to teach their own music, *but with a definite requirement of ability to teach music* applying in the selection and employment of the teachers. If teacher shortages exist, such abilities cannot be insisted upon and the plan is not practical. It should be noted that this plan necessitates available and adequate supervisory personnel.

Plans as above, which provide teaching in music, art, or physical education by talented, trained, and competent teachers also make possible the scheduling of a given group of pupils with one teacher for an entire half day in the core curriculum. Thus, these plans have the advantages of both the self-contained classroom in the core subjects and limited departmentalization by providing expert training in the arts, with minimum requirements for supervisory outlay.

Despite the present emphasis on the "self-contained classroom," there is a noticeable trend to provide specially trained teachers in music in the intermediate grades.

Music Supervision in Secondary Schools

The need for music supervision is undoubtedly greatest in the elementary schools; however, in communities large enough to have several junior and senior high schools, there is need for over-all guidance and coordination, besides in-service training for the continuing turnover of young and inexperienced teachers replacing the veterans.

The need for supervision is seen in the problems of "bridging the gap" from the junior high school to the senior high school where music instruction is concerned with performance in fine musical organizations. The very complexity and breadth of the technical skills required of secondary school music teachers calls for a supervisor who is at the same time a versatile musician as well as a mature educator and administrator.

The superintendent and principal must look to a staff member who, as a music specialist, knows the field completely and thoroughly. This expands the important functions of the supervisor to include responsibilities definitely administrative in character, such as are listed under the duties of a director of music education. Unfortunately, expanding administrative duties reduce the amount of time and energy the director can give to his most valuable service, which is to the pupils in the classrooms in the form of improved music instruction through classroom visitation. Since the preceding chapter deals with the Administration of Music Education, the concern here has been with but one of the director's duties, that of supervision.

Present Philosophy of Supervision

In our school systems which are responsible for educating the youth of the land, democracy should be demonstrated and practiced. There has been a gradual departure from the traditional authoritarian supervision in the direction of a more democratic procedure. The quasi-military "line and staff" authority has been eased in favor of a system of cooperation based on good human relations between teachers, principals, supervisors, and all school personnel. It was natural that there would be the inclination to seek a different job title, which would be free from undesirable connotations and which would fit more happily into the democratic administration of today. While the term *supervisor* is still used widely, there is considerable use of the terms *consultant, coordinator, counselor, teaching supervisor, supervising teacher, resource teacher, helping teacher, chairman,* and the like.

Regardless of the title, it is rather well understood that the greatest value of the music expert is as a helper to the teacher, and certainly their relationship should be one of willing cooperation. This assumes that the music supervisor is himself or herself an expert and mature teacher with a wide range of training and experience, and one possessed of personal qualities which promote friendly relationships.

Successful principals are quick to make use of the help of available supervisors of music, when such supervisors demonstrate their ability to be of genuine assistance to classroom teachers. Supervisors and principals should work together with genuine regard for the morale and self-confidence of the classroom and special music teacher.

The modern philosophy of school administration has emancipated not only the teacher but the supervisor as well. The supervisor, once charged with responsibility for music instruction itself in every classroom, and required to inspect, make reports, and rate teachers, is now usually freed from such obligations.

Qualifications of a Music Supervisor

(1) *Demonstrated Success as a Teacher.* While not all fine teachers may have the qualities necessary for success in supervision, a person who is *not* a successful teacher *cannot* possibly be expected to be successful in helping others to teach. Therefore, a supervisor must be, first, a thoroughly good teacher of the phases of the subject to be supervised.

(2) *Some Degree of Maturity.* Any person qualifying as a teacher of demonstrated success may be expected to have had some experience and, consequently, some maturity. Maturity in this sense may not necessarily refer to one's age or years of experience, but refers to emotional maturity and general outlook as a person and as an educator.

(3) *Personal Qualities Indicating Good Human Relations.* Since the mission of the supervisor is helping other teachers, it is necessary that the supervisor be a friendly and likable person able to communicate enthusiasm for the subject, able to take genuine pleasure in the accomplishments of others, able to make suggestions in a tactful yet straightforward manner without damaging the self-confidence of the teacher.

(4) *Recognized Skill as a Musician.* Since music education involves singing and, to a lesser extent, playing orchestra and band instruments, it is preferable that a supervisor of music have a background of *singing.* This is particularly necessary for music supervisors in elementary schools, where vocal music is a most important musical expression.

Musicianship for the city director of music may lie in the field of singing, band or orchestra, or conducting. Concert pianists may be totally unprepared for the work of music supervision unless the pianist has also gained a background in singing or in the other ensemble instruments, not to mention general education.

(5) *Professional Training Above That of the Average Teacher.* It is likely that most school systems expect their supervisors to hold the master's degree or its equivalent, and it is probably true that at least five years of study are required to enable a music supervisor to have the necessary minimum background in music and education. Further study in any field of music or education would be desirable, especially as it contributes to the over-all qualifications of supervisors.

(6) *Broad Educational Understanding.* Since music education is a part of the education of American children, it follows that music supervisors must understand the place of music in all education. Knowledge of all school subjects and of all school levels is important to supervision in any field of subject matter. Broad educational understanding can only come to a music supervisor who knows much more than music, and who remains a student of education every day of his life.

The Way Music Supervision Functions

For several years, representative music educators throughout the country have cooperated in finding out just how music supervision is being accomplished today.[1] These educators have set down the following statement of implements and devices, listed in the order of their relative effectiveness, by which supervisors go about their work of helping teachers teach music better.

(1) Planned classroom visits by a supervisor with preparation and follow-up at individual conferences.

(2) Teacher meetings of various types.

---

[1] Music Education Research Council Bulletin No. 18, *Music Supervision and Administration in the Schools,* pp. 11-14.

(3) Demonstration teaching for groups of teachers by other teachers or supervisors.

(4) Bulletins, suggestions, outlines, and various written communications offered by supervisors.

(5) Committee participation by teachers under supervisory leadership.

(6) Teachers individually permitted to visit and observe experienced teachers.

(7) Participation in preparing pupils for joint festivals or all-city programs.

(8) Encouragement of special study by teachers with recognition through salary increments.

(9) Teacher participation in textbook adoption committees.

(10) Use of audio-visual aids in improving instruction.

(11) Attendance at music conference meetings—national, state, county, and local.

(12) Professional reading, directed and suggested by supervisors.

(13) Attendance at concerts—artist series, college and school programs.

(14) Preparing and presenting programs and broadcasts.

(15) Music contests and clinic festivals.

Supervision on a Consultant Basis [1]

Music supervision on a consultant basis deals primarily with the classroom teacher in the self-contained classroom. Some classroom teachers seem to prefer the consultant or "on call" type of assistance. Full cooperation and understanding on the part of the principal is a primary requisite. Suggested ways in which the music consultant may operate are:

Teachers learn the type of consultant service available through:

—Meetings with administrative groups and consultants.

—Orientation of teachers new to a system.

—Faculty meetings at the school buildings.

—Principal-teacher conferences.

Consultant services are made more effective by:

—A flexible service.

—Time for meetings and office work.

—Conditions which tend to create a strong feeling of teacher-pupil-consultant rapport.

—Conferences on school time or after school hours if requested by the teacher.

Teacher improvement through in-service training:

—Music consultants assume the responsibility of leadership in the in-service training program.

—A fully organized in-service training program with college credit is desirable on a voluntary basis.

Consultant as a resource person.

—Consultant keeps informed on new methods and materials and the underlying educational principles involved in their use.

—Materials are kept constantly available to allow for integration within the music program and with other subjects.

---

[1] From the report submitted by Charles F. Lehman, Fort Worth, Texas, Southwestern Division Chairman, Music in American Education Committee on The Supervision of Music Education.

—The consultant should be qualified and immediately available to act as an adviser in the selection of equipment, such as pianos and audio-visual aids.

The consultant should also act as a liaison person in the preparation of performing groups in interschool programs, and should maintain public relations through the press, radio, television, festivals, community sings, and civic organizations. He should establish contact with other educational organizations, such as the Association for Supervision and Curriculum Development.

Summary. For the achievement of objectives sought under the present-day philosophy of education, it is necessary, even in the small school system, that in the primary grades a competent music supervisor or consultant should be available to assist classroom teachers.

In intermediate grades, it is recommended that music teachers of special training and ability be provided. If classroom teachers are expected to teach their own music, considerable supervisory help must be regularly available.

In cities of 60,000 population or more, it is desirable that a music director be assigned over-all responsibility as the head, coordinator, consultant, or supervisor. In the larger cities it will be necessary to provide supervisors of vocal music, of instrumental music, and of music in the elementary schools. It is strongly recommended that a head or director be selected. It has been demonstrated that avoiding the selection of a head, and depending upon two or more persons to share the responsibility for music leadership, does not make for satisfactory professional relations or satisfactory working conditions in general.

Music Consultant Service for the Self-Contained Classroom [1]

It is generally appreciated by school administrators that music is necessary for a well-rounded education, and that music can enrich classroom experiences of children. Leaders in the field have recognized the truth of this statement and have promulgated it in speech and in print. Local superintendents and principals may believe it, too, but they have been at a loss to know how to implement a music program in their classrooms. It is the thesis of the present writers that such implementation can be realized only through competent consultant service.

If the elementary classroom teacher should or must teach music, she ought to have help from someone who has expert knowledge and experience in school music. Call that "someone" supervisor, coordinator, helping teacher, or consultant in music, he must be available to assist, no matter how large or how small the school system. If such a person is not available the burden of teaching music is too great for the average classroom teacher. Music *is* a "special" subject requiring a know-how not to be expected of everyone. To lighten the teacher's burden, and especially to *make music meaningful to every child*, a supervisor or consultant must be on call to help in planning lessons and projects, to demonstrate, to evaluate new methods and materials, to provide resources, and to stimulate.

It is not the intention here to take issue with those who believe that the classroom teacher can and should teach music. The ideal situation for American schools is that every classroom teacher be talented and trained in music to the extent that she can make music a meaningful experience every day in the lives of the children under her guidance. Educators know that this ideal may never be realized, especially in those school systems which are being overwhelmed by the very numbers of children entering the elementary grades. It is difficult enough to find teachers to

---

[1] By Lawrence W. Chidester, Chairman of the Department of Music, Texas College of Arts and Industries, Kingsville, and Christine B. Rockefeller, Principal of the Prescott School, Corpus Christi, Texas. This material is a summary of items discussed in detail in a book manuscript by the authors. *Music Educators Journal*, January 1955.

man the ever-increasing number of classrooms in America, without insisting u̲ₓ
complete qualifications from each and every one of them.

In a recent survey in a large city school system only twenty-six per cent oₓ
the classroom teachers felt they were competent to teach music without assistance.
However, sixty-one per cent felt they could teach music with help (nine per cent
felt totally incompetent). Thus, the problem is a real one—of vital importance. If
children are to receive experiences in music, the schools must provide competent
supervisory or consultant service.

There need be no quibbling over terminology, that is, what to call the person
who performs this necessary service. The Music Education Research Council says
that the term "supervisor" should be applied only to a person responsible for guiding
the teaching of others; that the term "consultant" or "resource teacher" should be
applied to one who assists upon call. Because of recent economic, social, and
educational changes, current practices in supervision have been undergoing keen
scrutiny. If the classroom teacher needs the type of assistance embraced by the
term "consultant," so label the expert and allow him to go about his business.

The fact must be faced that the need is here, that it must be met. "Regardless
of controversy over the need for general supervision, it seems obvious that the
average classroom teacher will continue to require specific help in the fields of
music and art." [1] Thus concludes the Music Education Research Council.

Two important questions arise from the above discussion: What are the specifics
of the task, and what are the ways and means of accomplishing them? The following outline attempts to answer only the first question. It is a summary of some of
the services which the classroom teacher, the principal, the music director, and the
community may expect from a music consultant.

As to the relative importance of the various services, it is likely in the initial
stages of music consultant service in a school system that actual demonstrations
in the classroom will be most in demand. However, as classroom teachers become
more proficient in music teaching there will be more conferences, more teacher-
pupil-consultant planning sessions rather than so many actual classroom appearances
by the consultant.

SERVICES FOR THE TEACHER IN THE CLASSROOM

Teacher-pupil-consultant planning.
(1) Sequences of music activities for a period of time.
(2) Appropriate music to correlate with a subject.
(3) Programs.

Actual participation with the class.
(1) Teaching a new song, by rote or by note.
(2) Introducing new materials and equipment.
(3) Introducing a new area in music, such as rhythms, autoharp.
(4) Improving choral numbers already in progress
(5) Aiding with any phase of the music program as requested.

Assistance as a resource person.
(1) Finding supplementary songs and dances for units.
(2) Locating unusual items of interest for correlation.
(3) Evaluating new materials and equipment and helping to make them available to teachers.
(4) Preparing source materials units for the use of teachers.
(5) Acting as a liaison person in contacting outside resource people who will
come to the classroom.

---

[1] *Music Supervision and Administration in the Schools.* Music Education Research Council Bulletin
No. 18.

Evaluation of group activity.
(1) Evaluating music units in progress by discussion with class and teacher.
Helping the individual child.
(1) Aiding the uncertain singer.
(2) Listening to individuals who are learning independence by individual performance.
(3) Giving the unusually bright child an opportunity for more expression.
(4) Helping the slow child find activities in which he can excel.

SERVICES FOR THE TEACHER IN CONFERENCES

Individual conferences.
(1) Preplanning with the teacher before consultant works with class.
(2) Preplanning with the teacher for projects, long or short.
(3) Giving individual instruction when the teacher feels the need.
(4) Suggesting the location of materials.
(5) Giving help over the telephone during the day and at night.
Group conferences.
(1) Planning by grade level for a particular phase of music.
(2) Planning an entire school music program, all levels.
(3) Assisting special-interest groups of teachers who wish to learn a certain aspect of music.
(4) Advising faculty meetings where common problems such as scheduling are discussed.
(5) Orienting groups of new teachers to the music program.
(6) Assisting interschool groups of teachers in finding materials suitable for their classes.
(7) Demonstrating new materials and equipment to any group.
(8) Planning programs.

SERVICES FOR THE TEACHER IN THE
USE OF AUDIO-VISUAL MATERIALS

Assistance in the use of the phonograph.
(1) Helping the teacher plan listening lessons.
(2) Demonstrating the use of records for teaching a rote song.
Assistance in the use of the tape recorder.
(1) Demonstrating the use of the tape recorder.
(2) Preparing tape recordings for teaching songs and entire programs.
Evaluation of commercial phonograph and tape recordings.
(1) Visiting music stores to find new recordings.
(2) Preparing bulletins evaluating new recordings.
(3) Locating specific recordings for particular needs.
Assistance in planning live radio programs.
Assistance in selecting recorded programs for broadcasting to schools.
(1) Evaluating commercial series available to radio stations.
Assistance with resource materials to be used in preparation for listening to radio or television programs.

SERVICES FOR THE TEACHER IN
IN-SERVICE PROFESSIONAL GROWTH

Participating in group consultant planning.
Group leadership.
Demonstrations or actual teaching of music when requested by group.
Assistance to teachers who prepare classes for observation by others.

Presentation and evaluation of new materials and equipment.
Assistance as resource person to any group.
Assistance in the orientation program for new teachers.

SERVICES FOR SCHOOL-COMMUNITY RELATIONS

Liaison agent between school and community.
(1) Bringing school performing groups to the attention of community service organizations.
(2) Helping civic-sponsored performing groups arrange concerts in schools or to present special children's concerts.
(3) Arranging field trips to places of musical interest.
(4) Stimulating community attendance at school music programs.
(5) Arranging interschool music programs.
(6) Enriching in-service education of teachers through community contacts.
(7) Finding community resources which may be used to enrich classroom music experiences.

Generator of public relations.
(1) Supplying the press with accurate information about school music programs.
(2) Working with radio stations on programs of interest to schools.
(3) Giving talks on the school music program to various civic groups.
(4) Assisting the teacher with P.T.A. programs.
(5) Helping the P.T.A. with their community-wide activities.
(6) Stimulating interest in school visitations.
(7) Assisting the teacher and children in arranging exhibits.
(8) Aiding individual schools in preparing for all-school and all-city music festivals.

A member of the community himself.
(1) Taking an active part in community musical organizations.
(2) Establishing good rapport between the schools and the community.
(3) Encouraging teachers to find their places in the community.
(4) Representing the music staff wherever he goes.

SERVICES FOR THE SCHOOL PRINCIPAL

Conferences with groups of principals.
(1) Participating in joint consultant-principal meeting to discuss ways of improving consultant service.
(2) Participating in committee conference studying methods of working together.

Conferences with individual principals.
(1) Preplanning with the principal in September.
(2) Conferring with the principal during the school year.
(3) Assisting in preparation of music budget, purchasing music supplies, evaluation of materials, preparation of inventory, scheduling.

SERVICES WITH THE MUSIC STAFF

Cooperation with the music director.
(1) Arranging the all-city music festival.
(2) Attending weekly music faculty meetings.
(3) Suggesting materials for the resource library.
(4) Serving as liaison agent between elementary classroom teachers and junior high music teachers.

Cooperation with other music consultants.
(1) Coordinating all elementary school music activities.
(2) Arranging interschool programs.

(3) Preparing resource materials bulletins for teacher.

(4) Evaluating new materials and equipment.

(5) Issuing idea bulletins concerning teacher music activities.

Contemporary philosophy of education for the elementary school is focused on the self-contained classroom. Even the teaching of "special" subjects such as music is now the duty of the classroom teacher. Most of these teachers are inadequately prepared; they need help in making music meaningful in the classroom. Such help must come from music educators who are prepared to supply at least a minimum of the services outlined above. Only thus will be realized the goals of education through music. It becomes a challenge and an opportunity.

Selected Bibliography—Music Supervision

GENERAL EDUCATION

Adams, Harold and Dickey, Frank. *Basic Principles of Supervision.* New York: American Book Company, 1953.

Barr, A. S., Burton, William, and Brueckner, Leo. *Supervision.* New York: D. Appleton-Century Co., 1947.

Fitzpatrick, E. *Philosophy of Education.* New York: Bruce Publishing Co., 1953.

Gordon, Lee. *An Introduction to Education in Modern America.* New York: Henry Holt and Company, Inc., 1953. Part V.

Klausmeir, H. J. *Principles and Practices of Secondary School Teaching.* New York: Harper and Brothers, 1953.

Leonard, J. P. *Developing the Secondary School Curriculum.* New York: Rinehart & Company, Inc., 1953.

McNerney, Chester T. *Educational Supervision.* New York: McGraw-Hill Book Company, Inc., 1951. Chapters VI, VII, VIII, and XIII.

Unstattd, J. G. *Secondary School Teaching.* Boston: Ginn and Company, 1953.

Wiles, Kimball. *Supervision for Better Schools.* New York: Prentice-Hall, Inc., 1950.

MUSIC EDUCATION

See: "Music Education" and "MENC Publications" bibliography listed for "Administration of Music Education," p. 27.

CHAPTER IV

MUSIC EDUCATION AND INTERNATIONAL RELATIONS

THE CONTINUING PURPOSE of those working in the area of music education and international relations will be to assist executive officers and members of the MENC in maintaining continuity and sustained direction in the conduct of its steadily expanding program of international activities and intercultural exchanges.

These intentions have been translated into practical action in the past few years and will continue to guide future projects by:

—Assembling and making available sources of information that apply to immediate needs.

—Bringing the MENC membership not only up to date on events but abreast with MENC achievements, commitments, and obligations in foreign cultural and educational affairs.

—Suggesting possible extensions and improvements in the continuing development of long-term projects.

—Offering constructive suggestions in reference to provisional ventures.

American Music—The Government's Cultural Ambassador [1]

If you, a musician, had been traveling in Europe, Latin America, or certain areas of the Near East and Far East in the last few years, you would have been much pleased at the increasing interest in the music of your fellow countrymen. It is possible that in 1952, for example, you might have visited Austria. In Vienna you would have noticed the Kosmos Theater operated by the United States Information Service, the overseas arm of the U. S. Information Agency. Playing there was a show entitled "Broadway Calls." After a number of selections from current musical shows, you could have heard Menotti's *The Telephone*. Had you followed the production on tour, you would have heard this work performed no less than eighty-seven times.

In Paris you might have attended a referendum concert and heard Paul Creston's *Second Symphony* win first place in an international contest. Were choral music your interest, it is possible that you might have attended a concert of American music at the Schoenbrunn Palace in Vienna. You would have heard works of Randall Thompson, Samuel Barber, Walter Piston, and Virgil Thomson. As a special attraction, American conductor William Strickland could have been heard leading the Piston *Concertino for Piano and Chamber Orchestra*.

Should your travels have taken you to the Far East during a Christmas season of the past two years, you might have attended concerts sponsored by the Young People's Symphony Society of Tokyo. Among the American works played were Berezowky's *Christmas Festival Overture* and the *Serenade of Carols* of Morton Gould, both first performances for Japan. Closing the program, the *Hallelujah Chorus* in Japanese could have been heard, performed by seven hundred high school students in a manner which would rival that of any of our fine high school choruses.

A detour to Saigon, Viet Nam, would have given you a chance to see one thousand Vietnamese listen with rapt attention to a song recital by the radio officer

---

[1] By David S. Cooper, Chief, Music Section, Information Center Service of the U.S. Information Agency, Washington, D. C. Reprinted from *Music Educators Journal*, September-October 1954.

of the U. S. Information Service there. Enthusiastic applause greeted the program composed of Negro spirituals, American folk songs, ballads of the 19th and 20th centuries, and selections from the current Broadway musicals.

In 1954, a trip through Spain might have coincided with a Week of North American Culture in Madrid. As part of this ambitious project there was given an orchestral concert of American music, which included four well-known works by our composers: *Festival Overture* of William Schuman, the *Afro-American Symphony* of William Grant Still, the *Fifth Symphony* of Peter Menin, and the beloved *Concerto in F* of Gershwin.

In Athens the police were required to direct the eager audience thronging to witness one of the most exciting music projects now in progress overseas. You would have been lucky to get a seat in the largest auditorium in Athens where, under the sponsorship of the U. S. Information Service, a program of Greek and American music was to be given. An offshoot of an earlier series in which only the Greek compositions were given live performances, while the American works were recorded, the present series included live presentations of the works of both countries performed by distinguished Greek artists. Critical acclaim has been universally enthusiastic, and you would have seen graphic evidence of the friendship that can be generated through joint presentation of the musical art of two nations.

A LONG-RANGE CULTURAL PROGRAM

The question might well be asked, "How does all this music by such a variety of American composers come to be played in so many parts of the world?" The answer is that these performances are by no means accidental but are part of a long-range cultural program conducted by a recently established government agency, the U. S. Information Agency. Nearly everyone is familiar with the radio phase of our overseas information program, the Voice of America. People do not always realize, however, that radio is only one branch of that effort and through such related media as press, motion pictures, and information centers, an overseas audience of millions is given a picture of the United States and what it represents.

One of the stated aims of the U. S. Information Agency is to delineate "those important aspects of the life and culture of the people of the United States which facilitate understanding of the policies and objectives of the Government of the United States." The use of music in the Agency's program is designed to give all people of the world evidence of one phase of the "culture of the people of the United States." We seek to dispel the impression, held too firmly by many of our friends and vigorously propagated by our enemies, that we are a materialistic nation, unconcerned with spiritual or cultural values. Evidence of our contributions to music cannot fail to strengthen cultural ties with countries which place strong emphasis on music and whose traditions in this art are deep and long standing.

Music programs are carried on in two areas of the U. S. Information Agency: the International Broadcasting Service (the Voice of America) and the Information Center Service. The Voice of America presents a comprehensive picture of musical activities in the United States that reflect American culture, achievement, and progress in the world of music and its allied arts. The Voice obtains its musical material from live performances as they occur throughout the nation. This material is produced for rebroadcasting over local radio stations overseas.

Responsibility for the other aspects of the Agency's music program lies with the Information Center Service, the area of the Agency which administers our network of overseas libraries. Before proceeding further it might be of interest to consider briefly the nature of our Information Centers.

U. S. INFORMATION CENTERS

Information Centers are basically special purpose libraries and may be found in almost all the major cities of the world. They contain a wide assortment of books and periodicals on all aspects of American life, as well as collections of music and phonograph records of American works or foreign works by American artists. An Information Center is also headquarters for such related activities as the translations, presentations, and exhibit programs. In a very real sense these centers are establishments where people may come and absorb the spirit of this country in an institution exemplifying the best of our democratic tradition.

The focal point of the Agency's music program is the Music Section of the Information Center Service in Washington. Periodically, the Music Section sends abroad packets of scores and recordings of American works to keep our overseas posts supplied with the best of the latest releases. It also answers hundreds of requests for services and materials not covered in the packets. As an indication of the use our record collections receive, several posts have complained there has been such a demand that every disc in the Center needs to be replaced. These recordings are in constant use for concerts at Information Centers and for loan purposes to private individuals or groups.

Naturally, the library operation in a field such as music is only the beginning, and the use of our musical material is by no means limited to the four walls of an Information Center. Perusal of various items in the music collections by professional musicians often results in concert performances which might otherwise never have taken place. Our staffs are constantly on the alert to stimulate interest on the part of orchestral and choral conductors, chamber music groups, solo artists, and amateurs. To assist in the performance of orchestral works, the U. S. Information Agency maintains depositories of orchestral scores and parts in certain of the major capital cities of Europe, the Far East, and Latin America. These collections are available to local orchestras on a loan basis and include works which are not directly controlled by the foreign agents of American publishers.

VARIED ACTIVITIES OF INFORMATION CENTERS

Often, even though a performance is initiated by private arrangements between the publisher and the performing group, the Information Center will come into the picture. A case in point recently took place in Zagreb, Yugoslavia. Stravinsky's *The Rake's Progress* was presented for the first time by the opera company of that city. The conductor and leading members of the cast made frequent trips to the Information Center to study the only recording in Yugoslavia.

An astonishing variety of correspondence passes over the desk of the Chief of the Music Section in the course of a day. Requests for every conceivable type of service keep the staff busy. Vienna, for example, may read in the *New York Times* of an interesting concert of chamber music by composers whose works are in manuscript. The Music Section sets about locating the composer, obtaining his permission to use his music, and finally making arrangements for the reproduction and shipment of parts. A contemporary music society in London is interested in performing works by American composers. Can the Music Section help? All Information Centers have received recordings of the Music in America Series issued by New Records, Inc. Many listeners abroad are astonished that in the late 18th and early 19th centuries we had some very respectable but little known composers who, though no Haydns or Mozarts, still made a distinct contribution. Can the scores and parts of these works be obtained for Geneva, Ankara, or Paris? Yes. Photostats of the original manuscripts are run off, and chamber music groups abroad present for the first time a portion of a historic period in American music.

The director of a national radio network of a prominent Latin American country heard the *Waltzing Cat* of Leroy Anderson while visiting the United States on a grant from the Department of State. He fell in love with the music and was anxious to obtain the materials for performances at home. Was there anything the Music Section could do to help? Through the presentations program of the Information Center Service, which is designed for just such purposes, the Music Section was able to furnish him with the requested material. The result was one more friend for the United States.

One of the most unusual of the varied projects in which the Music Section becomes involved took place two years ago when our ambassador to the Associated States of Indo-China returned to this country for consultation. He brought with him several melodies composed by the King of Cambodia with the request that they be arranged for dance orchestra. (The King, by the way, is an accomplished musician and plays the saxophone in his own band.) The Music Section undertook the problem and approached Colonel George Howard, commanding officer of the Air Force Band. Through his good offices the melodies were not only arranged for dance band but were put in the form of an orchestral suite by his able staff of arrangers. In August of 1952 the first performance of the king's music was presented by the Air Force Symphony Orchestra. Later the suite was commercially published by private arrangements between the king and a publishing firm.

Scarcely a week passes without the chief of the Music Section welcoming to his office distinguished conductors, performers, and educators from other countries who have come to study the musical life of this country, or their American counterparts, eager to help the government promote a wider appreciation of our land through their art.

INTERNATIONAL EDUCATIONAL EXCHANGE SERVICE

No discussion of the music activities conducted by the United States government would be complete without mentioning the work of the International Education Exchange Service of the Department of State. As the name implies, this service is responsible for bringing to this country foreign leaders of outstanding merit and sending abroad a limited number of highly qualified American specialists. Musicians of various sorts are, of course, included.

On rare occasions the Department of State becomes involved in actual sponsorship of a musical project though these situations are the exception rather than the rule. Probably the best-known example of our official participation in a large scale musical production was the series of performances of *Porgy and Bess* at the Berlin Festival of 1952. The company toured Europe extensively as a commercial venture, and everywhere it was hailed as one of the most outstanding cultural achievements ever presented by this country.

More commonly, the Department "facilitates" the official appearances of American artists traveling on their own or on commercial tours. When an outstanding artist or performing group going abroad at personal expense advises the Department of its itinerary well in advance, our Embassies and Information Centers are often informed. If the artist is willing to donate his services for concerts at Information Centers or for those sponsored by our missions overseas, the Embassy or Consulate may, at its discretion, facilitate such performances as part of the Government's cultural effort.

Many distinguished artists have given generously of their talent as a public service to their country. Marian Anderson's appearances in Korea and Isaac Stern's tour of the Far East are but two recent examples. This past winter Shura Cherkassky gave a concert in Ankara under the auspices of the U. S. Information Service. He generously donated the proceeds of the concert to the widows and families of Turkish soldiers killed in Korea. Such gestures, far beyond the call of duty and coupled with first-rate music making, speak for themselves. Groups, too, going abroad at their own expense have received facilitative aid from the State Department

REPERTOIRE OF AMERICAN GROUPS

It might be of interest to share with music educators a few conclusions I have reached by talking to dozens of conductors, artists, and groups going abroad to perform, and by examining hundreds of programs of concerts they have given. My prime concern is the problem of repertoire and its relationship particularly to the European audience.

Though we are a young country without the long musical tradition of Europe, we may well take keen pride in many aspects of our music participation on all levels. For this reason, I believe it essential that when we perform abroad, we take great care to see that the quality of our repertoire matches that of our standard of performance. On several occasions critics have had the highest praise for our technical standards, which have been the result of excellent training and painstaking effort. They complain, however, that the compositions selected are more suitable for the cabaret than for the concert hall. It would seem imperative, if we are to show the best of our musical culture, that we gear our repertoire to the cultivated tastes of the extremely sophisticated audiences we seek to reach abroad.

As to the presentation of American music overseas, whether by private individuals or under the auspices of the United States Government, I trust that I will not be accused of contradicting myself if I state my belief that we do not best serve our ends by *over* emphasis of our own works. (I refer, of course, to general concerts; not to special concerts of American music.) Our goal should not be to proselytize but to place American music alongside that of other nations. By so doing we would hope to achieve the same end we wish to gain by performing American music in this country—giving that which is worthy of further hearing a chance to become part of the world-wide commonwealth of music.

We who are constantly working with various phases of musical activity under the auspices of the United States Government are proud of what has been accomplished thus far. We realize, however, that much remains to be done. Three areas of activity need consideration: (a) Presentation of some of the techniques of music education in all levels of education which have been so extensively cultivated in this country. (b) More vigorous promotion of American music abroad, together with assistance to those wishing to perform it. (c) Actual government sponsorship of some of our most outstanding performing groups, which compare very favorably with those of other nations.

It is gratifying, however, that music *is* a part of our over-all cultural program overseas, and we hope that it will continue to play its role as a unifying factor among the nations of a troubled world.

The International Society of Music Education [1]

UNESCO convened an International Conference on "The Role of Music in the Education of Youth and Adults" which met during 1953 in Brussels; it was there that the International Society of Music Education came into being. As chairman of the Preparatory Commission I had the privilege of opening the proceedings and of defining the purpose of the Conference. What I said on that occasion is equally applicable to the Conference, which is now a thing of the past, the International Society, which belongs to the future, and American music educators. I said:

> *We believe* that music is more than a gift of the Gods to the few: that the common man has a right to it as a part of that happiness which was once so unforgettably linked with life and liberty itself;

[1] From an address by Arnold M. Walter, Director, Faculty of Music, University of Toronto, Canada, given at the MENC Biennial Convention, Chicago, 1954. Mr. Walter was President of the International Society of Music Education, 1953-55.

We believe that music discloses its true meaning only to those who know its right use;

We believe—for historical, sociological, technological reasons—that right use depends, more than it ever did before, on teaching;

We believe that this all-important teaching has been handicapped by an astonishing lack of collaboration on an international basis.

It is unthinkable that any scientist would work today without being fully aware of discoveries made or techniques developed in other countries. Music itself has been internationalized in some of its aspects such as in composition, in performance, but certainly not in education.

So this is simply what the UNESCO Conference is for: to find out what we can learn from each other and to discover what we all have yet to learn; to find out which problems are solved already, and to discover which it will be our common task to solve.

To put it differently, it was our hope that a "Global picture" would emerge— that the present state of music education in the Americas, in Europe, Asia, and Australia, would be sufficiently described to enable us to compare, to select, to exchange, to embark on coordinated and cooperative action. A comprehensive plan, no doubt, and certainly no easy assignment.

Perhaps it was too much to expect from a single gathering, the first one of its kind, to cope with so many difficulties, to solve so many problems, to do in a few days what ought to have been done over the years.

The UNESCO Conference was brilliantly successful in bringing together delegates from almost forty countries, each and every one anxious to contribute his own knowledge, to learn from the experience of others. There was no lack of informative lectures, ingenious suggestions, valuable recommendations; yet there was a marked reluctance on the part of lecturers to comment on anything beyond their own personal experience; an almost total absence of comparative studies. It must be confessed that the "Global picture" hoped for did not materialize. It became evident that the work of the Conference had to be continued by some permanent body, which led to the establishment of the International Society of Music Education.

The task of the Society, then, is clearly defined: it must start right where the Conference left off. It must concern itself with the condition of music education in the world of today; with its impact on life; its major trends; its role in education; its function in a world dominated by science and technology.

The Society will, *first* of all, be a fact-finding body. "If we could first know where we are and whither we are tending, we could better judge what to do." *Second*, the Society must embark on comparative studies to select the best and most adaptable forms of organization, methods of instruction, and materials. *Third*, the results of such studies must be made available and applicable which, *fourth*, will lead to the desired increase in common knowledge and awareness, to an exchange of ideas and an exchange of teachers and students.

All nations have contributed to the common store of music and are the better for it; to pool the resources of music education will be equally beneficial. There is much that cannot be translated, adapted, exported or exchanged, but it will be a great step forward if we find a common denominator as a starting point. Two questions present themselves: (a) How is such an ambitious program to be accomplished; and (b) who will benefit by it?

To take the second one first, every music teacher in the world should benefit by it. It will comfort him to learn how his colleagues in other lands are striving and struggling. He will be tempted to try novel methods, to experiment with new material, to revise his fundamental concepts. The Society [1] ought to become a Music

---

[1] Membership in the International Society of Music Education is open to all interested in furthering the cause of music education on an international basis. For "Resolutions" of the International Conference on Music Education send a stamped, self-addressed envelope to Music Educators National Conference.

Educators International Conference attempting in the international sphere what is so splendidly done in the national sphere by the Music Educators National Conference.

As to the program itself, it is obvious that biennial or even annual meetings could not hope to cope with it. This is the reason for our ambitious plan to establish an International Institute for Music Education if sufficient funds can be raised. Perhaps they will be raised; but all these plans, blueprints, and organization charts will be merely bits of paper solemnly signed and soon forgotten if the music educators themselves do not help to make our dream come true. It would not be the first time in human affairs if the success of an undertaking failed to come up to the lofty phrase of the manifesto. What the Society needs are members who are willing to cooperate with their colleagues in other lands to share their respective heritage by mutual exchange—men and women who share our ideal and are willing to work for it.

Trends in Music Education [1]

I. *Developments and New Trends in Music Education in the United States.*

The over-all purpose of this session is to present to you, an audience made up of nationals from many countries, new trends in music education in certain parts of the world. This contribution could be made most ideally by including facts and supporting data concerning new trends in music education in the Western hemisphere, including Canada, the United States and Latin American countries.

There is much in common among the countries of the western hemisphere in their philosophy and in their objectives of music education. There is considerable professional compatibility among music educators from Canada in the North to Argentina and Chile in the South. Yet there are some basic differences in the framework of the society and in the organization of systems and patterns of education in these countries which would make overambitious any attempt to include all of the New World countries in this presentation. Assuming that many of these developments described can be seen in many countries of the Western hemisphere, this presentation concerning new trends should be regarded as applying particularly to the United States.

II. *Music Education in the United States Prior to 1900.*

For the present purpose, it is not necessary to dwell on music in the United States prior to 1900. However, it is necessary to realize that although there were great economic and certain political developments attained by the United States by 1900, our cultural moorings and concepts were those of a colonial people. Music instruction in the schools was scattered. It was without focus or plan and was largely in the hands of professional musicians whose imaginations were stirred by the necessity of professional adjustments but whose best efforts did not take them beyond some valiant attempts to imitate European traditions in methods of teaching and in materials as well. This statement intends to cast no aspersions whatsoever on our magnificent European heritage. The situation was such that, with the advent of the opportunity for expanding the program of music teaching in the schools *as a part of the educational program, imitations* of methods used under entirely different circumstances on the European scene, were inadequate. Materials which were prepared for the schools as *imitations* of European materials were similarly inadequate. The result was that around the period of 1900, there was a static quality in the teaching of music in the schools—sort of a calm before the door to a new era and a new profession in the field of music began to open.

[1] Presented by Vanett Lawler, Associate Executive Secretary of the Music Educators National Conference and Secretary General, International Society of Music Education, at the International Conference of Music Education, Brussels, Belgium, 1953.

III. *Two Conspicuous Developments in the Field of Music Education in the United States Since 1900.*

At the turn of the century, many of the same people who prior to 1900 had been making sporadic attempts to adapt to the public school system in the United States a way of teaching music which clearly belonged to the individual teacher whose principal work was the training of the professional student in music, many of these same people laid the foundation for what now can be said are the two most conspicuous developments in the United States in the field of music during the first half of this century:

(1) Emergence of the professional, voluntary and non-governmental organization belonging to the music teachers in the schools as the symbol of unity and authority within the profession and as the recognized spokesman for the profession of music education in the United States; and

(2) Recognition of music education as a profession in the field of music along with the other fields of music—musicology, professional music, conducting, and composition.

The order in which these are given—*first,* the professional organization, and *second,* the recognition of the profession—is the sequence of these developments. The recognition of music education as a profession very gradually emerged from the founding, the growth, and the leadership which was fostered *within* the professional organizations. To this day, the prestige of the profession of music education is enhanced and its stability is maintained through this symbol of unity within the profession which is manifest in the professional organizations.

IV. *Trends and New Trends Evolved from These Two Developments.*

Any thoughtful presentation and evaluation of evident trends and tendencies toward new trends in music education necessarily needs to assume the premise that there have been these two important developments—which in the process of their growth have been trends in themselves. It also follows that the consistent and parallel growth of the professional organizations and the profession of music education in the United States has been the result of:

—Trends which have been indicated from within the profession,

—Trends which have been accelerated as the result of experimentation by the music educators themselves,

—Trends in the changing pattern of general education toward broader curricula, and

—Trends which gradually became accepted practices and objectives of the profession, only to inspire further experimentation and exploration of new techniques, new materials, and new objectives.

Within a span of fifty years a new profession has been added to the American scene of music and education, has become of age, and is facing its future fully alert to its professional responsibilities.

V. *Music Education as a Part of the Development of Public Education.*

Music education has developed and is continuing its development as a part of the total education program. To appreciate the growth of the music education profession and the professional organizations, it is well to understand the processes inherent in the development of the public school system in the United States.

Since the beginning of the century there has been increased emphasis to provide more and broader educational opportunities for more people. Obviously this development in general education had considerable influence in the organization of a music education program which would be worthy as *a part of the total program of education.* Schools are concerned with the education of groups of people and at the same time with the development of all individuals in the groups. If music is to be a real part of education, then it too has to be concerned with a similar process. This emphasis in the general education program to provide increased and broader opportunities for more and more people varied, and continues to vary, both from the standpoint of geographical areas and educational concepts.

There has been one factor common to the entire development—namely, decentralization. The schools in the United States are not under Federal control. There is a certain uniformity in the instructional program, but great latitude prevails as to the processes and the machinery in attempting to attain the desired objectives. If there is uniformity, it is by common consent and not by top level control.

In fitting into the ever-widening and decentralized school program all over the United States, music education would also develop along lines of decentralization, with the result that there is a wide variety of techniques of instruction, a wide variety of materials, different philosophical applications concerning objectives, and an appreciable variance in the acceptance of music as part of curricula.

One should not infer from this that there is any Utopia in the United States. To visiting music educators from other countries, the situation might seem completely confused and without focus. The visitor would hear some excellent performances of music which would have the approval of any professional musician or music scholar. He would hear some magnificent performances of music which would not have the approval of professional musicians and music scholars. He might criticize severely what would seem to be diminished emphasis on note reading in the primary and intermediate grades in the elementary schools. It is possible he would not be sympathetic with many music educators who are partisan to the oral and rhythmic and creative approach in the early grades in the elementary schools. There is this variety in music education in the schools in the United States at the present time due to:

—Our decentralized system of public education, and

—The broadening school curriculum which is concerned with the training of the mind and the training of the emotions.

What trends have been accepted as practices in this developing process of music education in the United States? What are some of the new trends which may be on their way to becoming accepted practices and thinking?

(1) Increased professional autonomy enjoyed by music educators in the fields of music and education.

(2) Increased realization of the fact that the music education profession demands teachers trained in two professions—music and education.

(3) Increased recognition by music educators, administrators of school systems, boards of education, and directors of curriculum of the importance of a *well-balanced* program of appropriate music courses which will contribute to the objectives of general education.

(4) Increased utilization of school music performing groups as functional parts of total school programs.

(5) Increased recognition by administrators of Schools of Music and Schools of Education within State Universities and Colleges of Education, of the professional organizations, the Music Educators National Conference, the Music Teachers National Association and the National Association of Schools of Music, as the source for guidance in developing curricula for the education of music teachers.

(6) Increased insistence upon balance in education of the music teachers, as Musicians and as educators. In the United States it is not the conservatory which is the principal center of supply and training for music educators. The majority

of music educators receive their training in Schools of Music of State Universities and in State Colleges of Education in which there are offered courses in music, courses in education, and courses in the humanities.

(7) Increased recognition of importance of quality of materials used in the schools. Inherent in this tendency is the problem of the development of mass taste which is essentially the development of people themselves. United States music educators are devising their own criteria. They are working out their own standards which may or may not agree with European standards. There is no necessity for uniformity of standards or criteria among music educators all over the world. One of the fundamental purposes of this Conference in Brussels is to provide opportunity for an exchange of information on such matters.

(8) Increased opportunities for cooperation between music educators and musicologists, composers, private teachers, and professional musicians. This was not true to any appreciable degree twenty years ago or even immediately prior to the last war.

(9) Increased awareness of the public relations aspects of music education— of the importance of a nonisolationist policy of the music educators as regards their community.

(10) Increased attention by music educators and administrators of school systems and colleges of the pre-service training (before entering the profession) and in-service training (after entering the profession) *of the general elementary school teacher.*

(11) Increased attention to the importance of music education for exceptional children, including the physically handicapped and the mentally retarded, as well as the gifted child.

(12) Increased interest throughout the music education profession in the United States of the importance and effectiveness of music education in international relations and intercultural education.

What has been the means whereby such a highly decentralized music education program has been brought into focus in order to present to the music educators of the United States reasonable unity of purpose and action and to insure for them their position of prestige?

The continuing thread throughout the development of these trends which has made possible such a far-flung development for such a young profession has been the professional organization, the Music Educators National Conference. The MENC has been the proving ground for all that has happened. This little commonwealth of music education has been built up, sustained, and is being maintained in the United States because there has been this vehicle of the professional organization which has been created by the profession itself. The MENC has provided the music educators with a framework and foundation on which to build their profession, their professional practices, and standards. It has been for them a symbol of unity and authority which they and others have recognized.

Through the organization, and within the organization, the music educators have worked out their differences. These varieties of techniques, of materials, and objectives have been thoroughly discussed and have been demonstrated year after year on a state, regional, and national level at the meetings of the MENC since it was founded in 1907. The inclusion in the name of the organization from the very beginning the word "Conference" indicates the underlying purpose of the organization. At the meetings, local, regional, or national, the generalist in music education confers with the specialist—the person who is particularly concerned with *what* is taught and *how* it is taught confers with someone who is concerned with *why* music is taught. From this melting pot which is provided by the professional organization comes inevitable trends toward uniformity.

The United States has no monopoly on the idea that a professional and voluntary organization can be extremely effective in the field of music education. Chile can tell some fine things about the Asociación de Educación Musical which has been such an important ally in the development of music education in Chile. There is a new and effective organization in Peru, the Asociación de Profesores de Música, and there is another in Guatemala. The Nordic countries should be asked to tell about the Nordic Music Teachers Association, which has been an inspiration to the teachers of music in those countries for several years.

Summary. This has been a kaleidoscopic view of "where we were," "where we are," and "where we hope to go" in the field of music education in the United States. It is a new profession. Through the professional organization which is at the present time is at the strongest point of development in its history, and through the vitality of the profession whose members are in the profession for the principal reason of contributing to the intellectual, emotional, and spiritual growth of the girls and boys in the schools through music, it is felt that American music educators will continue to be worthy of taking their place, making what contributions they can, discharging obligations, and meeting responsibilities at future international conferences of music education.

Recommended Sources of Information on the United Nations and the United States National Commission for UNESCO [1]

THE UNITED NATIONS

UN Department of Public Information, New York, N. Y. Leaflets, pamphlets, lists of films, radio broadcasts and recordings; study guides and visual aids, general documents, etc.

UN Information Center, Official Branch Office of UN Department of Public Information, 2000 Massachusetts Ave., N.W., Washington, D. C.

International Documents Service, Columbia University Press, 2960 Broadway, New York 27, N. Y. Official sales agent for all publications of the UN and UNESCO. A complete checklist of publications is available on request.

THE UNITED STATES GOVERNMENT

U.S. National Commission for UNESCO Relations Staff, Department of State, Washington 25, D. C. Leaflets and pamphlets; a monthly *Newsletter*, reports on the *Third and Fourth National Conferences of the U.S. Commission for UNESCO*, held in New York, January 1952, and in Minneapolis in September, 1953, respectively; special materials and documents on international affairs. Address all inquiries to the UNESCO Relations Staff, Department of State, Washington 25, D. C.

U.S. Department of Health, Education and Welfare—Office of Education, Washington 25, D. C. Bibliographies, sample materials, teaching guides and consultation services.

NATIONAL EDUCATION ASSOCIATION OF THE UNITED STATES

Study guides; catalog of films; radio scripts and recordings; periodicals and special services. Address inquiries c/o NEA Committee on International Relations, 1201 Sixteenth St., N.W., Washington 6, D. C.

SPECIAL VOLUNTARY ORGANIZATIONS

American Association of University Women, 1645 I St., Washington, D. C. Pamphlet, *Guide to UN Agencies*. 35¢.

Foreign Policy Association, 22 E. 38th St., New York 16, N. Y. Pamphlet on Human Rights. 25¢.

General Federation of Women's Clubs, 1734 N St., Washington, D. C. Pamphlets on UN Agencies; speakers, radio scripts, recordings and special projects.

Music Educators National Conference, 64 E. Jackson Blvd., Chicago 4, Ill. Provides bibliographies, lists of audio-visual and song materials, assistance on special projects, and sources of pertinent information concerning intercultural relations.

Pan-American Union, Music Division, Washington, D. C. Collections of Latin-American songs; information on sources of cultural materials for inter-American units of study; bibliographies, pamphlets, reports, etc.

EDUCATIONAL EXCHANGES AND GRANTS

a. *U.S. Department of Health, Education and Welfare—The Office of Education.* Booklet, "1954-55 Exchange Teaching Opportunities Under the Educational Exchange Program," authorized by Public Law 584, 79th Congress, the Fulbright Act and Public Law 402, 80th Congress, the Smith-Mundt Act. Announced by Board of Foreign Scholarship, Department of State, Office of Education, Washington, D. C.

---

[1] From Information Bulletin No. 1 prepared by Lilla Belle Pitts, New York, New York, National Chairman, Music in American Education Committee on Music Education and International Relations.

b. *Private Agencies.* Institute of International Education, Inc., 1 E. 76th St., New York 21, N. Y. Issues information, handbooks, pamphlets, as well as administering exchange-of-persons programs between the U.S. and seventy-four countries.

Rotary International, 35 E. Wacker Drive, Chicago 1, Ill. Rotary Foundation Fellowships granted; additional grants given by individual clubs to foreign students coming to the U.S., and to Americans for study abroad.

Selected Bibliography [1]

American Junior Red Cross School Music Project, Its Plan, Its Purpose, Its Activities. Washington, D. C.: American Junior Red Cross. Free.

Exchange Teaching Opportunities Under the Educational Exchange Program. 1954-55. Washington, D. C.: U.S. Department of State.

Information Bulletin No. One. Chicago: Music Educators National Conference, 1952. 15¢.

Information Bulletin No. Two. Includes listing of representative collections of folk music. Chicago: Music Educators National Conference, 1954.

The International Music Council, What it is, What it does. Paris XVI: UNESCO House, 19 Avenue Kleber. Free.

The UN and UNESCO and the American Schools. Washington, D. C.: Educational Policy Commission, National Education Association, 1952. Free.

UNESCO in 1950, Outline of work 1947-1950, inclusive. Washington, D. C.: U.S. National Commission for UNESCO, Department of State. 35¢.

---

[1] A valuable source for reference material will be found in back issues of the *Music Educators Journal*, which has carried in almost every issue articles pertinent to various phases of international relations through music education.—Ed.

Preschool and Kindergarten Elementary, Rural

Music for Childhood

Coordinating Chairman: Mary Tolbert, Columbus, Ohio

Preschool and Kindergarten

Adeline McCall, chairman, Chapel Hill, N. C.

Elementary School

Earluth Epting, chairman, Atlanta, Ga.

Rural School

Thomas Annett, chairman, La Crosse, Wis.

Music for the Elementary Teacher

Charlotte DuBois, chairman, Austin, Texas

CHAPTER V

MUSIC FOR ELEMENTARY SCHOOLS

T HE ELEMENTARY LEVEL of our school system has become a national concern to many people during the past decade. The unprecedented number of children entering school has created problems throughout the country in all phases of the instructional program. New buildings of modern design now stand as evidence of an effort by the American public to provide physical facilities needed by growing communities. The staffing of these added classrooms has revealed the difficulty of finding and holding qualified teachers. Needs for materials and equipment for additional groups of children have mounted steadily. Statistics show that during the next ten-year period the enrollment in elementary schools will be the largest in the history of education in America.

As schools move into new or remodeled buildings, the content of the curriculum both in the elementary classroom and in schools for teacher education is coming under closer examination for essential values. Adults who are working with children want to understand more about how children learn and how they grow, as well as their needs for citizenship in today's world. Modern school programs are being built on a knowledge of children and the problems they face when learning and living together.

Music for Childhood in Education Today [1]

Music for childhood as a part of this educational picture is confronted by perplexing problems throughout the country. Elementary schools show wide differences in the music experiences provided for in their program. Some schools and communities encourage the development of musical activities because they are valued for their rich potentialities for human development. In other schools and classrooms there is a complete lack of opportunity for children to grow with and to learn about music. With extremes such as these, music for childhood necessarily reflects differences in educational possibilities. How music is a part of the school depends largely upon the insights and vision that administrators, teachers, and parents have developed through their own accumulated background.

OUR BELIEFS ABOUT MUSIC FOR CHILDHOOD

Interest in music for childhood is spreading among parents and school people who see that music is closely akin to life itself. They believe that music provides important experiences children need for personal growth, family membership, and community citizenship. They recognize in it avenues for developing potential strengths necessary for intelligent living in this age where scientific advance in mechanical and industrial skills has reached amazing possibilities. They know that the improvements in record players, recording devices, radio and television, as well as the availability of this equipment to a majority of families, mean that most children have numerous contacts with commercial uses of music, and that choice and discrimination as consumers of music are now factors in a child's world. They want a school program which provides for music as an important part of a balanced curriculum serving the developmental needs of boys and girls as well as the rapid changes in daily living. They have faith that musical experiences planned con-

[1] From the report submitted by Mary Tolbert, Columbus, Ohio, National Chairman, Music in American Education Committee on Music for Childhood.

sistently with human values in mind can help children develop attitudes which enhance the ideals and welfare of mankind in contemporary living, for:

(1) *Strengthening Beliefs* (Spiritual and Moral Values). Beliefs are often felt rather than thought through in a rational way. Children absorb many of these ideals emotionally through direct contact with great music.

(2) *Understanding Other People* (Intercultural Values). Through firsthand participation in their music, children learn to appreciate and understand the various cultural groups that have settled in America as well as people of other countries.

(3) *Living Together Happily* (Social Values). Each child enacts a dual role—that of an individual who has the right to expect a variety of musical opportunities in which he may participate freely and fully in satisfying ways, and that of a responsible member of a group striving toward a common goal.

(4) *Knowing How* (Intellectual Values). Children thrive in a rich musical environment that provides for growth in musical understandings and skills when they are needed. Children achieve a better quality of musical growth when a sequence of experiences provides for the gradual development of musical insight and skills as they are directly related to their need and the immediacy of their use.[1]

When the home, the school, and the community together foster a climate that encourages rather than blocks or diverts children in pursuing their enjoyment of music, their interests and abilities widen and unfold along with understanding and participation. Seeking outlets for their feelings and for their curiosity about life around them, young children delight in sound and movement as well as imaginative expressiveness of various types. They demonstrate in countless ways that they are spontaneous musicians by nature. Their inquisitiveness leads them to explore the numerous tonal and rhythmic experiences surrounding them daily. Their responsiveness shows that music tuned to their natural impulses and levels of interest can contribute to their development as happier, better balanced, and more creative persons.

What happens to children in their earliest years is being recognized by a wider circle as an important part of the whole educational picture. More attention is being given to growth through music at the preschool age.

POINT OF VIEW [2]

(1) All children possess innate musicality and have a need and desire for music.

(2) Music experiences are for all of the children of all of the people.

(3) Every child in every grade should participate in school music activities.

(4) Music experiences in the classroom should be enjoyable for both the teacher and the children.

(5) Through a rich variety of musical experiences, music serves as a means of integrating the child's personality.

(6) Music is a social art and the majority of musical experiences offered young children involve social responsibilities and growth.

(7) Music fits into many activities throughout the school day in addition to those of the formal music period.

---

[1] From Music for Childhood Committee Report, California-Western Conference, Tucson, Arizona, 1953. Mimeographed.

[2] "Music Section" *Curriculum Guide, The Elementary Program* (San Diego, Calif.: San Diego City Schools, reprinted 1953), p. 221.

(8) Teachers should aim to give children the world's best in music, both in quality of literature and in quality of media through which it is presented.

(9) All children should have opportunities to participate in music programs. Opportunities should be provided in school for talented children, but they should not be exploited.

(10) When public school music accomplishes its purpose it becomes a part of the daily lives of both children and adult members of the community in many of their activities in and out of school.

(11) Music, the universal language, is an effective means for achieving high ideals and the realization of a true interchange of all cultures and creeds.

(12) Folk music of all cultures makes pupils proud of their heritage and gives them an understanding of the oneness of the human race.

MUSICAL EXPERIENCES FOR CHILDREN [1]

Believing that . . .

1. *Young children are by nature and inclination among our most active music lovers and music makers.*

2. *All children are musical, but they differ individually in kind and degree of musical response, even as they differ in other areas of growth.*

3. *Children grow musically through direct, active, and enjoyable participation in music.*

4. *Children tend to use music spontaneously and naturally as a part of their daily living.*

Therefore, children's musical experiences should . . .

1. Provide extensive and continuing opportunities for children to explore, voluntarily, musical sound and rhythmic movement, individually and in groups.

2. (a) Invite the active yet individually differentiated, musical participation of *all* children in varied and appealing musical activities involving singing, playing, rhythmic movement, listening, making up.

   (b) Be based upon flexible standards of musical growth evolving from individual interests and abilities rather than upon fixed levels of music expectations for all.

3. (a) Emphasize opportunities for children to be active and interested participants rather than mere learners *about* music.

   (b) Take into account gropings for musical understandings and musical skills shown by individuals and groups and provide for fulfillment of these needs through experimentation, explanation, practice, supplementary reading, always with direct reference to the music itself.

4. (a) Thread the school day with many opportunities for music making.

   (b) Cultivate close associations in many musical ways within a school, between school and home, school and church, school and community.

---

[1] From Music for Childhood Committee Report, California-Western Conference, Tucson, Arizona, 1953. Mimeographed.

5. *Children's musical growth is so closely allied to their over-all growth as to be inseparable from it.*

5. (a) Use as guides the significant patterns of child growth and development within broad, chronological age levels.

(b) Ensure feelings of security, success, and group-mindedness as a result of personal satisfaction through music.

6. *Children's lives are enriched whenever musical values are realized simultaneously.*

6. (a) Attest to belief that music serves human needs: physically, socially, emotionally, spiritually, aesthetically, intellectually.

(b) Consider and respect the musical status of children at every stage in their musical growth; provide for a gradual widening of children's musical horizons; provide for a parallel, gradual rise in individual and group musical taste; consistently high light the musical values inherent in each song, instrumental selection, recording.

(c) Stimulate and maintain opportunities for children to express freely their thoughtful, sincere, and gradually changing preferences as to music literature, interpretation of musical selections, and the like.

THE TEACHERS OF MUSIC FOR CHILDHOOD [1]

In some elementary schools today, the music program is being carried by teachers who have studied both music and children as major interests in college. They are fully qualified in musical skills and resources to make this area alive and meaningful. Other schools rely upon the general teacher to use and develop his own musical resources. Less than half of these classroom teachers have the direct help of music teacher advisors. A traveling music teacher in some localities must divide his teaching time among many classrooms and children, while still other schools employ a music teacher to give private or small group instrumental lessons to a few children. In some rural areas a music teacher visits five one-room schools per day carrying materials to each school for their use during the weekly visit.[2]

Coming more and more into the national picture are classrooms where one teacher is urged to be responsible for integrating all learning situations of the students. These teachers usually need, and some of them ask for, help with materials, ideas, and procedures which will enable them to draw upon the variety of learning possible through music. Music materials designed especially for classroom teachers are becoming increasingly available and are critically needed in most schools, such as recordings, simple instruments, attractive songbooks, and suggestions for teaching.

Cooperative help is supplied in a number of places by music teachers and supervisors who work as consultants, demonstration teachers, workshop leaders, and organizers of resource material. Some are on call as needed, others visit classrooms with regularity to add their special help and to keep in touch with children's needs

---

[1] See Music for the Elementary Teacher, p. 89.

[2] Report of Walworth County Music Program, Elkhorn, Wisconsin, for Music in American Education Committee on Music in Rural Schools.

and interests. Keeping contact with children is particularly important for a special teacher to work adequately in this helping capacity.

Teachers who have been certified to meet the emergencies of teacher shortages, and teachers who have been accelerated through an educational training program in college to fill the job demands, usually feel unprepared to work in a situation involving music.

In many schools inadequate music preparation of the classroom teacher has curtailed the music experiences of boys and girls who are eager participants when there is skillful use of material.

More than half of the classroom teachers who have cooperated in surveys state that music was limited or omitted in their college training. Colleges of teacher education vary widely in how they are meeting the music needs in elementary classrooms. In-service education for teachers is a necessity if children are to be given musical opportunities commensurate with their potentialities. Music for childhood must stress workshops, clinics, conferences, and other means of group work in schools and professional organizations.

Each Division of the MENC has instigated workshop meetings which involved music education with classroom teachers experiencing, analyzing and evaluating techniques and procedures of group work.

ADMINISTRATORS GUIDE THE MUSIC PROGRAM

Enlisting the sympathetic cooperation and support of administrators is imperative in establishing a workable plan for music. In elementary schools where the principal takes an active part in the self-educative process, he joins general and special teachers in studying what is needed. Such situations give more hope that boys and girls will not be deprived of their rightful musical opportunities. The administrator who increases his understanding of the musical arts is better able to help teachers see ways in which these experiences may be both functional and inspirational.

The elementary principal who is sensitive to the values of music as a positive force in his school: [1]

- —*Understands* the over-all philosophy of the music program, how children learn and grow through music experiences.
- —*Recognizes* music needs of his student population, background and abilities of individual teachers.
- —*Utilizes* materials which are available and desirable, music resources within the community.
- —*Helps* teachers plan an effective music program, schedule and circulate music equipment and materials.
- —*Encourages* effective use of in-service education, workshops and meetings, and university courses.

The principal provides adequate materials for the elementary music program. He sees that:

- —Teachers have a record player, autoharp, piano, etc.
- —The school has a library of well-selected recordings of all kinds easily available.

---

[1] *The Principal Guides Music Education in the Elementary School* (San Bernardino, Calif., City Schools, 1953). Mimeographed pamphlet.

58

—Each class has access to music texts' accompaniment books, and many supplementary books.

—A tape recorder and radio is available.

—Melody bells and rhythm instruments are available to all teachers.

—Materials and facilities for instrument construction and repair are available.

—A workable system for circulating and replacing these materials is established.

—Teachers have continuous opportunities for in-service education in the use of this equipment and materials.

The principal encourages enrichment opportunities as an extension of classroom music experiences. For example:

—*Assembly Sings.* Periodic opportunities for large groups of children to sing together.

—*Choral Groups.* Additional singing opportunities for interested children, stressing musical refinement and using part-singing, interpretation, song material not ordinarily used in the classroom. Such groups should not substitute for classroom music.

—*Instrumental.* Piano classes, beginning orchestra, band, orchestra, ensembles. Regular class lessons given by trained teachers to interested students. Experiences should lead to enrichment of the classroom music program, opportunities to play with larger and more accomplished groups, and to periodic performances.

Boards of education should be encouraged to hire teachers who have musical ability, a liking for music, and as much training in music as possible. They should be shown that the teaching of music is as important for the child's total growth as the teaching of the three R's.[1] Teachers, too, need to understand how music contributes to other areas of the child's learning.

Correlation of music with other school subjects or activities contributes to improvement of the total school curriculum. Classroom teachers and music instructors should be careful not to force music into all curriculum units. Music is a subject with its own form and content. Music must be protected from exploitation when used improperly in other curriculum activities. Pupils discover quickly the meaningful contribution music may make to improved learning in other curriculum subjects.[2]

Where state music supervision has functioned, greater use of music is apparent in schools. There is critical need for coordination among teacher-education institutions, state departments for certification, superintendents and school boards who employ teachers, and in-service education programs.

SUMMARY: AREAS FOR CONTINUED EMPHASIS

(1) Making music a vital influence in each child's life.

(2) Helping each child learn in multiple ways through music.

(3) Relating all music experiences to the child's abilities and development at various growth levels.

(4) Helping children use music to express their ideas.

(5) Encouraging both children and their teachers to enjoy being musically alert and responsive.

---

[1] From the report submitted by Ruth Lawrence, Fargo, North Dakota, State Chairman, Music in American Education Committee on Music for Childhood.

[2] From an address by E. T. McSwain, Dean, School of Education, Northwestern University, Evanston, Illinois, given at the MENC Biennial Convention, Chicago, 1954.

(6) Considering classroom teachers a vital part of music program and planning with them.

(7) Guiding classroom teachers in building their understanding and grasp of music and its resources.

(8) Keeping good materials and equipment readily available in classrooms and libraries.

(9) Urging school superintendents and boards of education to hire teachers adequately prepared for teaching music.

(10) Evaluating the performance and progress in expressive and receptive musical behavior.

A well-balanced program which has positive approach and direction is an important consideration. It must consist of a variety of musical experiences so planned as to widen musical horizons and develop a greater appreciation and understanding of music. It includes the expressive singing of many beautiful songs appropriate to the various stages of child development and interest. Many of them will be taught by rote and later by reading. There will be opportunity for dramatization, creative response to rhythm, singing games and folk dancing. Experimenting with sound, especially on the primary level, and the playing of simple melody and recreational instruments for general musical experience provide stimulation and interest for further growth. All through the grades there will be much discriminating listening to beautiful music performed by artists in person, on recordings, on the radio, and in moving pictures. Creative self-expression will be a part of all work, whether singing, dancing, playing, or making original tunes and rhythms. The musical score will be interpreted with knowledge of the facts about music, theory, skills, and reading, merely as the means to greater enjoyment and not as an end in itself. Naturally, children will be interested in an acquaintance with the musicians whose music they sing, play, and hear. Special talent will be discovered and directed into proper channels. Opportunity will be provided for class instruction in piano and instruments of the orchestra and band.

As a result of this program school choruses, choirs, orchestras, bands, and ensembles will be possible. Music is important for its own sake and has many possibilities for enriching other areas of instruction. If given proper emphasis, it will provide experiences which meet the interests and needs found in all groups of children. Opportunity should be provided for the recreational use of music and for the sharing of out-of-school music experiences such as concerts, music on the radio, in movies, in church, and in the home.[1]

Areas for Continued Study. An integrated project needs to be carried forward which would include music for early childhood, preschool, kindergarten, elementary school, and rural school. The following questions require additional investigation and clarification.

(1) *Child Growth.* What music experiences contribute most to desirable child growth in general education terms?

(2) *Scope of Music Experiences.* What music experiences comprise a full, well-balanced program of activities in today's schools?

(3) *Best Learning Situations.* What controllable factors contribute to the child's musical development?

(4) *Available Materials and Resources.* What materials are needed and what are now recommended to carry on a broad musical program?

(5) *Forward-looking Practices.* What anecdotal material can be collected to show practices which provide both worth-while educational and musical experience?

[1] Ohio Elementary Music Guide, *The Music Program* (Columbus, Ohio: State Department of Education, 1949), p. 12.

(6) *Techniques of Group Dynamics.* What techniques of group work can be useful to activate classwork, in-service teacher education, and professional meetings?

(7) *National-Divisional-State Committee Work.* What two-way relationships can be established to provide leadership and inspiration from the MENC committee structure, at the same time recognizing and meeting problems from local situations?

(8) *Problems for Future Committee Work.* What problems can be defined and assigned to conference meetings, publications, research studies, volunteer workers, work centers?

(9) *Relation With Other MENC Groups.* What division of responsibilities will best serve the progress of work needed in this level of Music for Childhood?

Selected Bibliography—Music for Childhood

A Description of Curricular Experiences, The Music Program (Revised ed.). Columbus, Ohio: Ohio State University, 1952.

Anderson, Walter A. "What Makes a Good Workshop?" *Journal of Educational Sociology* (January 1951), pp. 251-281.

Cole, Natalie R. *The Arts in the Classroom.* New York: John Day Co., 1940.

Curriculum Guide, the Elementary Program. San Diego, Calif.: San Diego City Schools. Reprinted 1953.

Diedrich, Paul B. and Van Tie, William. *The Workshop, Guides* and *Teachers Manuals for All Basic Music Textbook Series.* New York: Hines, Hayden, and Eldridge, Inc., pp. 1-32. Pamphlet.

Krone, Beatrice and Max. *Musical Participation in the Elementary School.* Chicago: Neil A. Kjos Music Co., 1952.

Landeck, Beatrice. *Children and Music.* New York: William Sloane Associates, Inc., 1952.

McSwain, E. T. "Improving the Music Curriculum in the Elementary Schools," *Music Educators Journal* (June-July 1954), pp. 23-25, 44.

Madison, Thurber, Kelley, Dorothy, and Fox, Lillian M. *Music in the Elementary Schools in Indiana.* Division of Research and Field Services Bulletin (Vol. XXV, No. 4). Bloomington: Indiana University, 1949.

Mathews, Paul W. *You Can Teach Music.* New York: E. P. Dutton & Co., 1953.

Morgan, Russell V., and Morgan, Hazel B. *Music Education in Action.* Chicago: Neil A. Kjos Music Co., 1954.

Mursell, James L. *Music in American Schools.* New York: Silver Burdett Company, 1943.

———. *Education for Musical Growth.* Boston: Ginn and Company, 1948.

———. *Music and the Classroom Teacher.* New York: Silver Burdett Company, 1951.

Music in Elementary Education. Chicago: Music Educators National Conference, 1954. Mimeographed pamphlet.

Myers, Louise K. *Teaching Children Music in the Elementary School.* New York: Prentice-Hall, Inc., 1950.

Ohio Elementary Music Guide. Columbus, Ohio: State Department of Education, 1949.

Sheehy, Emma Dickson. *There's Music in Children.* New York: Henry Holt and Company, Inc., 1947.

The Arts and Children's Living. Washington: Education International, 1945.

The Child Experiences Music [1]

Through Bodily Movement and Dramatization. Movement to music is essential in the program of the classroom. It develops imagination in expressing ideas and emotions and provides opportunities for physical and social growth.

Movement to music satisfies the child's love of and need for motion, and brings about an understanding and appreciation of music through imitation and dramatization, through patterned physical activity, and through free interpretation.

Movements can describe feelings more effectively than words. A shrug of the shoulders or a sweep of the hand can convey ideas which children might not be able to express in words. Movements to music should involve not only the feet and legs but also the use of the head, arms, hands, and torso.

There is a developmental sequence in muscular coordination, progressing from the use of large muscles to a more refined control of the large and small muscles.

---

[1] Submitted by Mary Tolbert, University of Ohio, Columbus.

Therefore, emphasis on big movements is most important. Coordination of big muscles must be developed before coordination of the smaller muscles is possible.

Through Listening. An important function of the listening activity is to provide experiences from which children can gain an insight into the realm of music and develop an awareness of the "structural or continuitive elements" in music. This would include identification of:

(1) Intensity (loud, soft, medium, changing).

(2) Tempo (fast, slow, medium, changing).

(3) Rhythm (strongly accented or smooth meter).

(4) Pitch (high, low, up and down).

(5) Style (dramatic, lyric, florid).

(6) Structure (repetition of melodies and rhythms).

(7) Mood (gay, dreamy, weird, sad).

It is most important that children be led to notice the elements of beauty and of expressiveness in music, and in this way add to the enjoyment of music they hear.

Listening to music is not an experience which should be confined to the classroom alone. The listening experience might well begin with an exploration of the opportunities for listening to music. Then, in planning together for the listening activity within the classroom, discussion might center first around the different ways of listening.

Sometimes children listen to music in order to be able to respond through bodily movement, often in vigorous physical activity. Sometimes children listen to music very quietly in either a relaxed, recreational situation, or in a formal situation demanding their very best concert-audience manners.

There are significant psychological differences between shared listening and solitary listening. Children need to experience both. It is important as a growth experience for the child to make his own musical discoveries through listening and, at times, it is important that he share these discoveries with the group.

When listening experiences are thoroughly organized and when contacts with music are sufficiently varied and stimulating, they will reveal to the child what there is in music and will arouse in him a desire for continual contacts with music through listening activities.

Through Singing. The child's voice is a personal instrument and he enjoys using it. The child should have opportunities to experience the joy of singing, singing alone and with others. Special attention should be given to the use of the child's voice as related to the range of the songs chosen, to the "singing ease" of the melodies, and to the suitability of the text content and text vocabulary to the maturity of the child. The classroom teacher can rely on the selection of materials as found in the state adopted basic music texts.

Small children should sing for the sheer joy of singing, sing with spirit about the things that are going on within the classroom, and sing often.

For the classroom teacher who does not feel vocally secure, there are excellent recordings of songs in the basic music texts which make singing a free, joyous experience in the classroom.

Through Playing Instruments. Children who have the opportunity to play instruments as part of their classroom activity experience unlimited joys in such participation. The playing of instruments is often a medium of participation for children who are not successful in other areas of music activity.

Teachers without technical instrumental training can be successful in using the following instruments in the classroom:

Rhythm Instruments	Melody Instruments	Accompanying Instruments
rhythm sticks	tuned water glasses	autoharp
jingle sticks	xylophone	ukulele
tambourines	bells	banjo
castanets	piano	guitar
drum	flute-type instruments	piano
and others	and others	

It is not always necessary to have costly instruments. Children can often contribute to a group activity with much satisfaction and personal benefit using a homemade instrument.

Through Creative Music Activities. Elementary children are far more capable of expressing original ideas than teachers sometimes realize. If given the opportunity, children are capable of expressing their moods, their reactions, and their imaginative adventures through words and melodies of their own creation, through bodily movement and rhythmic dramatization and through the playing of instruments. Through creative activities, music becomes alive, vital, and dynamic. Music becomes their very own expression, an outlet from within.

Creative musical activities are experimental activities. Children should be given opportunities to play and sing and dance to their own music.

THE ELEMENTARY TEACHER

Analyzes the Child. Regardless of the area of learning, the competent teacher starts with a study of the characteristics of the individuals and of the group which is to be taught. Many factors have made the boys and girls the individuals they are, and the class the group it is. The intellectual abilities, emotional status, and social maturity, the level of school achievement of the group and the special abilities and disabilities of each individual child are important to the teacher. The socio-economic status, the type of home and neighborhood from which the children come, determine to some extent the special intellectual, emotional, social and physical needs of individuals and the group.

Mindful of these factors, the teacher looks at the music program, with its many diverse learning activities, in order to adjust activities and materials to meet individual and group differences in need, ability, and social maturity. In determining the actual status of children's attitudes, interests, and skills as related to the various phases of the music program, the teacher might ask:

Of Singing:
—Does the tone quality need improving?
—Is more precision in attacks and releases necessary?
—Would a specific study of notation be helpful?
—Does each child enjoy singing?
—Would a different selection of song material create more enthusiasm toward the singing activity?
—Has at least half of the class learned to repeat a short melodic idea after hearing it once?
—How many really poor singers are there in the class?
—What factors contribute to each; lack of experience, emotional, intellectual, or social adjustment?

Of Rhythms:
—Can they use the big muscles freely with well-coordinated rhythmic response?

—Can they clap, step, skip rhythmically?

—Can they recognize rhythmic patterns in music they hear?

—Can they transfer rhythmic patterns into notation?

—Can they follow through on singing games and folk dances?

Of Creating:

—Have they had experience in expressing original, imaginative interpretations of rhythms?

—Can they write words and melodies for songs?

—To what extent can they develop and present dramatic interpretations of music with freedom and ease?

Of Listening:

—What is the span of attention when listening to recorded music?

—Does it vary with types of musical composition, instrumentation, thought content?

—Do they enjoy listening to music they have not studied or been guided through several times?

Of Playing Instruments:

—What instruments have individuals learned to play outside of school?

—Are there those who manifest the need for participating through classroom instruments?

Since the patterns of growth and development through music, like all other aspects of growth, are relative to the situation in which they develop, the questions the teacher will ask in determining "where to start" will vary with classes of differing ages, abilities, and experiences.

Stimulates Interest and Activity. One question which confronts most beginning teachers is: How do you create or develop in children the desire to study, to work, to learn? Many experienced teachers are confronted with the task of discovering ways to create a willingness to learn in lazy, indifferent, or defiant pupils. The real problem of all who are responsible for guiding children in any area of learning is the discovery of means of motivation—ways of stimulating interest and active participation.

When the learning experience is geared to the interests, the activities, and the maturities of the learners, as individuals and as a group, active interest follows as a natural corollary. When a teacher is thoroughly aware of the characteristics of her class and is ingenious in linking the learning activity with those individual and group traits, motivation is no problem.

Teachers often develop a lasting interest in an activity by inviting pupil participation in planning the development of a learning situation. The learning of a group of songs or folk dances becomes more meaningful when the class or a group from the class has helped the teacher develop criteria for determining which activities best fit their immediate needs, and which materials are best suited for the activity.

When children have participated in the developmental pattern of any activity, whether it is singing or listening to music, moving bodily to rhythm in music, expressing ideas in original songs and dances, or experimenting with musical instruments, the activity will be more appropriate to the maturity of the group, it will be more challenging to them and achievable by them, and it will lead to new learnings and provide for the application of old learnings.

Children will move willingly and enthusiastically through any learning experience when they recognize the activity as usable and purposeful, where its

64

goals are achievable, and when the activity is varied enough to challenge and provide for individual abilities within the group.

Provides for Individual Differences. The intellectual limits of learning for most normal people are relatively wide; yet, every teacher recognizes the fact that pupils differ materially in many ways. A teacher must become constantly mindful of the outstanding ways in which individuals differ in order to provide for the needs of individuals while working with the group.

No two children in a class have exactly the same inherited tendencies, the same home, school, or community environment; group instruction is possible because children of any given age have certain broad fundamental characteristics.

There is no real difference in mental ability between the sexes. The seeming differences can be accounted for by the pressures of training and pressures of the social group. However, the sexes do differ in interests and special abilities. At certain ages girls excel in memory while boys excel in motor control and in dealing with mechanical situations. At certain ages girls are more interested in people while boys are more interested in things.

The alert teacher exerts every effort to provide for the individual differences in ability and interest within the classroom through a variety of types of assignments, through special reports and extracurricular activities.

In planning for singing sessions, pupil interest will often govern the selection of songs. Song texts and melodies which match the level of interest and maturation of children will help and encourage them to realize to the fullest possible degree their natural tendency to express themselves in song.

It is very evident to anyone who will observe children of approximately the same chronological age that they have not attained the same physical and social maturity. In planning for "rhythmic activities" (moving to music), groups may be organized to utilize the energy of the children who are strong and give activity without strain to those who are languid and do not abound with physical energy. Singing games and folk dances are valuable aids in drawing out the child who is retiring and reticent.

The class might be divided into groups when working on certain musical skills and techniques and brought together as a whole for recreational group singing and for listening.

The music period should be less a period for testing for information but more of a time for sharing, with the children helping each other learn.

A wise teacher will strive at all times to give music such a variety of meaning that it will touch the experiences of each child and bring to each child the joy and exhilaration which results from the knowledge of having achieved.

Utilizes Community Resources. Pupils taking an active part in a large number of community enterprises add meaning to their education since such participation introduces them to "adult affairs" in the society in which they are to live. The activities which will bring pupils and the community into interaction with each other may be observational, participatory, or contributory.

In order to choose wisely the educational opportunities within the community, the elementary teacher needs to secure adequate information about local needs, local resources, and influences within the community. What occupational services can be helpful, what the libraries have to offer, church activities, recreational activities, and commercial activities which offer opportunities for observation, for participation, and for contribution need to be investigated.

Until quite recently, the contributory type of school-community relation was seldom used in the traditional school. Learning through contributory contacts enables children not only to acquire knowledge and to better understand the community, but it also enables them to make an actual and effective contribution of their own to the community.

Carelessly selected activities are a waste of time and may have very undesirable results. The teacher might judge the value of any community activity by using the following questions as criteria for an evaluation of the activity.

(1) *Does the music activity acquaint the pupils with the resources of their own community?*

—Does it relate to a phase of community life?
—Is it typical of community life?
—Is it related to life in other communities?
—Can it be related to several phases of community life?

(2) *Does the music activity emphasize the community as a social organism with human interrelations?*

—Does it offer contacts with persons who are seen as human beings with needs, desires, and ideals?
—Does it relate to a basic continuing community problem?
—Does it actually contribute to the community rather than use the contributory contact as an opportunity for bolstering self-esteem in the community?

(3) *Does the music activity afford specific educational opportunities for the pupil?*

—Can the community be brought to accept it as a legitimate phase of the school program?
—Can it be related to the present living experiences of boys and girls?
—Is it interesting and challenging to boys and girls?
—Are pupils sufficiently mature to understand the social significance?
—Do the pupils participate in planning?
—Is provision made for differences in abilities and interests of pupils?
—Is the activity on a level of maturity in keeping with the pupils?
—Does it promote critical thinking?
—Does it contribute to the growth and development of habits, skills, knowledges, procedures, and ideals which are normally used by boys and girls in the important activities of life?

Seeks Consultative and Professional Help. There are many sources of help at the teacher's command. The staff members of music education departments of nearby colleges and universities are in contact with new materials, know specialists in the field, and have had practical experience. Usually they are glad to assist.

Clinics and workshops are held frequently. Workshops are offered during summer sessions at the colleges. Specialists from many parts of the country present demonstrations and conduct methods and materials clinics at these workshops.

The MENC has state, divisional, and national committees on elementary music education. A letter of inquiry will bring available materials.

Publishing companies employ full-time music consultants who may be called upon for help. They will help plan programs and suggest sources of materials. Some of the record companies offer the services of their consultants to educators. Most manufacturers of musical instruments make available free and inexpensive classroom materials such as charts and pamphlets.

When schools do not have music supervisors or consultants, it is advisable that each school have a music committee which should not only plan school programs for public presentation but should study and plan for the over-all music program so that it will progress from grade to grade. This type of group study, when shared with other members of the staff, will enable each teacher to know what is done in previous grades and what should be done in succeeding grades.

THE SCHOOL ADMINISTRATORS [1]

The Superintendent. The role of the superintendent in administering the music program is of basic importance. He provides a permissive framework within which the supervisory and instructional staff may plan and develop a program.

The discerning, competent superintendent is as proud of his knowledge in the field of music as in any other area of learning. Even though he may not be able to produce music himself, he can develop an understanding and appreciation of music as it relates to the total growth and development of the child by attending workshops and clinics.

Insofar as is possible, the superintendent has a real responsibility to employ classroom teachers who can direct music activities within their own classrooms. He will recognize the need for all teachers to continue professional growth through in-service teacher-education programs, in which they have a share in planning the areas of study, time and place of meeting, and consultative help needed. Since much inspiration and help can be derived from state or regional clinics and conferences, superintendents will find that it pays in results to provide some time during the school day, or an entire day or two off with pay, for teachers to attend such meetings.

The discerning administrator recognizes the need of those who actually carry on the program and provides space and facilities which are adequate. In long-range planning for the expansion of the music program, he will confer with music educators as well as architects in designing physical facilities. If the school system employs a music specialist, that person, with the superintendent, instructional supervisor, a principal, and a classroom teacher, might form a satisfactory committee for the selection of materials and equipment which meet the needs and interests of children.

The Principal. The elementary principal determines to a large extent the emotional climate of the school. He can take the leadership in making school a place where children have stimulating value-rich experiences in an atmosphere of warmth and friendliness. He can make it possible for teachers and children to feel free to be creative.

It is the responsibility of the principal to help the supervisory staff and teachers to recognize music experiences as a basic need in the total curriculum, to decide what constitutes a well-rounded program, and to provide time for many varied music experiences. Since music activities are curricular, they merit an adequate place in the schedule of the regular school day. All programs should be flexible to provide for creativity and spontaneity of expression.

Adequate space within the existing building needs to be made available by the principal. Access to the auditorium or gymnasium or other large areas for big bodily movements should be allowed. In a school which has no auditorium or gymnasium, provision can be made for the use of any room with enough space uncluttered by desks for the motion and rhythmic expression which is so much a part of music.

The relative value of a well-developed classroom program of music activities as against a "big performance" with emphasis on audience appeal, should be carefully studied by this group. If the performance is a sharing with parents' groups, it could well grow out of regular classroom activities. The best picture parents can

---

[1] See Chapter II, "Administration of a Music Education Program."

have of the music opportunities offered in the school, however, is through increased happiness which music brings into the lives of their children.

Each teacher needs to feel that music is not necessarily confined to a thirty-minute period, that it may permeate all the day's activities and may find expression at any time or several times during the day. The teacher needs assurance from the principal that this is an acceptable practice and that the timing of activities centered around music, as around any other subject area, are at her discretion as revealed by the needs and interests of the children.

There are often special abilities within the faculty which can be used to advantage. Special abilities of the staff often may be used to advantage in in-service groups and demonstrations. Sometimes it is thought advisable for teachers to exchange groups for certain activities. In so doing, however, the principal should not lose sight of the fact that the classroom teacher knows her own group and the needs of each individual child so much better than anyone else that such a practice might be questionable.

The principal will grow in an understanding of the well-balanced music program by observation, professional reading and study, and by participation in music activities.

The Elementary Instructional Supervisor. As a resource person, the instructional supervisor works with administrators, teachers, and parents in providing a school program that will improve the quality of living in the community. The supervisor creates an atmosphere and relationship which inspires critical and creative thinking and action.

The elementary instructional supervisor is concerned with the total program of the school and community. In systems where there is a music supervisor, they work together in the development of a program which includes a balance of musical activities in relation to the total program of the school and the individual abilities and needs of the children.

In systems where there is no specialist in the field of music, the responsibilities of the instructional supervisor for planning with administrators and teachers in the development of the music program are greater. Together they plan for in-service study, clinics, demonstrations, and visitations which may promote professional and cultural growth in this area of learning.

The wise instructional supervisor brings administrators, teachers, parents, children, materials, and resource people together in the process of developing a well-balanced educational program in which music is a necessary and vital part.

The Elementary Music Supervisor. [1] Some years ago, the classroom teacher looked on the music supervisor as a special music teacher and expected the class to be taken over and taught on visits to the classroom. These visits often constituted the whole music program for the children. In some instances, the teacher even left the room while the music supervisor was there, thus depriving herself of an opportunity for professional growth and the advantages the children might gain through follow-up.

Fortunately, this idea has given way to the broader concept of the music supervisor as a resource person, one who may teach a demonstration lesson at times, but whose greatest contribution lies in making herself and her special skills available to teachers in meeting their needs as they work with children. She meets these needs by arranging conferences which may follow visits in the classroom, by locating materials, and by providing instructional sessions for teachers in which she actually teaches them how and what to teach children at various levels of

---

[1] See Chapter III, "The Supervision of Music Education."

development. These sessions should be scheduled as teachers express a need for them.

The elementary music supervisor is eager to help teachers plan a flexible program that will be within the range of the teacher's ability and the children's interests, yet one which is challenging and vital in that it provides a variety of activities. She stimulates and encourages the individual teacher to use her own creativeness at all times, and she is ever sensitive to the needs of the community.

The competent elementary music supervisor is alert to all opportunities for professional and cultural growth. Supervisory leadership and skillful guidance will be reflected in continuous interest and development of musical skills on the part of both teachers and children.

EVALUATING THE ELEMENTARY MUSIC PROGRAM

Establishing Criteria for Evaluation. The "good" elementary school views its task of education broadly and conceives its major functions to be those of utilizing various capacities and interests, and providing situations and experiences which promote democratic human relationships and serve basic human needs.

In establishing a criteria for the evaluation of any part of the elementary school program, a faculty looks to the following as a general organization of the elementary school program and as a general organization of the criteria:

Viewpoint—values, outcomes, and how these are interrelated.

Function—goals, tasks, and opportunities of the elementary school.

Program—broad aspects, scope and organization, teaching-learning, evaluation.

Resources—plan, permanent facilities, materials, staff.

Planning—school-community planning; pupil-parent-teacher planning; faculty planning, etc.

Evaluation of the Elementary Music Program. The faculty and administration of any school can profit much through self-evaluation by reviewing the degree to which established functional learning experiences have been translated into actual practice. Only by careful consideration of the purposes of music in the elementary curriculum and by an objective evaluation of the degree to which their area of the curriculum is meeting basic human needs of utilizing capacities, can a faculty or administrators ascertain the degree to which music in the elementary school program is discharging its obligation.

The following outline points to some ways of analyzing capacities, needs, democratic relationships, and experiences provided in areas of living. All have direct bearing on the extent to which the elementary school, and particularly the music education program in the elementary classroom, is meeting its responsibilities.

The Child

I. Development of the capacities of the child as an individual and meeting basic needs of the individual:

    A. By developing physical well-being through

        1. A sense of security,

        2. Emotional health, and

        3. Mental health.

    B. By developing intellectual power through

        1. A sense of adequacy by the acquisition of factual knowledge,

C. By developing social growth through
   1. A sense of belonging,
   2. Guiding patterns of conduct,
   3. Nonsectarian and spiritual values, and
   4. Proper moral values.

II. Development of the child as a democratic individual with wholesome group attitudes:
   A. By clarifying democratic human relationships through
      1. A respect for individual ideas and
      2. A sense of responsibility to the group.

The Teacher, Supervisor, Administrator

I. Application of broad concepts of the instructional program:
   A. By providing facilities and materials essential to the program,
   B. By developing guiding patterns for staff, supervisor, and teacher preparation, and
   C. By use of community resources.

II. Application of recognized basic principles of scope and organization to provide opportunities for learning through:
   A. Teaching-learning processes, and
   B. Facilities and materials.

CHAPTER VI

MUSIC FOR EARLY CHILDHOOD— AGES TWO TO SIX[1]

THERE HAS BEEN an effort to point out the necessity of understanding the pre-school child's growth and development in relation to the musical experiences which are a part of his daily living. Music in nursery schools and kindergartens, music in church and community groups and in the home, for children under six, has been considered. Cooperation of the National Association for Nursery Education and of the Association for Childhood Education International proved to be invaluable. Kindergarten and nursery teachers, recruited through these two organizations, have taken an active part in music programs, workshops and study groups held in various communities from time to time throughout the year.

SUGGESTIONS FOR ENHANCING MUSIC FOR YOUNG CHILDREN

(1) Create a free and favorable environment through shared enjoyment, participation, exploration, experimentation.

(2) Allow for individual musical development and growth.

(3) Encourage singing at any time and about anything—familiar songs, created songs, and vicarious participation in songs of older children and grown-ups. Songs should be learned through appropriation rather than by direct rote teaching.

(4) Provide for space in which to enjoy free rhythms. Singing games and creative dancing which allow the child to respond as he feels rather than to directions should be used.

(5) Provide good instruments: Piano, phonograph, radio with FM, percussion instruments, simple pitch instruments such as chimes, bells, psalteries, autoharp. Percussion instruments should be used freely in connection with songs, instrumental music and activities not directly connected with music. Exploration and experimentation with one instrument at a time is important. Others should be added as interest and skill develop.

(6) Introduce standard instruments, such as violin, flute, French horn, etc., so that child can see, hear, and ask questions.

(7) Before starting formal lessons on any instrument, be sure that the child has had much first-hand experience with music—singing, realization of rhythms with large body movements, listening, and playing simple percussion and melody instruments.

(8) Provide for listening to music without distraction—music on radio or phonograph, skilled musicians in person, members of the school or family group, no matter how simple the skills.

(9) Build the child's own record library recording by recording rather than a large number at a time.

---

[1] From the report submitted by Adeline McCall, Chapel Hill, North Carolina, National Chairman, Music in American Education Committee on Preschool and Kindergarten Music.

MUSICAL EXPERIENCES AND LEARNINGS FOR THE PRESCHOOL AND KINDERGARTEN CHILD [1]

Singing

Having fun with singing.
Finding singing voice as different from speaking voice.
Singing simple, short songs.
Tone matching and tone games.
Singing in tune.
Integrating songs with home and school experiences.
Singing individually and in groups.
Recognizing and expressing moods in music.
Growth and development through group participation.

Rhythmic

Learning to move about in time to music.
Developing free rhythmic responses to music.
Responding in singing games and folk dances through directed rhythms.
Enjoying a variety of experiences in rhythm: fast-slow; heavy-light; smooth-jerky.
Interpreting the story of the music.
Acting out nursery rhymes.
Impersonating characters.
Playing singing games, action songs, finger plays, mimetic play.
Making and playing rhythm instruments.
Bodily coordination through rhythmic experiences.

Listening

Learning to listen to music.
Acting out what they hear in music.
Distinguishing between slow and fast; loud and soft; high and low.
Recognizing familiar melodies.
Identifying familiar instruments of the orchestra.

Instrument Playing

Listening to the music to be played.
Clapping or tapping the music to get the feel of the rhythm.
Choosing proper instruments for the music; soft-loud; heavy-light; high-low; smooth-jerky.
Selecting instruments to interpret songs.
Playing phrases or calls on melody instruments.
Developing self-control and self-reliance.
Becoming aware of starting and stopping at the right time.
Listening to and appreciating the efforts of others.

Creative

Feeling free to interpret own responses.
Learning to listen and to see mentally, color, sound, beauty of sight and sound, space and movement.
Developing own expression in verse, poetry, melody, rhythm, story, or dramatization.
Allowing imagination to develop.
Gaining self-confidence.
Enjoying free and dramatic play.
Creating own stories, dramatizations and interpretations.

---

[1] Prepared by Sylvia Ostrow, San Antonio, Texas.

FIELDS IN WHICH PRESCHOOL AND KINDERGARTEN CHILDREN PARTICIPATE IN MUSIC [1]

Homes. (a) Those of parents with good musical background in which children may be surrounded with good music; and (b) those in which no thought is given to worthiness of good music either because of the lack of knowledge of it or the lack of time to foster it.

Churches. (a) Here, too often emphasis is upon volume rather than quality. (b) Instrumental music is almost completely ignored. Children are sometimes taken into the sanctuary to hear a short selection played on the pipe organ.

Nursery Schools. (a) Those in which some person on the staff has good musical background and adequate training and interest in children; (b) those in which music is handled in any fashion with emphasis placed upon volume in the vocal field, and no use made of instrumental works.

Dancing Schools. (a) Most of the music used is popular music. The use of it for rhythmic purposes is not so bad, but for the singing material the texts are unsuitable for children 2-6 years of age. (b) Individuals and groups are commanded to "sing out" resulting almost in yelling. Ranges of songs are usually too low, or with too wide a range.

Influence of Radio and TV. There are radios in 90% of our American homes and television is following closely. Music is heard many hours each day. Children absorb music language just as they absorb the spoken language with which they are associated.

SUGGESTIONS FOR IMPROVING THE MUSIC PROGRAM FOR PRESCHOOL AND KINDERGARTEN CHILDREN [2]

Homes. Music educators should seek opportunities to speak at Mothers Clubs, Parent-Teacher Associations, etc., concerning music for these children. Talks might well include information on proper use of the singing voice, appropriate music, both vocal and instrumental, a list of good recordings and musical games for the children, and a list of books and magazines for the parents to use.

Churches. Music educators can take active part in Sunday Schools, directing the assembly singing and organizing children's choirs.

Nursery Schools. Recommendations could be made through the State Music Educators Association and local boards of education to all organized nursery schools as to how a well-planned and carried-out program could be of great benefit to the child's future in school.

Dancing Schools. Music educators could work toward personal contact with dancing school teachers. Invite attendance to school programs to establish friendly contacts.

Radio and TV. Recommendations could be made through national education groups to the major broadcasting companies that music used in the programs for these "tots" be kept at high level. This is a power far too potent to be ignored.

EXAMPLE OF A GROWING PROJECT IN SONGS AND PICTURES

September: To illustrate a song the children were learning, the teacher pasted an appropriate picture on tag stock and placed it on display. Children began bringing in pictures for songs being sung or pictures for which the teacher found appropriate songs.

October: The magazine pictures were discarded and the children began illustrating the songs in their own ways.

---

[1] From Missouri report on Preschool and Kindergarten Music.

[2] *Ibid.*

November: Thanksgiving songs and illustrations.

December: A song book with pictures by the children ; songs selected by the children for a Christmas present for parents ; the mimeographed music with words supplied by the teacher.

Spring: Songs created and illustrated by the children.

Selected Source Materials for the Child's Early Years [1]

GENERAL—THE CHILD'S DEVELOPMENT

Association for Childhood Education. *Nursery School Portfolio.* Washington, D. C.: 1200 Fifteenth Street. 1953. 75¢. Send for other titles.

Gesell, Arnold and Ilg, Frances. *The Child from Five to Ten.* New York: Harper and Brothers, 1946.
————. *The First Five Years of Life.* New York: Harper and Brothers, 1940.

Horwich, Frances. *Curriculum for Nursery Schools and Kindergartens.* New York: Hines, Hayden and Eldredge, 1947.

Hymes, James L., Jr. *Enjoy Your Child—Ages 1, 2 and 3,* Pamphlet No. 141. New York: Public Affairs Pamphlets, 22 E. 38th Street. 1950. 25¢.
————. *Understanding Your Child.* New York: Prentice-Hall, Inc., 1951.

Jenkins, Gladys G., Schacter, Helen and Bauer, William W. *These Are Your Children.* Chicago: Scott Foresman & Co., 1949.

Meek, Lois Hayden. *Your Child's Development and Guidance* (Rev. ed.). New York: J. B. Lippincott, 1951.

Mitchell, Lucy Sprague. *Our Children and Our Schools.* New York: Simon and Schuster, 1950.
————. *Know Your Children in School.* New York: The Macmillan Company, 1954.

National Association for Nursery Education. *Some Ways of Distinguishing a Good Nursery School.* Kingston, R. I.: Distribution Center, NANE, University of Rhode Island. 5¢.

New York State Department of Education. *Some Ways of Distinguishing a Good Kindergarten.* Albany, N. Y.: Bureau of Child Development and Parent Education.

Ridenour, Nina and Johnson, Isabel. *Some Special Problems of Children—Aged 2 to 5 Years.* New York: National Association for Mental Health, Inc., 1790 Broadway, 1951. 25¢.

Spock, Benjamin, M.D. *The Pocket Book of Baby and Child Care.* New York: Pocket Books, Inc., 1946. 35¢.

BOOKS FOR THE TEACHER

Association for Arts in Childhood. *Arts in Childhood Bulletins:* "Creative Movement" and "Enjoying Music." Nashville, Tenn.: Fisk University, 1952.

Barrett, Mary. *Living Music With Children.* Kingston, R. I.: National Association for Nursery Education, 1951. Pamphlet, 20¢.

Cole, Natalie Robinson. *The Arts in the Classroom.* New York: John Day Co., 1940.

Hunt, Evelyn H. "What We Do About Music for Young Children," *Progressive Education Magazine.* New York: Progressive Education Association, January, 1940.

Landeck, Beatrice. *Children and Music.* New York: William Sloane Associates, Inc., 1952.

Pillsbury Foundation Studies: "Chant" (I), "General Observations" (II), "Musical Notation" (III), "Free Use of Instruments for Musical Growth" (IV). Santa Barbara, Calif.: Pillsbury Foundation for the Advancement of Music Education, 1941-1944. 50¢ each.

Sheehy, Emma Dickson. *There's Music in Children.* New York: Henry Holt and Company, Inc., 1946.

Thorn, Alice G. *Music for Children.* New York: Scribner's, 1929.

Thorne, Margaret. *The Young Child and His Music.* New York: Arts Co-operative Service, 1950.

BOOKS—SONGS AND RHYTHMS

Aitken, Geraldine. *Music in the Home Before Lessons Begin.* New York: Carl Fischer, Inc., 1951.

Bailey, Charity, Abeson, Marion and Michel, Sally. *Playtime with Music.* New York: Liveright, 1952.

Bradford, Margaret. *Keep Singing, Keep Humming.* New York: Wm. R. Scott, 1946.

Buttolph, Edna. *Music in Motion.* Cincinnati: Willis Music Co., 1953.

Coleman, Satis N. *Dancing Time.* New York: John Day Co., 1952.

Coleman, Satis N. and Thorn, Alice G. *Another Singing Time.* New York: John Day Co., 1937.
————. *Singing Time.* New York: John Day, Co., 1929.
————. *A New Singing Time.* New York: John Day Co., 1952.

Coit, Lottie E. and Bampton, Ruth. *Follow the Music.* Boston: C. C. Birchard & Company, 1948.

Crowinshield, Ethel. *Stories That Sing.* Boston: Boston Music Co., 1945.

Diller, Angela and Page, Kate S. *A Pre-School Music Book.* New York: G. Schirmer, Inc., 1936.

Landeck, Beatrice. *Songs to Grow On.* New York: Marks and Sloane, 1952.
————. *More Songs to Grow On.* New York: Marks and Sloane, 1954.

MacCartney, Laura P. *Songs for the Nursery School.* Cincinnati: Willis Music Co.

McCall, Adeline. *Timothy's Tunes.* Boston: Boston Music Co., 1943.

Nelson, Mary Jarman. *Fun with Music.* Chicago: Albert Whitman & Co., 1941.

Nelson, Mary Jarman and Tipton, Gladys. *Music for Early Childhood.* New York: Silver Burdett Company, 1952.

Seatter, Elizabeth, et al. *Romp in Rhythm.* Cincinnati: Willis Music Co., 1944.

Seeger, Ruth Crawford. *American Folk Songs for Children.* New York: Doubleday & Company, Inc., 1948.

Songs Children Like, Folk Songs from Many Lands. Washington, D. C.: Association for Childhood Education, 1954.

Wessells, Katherine T. *Golden Song Book.* New York: Simon and Schuster, 1945.

---

[1] Prepared by Adeline McCall, National Chairman, Music in American Education Committee on Preschool and Kindergarten Music. For additional bibliography see pp. 91-93.

CHAPTER VII

BASIC MUSIC IN THE ELEMENTARY SCHOOL[1]

I N THE ELEMENTARY SCHOOL, where the emphasis of the total school is on the physical, intellectual, social, and emotional growth of each individual child, music, with its variety of activities, is just another experience which contributes to these phases of child growth and development.

In the elementary school children should become aware of music, develop an understanding of music through a variety of experiences, and find enjoyment through participation in some phase of musical activity.

For some children, *singing*, either alone or in groups, is a happy, satisfying experience. Other children find much more pleasure in *moving bodily* to the rhythm of music in singing games and dances. *Playing instruments* may be the most satisfying musical experience for some children, to other children just *listening* with a musical "awareness" seems to be the most pleasant musical experience. Other children with keen imagination and a spark of *creative* ability will use music as one more medium for the expression of their ideas.

The purpose of the elementary school is, therefore, to guide children through a pattern of varied experiences in musical activity so that each child, to the extent of his or her ability, will enjoy using music as a means of self-expression and will develop a consciousness of music as an art and an understanding of the musical expression of others.

Singing. Singing is perhaps the most important and the most universally developed music activity in the elementary school. Practically all children can learn to sing with some degree of pleasure so they should have opportunities to experience the joy of singing alone and with others. It is of utmost importance in the primary grades to sing for the sheer joy of singing, to sing with spirit about the things that are going on within the classroom and at home, and it is important to sing often within a school day.

With older elementary children it is important to achieve through singing a growing appreciation of music as something bringing brightness and beauty into daily living. It is important to develop the skillful use of the singing voice through a growing sense of tonal relationships, to acquire a knowledge of music fundamentals, and to increase skill in reading music from notation.

The classroom teacher, and the special music teacher as well, should be careful in the selection of song material for the elementary school. The teacher should give special attention to the use of the child's voice as related to the range of the songs and to the singing-ease of the melodic line. The text content and text vocabulary should be suitable to the maturity of the child because through the selection of materials, the teacher will prepare for and provide for the changing boy voice and will develop part-singing. Song material is a proper means for developing an appreciation of and a love for music.

Reliance can be placed in the selection of materials as found in most standard, current music texts. The teacher guides or manuals for the basic elementary music texts have excellent directions for ways of making music a part of the daily class-

---

[1] From the report submitted by Earluth Epting, Atlanta, Georgia, National Chairman, Music in American Education Committee on Elementary School Music.

room activity and suggest varied types of teaching techniques for the teacher who wants help in "what to do and how to do it."

For the classroom teacher who feels vocally insecure, excellent recordings of songs from the basic music texts are available. Several recent books have been written especially for the classroom teacher.

Rhythmic Activities. Moving to music satisfies the child's love and need for motion. It can bring about an understanding and appreciation of music by developing an awareness of rhythmic patterns and melodic ideas as well as mood and dynamic expression. Movement to music in the program of the classroom should make use of a variety of means of expression—*imitation and dramatization, patterned physical activity, and free interpretation.*

Through careful teacher-pupil planning a variety of "things-to-do-to-music" should be developed. The teacher's manuals for the basic music series include singing games and dances suitable for various stages of physical and rhythmic development, suggest means of motivating free responses to music, ideas for dramatization of songs, and instrumental music.

The classroom teacher, aware of the developmental sequence in muscular coordination, will realize that coordination of big muscles must be developed before coordination of smaller muscles is possible. Recently published books should be consulted to find suggestions of materials and techniques.

Listening. Listening to music is actually present in a sense in all musical activity and is a basic phase of music development. Sometimes children listen to music in order to be able to respond through bodily movement, or in order to be able to join in singing timely songs. At times children may listen to music in a formal situation which demands best concert-audience manners, or they may listen to music quietly in a relaxed, recreational situation.

An important function of the listening activity is to provide experiences through which children may become aware of music; its intensity, tempo, rhythm, structure, style, and mood.

(1) *Listening to dance.* Little children love activity and in their first musical experiences may express themselves by clapping, marching, skipping, galloping, swaying, or other muscular movements. In the primary grades it is necessary that the compositions be simple and of short duration if the children are to understand them sufficiently to respond rhythmically.

(2) *Listening to sing.* Singing is dependent upon listening. If the teacher has developed the right listening attitude, off-pitch singers, through listening, find their voices; new songs are learned; tone quality is improved; discrimination is established; and a real love for music is developed. While listening is a basic factor in singing and playing, such performance, in turn, makes a real contribution to listening. Children develop musicianship to a certain degree by listening to their own performances and to the performances of others.

(3) *Listening as an audience.* Listening to fine music on the air should be encouraged whether the broadcasts are received at home or at school. Many schools carry on a program for home listening with splendid results. Bulletins are prepared which give a résumé of the best programs for the week; the children listen to some of them and report. Home listening to suggested programs not only enriches the child's musical background, but through it many parents become interested in better music and thus are more interested in the musical development of their children, as well as in the entire music program of the schools.

Artists' concerts for children should be a part of the listening program, and a school concert series should be conducted in every community where it is at all possible. In case the school is too small to support such a project, children should be taken occasionally to a nearby town or city where there are concerts. Attending a concert not only stimulates interest in the listening lesson at school, but provides a beautiful experience which will remain long in the memories of the children.

Music in the church and in the movies is important. Here the teacher has an opportunity to teach the children to listen appreciatively to the music they hear at church and to develop an ability to evaluate music heard at movies.

(4) *Just listening.* There are significant psychological differences between shared listening and solitary listening. Children need to experience both.

The question frequently arises with teachers as to the amount of assistance children need in developing an understanding of the music they hear. Some teachers give too much assistance; others, too little. To leave the average child free to make his own interpretation usually results in neither thinking nor feeling but in "listless" listening; to impose too many ideas upon the child is to inhibit his growth and development. There must be a happy medium. Little children will need more guidance than older children.

The intelligent teacher will know thoroughly the music to be studied; she will know how and when to present it. Through skillful guidance she will stimulate thinking on the part of the children as to what the music really means. Opportunity should be given to children to express in their own way their feelings and appreciation of the music heard.

Children enjoy playing favorite recordings, and should be permitted to do so during free periods in school; at recess, noon, or before and after school. Many times there will be more active listening and more interest during these free periods than during the listening lesson. Any experience which creates interest in music and helps to develop a love for it, should be included as part of the listening program.

To develop an enriched listening program, a piano, a phonograph, a library of carefully selected records, and a radio need to be available. There should be recordings of songs for little folks and for older boys and girls which are both familiar and new; recordings for physical expression, for form, and for mood; music which suggests a story, both in major and minor modes; music in which harmony is predominant; the orchestra with its instruments; voices both in solo and ensembles; music of other lands; and, above all, music for music's own sake.

(5) *Recordings.* Many fine suggestions for an elementary school library are to be found in books and manuals for the basic texts in series listed previously.

Teaching Music Reading as a Skill [1]

If the ultimate aim of music education is for children to "appreciate the beauty and joy of music through participation," teachers should be aware of the place the skill of reading has in the elementary music program. The purpose of music reading is to open up for the child new musical insights and understanding that will increase his enjoyment of music. It becomes an integral part of his equipment to experience music. It must make sense for him as an individual regardless of his background. Therefore, the student must be shown the function music reading has in his everyday participation in musical activities.

Modern programs of music instruction include many activities, such as rhythms, dramatizations, and creative experiences, that are designed for the child to discover enjoyment and appreciation. Reading should be a part of this program even though there may be wide ranges of individual differences.

Teachers should realize that ever since music has been taught in the common schools of our country there have been some children who have been good music

[1] By Joseph C. Hartley, Principal, Peninsula Elementary School, Portland, Oregon. This article appeared in the *NEA Journal*, November 1954, and is included here as an indication of administrative understanding and cooperation.—Ed.

readers. Recently, there has been a tendency to avoid this important area of music education. Teachers at times have felt that in a modern music program, reading skills did not have a place. As a result some children have been denied a most pleasurable experience.

It should be recognized that elementary music is of necessity a teacher-centered activity, and that a child after progressing through the primary and early intermediate grades is more demanding of the teacher. Some teachers have had difficulties with classroom control at this point because they taught one activity at a time for *all* of the class. This meant that some members of the class were vitally interested, some passively interested, and others just bored with the whole situation. If a good proportion of the class activity was in the two last-mentioned groups, a distressing situation usually arose for both the students and the teacher. Music educators should devise means of working with small groups within a class.

A Survey of Student Preference. Students often feel a need for more extensive instruction in notation. In an experimental seventh grade class at Peninsula School, Portland, Oregon, twenty-seven pupils were interviewed personally concerning what they would like to do in a general music class for their level. Of the questions pertaining to reading and singing, twenty-two replied they would like to learn more about notes and how to use them. Twenty wanted to know how they might produce a better singing tone. Of the others, five felt they were having adequate music experience and were quite satisfied with their own performance. Two of the class just didn't care. After five months of instruction the questions were asked again. Of the twenty-two students wanting to know about notation, seven stated they had learned how to read music. This was verified by the teacher who observed increased interest and participation on the part of the seven. The teacher also observed that the other fifteen showed various degrees of growth. Nine of the twenty students who wished to produce a better singing tone stated they had improved and enjoyed singing more than they did previously. These replies are an indication that children of this age sincerely demand more refinement of instruction and deeper understanding of the musical offerings of the curriculum. Music reading should be a part of the offering.

It should be realized that background for music reading begins in the primary grades when the child first takes part in a musical activity. As he grows and develops in musical understanding he shows many signs of readiness for music reading that the teacher should observe, such as:

An interest in wanting to learn new songs.
An awareness to tonal and rhythm patterns that are similar and can be found in many songs.
An awareness of loud and soft tones, high and low tones, long and short tones, and songs that may be sung quickly or slowly.
Participation in rhythmic activities such as dancing, marching, singing.
Active participation in singing.
A desire to know about instruments, their tones, mechanical manipulation.
A desire to play an instrument.
A desire to learn to read music.

It is obvious that the first experiences in music should be of a broad nature to develop readiness for music reading. At the intermediate grade level the teacher must carefully observe the reading readiness of each child. The program of music instruction that has taken place in the primary years should be understood by the teacher so that the child's musical needs may be fully grasped.

A Problem Arises. How, within the organization of an ordinary classroom, may a teacher plan instruction for the children ready to find music? Here are a few suggestions that might be helpful:

(1) Bring those children who are to be introduced to music reading together in one group. If the teacher is a homeroom teacher and has to care for other children in the class, give the class something to do of an independent nature, such as an art project.

(2) Tell the children who are not participating in the group that they may listen and watch and even take part if they wish. No child should feel left out of any kind of music class experience.

(3) Work with the group as if it were pleasurable and not a drill type of activity.

(4) If the school is large enough, it may be possible to group children from other rooms or grades who show reading readiness. Those left could be grouped with some other teacher.

In the past, some teachers have thought that teaching music meant knowledge of key signatures, notes, and other abstract facts. Knowledge of this kind does not lead to reading skill. It may be helpful to the student to better understand musical notation after he can perform independently. Reading is the coordination or training of the ear and eye to transfer the symbol to music production. Each child must discover a method of making his voice or instrument do what the symbol says. He may use a combination of "sol fa" syllables along with a number system, or he may read by position alone. Regardless of what system he uses, it must be discovered and used as his very own. This is the reason that teachers should recognize the factor of individual differences and plan their instruction accordingly. It would be futile to try to get all children of an age group to perform exactly to the same degree of mastery. There is not a "one-way" or technique of teaching music reading. Each teacher must discover different techniques to fit different groups of children.

It is important also to guide music reading activities into as many channels of musical expression as possible. Therefore, it is imperative that a variety of approaches be made to meet the problem of individual differences. Above all, the reading experiences must be kept simple and understandable to provide success. Children love to succeed and see progress in their own development. This factor is very influential in sustaining interest regardless of the type of guidance a teacher gives to the pupil.

The focal point of any music program revolves around the teacher. Therefore, her expressions of feelings and attitudes about music and musical problems that children bring to the classroom will have much to do with the success of her teaching. If she is sincere and willing to learn with the children even though she does not have too much musical background, the chances of giving the children a pleasurable experience are many.

Teaching music reading is not difficult. Here are a few suggestions:

(1) Begin with very simple tonal patterns that are made by the teacher. These might contain only four quarter notes arranged in a 1-3-2-1 pattern. These tonal patterns might be taken from familiar songs the class has learned. Write them in notation on the blackboard or staff card *without words*. The class should sing them with some easy neutral syllable. Words or stories have a tendency to detract the eye from the musical symbol.

(2) Copy from familiar songs the repeated phrases for comparison. This technique can be varied by discovering likenesses, differences, and similarities.

(3) Give opportunity for the children to read at sight many songs that are not familiar to them. If possible, use an old set of books and cover up the words.

(4) Attempt many reading songs with words after tonal and rhythmic patterns have been established, making sure that no problem arises that has not been studied and understood by the children.

(5) Make the school chorus a very select group for the skillful and talented.

Emphasize quality rather than quantity. Mass groups tend to cover up many musical weaknesses. This select group can be used as a motivator for reading.

(6) Give the students opportunity to be creative by composing their own melodies. This gives them a chance to use notation, and to become familiar with some of the mechanics of music reading.

(7) Sing many songs in unison before attempting independent part-singing.

(8) Establish a room quartet or ensemble from the reading group which shows rapid progress.

(9) Give opportunity for the reading group to perform at special programs.

The teaching of music reading is only a small part of the total music experience a child should receive. With the broadened scope of the music program to include all of the possible activities inherent in a program of good instruction, music reading can enhance enjoyment. Some children have the ability to become excellent independent readers. It is important that they be given opportunities to realize fully their capabilities. Other children have the ability to become partially independent readers, and still others will never be able to read music securely. However, all children can develop to a degree a minimum ability to follow the printed score. Music reading is fun, and the approach should be made with that attitude by the teacher. It is incidental to the total musical experience of the child, but it is important. When children are exposed to music reading activities as a part of a gradual process throughout the grades, participation in singing becomes a real joy and many new avenues of musical experience are opened to them.

Music Comes Alive [1]

In the beginning, there is the growing child—a human being filled to the brim and overflowing with feelings and responses toward life that find satisfying outlets in musical expression. Music is "a way of life" in childhood, for much of child play is close kin to music.

Music comes alive in the flesh, bones, and tissue as well as in the hearts, voices and expressive movements of children who identify themselves completely with music that is enjoyed. Who has not heard from some child, "I am the music when I sing and dance"? Music comes to life in the schoolroom whenever the teaching situation utilizes the spontaneous music-making that fits into the many expressive play activities which the young engage in without benefit of parents and teachers.

Remember this: All on their own, young children and older boys and girls are busy finding out many fascinating things about the variety of tonal qualities and rhythmic movements that are in themselves and other people; in the world of animals; in the great out-of-doors; and in hundreds of mechanical things, all the way from scooters and skates to planes and trains. Furthermore, anything and everything that catches the fancy of a lively youngster is reproduced with voice and gesture, be it the "swoosh" of a jet plane or the squeak of one's own new shoes.

The young, however, need the help of their elders in becoming alive to the fact that music can be applied to their everyday play interests and activities. Children have a *feeling* for the meanings in music. However, because what they *feel* is sensory and nonverbal in character, children need assistance in becoming aware of the musical values that are in their singing voices, their rhythmic bodies, and their eager hands and fingers, as well as in their special curiosities and likings.

Growth—musical or otherwise—is an active, not a passive, process. A child learns to sing by singing; he learns to move expressively by moving; he learns to play an instrument by manipulating a given instrument; and he learns *to think* in musical terms by "acting out" the music that is in himself in as many appealing and enjoyable ways as possible.

[1] Lilla Belle Pitts. *Music in Elementary Education* (Music Educators National Conference). Distributed at the MENC Biennial Convention, Chicago, 1954.

Action songs may open the way for one kind of child, playing on a drum can awaken the interest of another. Still others come to life when the opportunity comes to go "galloping off to town"; or "skipping out to the orchard to pick apples"; or "down the track, clickety-clack," etc. The point is to provide means for every kind of child to get into the thick of things, body and soul.

At every level of growth, a child should enjoy the feeling of success which comes from *taking part*, from making his contribution in at least one musical activity. The child who is timid about singing may be self-confident with an instrument. Another may be indifferent about rhythmic play but interested and resourceful when it comes to musical dramatization. No child, however, ought to be forced or urged to do what others are doing. In music, there are children who must be given time to feel comfortable in situations which are, to the ear, strange and sometimes confusing and frightening.

Training a child in the complex techniques of skillful musical performance before he has reached the degree of maturity which prepares him to assimilate what is learned through its purposeful use day after day is not only time wasted, but more often than not it is a positive detriment to uninterrupted progress in their mastery.

Successful teaching and learning in the field of music calls for a point of view that is sound with regard to the fundamental nature of both *children* and *music*. In child growth the active precedes the passive; imaginative interpretation precedes intellectual understanding; and *sensing* meanings comes before attempting to translate abstract symbols (notes, letters, numerals) back into the meanings for which they stand merely as reminders.

Musical notation is *not music*. It simply pictures for the eye those musical experiences that are already alive in children, therefore *known* to them. No child can read printed words that stand for something or some idea that he has never lived into *knowingness*. Similarly, no child—or adult—can think or read the printed patterns of notation unless he has had living experiences with the melodic-rhythmic motives or phrases which groups of notational symbols picture for the eye.

Part-singing is a problem in many instances because an attempt is made to have boys and girls "read" harmonic notation before they have had sufficient experience either in *sensing* chord "color" or in responding imaginatively to the emotional effect of harmonic singing. Young people who are encouraged to "make up" harmonies to familiar songs are responding to a color, texture, and richness that is giving added emotional and imaginative values to what the voice sings, the fingers play, and the ear hears. Experiences of this kind must precede any attempt either to "read" harmonic notation or to "spell" major and minor triads. *Knowing* and *naming* are not effective approaches to harmonic development. Each of these aspects of learning follows as a normal aftermath of enjoyable and successful undertakings.

After all, the big point is not what the learner can do in producing more and better musical performances. The crucial question is what has music to contribute to growing better, happier, and more vitally creative boys and girls and men and women. Therefore, the major aim of classroom and special music teachers alike is to work together for the fullest development of each child—physical and emotional, mental and spiritual.

Music is for life's sake. And music comes alive most importantly when it becomes a way of getting more out of life for the greatest number of people. The realm of music is rich and varied, and in its broad domain there is room enough for all.

NOTE: For additional reference see *Music in the Elementary School,* MENC reprint of *The National Elementary Principal* Special Music Issue, February, 1951. Bibliography prepared by the MENC Committee on Elementary School Music, 1951. 56 pp. 50¢.

CHAPTER VIII

MUSIC IN THE RURAL SCHOOL[1]

THE SOCIOLOGIST'S DEFINITION of a rural school includes any school system in a community of under 2500 population. A rural school curriculum should have general goals of achievement for larger areas than single grades, based upon the needs and maturity levels of the children concerned. The curriculum should not differ in essential content from that of the urban elementary school. Areas of musical experience and activities should be outlined specifically as adaptable for the small ungraded school. This should consider child growth rather than subject matter and should attempt also to meet the needs of the vast body of transient, underprivileged children whose irregular attendance increases the already difficult situation in the rural school. These larger areas may be defined as primary, intermediate, and upper grade. On each level there should be vital experiences in singing, listening, playing, creating, and evaluating in order to provide a satisfying experience for each child.

Because Wisconsin has re-established the position of State Music Supervisor, the following material has been used to illustrate activities which may be helpful.

Rural School Music in Wisconsin. [2] According to the above definition, with the exception of the southern half of the Lake Michigan shore, Wisconsin is a rural state. Some rural communities have comparatively fine music education programs. Usually, the high school music program in these communities is much stronger than the music in the elementary school. The concern is mainly with the one-teacher school having eight grades because Wisconsin has about four thousand such schools, and over one thousand rural elementary schools with four teachers or less.

Only two counties have music supervision. Most Wisconsin counties are not ready to finance supervision of rural schools.

There are seventy-two county superintendents elected and financed by their individual counties. Each one appoints a general supervisor for each one hundred teachers. The salary of this supervisor is subsidized by the state. Little, if any, of the money for supervision comes from the county served.

Some reasons for pleasure in state music supervision are:

(1) Remote areas seem to make particularly fine efforts to educate their children in spite of financial handicaps.

(2) Rural teachers generally are tireless and devoted workers. For example, in a northerly county there was 100% attendance at an evening music workshop with the temperature 30° below zero and some having to drive forty miles.

(3) Unusually fine spirit and hospitality.

(4) The children seem so appreciative.

A little less than 10% of these schools recently have become part of the decentralized type of reorganized district, which is an administrative unit having a village or city high school and grades along with several outlying rural schools. Through setting up six experimental decentralized districts comprising one entire county, there evolved a flexible plan by which special services in music are now being offered the rural outlying schools. Most of the approximately forty new

---

[1] From the report submitted by Thomas Annett, LaCrosse, Wisconsin, National Chairman, Music in American Education Committee on Rural School Music.

[2] Prepared by G. Lloyd Schultz, Wisconsin State Supervisor of Music.

districts of this kind offer instrumental as well as special vocal opportunities to the children in the outlying rural schools.

Using an idea borrowed from Waukesha county, an experimental unit was established in Walworth county. In this plan the individual schools contribute to the county office a fixed sum for the employment of music specialists and for the purchase of music equipment. The county superintendent then provides one specialist for each twenty to twenty-three schools with one serving as chairman. The duties of the specialists include direct teaching, supervision, leadership for music curriculum planning, and leadership for county-wide musical activities. The three music broadcasts of the state-wide radio networks are usually used as a core of the curriculum. Ultimately, the plan is to include instrumental music. In initiating such a program it becomes the duty of the state supervisor to present this plan to school board members on a county-wide basis.

A most important item in the revised plan is that about one-fifth of the specialist's time is spent in consultation with rural classroom teachers who are responsible for the major portion of the music program. This plan is similar in many ways to the circuit teacher plan of some other states.

A most valuable project in terms of improving the rural school music has been the County-Wide Music Curriculum study project, which follows the curriculum philosophy of Wisconsin. The state music department issues only brief curriculum guides, and with state staff assistance the actual development of the curriculum takes place on the county or local level.

The state supervisor of music works with the county-wide groups of school boards to stimulate school boards to purchase musical equipment and books, as well as to evaluate the music curricula in their schools. Boards are urged to combine to purchase such large items as tape recorders and film projectors.

In-service training of teachers by means of county teachers' institutes and workshops are a major activity of the state supervisor.

The state music department co-sponsors, coordinates, and promotes music clinics and workshops by the university, and teachers' colleges stimulate extension courses in elementary school music where needed. It is important then that rural classroom teachers have music in pre-service training. Wisconsin has twenty-three county normal schools offering a two-year rural curriculum and eight teachers' colleges offering two-, three- and four-year rural elementary curricula. Constant efforts have been made to raise the music requirements until, with a few exceptions, six semester hours in all four-year elementary and rural curricula, and four semester hours in most two-year curricula are required.

The ultimate goal is to bring to the rural child the same musical opportunities as afforded those who live in the cities. In the musical education handbook of the state music department there is no distinction between the program for the rural child as compared with the city child.

If the rural teacher can be helped to see the need for music in the lives of boys and girls, to lose any fear regarding the teaching of music, and to acquire and use the few tools needed, the lives of many children will be enriched musically.

The Status of Rural School Music—A Survey [1]

A survey of the rural situation in the United States was conducted in 1952-53. A questionnaire was sent to all state supervisors of music and to State Departments

[1] Report of a survey made by Thomas Annett, National Chairman, Committee on Rural School Music.

of Education of those states not having state supervisors of music. Replies were returned from forty-six states which yielded the following information.

Number of One-Room Schools. There was found to be a total of 45,784 one-room schools. Nebraska and Iowa each reported over 4,000 one-room schools while Connecticut has none and New Hampshire has only four.

Grades Covered in These Schools. Most states reported eight grades in the one-room school; Delaware reported only six and Virginia, seven grades. Several states reported one- and two-room schools with a varying number of grades: Three, four, five, six, seven and eight.

Number of Two-Room Schools. The total of two-teacher schools was 11,555. Tennessee reported 1,019 and Washington, 998. Delaware has sixteen, Hawaii, ten, and Connecticut "very few."

Nearly four times as many one-room schools were reported as two-teacher schools.

States Requiring Teaching of Music. It was interesting that many states legally require the teaching of music. Replies from forty-four states indicate that 43% require the teaching of music in the schools and 57% do not require the teaching of music by law. Thirty-six per cent of those states not legally requiring music to be taught, specifically stated that music is recommended or in the course of study. This implies that music is considered important even though it is not required by law. There was no significance between the legal requirement and issuing of music bulletins.

Schools Under Music Supervision. Of the forty-six states reporting, 36% have state supervisors of music. One other state, from which a reply was not received, has a state supervisor. All states with state music supervisors have at least a general over-all supervision of music. Among these states, Delaware, Massachusetts, Montana, New Mexico, New York, Ohio, and Wisconsin report that all schools are supervised. Among states with no state music supervision, Connecticut reports that all schools are supervised. However, Connecticut has no one-room schools and few two-teacher schools.

Iowa, with no state music supervisor and with 4,052 one-room schools, reported that all schools have supervision in music. The Fullerton Choir plan has been in operation in Iowa schools for many years and it was presumed that this type of supervision was meant. Illinois reported that 992 schools are supervised; Tennessee, 623; and Florida, 608. Michigan, Vermont, and West Virginia reported that one-third of the schools in these states are supervised in music. North Carolina has 30% supervised, and in New Jersey fourteen counties are supervised out of twenty-one.

Number of Hours in Music Required of the Rural Teacher. Great differences in the amount of music education required of the teacher of the rural school were evident. Georgia headed the list with a requirement of "seventy-five quarter hours in the field of music." New Hampshire specified twenty-four hours. Massachusetts listed "fifteen to thirty hours." Oregon and Wyoming specified nine hours; New Jersey, eight; Vermont, six to twelve; and Virginia, five to nine hours. About 20% of the states reporting indicated no regulation as to the number of hours of music required in the preparation of a rural teacher.

Bulletins. An impressive list of bulletins are issued by the various states. It was noted that almost no publications are published specifically for the teachers of the one-room and two-room schools. It would seem advisable to issue more material that directly applies to the great number of teachers in these schools.

Summary. This study shows that there are still many one-room and two-room schools with a concentration in the middle western states. There is evidence of interest and recognized value of music whether or not it is required by law. On the basis of this study, the teaching of music in rural schools needs considerably more attention from the profession than it is now receiving, and the music requirements for the training of rural teachers needs scrutiny.

Practical Experiences in Rural School Music

The following are selected examples of practical experiences in teaching music in the rural school, which may have general application or suggestive activities.

Grundy County, Illinois. Lucile Aarrestad, music supervisor of fifteen rural schools in Grundy County, Illinois, visits each school twice a week for thirty minutes. At Christmas, each school presents an operetta. In the spring, the schools come together at the county seat for a music festival, each school presenting one number. Themes of the festivals have been: 1950, "This Is My Country"; 1951, "A Prayer for Peace"; 1952, "South of the Border"; 1953, "I Like It Here."

Berkeley County, West Virginia. Mary Emma Allen of Berkeley County, West Virginia, states that she tries to assist the classroom teacher in taking the responsibility for the music in her classroom with encouragement and help from the music supervisors. Their program is supplemented by weekly broadcasts to the classroom, giving one music lesson each week for the lower grades and one for the upper grades. This has proved helpful within its limitation.

The children enjoy their music. The schools, even the one-room schools, are equipped with radios, phonographs, recordings, pianos, and rhythm band instruments. All these supplies are supplemented by the library at the county office.

Los Animas County, Colorado. James W. Chandler, director of music of Los Animas County High School, Trinidad, Colorado, describes the instrumental music program in the county school system. Though organized only four years ago each county high school has a band, and there is an all-county band composed of the better musicians from each of the school bands.

Woodbury County, Iowa. Lois Grammer of Morningside College reports that in Woodbury County, Iowa, an effort has been made to take music to the rural school boys and girls by utilizing available resources. The problem was simplified by the fact that nearly all of the one-room rural schools have consolidated with a nearby small town school. There are several qualified music teachers who live in Sioux City. They have contracted to teach in two or three of these small towns, each on a part-time basis. They drive out to one of the schools each day, usually to the same school twice per week. The combined salary from this "circuit" is good. The teacher has the advantage of living at home, and the small town has the benefit of help from an experienced and trained music teacher. These teachers have begun high school choral work, bands that include grade school, junior high and senior high school pupils, and they have helped the grade school classroom teacher to bring some music to her pupils.

Morningside College, located in Sioux City, has helped music students who are seniors to arrange a schedule that will permit them to go to some of these outlying towns to teach music on a part-time basis. By the time these students are seniors they have had sufficient academic work to be granted a temporary certificate to teach in the state. Sometimes two students drive together and divide the work to visit all classes in the amount of time available. College friends sometimes are taken along to help the school children gain a concept of various new musical ventures. The college music faculty responds to calls from rural teachers for assistance in planning their work or in solving their problems. The senior students are doing their student teaching at the same time in Sioux City where they are closely supervised. They receive college credit only for their supervised student teaching but are paid by the school district where they serve. They gain very valuable experience in this plan while giving the people in the rural communities something very worth while. The superintendents and the people in these small towns are most cooperative in this musical venture.

Walworth County, Wisconsin. Patricia McConaghy states that Walworth County began its rural music program in 1950, with the chief aim of helping children to enjoy music.

The music program is on a voluntary basis. Any school that desires a music teacher pays a certain yearly fee (1953-54, $170) into the Walworth County Music Fund. This fund pays for the teachers' salaries and transportation and for the purchase of books, phonographs, recordings, and rhythm instruments. A tape recorder and an autoharp have been bought. Each music teacher carries these materials to the schools for use during the weekly visit. Classroom teachers are encouraged to follow the music instructor's work, and many schools have purchased books or phonographs.

A music teacher visits five one-room schools per day, three in the morning and two in the afternoon. In order to accomplish the most in the allotted time, the lower four grades are combined, and the upper four grades become a group. This plan is flexible and adapted to the needs of each particular school.

A varied and interesting program adapted to each school's needs, interests, and abilities is presented. Some activities in a lower group are: Action songs or finger plays, rote songs appropriate to the season, singing games, listening to and discussing recordings, learning songs from music books, and locating simple music patterns and notes.

In the upper group, children are encouraged to listen to a weekly half-hour radio program of music designed for rural children.[1] Work is continued on the songs presented in these radio programs. Other activities include songs from regular music books, use of tonettes, square dancing, circle games, broom dances, and some two- and three-part singing.

In the spring of the year parents are invited to see a regular music class. The culminating activity for the year is a county-wide music festival in which 1200-1500 children participate.

The Walworth County Music Plan started with thirty-eight one-room schools, two state-graded schools and forty-three rural schools. Ninety-five per cent of all the country schools are served by four teachers.

Waukesha County, Wisconsin. Ruth Winter, music supervisor, outlined their plan as follows:

About 80% of the schools in Waukesha County join and support the county music plan each year. To be a participant, a school board signs an agreement sent out by the county superintendent of schools in the spring of the year in which the board agrees to pay a specified amount for the services of a music teacher's salary and mileage, and for the purchase of necessary supplies and equipment. Each supervisor is employed on a full-time basis.

According to the terms of the agreement, the supervisor visits each classroom once a week, spending forty minutes in a one-room rural school—twenty minutes with the lower grades and twenty minutes with the upper grades. Thirty minutes is allotted for each room of a multiple-room school. The music supervisor teaches

---

[1] Professor E. B. Gordon's "Journeys in Musicland," Madison, Wisconsin.

the class and leaves with the classroom teacher a lesson plan for the "follow-up" music work between visits.

Music supervisors' meetings are held before the school term begins at which time one general curriculum plan for the year is worked out. Monthly meetings are held to make specific plans to meet the needs of each school and classroom, and to correlate the music with other classroom activities. Because these music supervisors work on a full-time basis, their interest is completely in the Waukesha County Music Plan.

Since 1947, the per cent of schools participating in this music plan has risen from 50-60% to an average of 75%.

Iowa State Teachers College Extension Service. John W. Mitchell indicated that the work in music in Iowa rural schools is delegated largely to the Extension Department of Iowa State College. It consists of a "limited, but good as far as it goes, means for getting singing in rural schools." He feels that some headway is being made in getting other aspects of music taught in the schools and hopes that rhythm and listening materials will be added next year.

Michigan State College Extension Service. Mabel Olive Miles gives the following résumé of the rural school music work carried on in the Music Extension Department of the college:

The service reaches nineteen counties in the state. Three full-time music supervisors are employed by the college, working with the schools of these counties. During 1950-51, some 1,385 rural teachers attended extension music classes; 1,142 schools carried on the music program; and 37,219 children received instruction through this supervision. Forty-eight music programs were given in the nineteen counties as a culmination of the year's work, and 929 schools participated in final school programs. The choruses numbered 10,917 children and 6,286 participated in the rhythmic work of the programs.

General Suggestions

(1) That the improvement of the quality of instruction in college music courses for rural teachers will do more to aid the situation than the addition of more courses.

(2) That provision should be made for practice teaching in music for those intending to teach in the rural schools.

(3) That further consideration be given to the use of the phonograph, also of films and filmstrips as means of furthering the rural school music program.

(4) Encourage educational music programs by radio and television which are broadcast especially for rural school reception. This should include both in-school and home listening.

(5) Furter emphasize all phases of in-service teacher training from two major sources: (a) county and state supervision, (b) teachers colleges and universities.

(6) Further the work needed on minimum rural school curriculum content and specific teaching aids.

Bibliography—Rural School Music [1]

GENERAL—MUSIC EDUCATION

Annett, Thomas. *Music in the Rural School.* Boston: Boston Music Co., 1938.
Kinscella, Hazel and Tierney, Elizabeth. *Music in the Small School.* Lincoln: Nebraska University Extension Division, 1939.
McConathy, Osbourne, et al. *Music in Rural Education.* New York: Silver Burdett Company, 1923.

[1] Major music textbook companies have one-book and two-bock courses for rural school use. These teachers' manuals should be investigated.
For additional bibliography see pp. 91-93.

Morgan, Russell V. and Morgan, Hazel B. *Music Education in Action.* Chicago: Neil A. Kjos Music
Co., 1954. Chapter 23.
Music Education Source Book (4th printing). Chicago: Music Educators National Conference, 1951.
Chapter VIII, p. 45.

INSTRUMENTAL

Bolet, Jan. *What Makes an Orchestra.* New York: Oxford University Press, Inc., 1951.
Huntington, Harriett E. *Tune Up.* New York: Doubleday & Company, Inc., 1942.
Lacey, Marion. *Picture Book of Musical Instruments.* New York: Lothrop, Lee & Shepherd Co., 1942.
Posell, Elsa. *This Is an Orchestra.* Boston: Houghton Mifflin Company, 1950.
Stoddard, Hope. *From These Come Music.* New York: Thomas Y. Crowell Company, 1952.

CHAPTER IX

MUSIC FOR THE ELEMENTARY TEACHER[1]

MUSIC FOR THE elementary classroom teacher needs to be defined in terms of goals rather than skills. The *first* goal is to understand the child, how he grows musically and how music affects his personality. The *second* goal is to understand the musical environment, how it can bring human enrichment in the school, home, and community.

With such a basic understanding of musical goals, it is evident that skills will fall into their proper place according to individual interests and capacities. Skills vary according to individual differences among teachers just as they do among children. Yet *all* can make music regardless of differences in skill.

The important problem for the classroom teacher is to foster musical growth through a rich musical environment. In order to do that, every musical resource in and out of school needs to be used. The real task is to lead people to select the best of music that surrounds them every day through radio, television, cinema, concert hall, fireside sing, and all musical pursuits.

A keen musical awareness will lead to musical growth of both pupil and teacher. Teachers and administrators of elementary teachers need to provide the stimulus to grow. Music is every man's heritage. Every person uses music in his own way for his own personal satisfaction. This is the way music should be presented in elementary education.

Much more is needed than is now being done to build a musical awareness among young people now in the elementary schools who will some day teach in the elementary schools. A continuity of general musical experience is needed for the layman, from elementary through high school to college and on into adult life. This can be accomplished, not so much through *courses* as it can through musical *opportunity* for 100% of our population. This problem concerns the specialist as well as the generalist in music education. The present accomplishments in general music education for *all* will bear fruit among the next generation of elementary classroom teachers.

In considering the development of specific teacher competencies, the following elements are accepted quite universally:

(1) That the elementary teacher is a professionally competent educator who is interested in the total development of the child. Music, to this teacher, is one of the *many* experiences that can enrich the lives of boys and girls.

(2) That capacities, needs and interests differ among teachers as among children. Some teachers are musical performers, others are musical consumers. The problem is to discover individual competencies, whatever they may be, and to direct these competencies into channels of musical growth. In light of the above, therefore, a flexible and varied program of music education is needed wherein the teacher can find success within a wide range of musical activities.

The self-contained classroom is in an ideal position to provide a rich environmental setting for child growth and teacher growth. However, the self-contained classroom needs the services of resource people and consultants who are trained in special areas such as music. Consequently, the ideal self-contained classroom is

---

[1] From the report submitted by Charlotte DuBois, Austin, Texas, National Chairman, Music in American Education Committee on Music for the Elementary Teacher.

not an entity unto itself. It is the center of child activity, constantly reaching out to available resources for cultural enrichment.

AREAS FOR GROWTH

"Successful music teaching results from pleasurable musical experiences and technical competence. Therefore, teacher-training institutions should provide an environment which will assure a continuing growth in each of these areas." [1]

Experiences. College courses need to provide for enjoyable creative experiences in singing, playing, listening, and moving to music. Within these areas each elementary-teacher-to-be will discover some means for successful musical expression. Through these enjoyable and successful experiences with music itself, an understanding of the elements of music (melody, rhythm, harmony, and form) will evolve. Materials used will include those which are directly related to the musical experiences of the elementary school child.

There is an obvious need for clarification and revision of titles and course descriptions in college and university catalogues. Because of the wide variation in state requirements, it is difficult to set up requirements as to minimum hours. Moreover, such a procedure is not desirable since attitudes and competencies, which are the true goals, cannot be expressed in terms of credit hours. Faculty members who teach music courses for classroom teachers must be not only sound musicians but persons who have an understanding of the needs of the classroom teacher, *born of actual teaching experience.*

Understandings. The process of growth in musical understanding is different for each individual, yet it is orderly and planned. Musical understandings are concerned *first* with musical concepts and *second* with musical symbols. Symbols are meaningless without a basic understanding of simple concepts. Bodily response and aural association precede the recognition of pictured symbols on the musical page. The large concept of musical growth is from experiences, to visual images of these experiences, to interpretation of the experiences. Concepts of sound are expressed in terms of high and low, long and short, fast and slow, loud and soft, like and unlike, etc. These concepts are represented in symbols of notation. Very gradually the classroom teacher will learn, as children learn, through evolution from experience to expression.

Guidance (Teaching-Leadership). Musical understanding accompanies musical expression but does not precede it. Successful musical guidance depends upon a knowledge of the growing child within his musical environment. The teacher needs to understand the changes in child growth and how to use musical materials which are appropriate to this growth. Therefore, it is strongly recommended that music be included in the student teaching experience of the elementary classroom teacher. Self-confidence stems from knowledge and experience.

In-service training is currently being provided in many ways. These programs are designed to (a) stimulate interest, (b) develop self-confidence, (c) develop specific abilities, and (d) offer opportunities for active participation within a music group.

The following types of in-service training will implement the needs stated above.

(1) Workshops held for one- or two-week perods at the beginning or end of the school year.

(2) Summer orientation workshops.

(3) Study groups.

---

[1] From the report of the Committee on Music for the Elementary Teacher, MENC Biennial Convention, Philadelphia, 1952.

(4) Extension courses.

(5) Week-end workshops on college campuses.

(6) Demonstrations at state and district professional meetings.

(7) Intervisitation. (Strongly recommended.)

(8) Visitation of music education consultants from various publishers of basic music series.

(9) Development of the ability of classroom teachers to use the piano as a basic tool of music. (Several school systems are now offering free instruction in piano classes to teachers in service.)

Through a vital interest, elementary teachers will learn to use elementary music materials which are musically worthy and which they can interpret with enthusiasm and confidence. A broad experience with available materials, resourcefulness, sparked with each individual's creative imagination, will bring living music to elementary children.

Selected Bibliography—Elementary School Music

UNDERSTANDING CHILDREN'S GROWTH AND NEEDS

Adams, Fay. *Educating America's Children.* New York: The Ronald Press, 1946. Part V.
Child Study Association. *Our Children Today.* New York: The Viking Press, 1952.
Cole, Natalie R. *The Arts in the Classroom.* New York: John Day Co., 1940.
Gesell, Arnold L. *The Child from Five to Ten.* New York: Harper and Brothers, 1946.
Lowenfeld, Viktor. *Creative and Mental Growth.* New York: The Macmillan Company, 1947
Macomber, Freeman S. *Guiding Child Development in the Elementary School.* New York: American Book Company, 1948.
Millard, Cecil V. *Child Growth and Development.* Boston: D. C. Heath Co., 1951.

FOR THE TEACHER'S UNDERSTANDING OF MUSIC

Copland, Aaron. *What to Listen for in Music.* New York: McGraw-Hill Book Company, Inc.; Whittlesey House, 1939.
Diller, Angela. *First Theory Book.* New York: G. Schirmer, Inc., 1921.
Leonhard, Charles. *A Song Approach to Music Reading.* New York: Silver Burdett Company, 1953.
Myers, Louise Kifer. *Music Fundamentals Through Song.* New York: Prentice-Hall, Inc., 1954.
Stringham, Edwin John. *Listening to Music Creatively.* New York: Prentice-Hall, Inc., 1946.

THE TEACHER'S APPROACH TO MUSIC FOR CHILDREN

Christianson, Helen. *Music and the Young Child.* Washington, D. C.: Association for Childhood Education, 1936.
Krone, Beatrice Perham. *Music in the New School* (Rev. ed.). Chicago: Neil A. Kjos Music Co., 1950.
Krone, Max and Krone, Beatrice Perham. *Music Participation in the Elementary School.* Chicago: Neil A. Kjos Music Co., 1952.
Mathews, Paul W. *You Can Teach Music.* New York: E. P. Dutton & Co., Inc., 1953.
Morgan, Russell V. and Morgan, Hazel B. *Music Education in Action.* Chicago: Neil A. Kjos Music Co., 1954. Parts I and II.
Mursell, James L. *Music and the Classroom Teacher.* New York: Silver Burdett Company, 1951.
Music Education in the Elementary Schools. Sacramento: California State Department of Education, 1944.
Myers, Louis Kifer. *Teaching Children Music in the Elementary School.* New York: Prentice-Hall, Inc., 1950.
Nye, Robert and Bergethon, Bjornar. *Basic Music for Classroom Teachers.* New York: Prentice-Hall, Inc., 1954.
Pitts, Lilla Belle. *The Development Approach to Music Reading.* Boston: Ginn and Company, 1950.
Seeger, Ruth Crawford. *American Folk Songs for Children.* New York: Doubleday & Company, Inc., 1948. See Introduction.
Sheehy, Emma Dickson. *There's Music in Children* (Rev. ed.). New York: Henry Holt and Company, Inc., 1952.
Teachers' Guides and Manuals for Basic Music Series:
A Singing School. Boston: C. C. Birchard & Company.
New Music Horizons. New York: Silver Burdett Company.
Our Singing World. Boston: Ginn and Company.
The American Singer. New York: American Book Company.
Together We Sing. Chicago: Follett Publishing Company.

FOR THE CHILDREN'S UNDERSTANDING OF MUSIC

Annotated List of Phonograph Records, Kindergarten to Senior High School. New York: Children's Reading Service, 1954.
Bakeless, Katherine. *Story Lives of Great Composers.* New York: Frederick A. Stokes, 1941.
Baldwin, Lillian. *Music for Young Listeners.* Blue, Red, and Green Books. New York: Silver Burdett Company, 1951.

——————. *Music to Remember.* New York: Silver Burdett Company, 1951.
Balet, Jan. *What Makes an Orchestra.* New York: Oxford University Press, 1951.
Buchanan, Fannie R. *How Man Made Music* (Rev. ed.). Chicago: Follett Publishing Co., 1951.
Burch, Gladys. *Modern Composers for Young People.* New York: Dodd, Mead & Company, 1941.
Burch, Gladys and Wolcott, John. *Famous Composers for Young People.* New York: Dodd, Mead & Company, 1945.
Coit, Lottie E. and Bampton, Ruth. *Composers' Lives.* A Series. Philadelphia: Theodore Presser Company, 1942-45.
Cotton, Marian and Bradburn, Adelaide. *Music Throughout the World.* Boston: C. C. Birchard & Company, 1954.
Dike, Helen. *Stories from the Great Metropolitan Operas.* New York: Random House, 1943.
Emrich, Marion V. and Korson, George. *The Child's Book of Folklore.* New York: Dial Press, 1947.
Handbook on 16 mm. Films for Music Education. Chicago: Music Educators National Conference, 1952.
Hartshorn, William C. and Leavitt, Helen. *Making Friends With Music; The Pilot and The Mentor.* Boston: Ginn and Company, 1940.
Kinscella, Hazel Gertrude. *History Sings,* Background of American Music. Lincoln, Nebr.: University Publishing Co., 1948.
——————. *Stories in Music Appreciation* (Rev. ed.). Kinscella Readers. Lincoln, Nebr.: University Publishing Co.
Lawrence, Robert. *Illustrated Stories of Operas* (Single volumes). See catalogs of Silver Burdett Company and Grossett and Dunlap.
Posell, Elsa. *This Is An Orchestra.* Boston: Houghton Mifflin Company, 1950.

RHYTHMIC EXPERIENCES

Basic Music Series. See "The Teacher's Approach to Music for Children."
Burchenal, Elizabeth. *Folk Dances and Singing Games,* Volumes 1, 2, and 3. New York: G. Schirmer, Inc., 1909-1922.
Christianson, Helen. *Bodily Rhythmic Movements of Young Children in Relation to Rhythm in Music.* New York: Teachers College, Columbia University, 1938.
Coit, Lottie E. and Bampton, Ruth. *Follow the Music.* Boston: C. C. Birchard & Company, 1948.
Crowninshield, Ethel. *Songs and Stories About Animals.* Boston: Boston Music Co., 1947.
——————. *Stories That Sing.* Boston: Boston Music Co., 1945.
——————. *Walk the World Together.* Boston: Boston Music Co., 1951.
Dixon, Clarice M. *The Power of Dance: The Dance and Related Arts for Children.* New York: John Day Co., 1939.
Driver, Ann. *Music and Movement.* New York: Oxford University Press, 1947.
Driver, Ethel. *A Pathway to Dalcroze Eurythmics.* London, New York: T. Nelson, 1951.
Flagg, Marion. *Musical Learning.* Boston: C. C. Birchard & Company, 1949.
Glenn, Mabelle, Leavitt, Helen and Rebmann, Victor. *Play a Tune.* Boston: Ginn and Company, 1936.
Gordon, Dorothy. *Treasure Bag of Game Songs.* New York: E. P. Dutton & Co., Inc., 1939.
Hood, Marguerite V. and Schultz, E. J. *Learning Music Through Rhythm.* Boston: Ginn and Company, 1949.
Hughes, Dorothy. *Rhythmic Games and Dances,* Basic Activities for Elementary Grades. New York: American Book Company, 1942.
Hunt, Beatrice and Wilson, Harry R. *Sing and Dance,* Folk Songs and Dances including American Play Party Games. Chicago: Hall & McCreary Company, 1945.
Landeck, Beatrice. *Songs to Grow On.* New York: Edward B. Marks Music Corporation, 1950.
La Salle, Dorothy. *Rhythms and Dances for Elementary Schools,* Grades One to Eight. New York: A. S. Barnes and Company, Inc., 1939.
Seeger, Ruth Crawford. *American Folk Songs for Children.* New York: Doubleday & Company, Inc., 1948.
Waterman, Elizabeth. *The Rhythm Book.* New York: A. S. Barnes and Company, Inc., 1936.
Whitlock, Virginia. *Come and Caper,* Creative Rhythms, Pantomimes and Plays with music by various composers. New York: G. Schirmer, Inc., 1932.

CREATIVE EXPERIENCES

Basic Music Series. See "The Teacher's Approach to Music for Children."
Brooks, B. Marian and Brown, Harry A. *Music Education in the Elementary School.* New York: American Book Company. Chapters III, VI, XIV, and XV.
Coleman, Satis N. *Creative Music for Children.* New York: G. P. Putnam's Sons, 1922.
——————. *Creative Music Series.* New York: John Day Co., 1930.
——————. *Creative Music in the Home.* New York: John Day Co., 1940.
Fox, Lillian M. and Hopkins, L. T. *Creative School Music.* New York: Silver Burdett Company, 1936.
Hartman, Gertrude and Shumaker, Ann. *Creative Expression.* New York: John Day Co., 1932.
Mearns, Hughes. *Creative Power.* New York: Doubleday & Company, 1929.
Murray, Josephine and Bathurst, Effie. *Creative Ways for Children's Programs.* New York: Silver Burdett Company, 1938.
National Society for the Study of Education. *Creative Activities,* Part II. Bloomington, Ill., 1936.
Nordholm, Harriet and Thompson, Carl. *Keys to Teaching Elementary School Music.* Minneapolis: Paul A. Schmitt Music Company, 1949.

MISCELLANEOUS

Basic Music Series. See "The Teacher's Approach to Music for Children."
Coleman, Satis N. and Jorgensen, Elin. *Christmas Carols from Many Countries.* New York: G. Schirmer, Inc., 1934.
Coleman, Satis N. and Thorn, Alice G. *Another Singing Time.* New York: Reynal and Hitchcock, 1937.
Davison, Archibald and Surette, Thomas. *140 Folk Songs.* Boston: E. C. Schirmer Music Co., 1921.

92

Fitch, Gladys. *One God, The Ways We Worship Him*. New York: Lothrop, Lee and Shepard Co., 1944.
Fox, Lillian M. *Autoharp Accompaniments to Old Favorite Songs*. Boston: C. C. Birchard & Company, 1947.
Heller, Ruth. *Christmas, Its Carols, Customs, and Legends*. Chicago: Hall & McCreary Company, 1948.
Hunt, Evelyn H. *Music Time*, Songs for Children from Two to Seven. New York: The Viking Press, 1947.
Krone, Beatrice Perham. *Growing Up With Music*, Volumes I and II. Chicago: Neil A. Kjos Music Co., 1937-44.
Krone, Max and Krone, Beatrice Perham. *A World in Tune Series*. Chicago: Neil A. Kjos Music Co., 1941-50.
Lomax, Alan and Lomax, John A. *American Ballads and Folk Songs*. New York: The Macmillan Company, 1934.
MacCarteney, Laura P. *Songs for the Nursery School*. Cincinnati: Willis Music Co., 1942.
Marais, Josef. *Songs from the Veld*. New York: G. Schirmer, Inc., 1942.
Martin, Florence M. *Songs Children Sing*. Chicago: Hall & McCreary Company, 1943.
McCall, Adeline. *Timothy's Tunes*. Boston: Boston Music Co., 1943.
Nelson, Mary Jarman. *Fun With Music*. Chicago: Albert Whitman and Co., 1941.
Sandburg, Carl. *The American Songbag*. New York: Harcourt, Brace and Company, 1927.
Seeger, Ruth Crawford. *Animal Folk Songs for Children*. New York: Doubleday & Company, Inc., 1950.
──────────. *American Folk Songs for Christmas*. New York: Doubleday & Company, Inc., 1953.
Siegmeister, Elie. *Work and Sing*. New York: W. P. Scott, 1944.
Twice 55 Series, Six books of community songs. Boston: C. C. Birchard & Company, 1923.
Van Loon, Hendrick W. and Castagnetta, Grace. *Christmas Carols*. New York: Simon and Schuster, 1937.
──────────. *The Songs America Sings*. New York: Simon and Schuster, 1939.
Wheeler, Opal. *Sing for America*. New York: E. P. Dutton & Co., Inc., 1944.
──────────. *Sing for Christmas*. New York: E. P. Dutton & Co., Inc., 1943.
──────────. *Sing in Praise*. New York: E. P. Dutton & Co., 1946.
──────────. *Sing Mother Goose*. New York: E. P. Dutton & Co., Inc., 1945.
Wilson, Harry R. *Rounds and Canons*. Chicago: Hall & McCreary Company.
──────────. *Sing Along*. New York: J. J. Robbins & Sons, Inc., 1948.
──────────. *Songs of the Hills and Plains*. Chicago: Hall & MCreary Company, 1943.
Wyckoff, Marjorie E. *A Child's Book of Hymns*. New York: Random House, 1945.
Zanzig, Augustus. *Singing America*. Boston: C. C. Birchard & Company, 1940.

SECTION THREE

Junior and Senior High Schools

Music for Secondary Schools

Coordinating Chairman: E. Lawrence Barr, Kalamazoo, Mich.

✠

Junior High School

Eleanor Anifantis, chairman, Arlington, Mass.

✠

Senior High School

Russell Williams, chairman, Norfolk, Va.

CHAPTER X

MUSIC FOR SECONDARY SCHOOLS[1]

IN FORMULATING A BASIS for the discussion of music in the secondary school it is important that we should consider as a major problem the development of a positive attitude toward music. Throughout most of the country the high school is the top rung in the ladder of compulsory education. It is at this level that we have our last concentrated opportunity to make music important and functional to the citizens of tomorrow.

We cannot escape our share of the responsibility for the fact that though more pupils have been studying music both privately and in school than ever before, a recent survey of ten cities having 200,000 population showed the concert audience to be less than one per cent. A similar survey showed the New York City concert audience to be less than 40,000 or about one-half of one per cent. Of course there are changes in our living pattern including the advent of radio and television which undoubtedly bear upon this picture, but these figures are still cause for concern.

As salesmen we apparently do not have the ability to retain our customers. James Mursell once wrote that music teaching is more than salesmanship, but that poor salesmanship kills effectiveness in teaching. This ineffectiveness can be highlighted by examining what seems to be certain fundamental weakness in secondary music education. *First*, we tend to stress showmanship and superficiality instead of sincerity. This is a criticism which pertains to much of our work in the performance class. I do not wish to minimize showmanship for it is an important ingredient in public performance, but I think certain aspects of it are sometimes stressed at the expense of musical expression.

Second, we tend to glamorize virtuosity and technical display instead of the communicative and expressive aspects of music. Whether or not the conductor uses a score, a baton, a podium, the conductor's gestures, his seating arrangement—these often become the center of our attention. Sometimes we even consciously try to affect mannerisms. In the professional concert world, though it is a known fact that the best performances are often given by artists of lesser renown, the fact remains that auditoriums tend to fill because of "names" rather than because of music. Musical personalities are considered as more important than musical expression. The press plays up the idiosyncrasies of musicians and they in turn play along with exhibitionism. In too many high school performance groups the material used may exhibit a bigness of sound or give momentary amusement to performer and listener, but fail to say anything musically significant.

Third, the traditional approaches in music appreciation are directed toward the periphery instead of the heart of music. Endless information about the composer is used. Many adults today say they would enjoy music if someone would "tell them the story." They have been conditioned to a story approach. Do you ever have people talk with you after a concert to find out how *they* liked it? Pupils are too often told about music—what is good, what is poor—on the basis of tradition. Though they may not understand what is considered good they grow up thinking "this is good because the expert said so." This is a superficial acceptance and they become increasingly frustrated about musical tastes.

---

[1] From an address by Karl D. Ernst, Chairman, Division of Fine Arts, San Jose State College, San Jose, California, given at the MENC Biennial Convention, Chicago, 1954.

They feel insecure and decide that music is for the expert. They often are afraid to express honest opinions or to ask simple questions for fear of ridicule. This is one of the primary reasons why so many otherwise intelligent men stay away from concerts. They do not wish to appear unintelligent, and they would like to express their own criticism freely. They have developed a false concept which says that music must mean the same thing to all people. Somehow our students must be led to the expressive core of music as an intense personal thing, rather than to its superficial externals. The listening experience must be active instead of passive. Why not begin more often with the music itself instead of elaborate explanations, utilizing pertinent and direct questions relating to mood and general expressive qualities, and which lead to lively discussion and even disagreement. Students should be helped to build their own standards of musical values. They may be different from ours, but they will be real and will hold meaning. The foundation will be there, too, for them to revise these standards as they gain more experience.

Finally, we have failed to make significant enough those classes which are made up mostly of average and below-average students. Most of our energy and creativeness goes into classes for the able, the performance classes. There is a very important reason for this. Our reputation and even our job often depends solely upon the end products of such groups, hence the tendency is to teach our classes with little or no preparation. They are often called dumping grounds and the students are there only because the counselor couldn't find another place for them. Related to this problem is the fact that teacher-training programs develop competencies primarily for the performance type of class. There is an obligation to find a more dynamic approach to music for these general students who lack the ability for the top classes. As someone has aptly said, we not only need to train capable students but also to people the realm of music with musical beings. Some of the school administrators who are the most unsympathetic to our cause are the ones who were once members of those classes.

Thousands in our high schools today will be teaching in the primary and intermediate grades in a few years and they will probably be teaching their own music. What attitude will they have toward music? Secondary teachers frequently complain about the musical illiteracy of the pupils who come from the grades below. There is a practical way to do something about it.

Another major problem at the secondary level is in the area of curriculum. Can we describe to an administrator or parent the specific goals and objectives for each class? What understandings, skills, appreciations, and attitudes are we striving toward, and have we developed ways of measuring them? Do we see to it that a youngster who stays with us for four years is getting a broad music education, or does he just learn to play or sing his part in given pieces? How long can a pupil register for one of our classes and continue to learn music in the broad sense? Do we exploit or do we educate? Do we use our time to best advantage? Is there waste motion such as needless overlapping between classes—not in the music used but in fundamental understandings and skills? Do we rehearse endlessly passages which the group knows? Do we plan interpretations ahead of the rehearsal or in front of the class? One of the reasons students read poorly is because as teachers we don't demand enough the first time through a new selection. The student knows he will encounter the piece daily for several months so why should he deliver with maximum concentration the first time.

The general secondary curriculum becomes more crowded each year with requests by pressure groups for additional required courses—driver training, consumer education, family living, new science courses, undiluted American history, etc. Unless the school day or year is lengthened, the solutions to the problem for the elective areas such as music is to make better use of the time we already have. In the Interim Report of the Ford Foundation's Fund for the Advancement of Education is this statement:

"Waste which the investigation found was of three main kinds: Doing much the same thing twice; dropping a subject before it has really done much good; and concern with less important aspects of a subject at the expense of the more important. Such waste was doing double damage, most often to the ablest students, in loss of time and loss of interest and momentum."

A committee working on an articulation study between high school and college found that of the 344 students whose school and college records were studied, 209 took physics, chemistry, or biology in college. Of this number almost half took in college the beginner's course in the same science they had taken in high school. Yet comparison of the grades of the repeaters with those of students from the same schools who took physics or chemistry for the first time showed that the repeaters had only a very negligible advantage.

In the elementary school we have been more articulate about a sequence of learnings, but in the high school just what does tenth grade choral or eleventh grade instrumental music mean in terms of skills, understandings, attitudes, and appreciations. In other secondary areas these are pretty well delineated. As the curriculum becomes more crowded and time becomes more important, we will need to be more articulate in this regard. A high school principal once asked me, "How long am I justified in programming a boy for choral music? Isn't two years enough? What can he learn in music the third and fourth years that he didn't learn during the first two years except a few more pieces? If we think of music in school as something more than learning to perform various pieces, shouldn't we develop courses of study which contain certain specifics toward which we direct our efforts? What are the skills that a high school student ought to be developing in a third-year music class? In reading? In tone quality? In technique? In ear training? What are the understandings that he ought to be developing about musical literature of various periods and styles? What are the attitudes he ought to be developing about the place of music in our time?"

During the past decade we have talked a great deal about general music classes and in some places they have been established with excellent results. However, there are many schools, perhaps the majority, that cannot offer general music classes. May I suggest a solution which I think can go part way in bringing general music to at least a majority of students in every high school which offers music of any kind. In my own city [1] we find from studying enrollment statistics that during each school year approximately thirty per cent of the students are enrolled in some type of elective music class. This means that over a four-year span, perhaps between fifty and sixty per cent of all our students participate in some kind of music. This is possibly a median figure, but in many smaller schools the average would be much higher. Have you ever stopped to think what a challenge this is for general music? Within the framework of the regular vocal and instrumental classes we could give a well-balanced course in general music with specific goals for each year. The first two years would be more basic in nature, while the last two years would aim particularly at the needs of the talented with greater stress in the area of music theory. It would obviously be important to plan the material for a year's work so as to include certain periods, styles, forms, composers—much as we would in a class in music literature except that in this case most of the material would be performed. In learning to perform them we would aim toward developing also an understanding and appreciation of them. Too often the typical year's work is

---

[1] At the time this article was written, Mr. Ernst was supervisor of music in the Portland, Oregon, Public Schools.

planned haphazardly with only holiday and festival programs in mind. In line with good education practices in other areas such programs should be the outcome of regular class activities.

Are our students only performing members of choirs, bands, and orchestras, or are they able to realize through such performances some of the broad implications and understandings of music as an art? Are we as their teachers primarily interested in instrumental and choral conducting in the professional sense or are we music educators? I am not suggesting any de-emphasis upon performing excellence for I fully believe that this kind of understanding will improve performance.

We should bring the art of music in its broadest sense into all music classes. They should be planned so that those pupils who enroll for four years have an opportunity to participate in a connected series of experiences where the primary emphasis is upon musical understanding and growth. Special classes in appreciation, history, and theory can promote this but in most schools they are impractical. Too often we try to improve the curriculum by adding new courses. Unfortunately, this has been the method used to improve teacher training. What is needed is to revitalize the present courses. In many cases we already reach over half the student body. Let's learn to do a better job with those pupils we already have before developing new courses designed to attract more pupils. One concomitant outcome of this kind of course revitalization would be that the whole matter of better music materials would be solved. We need to be constantly reminded of that weakness in music education. This has been forcefully brought to our attention in numerous ways through the columns of various periodicals, sometimes from unfriendly critics from outside our ranks but more often from our own members.

The teacher is the key to the quality of education. Good facilities, sympathetic administrators, adequate salaries—these are all helpful, but without a good teacher the results are disappointing. We must work more diligently to encourage people with contagious musical personalities to enter the teaching profession. We should evaluate our teacher-training programs to see what might be done to develop dynamic teaching personalities.

Too often we seek to improve our schools by external means—a new course, a new method or technique, a reorganization of the curriculum, a new course of study, bulletins from the supervisor—but what is so urgently needed is to change teachers as persons. I am not so concerned with the methods a teacher uses, traditional or modern, if he has the ability to ignite that spark of interest and enthusiasm which continues through life. When I attend a high school music performance and observe many graduates of previous years in the audience, I am reasonably sure there has been a good teacher at work. How many of your former high school students have entered music teaching as a profession? The answer to this question, too, probably bears a close relationship to effective teaching.

With all public programs we need to consider the necessity of helping increase the musical understanding and enjoyment of our parent audiences. Many of them lack the musical background of their children. They are not a typical concert audience. Informal yet dignified program notes, either written or narrated with student help, often are valuable. We would use better music material if we thought in terms of program notes. Audience participation is another effective ingredient. There is also a place at some public performances to help parents understand the aims and objectives of music in the school. An occasional sight reading number is good for both parents and the performing students, along with short illustrations of various stages of student musical development.

The time will come when the common-learnings teacher at the secondary level will have a richer background in the arts. Changes in teacher education will gradually bring this about, but the school itself should assist present staff members in those areas where their training has been limited. Music educators should not leave this to chance, but should take an active part in helping those who are responsible for its teaching. We should make our services available as resource people during the present interim period while the core teacher must proceed on the basis of a limited background. We should help administrators recognize the importance of music in the common-learnings class so that they will provide time in the schedule of the music teacher to assist in its planning.

A year spent in administering a Ford Foundation financed project for the gifted children in the Portland (Oregon), schools has sharpened my own thinking in this area. According to the Educational Policies Commission: "Tests given to fifteen million young men who entered the armed forces during the Second World War revealed that many gifted men had not been recognized as such." There are many evidences in our society of wasted talent. As a people we are greatly concerned about conservation—of minerals, forests, water, wildlife, soils—but our most important resource is our human resource and its conservation is of the greatest importance. Sometimes as music teachers we have been accused of exploiting the talented at the expense of other students, and sometimes we have been guilty. But there is considerable research today which emphasizes that we have not provided enough opportunities for our talented youth. If you are interested in further evidence read *The Education of the Gifted* by the Educational Policies Commission.[1] If we are neglecting the development of the ablest students, we must intensify our efforts to improve the quality of our performing groups. Gifted pupils in music should never be allowed to get by with mediocrity. Provision for the gifted must be a part of the regular school program. In addition to the present opportunities for talented music students to perform in our best school groups, ways must be found to augment the kind of experiences they receive in all-state and all-conference groups.

Music teachers can be more resourceful in utilizing the talents of gifted students even within the framework of the regular music classes—from the opportunity for conducting, sectional rehearsal leadership, solo and ensemble performance, and counseling into purposeful individualized study which would go beyond those activities usually carried on in the large class. This might include learning to play additional instruments, special reading assignments, theory study, keyboard harmony, etc.

When music first began to develop in the high school, adequate physical facilities were unavailable. Teachers in general areas have in the meantime discovered many individualized methods of instruction. The single text with its rigid and uniform assignments is no longer accepted in academic fields. Without special ensemble and practice rooms, music teachers have been limited in dealing with the needs of individuals. However, the enrollment growth which is upon us with its need for space is bringing new facilities and we are now in a position to individualize much of our instruction. As I visit new music quarters I seldom observe complete or effective use of them. We must become better acquainted with our students as individuals and plan our work so as to allow more opportunities for individual growth. Student section leaders can assist teachers and at the same time have an outlet for their own talents. In Portland we have used talented high school juniors and seniors to advantage in summer and in Saturday elementary instrumental music classes. The students work under the supervision of experienced master teachers, performing with the younger children and assisting with sectional rehearsals, thus affording to the enrollees a greater measure of individualized instruction. Many of these high school students have since become interested in teaching as a career and are now enrolled in training institutions. Gifted instrumental students often become

---

[1] National Education Association, 1950, p. 21. See also Chapter XXIX, "Exceptional Children."

bored with being held back to the level of the large group. Some of the turnover in such classes is due to the fact that the very talented are held back to the progress level of the least talented members of the class. Availability of practice rooms should result in a great development of small ensembles and an improvement in kinds of material for various types of ensembles.

The larger percentage of pupils now enrolling in high school, giving us a much wider range of abilities, is responsible for many of our problems. We are now on the threshold of an even greater period of growth and change. Enrollments in many communities will more than double in the next decade. This will mean new buildings, modernized facilities, more teachers. It is a real challenge. Will we capitalize wisely on this opportunity or will we be content to encamp on our present site, resting on the accomplishments of the past, which have been tremendous and unparalleled in curriculum movements? Will we recognize more fully the needs of individual pupils as we plan ahead or will we sit and defend what we have already built? Unfortunately, the history of high school curriculum development has tended along the latter lines and high schools, as a whole, have lagged behind the elementary schools in adapting themselves to change.

Music educators must be informed persons who see clearly the total curriculum needs of the modern high school for, increasingly, subject matter areas will be drawn more closely together. The respect of our professional colleagues and our administrators must be earned; unfortunately, they often feel we are narrow-minded and biased. As already mentioned, increasing demands for more required courses will make it difficult for students to elect music, and it will require something beside negative emotional outbursts of frustrated music teachers to solve this problem.

If music is taught as a vital and active ingredient of happy and successful living, if we can recapture its essential eloquence, if we can highlight its power to communicate so as to lift the quality of life, if we can channel this power toward releasing the pressures and tensions of our time, if we will not allow ourselves to be lulled into self-satisfaction and complacency by the magnificent achievements of the past but will continuously seek new horizons, then music in our schools and in our culture will become of age.

An Overview of Secondary School Music [1]

The following five statements indicate an over-view of the area of music in grades seven through twelve. [2]

(1) *The Importance of Music Education for all American Youth.* Music education in the junior and senior high school contributes in three important ways to the cultural growth of all youth: (a) educational development, (b) functional achievement, and (c) artistic performance.

The functional achievement should include inspiration toward good citizenship, initiative, self-reliance and assurance, respect for the abilities and interests of others, wholesome recreation in the home and community, and higher moral and spiritual values.

Through artistic performance, whether in a class or public concert, students experience intellectual and emotional release, and the satisfaction derived from success.

---

[1] From the report submitted by E. Lawrence Barr, Kalamazoo, Michigan, National Chairman, Music in American Education Committee on Music for Secondary Schools.

[2] Sadie M. Rafferty and J. J. Weigand, *The Function of Music in the Secondary-School Curriculum* (MENC reprint of *The Bulletin* of the National Association of Secondary-School Principals, November, 1952). Reprint available from Music Educators National Conference. $1.00.

101

(2) *The Importance of the Junior High School Grades.* The musical experiences of the seventh-, eighth-, and ninth-grade years are of vital importance in the social, emotional, and intellectual development of youth. Boys and girls with subtly changing voices, bodies and minds, need music's continuing stimulus and inspiration. Enthusiastically taught and properly administered, the music program of these years will be the key to future individual and group musical success and satisfaction.

(3) *The Maturing Experiences of the High School.* Music should be an essential part of the senior high school curriculum, organized and taught on a basis of equal importance with other subjects.

The high school music program should provide an opportunity for every student to participate in some musical experience each year. Students should be provided with experiences in as many phases of music as possible. This implies that the teacher of general music classes will provide challenging vocal and instrumental experiences in addition to listening, creative, rhythmic, and integrated activities; and that teachers of special music groups will provide many general experiences related to music understanding and knowledge.

(4) *The Golden Thread of General Experiences in Music.* Opportunities for challenging general experiences in music are present in all music classes, whether they be performing or general music groups, when basic concepts of musical theory, history of music and mankind, and appreciation of beauty are incorporated in teaching. All teachers have a great responsibility to youth in this respect.

(5) *Music Activities for Every Student.* The varied needs and interests of students call for school programs which include many different types of musical offerings, i.e., singing, playing, listening, and creative opportunities on varying levels of ability and experience. Required and elective general music or similar type classes (varying with grade level) should be considered basic to the well-rounded junior and senior high school music program. They should include experiences of a broad and challenging nature in which the consumer as well as the performer of music can discover adequate outlets for his interests.

Instructional Music Program in Secondary Schools [1]

JUNIOR HIGH SCHOOL

(1) *General Music Course* open to all students regardless of previous musical experience. A course offering a variety of musical activities such as playing, singing, listening, reading music, creative activity, etc.

(2) *Vocal Music.* Boys' and girls' glee clubs, chorus or choir, small vocal ensembles, assembly singing for all students.

(3) *Instrumental Music.* Orchestra, band, small instrumental ensembles, class instrumental instruction (wind, string and keyboard) for beginners and more advanced students, applied music study for credit available in Grade 9.

(4) *Special Electives in Music.* In some junior high schools there is need for special elective classes in Music Appreciation and in Music Theory, especially in Grade 9.

SENIOR HIGH SCHOOL

(1) *Vocal Music.* Boys' and girls' glee clubs, chorus, choir, small vocal ensembles, voice classes, applied music credit for private lessons. Some of the large

---

[1] From Recommendations of the North Central Association of Colleges and Secondary Schools adopted in 1951. Copies of the complete report and recommendations pertaining to music, *Music in the Secondary Schools,* available from MENC.

102

choral groups selective and others open for election by any interested student, unless the school is too small to allow for more than one group.

(2) *General Music.* Open to all students, regardless of previous musical experience. A course similar to that described above under junior high school, but adjusted in its content to senior high school interests and needs.

(3) *Instrumental Music.* Orchestra, band, small ensembles, class instrumental instruction, wind, string, percussion and keyboard for beginning and advanced students, dance band. Orchestra and band should be divided into beginning and advanced sections, or first and second groups, if the enrollment warrants such division.

(4) *Elective Course Offerings.* Music theory, music appreciation, music history. Many high schools find it feasible to offer several years of instruction in each of these fields.

FOR ALL STUDENTS IN JUNIOR AND SENIOR HIGH SCHOOL

(1) *Assembly Programs.* Music programs with singing by all the students, the appearance of school musical organizations, and the appearance of outside artists.

(2) *Recitals and Concerts* by student performers.

(3) *Educational Concerts.*

(4) *Music Clubs.* Clubs devoted to those interested in certain phases of music study or related areas: Record Collectors' Club, Conducting Club, Folk Dance Club, Recorder Club, etc.

CHAPTER XI

JUNIOR HIGH SCHOOL MUSIC[1]

THE AGES FOUND in the seventh, eighth, and ninth grades are usually regarded as transitional and unstable because the boy or girl is passing through the years of rapid development. Abundant enthusiasm and vitality, emotional impulses, individual variations, and instinctive desires, combined with the consideration needed to cope with voice problems of these individuals, makes it highly important that the junior high school level receives special emphasis in the vertical continuity of music in education.

General Aims and Objectives

The general aims and objectives of music education in the junior high school may be stated as follows:

(1) Provide opportunities for the child to explore music as a means of further development of musical talents according to individual abilities.

(2) Increase the students' enjoyment of, sensitivity to, and appreciation for music, both as a performer and a listener.

(3) Provide musical experience that will contribute to a realization and development of spiritual and moral values.

(4) Provide through music for social, emotional, and physical outlets and experience for every student through self-expression, creative effort, and enjoyment.

SPECIFIC AIMS IN JUNIOR HIGH SCHOOL MUSIC

(1) To continue the development of music skills.

(2) To provide a singing program of unison and part songs.

(3) To recognize the importance of changing voices.

(4) To provide a variety of instrumental music experiences, to include social instruments.

(5) To develop a discriminating taste through a well-organized listening program.

(6) To provide opportunities for creative self-expression in all areas of the music program.

(7) To stress the importance of our musical heritage and its effect on present-day culture.

(8) To offer challenging experiences for gifted children through participation in solo, choral, and instrumental ensembles.

(9) To understand the adolescent in relation to his musical development.

Current Issues Facing the Junior High School Music Program

What procedures could be recommended for use in the handling of groups having changing voices?

[1] From the report submitted by Eleanor Anifantis, Arlington, Massachusetts, National Chairman, Music in American Education Committee on Junior High School Music. The material was assembled on the basis of a decision made by the MENC Junior High School Committee at the 1950 MENC Convention at St. Louis, namely, to consider topics which have been requested frequently by junior high school music teachers, concentrating on topics which have not been adequately covered previously.

A thorough understanding of the vocal range and voice qualities peculiar to junior high groups is of paramount importance. In order to classify voices according to various vocal ranges and separate into singing groups, the following procedure is suggested:

Sing unison songs such as "Swanee River" and "Old Black Joe" in various suitable keys. This will identify the boy baritone. Segregate these and establish a key where they can sing the tune of the song comfortably.

Then sing the same song in a key about a fifth higher, which will identify both the high and low unchanged voices. It follows that the remainder of the group will consist of the changing voices. When the full potentialities of the group have been discovered there should be a place for each pupil.

The criteria for selecting materials for these groups are: (a) Proper range and tessitura, (b) interest of tune and text, (c) length of selection, and (d) pupil interest.

What good reasons can be given to substantiate the recommendation that general music be required?

(1) Discontinuing guided musical growth at the end of the sixth grade would deprive the student of many enriching musical experiences because we believe that music is one of the most all-enriching contributions to human living and understanding.

(2) Adolescent pupils, who are immature and at their most impressionable stage, need the guidance and exploratory experiences of general music classes to help develop their musical ideals which will carry over not only into the high school music program, but throughout adult life.

What is the place of performing groups in the junior high school and their relation to the total school program?

(1) To give musical pupils an opportunity to participate in a type of musical activity beyond the ability of general music groups.

(2) To develop a more sensitive aesthetic appreciation by singing and playing the very best in vocal and instrumental music.

(3) To develop poise, self-confidence, a sense of service and responsibility, and a feeling of pride and accomplishment.

(4) To give pupils the needed specialized background so that they will be better able to participate in senior high school performing groups.

(5) To create a culminating activity which would act as an integrating force for the entire school program.

Should instrumental music be started in junior high school, or should it begin in the earlier grades?

No set age for starting instrumental music can be given because the beginning of this training is determined by the musical maturation of the child; therefore, beginning classes should be offered in junior high as well as in elementary school. Some instruments, such as tuba and string bass, whose playing demands arm length, stature, strength, etc., can well be begun in junior high school.

What suggestion can be made for remedying the lack of suitable music for junior high school use?

Publishers, editors, and arrangers need to know the abilities and limitations of junior high school music groups. This applies specifically to range, interest of tune and text, length, legibility of printed page, and making all parts interesting by moving the melodic line.

What can be done to make more effective the carry-over of the music program of the junior high to the senior high school?

The program director must be able to stimulate the pupils to desire more advanced musical activity as they go from the junior high to the senior high school. The music teacher and the guidance department should follow up junior high school pupils as they enter high school so that there will be continuous musical growth. Opportunities for musical growth should be made available to suit the varied interests of pupils entering the senior high school. An interchange of performing groups between junior and senior high schools is a fine way to bridge this gap. Periodic planning meetings of junior and senior high school teachers should be held to consider mutual problems.

What part does music play in the total integrated program for junior high school?

Music is vital to the child and should be integrated with all phases of his activities. Music readily correlates with other school departments and activities and should be organized around pupil-teacher planning wherever possible. Through an integrated program, music should give the child the tools and values for better use of his out-of-school experiences.

What can be done to meet the challenge of outside influences of today (television, radio, etc.) so that the junior high school music program fills the needs of today's student?

Radios and television sets should be utilized in the school day and incorporated as aids to the music program. Effort should be made to increase the number of worth-while programs on television and radio through active criticism of existing programs, and through active cooperation with civic and parental organizations.

Worth-while music from movies are splendid classroom activities. For example: *A Song to Remember, The Great Caruso, Rhapsody, Rose-Marie, The Glenn Miller Story,* etc.[1]

Standards for evaluating programs should be established by class discussion. Information may be obtained about good television and radio programs in advance and discussed with students so they are informed about what they are going to hear and see. Opportunities for class visitation to music programs in the school, church, and community should be utilized. Guided listening and discussion are profitable for dance music as well as the more traditional aspects of operatic and symphonic music, also sacred and secular choral mediums. Acquaintance with the music section of the school and public library may be had from supervised visits. Students should be encouraged to read the music sections of local papers and of magazines. Many children have personal record collections and deserve interest from the junior music instructor in this project.

What is the place of music in the junior high school core curriculum?

Music should be retained in the core provided that, in addition, general music classes are required, and adequate elective music is offered.

What recommendations can be made for adequate teacher training on the junior high school level?

Psychology and education course requirements should be interrelated with methods courses so that the trainee is prepared for handling both pupils and course content. Recognizing that junior high music teaching requires special training and a creative personality, those having this combination should be encouraged to enter the junior high school field. Special emphasis should be placed on more music education courses dealing directly with junior high school. Stress should be placed on the general music class including methods and materials. Student teaching

[1] See "Films," p. 216.

106

should be as continuous and concentrated as is practical. Provision should be made for more opportunity to participate in activities of the school and community.

Topics for Future Studying and Planning. It is hoped that in the future, junior high music teachers may be supplied with proven usable advice, and materials that have been recommended by successful people actively engaged in teaching junior high school music. It is suggested that attention be given to the following projects:

(1) A study of how to carry out the specific aims and objectives previously listed.

(2) Sponsor research projects in new curriculum developments for the junior high school level.

(3) Encourage further additions to the recommended lists of junior high materials.

(4) Continue collecting sample units of study, resource guides, and schedules.

Recommendations

(1) For greater ease in studying the problems pertaining to the junior high school, separate future publications dealing with music in secondary schools into two categories namely junior high school and senior high school.

(2) Continue emphasis on adequate training for teachers at the junior high level.

(3) Encourage workshops, clinics and demonstrations.

(4) Include more sessions specifically designed for junior high school at division and state meetings sponsoring festivals.

In order to have a truly satisfactory and functioning music program at the junior high school level, it is recommended that the following be given careful consideration:

(1) The major purpose of music at the junior high school level is to continue the educational and cultural processes begun previously rather than the exploitation of groups for public performance. Small performing ensembles are very desirable.

(2) To the degree that it is possible, in all planning there should be student-teacher collaboration but with definite teacher guidance.

(3) The junior high school program should be planned within the limits of administrative advisability to permit the student to have both vocal and instrumental experience.

(4) At least five periods per week should be included, if necessary, dividing the time among instrumental, vocal, and general music activities.

(5) A minimum of six periods per day (preferably seven) should be in effect in the junior and senior high schools in order that the student may have enough time for a variety of activities. Naturally, this includes all activities and not merely those pertaining to music.

Singing in the Junior High School

The junior high school presents a diversity of vocal problems. Both girls' and boys' voices change and partially mature in these grades, but no two voices change at the same chronological age. The student body includes, therefore, the girls with unchanged and maturing voices and boys with unchanged, changing, and changed voices. The last named are few in number. Huskiness in the upper tones, and a disinclination to sing them, is regarded as an indication of the approaching voice change in the boy.

Whether the junior high school music classes are mixed or segregated groups, the utmost care should be exercised to protect the growing voices. The pupils should be carefully watched in order to avoid all straining or forcing. Voices should be tested at the beginning of the semester and frequently thereafter, and pupils assigned to the voice part which the range and quality of their respective voices indicate. Re-classification takes place from time to time, as the development of the voices warrants. The practice of placing either boys or girls on any part because they can carry it well, or for the sake of tonal balance, is inadvisable. School music educators realize that the growing voice must be protected, even at the sacrifice of musical results.

The junior high school is the logical place for beginning three- and four-part singing. The latter is not always possible, since not every group will include a sufficient number of either alto-tenors or boy-basses. Singing in three parts—either three unchanged voices, or soprano, alto, and bass, is practical in most schools.

Survey and Analysis of the Problem of Junior High School Music [1]

All junior high school music teachers in the MENC California-Western Division, plus 153 college music educators, took part in a survey which yielded the following conclusions:

According to *junior high school music teachers*, the five most important problem subdivisions, in descending order of importance were as follows: (a) How to secure good discipline. (b) How to fulfill the necessary business management requirements of a music department. (c) How to conserve music equipment. (d) How to treat sight-singing. (e) How to provide for individual differences.

According to *college music educators*, the five most important problem subdivisions, in descending order of importance, were as follows: (a) How to handle boy changing-voice problems. (b) How to handle problems of the general music class. (c) How to guide student interest outside of school. (d) How to treat sight-singing. (e) How to plan the curriculum for the general music class.

The main categories that should be emphasized, in order of their importance, are as follows: (a) Classroom management problems. (b) Problems concerning techniques of teaching. (c) Curriculum planning problems. (d) Problems concerning motivation and the development of interests. (e) Administrative problems. (f) Interpersonal relationship problems.

An Administrator Looks at Junior High School Music [2]

The junior high school is a place for general education—the providing of a fairly common background in basic skills, knowledge, and attitudes for people of this country, and to provide wide exploratory experience in order to enable students to choose better in more specialized interest and occupational fields of the senior high school and college.

Our major role is to build on the universal appeal inherent in music. The spirit of music, not the technique, should be the guiding force at this level.

The administrator must keep the class size to a level that a normal, reasonably well-trained music teacher can handle effectively. The tools with which to work must be provided. The administrator must be concerned with the weaknesses of the program and be ready to share responsibility with the music educator for planning the content of required courses. He must admit the music program to the curriculum and to the class schedule on equal terms with the more traditional subjects.

[1] Summary of a study made by Lorn E. Christensen, University of Southern California.

[2] From an address by Edwin C. Mustard, Principal, Amherst Central Junior High School, Amherst, New York, given at the MENC Eastern Conference, Buffalo, New York, 1953.

Music people could stimulate interest in music as well as help vitalize traditional subject courses by going out of their way to seek ways to introduce music to the classroom. The administrator must arrange a flexible schedule for music teachers to give them time to go into classrooms on an informal basis and serve, if necessary, as the link between unconvinced members of the staff. He must encourage, at every turn, students and faculty alike to accept this as a normal part of their classroom experience.

At this level the primary aim should be opportunity for all to find a place in music. This means band, orchestra, quartets, ensembles of all kinds, instrumental classes, boys' chorus, girls' chorus, and mixed chorus. Time and adequate personnel and equipment are paramount.

Part of the administrator's responsibility lies in finding audiences for his music groups—assemblies, parents, general public, other schools. With it, of course, goes the responsibility of transportation, time from school, and all other physical arrangements. Administrators should avoid exploitation, but they should be the spearhead of interpreting the music program to the community and to the board of education. The music teacher may have a continuous struggle for equipment, for help, for space. These things can be overcome to some extent in most situations by administrative cooperation.

Many music teachers come into the junior high field with great reluctance. Even people who teach in both junior and senior divisions often almost ignore the junior high program. They do not seem to realize that the success of the entire senior high program, especially the performing groups, depends on the love of music instilled in junior high students. Where better than at this level will one find the basic elements of a good music teaching situation—inherent interest in music on the part of the pupils' great vitality and enthusiasm, the driving force of wanting to belong to a group and engage in group activities, the desire on the part of pupils to run their own show, the great curiosity of the pre-adolescent for new experiences, and the friendliness inherent in most students if you will let them be friendly. *Probably the greatest challenge in public education today lies at the junior high level.* Its curriculum is not static, nor does it have the great weight of tradition as is true in the senior high.

If you have patience, if you have a sense of humor and friendliness, if you are willing to accept the students' idea of music in return for their acceptance of yours, if you are big enough to get rid of preconceived ideas of what is acceptable music, if you can drop traditional methods, and if you enjoy moving into unexplored areas, then you belong in the junior high school. If, on the other hand, your primary interest is in finished performance, technical competence, traditional methods, and subject matter, you will not be successful, nor will you be happy teaching music in the junior high school.

No community, no school, no administrator will ever hand you the program about which you dream on a silver platter. To get a good music program in any school *you* must educate the administration, the school board, and the community— your vision must always be ahead of the school at any given time. Above all, you must sell music so completely to your pupils that the pupils themselves become the emissaries for your vision. They are the best pressure you can bring to bear for anything pertaining to a school.

Selected Bibliography—Music in the Junior High School

GENERAL EDUCATION

Boyles, Ernest E. *The Theory and Practice of Teaching.* New York: Harper and Brothers, 1952.
Gruhn, W. T. and Douglas, Harl R. *The Modern Junior High School.* New York: The Ronald Press, 1952.
Havighurst, Robert and Taba, Hilda. *Adolescent Character and Personality.* New York: John Wiley and Sons, Inc., 1949.

Noar, Gertrude. *The Junior High School Today and Tomorrow.* New York: Prentice-Hall, Inc., 1954.
Woodring, Paul. *Let's Talk Sense About Our Schools.* New York: McGraw-Hill Book Company, Inc., 1953.

MUSIC EDUCATION

Andrews, Frances and Leeder, Joseph A. *Guiding Junior High School Pupils in Music Experiences.* New York: Prentice-Hall, Inc., 1954.
Beattie, John, McConathy, Osbourne and Morgan, Russell V. *Music in the Junior High School.* New York: Silver Burdett Company, 1930.
Dykema, Peter W. and Cundiff, Hannah. *New School Music Handbook.* Boston: C. C. Birchard & Company, 1939. Part III.
Dykema, Peter W. and Gehrkens, Karl. *The Teaching and Administration of High School Music.* Boston: C. C. Birchard & Company, 1941. Pp. 54-69.
Gehrkens, Karl W. *Music in the Junior High School.* Boston: C. C. Birchard & Company, 1936.
Morgan, Russell V. and Morgan, Hazel B. *Music Education in Action.* Chicago: Neil A. Kjos Music Co., 1954. Part II.
Nordholm, Harriet and Bakewell, R. V. *Keys to Teaching Junior High School Music.* Minneapolis: Paul A. Schmitt Music Company, 1953.
Pitts, Lilla Belle. *Music Integration in the Junior High School.* C. C. Birchard & Company, 1935.
Rafferty, Sadie and Weigand, J. J. *The Function of Music in the Secondary-School Curriculum.* Chicago: Music Educators National Conference, 1952.
Rorke, Genevieve. *Choral Teaching at the Junior High School Level.* Chicago: Hall & McCreary Company, 1947.
Squire, Russel N. *Introduction to Music Education.* New York: The Ronald Press, 1952, p. 70.
Ward, Arthur E. *Music Education for High Schools.* New York: American Book Co., 1941. Chapter III.
NOTE: Many helpful articles dealing with music in the junior high school have appeared in the *Music Educators Journal.*

Suggested Book List for Junior High School
General Reference and School Library

[NOTE: The following list prepared by Eleanor Anifantis, National Chairman of the Committee on Junior High School Music, does *not* duplicate any books given for junior high school under "Minimum Library Books About Music, Musicians, and Instruments" in *Music Education Source Book*, p. 247.—Ed.]
Baldwin, Lillian. *Music to Remember.* New York: Silver Burdett Company, 1951.
Barnard, Bernice and Jones, Archie. *Introduction to Musical Knowledge.* Minneapolis: Paul A. Schmitt Music Company, 1935.
Boni, Margaret B. *Fireside Book of Folksongs.* New York: Simon and Schuster, 1952.
Buchanan, Fannie R. *How Man Made Music* (Rev. ed.). Chicago: Follett Publishing Co., 1951.
Cott, Ted. *Victor Book of Musical Fun.* New York: Simon and Schuster, 1945.
Ewen, David. *Music for the Millions.* New York: Arco Publishing Co., 1950.
Ewen, David and Slonimsky, Nicolas. *Fun with Musical Games and Quizzes.* New York: Prentice-Hall, Inc., 1952.
Herman, Michael. *Folk Dances for All.* New York: Barnes and Noble, 1947.
Hood, Marguerite and Perry, Lawrence. *Let's Sing.* New York: Carl Fischer, Inc., 1952.
Kaufmann, Helen. *Minute Sketches of Great Composers.* New York: Grossett and Dunlap, 1932.
Kinscella, Hazel G. *Music and Romance for Youth.* Camden, N. J.: RCA Victor, 1940.
————. *Tales of Olden Days.* Lincoln, Neb.: University Publishing Co., 1939.
————. *Around the World in Story.* Lincoln, Neb.: University Publishing Co., 1939.
————. *Music On the Air.* New York: The Viking Press, 1934.
Kolb, Sylvia and Kolb, John. *A Treasury of Folk Songs.* New York: Bantam Books, 1948.
Krevit, William. *Music for Your Child.* New York: Dodd, Mead & Company, 1946.
Lacy, Marian. *Picture Book of Musical Instruments.* New York: Lothrop, Lee and Shepard Co., 1942.
Lawrence, Robert. *Metropolitan Guild—Stories of the Operas.* New York: Grossett and Dunlap, 1938.
Lyons, Henry. *Stories of Our American Patriotic Songs.* New York: Vanguard, 1940.
McCutchon, Robert G. *Our Hymnody.* Nashville, Tenn.: Abingdon-Cokesbury, 1937.
McGee, Thomasine. *People and Music.* New York: Allyn and Bacon, 1931.
McKinney, Lawrence. *Music and Man.* New York: American Book Company, 1948.
————. *People of Note.* New York: E. P. Dutton & Co., Inc., 1940.
O'Connell, Charles. *The Victor Book of the Symphony.* New York: Simon and Schuster, 1935.
Purdy, Claire L. *Victor Herbert.* New York: Messner, 1944.
Sholes, Percy. *The Concise Oxford Dictionary of Music.* London: Oxford University Press, 1952.
Smith, Harold D. *Instruments of the Orchestra.* Camden, N. J.: RCA Victor, 1940.
Sousa, John Philip. *Marching Along.* Boston: Hale, Cushman and Flint, 1941.
Spaeth, Sigmund. *Great Symphonies.* Garden City, N. Y.: Garden City Publishing Co., 1936.
————. *Opportunities in Music.* New York: Grossett & Dunlap, 1950.
Thomas, Cloea and Leeder, Joseph. *The Singin' Gatherin'.* New York: Silver Burdett Company, 1939.
Victor Book of the Opera. (Rev. ed.). Camden, N. J.: RCA Victor, 1950.
Wheeler, Opal and Deucher, Sybil. *Sebastian Bach.* New York: E. P. Dutton & Co., Inc., 1937.
————. *Beethoven and the Chiming Tower.* New York: E. P. Dutton & Co., Inc., 1942.
————. *Stephen Foster and His Little Dog Tray.* New York: E. P. Dutton & Co., Inc., 1941.
————. *Joseph Haydn.* New York: E. P. Dutton & Co., Inc., 1945.
————. *MacDowell and His Cabin in the Pines.* New York: E. P. Dutton & Co., Inc., 1949.
————. *Mozart, the Wonder Boy.* New York: E. P. Dutton & Co., Inc., 1941.
Wilson, Harry; Leeder, Joseph; and Gee, Edith. *Music America Sings.* New York: Silver Burdett Company, 1949.

CHAPTER XII

SENIOR HIGH SCHOOL MUSIC[1]

THE IDEALS AND PHILOSOPHY which serve as a foundation for the content of the secondary school music curriculum continue more or less constant in this era of shifting trends. The maintenance of usual high standards of quality, usefulness, and suitability remain in the forefront as acceptable guiding factors. The good teacher will be exceedingly alert to adapt teaching content and methods to the specific needs of the pupils and the community concerned. It should be the aim during high school years to build up reservoirs of songs, instrumental selections, etc., which will carry over into after-school years as an infectious enthusiasm for music for fun and for genuine enjoyment.

Suggested Courses and Activities

The primary aim of the senior high school music program should be to offer many musical experiences to *every* student so as to build for continuing growth and expansion of participation and appreciation. The musical experiences offered every child should, of course, include either participation in or frequent listening to the fine high school bands, orchestras, and choirs which for so long have been a matter of great school pride. But in addition to this, and in order to meet the varying needs of the majority of the student body who have not the necessary qualifications for membership in organizations, greater emphasis is recommended for the following suggested courses and activities.

(1) *General Music Course.* [2] There is a feeling on the part of music educators that courses should be offered in the secondary schools which would interest all students who elect them. This general music course is intended for the mass of students and should have no prerequisites. The content of this course should be limited to what reasonably might be considered within the range and capacity of the average student. The choice of material would be conditioned largely by the interests and needs of the class and should be selected from unison, two-part, three-part, and four-part songs.

A general course is recommended which will bring every high school student into contact with modern architecture, drama, radio arts, painting, dancing, and music, that is, all of the communicative arts. In a school with an integrated program, the arts can be drawn into all the areas where valid relationships can be found. The infinite richness allowed by this program may not be possible in conventional high schools, but some schools have introduced a course in *the arts* which serves as an introduction to the modern arts in adult living. A well-selected library shelf of books should be available for those students interested in any and all of the allied arts.

The objectives of the general music course should be to (a) arouse and develop interest in music, (b) give further contact with music and some experience in producing it, (c) give information about music that the well-informed person should have, (d) provide exploratory experiences in singing, listening and playing, (e) further desirable musical skills, and (f) provide opportunities to discover musical skills.

---

[1] From the *Music Education Source Book* (Chicago: Music Educators National Conference, 1947), pp. 13-16.
[2] See Chapter XVIII, "General Music Classes at the Secondary Level."

It is suggested that, in schools where general music has not been popular and so has partially failed of its purpose, the name of the new course might well be changed as the content of the course and the teaching methods are improved and brought up to date. Possible titles which seem to have more student appeal are *Music and You, Music for Everybody,* and *Enjoyment of Music.*

Further suggestions regarding the content and procedures for such a course are: (a) More unison singing of interesting songs of all classifications. Songs with strong melodic or rhythmic appeal seem especially desirable. (b) Enough voice training to enable each student to use good tone quality and good diction, and to understand the possibilities in the use of his singing and speaking voice. (c) Much use of attractive illustrative material of all kinds. (d) Attention to the development and use of varied techniques in teaching this course, for example, demonstrations, discussions, programs by visiting artists or speakers, class concerts, and class expeditions to places of musical interest. (e) A tie-up of subject matter as far as possible with the students' other in- and out-of-school interests such as topics or projects which interest them in social science, English, art, or modern language; music they have heard and enjoyed in radio, in concert performances, or in motion pictures. (f) Frequent use of all audio-visual aids and other new teaching devices.

The course in general music must be flexible because of varying local conditions and pupil needs. It will *not* be an easy class to teach. The classes should not be larger in size than classes in other fields having similar objectives. The teacher must be broadly trained in music, ever alert to evidences of interest and personal growth in the students. It is felt that the kind of course described offers so much of value for general educational purposes, for orientation in the field of the arts, for the development of the personality of the individual, that it would justify listing as a requirement, preferably in the ninth or tenth grade.

(2) *Assembly Singing.* Music educators have recognized for a long time that well-developed assembly singing is an ideal activity toward the end of participation by all. At the same time, the production of effective group singing has proved most challenging to the ingenuity of the teacher. Lack of interest on the part of many music teachers and/or a feeling that they are not prepared to cope with this challenging opportunity are the factors in the main responsible for the fact that very few schools show much activity in assembly singing.

Singing by the student body during the assembly or convocation can be very inspirational. It will be inspirational if the person who directs it has a genial personality, plans carefully and in detail, and has a fine accompanist trained to work in close cooperation with the director. Assembly song material needs to be well selected to meet the broad interests and tastes of the wide variety of individuals. This material must be pleasurable enough to keep the interest, and instructive enough to give some musical training.

In addition to the especially planned and programmed music assemblies which have been productive of good results in many schools, it is urged that music teachers seek opportunity for group singing of even one or two songs in home rooms, during recreation periods, and in general assemblies.

(3) *Performing Groups.* There are those students who like to make music for themselves, and for them the course should provide for performing groups of all kinds. These groups should be set up on a broad base to reach all who are interested in singing or playing and advancing by levels, so that the best students in the school can pace themselves by others of equally fine ability and experience. School groups, large and small, should be available to suit the experience of any student who wishes to enroll.

The instrumental groups, from the smallest chamber music group to the school symphony orchestra and concert band, should have special attention. Small vocal ensembles, madrigals as well as choirs, choruses and glee clubs should be available for the vocal students.

The high standard of performance of choirs, orchestras and bands, which has been established in many high schools, should be maintained. More schools should organize such groups in order that these selected students may be provided with experiences in significant music. These organizations promote favorable relations with other pupils of the school and with the community. Students in these groups should be encouraged to perform solos and play and sing in small ensembles. If possible, every member of these large organizations should play in a small group. Each ensemble may have its own student leader and should have regularly scheduled rehearsals.

(4) *Individual and Group Lessons.* In *voice*, the scientific production of tone should be stressed, with emphasis upon a systematic way of singing which preserves and improves the voice. In addition, good speech habits (diction) and experience with the best song literature should be emphasized. Any student should have the opportunity to study an *instrument* at public expense. Experience in a band or orchestra which has achievement standards on the student's level should be available to him. In smaller high schools, an ensemble of any combination of orchestra or band instruments could furnish experience for students in these schools.

Every student in choir, orchestra and band should have instruction on his instrument or in voice. Those who do not study with a private teacher should receive individual or class instruction from the music teacher in the school during school hours.

(5) *Music Appreciation.* Since a large number of pupils will be listeners to music, it is desirable to require a listening course of most students. Such a course should be offered for a semester or a year. The musical compositions used should be varied and of high standard. Attitudes toward the music are of prime importance.

This should be an enrichment course for required general music courses. Music majors and minors should take this course. Emphasis should be placed upon hearing the music. Information (history and biography) about the music played should be incidental and should emphasize the interrelationship of music with the other arts— with literature, geography, government, economics, etc.

Provision should be made for students to rehear music played in the classroom. The use of the school library for the installation of muted record players, for example, would step up the good results considerably. It must be remembered that one presentation of the music in class is not sufficient. It must be accompanied by the stimulation of desire for further listening. It is this follow-up part of the teaching of appreciation which seems to have been overlooked generally.

(6) *History of Music.* As much illustrative material as possible should be used, including thorough analysis of *things for which to listen.* This course should be on a par with other academic courses in history. Teachers of music history courses will profit by a familiarity with contents and techniques used by general classroom teachers of history.

(7) *Theory and Harmony.* [1] A class in harmony, especially keyboard harmony, should be provided for instrumentalists. Training in transposition, harmonization of melodies, and other practical applications of the student's knowledge should be a part of any theory and harmony course. Ample opportunity should be given for original work emphasizing good melody writing. Creative work should be arranged only for those who are gifted and interested in such larger original projects.

---

[1] See Chapter XXII, "Music Literature, Theory, Harmony and Composition."

Minimum Activities

(1) Assembly singing should be scheduled for all students. If no other music activities are available, at least recreational singing should be provided.

(2) Special instrumental and vocal performance groups should be encouraged. Those students showing marked talents and abilities should be organized to provide enriched musical experience both for themselves and others in the school.

(3) There should be provision for ability segregation. Students should be grouped, both vocally and instrumentally, according to their ability, rather than by academic grade level.

(4) Theory classes should be provided for the specially gifted and interested students.

(5) The playing of the informal instruments should be encouraged as an extra-curricular activity.

Selected Bibliography—Music in Senior High School

GENERAL EDUCATION

(NOTE: See additional bibliography on Secondary School Administration and Supervision, pp. 27, 28, 40.

Alcorn, M. D. *Better Teaching in Secondary Schools*. New York: Henry Holt and Company, Inc., 1954.
Alexander, Wm. and Saylor, J. Galen. *Secondary Education, Basic Principles and Practices*. New York: Rinehart & Company, Inc., 1950.
Bremeld, Theodore. *Ends and Means in Education*. New York: Harper and Brothers, 1950.

MUSIC EDUCATION

Dykema, Peter W. and Gehrkens, Karl. *The Teaching and Administration of High School Music*. Boston: C. C. Birchard & Company, 1941. Pp. 54-69.
Morgan, Russell V. and Morgan, Hazel B. *Music Education in Action*. Sections II and III. Chicago: Neil A. Kjos Music Co., 1954. Part II.
Music Education Source Book (Rev. ed.). Chicago: Music Educators National Conference, 1951. Sections II and III.
Rafferty, Sadie and Weigand, J. J. *The Function of Music in the Secondary-School Curriculum*. Chicago: MENC, 1952.
Squire, Russel N. *Introduction to Music Education*. New York: The Ronald Press, 1952. Chapters V to IX.
Ward, Arthur E. *Music Education for High Schools*. New York: American Book Company, 1941. Chapter III.
Wilson, Harry R. *Music in the High School*. New York: Silver Burdett Company, 1941.

INSTRUMENTAL MUSIC

Abbott, George J. *Instrumental Music in the Public Schools*. Boston: C. C. Birchard & Company, 1935.
Dvorak, Raymond F. *The Band on Parade*. New York: Carl Fischer, Inc., 1937.
Goldman, Richard Franko. *The Concert Band*. New York: Rinehart & Company, Inc., 1946.
————. *Band Betterment*. New York: Pitman, 1938.
Hindsley, Mark. *Band Attention*. Chicago: Gamble Hinged Music Co., 1924.
————. *School Band and Orchestra Administration*. New York: Boosey & Hawks, Inc., 1940.
Hjelmervik, Kenneth and Berg, Richard C. *Marching Bands*. New York: A. S. Barnes and Company, Inc., 1953.
Hovey, Nilo. *The Administration of School Instrumental Music*. New York: Belwin, Inc., 1952.
Jones, L. Bruce. *Building the Instrumental Music Department*. New York: Carl Fischer, Inc., 1949.
Kennan, K. W. *Techniques of Orchestration*. New York: Prentice-Hall, Inc., 1952.
Malstrom, George N. *The Drum Major's Manual*. Chicago: Ludwig and Ludwig, 1928.
Newton, Leonard G. and Young, T. C. *The Book of the School Orchestra*. London: Oxford University Press, 1936.
Normann, Theodore. *Instrumental Music in the Public Schools*. Philadelphia: Oliver Ditson Company, 1941.
Prescott, Gerald and Chidester, Lester. *Getting Results with School Bands*. Minneapolis: Paul A. Schmitt Music Co., 1938.
Righter, Charles B. *Success in Teaching School Orchestras and Bands*. Minneapolis: Paul A. Schmitt Music Company, 1945.
Rogers, B. *Art of Orchestration*. New York: D. Appleton-Century Co., 1951.
Skeat, William; Clarke, H. and Morgan, R. V. *Fundamentals of Band Arranging*. New York: Sam Fox Publishing Company, Inc., 1938.
Woods, Glenn. *School Bands and Orchestras*. New York: Ditson, 1920.

VOCAL MUSIC

Cain, Noble. *Choral Music and Its Practices*. New York: M. Witmark & Sons, 1932.
Christy, Van A. *Glee Club and Chorus*. New York: G. Schirmer, Inc., 1940.
Clippinger, David A. *Collective Voice Training*. Chicago: S. F. Fearis, 1932.

Davidson, A. T. *Choral Conducting*. Boston: Harvard University Press, 1940.
Earhart, Will. *Choral Techniques*. New York: M. Witmark & Sons, 1937.
Fields, Victor A. *Training the Singing Voice*. New York: King's Crown Press, 1947.
Johnson, Claude E. *Training of Boys' Voices*. Philadelphia: Oliver Ditson Company, 1935.
Kagen, Sergius. *On Studying Singing*. New York: Rinehart & Company, Inc., 1950.
Nicolí, Irene and Dennis, Charles M. *Simplified Vocal Training*. New York: Carl Fischer, Inc., 1940.
Pierce, Anne and Liebling, Estelle. *Class Lessons in Singing*. New York: Silver Burdett Company, 1937.
Pitts, Carol. *Pitts Voice Class Method*. Chicago: Neil A. Kjos Music Co., 1936.
Shaw, W. Warren and Lindsay, George L. *Educational Vocal Technique*, Vol. I & II. Philadelphia: Theodore Presser Co., 1936.
Sunderman, L. F. *Some Techniques for Choral Success*. Toledo, Ohio: University of Toledo Press. 1954.

CONDUCTING

Bakalenikoff, Vladamir. *Elementary Rules of Conducting*. New York: Boosey, Hawkes & Belwin, 1938.
Branthwaite, W. *Conductor's Art*. London: Williams & Norgate, Ltd., 1952.
Fuhr, H. M. *Fundamentals of Choral Expression*. Lincoln, Nebr.: University of Nebraska Press, 1944.
Goldbeck, F. *The Perfect Conductor*. Toronto: George T. McLeod, Ltd., 1951.
Jones, Archie N. *Techniques in Choral Conducting*. New York: Carl Fischer, Inc., 1948.
Krone, Max. *Expressive Conducting*. Chicago: Neil A. Kjos Music Co., 1945.
Van Bodegraven, Paul and Wilson, Harry R. *The School Music Conductor*. Chicago: Hall & McCreary Company, 1942.
Van Hoesen, K. *Handbook of Conducting* (Rev. ed.). New York: D. Appleton-Century Co., 1950.
Whiteman, P. and Lieber, L. *How to be a Bandleader* (Rev. ed.). New York: McBride, 1948.

NOTE: For additional instrumental, vocal, and conducting references, consult appropriate chapters for books listed under "Music Education."

Colleges and Universities

Music in Higher Education
Coordinating Chairman: Earl E. Beach, Athens, Ga.

☩

Junior College
Hal D. Dellinger, chairman, Joliet, Ill.

☩

Music for the General College Student
Clel T. Silvey, chairman, Indiana, Pa.

☩

The Education of the Music Teacher
Leo J. Dvorak, chairman, Charleston, Ill.

☩

Graduate Study in Music Education
Theodore F. Normann, chairman, Seattle, Wash.

CHAPTER XIII

MUSIC IN COLLEGES AND UNIVERSITIES[1]

MOST COLLEGES AND UNIVERSITIES in the United States offer education in music, much of it characterized by high standards of excellence. Orchestras, bands, choruses, a cappella choirs, operatic and chamber groups—all are commmonly found in the United States college or university. Intensive training for a professional career in music is readily available in the college or conservatory. Advanced studies in theory, history of music, and compositions are found in numerous graduate schools. Thousands of teachers and supervisors are trained annually to meet the demands of a broad music program in public and private schools and colleges. The church musician finds an ever-increasing provision for his preparation in many institutions. These extensive music activities have focused attention on universities and colleges as the providers of leadership in the field of music.

The Music Profession. A sizable number of persons are engaged in the music profession. While the profession as a whole has not been growing rapidly in recent decades, certain segments in the field of music, notably music education from preschool through college and university, have grown appreciably within the last quarter century.

The variety of opportunities for performing musicians is great, but the number of musicians who can subsist on earnings from music performance is comparatively small. Symphony orchestras and a few ballet and opera companies provide employment for instrumental musicians who supplement their incomes by occasional work in musical comedy, operettas, or other musical shows. Radio and television orchestras offer limited employment. The growth of good orchestras in smaller cities throughout the country has afforded new opportunities but not sufficient to do away with the need for supplemental employment from teaching or other professional work. Many musicians find semipermanent work in dance bands and orchestras. The opportunities in the concert field or operatic stage are extremely limited despite the number of singers who aspire to such careers. An expansion of these opportunities has been provided through television.

Churches employ a large number of organists, choirmasters, and singers. The minister of music found in many churches is a well-trained musician and, in many cities, receives an excellent salary.

Conducting offers a limited field of opportunity to a highly specialized group. In former years, conductors for major musical organizations were secured from abroad. At present numerous important conducting posts are held by men who received their training in this country.

Composition, writing and arranging for radio, television, movies, recording, arranging for dance bands or for school bands and orchestras, newspaper criticism, music librarian, music publishing, music merchandising, and music therapy are various areas of the profession for which an education in music may prepare.

The Teacher of Music. The virtuoso whose interest is primarily in performance and the training of performers is attracted to a music school or conservatory, or to the establishment of his own private studio—or both. The performing artist in

---

[1] Robert A. Choate, from *Higher Education*, monthly publication of the U. S. Department of Health, Education, and Welfare, December, 1953. Reprint, under title *Music in Higher Education*, available from Music Educators National Conference. 30¢.

118

his later years generally turns to teaching as a means of livelihood or continued professional interest. As a sideline, many symphony musicians, artists, school teachers, and church musicians supplement their income by establishing a private studio.

Doubtless the greatest number of vocational opportunities for the musician exists in teaching. The added compensations of income certainty, domestic stability, retirement benefits, and desirable environment have greatly increased the stature of this professional activity during the past thirty years. Since music is commonly accepted as an integral part of the child's education, teacher-demand pyramids with that of school enrollments. Thus, the greatest opportunity lies in the elementary school, and diminishes toward the college level. Conversely, increased preparation of the teacher, particularly at the advanced graduate level, tends to invert the pyramid of supply, creating a surplus of teachers aspiring for positions in higher education.

State departments of education require the public school music teacher to be prepared in educational philosophy, teaching processes, and growth and development of the child, as well as in his musical art. Private schools generally are not held to such certification requirements. The baccalaureate is commonly required with course stipulation for a teaching certificate, although many states issue temporary certificates involving lower requirements.

Advanced degrees are usually necessary for obtaining administrative positions or instructing academic and theoretical courses at the college level. In applied areas, professional proficiency and successful experience remain as principal criteria for employment. Certain state institutions, however, because of the necessity for standardization of procedures for determining faculty promotion, salary schedules, and tenure by state legislation, have established advanced study and degrees as objective criteria.

Organizations of Musicians; Publications. The growth of the profession of music, particularly those segments which concern higher education, is indicated by the coincident rise of professional organizations and the literature of the profession. Earliest of such organizations was the Music Teachers National Association (MTNA), founded in 1876. The MTNA holds annual meetings and is concerned with problems related to the private music teacher, music in schools and colleges, community music, and research in numerous fields. It has exerted considerable influence in music teaching through its permanent committee organizations. The proceedings furnish invaluable records of the musical development in the country. *American Music Teacher* is issued five times annually.

The Music Educators National Conference (MENC), founded in 1907 as the Music Supervisors National Conference, has afforded leadership in the development and formulation of music instruction in the public schools and colleges of the United States. The Conference functions as a national organization with six divisions, fifty affiliated state and territorial units, and several auxiliary and associated organizations. National and divisional conventions are held biennially in alternate years. State units hold at least one annual meeting. The growth of the Conference has been rapid, consisting at present of almost 25,000 members, and its influence has been notable in setting instructional patterns, raising the standards for music instruction, establishing adequate equipment standards, defining methods of credit for music study, advancing instrument study, correlating school and college programs, and promoting interest in community music as well as international relations and understanding through music. The *Music Educators Journal* is issued six times yearly. The first issue of the *Journal of Research in Music Education* was released in the spring of 1953. Numerous books and pamphlets dealing with specific areas are published by the MENC. Serving as the Department of Music of the National Education Association, the Conference maintains an office in Washington, D. C., as well as its national headquarters in Chicago.

The American Musicological Society (AMS) is an organization for the advancement of research in the various fields of music. Organized in 1934, the society is divided into regional chapters which hold regular meetings at which papers of musicological interest are read. The *Journal of the American Musicological Society* is published regularly.

The National Association for Teachers of Singing (NATS), founded in 1944, has contributed significantly in helping to guide curriculum developments in vocal instruction. Especially of benefit is the clarification of fundamental aims and procedures in voice training, establishment of codes of ethics, and the compilation of teaching literature of a high quality. NATS sponsors national and sectional meetings and summer workshops; publishes a periodical.

The National Association for Music Therapy (NAMT) was organized in 1950 to coordinate the wide activities and research in this vital area. Publications issued by the Association include a periodical.

Although not as closely associated with the colleges as the above-named organizations, the American Guild of Organists exerts a great influence in musical standards and accomplishments of organists in the United States. Examinations covering performance and general knowledge of music are given for the certificates of associate (AAGO), and fellow (FAGO). The guild is subdivided into numerous chapters which meet regularly and administer examinations. The *Diapason* serves as the official magazine for the Guild.

As a result of the first International Conference on Music Education, which was held in Brussels, Belgium, in midsummer 1953, an International Society of Music Education was formed. This organization has as its aims the exchange of philosophies, objectives, and materials in music teaching, the furtherance of understandings and relationships through music, and the projection of further international conferences.

Development of Music in Higher Education. Music was relatively late in entering the curriculum of the American college. Although there are numerous records of musical activity in early colleges, the first professorship announced in music was in Oberlin College in 1835—a "Professorship of Sacred Music." The Harvard Musical Association was established in 1837, although the Pierian Sodality (which still flourishes at Harvard) was founded as early as 1808. The first recorded bachelor's degree in music was that given by Boston University in 1876. The gap of 200 years from the founding of Harvard College (1636) to the earliest recognition of music in higher education is understandable when colonial living conditions and the Old World influences on American education are considered. There was little place for music in these first institutions which were largely prototypes of English or continental schools concerned with training men for the learned professions or the ministry.

The numerous forces affecting higher education predestined its institutions to a characteristically different role both in scope and influence. Among these forces were the pioneers of musical education and the societies dedicated to its future. After 1870, music professorships and departments of music were established in several of the leading colleges, and numerous conservatories were founded. From 1870 to the present, establishment of university schools of music has been nationwide. Music departments constitute an integral division of the liberal arts colleges, and noted musicians have been appointed to professorial chairs, indicating the recognition of music instruction.

A coordinate development in the early years of this century was the attention given to teacher preparation in the field of music. Although music instruction had begun in the public schools of Boston as early as 1838 and had spread rapidly to other cities throughout the United States, training of the music teacher was supplied by conventions and institutes sponsored largely by various book-publishing concerns. These companies contributed significantly to the remarkable growth of early music and supplied training not to be found in the college of that day. As the public school music program expanded, the need for increased emphasis on teacher training and the responsibility for assuming leadership in this vital area became evident. Courses in music pedagogy, methods, and materials were added to the college curriculum, and teacher-training departments were organized.

In the present century, music has risen steadily to a place of equal status with other subjects in the liberal arts curriculum. Most of the 1,400 or more colleges accredit courses in music, and adequate recognition is given in both undergraduate and graduate degrees.

CHAPTER XIV

THE JUNIOR COLLEGE

THE JUNIOR COLLEGE occupies a unique position in the realm of education because its inception was for both the practical and aesthetic needs of the people of the community. Generally speaking, this educational institution has prospered to the degree that it has continued to provide for the local needs.

A New Look at the Junior College Music Program [1]

Democracy at work as expressed in the phenomenal growth of the junior college movement in the United States is but one manifestation of the importance of the individual. Youth's enthusiasm for more education is finding expression through increased educational opportunities made possible by present day philosophies of the junior college.

Objectives. College music teachers and administrators should be fully aware of the main purposes and objectives of a junior college. They are generally stated as follows:

(1) The *Terminal Function* serves students wishing to complete a type of college education in two years. The curriculum may be either vocational or general.

(2) The *Preparatory Function* supplies two years of lower division work to precede the upper division of a college or university.

(3) The *Community Education Function* essentially serves the needs within the community with worthy use of leisure time and personality development frequently incorporated into such a program.

(4) The *Adult Education Function* serves as a composite of the above three functions for those who otherwise might postpone their education or who believe that education is an ever-expanding experience.

Some junior colleges are so geographically situated that the terminal or community functions are more important than the preparatory or adult education ones, while other schools may find it more desirable to emphasize other functions.

A Study of Trends. A survey of 75 junior college music program offerings was made in 1942 which included representative junior colleges from California, Florida, Illinois, Kansas, New York, Pennsylvania, and Massachusetts. Catalogs from these schools were studied and analyzed. An attempt was made recently to resurvey the same schools as were graphed in the data assembled in 1942 and to make a comparative study of trends. Some interesting changes have occurred during this twelve-year interval from 1942 to 1954. Courses were grouped under the following headings: (a) theory, (b) appreciation, (c) vocal, and (d) instrumental.

Six hundred eighty courses are now being offered as compared with 539 in 1942. The theoretical offerings reveal that harmony is the most frequently taught subject in the area of music, with ear training and musicianship ranking second. To a lesser degree, fourteen offer counterpoint and orchestration; nine, form and analysis; six, composition; and one, keyboard harmony. Although not a theory course in itself, school music, as such, is being taught in fourteen junior colleges, notably in Kansas.

---

[1] From an address by F. Anthony Viggiano, Los Angeles, California, given at the MENC Biennial Convention, Chicago, 1954.

In the field of music history and appreciation, the trend has been to offer more courses combining history with appreciation than as a separate course. Approximately one-half of those who formerly taught courses separately now fuse them into one course.

Some interesting titles and descriptions of courses include: Adventures in Listening; Layman's Music Course; Music Orientation; Survey of Music; The Symphony, Opera, Oratorio; Symphonic Literature; Early Music for Listeners; Modern Music for Listeners; Men in Music; Gregorian Chant; History of Jazz; American Music.

The descriptions of some courses were interesting. For example:

"*Music in American Culture*. A study of music in American life from Colonial days to the present time. The three broad divisions covered are: The music the colonists brought and what they created; folk music from various sections of the country; our important composers with an examination of the fields of opera, concerts, radio, and television in our life today."

"*Music in Family Living*. How music may be used effectively in the home. Study will be made of how to buy, operate, and care for musical instruments such as the phonograph and tape recorder; how to build record libraries; what kind of music is effective for child development; kinds of music desirable for different social occasions and times of the day; the citizen's responsibility in supporting civic music organizations."

In the field of vocal music, titles have changed more significantly than the increase in the number of offerings. The increase has been from 155 to 160 in 1954. The use of the term a cappella choir, *per se*, has changed from twenty-two schools using that term in 1942 to five in 1954. Choral groups still exist in great numbers but are referred to as chorus, vocal ensemble, choir, concert choir, college singers, choral club, and madrigal singers. Of significance is the growth in courses referred to as "Opera Production," from one in 1942 to nine in 1954.

In the field of instrumental music, a more dramatic trend and change was observed. Course offerings have increased from 175 to 254. The largest change occurred in beginning instrumental classes, which have increased from twenty-six to sixty-three. The general terms "band" and "orchestra" were used most frequently, with the terms "symphony," "little symphony," and "community orchestra" being used much less. Conducting courses were offered by sixteen colleges as compared with twelve in 1942. Only one college offered a formal class in dance band twelve years ago. Seventeen now present such a course, sixteen of them being from California.

Some interesting titles of instrumental activities are:[1] Accompanying (2); Harp Ensemble (1); Coordinated Show Band Techniques (1); Chamber Music (2); Radio Ensemble (1); Pep Band (1); and Marching Band (2). The frequency of courses in organ has about doubled, from ten to eighteen, and is probably due to the popularity and accessibility of electronic instruments.

More important than these statistics was the content, methods of presentation, and materials used. The question to be answered now is, "Do these courses provide adequate training to students preparing for the music professions, for school music teaching, and for the general college student?"

The increasing interest in music which is evident can be used to reach general college students. They can be inspired and shown ways for developing personal musical tastes. This strong love for the arts can be enhanced by streamlining the

---

[1] Numbers in parentheses indicate frequency.

courses without diluting them. This may call for redesigning and rebuilding over the solid foundations already present. These changes can give energy and life to courses so that young people may better understand art values.

Many administrators are aware that the present age indicates a need for the humanities. The role music can play in meeting this need is no mystery and the many opportunities to help America fulfill its cultural destiny are constantly asserting themselves. The humanism of man must be placed in proper balance with science. In this simple idea lies the greatest opportunity for the junior college.

Music in the Junior College

The music program in the junior colleges of America should further the general goal of music education for everyone according to his interest and ability by providing challenging musical experiences for (a) the future professional musician, (b) the student for whom music is an avocational or recreational outlet, and (c) the residents of the community who desire additional sources for developing and stimulating their musical interests.

QUESTIONNAIRE SURVEY [1]

A questionnaire was submitted to divisional and state chairmen of the junior college subcommittee of Music in American Education during 1953-1954 in an attempt to get a representative national picture of the present situation involving the musical activities of America's junior colleges. No claim is made as to the validity of the results of the questionnaire; however, it is believed that certain trends and deficiencies are recognizable. The data following are a compilation of replies from ninety-eight junior colleges in fifteen states. [2] Some states are not represented because not all states have junior colleges. The new Illinois state chairman was appointed too late to participate. Kansas did not report, but it is well known that much is being accomplished there in the junior college field.

Of the fifty-four junior colleges sponsoring community vocal groups, most emphasis seemed to be on secular and small musical groups and ensembles. While this is exceedingly worth while, it is evident that community choirs and oratorio societies sponsored and supported by junior colleges need to be developed. There are many ways of organizing community assets. Those communities having best results seem to operate along the following general lines. [3]

(1) Initial organization of the community chorus or oratorio society should be approached through an advisory committee recruited from local community leaders in vocal music (teachers, singers, church choir directors, etc.). Such a plan has great value especially to directors who are new to a community. It should be remembered that it takes time to establish a great tradition and the foundations must be firm and based on good music, advice, and sound musicianship.

(2) Administration of the financial affairs of a good community-college music program should be handled through the school financial office. Two separate accounts usually are established:

Regular Budget. To include salary appropriation for the director, as well as the music department allotment for supplies, repairs, replacements, equipment, etc.

---

[1] From the report submitted by Hal D. Dellinger, Joliet, Illinois, National Chairman, Music in American Education Committee on Music in the Junior College.

[2] Maryland—3 ; New Jersey—3 ; Oklahoma—5 ; Michigan—5 ; Minnesota—5 ; Mississippi—6 ; Missouri—6 ; Colorado—7 ; Washington—11 ; Idaho—11 ; Oregon—11 ; Montana—11 ; California—14 ; Iowa—14 ; Texas—19.

[3] See Chapter XXVIII, "Music Education in the Community."

Activity Account. Admission receipts from all college music activities, including the community and regular student concerts. In addition many colleges assist this fund by depositing a percentage of the activity fee charged each student at time of enrollment. Some college music departments finance the entire expense of these community musical activities, furnish the music library as a part of its yearly budget, and engage the director.

Many schools combine their yearly musical offerings into what might be generally termed a Greater (name of city) Concert Series which offers a full season of musical events for a season or budget price. Individual program admissions should be made available also. Such a series would place emphasis on *local* talent. Community-sponsored instrumental groups appear not to be supported by junior college music departments as much as vocal groups.

Academic Courses. Academic courses for adults in junior colleges are primarily centered in the field of music theory. A little more than fifty per cent of the colleges reporting offered courses for adults. There is much room for expansion especially in the field of arranging and course offerings for elementary and high school classroom teachers.

One of the most obvious deficiencies shown in this survey is the lack of adequate music library facilities available to the community and the regular student body. Most colleges do not make their music libraries available to the public. Library facilities are, on the whole, inadequate to meet the needs of the community. Junior college music educators need to promote and increase the range of availability of texts, recordings, and scores.

Terminal and Professional Courses. Most needs are being met with course offerings for the first two years of college training. In the category of psychology of music education, it has been common practice to place such studies somewhere in the junior or senior years of undergraduate training. Although this is a common practice, junior colleges would do well to offer some sort of orientation course at the beginning of the freshman year. Most students preparing for professional training have a great need for studying the qualifications, requirements, expectations, and musical values of their art. They need to know from the beginning how to go about the job of learning to be a music educator; to be better informed how to practice, how to use technique for the expression of musical purpose, and in general what to expect as they are to follow the trail leading to a professional degree.

Individual Instruction. The data shows that private instruction is emphasized rather than class techniques. There is a feeling that too many private teachers fail to teach from a creative point of view, i.e., improvization through an understanding of scales and their tonal tendencies together with fundamental chords and their relationships. Expansion of class instruction of applied music seems to be needed.

Only three of the colleges reporting are affiliated with the National Association of Schools of Music. This may be due to the general feeling on the part of most junior college school officials that their own regional accrediting agencies have set the necessary standards for transfer of credits.

It is recommended that junior college music educators be encouraged to adopt a creative point of view in developing the unique resources of their own communities and to enlarge the scope of musical activities wherever possible.

The Junior College Curriculum [1]

A music education program which seeks to extend general education and so create human understanding and harmonious relationships will find practical appli-

[1] From the *Music Education Source Book* (Chicago: Music Educators National Conference, 1947), pp. 26, 27.

cation in the junior college music program. This policy implies that music experience is the rightful experience of every student on the thirteenth- and fourteenth-grade levels as well as in the preceding twelve grades. Thus the integration of music into the general education pattern should be the guilding principal of the junior college music department. Music departments which continue to make performance the guiding policy seem to be encouraging the exclusion of music from the general education pattern and to place music in an isolated area to be regarded as a fine art accessory. Active participation in music by a select few while the student body becomes merely consumers of music does not constitute an adequate junior college music program. The junior college can and should be the flowering of many years of music training and activity. Numerous items, however, will influence the curriculum.

(1) *Any Curriculum Must Be Determined by*
  a. Demand (there must be a sufficient registration).
  b. Equipment.
  c. Teaching staff (size and particular strength).
  d. The type or plan of organization of the college (two or four years; in conjunction with high school, college, or separate school plant).
  e. The types of student interest—terminal (vocational and cultural), professional (lower division studies), professional skills.
  f. Nature and standards of the senior college or any other institution for which the junior college makes preparation.

(2) *Any Program Must Provide for a Transient Situation.*
  a. For certain irregularities in entrance and attendance.
  b. The necessary special tutoring attending these irregularities, etc.

It has been pointed out that the junior college, due to its comparative newness, is the most flexible area in the entire educational scheme, hence, less bound to tradition and freer to adjust its curricula to rapidly changing conditions and needs. Its intimate contact with adult community life makes it possible to know the needs of the public and to revise curricular offerings accordingly. Conditions such as these place the junior college in a unique position of educational service to the community which is dominated neither by the traditional high school nor university and college standards. However, the establishment of a music program which will be functional for the mass of students and also for the specially talented may require some daring innovations.

SAMPLE JUNIOR COLLEGE MUSIC CURRICULA[1]

Curriculum I

Assumptions: (1) Size of institution, 150 to 350 students. (2) Only one instructor available. (3) Objective, to serve the needs of the general student.

COURSE TITLE	SEMESTER HOURS	TEACHING HOURS	NO. OF SEMESTERS
Music Appreciation or Survey of the Arts	2 or 3	2 or 3	2
Elementary Musicianship	2 or 3	2 or 3	2
One vocal group: Choir, Men's Glee Club, etc.	?	3	?
One instrumental group: Band, perhaps Orchestra	?	3	?
Beginning Voice, Instruments or Piano, depending on instructor's interests and abilities	?	4 to 6	?
Chamber Music	?	4 to 6	?
Total	?	18 to 24	

[1] From an article by Neil M. Daniels, *Music Educators Journal*, March 1946, p. 80.

Curriculum II

Assumptions: (1) Size of institution, 200 to 400 students. (2) One instructor available. (3) The primary interest is to offer the minimum of essential courses for vocational and pre-professional training on the junior college level.

COURSE TITLE	SEMESTER HOURS	TEACHING HOURS	NO. OF SEMESTERS
Elementary Musicianship	2	2 to 4	2
Intermediate Musicianship	3	3 to 5	2
*Advanced Musicianship	3	3 to 5	2
History and Literature of Music	3	3	2
Beginning Piano Class	1	2	2
*Beginning Voice Class	1	2	2
*Beginning Instruments	1	4 to 8	2
Concert Band	1	3	?
*Chamber groups for string players	1	4	?
Choir	1	3	?
Total	17	29 to 39	

*Note: If only one instructor is available, one or more of the courses marked with an asterisk will have to be deleted.

Curriculum III

Assumption: (1) Size of institution, 400 or more students. (2) Two or more instructors available. (3) Objective, an adequate but not elaborate curriculum to serve the needs of all types of junior college music students.

This curriculum will be a mixture of I and II. Some advanced work in voice and instruments should be available.

Selected Bibliography—Junior College

BOOKS

Bogue, Jesse P. *The Community College.* New York: McGraw-Hill Book Company, 1950.
Eells, Walter C. *The Junior College.* New York: Houghton Mifflin Company, 1931.
Jeffers, Edmund V. *Music for the General College Student.* New York: Columbia University Press, 1944.
Jones, Vincent. *Music Education in the College.* Boston: C. C. Birchard & Company, 1949.
Koos, Leonard V. *The Junior College.* Minneapolis: University of Minnesota Press, 1924.
Sexson, John A. and Harbeson, J. W. *The New American College.* New York: Harper and Brothers, 1946.
Starrak, J. A. and Hughes, R. M. *New Junior College.* Ames: Iowa State College Press, 1948.
Ward, Phoebe. *Terminal Education in the Junior College.* New York: Harper and Brothers, 1947.

PERIODICALS

Daniels, Neil M. "The Junior College Music Curriculum," *Music Educators Journal* (March 1946), p. 54.
Hodgson, Walter. "Problems of Music Administration in Colleges," *Education* (September 1951), p. 13.
Lindsay, Frank B. "California Junior Colleges, Past and Present," *California Journal of Education* (March 1947).
Reiss, Muriel. "The Place of the Junior College in Training Musicians," *Music Educators Journal* (January 1950), p. 20.
Stover, Oscar. "Problems of the Junior College Band," *Proceedings: Southwest Division, College Band Directors National Association* (December 1951).
Swartz, Jack. "Civic Music Life and the Community College," *Junior College Journal* (April 1950).

ARTS AND HUMANITIES

[NOTE: Those who deal with junior college students will need especially to have a broad concept of the place of music as an art in its relationship to the humanities. The following bibliography is indicative of this aesthetic aspect.]

Allen, Warren D. *Philosophies of Music History.* New York: American Book Company, 1939.
Barlow, W. B. *Foundations of Music.* New York: D. Appleton-Century Co., 1953.
Barnes, Harry E. *An Intellectual and Cultural History of the Western World* (Rev. ed.). New York: Random House, 1937.
Barzun, Jacques. *Of Human Freedom.* Boston: Little, Brown & Company, 1939.

Brown, Calvin S. *Tones into Words*. Athens, Ga.: University of Georgia Press, 1953.
Burke, Cassie; Meierloffner, Virginia, and Phillips, C. A. *America's Musical Heritage*. New York: Laidlow Bros., 1942.
Copeland, Ralph. *Music and Imagination*. Cambridge, Mass.: Harvard University Press, 1952.
Cotton, Marian and Bradburn, A. J. *Music Through the World*. Boston: C. C. Birchard & Company, 1953.
Dewey, John. *Art as an Experience*. New York: Minton, Balch & Co., 1935.
Edman, Irwin. *Arts and the Man*. New York: W. W. Norton & Company, 1939.
Everett, Millard S. *Ideals of Life—Introduction to Ethics and the Humanities*. New York: John Wiley and Sons, 1954.
Ewen, David. *European Composers Today*. New York: The H. W. Wilson Company, 1954.
Ferguson, Donald. *History of Musical Thought*. Minneapolis: University of Minnesota Press, 1936.
Finkelstein, Sidney. *How Music Expresses Ideas*. New York: International Publishers, 1952.
Flewelling, Ralph T. *The Survival of Western Culture*. New York: Harper and Brothers, 1943.
Gradenwitz, Peter. *The Music of Israel*. New York: W. W. Norton & Company, Inc., 1949.
Greene, Theodore M. *The Arts and the Art of Criticism*. Princeton, N. J.: Princeton University Press, 1940.
Hughes, Charles W. *The Human Side of Music*. New York: Philosophical Library, 1948.
Kallen, Horace M. *Art and Freedom*. New York: Duell, Sloane and Pearce, 1942.
Lang, Paul H. *Music in Western Civilization*. New York: W. W. Norton & Company, Inc., 1941.
Livingstone, Sir Richard. *On Education*. New York: The Macmillan Company, 1944.
MacCarthy, Desmond. *Humanities*. London: Oxford Press, 1954.
McKinney, Howard D. *Music and Man*. New York: American Book Company, 1948.
Meier, Norman C. *Art in Human Affairs*. New York: Whittlesey House, 1942.
Mumford, Lewis. *The Culture of Cities*. New York: Harcourt, Brace and Company, 1938.
Munro, Thomas. *Scientific Method in Aesthetics*. New York: W. W. Norton & Company, Inc., 1928.
Reese, Gustave. *Music in the Renaissance*. New York: W. W. Norton & Company, Inc., 1954.
Saminsky, Lazare. *Living Music of the Americas*. New York: Howell, Soskin & Crown, 1949.
Schoen, Max. *Art and Beauty*. New York: The Macmillan Company, 1932.
————. *Understanding Music*. New York: Harper and Brothers, 1945.
Seashore, Carl E. *In Search of Beauty in Music*. New York: The Roland Press, 1947.
Sessions, Roger. *The Musical Experiences of Composer, Performer, Listener*. Princeton, N. J.: Princeton University Press, 1950.
Spaeth, Sigmund. *The Art of Enjoying Music*. New York: McGraw-Hill Book Company, Inc., 1942.
Ulrich, Homer. *The Education of a Concert Goer*. New York: Dodd, Mead & Company, 1949.
Weinstock, Herbert. *Music as an Art*. New York: Harcourt, Brace and Company, 1953.

CHAPTER XV

MUSIC FOR THE GENERAL
COLLEGE STUDENT[1]

THE GOLDEN AGE of American education, when every college student was a well-rounded scholar, seems to have ended in the last half of the nineteenth century. This change was influenced by Charles Eliot (Harvard 1869-1908) who founded the elective system. He came under the natural influence of his age with the flood of specialized knowledge that had come to our shores from European universities. It appears that the secondary schools of Europe usually have succeeded in better preparing their graduates for college specialization than has been true in America. The general education movement in the colleges of the United States is essentially a recognition of this need. The first two years of college can supply the necessary foundation.

The Harvard report on general education (1946) took direct issue with the philosophy of Dr. Eliot. This report issued an indictment of undergraduate majoring at the expense of a more general cultural background. Between the student's major and his electives, according to the report, the basic courses which were left shrunk to almost zero. Thus, there resulted an ignoring of liberal studies and a unifying force within the curriculum.

The adjective "general" has all but displaced the word "liberal" in educational discussion, but the movement represents more than a name. It is a movement which began with a reexamination of the nature and purposes of liberal education and one which is leading toward a revitalization of the liberal arts.

From its earliest inception, general education was a reaction against over-specialization. It has been a cry against the unbalance between the pursuit of special interests and the broader training needed for the liberally or broadly educated man.

The curriculum had grown into a plethora of fragmentary compartments. It was becoming more and more difficult for scholars to keep the student in mind at all, much less to see him as a whole. Technical matters were crowding out humane considerations. Each college department began to treat *all* students, even in elementary or introductory courses, as potential specialists.

Thus, general education was and is a reaction against formalism in liberal education. Sir Richard Livingstone warned that "Education may lose contact with the human spirit; it may degenerate into something perfunctory, narrow or stilted . . . the humanities can lose their humanity . . . by its very nature education tends to degenerate into technique and the life goes out of all subjects when they become too technical . . . education can so easily decline into routine and mechanism . . . knowledge may become an end in itself irrespective of whether it is worth knowing." President Seymour of Yale argues that we should make learning "functional and living in our time."

Present Concern. The present concern has been chiefly with the type of contributions that college music teachers may or may not be making to the broad foundations hoped for in the humanities field. Some of the B.A. curricula in liberal arts colleges still prefer less breadth of training. For example, a student in business

---

[1] From the report submitted by Clel T. Silvey, Indiana, Pennsylvania, National Chairman, Music in American Education Committee on Music for the General College Student.

administration can graduate from some colleges without history, philosophy, or natural sciences. Likewise, a student majoring in one or more of the related humanities will pursue more detail and exactness of training, made possible in many instances because of a more highly selective screening process in the selection of students taking the course. Thus the curricula planners for their respective B.A. and B.S. degrees have not as yet agreed upon a need for certain liberalizing courses.

The three major fields of liberal learning which provide a basic general education are (a) the humanities, (b) the social sciences, and (c) the natural sciences. Many general education programs place emphasis upon the development of *all* phases of the individual's personality—intellectual, social, physical, and emotional.

The Course Plan. Perhaps the most logical way to plan courses in general education would be that the purposes be determined first and then content or learning experiences be selected in terms of them. Possibly too many start with content and then try to make it significant to students. Regardless of how the attack is planned, the basic problems of general education have to do with the ends to be attained together with the most economical means of achieving the objectives for individual students.

It could be that there is too much concern about the organization of content as presented to the general student. The way the learner organizes his own experience is more important than the organization imposed by others. The psychology of general education is more concerned with means than ends. The best laid plans for an adequate general education program are likely to go awry if the *teachers* are unsympathetic with the purposes. Unfortunately, most college and university teachers have been educated, selected, and appointed as specialists, and most institutions must rely on these same specialists for breadth of vision.

The Aims. The aims in an introductory music course for the general college student should have some semblance to those programs of general education which aim to be practical or useful. It is agreed generally that college graduates, because of their education, should want to improve society. The majority of our "Introduction to Music" texts and syllabi hold to the conservative view of the past in prescribing a program of studies based solely upon content and historical sequence. They emphasize a description of subject matter to be studied critically and feel that, as a result of pursuing such a method, intellectual development will occur. There are others who advocate (a) a curriculum flexibility which allows for wide differences among college students, and (b) a consideration of the needs of students or a "student-centered" program.

Music can and should contribute much to the program of humanities in general education. The humanities are needed as a balance to the natural and social sciences. Knowledge and appreciation of the material products of our twentieth century scientific culture need to be balanced by a knowledge and appreciation of man's non-materialist achievements. The descriptive and statistical methods of the science need to be supplemented by the normative and philosophical approach of the humanities. Courses in the humanities undertake to develop a reasoned philosophy of values and ends.

Historical knowledge in and for itself is a desirable thing but must take a place below other objectives (aesthetic and philosophic) in the study of the humanities. It is true that the traditions of lectures, textbooks, and examinations affect the modes of undergraduate teaching—especially in general education courses. The tendency is unquestionably away from the textbook and lecture method and in the direction of group discussion and activity. Improvements in the methods of instruction will not result from an invention of new devices, but rather from them will result a clearer formulation of (a) the nature of the humanities, and (b) the ends in view.

Types of Offerings. Practically every American college and university today offers two general types of music for the entire student body (the general college student) : (a) the one- or two-semester introductory music course, and (b) vocal and instrumental groups. The present-day American college that fails to provide music activity groups is a rare exception. Many, unfortunately, stress a high degree of group performance ability at the expense of many general college students. Excellence of performance ability is a worthy goal even though the personnel of such groups must necessarily be limited to students with a high degree of talent. But the more farsighted college music program today is not content with the one or two superior performing groups. They provide for intermediate and beginning groups so that the general college student—the non-specialist, who has had limited musical opportunities—will not be denied his inherent rights. The most noticeable weakness, however, in our American college music education program today for the general student is the shortsighted policy in providing for the introductory music course.

While college curricula for the music major reveals commendable growth and alert thinking during the past decade, there is a serious obligation for the musical activities of the general college student—those students today who will want to listen to the concerts of tomorrow, and those students today, who will be school and college administrators tomorrow.

Some Questions. Those in music education who are dealing with music for the general college student will be needing to search for answers to the following questions. Is your approach functional? Is music being taught as a way for happy living or is there danger of the professional musician teaching it as he would use it rather than as the layman would be able to use it? Should it be admitted that our *status quo* is one of selfish self-containment, or may a brighter future be in store where teachers and students become partners in a growing venture which can be best described as the general education movement?

An AACTE Questionnaire. A committee of the American Association of Colleges for Teacher Education undertook in 1950 to discover by questionnaire the desirable traits which the college executive preferred in college teachers of the lower-division students. The question asked was, "What personal and teaching traits should the administrator look for in assigning music educators to teach the general college music course?" Four hundred nineteen respondents listed the following:

Inspires students to think and express own ideas.

Emotionally stable and mature.

Organizes materials and prepares carefully for each class.

Is friendly, tolerant, and democratic.

Understands the problems met by college students.

Behavior reflects high ideals.

Takes broad view (not departmental) of educational problems.

Leads students to take responsibility to plan and check progress.

Has infectious enthusiasm for teaching.

Shows active interest in constructive professional study.

Regards self as a college teacher rather than as a subject-matter specialist.

Demonstrates skill in methods of instruction appropriate to his field.

Has successfully taught his subject in college.

Academic record in his special field was unusually high.

Has genial personality and sense of humor.

Survey by Southern Division [1]

The Committee on Music for the General College Student of the Southern Music Educators Conference set up two steps of procedure to assemble information which can assist institutions of higher learning to improve their opportunities in music for the general college student.

First, during the school year 1952-53, a survey was sent to all institutions of higher learning in the Southern Division of MENC. The purpose of this initial survey was to reveal what the colleges and universities were offering in music for the general college student. Of these 202 institutions, 61 returned the surveys furnishing the requested information.

Second, during the school year 1953-54, the committee made a survey of 37 institutions selected from the 61 who had returned the first survey. This second survey requested specific information from these selected institutions revealing how each school had been able to provide a fine music environment and unusual music opportunities for the general college students in that institution.

Institutional Music Environment. The second survey, made in 37 selected institutions of which 26 reported, revealed many factors which contribute to a fine institutional music environment, the most predominant of which were as follows:

(1) Music is actively supported, both financially and by attitude, by the administrative officers.

(2) Music is actively supported by the entire faculty of the institution, and particularly by those who advise students in making schedules.

(3) Adequate music facilities and equipment are provided.

(4) *All* students are permitted membership in campus music organizations if they can qualify.

(5) Students participate in the planning of nonclass campus music activities.

(6) Music is a regular part of the convocation or assembly programs.

(7) There is a close interrelationship between the departments of the institution so that music majors and nonmusic majors actively participate together in both music and nonmusic activities.

(8) Applied lessons, whether with or without extra charge, are in great demand by many general students and contribute greatly to an increased interest in music by the general students.

(9) Concerts, programs, recording library, and community music enterprises all increase the enthusiasm the general college student has for music.

(10) Elective courses of high music caliber but of a nontechnical nature (as compared to the courses taken by music majors) are offered by the institution.

(11) Music is integrated and correlated into courses of a general cultural nature, such as the humanities courses.

(12) The personality of the individuals who teach and direct the music courses and activities is an important factor which the general college student considers in choosing his electives and activities.

(13) The quality of the teaching as evaluated by students who have already taken the course(s) is important.

(14) Opportunities for student leadership and responsibility are provided, particularly in the performing organizations.

---

[1] From the report submitted by Clifford W. Brown, Morgantown, West Virginia, Southern Division Chairman, Music in American Education Committee on Music for the General College Student.

Survey by Northwest Division [1]

A questionnaire survey dealing with musical opportunities available in the colleges located in the states which comprise the Northwest Division of MENC was made during the first three months of 1954. The following data are based upon an 80% return.

(1) *Music activities of a nonclass type were provided by colleges as follows:*

80%—Student recitals and faculty recitals, free of charge.
66%—Record library open to all students.
54%—Free concert series.
50%—General listening rooms, headphones.
33%—Private listening rooms, phonographs.
20%—Portable phonographs with checkout privileges.

(2) *Audio-visual aids used in teaching general music courses include:*

96%—Phonographs.
79%—Charts, etc.
70%—Tape or wire recorders.
50%—Moving pictures.
38%—Film strips.
29%—Radios.

46%—Found movies of orchestral instruments effective.
33%—Found movies of opera effective.

(3) *General Music Course.*

a. The responsibility for planning the content of the general music course was as follows.

88%—Teacher in charge of course.
29%—Music department head.
20%—Committee of teachers who are teaching the course.

b. Methods of presenting material in the course were listed by the schools in order of importance, as follows: Lectures by the teacher; listening to recordings in class; assigned reading; listening to records outside of class.

c. With the exception of one school, the instructor responsible for the general college music course was from the local department of music. The specialized fields within the music department were:

42%—Teachers of music theory and composition.
42%—Music education.
29%—Piano teachers.
25%—Directors of orchestras.
20%—Directors of bands.
17%—Directors of choirs.

(4) *Basic Texts.* 54% reported a basic text used in such courses; 29% used no text; 17% omitted reply.

Textbooks mentioned: *What to Listen for in Music,* Copland; *Introduction to Music,* Bernstein; *Discovering Music,* McKinney and Anderson; *Music and Man,* McKinney; *From Madrigal to Modern Music,* Moore; *Listening to Music Creatively,* Stringham.

In this introductory music course, an attempt was indicated to teach basic music skills, as follows:

50%—Read musical notation.
42%—Sing.
42%—Conduct organized community group singing.

25%—Play orchestral instruments.
25%—Piano playing.
13%—Folk dancing.

[1] From the report submitted by R. F. Goranson, Pocatello, Idaho, Northwest Division Chairman, Music in American Education Committee on Music in Higher Education.

133

CHAPTER XVI

EDUCATION OF THE MUSIC TEACHER[1]

THE PROBLEM of teacher education in music obviously is concerned with just how the course offerings may be geared to attain desirable ends. Within the limitations of the undergraduate degree, the problem becomes complex. Many teachers-to-be come to training institutions with a background for their particular field. However, in many cases the precollege training is not adequate for continuation at the college level. Much time is lost in the preparation of teachers of music because it is necessary to bridge the gap between the secondary school experiences in music and the standards advisable and expected of incoming college freshmen. This gap is usually concerned with the theoretical aspects of music, although often the student is also lacking in technical proficiencies of a performing medium.

What is wanted in the teacher of music? A good teacher, aside from competence in his special field, must have an understanding of the whole area of general education as it applies to the training of all pupils in the public school. He must understand children, how the learning process operates, and understand and practice the methodology of enlightened teaching. The teacher must attune his field so that it contributes to the cultural understanding and feelings of the pupils, and becomes an integral part of the school program. Techniques and knowledge must serve aesthetic values and realizations so that auditory stimuli resolve into meaningful experiences.

The program of musical training at the college level may be generally described as follows:

(1) Development of basic technical skills giving opportunities for personalized expression in music in gaining experiences for teaching.

(2) Development of understandings, uses, and ability to respond to visual, auditory, and aesthetic considerations in music.

(3) Experiences to develop understandings and the abilities to use techniques of the classroom in the teaching of music.

The problem has become confused because of the need for broad experiences in the fields of general education. It is expected that in the very near future, with the general improvement in the teaching of music in the public schools, better prepared students will come to college for training in music education.

The following observations are quite universally accepted:

(1) Students preparing for teacher education in music should be a highly selective group.

(2) The program of training should emphasize a broad base in general education.

(3) The human element should be an important factor in the selection of prospective teachers for training.

(4) Student-teaching experiences should be given on a broad plane to include classroom, community, and other pertinent experiences.

(5) Teacher preparation in music should include recognition of the consumers of music as well as the producers.

---

[1] From the report submitted by Leo J. Dvorak, Charleston, Illinois, National Chairman, Music in American Education Committee on The Education of the Music Teacher.

(6) The program of teacher education in music education should be subjected to constant reappraisal and evaluation to insure growth.

The Attributes of an Effective Teacher [1]

Questions. What are the qualities that distinguish our successful music teachers? What are the traits, the peculiarities of excellence, the capabilities, the refinements that make of a teaching personality one which produces the ultimate in student growth, student attitudes, student capabilities and artistry? And, in terms of an identification of these, what are the characteristics the college student, who is to be the teacher of tomorrow, must cultivate?

First, it is necessary to recognize the fact that there are certain constants among the attributes of effective teachers no matter what the individual teacher's immediate sphere of influence. The successful teacher of first-grade music needs to possess these qualities just as surely as does the effective teacher of applied music at a conservatory of music. Area of music specialization and degree of specialization are the variants.

Foremost among the constants might well be the indefinable quality known as vision—vision to see potentialities in people individually and collectively, children, adolescents, and grownups; vision to see potentialities in situations, in music, and, not least of all, in self.

Feeding the artery of vision are such intangibles as capacity for friendship, love and respect for fellow-man, superior intelligence, an inquiring mind, creative artistry; among the tangibles is a manifestation of the acceptance of the Golden Rule in its most idealistic implications as a working philosophy.

Second, among the attributes of a good teacher one finds knowledge of teaching techniques and ability to use those techniques in awakening others to an awareness of their own potentialities and a desire to do something about them, whether those potentialities be for richer human relationships; for greater cultural wealth; for better physical health; or, musically speaking, for more intense enjoyment of music through amateur or professional performance, through creativity, or through more acute listening.

Underneath the second constant lie such illusive qualities as charm of personality; dynamic but controlled leadership; taste in dress, manners, speech, and music; a flair for varying degrees of showmanship; and a sensitivity to public relations procedures.

The *third* constant would be the ability to direct growth in a very subtle way toward the realization of the envisioned and ever-expanding potential.

This ability is fed by an understanding of the nature and needs of children, adolescents, and adults; an understanding of pedagogical and psychological principles and their application; an ability to discipline self and promote self-discipline among others; ability to plan, carry through, and evaluate objectively; and ability to impart an unquenchable enthusiasm for teaching and learning.

The *fourth* constant would be that of faith in self as a person and as a musician, and an ability to impart that faith to others.

This faith is derived from a growing competency in maintaining personal integrity; competency in a performing medium or mediums; competency in an expanding scholarship in music literature; competency in the use of method and materials.

The *fifth* constant would be the teacher's pride in his profession and his sincere belief that his art, music, was intended to serve mankind as a vehicle of individual

[1] By Lois Laverne Schnoor, Florida State University, Tallahassee. Reprinted from the *Music Educators Journal*, April-May 1953, p. 58.

and group expression. Belief in music as a servant of mankind is the warp and woof of effective teaching.

Lastly, a never-varying attribute of the good teacher would be that of holding steadfastly to high musical ideals, and yet being able to extract joy from the nearest approximation of those ideals of which his groups are capable in the light of their background.

These six constants are all veined with an underlying network made up of a host of qualitative and quantitative tangibles and intangibles.

Special Competencies

The qualified music teacher appraises his environment objectively. It is easy for a music teacher to be so carried away by his own work and plans that he fails to see the forces in his environment that would aid or thwart him. With this skill he can choose the proper job, initiate activities at the most propitious moment, and estimate soberly the effects of his program. Every citizen needs this ability, but the music teacher fails without it.

The qualified music teacher understands the relationship of the music program to society. The schools are an agent of society, existing in order to create adults who are qualified to carry on and improve society. Music is an integral part of that educational program. Thus the teacher's daily course is shaped by his understanding of the functional role which music plays in social and cultural institutions.

The qualified music teacher participates in community activities. The distinctive relationship between the music teacher and the community is strengthened greatly by whole-hearted entrance into local activities for which he may be qualified. The school music program demands public support, which the teacher may not gain without evidence of interest in the daily affairs of the community.

The qualified music teacher foresees his problems and plans accordingly. Many music teachers have demonstrated that thinking and planning can carry them far on the road to success. People, duties, and coordination are involved.

The qualified music teacher promotes his interests vigorously, yet considerately. The music program undoubtedly has inherent public relations value for the school, and proper use of this advantage may enhance the attainment of musical objectives. Shallow publicity, however, built on nothing substantial, brings disillusionment. The teacher may not long push his interests to the detriment of his colleagues.

The qualified music teacher works cooperatively toward common ends. Since the school music program or any aspect of it does not stand alone and apart from the general educational program, the music teacher necessarily works with associates in joint undertakings. Perhaps more often than other teachers he must go more than halfway since some believe his program to be an educational luxury.

The qualified music teacher adapts to the customs of his community. One may keep a personal sense of integrity without offending the sensibilities of the community. Those who feel that their personal liberty is infringed or restricted do not realize that it is the way they react rather than what they do or believe that is at issue. The successful music teacher does not become a carbon copy of the local pattern but respects and learns to understand that pattern for the betterment of his program.

The qualified music teacher leads groups effectually. True group leadership is an ever-changing function since it depends upon relative qualifications or expertness on points of immediate issue. Thus actual, if not nominal, leadership is thrust upon the music teacher on many occasions. He must be prepared to discharge these responsibilities in a democratic spirit, as an indispensable servant of the group.

The qualified music teacher functions smoothly on public occasions. In the spotlight on so many programs, the music teacher needs confidence, a sense of fitness, and command of crowd psychology. Whatever is said should be well chosen and clearly spoken. In organizing the public appearances of his performing groups he needs to plan well the sequence of events and exhibit that serenity of spirit which will be communicated to students and audience.

The qualified music teacher deals ethically with people. There is a code of ethics for teachers, another for music teachers, and an unwritten code for general social use. Music teachers deal with large numbers of people in many different circumstances and have need of honest, consistent, and ethical behavior.

The qualified music teacher respects the endeavors of his associates. Credit should be given where credit is due—to musical colleagues, fellow members of the teaching staff, and all associates who are sincerely engaged in gaining their own objectives. The cynical, self-centered attitude, the belief that no one else seems to be doing anything valuable, is not for the successful music teacher.

The qualified music teacher accepts and values his role in society. It is manifestly impossible to produce good teaching if one feels that his talents are being wasted, or that his job is really superfluous. The music teacher's job is one of the most important in producing cultural continuity and finding common values for society. The music teacher may be underpaid and unsung, but he should apprehend this possibility before he is committed to teach and work to improve society's valuation of his job.

Curriculum for the Education of Music Teachers [1]

It is recognized that teacher-training institutions throughout the country vary greatly in outlook, personnel, opportunity, equipment, and clientele. Such differences are not only inevitable but healthy and desirable, so long as the staff of the institution accepts the responsibility for dealing with its special problems effectively. Out of the work and study of such local staff groups, new and better ideas and practices may be expected to emerge, which will be found helpful elsewhere. This is by far the most promising means of improving the training of workers in music education throughout the country, as indeed it has been and still is the characteristic means by which American education as a whole has brought about improvement. It is evident that an over-all standard plan, even if a suitable one could be drawn up, would tend to discourage the local planning which can and should be so fruitful and important. However, common experience has already shown that the staff of any local institution which undertakes to better and replan its work benefits greatly by guidance, assistance, and the encouragement and stimulation which comes from the backing of a national body. It is precisely this which the following material hopes to supply.

THE STARTING POINT

The Basis for Planning. The proper starting point for the planning of the training curriculum is a clear conception of the duties and functions of the worker in music education. To build a teacher-training curriculum out of courses in applied music, theory, history, and so forth, patterned on the standard offerings of conservatories and academic departments of music with courses in music pedagogy super-added, is a serious error. This leads to an incoherent and ineffective program because the aims and practices of conservatories and academic music departments are in important respects irrelevant to the training of workers in music education,

---

[1] By James L. Mursell, Teachers College, Columbia University, New York, New York, and Bjornar Bergethon, University of Illinois, Urbana. Adapted from "Teachers College Curriculum," *MENC Committee Reports, 1944.*

and legitimately so. The curriculum should be a coherent whole, focused explicitly upon the type of professional worker considered desirable.

The Profession of Music Education. The striking evolution of music in American education has brought about a demand for what is in effect a new type of professional worker. Such a worker is called upon to be something more than, and different from, a teacher of voice, or piano, or orchestral instruments, or history, or theory, or a director of choral and instrumental ensembles. To be sure, he needs to be an efficient and versatile teacher, able to get tangible and creditable results. But beyond, although including this, he needs to be an organizer, a promoter, a musical educator in the widest sense. He should be capable of working resourcefully and adaptably both in the schools and the community to make the art of music a living force. Such social and educational leadership in the interest of music is indeed his most essential function.

Music education has reached a stage of maturity where service of this kind is a practical possibility, and not a mere utopian dream or idealistic theory. In many American communities a worker who understands his function in these terms and discharges it effectively can achieve an outstanding success and exercise a most valuable influence. He will find that the key to success lies in being able to deal with a service situation with initiative, resourcefulness, confidence, and good judgment. This should be the focus of the training program.

Guide Lines for Planning. The preparation of workers should enable them to take hold of a service situation and to shape it constructively; and to develop in them the personal, professional, pedagogical, and musical resources necessary for such an undertaking. This leads to certain general ideas which should be taken as guide-lines in planning the curriculum.

(1) The training program should exemplify under favorable conditions and at the highest possible level the very things which the worker himself will be called upon to do. It is a capital error to suppose that a teacher-training curriculum can be effective if it violates or ignores in itself the very principles and practices which it recommends.

(2) Above everything else it must be an inspiring and convincing personal experience. It should reveal to the student by first-hand experience how music can function in human living, both individual and social. Curricular and extracurricular activities, and the attitudes and professional activities of the staff of the teacher-training institution should be shaped to this end.

(3) It should equip the student with practical pedagogical expertness, that is, the ability to develop in children, adolescents, and adult learners tangible musical skills, insights, and backgrounds. Without this the best of intentions become nugatory, and music leadership either fails completely or is crippled. The building of such pedagogical expertness is by no means the sole function of the methods courses. It should be brought about by all the instruction the student receives in his training —instruction in applied music, theory, history, appreciation, and so forth. The entire training program should reveal to the student what good teaching of music means as a practical possibility.

(4) It should develop in the student not only pedagogical expertness, but pedagogical versatility. No doubt it is desirable for him to possess special teaching expertness in some one field—piano, violin, voice, theory, history, appreciation, and the like. But if this is all he has, he is severely limited. He should be familiar with the basic teaching problems and the best teaching practices in a number of fields. Once more he should gain this not by way of methods courses only, but in and through his own learning under expert instructors.

(5) The training program should include and exemplify what the staff considers the best and most desirable practices in music education. Instances would be class work in piano or instruments or voice, rhythmics, folk dancing, an all-school chorus, and so forth. If the staff considers such practices worth while, it should not be content to have the student merely hear or read about them. He should learn by first-hand experience what they amount to when well handled. Such experience can be a most important professional resource.

(6) The net outcome of the student's training should be a convinced and enthusiastic awareness of what a practical and creative musical leader can and ought to do, of how he can and should work in a social and educational situation. This enthusiasm and belief is the true and decisive agency for bringing about a transfer from his work in training to his service in the field. The program can generate such enthusiasm insofar as the student finds in it a musical and human experience which has a commanding value for him and which, accordingly, he wishes to transmit to others.

MUSICIANSHIP

Type of Musicianship Desired. The ideas just set forth have a direct bearing upon the type and standards of musicianship which the training program should develop. Everyone readily agrees that the worker in music education should be a good and competent musician. But here we have a term of many meanings, so much further definition and specification is required. As a result of many years of music study a person may be able to perform a limited repertoire with credit; or to produce grammatically and formally correct compositions; or he may have gained considerable knowledge of the history and traditions of music. He may have achieved a genuine musicianship in any one of these senses, and yet it may not fit him at all for the promotion of the art of music in the schools and the community. So there are types of musicianship which are not well suited to the practical needs of the worker in music education, and the musical standards of the training program should not be set up as milestones along the road to their attainment.

In general what the musicianship of the music educator ought to mean is versatility, flexibility, and self-confidence with the art of music. The first question is not whether he is a good pianist, or violinist, or vocalist, whether he has mastered chromatic harmony or taken a good deal of work in the history of music. The first question is whether he has the skill, the knowledge, the disposition, the initiative— and all four are important—to take hold of varied groups and individuals and open up the art of music for them and with them. This is what a sound training program should accomplish in the way of musicianship.

Musical Performance. Here the primary aim is to produce not fairly good virtuosi, but persons able to use the skills of musical performance in dealing with human, social, and educational situations. Thus a person may be a fairly good solo pianist but quite unable to lead group singing, to handle a vocal or instrumental ensemble, to extemporize a brief passage on the piano, to transpose, or to improvise a simple accompaniment, or even to read fluently and confidently. Then one can only conclude that his many hours of piano study, centered on a limited *memoriter repertoire* and to the exclusion of other facilities, have been leading him away from effectiveness as an educational and musical leader.

It is helpful to think of performing musicianship as falling into two types, extensive and intensive. By extensive performing musicianship is meant ability to perform on a reasonable though elementary level in many media—piano, strings, woodwinds, brass, percussion, and voice. It should be noted that the writers consider ability to rehearse and direct vocal and instrumental ensembles as belonging to the classification of musical performance. By intensive performing musicianship is

139

meant high competence in a single medium. Both intensive and extensive performing ability are necessary for a well-trained worker in music education.

EXTENSIVE PERFORMANCE

The training program should equip the student to meet the following standards of extensive musical performance.

—To play the piano sufficiently to read at sight material of the difficulty of hymn tunes.

—To play the piano sufficiently to execute fluently and with musicianly feeling material on the level of his contemplated teaching.

—Have sufficient command of one or more representative instruments from each of the four choirs (string, woodwind, brass, percussion) to be able to play material of the difficulty of elementary school songs.

—To demonstrate the basic techniques and manipulative problems of such instruments.

—To sing simple melodic material with musicianly feeling, and with the voice consciously controlled according to good production principles and practices.

—To demonstrate the basic techniques of good voice production.

—To use basically sound practice in rehearsing and directing vocal and instrumental ensembles, including community and assembly groups.

—To use and to demonstrate a basically sound baton technique.

—To make simple repairs and adjustments on band and orchestral instruments and pianos.

The above are basic minimum standards without which no worker can be considered properly equipped for service in music education. It should be noted in the first place that they are not stated in terms of length of time spent in study, but of actual achieved competence. In the second place, achievement is stated in terms of ability to deal with music, not of formal technical competence, such as the ability to play the scales in various patterns up to a designated tempo.

The following are comments and suggestions with regard to the standards proposed above:

(1) They are to be regarded as minimum standards necessary for effective work in music education. It may well happen that certain institutions will find it possible to go beyond them.

(2) The teaching of extensive performance must be expert and efficient. That is of great importance for two reasons: *First,* rapid progress is essential if the student is to achieve the indicated standards within the time available. Experience indicates that this is possible, but only under instruction efficiently geared to the problem. *Second,* work in extensive performance should reveal to the student what highly expert music teaching means, how it is conducted, and what it can accomplish. Here we have an application of the first of the guideline ideas mentioned previously.

(3) The teaching of extensive performance should in the main be social. Class instruction should be the mainstay, both for economic reasons and also because when well conducted it can yield rapid and excellent results. But social opportunities for acquiring and consolidating performing skills should go far beyond the instrumental and vocal classes, through the organization of singing circles, semiformal and informal instrumental groups, and the like. Here again the first of the general guideline ideas is exemplified.

(4) A large proportion of the material used should be that actually in use in the schools. This gives the student a body of music which can be drawn upon in

his own work, and if it is followed as a widespread policy it is likely to have a beneficial effect upon the quality of school music.

(5) The work should be dominated by a spirit of cooperation, helpfulness, happiness, and encouragement. Mutual help among the students themselves should be fostered, both to promote their own learning and to provide a valuable clinical experience. It is of great importance that the student who comes to the teacher-training institution should find there a new and wider joy in performing music for others and with others, and in learning to do so.

INTENSIVE PERFORMANCE

The training program should equip the student to meet the following standards of intensive musical performance.

—To perform a repertoire of the standard concert works of his chosen medium sufficient for three one-hour recital programs.

—To read with reasonable technical mastery and musicianly feeling a much larger selection of the standard literature of his medium.

—To take a composition of some length, somewhat below the upper limit of his technical ability, and work it up for creditable performance in a week's time without the aid of an instructor.

—To give evidence that the intensive study of his special medium has developed in his keen and practical musicianly insights. This evidence can be given (a) directly through his performance in his own medium; (b) indirectly through his ability to criticize the musicianly values of a performance in another medium, and to suggest ways for improvement of them.

—To read fluently, and with musicianly insight and feeling, compositions in his chosen medium considerably below his upper technical limits.

—To give evidence of poise, control, and good personal rapport both in formal concert performance and in playing for informal groups and occasions.

Certain additional standards of achievement relevant to intensive performance will be found listed under musical theory.

COMMENTS AND SUGGESTIONS

(1) The foregoing scheme of basic standards is in contrast to an intensive performing musicianship which centers in a single terminal recital offering a limited repertoire which has absorbed an undue proportion of the student's time.

(2) It is clear that such a scheme of standards requires much more than a snapshot evaluation depending on a terminal recital or examination. The student's work must be observed and appraised over a period of time in order to determine whether such standards have in fact been achieved.

(3) The examining or appraising body which passes on the student's achievement should consider him not as a prospective solo virtuoso, but as a prospective worker in music education. Moreover, it should consist of persons fitted by experience and outlook to do so. This follows at once when it is seen that the proposed standards by no means center on an externalistic demonstration of performing skill alone.

(4) It is of considerable importance that intensive performing ability should not be regarded as an absolute, or sacrosanct, of independent requirement or as the only desirable type of musicianship. The highest possible standards are of course desirable, but it must be recognized that when they become excessive they can be purchased at an undue price and can throw the total training of the student

seriously out of balance. Like every other element in the curriculum they must be considered in terms of their practical values, and in relationship to the whole pattern of the student's training.

Musical Theory. The training program should equip the student to meet the following standards of what may be called theoretical competence:

—To modulate at the keyboard from any key to any key.

—To transpose at the keyboard material of the level of simple song accompaniments from any key to any key.

—To extemporize material of the level and general type of simple song accompaniments at the keyboard.

—To notate from dictation material of the level and general type of the creative melodies of children.

—To rearrange the parts of a vocal ensemble to secure more ready and effective performance by groups of young singers.

—To arrange for performance by instrumental ensembles of varied types and components the type of material found in collections of music for high school use.

—To reorchestrate and rearrange standard instrumental works for effective performance by small, ill-balanced, or unusual ensembles.

—To write effective descants.

—To write effective piano accompaniments for vocal numbers.

—To take compositions of the type likely to be produced by high school and college students and correct and improve them for effective sound.

—To compose work of the type of school and assembly songs, simple marches, and the like.

✓—To work freely in the idiom of the pentatonic scale.

—To analyze by ear compositions of the level of the Haydn and Mozart piano sonatas, indicating their main structural elements and identifying their type (sonata form, rondo, etc.).

—To analyze similar compositions rapidly from the score, making similar indications.

—By dint of more intensive study, to identify the harmonic and contrapuntal content of music of this level of complexity.

With regard to the teaching of theory to secure practical outcomes of this kind, the following suggestions and comments are offered:

(1) It is clear that the conventional courses in diatonic and chromatic harmony and elementary counterpoint by no means secure them. This is probably because the work is excessively grammatical, and too divorced from practical musical considerations and problems. Since the aim of the whole training program is to equip the student with actual working abilities, it is urged that experiments in the teaching of theory be set up to discover the most effective means of attaining the standards listed above.

(2) One type of experimental approach would be to organize basic courses in theory of what may be called the workshop type. The essential idea here would be to organize the course, not about the conventional sequence of grammatical topics but about the actual functions it is desired to develop, namely, those listed above. No doubt there may properly be many variations in the practical working out of this idea. Such courses make very considerable demands upon the teacher since ready-made materials do not exist. It is urged that teaching groups who feel able and disposed to do so set up experimental approaches along this line as a

promising solution to one of the least satisfactory problems in the training of workers in music education.

(3) Another type of experimental approach is to enrich the systematic or grammatical treatment of theory with large amounts of actual composed music, and more particularly with the kinds of music likely to be used in school situations. Along with this may well go the interpolation of various projects to be carried out by the students, such as setting poems to music, writing accompaniments, and the like. This might be considered a compromise between the workshop approach and the purely grammatical approach.

(4) Yet another type of experimental approach would be to scrap the terminology of the present theory methods now in use, substituting for them a basic theory similar perhaps to basic English. This would eliminate the hardship put on the student who changes from one so-called system to another. It would also mean that the theory teacher would have to create a large part of his own course text, taking his material from composed music rather than having the material constructed to fit formal definitions.

(5) It should be pointed out that the attainment of standards such as those listed above need not be considered solely the responsibility of the work in theory as such, and that properly directed study of musical performance can and should contribute greatly to it.

Musical Culture. This term is used to designate familiarity with the literature of music, its manifestations in everyday life, its personalities, traditions and history, its social and cultural affiliations, and its aesthetic significance. Very obviously musical culture in this sense is an essential resource for anyone who wishes to work effectively as a musical leader and organizer.

The training program should equip the student to meet the following standards in musical culture:

—To recognize by ear and from the score a large body of works of various types, and to identify them by composer and period.

—To comment upon and discuss the outstanding masterpieces of the musical art, illustrating his remarks by excerpts played on the phonograph or otherwise.

—To characterize the lives and works of the major composers, placing them in their historical and social setting, and illustrating his remarks by suitable selections from their music.

—To characterize and illustrate the main periods of musical history.

—To characterize and illustrate a variety of typical musical styles.

—To indicate coordinations—historical, cultural and aesthetic—between musical periods, styles, and masterpieces, and other artistic manifestations, such as those of painting, sculpture, architecture, the dance, drama, and poetry.

—To characterize and discuss modern and recent musical manifestations and phenomena, including musical organizations and personalities and more general social manifestations, and to illustrate his comments by musical examples.

—To present competent and instructed critical reviews of musical performances and musical compositions.

In regard to these proposed standards, the following comments and suggestions are offered:

(1) Such standards of culture can and should be to a considerable extent developed incidentally. The training program as a whole offers very rich opportunities along these lines, which should be capitalized. Classes in musical perform-

ance and theory should by no means be limited to the acquisition of skills. Students should be furnished lists of books and records, and part of the time the course should be devoted to consideration of such materials. The same should be done in connection with all vocal and instrumental ensembles. Part of every student's work in his chief performing medium should turn on a study of its history, significance, general significance, and literature. The advantages of such a policy are many sided and obvious. In general it means that musical culture is made an integral part of the student's developing musicianship. To impart such cultural resources as vital and usable material is clearly a function of the whole training program, and no aspect of it should be unrelated to the undertaking.

(2) It is desirable to set up certain standard courses which deal directly with this material. There can be no reasonable objection to a sequential course in the history of music systematically presented. There is, however, the greatest possible objection to a course of this type which deals wholly in verbalizations and the printed page. It must certainly involve rich and varied direct contact with music if it is to have any considerable value. What the prospective teacher will need in his work is the widest possible familiarity with musical literature at first hand, and this the history course should supply. Moreover, it should not be narrowly concerned with nothing but the names, dates, and works of composers, the chief epochs of musical art and the like. One of the commanding advantages of the systematic presentation of musical history is the opportunity it offers for making the student aware of the place and significance of the art in human affairs, and of its wider cultural and social ramifications.

(3) It may well be that a course of quite a different type may be found desirable for dealing with materials of this type. This can be a laboratory or workshop course in musical culture. It should carry ample credit allotment and command a good deal of the student's time. It should involve systematic listening to recorded music, radio listening, concert attendance, the reading and discussion of important books, demonstrations of various kinds, and so forth. Particular emphasis is placed upon the provision of opportunities for phonograph listening and the motivation of their use as an essential part of the training program. Such a course takes the basic idea of what has been called music appreciation and greatly amplifies, enriches, and extends it. It can have a pivotal place in the training program and help to bring all other activities and aspects of that program into relationship.

(4) Besides all this, it is very desirable for the student to have some contact with arts other than music. And his contact should involve participation. He should paint, draw, do craft work, dance, write, act, and so forth, under competent direction. Such experiences can be very revealing and releasing, and have many and varied values. They can be prevented from becoming a mere unrelated scatter if their aesthetic significance is studied and developed, and this can bring about a deeper insight into the art of music itself.

EDUCATIONAL INSIGHTS AND TECHNIQUES

The following general considerations are presented as a guide to more detailed and specific analysis of educational insights and techniques.

The problem is that of the work in music education as such, and the work in general education. This latter has on the whole not functioned to the satisfaction of students and staff members in the field of music education. The student is apt to find it remotely related to his own interests and concerns, and to see little real point in it. The problem cannot be solved by the music staff alone for they do not control the offerings in general education. It can, however, be hopefully attacked by a clear formulation of policy and aims which can be discussed with those in charge of work in general education.

It is clear that the music teacher who is to exercise effective leadership and promote his art in an effective fashion needs to be aware of emerging educational doctrines and practices which affect the work of the schools. Otherwise, he will be unable to bring his own undertakings into relationship with them, and this may easily have most unfortunate practical effects. Many subject-matter areas have suffered in enrollment and general standing by getting out of line with developing educational policy, and the same can be true of music. When some new idea or practice is proposed, it is a great advantage for the music teacher to be able to understand it, to discuss it, and to shape it in relation to his work, and his work in relation to it. Moreover, he needs to be able to develop the work in music in conformity with the climate of ideas of a modern school system quite apart from any such specific new practices. This is one of the most important outcomes of the courses in general education and music education, and these courses should be geared explicitly to achieve it.

The prospective teacher needs to know what to do and how to do it when he faces a class. He needs, that is, self-confidence. But this should not be secured by teaching him a routine methodology set out in elaborate detail. Apart from the fact that there never is a "best" method, this is gravely limiting. He may find himself in a situation where the method he has been taught to use is inappropriate or unacceptable. Even if it helps him at the start, it may hamper him in the future and prevent his professional growth. He needs practical guidance, but it must be guidance calculated to make him into an educational and community leader in things musical rather than a routine-bound teacher. The position is taken that the training program should equip the student with good practical teaching techniques immediately upon graduation, together with the knowledge, the insights, and the attitudes of mind which will lead to continuing growth and favor adaptability and initiative.

The answer seems to be the close coordination of the courses in education in general and in music education with the entire teacher-training curriculum. Since only the latter are controlled by the music staff these shall be considered alone, but the principle applies also to the former. The courses in music education should be integrally related to that part of the program which seeks to develop a functioning musicianship. They should reflect back upon and expound this part of the work. They should explain the how and why of the teaching of performance and theory as the student himself has actually experienced it. They should show how the practices installed in the teacher-training institution can be made applicable at other levels, *mutatis mutandis*. They should reveal how the materials of musical culture can be utilized as teaching resources in varying situations and at varying levels. This by no means implies an irritating, awkward, mechanical coordination between courses in music education and work in musicianship. What it does require, however, is an essential unity of viewpoint throughout the entire training program, permeating all aspects of it. It requires that all members of the staff be aware of what each is doing, and that each be willing at all times to submit his work to the review and consideration of the rest. Everybody concerned—teachers of piano, voice, instruments, theory, history, and music education as such—is seeking to prepare effective, resourceful, creative musical leaders. And the work in music education is the place to bring the whole undertaking to clear and explicit formulation. All this, of course, implies the very best kind of intro-staff relationships, and the mutual interplay of ideas should go on in informal discussions, as well as in formal staff meetings.

This coordination of the whole program is the true answer to the problem of the courses in music education. It means that they become practical without a hampering and limiting specificity because the whole program is geared to show the student what to do in a service situation. Then the courses in music education are simply an opportunity for him to consider in general and in principle his proposed practices. Moreover, it is very likely that such a vitally unified training program in music education will, over a period of time, influence the institution as a whole and lead to a better coordination of the work in general education.

A word also should be said about observation and practice teaching. A considerable amount of such work is required for certification in many states; but too often it is continued simply because of legal demand, and treated as an unrelated tag-end to the program. Students observe and teach under some kind of nominal supervision, and probably get little of real value out of it. Clearly, the answer is to make all observation and practice teaching conscious, intelligently directed experimentation and appraisal in terms of definite ideas and principles. Observation and practice teaching should essentially be an intelligently directed clinic experience in how to secure good learning. The indicated policy is to focus and bring to bear the whole complex of principles and concepts for which the training program stands so that students are not distracted by irrelevancies and do not simply put in a number of hours to meet a state requirement. Once more the trouble with much observation and practice teaching is that the training program itself is not coordinated, that it does not add up to some definite body of doctrine and practice. This means that the student has nothing to guide him as an observer or practice teacher and, what is still worse, that he will have nothing convincing or reliable to guide him when he has to deal with practical situations as an independent worker.

THE PERVASIVE SPIRIT OF THE PROGRAM

The training of the school music teacher is a period when he lives with other musicians and educators, works to develop himself in new musical insights and skills, discovers new musical and educational horizons and new opportunities for constructive service, and has the privilege of sharing in a stimulating and inspiring milieu. It is of the utmost importance that there be throughout a pervasive spirit of friendliness, helpfulness, mutual concern, and genuine enthusiasm. It is a considered opinion that this is at least as important as any of the special aspects of the program discussed above. Such a spirit is the most potent single influence leading the student to carry forward into his own work the impetus and ideals gained in training. He should find in his work a revelation of the happiness and genuine human warmth which can mark cooperative musical living and learning. This can be to him an unforgettable lesson whose meanings he will never cease seeking to project throughout his whole professional career.

Here is something far more tangible than a mere pious wish or platitude. The pervasive spirit of the program should be a matter of constant and realistic concern to all those responsible for it. They should be at pains to maintain and develop ample avenues of natural and friendly intercommunication between students and staff. They should be active in supporting an adequate social organization. While this needs the backing of the staff, the chief responsibility should be in the hands of the students, and they should be encouraged to make decisions as they themselves see fit. The duty of the staff, in addition to general encouragement, is to guard the social life of the whole group from unfortunate developments and to keep it happy, healthy, and truly democratic. All this takes time and energy, but is is well worth it. Such activities are usually called extracurricular, and so they are, in the sense that they do not earn college credit. But they are every bit as important as any item in the formally recognized curriculum, and they should be treated as such in the allocation of time and facilities and the investment of personal energies. For a training program which exemplifies all that is best, most inspiring, most human, and most liberating in musical living is the paramount agency for the development of effective musical leadership.

Standards for the Evaluation of the College Curriculum
for the Training of the School Music Teacher [1]

As music becomes an increasingly powerful force in American life and education, it becomes increasingly necessary that the training programs of school music teachers be subject to periodic examination. The following schedules have been prepared to serve as a guide for such examinations, and to assist the school being examined and the visiting examiners in giving attention to both the broad and the specific needs of the training program for the student who is preparing to be a school music teacher. There has been a tremendous increase in the number of schools and colleges training music teachers. All such institutions have felt the need for specific information regarding criteria for the training program, and these schedules should be of value in answering the requests of these various institutions for such guidance.

It will be noted that while similar recommended schedules for the evaluation of teacher education in some other fields might be limited in scope to include either the elementary *or* the secondary level, the following schedules include *both*. This broad scope is written into these schedules because experience shows that in *most* areas of this country a school music teacher must have had training at both levels if he is to be prepared to meet the requirements of the teaching positions most commonly found.

While provision is made for opportunity for each individual to develop one major performance field, these schedules make possible for *every* student some training in both the vocal and the instrumental areas. This is included not only to broaden the general musical understanding of every student, but also because experience shows that many school music teachers in all parts of the country find it necessary to teach both vocal and instrumental music.

It should be noted that the approximate percentages suggested in these schedules for each area in the teacher education program are indicated as a *minimum* not a maximum requirement.

PRECOLLEGE MUSIC TRAINING

It is obvious from the study of any set of recommended schedules that the successful completion of a good music teacher education curriculum at the college level demands that the student shall have had previous musical training. For this reason it is recommended that high school music teachers study these schedules carefully and try to guide high school students who anticipate making music education their major field in college into the most valuable music study sequences possible. It is suggested that it is desirable that the student's high school training provide him opportunity to acquire some knowledge and develop some proficiency in the following areas:

1. Musical performance, including, if possible, the development of some degree of functional piano facility, of some proficiency on minor instruments as well as a

---

[1] These standards were developed by the MENC Commission on Accreditation and Certification in Music Education, Marguerite V. Hood, University of Michigan, Ann Arbor, Chairman. The introductory statements and subject content area outlines have been studied and revised by joint action of the MENC Commission and the Committee on Music Education of the National Association of Schools of Music. A group of members of both organizations did further study and revision of the outlines under "Subject Content Areas" and of Schedules II and IV in 1952, ending by voting acceptance of those sections. The same sections were discussed and accepted by the NASM General Assembly at its 1952 Convention. Later, a group of the principal executive officers of the National Association of Schools of Music, Music Teachers National Association, and Music Educators National Conference gave their joint approval as individuals of the principles involved in the setting up of these evaluation materials. The entire body of curriculum outlines and schedules was approved by the Board of Directors of the MENC. In 1953 the Committee on Studies and Standards of the American Association of Colleges for Teacher Education approved these materials and added them to the evaluation schedules of the AACTE for use in connection with its current intervisitation program.

major instrument, and of a variety of instrumental and vocal ensemble experiences, large and small.

2. Basic Music (Fundamental Theory).

3. Music History and Literature.

If the work of a student in these areas in high school has reached such a degree of advancement as to merit it, such work can be recognized by entrance proficiency auditions at the college level. This will enable the student to substitute other areas of study at the college level for those in which he is already prepared, to the end that he may have opportunity for an increased breadth of cultural experience and for the development of increased skill in many musical areas in which he is expected to be proficient.

Subject Content Areas in the Music Education Curriculum

It is suggested that entrance proficiency and achievement tests may be given in Basic Music and in Musical Performance, and that a student may be relieved of requirements which he has already completed and allowed to use the freed time for electives.

I. GENERAL CULTURE

Minimum requirement suggested: 33% of the total (120 semester hours) required for an undergraduate degree.

The purpose of this area of the curriculum is well stated in the National Association of Schools of Music By-Laws and Regulations, 1949, p. 20: "This area of preparation should assist the individual (prospective teacher) to take his place in a democratic society and a world order; to gain a cognizance of the scientific contributions to mankind; to recognize and accept the responsibility of living in a social relationship; and to evaluate the cultural heritage. He should be able to use, adequately, the English language and should acquire the ability to recognize and solve problems independently."

The courses in this area include the following, some of which may be specific institutional or state requirements:

1. Nonmusic subjects to include a nonmusic minor if required.

2. Any psychology course other than educational psychology.

3. Music literature, history, and/or appreciation.

4. The basic survey type of course, where required: Humanities, social sciences, natural sciences.
   (In some cases subjects listed under 1, 2 and 3 above are, or may be, included in certain surveys.)

II. BASIC MUSIC

Minimum requirement suggested: 14% of the total (120 semester hours) required for an undergraduate degree.

This area includes subjects such as the following in the area of music theory. These sometimes are taught separately and sometimes in combination courses which may include several subjects.

1. Music reading (sight singing, etc.).
2. Ear training and dictation
   (melodic, harmonic and rhythmic).
3. Keyboard harmony.
4. Harmony (part writing).
5. Eurhythmics.
6. Form and analysis
7. Instrumental and/or vocal arranging.
8. Counterpoint.
9. Composition.

The objective of the above courses should be to develop sound musicianship, with constant emphasis on the usefulness of this material in the classroom teaching situation. The use of various mediums of performance in addition to the piano is encouraged as being beneficial in achieving this objective.

III. MUSICAL PERFORMANCE

Minimum requirement suggested: 33% of the total (120 semester hours) required for an undergraduate degree.

The following subjects are included in this area: Conducting; ensembles, large and small; functional piano facility; major performance area (voice, violin, cornet, clarinet, etc.); minor performance areas.

In order to foster a broad understanding of the total music program, it is recommended that all music education majors receive some training in voice and also in band and orchestra instrument performance.

1. *Conducting:* It is recommended that the student be trained to read and conduct from both choral and instrumental scores of suitable school music materials.
2. *Ensemble Experience:* It is recommended that, insofar as practical, all music education students regularly participate in both large and small ensembles.
3. *Functional Piano Facility:* It is recommended that *all* music education majors be expected to demonstrate piano facility as follows:

   a. Ability to sight read songs of the type found in a community song book.

   b. Ability to harmonize at sight improvising a simple piano accompaniment for songs requiring the use of I, IV, V chords and some simple modulations; also to transpose the songs and harmonizations to other keys.

   c. Ability to sight read fairly fluently simple accompaniments, vocal or instrumental, and simple piano compositions of the type used for school rhythmic activities.

4. *Major Performance Area:* Each music education student should have one performance area in which he excels. It is recommended that the study of the major performance area be continued until the student is able to demonstrate satisfactory performance ability for use in school and community.
5. *Minor Performance Area:* It is recommended that every music education student in addition to his major performance area have the equivalent of the following as a minimum requirement:

   a. One year of voice study.

   b. One term or semester of violin.

   c. One term or semester of clarinet.

   d. One term or semester of cornet.

   e. One term or semester of percussion, emphasizing the fundamentals of the snare drum.

IV. PROFESSIONAL EDUCATION

Minimum requirements suggested: 20% of the total (120 semester hours) required for an undergraduate degree.

This area includes:

1. Music education, materials, observation and student teaching.
2. Professional educational courses aside from music education.

One of the chief objectives of the course work in this area should be to prepare music education students to take their proper place in the total school program. It is also important that the students become well acquainted through study, demonstration, observation, and laboratory sessions with the methods and materials for teaching instrumental and vocal music in elementary, junior and senior high schools. Furthermore, it is important that opportunity be provided for the student to do practice teaching on *both* elementary and secondary levels and, when he is qualified, in both vocal and instrumental music.

Professional education courses in general education and in music education (such as courses in Elementary Education and Elementary Music Education, Secondary Education and Secondary Music Education) should be integrated to avoid the duplication of areas which frequently exist and to prevent the resulting waste of the student's time.

The Role of the Teacher of Music in Counseling [1]

Many schools are staffed with a specialist whose primary duty is counseling students but others are not so equipped and, consequently, the students are given little or no guidance. In schools where a school counselor is available, the teacher of music can be of considerable help with those students under his supervision. Because of the innate quality of music itself, the teacher of music has a particular opportunity because of the personal relationships with students. In whatever situation, the teacher of music must accept certain responsibilities.

The techniques of counseling are complex and the teacher of music cannot be expected to become a professional counselor. The following suggestions or principles may serve as a basic guide:

1. Individual differences in musical needs, abilities, and interests must be recognized.
2. Musical training must be considered in light of the general welfare of the student.
3. Counseling implies guidance and not compulsion by the instructor.
4. Counseling seeks to assist the student to find himself and to make continuous growth.
5. Counseling is for all students and not for an obvious few at either end of the scale.
6. Counseling should begin at the lower grade levels and continue beyond the school years.
7. Planning and organization of information, materials, and experiences are necessary for effective guidance.

A student with ability would be encouraged to further his music. This pupil needs expert help in understanding his capacities, opportunities for future success, and the responsibilities of undertaking a vocation in music. The student with limited capacity for musical success should be guided into fields other than professional study in music.

The teacher of music could strengthen his position by incorporating a program of guidance for his students to a more purposeful plane of learning. Better musical results would be secured because teaching would be in focus and because musical objectives would be merged with general educational objectives. Student interest would be greater if the emphasis has been upon musical satisfactions and enjoyment in a functional environment. Remote dubious rewards would be eliminated in favor of immediate cultural learnings.

While the majority of students will become consumers, some will continue their interests into avocational channels, some will become community church choir leaders, organists, band leaders, etc. The more talented should be encouraged to choose teaching of music as a profession as this holds tremendous satisfactions for service.

---

[1] Submitted by Leo J. Dvorak.

Bibliography—Counseling [1]

GENERAL

Baxter, Edna. *An Approach to Guidance.* New York: D. Appleton-Century Co., 1946.

Blum, M. L. and Bolinsky, B. *Counseling and Psychology.* New York: Prentice-Hall, Inc., 1951.

Chisholm, Leslie L. *Guiding Youth in Secondary Schools.* New York: American Book Company, 1945.

Crow, L. D. and H. V. *Introduction to Guidance.* 1951.

Darley, John G. *Testing and Counseling in the High School Guidance Program.* Chicago: Science Research Associates, 1943.

Douglas, Harl R. *Secondary Education for Life Adjustment of American Youth.* New York: The Ronald Press, 1952.

Erickson, Clifford E. *Counseling Interview.* New York: Prentice-Hall, Inc., 1950.

————. *Basic Text for Guidance Workers.* New York: Prentice-Hall, Inc., 1947.

Froelich, Clifford P. *Guidance Services in Small Schools.* New York: McGraw-Hill Book Company, 1950.

Hamrin, S. A. and Paulson, B. B. *Counseling Adolescents.* Chicago: Science Research Associates, 1950.

Hiltner, S. *Counselor in Counseling.* Nashville: Abingdon-Cokesbury, 1952.

Meland, B. E. *Higher Education and the Human Spirit.* Chicago: University of Chicago Press, 1953.

Pepinsky, H. B. and P. N. *Counseling: Theory and Practice.* New York: The Ronald Press, 1954.

Rogers, C. R. *Dealing with Social Tensions.* New York: Barnes and Noble, 1948.

Strang, Ruth M. *Counseling Techniques in College and Secondary Schools.* New York: Harper and Brothers, 1949. Revised.

————. *Educational Guidance—Its Principles and Practices.* New York: The Macmillan Company, 1947.

Tyler, L. E. *Work of the Counselor.* New York: D. Appleton-Century Co., 1953.

Warters, Jane. *High School Personnel Work Today.* New York: McGraw-Hill Book Company, 1946.

Wrenn, C. Gilbert. *Student Personnel Work in College.* New York: The Ronald Press, 1951.

MUSIC

Anderson, W. R. *Music as a Career.* London: Oxford University Press, 1939.

Johnson, Harriet. *Your Career in Music.* New York: E. P. Dutton & Co., 1944.

Spaeth, Sigmund. *Vocations in Music.* New York: G. P. Putnam's Sons, 1951.

Sur, William R. *Your Future as a Teacher of Music in the Schools.* Chicago: MENC, 1954.

---

[1] Texts on music education in the secondary schools should be consulted for material on guidance and counseling. See pp. 110, 114.

CHAPTER XVII

GRADUATE STUDY IN MUSIC EDUCATION[1]

THE DEMAND for musicians with advanced degrees has arisen simultaneously with the growth and expansion of the music program in American educational institutions. The fact that musicians now practice their profession in close association with scholars of other disciplines, gives rise to at least two factors which underlie the demand for degrees.

The *first factor* is that administrative reasons (credits, academic rank and tenure, accreditation, etc.) has made it necesary to find a method of interpreting musical training in terms equivalent to those used in nonmusic fields.

The *second factor* giving rise to the demand for advanced study in music is at once more important and more complex than the first. It has to do with the fact that teachers of music, functioning as they do in an academic environment, must be expected to meet the standards set by the nonmusic faculties in general erudition and culture and, most important, in scientific objectivity toward their subject matter. In short, musicians must be scholars. This applies with especial force to music educators, theorists, and historians. For music educators themselves to question the value or need of advanced degrees in their field is to say, in effect, that their subject matter is unworthy of scientific study, that the rigorous techniques of scholarship cannot profitably be applied to it. It is to imply, further, that music teachers are incapable of utilizing such techniques. Such is not at all the case; and there is perhaps no single field as much in need of development in this direction as that of music education.

Resident Requirement for Advanced Degrees. It is recommended that graduates of four-year programs with a major in music education who fail to fulfill the undergraduate requirements of the program of studies jointly approved by the Music Educators National Conference, the National Association of Schools of Music, and the American Association of Colleges for Teacher Education, may be expected to spend sufficient time in residence for the removal of all deficiencies.

The doctorate should be granted only to those students who, having demonstrated a high degree of musicianship and a broad knowledge of musical literature, show a mature and intimate grasp of subjects in which they have specialized and contribute to musical knowledge by writing a dissertation containing the results of independent study. The committee recommends that only under most exceptional conditions should it be possible to complete these requirements in three years, and that under normal conditions the music education student should plan on approximately four years of graduate study for the attainment of the doctorate degree.

Admission to Candidacy for a Higher Degree. Each institution of higher learning offering a program of graduate studies determines its own administrative policy for the processing of graduate students. This policy may vary from institution to institution; however, the policy applies to all departments and schools within the college or university which have approved graduate standing. Beyond the minimum standards applicable to the institution as a whole there exist provisions for individual departmental requirements within the framework of the over-all institutional policy.

---

[1] A condensation of the report submitted by Theodore F. Normann, Seattle, Washington, National Chairman, Music in American Education Committee on Graduate Study in Music Education. For complete report see Fall, 1954 Issue of the *Journal of Research in Music Education* (Chicago: Music Educators National Conference).

It is comparatively simple to make up a long list of characteristics which a music educator should possess in order that he be admitted to graduate standing. It is simple and it is unwise. Artificial barriers may exclude worthy applicants and do not necessarily guarantee the worth of those who may be able to meet them. Departmental requirements set up to protect the standards of graduate study should be administered in their spirit perhaps rather than their letter. The essential elements that should govern decisions in the case of a candidate for admission are innate musical sensitivity, a high degree of intelligence, and promise of ability as a teacher and scholar.

A person holding a bachelor's degree with a major in music education should normally be admitted to graduate standing provided: (a) The scholarship requirements of the institution and the department of music education have been met and completed; (b) two years of successful teaching experience have been completed.

Before being recognized as a candidate for the degree the student should: (a) Be admitted to full graduate standing, (b) meet all departmental requirements, and (c) be approved by a committee charged with the supervision of the candidate's work.

SCHOLARSHIP

The following departmental requirements in music education are recommended:

(1) Present evidence of the completion of a four-year curriculum with a major in music education from a recognized school or college. Any deficiency in undergraduate preparation should be made up without credit toward the advanced degree.

(2) Demonstrate in audition and by examination, skills and capacities in the following fields:

a. Harmony—written, aural, and applied.

b. History and literature of music equivalent to that normally expected of the undergraduate major in music education.

c. Performing ability of a competent and musical nature in one field of applied music.

d. Piano—ability to use the piano in a musical manner to play easy accompaniments, folk songs, and chorales.

e. Voice—ability to use the voice in a pleasing manner giving evidence of breath control, principles of enunciation and pronunciation as applied to singing, tone placement and the essentials of a musical interpretation; ability to sing easily at sight unison and part songs.

f. Orchestral instruments—a playing acquaintance with one orchestral instrument in each section of the orchestra.

THE CANDIDATE'S COMMITTEE

The final acceptance of a graduate student and the guidance of his program of studies should rest in the hands of an appointed committee rather than a single individual. The membership of this committee should contain representatives from both the department of music education and the department or school of music together with representatives from such other departments as may seem advisable. It should be the responsibility of the candidate's committee to:

(1) Determine whether the student has the quality of mind, musical capacity, and personal fitness for advanced work which would justify study for an advanced degree in the teaching of music.

(2) Ascertain whether the student has the necessary foundation in the subject matter areas in which he will do advanced work.

(3) Pass upon a proposed program of studies and make modification of such a program when deemed advisable.

GRADES AND CREDITS

An over-all grade average of *B* or above is the minimum that should be acceptable for an advanced degree. Any work done for the master's degree should be invalidated after a lapse of six years. Any credit earned toward the doctorate should be invalidated after a lapse of ten years. Credit should not be granted toward higher degrees by advanced credit examination. The amount of credit which may be transferred from one institution to another should be governed by the policy of the graduate division in the institution concerned.

The Master's Degree. There are a wide variety of titles used by American institutions of higher learning to indicate the master's degree. In the field of music education alone some ten or more different titles are in current usage. In order to clarify the significance of the various masters' degrees the following suggestions are made:

(1) The Master of Arts is the degree traditionally associated with the graduation from a liberal arts college.

(2) The Master of Science degree should properly be granted only to those whose field of study lies in some province of the physical and biological sciences. This degree should not be used to indicate graduation from the humanities or fine arts.

(3) The Master of Education degree should be associated only with degrees granted by schools and colleges of education.

(4) The Master of Music degree should be limited to schools of music and conservatories of music.

The recommended requirements for the master's degree in music education are:

(1) A student who is a graduate of a four-year college curriculum in music should normally plan to spend three semesters or their equivalent as a registered student of graduate standing. In no case should the degree be granted for less than one full academic year in residence. Work done elsewhere should pass review by examination and should not reduce the residence requirements of the institution concerned.

(2) Completion of a course of study as determined by the candidate's committee at the time of admission to candidacy.

(3) Completion of a project or thesis which shall indicate the student's ability to organize, interpret, and develop the materials of music and of learning.

(4) An oral, or written, or oral and written examination covering the candidate's qualifications for the degree. This should ordinarily include:

    a. Musical performance above the level of that expected of the undergraduate major in music education.

    b. Interpretative analysis of representative musical scores as to style, structure, and chordal analysis.

    c. Adequate knowledge and understanding of musical literature and history indicating a growing awareness of critical, philosophical, and aesthetic questions pertaining thereto.

    d. The project or thesis.

The following curriculum is recommended as a basic plan for candidates for the master's degree:

Education 25%
General and music education depending upon the amount and kind of undergraduate courses submitted for admission to graduate standing. The program of studies should be so planned as to provide for a solid understanding of the over-all program of music education in all its phases rather than focusing upon technical aspects of rather limited areas.

Music Theory and Composition 15%
Selection should be made from courses beyond those required for the undergraduate major. Theory courses should go beyond mere textbook formulas and should lead to an insight into the use of the musical language. Such courses should be alive through an actively related musical experience.

Music History and Literature...15%
Advanced courses in the history and literature of music with predominant emphasis upon the illumination of the materials, forms, styles, and literature through musical experience.

Applied Music 15%
To be chosen from any of the standard instruments or voice, subject to the provision that study shall be at the upper division level and that credit is granted only for a minimum of one hour per week of individual instruction.

Ensemble Music...No Credit.
All students should be expected to participate in one or more ensembles during the period of residence. Graduate credit should not be permitted for such participation except when the ensemble is limited to faculty and graduate students, and the literature is studied for its own sake rather than preparation for public performance.

Electives 30%
To be selected from those subject areas which give most promise of rounding out the student's program in terms of his own needs as an individual and a teacher of music.

Total...One full academic year or equivalent.

The Doctor's Degree in Music Education. The requirements traditionally demanded of all doctoral candidates are as follows:

(1) Complete a program of studies and research as planned by the major department or college.

(2) Demonstrate the ability to use accepted instruments of research.

(3) Pass a creditable comprehensive examination in the major field and, when a part of the program of study, in the minor field or in supporting courses.

(4) Prepare a thesis which is a significant contribution to knowledge.

(5) Pass a final examination which is normally devoted to the thesis and to the field with which it is concerned.

To overburden the student with arbitrary credit hours to the extent that he is left little time to think through the matter of his own education under his own initiative is not the best educational policy. It should be noted that the doctorate is based not so much upon the completion of a list of courses in a catalog, but rather upon the attainment of those virtues which characterize full maturity of stature.

Core of Achievement. It would be well to recognize, however, that for any doctor's degree in music education there must be a solid core of achievement in the four phases indicated below. Much of this solid core should, ideally, be there before a student begins work on the doctorate. In any case, it should be allowed to expand, broaden, and deepen to the point where it would be well rounded and thoroughly satisfactory at the time of the general comprehensive examination.

Education 25%
The emphasis should be upon a thorough grasp of all phases of music education including not only philosophy, methods, curriculums, and materials of music suitable for the public schools, but acquaintance also with those problems of music in community life which influence directly or indirectly any part of the teaching of music. The student should have a comprehensive grasp of the place of music in American life. His knowledge of professional education should be sufficiently broad to enable him to discuss and to think clearly in terms of American public education. He should be able to utilize his knowledge of professional education to the end that he may give promise of functioning in an able manner in a wide variety of teaching situations in which music plays a major role.

Theory and Composition 15%
The student should possess a broad and sufficiently deep knowledge of music theory and enough experience with actual composition to understand the creative approach and its problems. He should be able to think and to analyze beyond the textbook to the more fundamental problems of theory and its value as a guide and mentor in the interpretation of music.

History and Literature 15%
   The student should possess a basic understanding of the music of all periods, a
   rather wide general comprehension with considerable amounts of actual music
   for the various mediums, and a rather thorough knowledge of the literature
   pertinent to his own performance field and to music education.

Applied Music 15%
   Since it is only through the medium of performance that one is basically a musi-
   cian, this can only mean artistic attainment and performance in one or more
   performance field (instrumental or vocal). Where the primary performance field
   is not piano, provision should be made for genuinely adequate use of the piano
   as a tool. Since conducting plays so important a role in music education, provision
   should be made for more advanced development of this aspect of applied music.

Electives and Supporting Courses 30%
   The amount of credit permitted for the dissertation should depend upon the nature
   and scope of the research involved. Sufficient latitude should be allowed to provide
   for broadening the education of the student and providing for his individual interests and needs.

Total minimum requirements .... Three academic years or equivalent.

INSTRUMENTS OF RESEARCH

Traditionally, the research tools expected of a doctoral candidate have been a
reading knowledge of two foreign languages, preferably French and German. In
recent years some graduate schools have permitted courses in statistics, histori-
ography, or other methods of research to substitute for one or both requirements
in foreign language. There seems to be a growing tendency to adapt such requirements to the particular needs of the student. This tendency should be encouraged.

THE THESIS OR DISSERTATION

Reluctant though one may be to admit the fact, anyone who has thoughtfully
examined many of the theses which have been submitted in partial fulfillment of
the requirements for the master's or the doctor's degrees in music education must
concede that they frequently fall considerably short of what might be termed
scholarly research. The present dearth of dissertations in music education which
command respect for substantial scholarship is not entirely to be laid at the door
of the student. Other factors play a significant part.

(1) Music education stands in need of a well-trained body of scholars, men
and women imbued with a fervor for exploration, a passion for logic, and a sincere
interest in creation. An advanced degree means little unless it be used as a stepping stone to further study, thought, and inquiry.

(2) There is a present danger in some quarters of expanding the graduate
program in a department to the point where personal contact is lost and the work,
as a consequence, tends to become increasingly more formalized with more importance being attached to completion of courses and the passing of examinations
than to the stimulation of true creative and investigative endeavor.

(3) Colleges of Education have, in many instances, taken over the major
responsibility for the advanced study of majors in music education as well as other
branches of knowledge. This may have certain advantages but the tendency has
been to require so many courses in professional education that the student is seriously deficient in his basic musical training. Coupled with this have been instances
where the guidance of the thesis project has been entrusted to an individual or a
committee with no training in the particular subject field in which the thesis is
written. It may be seriously questioned whether a specialist in curriculum construction, in guidance and counseling, in educational psychology, or other divisions
of a college of education is qualified, without some insight into the province of
music, to direct adequately a research investigation in music education.

(4) The term "music education" in itself leads to some confusion. This has
had its effect upon research and investigation. If housed in the school of music the
tendency has been to place strong emphasis upon historical research. If the divi-

sion is linked with the College of Education there has been an equal temptation to stress surveys and experimental studies. All types of research have a legitimate place in music education and, if graduate offerings are to be made, a staff should be provided which is capable of guidance in both historical and quantitative research.

(5) In their ambition to set up graduate departments many colleges and not a few universities have authorized graduate degrees in music without adequate facilities in staff or equipment to realize fully the traditional differentiation between undergraduate and graduate study. The result has not been graduate study in the real sense of the term but rather an extension in terms of courses of the undergraduate curriculum. In a competition for students to support an over-extended program of course offerings this has all too frequently led to a further depression of the standards which should be associated with graduate study.

The question arises as to what areas lend themselves to investigation by the music educator. This question may most easily be approached by a consideration of the methods of investigation which may be employed. The three major categories of research methodology are the historical, the quantitative (statistical), and the survey (case-study). The first is humanistic, the second scientific, and the third sociological. Since music education is both an art and a science, and since its purposes are sociological, the fact is obvious at the outset that research in music education can be restricted neither to one methodology nor to one area but must pursue a variety of paths and utilize as wide a variety of techniques as are available.

Nevertheless, it is the opinion of this committee that music and music education are pre-eminently artistic in nature and humanistic in significance. Insofar as possible, then, research in music education should largely comprise studies in which specifically musical considerations have the largest role, due provision being made for a certain amount of investigation into such ancillary areas as average salaries, acoustical properties of music rooms, interest inventories, and so forth. Topics should be chosen with the welfare of the research in mind, and their potential value should be judged in the light of such questions as these: Will the researcher make use of his musical judgment and sensitivity in making this investigation? Will this investigation be likely to develop a better understanding on the part of the investigator of music, the teaching of music, or of the function of music in our educational system?

SECTION FIVE

General and Special Areas in Music Education

General Music Classes
Chairman: Edith White Gee, Cleveland Heights, Ohio
Acting Chairman: Joseph Leeder, Columbus, Ohio

✠

Instrumental Music in the Schools—Band and Orchestra
Coordinating Chairman: Ernest E. Harris, New York, N. Y.

Strings
Gilbert R. Waller, chairman, Urbana, Ill.

Winds and Percussion
Myron E. Russell, chairman, Cedar Falls, Iowa

Piano
Fay Templeton Frisch, chairman, New Rochelle, N. Y.

Organ
Katharine Fowler, chairman, Washington, D. C.

✠

Vocal Music in the Schools
Chairman: Alex H. Zimmerman, San Diego, Calif.

✠

Music Literature, Composition and Theory
Chairman: Sadie Rafferty, Evanston, Ill.

CHAPTER XVIII

GENERAL MUSIC CLASSES AT THE
SECONDARY LEVEL[1]

IT IS A COMMON BELIEF that "all students should have the opportunity for continuing experiences with music of general nature, planned to meet their interests and needs. It is most important that *all* students have opportunity to continue these activities in keeping with their changing and developing interests and abilities in the junior and senior high school grades."[2]

What Is General Music? By "general music class" is meant a class of secondary pupils, most commonly composed of a particular grade in the junior high school and sometimes in the senior high school, meeting together to participate in a wide variety of music activities.

Values of General Music for Pupils. General music should aid in a continuing creative development of awareness to the responsibilities and privilege of living in a democracy through a belief that "every child has the right to full and free opportunity to explore and develop his capacities in the field of music in such ways as may bring him happiness and a sense of well being . . ." and "as his right, every child shall have the opportunity to experience music with other people so that his own enjoyment shall be heightened and he shall be led into greater appreciation of the feelings and aspirations of others."[3]

This philosophy may be realized by:

(1) Helping each pupil find some musical activity in which he can participate with satisfaction and some degree of mastery.

(2) Building a repertoire of songs, unison and part, which the group can sing with musical enjoyment.

(3) Building a listening repertoire that is both immediately satisfactory and of lasting musical significance.

(4) Developing *musical learning* (knowledge and skills) concerning instruments, voice types, and technical information through varied activities such as singing, playing on instruments, listening, rhythms, and reading literature concerning composers and music.

Personnel of General Music Class. The general music class should be made available to all pupils who care to elect it, with a minimum requirement during the seventh and eighth grades. It should not be used as a substitute for performance courses (choir, glee clubs, ensembles, band, and orchestra). Because of its varied activities, general music should serve the performer as well as the consumer. The grouping should be heterogeneous with no discrimination as to intelligence or talent ratings.

---

[1] From the report submitted by Joseph A. Leeder, Columbus, Ohio, Acting National Chairman, Music in American Education Committee on General Music Classes. Edith W. Gee, Cleveland Heights, Ohio, National Chairman.

[2] From "General Beliefs," from the Recommendations approved by the North Central Association of Colleges and Secondary Schools. The complete report, *Music Education in the Secondary Schools*, is available from the MENC office. 15¢.

[3] From the Prelude of *The Child's Bill of Rights in Music*, MENC Resolutions adopted at Biennial Convention, St. Louis, 1950.

Organization of General Music Classes in Secondary Schools. In the junior high schools, pupils of a certain grade level should be organized into various classes (seventh, eighth, and ninth), as far as possible. The tenth, eleventh, and twelfth grade pupils could be successfully combined if necessary; but when scheduling permits, a separate tenth grade section is preferable for social as well as musical reasons. One period per week is unsatisfactory for pupil growth. Two, three, or five periods per week are recommended.

In the junior high school, the size of the classes should be essentially the same as the academic classes. At the senior high school level it may be advisable to have larger groups. When instrumental activities are a part of the general music class of the senior high school, smaller laboratory sections may well be scheduled as a part of larger sections.

Accrediting General Music Classes. General music classes in the high school should receive academic credit. They may be accredited on the laboratory basis, one-half unit for one year's work, consisting of daily recitations, when no preparation is required outside the classroom. When classes meet fewer times a week, the amount of credit should be given accordingly. When the class meets daily, and outside preparation is required, full academic credit should be given which is usually one full credit per year. It is recommended that the pupil secure more than one-half credit in music activities in order to satisfy certain college entrance requirements.

Activities in the General Music Class. Because of pupils' individual differences, interests, and ability to participate, the activities in the general music class should likewise be varied. Following is a suggested list of suitable music activities:

(1) Singing of unison and part-songs (learning to use the voice well).

(2) Listening to music through all media: Recordings, films, live performance by school personnel and artists outside the school, television and radio.

(3) Rhythmic experiences, both creative and directed.

(4) Instrumental experiences: (a) Playing on social instruments (autoharp, recorder, etc.); (b) enriching the musical experience through demonstration, performance, and accompaniment by class members on band and orchestral instruments.

(5) Discussion and reports on concerts, radio, television, musical movies, assembly programs, etc.

(6) Preparation for listening through the use of books, magazines, newspapers, etc.

The interpretation of the symbols of the printed page should grow out of the aforementioned activities. The emphasis placed upon each category and the order of presentation will be dependent upon the over-all background of musical experience, the abilities and interests of the different classes being taught. These experiences should be interrelated and based on a center of interest which may be a part of present-day culture, our musical heritage or community and in-school life.

Illustrative Course

Argyle Central School District No. 1, Argyle, N. Y.[1]

There was a definite need for a new general music course which would be more in line with other subjects, more up to date, and correlated with other subjects, such as social studies, art, etc. The course was offered in grades 9-12, five

---

[1] Submitted by Stanley P. Trusselle.

periods a week for one year for a full unit of credit. The objectives of the course were:

—To discover an enjoyment in music that will carry over into adult life.

—To provide an opportunity for self-expression through participation in simple musical experiences.

—To develop an awareness of music as a cultural heritage.

—To develop a discriminating taste in music.

—To develop an understanding of the basic essentials of the music language and the mechanics of its production.

Suggested Topics for the First Semester:

(1) The types of music the pupil ordinarily hears every day, such as various dance rhythms, sacred music used in churches, band music used for parades, popular juke-box music. Attention should be given to accompaniment and background for motion pictures, radio, and television programs. The use of music as a therapeutic agent.

(2) Our national heritage, kinds of music developed in America. Music in each successive period in American history, correlating with social studies. Study of American composers from Francis Hopkinson to present-day composers. Another unit of study should include patriotic selections, folk tunes, etc.

(3) Music of other nations. Contributions of foreign countries to music development in America.

(4) Music makers—instrumentation of orchestras and bands; singers; dancers; conductors; and instrumentalists.

(5) Program music.

Suggested Topics for the Second Semester:

(1) Music and the stage, musical architecture, extension of music of other nations, history of music and present trends, church music of middle ages, etc.

(2) Supplementary study to include: String quartet, brass and woodwind ensembles, art and music, poetry and music, etc. Field trips to various churches to study the organs, especially the large Skinner five-manual organ at the Glens Falls Presbyterian Church. A visit to the Estey organ factory in Brattleboro, Vermont, visits to radio and television stations WGY and WRGB in Schenectady, New York.

The use of film strips and films is a feature of the year's course. The books for reference, purchased for the library, are used for lesson assignments.[1]

---

[1] For bibliography see pp. 109, 114.

CHAPTER XIX

INSTRUMENTAL MUSIC IN THE SCHOOLS
Band and Orchestra[1]

THE DEVELOPMENT of instrumental music in American schools during the past twenty-five or thirty years has been very impressive from many points of view, but from the standpoint of a well-articulated course of study that provides for continuous musical growth and one that is well organized through all grades, there is still much to be desired. Vocal music with theory and appreciation well integrated has had an articulated course from kindergarten through high school for some time, and wherever one finds a fairly well developed choral program this articulated course has come to be expected; yet this is not so in the instrumental field in most localities. The instrumental program is organized only in a fragmentary manner, and few places provide for the continuity that is so important if all levels of playing are to be provided for students. This, therefore, seems to be the proper starting place for the discovery of the "Basic Purposes of Instrumental Music in the Schools."

It would seem that the time has come to urge strongly, or even insist, that every program of instrumental music study should begin with the rhythm orchestra or toy band in the kindergarten and culminate in senior high school or college ensembles of symphonic proportions. This is being done in a few places at present, and if we believe that it is attainable and possible then we must advocate a complete instrumental music program for all schools at all levels.

To be complete, an instrumental music program must include rhythmic orchestras with toy instruments for young children. The toy orchestras of kindergarten, first, and second grades should gradually introduce instruments of pitch such as song bells and piano so that other melodic instruments may be used during the third and fourth grades. At the same time the percussion type of instruments should be eliminated gradually so that by grades five and six an elementary school orchestra with legitimate instruments will be possible. If violin and cello are started in fourth grade and clarinet, flute, trumpet, and trombone are begun in the fifth grade, a fairly well-balanced instrumentation will result and string techniques will be advanced far enough for adequate elementary orchestra playing. During this entire period *every child* should receive both *opportunity* and *encouragement* to study an instrument. Of course no one expects all students to become performers, but there must not be a neglect of talent-finding and interest-developing experiences at this period of growth.

Beginning in the junior high school, a program of variously graded instrumental classes and ensembles should be continued and expanded as the need develops. False enthusiasm and exploitation should have no part in such a program. Every boy and girl likes some kind of music and it is *our* problem to contact the responsive level of each individual and develop a consciousness of its place in the whole program of musical activity. Both by correlation and integration students need help to find a way to make music a regular part of sane and normal daily living. A provision for varying needs and capacities in music also must be present in the teacher's mind when attempting to point out the real values inherent in music education for all children.

---

[1] From an address by Ralph E. Rush, Chairman of Music Education, University of Southern California, Los Angeles, given at the MENC Biennial Convention, Chicago, 1954.

Such an articulated instrumental music program should in no way detract from nor compete with the continuing vocal program. Instead, if properly organized, both should and will become contributing factors toward an integrated and comprehensive music education program.

During the senior high school grades, regardless of whether it includes a three- or four-year span, both an orchestra and a band should be available in at least two and possibly three levels of attainment. For the more mature and advanced performers, the possibility of small chamber music groups should be considered. It has been most heartening to witness the enthusiastic response to the chamber music concerts. Fine high school small instrumental ensembles are flourishing in America!

If instrumental music teachers only knew clearly and definitely the objectives of the instrumental program and what the basic purposes of instrumental music in schools should be, then they could set up a basic course to follow. Their work would develop effectively to benefit all students performing, would alert the student body as a whole to the values of instrumental music, and would extend into the community instrumental music activities.

Basic Purposes. A summation of the above will show that the basic purposes of instrumental music in the schools should include:

(1) Music has something to say to the human race that no other *art* or *science* can express, and the outstanding literature for instrumental music, especially since the days of Haydn, most certainly should be a part of the literature that will be performed by students during days of growth.

(2) By both correlation and integration music teachers should strive constantly to find ways of making instrumental music a normal part of good daily living.

(3) Because of the varying needs and capacities of individuals, provision for these individual differences must be taken into account in the instrumental music classes.

(4) The real values inherent in instrumental music study and musical experiences must be faced squarely and there should be no bending to false enthusiasm and exploitation.

(5) Social values through instrumental music activity should be emphasized and extended.

(6) The development of a profound and thorough musicianship should be stressed more and more as higher levels of skill are attained by the gifted and talented instrumentalist.

(7) Since everyone likes some kind of music, the music teacher's primary problem is to contact the responsive level of each student and develop a consciousness of this place in the whole program of musical activity.

(8) The development of *a creative attitude, a determination to reconstruct,* that is, *re-create the innermost thought and feeling of the* composer rather than be content merely to attain the outward form of pitch, time, or any one single element in music, should be the constant long-range aim of every instrumental music teacher for his pupils.

(9) The school instrumental music program should be geared whenever possible to supplement and dovetail into the music organizations of the community.

(10) A good instrumental music program should result in recognition on the part of the students of the importance of the literature for orchestras, bands, and chamber music groups just as they consider English and American Literature to be representative of the artistic ideals of English-speaking countries.

It should be remembered that the two primary aims of the instrumental music program in the eyes of the administrator, the parents, the students, and their teachers ought to be concerned (a) with instilling within each participant an *appreciation of* and *love for* good music that will continue to develop throughout life, and (b) with cultivating the desire for worth-while citizenship in their group and community.

Instrumental Music in the Elementary Schools[1]

Instrumental music, properly experienced, contributes much to the total growth of the child. The instrumental music program affords opportunity to unfold creative talent, and allows each child the opportunity to gain, according to his individual capacity, certain knowledge, techniques, and skills pertaining to music as are appropriate and desirable for successful experiencing of music.

Educational Values. Observation of elementary school programs throughout America shows clearly that the opportunity to respond actively to natural love for tone and rhythm is desired by most boys and girls. Incidental musical experiences are followed in the kindergarten and primary grades with opportunities for making music with simple instruments. These instruments may be purchased, but many can and should be made by the children themselves.

From the fourth grade on every child wishing experience in playing a regular orchestra or band instrument should be afforded an opportunity in the line of his interest, talent, and physical fitness. Class instruction and ensemble participation afford a real sense of belonging, self-respect, and feeling of accomplishment. In some elementary schools the instruments used are limited to violins, flutes, clarinets, cornets, trumpets, mellophones, percussion, and piano. In other elementary schools additional instruments include violas, cellos, string bass, trombones, baritones, and oboes.

Patterns of Instrumental Class Organization. It is general practice to teach instruments to children in small classes, meeting from one to several times a week. There are three patterns of class organization with respect to kinds of instruments. The second type seems to be most prevalent. The three patterns follow:

—Classes consisting of identical instruments such as cornets, clarinets, violins, etc.

—Classes consisting of closely related instruments, such as woodwinds, brasses, strings, percussion.

—Classes consisting of any combination of instruments regardless of type.

In well-developed instrumental music programs, classes also are organized according to individual abilities and stages of advancement. In addition to the various instrumental classes there are both large and small ensembles that meet from one to several times per week. The large ensembles are usually in the form of a band or orchestra, even though the instrumentation is not complete nor finely balanced.

Exploratory keyboard experience for the whole classroom may be started in the kindergarten or first grade. It provides an excellent background and will develop a readiness for the instrumental program.

Piano classes continue the presentation of keyboard experiences, with added emphasis upon acquiring skill in the use of the instrument. These classes have come to be highly regarded and desirable in the elementary school program. The classes are usually organized according to age levels and pupil advancement. When

---

[1] From the report submitted by Ernest E. Harris, New York, New York, National Chairman, Music in American Education Committee on Instrumental Music in the Schools.

only one piano is available, the children take turns at the instrument while the others perform on silent keyboards. When this arrangement is necessary, it is best if the keyboards have movable keys. When two or more pianos are available it is common practice to seat two children at each piano, although it may be desirable at times to have only one at each instrument.

Materials. All printed material used should be of high musical worth and should be selected on the basis of its meaningfulness and technical appropriateness to the children who will use it. A wide range of musical materials should be available and provided by the school.

Equipment. The school should assume the responsibility of providing a reasonable supply of the instruments. These usually are available to pupils on a rental basis although some schools provide instruments on loan without charge. All musical equipment should be of good to very good grade. Anything less than a moderately good grade is usually a poor investment from the standpoint of durability, replacement, upkeep, etc. and, at the same time, seldom affords the child a satisfactory musical result.

GUIDING PRINCIPLES

(1) The instrumental music program should be embodied in the immediate set of educational experiences which form the pupil's curriculum. For this to be possible, instrumental instruction must be given during school time and in the pupil's own school. A program so conducted can also encourage the kind of music activities that will have a definite place in the local home life of the children and thus be of real value to the community. To justify a place in the curriculum, instrumental music must do more than teach a few children to play instruments for the purpose of developing a school orchestra or band.

(2) The opportunity for ensemble participation should be provided at all stages of instrumental study. If the program is to render the broadest educational service of which it is capable, attention must be given to the strong social appeal that is inherent in properly taught instrumental classes, especially those at the elementary level. Under certain conditions the less experienced performers can quite successfully be combined with those more experienced.

(3) The development of skills should be pursued primarily as an outgrowth of the immediate needs of the musical goals at hand, with a wholesome perspective of those required for future use. This is not to suggest that techniques are unimportant, for attention to correct performance habits and skills is essential if music is to provide the emotional satisfaction most desired. The enhancement of music through a functional approach and of acquiring technique should represent the guiding principles in dealing with this phase of the instructional program.

The Importance of Strings in Music Education[1]

In many schools of the United States string instrument instruction flourishes as a vital part of the musical activities of the community. In practically all of these places a good band as well as orchestra is maintained, and the administrators in charge are convinced that they are supporting a broad and well-balanced music program of real educational value, wherein every child is given the chance to participate in the musical experience best suited to his talents. In the schools where a large orchestra of fine quality has existed year after year in uninterrupted force, both school and community take a genuine pride in this accomplishment and make

---

[1] Prepared by Markwood Holmes, Kansas State Teachers College, Pittsburg.

sure each year that the program remains under capable, experienced supervision and that nothing interferes with its continued support.

Administrators in schools which maintain strong string programs are well aware of the significant part which music for strings and the orchestra plays in in the cultural life of a community. *First,* the increasing abundance of music of a high order, the encouragement being given contemporary composition, and the evidence of its greater appreciation on the part of the public should lead to the belief that music in America is indeed becoming the universal language. *Secondly,* good music can no longer be lightly brushed aside. In well-balanced proportions, as to orchestra, band, choir, ensemble, and solo appearances, it is not only a tremendous educational and esthetic force—it is big business. According to an article in the *Readers Digest,* a survey made in 1949 showed that more money was spent that year for admissions to symphony concerts, operatic performances, and recitals by topnotch artists than on baseball. This did not take into consideration the gigantic sales of fine recordings or the printed music itself—to say nothing of the costly presentations on radio and motion picture sound track.

From the discovery of the full possibilities of the string instrument family stems a considerable portion of the great musical development of the world. The opera, the symphony, the oratorio—all depend on the orchestra for full realization, and it is the string section, comprising seventy per cent of the personnel (the violins, violas, cellos and basses) which gives the orchestra its unique character.

Wealth of Musical Resources. The infinite variety of shading and tone color produced by a well-trained string group has attracted the best efforts of the greatest composers, and to the string quartet, called by some the most perfect of all instrumental ensembles, these composers the world over have entrusted their most precious creative productions. It is around these four instruments (two violins, viola and cello) that the fabulous wealth of chamber music—music designed to be performed in the home or in small auditoriums—has been written.

This appealing literature, which can bring children into a realm of music of high intellectual caliber and develop in them high standards of appreciation of the beautiful, is so vast and so varied in character that it offers a practical solution to some of the material selection problems of the thoroughly conscientious school music director. While it is true that the study of many of the master chamber music works challenges the best efforts of the most talented and accomplished musicians, there is also a wealth of material suitable for players in elementary and intermediary stages of development. Music for duo, trio, quartet, and on up to the chamber orchestra of from ten to twenty or more players, is available to groups of various sizes and in almost every conceivable combination of instruments.

Strings blend well with any and all instruments and are highly effective as accompaniment for other groups. Thus, as a nucleus for the organization of a school orchestra, the multiple string duo, trio or quartet, with or without piano, can be of great value.

Encouragement of the study of a string instrument is practical for at least two other reasons: (a) Violins, for example, are available at very reasonable cost, and for the young player, in small sizes. Violas and cellos, too, can now be obtained in half and three-quarter sizes, making possible the formation of a miniature string quartet for very young children. (b) No better ear training can be imagined than that which the study of string instruments affords, and under capable guidance a talented and ambitious member of such a group could, by the end of his high school career, emerge as a highly efficient ensemble and orchestral player, or even a brilliant soloist. The possibilities for individual accomplishment are limitless.

167

Ensemble Playing. The thrill of playing in a large ensemble is an experience not soon to be forgotten. Under proper conditions a spirit of cooperation and fair play, and an alert and sensitive attitude are developed to a high degree.

This is true also in the small ensemble, which is a necessary part of every well-organized school music program. The chance for personal expression is greater, almost demanded, in fact; and since each individual part is of such importance, the mediocre player in the trio or quartet has less opportunity to lean on other more proficient players, which is sometimes possible in a larger organization. Thus, the desirability for rapid advancement is immediately presented, and it is obvious that the more competent small ensemble players there are in the school system, the better will be the big orchestras and bands.

Size Is No Barrier. The size of the community should not deter the establishment of a string program. Many a small school supports an excellent orchestra as well as a band. The music director who knows little or nothing about strings is naturally reluctant to embark on a program which he feels might result in failure. However, there are many conductors who are not essentially "string men" who are at the head of systems maintaining strong string departments. They have been ingenious enough to enlist the help of local private violin or cello teachers or, if none are available, have interested enough students in private lessons to engage such a teacher from a larger community for one or more days each week. Such a conductor —musically conscientious, alert and ambitious, although knowing little about string technique at the beginning of his teaching career—will acquire, after a few years' experience, a most commendable understanding of string problems by observation, experimentation, and perhaps an occasional lesson with a competent teacher.

Obviously, this method, while better than neglecting strings completely, is far from ideal. Unfortunately, many music majors have been graduated from colleges and universities with such a scant knowledge of string instrument pedagogy that they will start an orchestra only under pressure. If there is no urging from administrators or community the situation is allowed to drift along with the result that many ambitious and talented students are deprived of a chance to become competent string players.

Competent Direction. Investigation has shown that an orchestra flourishes wherever there is an enthusiastic director of reasonably high musical accomplishment in charge—one who knows something about strings and therefore is in sympathy with the problems involved. Such a director sees to it that the orchestra plays many times during the year, thus requiring a high peak of interest and effort, and making the organization an indispensible part of the community's artistic life.

Teacher-training institutions need to prepare their graduates to handle orchestras as well as bands and choruses, and it is to this end that the Committee on String Instruction for the Music Educators National Conference has set up a suggested curriculum for music majors.[1] Administrators can help make the teacher-training institutions aware of the need for more adequately prepared teachers if, when hiring new personnel, they will require that applicants be thoroughly trained in all phases of instrumental music.

Signs of Progress. Within the last few years the string teaching situation has taken a tremendous turn for the better. String clinics have sprung up all over the country and are responsible in some areas for the gathering together of as many as 400 to 500 high school string players. The increase in the number of professional and semiprofessional symphony orchestras is amazing. A tabulation by the American Symphony Orchestra League shows that whereas there were but nine symphony

[1] See page 173.

168

orchestras in this country prior to 1900, in 1951 there were seven hundred and two—with one hundred and twenty-five of them in cities and towns of less than 25,000 population. Everywhere institutions of higher learning are strengthening their string departments, sponsoring chamber music concerts, and supporting world-famous string quartets in residence. The conductors of our great symphony orchestras have made it very evident that something drastic needs to be done to stem the threatened shortage of fine string players throughout the nation, and many of those vitally concerned have answered the challenge with active programs which have made fine starts toward bringing the strings to proper position in the music program.

During the past few years, there has been considerable improvement in the string situation in the schools. Not only has there been an increase in the number of students started, but the quality of work has improved. School administrators are more aware of the values of string instruction and of school orchestras; music teachers in general are encouraging string playing, and colleges and universities are placing more importance upon strings by: (a) sending string teachers into the schools to teach and to help the local string teachers; (b) sending string soloists and string groups into outlying communities for performances; (c) organizing on- and off-campus camps, all-state orchestras, clinics, etc.; (d) offering scholarships to string players; and (e) improving their teacher-training curricula and their methods courses in strings.

Many music magazines carry a string clinic column and many more carry good articles on string instruction. String teachers are searching for better ways of doing a superior job. New methods and materials offer a wider selection for instruction and performance. Music merchants, manufacturers, and importers are providing instruments of better quality.

Although there has been improvement, the string advancement program is really in its infancy. Good teaching still is the most important factor. The ability to analyze string playing problems immediately and to apply appropriate remedial treatment should continue to be the goal of both the private and group string teachers.

Two groups of string teachers, the MENC Committee on Strings and the American String Teachers Association, have been largely responsible for most of the publications, clinical and teaching materials. These groups, with much overlapping of membership, have worked exceedingly well together.

String Instrument Study and Playing[1]

Note: It has been quite common to use the terms *string, strings,* and/or *stringed* when referring to those instruments which have strings. The term *string instrument* has been used here to denote the members of the viol family only (string choir of the symphony orchestra), namely, violin, viola, cello, and string bass.

The present nationwide revival of interest in string instrument playing has great musical significance and has led to the development of fine school and civic orchestras. Far greater values than mere community pride will accrue to the individual child who studies a string instrument and participates in these orchestras. The values are very real, and the following exposition is an effort to explain some of them.

Performance. The first and most important effect of study of any instrument is that one ultimately learns to play the instrument. This is the real goal and is

---

[1] From the report submitted by Gilbert R. Waller, Urbana, Illinois, National Chairman, Music in American Education Committee on String Instruction.

the one which motivates most students, and herein lies the reward for time and effort spent.

Musical. In the orchestra is found all the instruments of the wind band plus the great body of strings with their limitless varieties of color, expression, and range. Because of this inclusiveness of the orchestra and its consequent ability to express, the great composers have chosen it as the medium for the performance of their works. Due to the fitness of the strings to carry the burden of technical and interpretive demands, these instruments form by far the largest and most important section of the orchestra. They also hold a place of prominence as chamber music instruments. Due to the character of the instruments and the music written for them, those persons who play the strings are naturally drawn into contact with great music.

Social. Perhaps the next most important value of string instrument study is social. Since stringed instruments form the backbone of the orchestra, string players usually seek a place in an orchestra of some kind. Ability to perform is a mark of distinction and social barriers disappear. Prestige, due to wealth or so-called social standing, fades before skill in performance. Because the parts of an orchestration are so mathematically built, there can be no shirking without the full knowledge of everyone. The acceptance of the responsibility for a particular part and the teamwork toward the whole performance are indeed valuable social attributes.

No one can deny that it requires perseverance, intelligence, and sensitivity to play a string instrument. A great deal of time is needed for the development of skills on a string instrument. A person who learns to play acceptably has not been a loafer and is not likely therefore to be an undesirable citizen.

Cultural. For the student who wishes to follow some vocation other than music the cultural values become more important. One may study an instrument and for some reason never play upon it again, yet there is left an understanding and an appreciation that varies directly with how far that person has progressed in his study. If one has played a great deal of orchestra literature or chamber music, this value will be very great. For the person who has progressed sufficiently to understand these works, even though he may not play them well, there is a joy and an appreciation that can never be gained by only hearing music or reading about it.

One cannot seriously study a string instrument without learning something of its history and its music, and of the composers who wrote for it. Each of these will open many channels of thought that otherwise would have remained entirely unexplored. Active participation on a string instrument is one of the best and most thorough routes to a cultural understanding of good music.

Personality. For mastery, the violin, viola, cello, or string bass require careful study, analysis, and drill. Through a daily practice routine, the student will find himself gradually growing in his sensitivity to pitch, rhythms, timbre, form, dynamics, orchestral color, and general artistic appreciation. Parallel with this musical growth there will be developed another value—patience in pursuance of an artistic ideal.

Through the study of string instruments and through performance in orchestras and chamber music groups, the student will constantly be responsible for meeting standards of musical excellence. The continuous association with people in groups at rehearsals, concerts, banquets, etc., gives the student an opportunity to develop many personality traits far removed from music. His manner and taste in dress, evaluation of friendships, and his ability to meet and converse with people will be influenced.

All of these personality traits merge when the student attains the soloist level. Stage deportment, judgment in the selection of the music for the occasion, perfect memorization, a clear auditory picture of how every note must sound, control of the emotions and muscles needed in drawing from the instrument a meaningful interpretation—all contribute to the personality of the soloist.

Physical. No doubt people differ widely at birth in their sensitivity to music and in the acuteness of their ears. The emotions develop as one's study embraces new and additional material, and the ear grows in both its pitch and quality discrimination abilities. The muscular system increases in sensitivity to rhythms as more muscles are called upon to play these rhythms. There comes a time when it can rightly be said that the string instrument player has a very sensitive ear, which means that the sounds existing about us mean more to the ear which has been trained and developed through playing a string instrument.

Professional. A professional symphony orchestra employs many string players who usually are able to augment their salaries considerably by extra playing— television, radio, summer opera, solo concert engagements, and teaching.

The public schools are in need of people to teach string instruments. In addition to the regular nine-month salary, these school music teachers often make considerable additional salary through private lessons and extra summer work.

Some string teachers prefer a connection with a college, university, or music school where duties consist mainly of giving private lessons; others establish private studios. Some may choose to direct orchestras, coach string quartets and ensembles, or teach other courses.

The well-trained person may be reasonably confident that he will be able to earn a comfortable living and enjoy a respected position in his community. It is increasingly evident that incomes of competent players and teachers of string instruments are fully comparable to those people engaged in other highly specialized professions.

Hobby. String instruments, because of their perfection of design and from an acoustical standpoint, are very fascinating. This interest is intensified by the knowledge that these instruments were made by hand, completely without modern science and machinery. Many people have spent a good portion of their lives and even fortunes in collecting and studying string instruments. Others have taken up the repair and maintenance of them, which is equally interesting and can become a lucrative sideline.

Some people like to study and to play folk dances of various lands. Some collect manuscripts, which may increase in value manyfold. Some make violins and experiment with varnish in an effort to duplicate the old masters.

The National Association of Amateur Chamber Music Players is a voluntary banding together of nonprofessional instrumentalists who love to play trios, quartets, quintets, or duo sonatas.

Due to the voluminous amount of small ensemble music available to the string instrument player, many amateur musicians meet in weekly or bimonthly meetings of neighborhood string quartets or other small ensembles. Those who have experienced these challenging and memorable occasions claim they are among the highlights of their lives.

Conclusion. The music teachers, the parents, or other persons having the responsibility for advising children in the selection of a musical instrument should give strong consideration to the strings. From the standpoint of musical merit and other lifelong values, these instruments hold an indisputably high position.

Improvement of Teacher-Training Curricula in Strings[1]

Although conditions vary widely in teacher-training institutions, making impossible the adoption of any standardized curricula, the following recommendations are offered with the hope that the administration of each institution preparing instrumental music teachers will strive to develop as fine a string teacher-training program as their facilities and staff will permit.

The basic competencies which should grow out of the recommended curricula are:

(1) Knowledge of the basic pedagogical principles upon which string instrument teaching rests.

(2) Understanding of procedures for successful classroom teaching of strings in homogeneous and heterogeneous groups.

(3) Knowledge of string instructional materials for individual and group instruction.

(4) Understanding of the mechanics of string instrument construction, care, minor repair, and alignment.

(5) Knowledge and understanding of educational psychology, principles of guidance and other phases of the general learning process.

(6) Understanding of the ways and means of advancing the string program in the school and the community.

(7) Adequate teacher performance on violin, viola, cello, string bass.

RECOMMENDATIONS[2]

Curriculum for Music Education Majors— Vocal Emphasis

1. At least one year of string class work.
   a. This to be started in the freshman year so that the student may use electives if he so desires for further string study during the remaining three years.
   b. It is suggested that the student remain on one string instrument for at least one year so that some degree of proficiency may be reached.
   c. The string class should be taught as nearly as possible like a similar class would be taught in the public schools. This involves a choice between or a combination of two plans, the homogeneous (like instruments) or the heterogeneous (all strings together) methods.
   d. The class should be a constant laboratory for showing how to correct the many pedagogical problems in string playing and teaching. The string classes should be scheduled to meet daily if possible.
2. A third semester of string class work, the student now covering one or both of the opposite pair of instruments (violin-viola or cello-bass) not previously studied. If all instruments are taught in the same class, this second course (on a different instrument) could be programmed to meet with the first-year string class. For the teacher, this would reduce the number of classes and for the student it would provide an opportunity to observe the teaching of his last year's instrument as he now learns a different one.
3. At least one semester of private instruction on a string instrument, preferably violin, with cello as secondary choice.
4. At least one semester (preferably two) of string ensemble, using materials at the students' level, which would have greatest educational value and which would be applicable to public school use.
5. At least one semester (preferably two) of music education orchestra experience on a string instrument, playing materials of value most suited for public school use.

---

[1] Prepared by W. Gibson Walters, San Jose, California, member of National Committee on String Instruction.

[2] These recommendations were developed by the combined efforts of the entire Committee on String Instruction (almost three hundred leading string teachers in the public schools, colleges, and universities), Gilbert R. Waller, chairman. It is obvious that programming problems will make it necessary to combine some of the courses here recommended.

6. At least one course in orchestral methods, organization, and procedure in which would be included as much information as possible about how to stimulate, start, encourage, and maintain the orchestra and also the necessary information on mechanics of string instrument construction, care, repair, and alignment. Teachers in the public schools should be able to make minor repairs on string instruments; they should know how to select tnem and be able to recognize defects, such as fingerboard buzzes, short necks in old violins, low or high saddles or nuts, improperly fitted pegs, bridges, sound posts, stripped threads in bow eyelets, etc. They should know where and how to send an instrument to a reputable craftsman to have it put in proper playing condition.

7. At least one course in student teaching, a portion of which should be devoted to string class and orchestra work.

Curriculum for Music Education Majors— *Instrumental Emphasis*

1. At least two years of string class work.
   a. One year on violin or viola, and one year on cello or bass. If the second-year class (covering the same material but on a different instrument) is programmed with the first-year class, the student might well cover both the cello and bass by alternating on them at successive meetings of the class. This can be done easily since the cello and bass are quite similar and since the student will already have developed some feel for string instrument performance.
   b. This class to be taught as outlined for vocal emphasis students.
2. If possible, a third year of string class work in which the student could alternate between assisting the teacher of the class and additional work on any string instrument where extra experience is desirable.
3. At least two years (preferably three) of applied instruction on string instruments, with particular emphasis on violin as first choice and cello as second.
4. At least two semesters (preferably four) of music education orchestra experience on a string instrument, playing materials of value most suited for public school use.
5. At least two semesters (preferably four) of string ensemble using materials at the student's level which would have greatest educational value and which would be applicable to public school use. It is further suggested that the student play the instrument with which he has up to this time had the least experience.
6. At least one course (preferably two) in orchestral methods, which would also include the information specified for students of vocal emphasis.
7. At least one course (preferably two) in student teaching, a portion of which should be devoted to string class and orchestra work with children in the laboratory or the local public schools.
8. Additional suggestions:
   a. All string classes of like level (unless they become too large) should be programmed together regardless of emphasis.
   b. All instrumental teachers sent into the public schools should play a string instrument (preferably violin or cello) with some degree of proficiency.
   c. Supervised student teaching is very necessary and all college students who intend to become teachers should be urged to have some experience with strings and orchestras in their student teaching assignments.

Curriculum for Music Education Majors— *String Specialist*

1. At least two years of string class work.
   a. To be begun in the freshman year as was suggested for vocal and instrumental emphasis, the student working on an instrument other than his major.
   b. These students should also be programmed with other music education string classes, the classes following a public school approach.
2. If possible, a third year of string class work in which the student would devote most of his time assisting the teacher by making corrections and suggestions to individuals as needed while the class plays. This should be a practical type of course, and for the music education string specialist would not involve much preparation. The purpose is to increase the student's ability to analyze string pedagogical problems and to continue his growth in string class procedure.
3. At least tnree years (preferably four) of private study on the student's major string instrument.
4. At least one year of private study on a secondary string instrument. This secondary instrument being one of the opposite strings, considering violin-viola as one type, and cello-bass as their opposites.
5. At least one semester of private study on each of the two remaining string instruments.
6. At least one semester with additional performance experience with music education string ensemble materials, playing the string instruments with which the student is least familiar.
7. At least one year (preferably two) of string ensemble experience with literature of college string ensemble level.
8. At last one semester with additional performance sessions of music education orchestra materials.

9. At least three years of college or university orchestra experience playing a string instrument.
10. At least one course (preferably two) in orchestra methods which would include the information specified for vocal emphasis.
11. At least one semester (preferably two) of student teaching, all of which would be devoted to string class and orchestra work in a laboratory or a public school situation.

Curriculum for String Majors [1]

1. At least one year (preferably more) of string class work with music education students on an instrument (or instruments) other than his major.
2. At least one semester (preferably more) of applied study on a string instrument of an opposite type than his major.
3. At least one course in orchestra methods with music education students.
4. At least one semester (preferably on his secondary string instrument) on music education string ensemble materials.
5. At least one semester of student teaching, all of which would be devoted to string class and orchestra work in a laboratory or public school situation.

Basic Principles of String Playing As Applied to String Class Teaching[2]

To teach strings in classes successfully, it is imperative that teachers know the basic principles involved in the playing of each instrument. Such teaching is greatly simplified, however, when one realizes that these principles are basically the same, are fundamental and inherent for all the strings of the orchestra. There is much variation in the application of these principles among players and teachers, and observation of several performances will reveal this fact.

It will be observed that some players play their respective instruments with less effort than others. This is an essential point to keep in mind in teaching youngsters to perform successfully on string instruments. The application of the basic principles of playing the instruments in a manner conducive to a relaxed, balanced playing position will achieve this purpose. To enjoy music from the start should be the objective of string class teaching. This is certainly one of its advantages.

When the body, arms, and hands are made to move with the greatest freedom, the whole technique of string playing can be greatly extended. Careful attention given to balancing the body as a whole and balancing the two arms and hands in their separate functions furnishes the key to this freedom. This can be carried out easily with groups as large as twenty to twenty-five in a class of combined strings.

Seating. It is important that the class be seated so that the teacher can give individual manual help to any child as the class works. Important factors to be considered are (a) plenty of space between players, and (b) a separate stand for each student. It is helpful to seat instruments with like strings, such as violins and basses or violas and cellos near each other. Since violins and violas will require more individual attention it is usually best to seat them near the front. Use of the piano as a stabilizing factor for pitch and rhythm is recommended, particularily in the early stages of string playing. With the myriad of problems (holding and drawing the bow, holding the instrument, correct left hand position, fingerings, etc.), the use of the piano can serve the students well while mastering the first complex problems of playing; too, the teacher is free to work with individual students. Fre-

---

[1] This contains only those music education items which should help the professional string person to handle a college teaching assignment, should he ultimately move in that direction instead of professional playing.

[2] Submitted by Robert R. Becker, Laramie, Wyoming, member of National Committee on String Instruction.

quently, the piano should be used as an independent accompanying instrument in order to avoid complete dependence on it for pitch and rhythm.

Instruction begins with the care of the instrument and the bow. It is important that the children know at least the following few simple rules before work begins:

—Keep the instrument and bow in the case when not in use.

—Leave the strings pulled up to pitch; do not loosen them.

—Wipe rosin dust from the instrument and bow stock with a soft cloth each time before placing in case.

—Never leave the instrument or bow near a radiator or in a cold draft as this may cause the instrument to crack or the bow to warp.

—Do not permit anyone else except your teacher to handle your instrument.

—Take good care of the bow; always keep the hair under a little tension. The hair should not sag.

Rosining the violin, viola, or cello bow presents no particular problem. Bass students should, however, be cautioned to allow the hair to leave the rosin at the end of each stroke in order to keep the hair from sticking to the rosin and possibly jerking out quantities.

Posture. Before beginning technical instruction the teacher should help the children understand the importance of, and what constitutes, good posture. By having the children stand erect then having them sit on the front edges of their chairs, retaining the standing position from the waist up with feet flat on the floor, a good posture will be achieved—straight spine, body away from the back of the chair, and shoulders erect but relaxed.

Balance—Right Hand and Arm. Because the bow arm is the means of tone production and because it is more difficult to develop, it is wise to keep its progress somewhat ahead of the other arm. There are many similarities in this technique for all the strings: (a) The right arm because of its ability to maneuver is able to bring the hand, wrist and fingers into such positions as may be necessary to accommodate the movement of the bow on each string. (b) Right hand balance and control of the bow is the same for each instrument, namely, the thumb remains opposite the finger load. The thumb, second and third fingers support the bow (holding fingers) while first and fourth fingers are controlling fingers in conjuction with the opposing pressure of the thumb. (c) The thumb position is curved and touching on its tip near the inside corner of the nail. (d) Wrist action complements the movement of the bow by allowing the fingers and hand to maintain their position on the bow.

Differences should be carefully explained. For *violin and viola* (a) the bow inclines slightly toward the outside edge; (b) the arched fourth finger is on its tip on top of the stick, comfortably close to the third, *not* out on the screw; (c) first finger at the middle joint placed on top of the stick next to second finger. For *cello and bass* (a) the bow inclines toward the inside edge; (b) because the approach to the bow is at a different angle (hanging downward from the hand and fingers), the second finger will usually extend over the ferrule about one-quarter or one-half inch; (c) the fourth finger will extend over the side of the frog about the length of the last phalanx, and the first finger will fall on the stick about midway between the first and second joints from the tip and somewhat away from second in order to provide more bow pressure.

As the teacher gives this information, demonstration of correct finger placement for each of the types of bow-holding should occur simultaneously. The seemingly minor differences between the violin-viola and cello-bass finger placement on the bow can easily be demonstrated by dropping the hand at the wrist to assume the

175

"reaching-down" position necessary for cello-bass as contrasted to the "reaching-out" position for holding the violin-viola bow. Then the teacher moves quickly from student to student, checking each hand carefully, reminding the pupils that in addition to placing fingers correctly they must relax fingers, hand, and arms so as to allow the flexibility necessary for drawing the bow. This is a very important teacher activity. If the student's hand is deftly manipulated into correct position at this time, the muscular or kinesthetic sensations are set up which are inherent in good bow control.

Balance—Left Hand and Arm. The left arm, hand, and fingers should be treated as a whole. The arm through its ability to maneuver is able to bring the hand into such positions as to make the fingers accessible to the finger board. For each of the string instruments, the thumb-to-fingers relationship in the left hand is basically the same, namely, the thumb remains opposite the finger load. While the fingers move constantly, the thumb does not have this same agility. It must, however, be a centering medium, accommodating the movements of the fingers either from string to string or up and down the finger board.

For *violin-viola*, the instrument rests on the end of the left collar bone nearest the throat, with the button pointed to the center, and the violin neck is supported by the second phalanx of the left thumb pressing upward, opposing the weight of the instrument as well as the action of the fingers on strings. The jawbone should rest lightly on the chin rest in such a manner as to keep the head straight.

The *cello* stands on the end pin, supported by the knees and resting just under the chest bone and above the stomach. The bottom of the scroll should not rest on the shoulder but should be slightly above it. The left hand is in a balanced position over the thumb, which acts in opposition to the finger action; fingers are poised above the fingerboard. The thumb is directly opposite the second finger, first finger points upward, fourth downward, and second and third are well arched on the tips. The thumb is not bent. This hand position is the same for *bass,* the instrument being supported with the back edge resting in the left groin, while the upper bout rests against the left side of the abdomen. The instrument can now be adjusted to and fro until it is perfectly balanced. This technique of balancing the bass is extremely important for future left hand freedom.

The teacher should now move from one student to another, checking first the holding of the violins and violas, then the cellos and basses. Again, here is the teacher's opportunity to start the desired kinesthetic sensations of arm and body balance. For violin and viola students, particular attention should be paid to the following: That (a) the neck and shoulder muscles are not tense; (b) the left arm is relaxed, permitting the elbow to swing to and fro easily under the center of the instrument; (c) the left wrist is straight; (d) the violin neck is supported by the second phalanx of the left thumb, extended outward and relaxed; (e) the left hand is not gripping through the fingerboard horizontally; and (f) that the jawbone is resting lightly on the chinrest but not grabbing or trying to support the instrument in springboard fashion.

Three problems most common in the balanced left hand position for cello and bass are: (a) Excessive pressure with the thumb tip, causing the joints to double in toward the hand; (b) the thumb placed too near the first finger, occasionally too far down near the fourth finger; and (c) lifting the fingers when crossing the strings.

Technique—Right Hand and Arm—Use of Bow. The next step in the class procedure following establishment of the correct methods of holding the instrument and the bows should be that of putting the instrument and bow together. The purpose is to form the essential control patterns necessary for the production of a good healthy tone. Since the bow is least difficult to control when playing in the middle, it is advisable to start development in this part.

To establish the correct position for *violin and viola* students, the following procedure is recommended: The right arm should be allowed to hang at the side; by bending the arm at the elbow, the forearm and upper arm will form two sides of a square; the bow will now form the third side and the instrument the fourth side, completing the square. For the average-size student, the bow will contact the E string (A string—viola) at about the middle. Then, as the elbow is raised, the bow will successively contact the other strings, the lowest when the upper arm and bow are about parallel with the floor.

Because the *cello* is held in an inclining position the bow arm angles will not be the same, but the principles of arm elevation for the various strings will be. With the *bass*, the hand is always in a downward, reaching position. The arm remains practically straight, with action only in the shoulder for the different string elevations; but for drawing the bow there will be action in both the shoulder and the wrist.

Full-voiced tone production on the string instruments is controlled by application of maximum pressure on the bow stick (plus weight of bow, which is small) plus speed of bow. *In the upper half* this pressure of added weight is applied by the first finger pressing down on the stick and by the tip of the thumb pressing up; *in the lower half* by pressure of the little finger downward and by the tip of the thumb upward. *The whole bow* combines these two controls and involves a transfer from one to the other at the balance point of the bow; e.g., at the start of the down-bow stroke, the weight of the bow is carried by the little finger and the thumb, continuing itself until the bow reaches the balance point where the pressure of first finger and thumb takes over and continues to the tip. This allows for a continuous, even pressure of the bow at its contact point on the string which is necessary to produce steady tone.

In connection with this pressure control, the use of the *violin-viola bow* involves the hinging action of the elbow and wrist plus some upper arm action at the ends of the stroke. *At the middle*, weight of the lower arm is applied to the stick through thumb and first finger. *At the tip*, arm weight is applied downward through the first finger. The wrist will now be much lower and rolled outward, more away from the body. *At the frog*, the thrust of the elbow forward is from the shoulder joint, the wrist bending laterally to keep the bow parallel with the bridge; arched thumb and second finger serve as a fulcrum, and the arched fourth finger exerts strong pressure downward on top of the stick for balance.

For use of the *cello bow*, the hinging action of the elbow and wrist is necessary with some upper arm action at the ends of the bow stroke. Note that the reach is downward because of the angle of the instrument; therefore the controls are easier. *At the middle, at the tip,* and for the *whole bow* the principles are the same as above; *at the frog* the arched wrist is necessary to align the stick with the bridge; pressure is transferred from the second finger-thumb-fulcrum more quickly to the first finger which rests against the side of the bow pressing inward toward the strings as the thumb presses outward. This creates a lever action, which enables the wrist to roll outward thus bringing arm weight into the stick.

The *bass bow* is handled the same as the cello bow except with a firmer grip since the stick is heavier and the bass strings require more pressure to start the tone. The use of the arm full length with the bow practically straight is necessary, the bow action coming from the shoulder joint and the wrist bent sufficiently to keep the bow parallel with the bridge.

Technique—Rote-Playing Period. After careful explanation of the above principles, the teacher should allow the students beginning trials with instruments and bows after carefully checking each student for correct position. This rote-playing period can provide the basis for skill in playing. The student's attention can be centered on the immediate problems of bow control and not be hampered by the added problems of reading from the printed page. To start playing, a simple exercise such as four quarter notes followed by four quarter rests on the D string is suggested. Since this is an inside string on all of the instruments, the students find from the beginning that elbow elevation must be watched carefully if the bow is to remain on only one string.

A steady tempo will provide for a group rhythmic response and the four rests afford an opportunity for the teacher to remind the students of the many details of this period. A solid chordal accompaniment provided by the piano during the four quarter notes followed by pianissimo chords or single notes during the rests will help to give emphasis and vitality to this first playing experience. The cycle of play-four rest-four should be repeated about ten times and then the students allowed to rest. At this beginning stage the practice periods should be short to avoid fatigue.

For variety employ the different strings, vary the number of notes and rests or vary the speed slightly; but keeping the tempo once it is established is important. The value of this rhythmic approach should not be underestimated; it is the basis for a good response as a class and later as an orchestra.

Starting first with the middle bow, the second step should be playing at the tip, then at the frog, and finally with the whole bow. With the latter, the note values should be enlarged to allow sufficient time for the change of controls from the lower to the upper part of the bow.

As this bow activity is proceeding on the various strings, principally on the inside ones, each child should concentrate on the right hand, working for the ideal pressure and speed to produce a resonant full-voice tone. Also, he should be made very conscious of the difference in control in upper half, lower half, and in combining these controls in the use of the whole bow.

Technique—Left Hand and Arm—Use of Fingers. Again, the basic principle for all the string instruments is the same; namely, the thumb provides the opposing pressure by the fingers on the fingerboard. (See Balance—Left Hand and Arm.) Well-arched fingers are necessary with the tips covering the string and pressing down firmly. The knuckles are approximately in line with the fingerboard and the fingers are poised above and close to the string. Finger action should be decided and firm, the fingers falling with weight. The release of fingers should be instantaneous and springy. Finger action should be from the knuckles and not from the second joints; especially is this true for the first finger. When second, third, or fourth finger stops a note, all the other fingers behind that finger are kept down also, for support.

Keeping fingers down while crossing strings is essentially important for all instruments; ascending, by holding fingers 2 and 3, or 2, 3, and 4 in place while the first assumes its place on the next string; descending, by holding first finger in second place while second, third, and fourth assume their place on the next string, or allowing all four fingers to fall in place on the next string. For *violin-viola* the thumb is approximately near the first finger or ahead of it, its tip pointing away from the instrument. For *cello* the fingers are spaced evenly, the first directed somewhat upward, the fourth slightly downward, second and third at right angles to the finger board, well arched and on their tips. The left thumb rests lightly against the neck approximately opposite the second fingers and is not bent inward but is usually about straight, sometimes arched away from the hand slightly. On the *bass*, the extension between first and second fingers is maintained, the first directed somewhat upward, the fourth slightly downward; second and third are well arched and nearly at right angles to the fingerboard.

For the *cello*, the extended or expanded left hand in a "stretched" position is soon required of beginning cello players. It consists of whole steps between fingers 1-2 and 2-4. As the hand moves forward, pivoting on the first finger at the knuckle, second, third, and fourth fingers move one-half step higher and the thumb remains under the second finger.

In establishing good left-hand position and intonation, it is well to introduce the fingers one at a time. Assuming that the bowing has been developed well ahead of the fingering, drill may be limited to two or three exercises with each added finger in order to get at least three fingers into operation for violin-viola and four fingers for cello and bass. Use of two or three simple pieces played slowly with good bowing and intonation should establish familiarity with note names and provide the first elements of reading. Careful attention should be given to the application of the hand and fingers to the fingerboard and neck. This is extremely important to fine left-hand development.

Following the introduction of new skills there should be a consolidation period during which these may be transformed into techniques through drill and disguised repetition. These periods should vary in length with the difficulty of the problems. In any case, this is the time for the teacher to do his best work.

As these skills are worked in, (a) observe over-all posture to keep freedom in the whole body; (b) keep the bow arm free by playing at the frog, tip, middle and with the whole bow, stressing the sharp differences in control in each area; and (c) check left hands and arms for tension, both in the direction of up and down the fingerboard and through from left to right. During these periods of assimilation, the progress of the class depends almost entirely on the ability of the teacher to analyze its needs and to use exercise material in such a way as to satisfy them.

Technique—Shifting. The technique of shifting, or change of position, involves the movement of thumb, fingers, and hand as a unit. The finger that is on the string last makes the shift, pressing the string sufficiently to contact the fingerboard. It is good practice to keep other fingers down to establish schooling of the hand.

On the *violin-viola* on the upward shift the whole hand moves up in one movement; on the outward shift the hand balance can be momentarily broken, immediately prior to the shift, by quickly adjusting the thumb toward the scroll. The *cello-bass* shift does not require advance preparation of the thumb; it remains even with the second finger as the hand moves.

After careful introduction of this procedure with the class, by explanation and example, simple exercises such as shifting in whole and half steps scale-wise, may be used. Start with first finger, up a whole step and back, single bows, then slur the two; use the same pattern for second finger, etc. This simply amounts to moving from first to second position and back with each finger. This pattern may be used on each string and after some proficiency is gained the same procedure may be used with first and third positions. Further development may be carried on with combinations of fingers, and with other positions.

Technique—Vibrato. One of the elements of a beautiful string tone is a fine vibrato, free and continuous. Since it is a motor skill, particularly in the beginning stages, it can be taught as successfully as the other skills; and it can be taught in large classes of mixed strings. Vibrato should receive its development along with the left-hand skills since they are closely related. Instruction may begin after fairly good establishment of correct posture, coordination of right and left hand techniques, and good tone production.

In general, vibrato is produced by the tip of the finger rolling back and forth on the string, raising and lowering the pitch. To begin, a thorough explanation of the basic motor activities, followed by preliminary practice of these movements away from the instrument, is suggested. The basic movement for *violin-viola* is a wrist action with the thumb resting securely on the neck of the instrument, allowing the hand to swing to and fro, lightly touching the edge of the fingerboard. The *cello-bass* movement is a coordinated movement of the forearm from the elbow, originating from a rotating action in the upper arm and including as a unit the wrist, hand, and fingers swinging in an arc over the fingerboard. The thumb serves as a pivot or an axis resting against the underside of the neck.

Further practice of the vibrato action should include (a) silent practice on the instrument with each finger in rhythmic patterns of two, three, four, six, and eight; (b) then with the bow to establish coordination; (c) slurring from finger to finger; (d) shifting to other positions maintaining a continuous, uninterrupted vibrato; and (e) scale practice in all forms. For best schooling of the hand and fingers, it is well to hold the fingers down behind the vibrating finger. Early stages of practice should be of short duration to avoid unnecessary tension in the hand or arm mechanism and a slow, wide, and relaxed vibrato in singing style should be cultivated rather than one which is fast, narrow and tense.

SUMMARY OF THE BASIC PRINCIPLES OF STRING PLAYING PARALLELISMS

Body Position or Posture

Erectness—weight generally to the left in order to accommodate the left arm and hand techniques (either standing or seated).

Minimum Holding of Instruments

Bass inclines, balances; cello between the knees, rests against the chest; violin rests on two anchors (collar bone and left hand). The left thumb and fingers maintain contact without squeezing.

Arm and Hand Balance

1. Left arm ability to maneuver brings the hand and fingers into such positions as will make the fingers accessible to the fingerboard using natural arm movements in balanced relationship without unnecessary muscular tensions (to the front for *violin-violo;* to the side for *cello-bass*).

2. Left hand thumb-to-fingers control. The thumb remains opposite the finger load utilizing the natural strength of the hand.

3. Right-arm maneuverability brings hand, wrist, and fingers into such positions as are necessary to accommodate the bow on each string, using the natural arm movements in balanced relationship without unnecessary muscular tensions.

4. Right hand thumb-to-fingers control. The thumb remains opposite the finger load utilizing the natural strength of the hand (downward position for *cello-bass*).

5. Law of lever and fulcrum operates in all right hands. Thumb and second finger fulcrum and third finger support the bow (holding fingers), while first and little fingers are controlling fingers in conjunction with the opposing pressure of the thumb.

6. The thumb position (under the second finger) is curved and on its tip.

7. Wrist action complements the movements of the bow.

8. The attack and release uses the same digital control for all, e.g., fingers press or release the stick or frog at start or at end of all bow strokes (greater for bass—larger string).

9. String crossing involves elevation of entire arm to accommodate bow levels for each string.

Tone Production

1. Full-voiced tone production is controlled by application of maximum pressure on the bow stick (plus weight of bow) plus speed of bow. Varies with size and length of string.

2. Bow control governed by the balance point of the bow (heavy frog, light tip). In the upper half, by use of first finger pressing downward (or inward, for *cello-bass*) and thumb pressing upward (or outward, for *cello-bass*). In the lower half, by pressure of the little finger, (or inward, *cello-bass*) and thumb pressing upward (or outward, *cello-bass*). The whole bow combines these two controls and involves the transfer from one to the other.

180

3. Fundamental approach to basic bowings is the same for all string instruments. Legato, detached strokes, either on the string or off the string.

4. Good left-hand tone production requires finger action which is decided and firm, the fingers falling with weight. The release of a finger should be instantaneous and springy. Finger action is from the knuckles, not from the second joints, especially the first finger.

5. Holding fingers down wherever possible, especially when crossing strings, is the same for all the strings.

Shifting

1. Whole hand is moved up in one movement to the new position. (Downward movement for cello-bass.)

2. The finger that is on the string last (before the shift begins) slides on the string.

Vibrato

1. Is produced on all the string instruments by tip of the finger rolling back and forth on the string raising and lowering the pitch.

2. The thumb serves as a pivot.

Conclusion. Class teaching and private teaching do not differ fundamentally. Both are concerned with the basic principles of good string playing which must be adhered to if the students are to learn.

First, and most important, is the teacher who above all must be one with musicianly qualities, sensitive to music in all its phases as an expressive art; *second,* there must be a well-planned and balanced approach to the acquisition of the physical movements necessary to play the instruments correctly, and to the musical apprehension and responsiveness of the students. To attain this it must be thoroughly understood that the learning of the performance skills, the detailed posture and technical drills, is a means, however necessary and fundamental, to fulfilling the desired objectives. This drill and technical work always should be meaningful to the students in terms of the musical results to be achieved.

With an understanding of class procedures, a teacher with a string background and thorough knowledge of the basic principles of string playing can teach groups of children to play the string instruments correctly and musical results *can* be obtained.

Basic Principles of Group Woodwind
Instrument Instruction[1]

In third and fourth grades, exploratory experiences should provide an opportunity for children to experiment with woodwind instruments. This opportunity should assure a fuller musical growth through instrumental class instruction as a part of school activities during the regular and summer sessions. These experiences often furnish the only opportunity the more gifted child may have to discover his musical potentialities.

Physical Requirements. Children and parents often come to a music teacher asking for guidance in selecting a wind instrument. There are many things which teachers should know in order to give the best advice possible. The following points should be kept in mind:

(1) Is the shape of the mouth and the formation of the teeth such that the child can learn to play the particular instrument in which he is interested? A teacher should not recommend any particular wind instrument for a child who is having his teeth straightened by an orthodontist. Parents should be encouraged to see their doctor and thoroughly discuss this problem before the child is allowed to start music lessons. This is important because a child playing a clarinet, trumpet, or trombone may be retarding or hampering improvement of the condition which the doctor is attempting to correct.

(2) It should not be taken for granted that a child who has a large physique will be able to play a wind instrument easily. Occasionally these children may have other problems which handicap them in learning to play a wind instrument. The teacher always should check the health record before permitting a child to start lessons.

(3) It is not necessary to have large hands in order to play the clarinet, although children with very small hands will find it more difficult in the beginning to cover the tone holes correctly. In many cases it has been found that small children having difficulty are holding the instrument incorrectly, making it impossible for them to cover the tone holes.

(4) Children who are small of stature, who have short arms, will find it difficult to extend their arms and fingers far enough to play the flute correctly. It should not be recommended that children who are extremely small begin with the flute. They will be confronted with additional physical problems which may discourage them in continuing the instrument.

Breath Control. Good breath control is the foundation of good tone production. The technical aspects of correct breath control and the physical functioning of the diaphragm need not be discussed with the beginning wind player, even though they are basic to good tone production. This does not mean that the beginning player should not be helped to make use of the diaphragm so that he may produce as good a tone as possible.

Most children when told to take a deep breath will pull in on the diaphragm, take an excessive amount of air into the lungs, expand the chest and raise the shoulders. In doing this, the muscles in the chest and throat are tightened thus cutting off the column of the air and producing a poor tone.

The following is suggested as a procedure which will help the beginning player to relax the chest, shoulders, and throat and bring into use the diaphragm without

---

[1] From a demonstration workshop conducted by Fred A. Graichen, Los Angeles, California, at the MENC Biennial Convention, Chicago, 1954.

discussing its physiological or technical implications. Immediately after the child has learned how to produce a tone with the instrument, he should be encouraged to practice long sustained tones. More breath and breath control will be needed. First have the child practice the following without playing the instrument:

—Sit in the correct playing position.

—Relax the shoulders and chest.

—take a deep breath, hold it without moving chest or raising shoulders.

—Exhale the breath through the mouth.

If the shoulders and chest remain in a relaxed position and a deep breath taken in, the diaphragm will automatically be brought into use. Repeat this exercise slowly several times without the instrument. Then have the child attempt it with his instrument, playing sustained tones.

The beginning woodwind player may not be able to achieve immediate success in the above procedure, but a few minutes' practice at each class lesson will help teach this skill. It should not be treated as an isolated study but as a regular part of each exercise the child is playing. Frequent reminding will help children remain constantly aware of the importance of correct breathing.

Sitting Position. Correct chairs for seating the wind instrument class are imperative. Each child should be seated in a chair which will permit him to assume comfortably the correct playing position. A good playing position is dependent upon the child sitting with his back well supported and his feet firmly on the floor. For the average class this will mean that it will be necessary to have chairs of various sizes. Too frequently the auditorium type of folding chair is used which makes it impossible for the child to sit correctly. A poor chair will allow the child to develop a poor playing position. Occasionally makeshift arrangements have to be made but they cannot be educationally justified. It is better to have each child bring his own chair from his classroom to the wind class than to have him use an inadequate one.

The children should be seated in such a way that the teacher may observe every player at all times.

How to Practice. If the child is to progress as rapidly as possible, it is important for him to know and understand not only the technicalities involved with his particular instrument, but also the best way to practice so that his time and effort will not be wasted. Mursell lists four outcomes resulting from having the student practice with definite objectives in mind:

—The pupil has standards with which to measure his development.

—Practice becomes intelligent because it has an aim.

—Interest is aroused because of the motivation.

—Additional results are obtained because of the goal in mind.[1]

Each assignment should be made with a definite purpose in mind. The lack of being definite in the assignment is often the cause of children losing interest. To be definite the assignment should be clearly explained.

Practice on a woodwind instrument involves much more than just playing through some music or spending a certain length of time with the instrument. The child should have a definite purpose and aim or goal toward which he is working. His practice should be planned to help him grow in particular skills. It will be necessary to repeat technical exercises many times to accomplish or learn a particular skill.

---

[1] James L. Mursell, *Education for Musical Growth* (New York: Ginn and Company, 1948).

Learning to play a woodwind instrument requires daily practice. The teacher should help the child to plan a regular schedule of practicing before and after school. Two fifteen-minute periods are better than one long period. As the child progresses he should be encouraged to lengthen the period, but should continue to play at least twice daily. If the following suggestions are discussed with the child it will help him to make the best possible use of the time spent in practicing his instrument:

—Choose a quiet room where one will not be interrupted.

—Use a straight chair.

—The feet should be able to touch the floor.

—The back should be well supported.

—Check constantly on the position of the instrument.

It should be remembered that any playing done in a poor position tends to establish bad habits which are difficult to correct. Occasionally, practice before a large mirror aids in checking the playing position. Begin with several minutes of sustained tones. Try to produce a full, rich tone and listen constantly for it. After playing the sustained tones, the exercises and pieces assigned at the previous lesson should be practiced. They should be played slowly and carefully. The counting should be steady and the playing should match the counting.

In everything practiced there is something that needs to be improved. Learn to recognize the most important problems or difficulties in each exercise. Practice them by themselves slowly until they can be played well. Practice with the mind as well as the body; with the ears as well as the hands. Listen constantly for good tone and be sure to play in tune. Careful listening is the key to successful practicing. Never hurry through an exercise. Careless playing is detrimental and correct practice will bring improvement.

Children should be aware of and understand these basic principles of how to practice. They are just as important as interest and innate ability. A pleasing personality is a great aid in helping students through the initial stages of learning to play an instrument. Children are willing to work for someone in whom they have confidence.

THE CLARINET

Assembling the Mouthpiece. The beginning clarinet player should start to play with just the mouthpiece. Unless he can produce a tone on the mouthpiece alone, he will find it almost impossible to produce a tone when the instrument is fully assembled. The reed should be taken with the fingers of the right hand and carefully placed in the mouth so that it can be dampened. A dry reed will not vibrate correctly and often will not produce a tone.

Producing a Tone. Children should be told that the playing of a wind instrument requires practically no breath effort on the part of the player. Beginning players will have the tendency to overblow. After the initial tone is produced, have the child attempt to produce the tone again without blowing too hard.

If the first tone produced by the child is a squeak or is coarse and blatant, the mouthpiece has been inserted too far in the mouth. If the tone is very thin or quivers, not enough of the mouthpiece has been inserted in the mouth. The child should be allowed to produce a tone several times, holding it for at last four to six slow counts before he is instructed to use the tongue to start the tone.

Playing Position. To assume the correct clarinet playing position, have the child pretend that he is grasping a large baseball in each hand. The clarinet is played with the soft pads near the ends of the fingers and not on the tips which are hard and small. By flattening the fingers and using the soft pads, a slight pressure will cause the pads to expand and cover the tone holes securely.

The position of the right thumb on the thumb rest will vary slightly depending on the size of the hand. In most cases, however, it will be approximately on the knuckle.

Playing the First Tone. Second line *G*, the first tone written for the clarinet in many class methods, is not the best starting tone for the beginner. This tone does not require the player to use any of his fingers. It will be difficult for him to balance the instrument between the right thumb and the mouth. Starting on a tone which will require the use of at least one or two fingers, the beginner will develop some feeling of security with the instrument before he attempts to play a tone where no fingers are required.

THE FLUTE

Introduction. Frequently the teacher will have more difficulty with the beginning flute player than with the child learning to play other wind instruments. Ideally, the beginning flute player should be given individual instruction until he is able to blow a clear sustained tone while holding the instrument correctly. In most cases it is impossible to arrange a schedule so that this may be done. The beginning flute player may have difficulty playing a tone if the entire instrument is used. For the first week or two the child should play on the mouthpiece alone, until it is possible for him to play a sustained, clear tone. The following suggestions may be helpful to the teachers conducting classes in which there are beginning flute players.

Holding the Mouthpiece. The mouthpiece should be held in the same manner that the entire flute is held when assembled; the right thumb should be on the bottom, with the four fingers on top placed at the lower end of the mouthpiece. The left thumb should be on the bottom and the four fingers placed on top approximately one inch from the point where the child will blow into the mouthpiece. This position will help him to assume the correct position for the hands and arms when the entire instrument is used.

Position of the Mouthpiece. In order to produce a tone it is extremely important that the mouthpiece be placed in the correct position as follows:

—The mouthpiece should rest in the cleft of the chin with the inner edge of the tone hole placed at the lower edge of the lip. This will allow the lower lip to cover approximately one-third of the tone hole.

—Extend the tongue out over the lower lip to find the outer edge of the tone hole. This is the point at which the child should blow.

—The jaws should be opened slightly so that the tip of the tongue can be inserted between the teeth. Draw the lip slightly back against the teeth and press the lips lightly together at the corners of the mouth. This will leave a small opening in the center of the mouth.

Producing a Tone. To produce a tone for the first time, have the child say the word "poo" and blow at the same time. If he is not able to produce a tone, rotate the mouthpiece slightly in either direction until the correct position is obtained and a tone produced. When the tone is produced have the child play it several times without taking the mouthpiece away from the lips. Before he removes it, instruct the child to again extend the tongue out over the lower lip to the outer edge of the tone hole. This will help him to find the correct position when the mouthpiece is again placed up to the lips. This sequence should be repeated several times until the child can place the mouthpiece to the lips correctly. Each time a tone is produced have him attempt to hold the tone longer.

Playing Position. To assume the correct playing position the child should be instructed to hold his hands as though he were grasping a large baseball. This will make it possible for him to rest the fleshy part of the fingers on the keys. It also helps the beginner to keep the wrists high, which relaxes the tendons in the back of the hand so that the fingers can be moved easily.

The chin should be up, the shoulders relaxed, and the arms and elbows away from the body. A beginning student should not be allowed to turn his head in order to help support the flute by placing the mouthpiece on the shoulder. This will tighten the muscles in the throat, cutting off the column of air which is necessary to produce a clear, steady tone on the instrument. In order to help the child overcome this tendency, he should be instructed to extend both arms to the right, keeping the head straight.

Playing the First Tone. The first tone the beginning flute player is instructed to play should be either *A* or *A flat*. This is an easy note for the beginner to play on the instrument. It also permits him to use some of the fingers of the left hand, which helps to balance the instrument.

The Brasses—Some Procedures for Improving Standards[1]

In general, throughout the country there is not a shortage of brass instrument players. In spite of the number of players, however, the quality of playing can and should be improved.

Any noticeable improvement of quality will be the result of a long, well-planned program. Some suggestions for a long-range plan for the improvement of the musical quality of the brass instruments are:

—Start beginners on school-owned instruments as the first consideration of "the right instrument for the right child." This permits a change of instrument without upsetting either the student or parent.

—Make use of rental plans for the school-owned instruments.

—Arrange for resale when a student is asked to change instruments.

—Start beginning brass instruction in small classes of four to eight students, regrouping at the end of a month, three months, and again after six months, if both the number of players and the schedule permits.

—Recommend that a student study privately as soon as possible.

—Stress musical growth, not the number of pieces learned or pages played.

—Increase attention given to quality of tone.

Percussion—Some Procedures for Improving Standards

The observance of the following suggestions should improve the standards of percussion playing:

—The teacher must be prepared in the fundamentals.

—Spend more time with percussion students.

—Select percussion players more carefully.

—Develop an attitude wherein each player is proud to be called a percussionist.

—Invite excellent percussion players to give workshops and demonstrations.

—Make a supreme effort to develop at least one fine player to inspire others.

—Make use of recordings of excellent percussion work.

---

[1] From the report submitted by Myron E. Russell, Cedar Falls, Iowa, National Chairman of the Music in American Education Committee on Wind and Percussion Instruments.

Drop-Outs[1]

The tendency to start instrumental lessons and then give up or change to another activity appears to be a problem for consideration. Before a solution can be suggested the fault or problem should be recognized. The following list is by no means exhaustive, but it may serve as a beginning check list.

SOME POSSIBLE REASONS FOR DROP-OUTS

Uninteresting music.
Too frequent change of directors.
Inadequate equipment.
Unsympathetic faculty and/or administration.
Other extracurricular activities introduced to the student before instrumental music has been given an adequate chance.
A too crowded daily schedule of classes.
Lack of adequate counseling.
Music not recognized as a credit subject.
Teacher required to spread efforts too thinly.
Lack of recognition of achievement of the individual or group by the student body, faculty, or community.
Not enough opportunities to perform before the public.
The student not physically suited to a particular instrument.
Lack of care in selection of player for particular instrument.
Teacher not prepared adequately.
Personality clash between the teacher and student.
Attitude of the parent towards music.
Too much or not enough marching band.
After school part-time work.
Too many social functions.
Progress too slow.
Music played is too difficult.
Poor teaching techniques.
Inadequate motivation.

SUGGESTIONS FOR ELIMINATION OF DROP-OUTS

Each one of the suggested reasons for a drop-out should also suggest some kind of remedial action. The following suggestion for the elimination of drop-outs should be considered only as a beginning list:

Improve the quality of the organization.
Give more personal attention.
More personal contact with the home.
Provide more opportunities to perform.
Make possible more concert trips.
Have individual instruction within the school day.
Start the instrumental program in the elementary grades.
A more adequate testing and selection program.
Better discipline.
A more sympathetic attitude on the part of counselors, administrators, and the community.

---

[1] Submitted by Myron E. Russell.

Selected Bibliography[1]

Brooks, B. Marion, and Brown, Harry A. *Music Education in the Elementary School.* New York: American Book Company, 1946. Chapter XIII.

Church, Norval L. and Dykema, Peter W. *Modern Band Training Series*, "Teachers Manual." Boston: C. C. Birchard & Company, 1939.

Dykema, Peter W. and Gehrkens, Karl W. *The Teaching and Administration of High School Music.* Boston: C. C. Birchard & Company, 1940.

Hindsley, Mark H. *School Band and Orchestra Administration.* London: Boosey & Hawkes, Ltd., 1940.

Jones, L. Bruce. *Building the Instrumental Music Department.* New York: Carl Fischer, Inc., 1939.

Morgan Russell V. and Morgan, Hazel B. *Music Education in Action.* Chicago: Neil A. Kjos Music Co., 1954. Chapters V and XVIII.

Mursell, James L. *Music and the Classroom Teacher.* New York: Silver Burdett Company, 1951. Chapter VIII.

——————————. *Music in American Schools.* New York: Silver Burdett Company, 1943. Chapter IX.

Music Educators National Conference. *Minimum Standards for Stringed Instruments in the Schools.* Chicago: MENC.

——————————. *Music in the Elementary School.* Chicago: MENC, 1951.

——————————. *Music Education Source Book.* Chicago: MENC, Fourth printing, 1951.

National Interscholastic Music Activities Commission. *Solo and Ensemble Lists.* Chicago: MENC, 1953.

Normann, Theodore F. *Instrumental Music in the Public Schools.* Philadelphia: Theodore Presser Co., 1941.

Prescott, Gerald R. and Chidester, Lawrence W. *Getting Results with School Bands.* Minneapolis: Paul A. Schmitt Music Company, 1952.

Sheehy, Emma Dickson. *There's Music in Children.* New York: Henry Holt and Company, Inc., 1946.

Van Bodegraven, Paul. *Organizing a School Band.* New York: Irons-Snell Printing Co., 1938.

Wilson, M. Emmett. *How to Help Your Child with Music.* New York: Henry Schuman Co., 1951.

---

[1] For additional references see p. 114, also Appendix p. 309.

CHAPTER XX

PIANO AND ORGAN INSTRUCTION IN SCHOOLS

PIANO AND ORGAN instruction is an integral part of the school instrumental program. Because there are certain phases of instruction in piano and organ playing which are common to both instruments, the following material was not integrated with the preceding chapter. It is important that the unique aspects of each instrument should be recognized and considered.

Piano Instruction in American Music Education[1]

An ability to play the piano is a social asset for music participation in the home, community, church, and in all music-making with other people. Piano experience, can be a fine foundation for all further music specialization. In a broad sense, piano belongs to everyone: (a) Keyboard experience belongs in every general elementary music class; (b) piano classes lead to making music on the instrument; (c) talented students should be encouraged to specialize; and (d) adult piano classes can take care of a great need in adult life.

Piano takes on the following emphasis in the training of teachers:

—For the school music teacher, there should be a functional application directed toward playing accompaniments and vocal scores.

—For the piano teacher, preparation should include flexibility in sight reading, accompanying, and harmonization.

—for the classroom teacher, piano may become a tool in making music effective for classroom music.

Purpose of Group Piano Instruction. Group piano instruction in the schools follows a basic principle of American education in offering equal opportunity to every student to explore vocational and avocational interests. It offers an enriching experience in the personality development of every student and contributes a foundation for future specialization in music. It supplies another means for creative self-expression and for the acquisition of desired skills in musicmaking. It complements and strengthens the vocal and instrumental music program of the schools.

Types of Piano Instruction in the Schools. There are three types of piano activities in music education—keyboard experience, classroom piano, and elective piano classes.

(1) *Keyboard Experience.* This is used by the regular classroom teacher or the music specialist to enrich and intensify other music learnings in the general classroom music program. It provides an equal opportunity for all children to learn something about the keyboard. It provides an excellent means of teaching pitch, rhythm, and music reading. It provides a firm foundation upon which to develop special skills under the vocal and instrumental specialist. It stimulates an interest in music and may arouse a desire for further exploration of the possibilities of the piano keyboard. Keyboard experience can function at all levels. Details concerning the use of keyboard experience in the classroom music program may be found in various current publications.

---

[1] From the report submitted by Fay Templeton Frisch, New Rochelle, New York, National Chairman, Music in American Education Committee on Piano Instruction.

Keyboard experience appeals to the school administrator because it can be included in the music program without increasing the school budget. It also offers an equal opportunity to all children for exploring the keyboard and provides a natural means of discovering special aptitudes.

(2) *Classroom Piano.* This can be a scheduled part of the elementary music program designed to give all children an opportunity to learn some of the basic fundamentals of piano playing and to aid in the further development of the objectives of the general music program with a broad background of musicianship. These classes should be taught by a specialist in group piano instruction.

(3) *Elective Piano Classes.* These are comparable to the elective violin or trumpet classes in which the fundamentals of music education are incorporated with the opportunity for specialized training in pianistic skills. Elective piano classes should be taught by a class piano specialist who understands group techniques as well as the philosophy and practices of music education.

The elective piano classes within the curriculum, or as an extracurricular activity, provide for greater development of abilities discovered in other types of classes. Piano ensemble playing in these classes develops real musicianship which can be carried over into other music activities in the school and the community.

Many have elected music courses in high school and college because of their piano ensemble playing experience in the grades and in junior high school. Some children never become a part of a choral or instrumental group. The piano classes supply the means for music participation for these children.

The effectiveness of a music program which includes piano classes is revealed in the reports from schools which have had a continuity of piano activities over a period of years. These reports indicate that elementary children who have had class piano lessons usually enter junior high school with the ability to play more than one instrument and that there is a greater enrollment in music courses in the senior high school.

Some high schools offer full credit for four years of high school class piano on the beginning, intermediate, and advanced levels. This provides an opportunity for those students who do not have pianos in their homes as well as those who do. It is interesting to contemplate what this type of program can mean to future college freshmen entering theory, harmony, and other special music courses.

The real effectiveness of a continuous piano program depends upon the teacher, and the cooperation of the school administrator and other members of the school music faculty. How universally they put action behind their convictions will determine when and where the piano activities are to be included.[1]

Many teacher-training institutions are re-evaluating their music curriculums and requiring adequate courses in group piano methods and pedagogy. Practice teaching is another requirement which is receiving attention.

ELEMENTARY LEVEL OF INSTRUCTION
Keyboard Experience[2]

Objectives:

1. To introduce children to another means for making music.
2. To heighten enjoyment in music and to develop self-confidence.

---

[1] Specific suggestions for qualification of teacher, for scheduling, operation, and materials for piano classes may be found in the *Handbook for Teaching Piano Classes* (Chicago: Music Educators National Conference, 1952).

[2] From the manuscript for *Keyboard Experience*, a projected publication prepared by the MENC Piano Instruction Committee.

3. To awaken an interest in creative expression.

4. To use the keyboard in connection with other music activities of the school and other classroom experiences.

5. To aid in developing the ability to sing on pitch.

6. To develop aural, tactile, and visual preparation for music reading.

7. To develop ability to find starting tone of classroom songs.

8. To develop the feeling for harmony and cadence.

9. To develop ability to use simple basic chord accompaniments to songs the children sing.

Suggested activities:

1. Locate black-key groups, high and low, soft and loud.

2. Use black-key groups for guides in locating specific white keys.

3. Children may play "accompaniments" of one tone to such songs as "Are You Sleeping" and "Row, Row Your Boat."

4. Children may play repeated short melodic patterns on the three black-key groups while the class sings. Patterns such as "ee-i, ee-i-o" in "Old MacDonald" can be done very easily. The black and white key patterns will develop the concept of key and tonality.

5. Write notation of tone patterns on the blackboard to show that the direction of the notes indicates the direction of playing on the keyboard.

6. Play rhythm instrument accompaniments to many types of melodies, and use the keyboard as a rhythm instrument.

7. Two or more pupils should be at the piano at all times during the activity. This will allow for frequent and equal participation, also will provide opportunity to develop a feeling for the rhythm of the phrase over the beat.

8. Five-tone or five-finger melodies can easily be learned.

9. The tonic, dominant seventh, and the subdominant triads may be presented for simple accompaniments.

Expected results:

1. A satisfying knowledge of the keyboard.

2. Interest in the piano with perhaps a desire for further study.

3. Greater interest in general music and an interest to continue the study of music.

4. An enthusiasm for exploring music literature.

5. Greater facility in hearing, reading, singing, and playing simple music.

6. Better understanding of basic principles of music.

Classroom Piano

Objectives:

1. To introduce children of all grade levels to the pleasure of playing the piano alone or with others.

2. To enhance the enjoyment of the general music program.

3. To teach the fundamentals of good musicianship.

4. To provide a background for further intensive study of the piano and other music instruments.

Suggested activities:

1. Play by ear favorite melodies in several different keys.
2. Use these familiar melodies to emphasize important aspects of general musicianship.
3. Learn the primary chords in the keys generally used in elementary song texts, G–D–A–E–C–F–B♭–E♭–A♭.
4. Use these chords to make simple accompaniments to familiar songs.
5. Elementary piano materials may be used with the classroom music texts.[1]

Expected outcomes:

1. An understanding of the keyboard and the ability to play simple melodies.
2. Ability to accompany the songs that require only the I, IV, and V chords.
3. Ability of most children to play and transpose into many keys.
4. Better understanding of notation and the ability to read music independently.
5. Development of self-expression according to individual capacities.
6. Development of discrimination in listening.
7. Stimulation of desire to continue piano study.
8. Use of piano background as a foundation for study in vocal and instrumental groups.

Elective Piano Classes

These classes are designed for specific training in pianistic skills to develop ability to perform in a musically satisfying manner. Expected achievements and lesson outlines may be found in the *Handbook for Teaching Piano Classes.*[2]

Junior High School Level of Instruction. Beginning piano classes also have an important place in the junior high school music program. Grades seven through nine should have an intensified development of the piano study begun on the elementary level. Suggestions for procedures and materials may be found in the *Handbook for Teaching Piano Classes.*[3]

Senior High School Level of Instruction. Three levels of study in the high school seem desirable—beginning, intermediate, and advanced. A reading knowledge of the repertory of the other students in the class should be emphasized and ensemble playing should be stressed. Materials and suggested achievements through four semesters may be found in the *Handbook for Teaching Piano Classes.*[4]

HIGHER EDUCATION—
AREAS OF INSTRUCTION AND EXPECTED ACHIEVEMENTS
For Piano Teachers and Performers

Performance:

1. Facility in sight reading, harmonizing, improvising, transposing, and accompanying.
2. Musically satisfying performance of standard piano literature.

---

[1] Refer to *Handbook for Teaching Piano Classes* (Chicago: Music Educators National Conference, 1952), p. 58.
[2] *Ibid.*, pp. 49-59.
[3] *Ibid.*, pp. 61-63.
[4] *Ibid.*, pp. 64-73.

Further knowledge and skills required of piano teachers:

1. Knowledge of the learning process and skill in effective teaching procedures.
2. Skill in planning and implementing a progressive sequence of music study, and in selecting appropriate teaching materials.
3. Skill in encouraging the creative impulse toward music.
4. Skill in evaluating musical achievement of students.
5. Skill in working effectively and dynamically with individuals and groups.

For Supervisors, Consultants, Coordinators, and Directors of School Music—Vocal, Instrumental, General

Facility in sight reading, harmonizing, improvising, transposing, and accompanying:

1. Sight reading community songs, simple vocal and instrumental accompaniments, rhythmic activity accompaniments, choral scores.
2. Harmonizing and improvising accompaniments to songs requiring I, IV, V chords and simple modulations.
3. Transposing these accompaniments to other keys.

For Preschool and Elementary Classroom Teachers

1. Facility in using the piano as a resource instrument in the general music program to illustrate pitch relations, rhythmic patterns, basic harmonies, and expressiveness, and to encourage the creative impulse toward music. This use of the piano is called "keyboard experience."
2. Additional facility at the piano is recommended for teachers in these early grades because of the many uses a creative teacher finds for the piano while enriching the children's daily classroom experience in music and other subjects.

For Other College Students

Offer service courses to meet the various needs of:

1. Physical education and recreation students.
2. General college students.
3. Special college students.
4. Students enrolled in extension courses.
5. Others in the college community.

Piano study is considered by many teachers of band and orchestra instruments as a necessary preliminary to the study of other instruments. Many instrumentalists state that piano training aids in such items as (a) finger manipulation, (b) hands together, (c) rhythmic transfer, (d) theory and harmony, and (e) the feeling for cadence. To be successful, students must listen, and piano study develops listening.

The potentialities of group piano instruction are beginning to be better understood. There are numerous stories of the success of group piano instruction with the physically and emotionally handicapped, with the gifted child, and with adults. Principals of elementary schools have sought the help of the class piano teacher in working with all types of exceptional children and the results have been most gratifying. Adult classes have become an important part of the adult education programs in many cities.

Piano classes are now an accepted part of the great instrumental program in music education.

193

EXTENSION OF PIANO INSTRUCTION IN OTHER AREAS

Radio and Television.[1] Radio and television have played an important part in a plan to educate the general public concerning the advantages of group piano instruction. Both mediums have been used to present demonstrations of class piano methods, to present persons in interviews who are authorities on group piano instruction, and to present distinguished groups of panelists who have discussed the place of class piano in American education.

On the first educational television station at the University of Houston, group piano instruction was given as a telecourse which carries credit in applied music as required by the Texas State Department of Education. Students also may take the course for their own enjoyment without credit. Students who take the course for credit attend seminars twice a month on the college campus. The course allows three hours of college credit and costs $40.00 for enrollment which includes material in mimeographed form. The fee for those taking the course without credit is $10.00, and this includes all of the music in mimeographed form which is mailed to the students weekly. The music includes more than 100 different easy arrangements of all types of music.

The telecourse is presented with four students at two pianos in a demonstration class, and viewers simply join the class in the privacy of their own home. The students have no inhibitions about trying new things which may be suggested during the lesson, which makes for an ideal teaching situation. Interest in these lessons has increased daily and enrollments continue to increase.

Entire families have been taking the course. It is not unusual for mother, father, and daughter to sit at the piano together and follow the telecourse. One father has been taking the course with his two sons, aged 11 and 13, respectively.

An interesting development is the fact that students taking the telecourse have made considerably more progress than those taking a similar course on the campus. It is no longer an experiment. The fact that piano can be taught successfully over television is a reality.

Audio-Visual. Tape and wire recorders are important tools in developing discriminating listening and, as such, have been used in piano classes for years. Listening to recordings of fine pianists can serve as a model and set up goals of attainment. Film strips of class activities are interesting to make. They provide a happy correlation with other school activities and give an opportunity for excellent integration.

Piano Festivals.[2] Piano festivals are held every year in various states. The piano festival affords group participation to the student comparable to performing in an orchestra or band. Multiple pianos are used and the music is usually chosen from duos, trios, quartets, two-piano arrangements for four hands, and two-piano arrangements for eight hands.

The festival may be merely an ensemble program presented annually in a school where class piano is taught. It may be an all-ensemble program including groups from all of the schools of a city, presented as a part of the spring programs of the music education department. Some festivals have featured parent-and-child teams. Sometimes there is a guest artist as soloist. One festival had several teachers and a professional pianist of the community playing on multiple pianos.

The festival may be sponsored by a music teachers association; e.g., the Southern California School Piano Association which sponsors a festival each spring in Los

---

[1] By George Stout, Houston, Texas, member of National Committee on Piano Instruction.
[2] By Marjorie T. Sellers, Phoenix, Arizona, California-Western Division Co-chairman, Music in American Education Committee on Piano Instruction.

Angeles. It may be sponsored by a piano dealer as at the festival in San Diego which is presented each fall. It may be a real community project representing a joint effort of several piano dealers and the local music teachers association as is done in Phoenix, Arizona. In some cases the festival director is a teacher in the community, or a guest conductor from out of town may be engaged. Piano dealers may cooperate by providing rehearsal facilities in their showrooms and lending pianos for the concert.

Another project of joint effort was the Mass Piano Festival with thirty communities, 300 pianists, fifty schools, several colleges, and a guest artist all participating in Fond du Lac, Wisconsin. The public school music department of Fond du Lac and its Parent School Music Association, with the cooperation of the Fond du Lac County Piano Teachers Association, the State Department of Education, the Music and Extension Departments of the University of Wisconsin, and the Wisconsin School Music Association presented the festival on a Saturday evening and Sunday afternoon. The program had variety with a choral group from one of the colleges, a trumpet solo, a vocal duet, and a fine pianist as guest artist.

Milwaukee, Chicago, New Rochelle (New York) and numerous other cities have presented a piano ensemble program or festival annually for many years as a part of the regular music education department projects of the city schools.

This group activity seems to offer valid educational advantages to the pupils. There is the incentive to qualify for an ensemble, the discipline of following a conductor's baton, the development of the listening ear, and the quickening awareness of rhythmic flow. It provides a means of developing excellent musicianship which is lacking in solo performance. If the programs are planned to show progressive levels of accomplishment, the pupil's horizons are broadened and his musical life is enriched. The cooperation of school piano teachers and studio teachers should be a means of promoting professional ethics and morale. Working together on a common project brings mutual confidence and respect.

CLASS PIANO FOR MUSIC EDUCATION STUDENTS[1]

It has been found that pre-teaching experience in functional piano accompanying for school music is of great assistance to all students of music education. Such accompanying requires an application not usually stressed in the formal piano lessons. A course, Class Piano for Music Education Majors, has been offered as a prerequisite to directed teaching. Music education students of junior standing with a background of four semesters of harmony and solfeggio, as well as a fair degree of piano facility, are admitted. The course is primarily for music education majors, although general education students who can meet the prerequisites in harmony and piano are welcomed. Panel examinations for each member of the class at the end of the eighteen weeks' session determine his ability to enter directed teaching in the field of music.

Class Organization. A class composed of fifteen students simulates many school music situations in which each student may practice the techniques of accompanying; *i.e.*, classroom music participation; the rehearsal of a vocal score with piano as a tool; a string or wind instrument sight-reading session with piano; student soloists, both vocal and instrumental, offering their services to class-member accompanists.

The musical-technical problems thus encountered includes harmonization at sight, suitable improvisation of accompaniments for a wide variety of folk music,

[1] Description of a course at the University of Southern California, contributed by Dorothy Bishop, California-Western Division Co-chairman, Music in American Education Committee on Piano Instruction.

music reading of typical accompaniments and vocal scores, transposition, and the abilities to "lead from the piano" or follow the soloist as the situation requires.

Final Panel Examinations. The final examination covers the following: (a) Harmonization of a melody at sight; (b) sight reading; (c) transposition of a simple two-staff score; (d) accompaniment for a singer or player; (e) free style accompaniment for a folksong; (f) playing from four-staff score (instrumentalists excepted); (g) playing The Star-Spangled Banner from memory.

Publications by the MENC Piano Instruction Committee[1]

Handbook for Teaching Piano Classes, MENC Piano Instruction Committee, 1952. $1.50.
Piano Instruction in the Schools. Report of a Survey, edited by William R. Sur, 1949. $1.00.
Piano in School by Raymond Burrows, 1949. 25¢.
Calling All Piano Teachers by Fay Templeton Frisch, 1949. 25¢.
Social Implications of Piano Study by John Crowder, 1949. 15¢.
The Advanced Piano Class by Raymond Burrows, 1947. 10¢.
Traveling the Circuit with Piano Classes, edited by Raymond Burrows, 1949. 50¢.

Organ Instruction in the Schools[2]

The opportunity for the study of organ should be made available to junior and senior high school students. It is felt that pupils with third-grade piano ability progress faster, but beginners in music have learned to play the organ. Organ classes during the school time are favored; thus the class becomes a part of the regular curriculum and is a recognized school subject with appropriate credit.

Qualifications of the Class Organ Teacher. A teacher of organ must be physically fit, have an attractive personality radiating hope, courage, and cheerfulness; have sincerity and assurance; have a broad musical knowledge; have at least a Bachelor of Music degree with special training in organ and modern methods for teaching organ.

There should be a well-organized plan of procedure which is followed. There should be definite goals to be reached by the pupils by a certain time and the teacher must know the orderly steps to reach these goals. An alert organ class teacher will develop a department which is indispensable to the school and community.

INCLUSION OF ORGAN CLASSES WITHIN THE SCHOOL PROGRAM

Three outstanding factors affect and determine the inclusion of organ classes within the school program. They are:

(1) *The Lack of Teachers Trained to Teach Class Organ.* There have been no methods established as yet for such classes. The closest approach to such methods are those utilized in piano class instruction. Until organ class methods are developed and established these should continue to be adapted.

No teacher-training colleges provide for instruction in how to teach class organ. Some music schools have classes in organ methods but these are for teaching organ privately.

Teaching class organ is not a new area. As many as twenty-five years ago the great Lynnwood Farnam taught his best pupils, who are now our most outstanding organ concert artists and teachers, by class organ methods. He instructed from three to five at a time, on an advanced level which is much more difficult than that of beginners.

---

[1] Available from Music Educators National Conference.
[2] From the report submitted by Katherine Fowler, Washington, D. C., National Chairman, Music in American Education Committee on Organ Instruction.

(2) *The Lack of Available Literature in the Field.* All teaching material for organ is based on private instruction. This material can be adapted, but instruction books written especially for class organ would greatly facilitate teaching. Such a fertile field should interest compilers and music publishers.

(3) *Lack of Instruments.* Of the three factors, the lack of instruments is the smallest need. In a recent survey of five hundred cities, thirty per cent of the secondary schools offered organ instruction. In the schools where organ was taught, ninety per cent used electronic instruments. With the advent of the electronic organ many more organ classes undoubtedly will open. The price range is within the budget of the larger school districts, and such related organizations as the Parent Teacher Associations have in several instances added this instrument for the use of their children.

Such factors as an overcrowded auditorium schedule, with patience and understanding, can be adjusted. Schedules which permit organ classes, organ practice, band and orchestra practice, play and assembly practice, can all be developed cooperatively. The benefit to the school and community from the inclusion of class organ instruction surpasses the inconvenience in making such a schedule.

OUTCOMES OF ORGAN CLASS INSTRUCTION

(1) Pupils enjoy organ study and will continue it over a period of years if they are taught adequately and have many opportunities to play.

(2) Performance before the class develops confidence; group training initiates a sense of belonging and teaches older members of the class to assist new members; caring for the instrument, locking it, turning the motor on and off, putting the keys away, etc., develops a sense of responsibility and an appreciation of the value of property.

(3) Young organists should be encouraged to use their skills on the organ whenever possible, at school assemblies, shows, recitals, at church for youth organizations, and for friends.

(4) All organ classes should be related not only to the school music program but to other school activities, such as background music for assembly programs, plays, and pageants.

(5) The study of organ is an aid to physical coordination because it involves the mind, the eyes, the hands, and the feet.

(6) The practical use of foreign languages is aided by the study of organ literature since much of the organ repertoire has instructions for registration in either French or German.

(7) Cooperation with local private organ teachers leads to a better understanding of modern teaching procedures.

(8) Talent may be discovered through the organ class. Many a pupil who has started the class in curiosity has continued study of organ privately or in music conservatories.

(9) Reading ability can be developed in organ classes where modern methods are employed. Horizontal or voice reading, as well as vertical or chord reading, must be developed in organ playing. Phrasing, chord progression, the repeated figure such as appears in the chorale prelude, the recognition of sequence, repetition, and contrast are all essential to good reading.

(10) Creative talents may be developed through instruction in improvisation. Using the I, IV, V, I chord pattern with an A, B, A form gives a good beginning in keyboard improvisation.

(11) Technical facility is developed to a higher level if the teacher demonstrates the need for such in the learning of organ literature. All organ students should be

encouraged to continue piano study while learning the organ so as to keep a flexible finger technique.

(12) Interpretative powers should be developed through class performance and constructive criticism. The exchange of ideas in class increases interpretative resourcefulness and encourages others.

(13) Memorization can be encouraged by group learning through organized methods of memorizing, opportunities to hear and think through a piece played by someone else, and the many repetitions of a piece played for class during the learning process.

(14) Pupils learn to play by ear, to harmonize at sight, and to improvise which can be used at home and elsewhere.

(15) Constant survey of improved teaching materials should be exercised by the class organ teacher in order to select the best of the old and the new sources to develop organ skills.

(16) Regular meetings of organ teachers should be held for the discussion of teaching problems and for the observation of good teaching procedures.

(17) It is suggested that colleges and conservatories develop in their organ departments a course for the teaching of class organ methods, and that many teachers of organ attend such a course to refresh and extend their professional equipment.

(18) Class organ lessons provide experience for children whose parents can not afford the cost of expensive organ instruction. Short lessons, short assignments, with short practice time require intense concentration during the time spent at the console and results in worthy achievement.

(19) Adults may be encouraged to study in organ class, either as beginners or for refresher courses.

(20) Opportunities should be utilized by the class organ teacher to present her pupils in auditions and festivals. These functions help maintain high standards of solo performances and further a universal interest in the instrument.

Survey of Organ Instruction in the Public Schools. In the spring of 1953 five hundred questionnaires were sent to selected schools, and on the basis of 107 replies, the following facts were revealed:

63% have pipe organs.

90% have electronic organs.

2.7% have organs but do not use them.

43 senior high schools have organs.

3 junior high schools have organs.

10 schools have organs which are used but provide no instruction.

28% have organ instruction in the schools.

In these schools 93% have organ instruction on school time.

57% receive credit.

98% provide for practice at school.

On the basis of this questionnaire it may be concluded that organ is being taught in the public schools; that credit is being given for the course; that most students studying organ practice at school; that all schools having organs do not utilize them to the fullest; that there are more electronic organs available than pipe organs; and that senior high school seems to be the logical place for class organ instruction in the public schools.

198

Compositions for Organ With Other Instruments[1]

Organ and Brass Quartet
    Bridge, F. *Flower of the Forest*. London: Hawkes and Son, 1919.
Organ and Trumpet Quartet
    Chladel, H. C. *Poem Fantasy*. Library of Congress, 1922.
Organ, Trumpets, Trombones and Timpani
    Karg-Elert, S. *Wunderbar Koenig*. London: Novello & Co.
    ————. *Chaconne*. London: Novello & Co., 1910.
    Reger, M. *Nun Danket Alle Gott*. New York: Associated Music Publishers, Inc.
Organ, Trombone and Tympani
    Strauss, Richard. *Festival Procession*. New York: C. F. Peters.
Organ and French Horn
    Homelius. *Chorale Prelude*. Library of Congress.
    Alfven, H. *Notturno eleguiaco*. Stockholm: Gehrmans, 1952.
Organ and Oboe (trumpet)
    Krebs, J. *Eight Chorale Preludes*. New York: Music Press, 1947.
    Miller, K. *Andante religioso*. Leipsig: Mersburgen, 1927.
Organ and Trumpet
    Purcell, H. *Ceremonial Music*. New York: Music Press, 1946.
Organ and Flute
    Gullon, N. *Recueillement*. Paris: Leduc, 1951.
Organ and English Horn
    Sowerby, L. *Ballade*. New York: H. W. Gray Co., Inc., 1950.
Organ and Violin
    Antonii, P. *Sonatas*. Zurich: Baumgartner, 1947.
    Besselaar, J. *Four Vielles Chansons*. Amsterdam: Seyardts, 1922.
    Reger, M. *Maria Wiegenlied*. New York: Associated Press Pub.
    ————. *Largo*, Op. 93. New York: Associated Press Pub.
    ————. *Aria*, Op. 103A, No. 3. New York: Associated Press Pub.
Organ and Cello
    Klongel, J. *Andante sostenuto*, Op. 51. New York: Breitkofpt & Hartel, 1946.
    Reger, Max. *Aria*, Op. 103, No. 3. New York: Associated Press Pub.
Organ and Viola
    Sowerby, Leo. *Poem*. New York: H. W. Gray Co., Inc., 1947.
Organ and Viola d'amour
    Martin, F. *Sonata da chiesa*. Vienna: Universal Ed., 1952.
Organ and Harp
    Arne, Thomas. *6 Favorite Concertos* (instrumental parts). London: Harrison, 1787.
    Grandjany, M. *Aria*. Library of Congress.
    ————. *Fantasie Chorale*. Library of Congress.
    Pinto, A. *Album of Duo's*. New York: International Music Pub. Co., 1922.
Organ and Ensembles
    Albinoni, Thomas. *Trio Sonata* (2 violins, cello, continuo). Vienna: Wissenschaft & Kunst, 1952.
    Bach, J. S. *Sheep May Safely Graze* (organ and strings). New York: H. W. Gray Co., Inc., 1944.
    Bachman. *Ave Maria* (organ, harp, violin, cello). Paris: Care Silva, 1914.
    Bingham, Seth. *Concerto*, Op. 57. 1953.
    Bossi, E. *Concert Study*, Op. 130 (organ and string orchestra). Leipsig: Reuter, 1938.
    Braunfels, Walter. *Concerto* (3 trumpets, bass, posaune, paube) (gross tromme and string orchestra). Library of Congress, 1928.
    Casella, A. *Concerto Romano* (organ, strings, timpani). Leipsig: Universal Ed., 1938.
    Ciampi-Lyrinzis. *6 Concertos* (organ, 2 violins, figured bass). London: Walsh, 1760.
    Coerne, Louis. *Concert Stuck in E Maj.* (organ, string orchestra, 3 horns, 2 harps). Library of Congress, 1892.
    Dubois, T. *Nuptual Hymn* (violin, alto, cello, harp, organ). Paris: Hugel, 1892.
    Felton, W. *Concerto in B Flat No. 3* (organ, string orchestra, and oboes). New York: H. W. Gray Co., Inc., 1942.
    Heidrich, Max. *Concerto in F Minor* (organ and small ensemble). Leipsig: Leuchart, 1911.
    Hindemith, P. *Concerto*, Op. 46, No. 2. Mainz: Schotte Sohne, 1928.
    Holler. *Concerto* (organ and chamber orchestra). Leipsig: Leuchart, 1932.
    Marcello, B. *Psalm XIX.*
    Miller, J. I. *Concerto*, Op. 20 (organ, 2 violins, viola, bass viol, 2 clarinets, horn, clarini, timpani). Library of Congress, c.a. 1800.
    Mozart, W. A. *3 Organ Sonatas, Nos. 9, 13, 15* (2 violins, organ, string orchestra). New York: Music Press, 1942.
    Parker, H. *Concerto* (organ, strings, brass, harp, drums). London: Novello & Co., 1923.
    Poulenc, F. *Concerto in G Minor* (organ, string orchestra, timbales). Paris: Deiss, 1939.
    Saint-Saens, C. *Lauriers* (organ and chamber orchestra). Paris: Durand, 1919.
    Salome, Th. *Berceuse* (string quartet and organ). Paris: Leduc, 1902. Weber, Karl. *Adagio and Rondo*. Berlin: Simon, 1897.

---

[1] Prepared by Katherine Fowler.

Organ and Full Orchestra
  Bach, J. S. *Cantato Sinfonie*. Mainz: Schotte Sohne, 1943.
  Bingham, Seth. *Concerto*, Op. 46.
  Copland, A. *Symphony*. L. C., 1924.
  Degan, H. *Konzert*. New York: Associated Music Publishers.
  Demesseux, J. *Poem*. Paris: Durand, 1952.
  Dupre, M. *Concerto in E Minor*, Op. 31. Paris: Bornemann.
  Gubstosi, E. *Chorale Sinfoniso*. Milan: Carisch, 1946.
  Guilmant, A. *Symphony No. 1*. Library of Congress.
  Handel, G. *6 Organ Concertos*. London: Preston and Smith.
  ——————. *Concertos 4-7-9*. London: Augener & Co.
  ——————. *Concerto 4*. Mainz: Schotte Sohne.
  Harwood, Basil. *Concerto D Major*. New York: Novello & Co., 1910.
  Hayn, K. *Introduction & Chaccone*. New York: Breitkoft & Hartel, 1916.
  Jongen, J. *Concerto*. Brussels: Cranz, 1932.
  Lefebvre, C. *Meditation*. Paris: Mackar.
  Miller, J. *6 Variations*, Op. 65 and 24. Library of Congress.
  Mozart, W. *Adagio & Rondo*. *The Glass Harmonica*. Library of Congress.
  Schroeder, H. *Concerto*, Op. 25. New York: Associated Music Publishers, 1939.
  Sowerby, L. *Medieval Poem* (women's or boys' voices in score). New York: H. W. Gray Co., Inc.
  Stohr, R. *Symphonies Fantasie*. Leipsig: Siegel, 1912.
  Vierne, L. *Adagio* (3rd Organ Symphony). Paris: Durand, 1927.
  Widor, C. *Sinfonia Sacra*. Paris: Hamille.
  Yon, P. *Concerto Gregoriano*. New York: J. Fischer & Bro., 1921.
  Zeuner, C. *Organ Concerto*. Library of Congress.
Organ and Piano
  Clokey, J. *Symphonic Piece* (5 movements). New York: J. Fischer & Bro.
  Demarest, C. *Ave Maria*. New York: H. W. Gray Co., Inc., 1946.
  ——————. *Rhapsody*. New York: G. Schirmer, Inc., 1925.
  Dupre, M. *Ballade*. New York: H. W. Gray Co., Inc., 1933.
  ——————. *Sinfonia*. New York: H. W. Gray Co., Inc., 1947.
  ——————. *Variations*. New York: H. W. Gray Co., Inc., 1938.
  Elmore, R. *Venite Adoremus*. New York: J. Fischer & Bro., 1951.
  Gershwin, G. *Rhapsody in Blue*. New York: Harms. 1945.
  Handel, G. *Hallelujah Chorus* and *Overture to the Messiah*. Dayton, Ohio: Lorenz Publishing Co.
  Kohlmann. *Silent Night*. Dayton, Ohio: Lorenz Publishing Co.
  Larson, E. *Dutes*. Rockville Center, N. Y.: Belwin, Inc., 1952.
  Lorenz, J. *Chancel Duets*. Dayton, Ohio: Lorenz Publishing Co., 1943.
  ——————. *Organ and Piano Duets*, Nos. 1 & 2.
  Malotte, A. *Lord's Prayer*. New York: G. Schirmer, Inc., 1950.
  Neidlinger. *The Birthday of a King*. Dayton, Ohio: Lorenz Publishing Co.
  Smith, E. *First Organ & Piano Duet Album*. New York: Ethel Smith Music Corp., 1952.
  ——————. *Second Organ & Piano Duet Album*. New York: Ethel Smith Music Corp., 1952.
  ——————. *Christmas Music*. New York: Ethel Smith Music Corp., 1952.
  ——————. *Easter Music*. New York: Ethel Smith Music Corp., 1953.
  Sowerby, L. *Classic Concerto*. New York: H. W. Gray Co., Inc., 1949.
Organ Duets
  Dickinson and Lockwood. *Organ Duets*. New York: H. W. Gray Co., Inc., 1927.
  Lorenz. *Sacred Concert Duets*. Dayton, Ohio: Lorenz Publishing Co.

Bibliography

MAGAZINES

The Diapason, Chicago, Illinois.
The American Organist, New York, New York.
The Hammond Times, Chicago, Illinois.
The Organist, Dayton, Ohio.

METHODS

Baranoski, S. *Organ Playing Made Easy*. Park Ridge, Ill., 1950.
Barnes, E. *School of Organ Playing*. Boston: Boston Music Co., 1921.
Cannon, T. *The Organists Manual*. Salt Lake: Deseret Book Co., 1952.
Carstens, H. *A Brochure for Young Organists*. Mason City, Iowa: Vance Music Co., 1951.
Crawford, J. *Organ Courses In the Popular Style of Organ Playing On the Hammond Organ*. New York: J. Crawford Organ Pub. Ascher, 1949.
Dickinson, C. *The Technique of Organ Playing*. New York: H. W. Gray Co., Inc., 1922.
Dupre, M. *Seventy-nine Chorales for the Organ*, Op. 28. New York: H. W. Gray Co., Inc., 1932.
Eigenschenk, E. *Organ Jazz*. Chicago: Fulco Organ Studies, 1927.
Gaumer, V. *How To Play Popular Piano Music on the Organ*. New York: Bregman, 1948.
Gleason. H. *Method of Organ Playing*. Rochester, N. Y.: Eastman School of Music, 1949.
Jennings, A. *First Elements of Organ Techniques*. New York: M. Whitmark & Sons, 1947.
Koeb, J. *Home Study for Pipe, Reed and Electronic Organ*. New York: U.S. School of Music, 1952.
Salvador, M. *Method of Organ Playing*. Toledo, Ohio: Gregorian Institute, 1949.
Stainer, J. *The Hammond Organ*. Bryn Mawr, Pa.: Theodore Presser Co., 1943.
——————. *Easy Organ Method*. Dayton, Ohio: Lorenz Publishing Co., 1952.

IMPROVISATION

Schlieder, F. F. *Improvisation at the Organ.* Decatur, Ill.: Church Music Foundation, 1949.
Stubington, H. *Practical Extemporization.* London: Epworth Press, 1940.
Whilmer, T. *The Art of Improvisation.* New York: M. Whitmark & Sons., 1941.

PEDAL STUDIES

Bach, J. Coates. *Bach Technique of Organ Pedaling.* London: Ashdown Ltd., 1953.
Buck, D. *Studies in Pedal Phrasing.* New York: G. Schirmer, Inc., 1895.
Dunham, R. *Pedal Mastery.* Bryn Mawr, Pa.: Theodore Presser Co., 1951.
Dupre, M. *Pedal Scales for Organ.* Paris: Leduc, 1924.
Nevin, G. *Twenty-five Advanced Pedal Studies.* Bryn Mawr, Pa.: Oliver Ditson Company, 1929.
————. *Swell Pedal Technique.* Bryn Mawr, Pa.: Theodore Presser Co., 1924.
Peeters, F. *Ten Pedal Studies* (air and variations). Boston: McLaughlin Reilly, 1946.
Sheppard, E. *Pedal Studies for Organ.* Bryn Mawr, Pa.: Theodore Presser Co., 1924.

SERVICE PLAYING

Christensen, G. *A Direct Approach to Service Playing.* Library of Congress. MT180.C5
Conway, M. *Church Organ Accompaniment.* London: Canterbury Press, 1952.
Lochner, M. *The Organists Hand Book* (guide to Lutheran service playing on small pipe organ, reed organ). St. Louis: Concordia, 1937.
Lovet, S. *The Use of Small Church Organs.* London: Oxford Press, 1953.

TRANSCRIBING AND TUNING

Bryant, N. *Tuning, Care and Repair of Reed and Pipe Organs.* Battle Creek, Mich: Niles Bryant School of Piano Tuning.
Ellingford, H. *The Art of Transcribing for the Organ.* New York: H. W. Gray Co., Inc., 1922.

STOPS

Audsley, G. *Organ Stops and Their Artistic Registration.* New York: H. W. Gray Co., Inc., 1921.
Boyd, C. *Organ Accompaniment and Registration.* Bryn Mawr, Pa.: Theodore Presser Co., 1932.
Grudin, M. *The Well-Tempered Hammond Organ.* Paterson, N. J.: Music Textbook Co., 1953.
Nevin, G. *A Primer of Organ Registration.* Bryn Mawr, Pa.: Oliver Ditson Company, 1920.

CHAPTER XXI

VOCAL MUSIC IN THE SCHOOLS[1]

CHORAL MUSIC can effectively provide that means of self-expression which every individual keenly needs and afford an opportunity for real social development. Group participation in choral singing can give the shy individual confidence and self-assurance necessary to make him an effective member. Such participation gives poise, develops an ability to appear at ease in public, and can make it possible for the student to operate effectively as a member of society.

The out-giving individual can come to know through choral performance the joy which is possible in group activity; can be made aware of the necessity of the individual to merge his own personality with that of the group, and can be taught the spirit of cooperation and group feeling. Choral activities provide not only for the development of individual leadership and initiative, but offer, in an equally unique fashion, a means whereby individual ability can be made to contribute to the achievement of the group as a whole.

Further, the choral group provides a channel through which all of the streams of our culture can mingle. Through the mutual joy which all participants in singing can experience, there comes voluntarily and without compulsion a tolerance and sympathy for other members of the group, an awareness which all men, of whatever race or creed, can experience in mutual enterprise.

Choral methods and procedures should be adapted to fit a changing situation, but the basic values must be retained. These basic values may be listed as (a) the enrichment of the life of the individual through vocal musical experience, and (b) the development of vocal skills and techniques which will enable the individual to use to the utmost of his ability his own aptitude for music.

School choral organizations have a responsibility not only to the individuals within the group, but also to the school itself and to the community at large. Choral groups should provide the school and the community with the opportunity of singing, hearing and becoming acquainted with fine choral literature. They should provide experience in fine music for audience, as well as participants. With an educational viewpoint on the part of the director, school music groups can do much to raise the standard of music throughout the community, as well as develop the child through the use of vocal music.

The Elementary School

While singing, listening, rhythms, playing and creative activities are all a part of the elementary music program, the first of these activities to become a part of regular school was singing. Singing is first for many reasons—because it can be started easily at any time; because very little preparation is required; because all pupils can so readily participate and because little equipment is needed.

Singing in the elementary schools emphasizes enjoyment. This does not mean boisterous, forced singing. Rather it means the pleasing, "floaty" tone of the child voice which comes naturally when the voice is not exploited. Young voices are not to be subjected to voice training devices which unthinking adults sometimes try to use with children.

---

[1] From the report submitted by Alex H. Zimmerman, San Diego, California, National Chairman, Music in American Education on Vocal Music in the Schools.

The problem of "uncertain singers" (not monotones) may be present. These are simply the children who need extra help. It is important not to set these children apart as being different from the others, but rather lead them patiently to achieve a successful finding of their voices.

The field of music materials is replete with countless basic and supplementary music texts well suited to elementary singing.

NOTE: Consult index for other elementary school material.

The Junior High School

The junior high school vocal music program includes general music classes, girls' and boys' glee clubs, and small ensembles. Mixed choruses are found particularly in the three-year junior high school.

Girls' groups adapt well to two- and three-part arrangements where the alto part is not too low.

The boys' glee club is composed of unchanged, changing, and changed voices. In the three-year junior high schools three- and four-part materials in varying arrangements should be used and carefully chosen for voice ranges.

The Changing Voice. There have been varying concepts concerning the potential of the changing voice of the boy. The psychological and physiological changes taking place in the adolescent boy present a unique situation. A valid concept must be based on the inherent qualities of the boy's voice itself inasmuch as the scope, range, and potential of this voice has already been determined by nature.

Several points of view related to the changing voice are presented here for consideration.

(1) "The voice of the junior high school boy has been considered a problem because the singing of boys preceding junior high school age has been developed *en masse*, while the voice of each boy in junior high school is an individual problem and must have individual attention. Junior high school boys vary considerably in size and physical development, and for that reason their voices should be classified into at least four divisions.

"Usually, boys from ten to twelve years of age, who are not overgrown, sing either soprano or second soprano, a soprano to *high A* and a second soprano not lower than *middle C*. These same boys, not overgrown, usually develop into altos at thirteen, and into rich alto-tenors at fourteen or fifteen. The range of the alto-tenor is likely to be from *middle C* to *two-line G* above *middle C*. This is the short-range period and often a teacher finds a boy who has only five tones in his singing voice at this time. The usual junior high school baritone sings in the *C* octave, although often a teacher finds a boy with a *low G* who is unable to sing *middle C*. Junior high school baritones range in age from thirteen to sixteen. Boy baritones of thirteen are usually overgrown.

"The speaking voice places a boy in one of three groups. He has an unchanged voice of soprano or alto quality; or he has a changing voice which indicates the alto-tenor part; or he has a changed voice which, in junior high school, almost certainly places him in the baritone group. The changed tenor in junior high school is a very rare voice.

"Classifying voices through the speaking voice and through the size and appearance of the boy may seem superficial, but in most cases it is accurate. When a boy moves into adolescence, there is a certain brilliancy which enters his soprano voice for a short period. When the teacher hears that celestial brilliancy coming into the boy's voice, he knows that it will be only a short time before the voice will be lower. That boy must be watched closely and when the first sign of strain or

203

out-of-tune singing appears, he must be moved into the second soprano part. From this time on there should be constant vigilance and reclassification into first alto, second alto, and alto-tenor, until the young baritone voice arrives. The respective ranges of these divisions are approximately as follows: *Soprano*—from *middle C* to *G* above the treble staff; *Alto*—from *B flat* below *middle C* to *D*, fourth line treble staff; *Alto-Tenor*—from *A flat* or *G* below *middle C* to *F*, first space, or *G*, second line treble staff; *Boy-bass*—from *C*, second space, or *B flat*, second line bass staff to *middle C*.

"Alto-tenors often have a very much more limited range than the one given, sometimes being able to sing only a few notes within the stated limits. This is true also of the boy-bass who sings his low tones with ease once the plunge to the lower octave has taken place, but needs to practice to enable him to sing the tones in the upper range indicated.

"The natural tendency of the voice is to sink little by little to a lower range. With the growth of the boy the thyroid cartilage pushes out, making the Adam's apple. The vocal bands are attached to this cartilage and must extend. With their gradual extension, the pitch is lowered. The boy, through this period, not only has a new body to manage, but a new vocal instrument presenting unfamiliar problems. Sensible singing through this period not only develops the voice but furnishes a wholesome means of self-expression so needed at this time.

"Very often the young baritone has a throaty tone to overcome. We must remember he has a new vocal instrument, and the more anxious he is to make beautiful tones the more likely he is to stiffen the base of the tongue. If his attention can be taken from his throat and placed upon his posture, deep breathing, firm abdominal muscles, and correct vowel definition, this throatiness can be avoided. A depressed tongue and rigid jaw always accompany a throaty tone.

"For testing the singing voice, it is wise to use the descending scale with boys who have unchanged voices. The teacher should observe where quality changes. A boy with a changing or changed voice may be asked to suggest the easiest tone in his voice. Using this tone as a starting note of a scale, he may sing as many tones in the ascending scale as are comfortable and consequently pleasant. Then taking his last comfortable tone as a point of departure, he may sing a descending scale.

"When a boy's voice is led carefully into the man's voice, there is no break and therefore there need be no cessation of singing. Indeed, regular vocal exercises to prevent stiffness are desirable through this period. A hoarseness is sure to result if small boys from ten to twelve years of age who possess soprano voices are allowed to force tones down to a low part. Often teachers, led astray by the term junior "high school," have been too eager to make small boys into mature singers. Vocal exercises used for adolescent boys should be similar to those used for beginning adult pupils. First attention should be given to posture—straight spine, firm torso and limbs, and deep breathing.

"If vocal ideals are built in the first seven years of school, a boy will be sufficiently intelligent through the period of voice changing to watch his own voice. The teacher must not shift responsibility, but if her teaching has been efficient, she will have developed many helpers."[1]

(2) One authoritative concept of the adolescent voice is that the boy's voice usually changes gradually, slowly sliding down the scale until it finds its own level.[2]

(3) Another concept classifies the changing voice as "alto-tenor" and restricts the range to about five notes centered around *middle C*.[3]

---

[1] *Music Education Source Book* (Chicago: Music Educators National Conference, 1947), pp. 10, 11.
[2] *Ibid.*, pp. 10, 11.
[3] Lilla Belle Pitts, *Music Integration in the Junior High School* (Boston: C. C. Birchard & Company, 1935), p. 17.

This same source suggests a range of one octave for the baritones and does not list the soprano range because of its great familiarity to all music educators. Thus, taking the suggested alto-tenor and baritone ranges, and the generally accepted soprano range and making an analysis of them, yields a composite unison range of a fourth, *B flat to E*.

(4) Still another author advises that the teacher excuse from singing those boys whose voices are in the process of change,[1] while another authority advises that singing through this period of change can result in decided benefits.[2]

(5) Yet another concept of the changing voice has been termed "Cambiata."[3] This similarly regards the boy's voice, in his pre-adolescent years, as comparable in range, articulation speed, and general characteristics with that of girls (*B flat* below treble staff to *F*, fifth line).

The belief is that in adolescence the boy's voice passes through stages of change. The first stage of this change may be noted by a new vocal range (*F*, fourth line bass staff, to *C*, third space treble staff) with a pronounced retardation of articulation speed and the quality of the voice becoming thicker and perhaps strident.

A second change takes place later (sometimes after only a few months, other times after a year or two) with a new vocal range (*B flat*, second line bass staff, to *F*, first space treble staff), and the vocal articulation speed again slows down. From this point, the boy develops into either a mature tenor or baritone. Every boy does not necessarily move into these exact ranges.

The ranges of the various classifications and the composite unison range becomes a ninth, from *B-flat* below *middle C* to third space *C*, treble staff. A unison song should lie within this range for its best performance by a junior high school vocal group. The slow articulation speed of baritone and Cambiata must also be taken into account when selecting suitable part songs for junior high school students. Further, because of the extended ranges assigned to the male parts, greater possibilities for melodic and polyphonic singing should be realized.

By a thoughtful understanding of the boy's voice during the changing period and a use of material within the limits of these voices, the choral director can develop a very rich and satisfying program for junior high school students. It is recommended that vocal directors familiarize themselves with all research and experimentation available on the changing voice and evaluate it in terms of their own communities, ethnic groups, and school organizations.

The Senior High School

Choral music flourishes in the senior high school because of the growing maturity of the voices and the boundless enthusiasm of youth which can be channeled into meaningful and effective choral experiences.

While the senior high school may have girls' and boys' glee clubs and general choruses, these groups are used not only as very worthwhile musical organizations in themselves, but serve as training groups which may lead to membership in selected choral organizations. The girls' groups usually use three-part and only occasionally four-part material. The boys' glee club functions on a more mature level than in junior high school and should use carefully selected materials which

[1] Grant Parks, *Music for Elementary Teachers* (New York: Appleton-Century-Crofts, 1951), p. 99.
[2] Peter Dykema and Hannah Cundiff, *New School Music Handbook* (Boston: C. C. Birchard & Company, 1939), p. 289.
[3] Irvin Cooper, *Letters to Pat Concerning Junior High School Vocal Music Problems* (New York: Carl Fischer, Inc., 1953). The changing voice range (*G*, fourth line bass staff, to *C*, third line treble staff) has been named "Cambiata" (from the Italian, meaning *changing*) to differentiate it from the range implied by the usual term "alto-tenor."

include unison, *TB, TBB* and *TTBB*. The use of more unison material to achieve greater vocal and technical development and a finer degree of musical understanding is recommended.

It is recommended that all choral directors, experienced as well as novices, explore the wealth of material available. New ideas are being found constantly which can be adapted to the established procedure of even the most experienced director.

The high school choral director should be cognizant of the fact that through physical growth and development, the voices undergo changes. For the protection and welfare of the immature voice constant voice appraisal should take place.

There is a rather general feeling among high school music teachers that the term *a cappella* has had some incorrect usage in high schools. The term should not be regarded as synonymous with *unaccompanied*. Further, it is believed that the *a cappella choirs* in some high schools have excluded the use of a great wealth of accompanied choral music which the high school mixed chorus or choir should be given the privilege of using.

Since music educators and school administrators agree that senior high school choirs can be combined very effectively and easily in music festivals, the type of festival where schools can participate individually and collectively is recommended.

Assembly Singing. The primary purpose of assembly singing should be the immediate enjoyment of it. The assembly sing can serve as a direct contributing force to the growth of the personality and character of each individual student, to his emotional stability, and to his regard for his fellow students.

Since good taste in vocal music increases with participation, the assembly sing can act as a stimulus for the increase of interest and participation in the formal music program of the school. The vocal music educator who will take time for careful planning can make the assembly sing of value to the entire school.

Organization of Choral Groups. The organizational aspects of choral groups in American schools and the routine management of these groups has developed in a most phenomenal way during the past quarter of a century. This high degree of efficiency in organization has come about largely because of the exacting demands an increasingly crowded schedule in the American high school has imposed. More and more has been required in less time than previously, and alert teachers have met the emergencies by increased efficiency.

It has been found that this increased efficiency has made good choirs better, partly from a psychological effect of impressing each individual choir member with the importance of his own individual contribution to the morale and spirit of his group. Young people are quick to sense the loss of time in needless detail and talk. Many choral groups are second rate simply because the director spends too much valuable time in needless and irrelevant talk. The best choirs are those which are singing fifty minutes out of each hour of rehearsal time.[1]

Student Officers and Executive Committee. If the choir is a large organization, a group of student officers and part-leaders will assist greatly in managing the choir. These officers usually consist of president, vice-president, secretary, treasurer, and librarian, and are elected by the group. In addition there should be a part-leader for each section. Since the secretary is charged with the regular routine of roll-taking each day, some directors prefer to appoint this officer. Some use an under-secretary who thus even gains experience to take over the secretary's duties.

It is well for the choir director to reserve the right to choose the part-leaders rather than have them elected. This gives the director the opportunity to appoint individuals who are deserving but who might not be elected.

---

[1] From an article by Truman Hutton. *Music Educators Journal*, February-March 1954, p. 53.

The wise choir director will not have officers elected the first day the choir meets. Rather, he will announce a date, possibly two weeks hence, when an election is to be held. At the first session, and repeatedly until the election, the director should keep before the group the high qualities necessary for a good selection of officers and will thus avoid officers elected by the mere whim of the group.

The officers, together with the part-leaders, form the executive committee which functions as a governing group. Executive meetings should be held during out-of-school hours so as not to interfere with the regular rehearsal schedule of the choir. The executive group may appoint committees as necessary for the regular function of the choir—robe committee, stage committee, hospitality committee, etc. The astute director will find wonderful assistance and encouragement in a good executive group.

Personnel Cards. Choral organizations in a school would do well to adopt a *personnel system* which keeps a cumulative record of choral students as they progress from glee clubs through choir into the alumni group. Upon graduation, the record of the student and his address should become available for future contacts. In some American high schools, overflow attendance at concerts is assured by the easy process of mailing a postal card to the alumni members.

A director maintaining and using a personnel file system becomes more familiar with the students and their individual personalities than any other teacher in the school, which enhances his work as a counselor and guide.

Taking Roll. Rehearsal time should not be used for calling the roll. The secretary merely turns the name card of each member in its respective pocket in the seating chart. When the student returns from his absence and presents proper slips from the attendance office, the card is again placed "face up" by the secretary.

Folio System. The efficiently organized choir will not take rehearsal time to pass and collect music but will use a folio system. Each folio may be numbered and a library sign-out card included so that the student may take the folio home for study by signing the library card and handing it to the librarian at the end of the rehearsal. Two sets of folios, usually of different colors, will avoid confusion. One set contains music of the concert in preparation, while the other may contain sight-reading and other instructional materials.

Choir Materials. In the matter of choral literature in use in American schools, there seems to be quite a general agreement on two important points:

(1) There are too many choirs and choral directors utilizing too few materials. If the same titles are used again and again, year after year, the choral program will stagnate.

It is the opinion of some choral authorities that while certain great pieces of literature are worthy of constant repetition, the list of these immortal works is so great that there is no excuse for repeating a number on the annual Christmas concert for example, each year for four or five successive years. Similarly, choirs have been known to appear at festivals using the same repertoire that was used the preceding year. School administrators question whether or not some choral groups should be a part of the regular curriculum since this needless repetition of music raises a question regarding the educational value of the undertaking.

There is a growing belief that reading techniques and other facets necessary to justify choral groups as a regular part of the curriculum depends upon a coverage of more and better literature.

(2) There is a wealth of fine publications being released constantly. However, the school choral groups must strive to bring to the student the representative literature of all periods as well as the best current materials. The madrigal,

spiritual, anthem, folk song, and standard classic selections, as well as new releases, should be included in the choir repertoire. Judgment should be used in deciding the amount of each type to sing. This decision should be based upon the needs and the background of the group. In program planning, unless it is one with a special theme, a variety of types and styles should be included.

(3) Music to be sung in the schools should have a range and tessitura comfortable and accessible to each individual section of the chorus. The average voice of limited training has a short range in which it can be used with an acceptable quality.

The Welfare of the Voice. In the classification of voices, the welfare of the individual should be placed above the desires for an ambitious performance or for balance of parts within the singing group. All voices should be re-examined or tested frequently, and the director should be willing to shift the individual to another section if such a change seems desirable from the standpoint of the student's vocal welfare.

Choral Techniques. The development of techniques and skills should be maintained in all choral groups. It should be remembered that techniques and skills should be developed not as ends in themselves, but as the means whereby the individual may be able to acquaint himself with a wider range of literature than would be possible without these skills. It is generally agreed that these skills should not be approached as isolated material, but rather in connection with fine literature which is being mastered.

Posture and Breath Support. Since vital, well-balanced body position is the fundamental basis of all singing, it must be maintained in all choral rehearsing. For those who rehearse their groups while seated, careful attention should be given to singing with relaxation posture. The practice of standing during a part of the rehearsal is strongly recommended. Breathing action patterns should be made consistent habits; the functions of inter-costal expansion, lower muscular activity and support, and a vitalized position of the upper chest should be maintained.

Tone Production. If adequate choral performance is to be secured, the choral director should have a definite concept of good choral tone. Careful analysis of syllables, consonants, vowels, and song phrase is a sensible recommendation toward achieving this goal.

Notation and Sight Singing. It is a fallacy to assume that those students who enter high school without the ability to read music cannot develop this skill during the period of the high school career. Good high school directors know how rapidly this skill can be achieved when approached from an aural and visual standpoint. The natural progression and resolution of chords are very practical devices in assisting with sightreading.

It is further believed that the development of music reading as a skill is a continuous process and the astute director uses the regular rehearsal as a constant opportunity to point up and perfect this important skill.

Voice Training Classes. While special voice training classes have been a part of the regular schedule in many American high schools for more than a quarter of a century, the practice is still far from universal. It thus becomes mandatory that many of the technical aspects of singing be given to the student in the regular choral groups. This is being done successfully in many major high schools of the country. A special voice class group formed for out-of-school hours may be successful. Some directors have made voice training classes a part of the procedure of small ensembles chosen from the choral groups.

The Small Ensemble. It is believed that ever-widening opportunities should be provided for selected students, and small ensembles can help to accomplish this.

Even though time on the regular daily schedule may not provide for ensemble classes, teachers throughout the country are taking time to formulate and train small ensemble groups of all kinds.

The girls' triple trio is a very popular combination, using three girls on each part (SSA); thus the group is very flexible, since it can be used as a single, double, or triple trio. Similarly, boys may be selected for double quartets, giving assurance that a single quartet would be available in the event of illness or schedule conflicts. Mixed groups are popular ensembles with the director encouraging double mixed groups.

SUMMARY

An adequate vocal program would achieve the following:

(1) Retain the innate enjoyment for singing and stimulate more active participation in self-expression through the medium of the voice.

(2) Include at the junior and senior high school levels general music classes which will form the foundation for all phases of music participation, and integrate through music, the humanities and the social sciences.

(3) Include further development through more advanced choral groups which will:

—Develop the ability to conduct oneself easily in public and induce tolerance and sympathy for other members of a group by experience in mutual enterprise.

—Develop vocal skills and techniques which will enable the individual to use to the utmost his ability, his own aptitude for music, and permit him to be versed sufficiently in these vocal techniques to take some responsibility for the care of his own voice, improving his own speech and posture habits.

—Utilize the wealth of choral materials for one, two, three, four or more voices—accompanied as well as unaccompanied—of all periods, including some of the best in the current period.

—Provide the student, the school, and the community with opportunities for singing, hearing, and becoming acquainted with an adequate variety of this store of choral literature.

CHAPTER XXII

MUSIC LITERATURE, THEORY, HARMONY, AND COMPOSITION[1]

IT SEEMED EXPEDIENT to clarify the terms used in the title of this area before presenting recommendations. The meanings and extent of the term "music literature" are particularly confused.

Music Literature

Music literature implies all the materials which give one musical experience whether one sings these materials, plays them, listens to them, reads about them, dances to them, creates them, or experiences them in some other way. While the word "materials" is especially confusing, the idea at this point is more important than the word.

Music literature is the medium through which music can be experienced. This involves all categories of participation—performing, listening, creating, and reading music. It includes the music which is performed, read, created, or heard at all age levels, regardless of breadth of experience or development. Literature about music is necessary, important, and helpful to the understanding and appreciation of music.

A study of the word "literature" shows that literature implies the body of writings having to do with a given subject. "Language" is any means, vocal or other, of expressing or communicating a thought. "Culture" which is also implied in this study, is defined as the art of developing by education, discipline, training, etc. It is the enlightenment and refinement of taste acquired by intellectual and aesthetic training. So the study of music implies the study as literature, as a language, and as a culture. In any case, *Music Literature* implies all music experienced.

Further, music literature is described as *music*, good, bad, or indifferent, whatever its purpose, at whatever age, grade, or ability level it is intended to be used.

Experience in music demands music literature whether that literature be the first lullaby which a child hears or the final symphony which a composer writes. Music experienced in the home contributes to the music education of an individual, whether he is a child or an adult. One's experience with music throughout life colors his appreciation of music in general.

In order to experience music, an individual also experiences the literature of music. Therefore, music literature becomes basic in music education if education is based upon experience, whether that education is received at home, in public schools, in private schools, from private teachers, in churches, at concerts, at movies, via radio, television, or recordings, through college or university study, through teacher training or wherever music is experienced. Music experience, *wisely guided*, through performance, study, listening, and creating, should lead to an understanding and appreciation of music.

Music educators have the opportunity to guide individuals into experiences which they would not otherwise investigate. Many music educators appreciate the

---

[1] From the report submitted by Sadie M. Rafferty, Evanston, Illinois, National Chairman, Music in American Education Committee on Music Literature, Theory, Harmony, and Composition.

broad field of music experience which it is possible to bring to students. Others are likely to narrow the field of music experience for the average student because of the limited interest of the educator, because the educator thinks in terms of performance only, or because of time schedules and taxing programs. Most educators are aware of the broad scope but are prevented from going far afield because of many factors which are very real. No doubt with more study and understanding of educational planning in music education, music literature in all its wide areas may be recognized as basic in music education.

At elementary levels, all phases of music may be woven together to emerge as an enjoyable and worth-while musical experience. This requires an ever-broadening background for the teacher. Music literature thus is studied by pupil and teacher in all its phases, as one relates to another, rather than in isolated areas.

At the junior high school level, students are particularly impressionable to music which is closely related to life as they know it or desire it. At this age, boys and girls are very receptive if they are properly approached.

In performance groups, it is possible to widen music experience beyond the music literature which the individuals are capable of performing. Here the teacher must be interested and capable of lending inspiration and guidance. Performance groups would no doubt perform more musically and with more enjoyment because of such experiences. The challenge and experience should have the resultant effect of performance, growth, and musical understanding. This field of music education needs much thought and study to arrive at "ways and means."

At the senior high school level, many students who have to concentrate on careers or college preparation are still interested in music and should have some opportunity for continued experience with music, if only through an audience participation technique. Intelligent listeners are needed.

All colleges, universities and teacher-training institutions should prepare teachers to meet the needs of guidance in music literature which leads to a better understanding and appreciation of music. Furthermore, a good teacher should, throughout his entire teaching experience, continue to broaden his own knowledge of all types of music literature. Music educators, while they are bound to stress their own preference and specialized field, should have as much knowledge and experience as possible in the entire field of music literature.

Is it possible, with able, understanding teaching and guidance, to have a musical America? Some say we have it now. Another says it will take generations. Still another says "only if applied with sufficient power to overwhelm the meretricious influence of music that is heard outside of school." Others might agree that music heard and experienced in school is far from desirable music literature.

Theory, Harmony, and Composition

These terms are not quite as baffling but their usage and development are somewhat controversial. It is possible and highly desirable to teach the theory of music so that technique becomes a fundamental part of an enjoyable musical experience; that enriching and refining all music experiences are the fields of study for theory, harmony, counterpoint, form, style, and composition.

Experience and enjoyment of music should precede the technical approach to music. That is to say the technical approach should not introduce the music experience. However, it is hardly possible to experience music without the technique being present, with or without the knowledge of the individual. Functional music theory should be presented when it may be applied in music experience. Enjoyment should grow from theory, and much depends upon the quality of the musical experience and how music theory is introduced.

If all teachers could guide pupils consistently and wisely through the elementary grades, most pupils would have a fair knowledge of functional theory. Music theory is cumulative and should grow as the pupil progresses from year to year. However, the theory must be related to its practicability and usage, and the fundamentals stressed over and over throughout musical development. As one educator states it, "insofar as the masses of pupils are concerned, we have only to begin at the beginning with each group and proceed a step further." Theory and participation should go hand in hand.

"Making up" music can be a natural expression of music experience. Such a process should start early and its techniques competently developed. The teacher must be a stimulating and wise guide, a person with imagination and initiative.

The development of a harmonic and melodic sense can be introduced very early in music education, in fact as soon as there is an accompaniment to unison singing or when there is part singing or playing. These should be introduced as such when they enter the student's experience. All melodic progressions have their own inherent harmonic basis, and teachers should not be reluctant to give such technical facts their true value.

There is no doubt a level of development, probably no earlier than junior high school and certainly no later than senior high school, when there should be opportunity for the study of theory, harmony, form, style, and composition as an art. The senior high schools and colleges should be particularly interested in this phase. Many experiments and studies are in the process of development.

There is a great need and demand for universities, colleges, and teacher-training institutions to prepare teachers to teach theory, harmony, composition, etc., as an integral part of music as well as an art and skill in itself.

Music educators desire to see basic theoretical courses as a part of the high school curriculum, and a number of high schools over the country successfully offer such courses. The program is started well in many grade school programs, but on entering high school performance is often stressed to the exclusion of other musical values. More basic knowledge of music, properly presented, should give students a carry-over appreciation of music throughout life.

Because theory is a very basic part of music, a technical musical education should result in a greater understanding and appreciation of the best in music.

Recommendations

Since the broad scope of music literature, theory, harmony, and composition embraces the entire field of music, it is suggested that all these areas be included in all other studies and plans.

There are a number of projects which should be beneficial to all music educators and which would be within the province of the Committee on Music Literature, Theory, Harmony, and Composition. The projects suggested are as follows:[1]

(1) A studied listing of "Great Music" which would correspond to a similar study which produced the listing of "Great Books"; "Great Music" at various age levels; a minimum "Great Music" recommended list for grade school teachers.

(2) A study of a broad integration of all phases of music education at various levels; a study of the closer integration of the technical aspect of music with music literature.

---

[1] These items are the outcome of a discussion at the MENC Biennial Convention, Chicago, 1954.

(3) A study for guidance in the selectivity of literature of music.

(4) Suggestions for music for specific purposes.

(5) A bibliography on books concerning music.

(6) Detailed plan for a specific course using music as one of the humanities, using music as the focal point of departure.

(7) Study of learning processes as applied to theory.

(8) A suggested course of study for Theory, Harmony, and Composition classes at high school level.

(9) Cooperation with other areas of music education in studies made by areas represented in this report; a cooperative study with the MTNA of the field of theory teaching.

(10) A study of the place of music literature, theory and composition in American music education, and current practices in these fields, with an end to establishing a basic philosophy of music education covering these fields and recommending a generalized course of study of these elements of music education which should be a part of every educated individual. This study could be approached in the following manner.

—A study of current practices in the teaching of music literature, theory, and composition in American music education with special attention to informal teaching of this material.

—Research, in conjunction with some university or research foundation, into the learning processes of people at all levels in regard to these subjects.

—Assimilation and valuation of the two preceding steps.

—Formulation of a complete program of courses of study embracing these areas so that, as in other fields, the American citizen may be well versed in aesthetics.

Arizona Music Theory and Composition Survey[1]

Questionnaires were sent to all high schools in the state and twenty-nine per cent were returned. On the basis of this data it was felt that a few definite trends toward facts could be established.

(1) There seemed to be no particular correlation between the size of the school and the amount of composition and theory taught, nor did any general area of the state report a dominating amount.

(2) It is the opinion of many of the music educators in the Arizona high schools that most of the theory should be taught through performing groups.

(3) The extent to which theory and composition is being taught depended upon the background of the teacher and not particularly upon the size, facilities, and time available in the particular school.

(4) In reference to the opinion of the teachers as to what should be taught, the following are listed in the order of preference: Knowledge of fundamentals (lines, spaces, key and time signatures, clefs); background of major scale; basic harmony; minor scales; sight singing; classical through romantic periods; preclassical; background of melodic dictation; modern through contemporary music; knowledge of modulation; form and analysis; harmonic dictation.

[1] From the report submitted by Pat B. Curry, Snowflake, Arizona, State Chairman, and Miles Dresskell, California-Western Division Chairman, Music in American Education Committee on Music Literature, Composition, and Theory.

The Function of Music Theory as a Service Course to Music Education[1]

Music theory has this twofold purpose: (a) To supply the novice musician with a sound core of musicianship and knowledge; (b) to equip the potential recipients of degrees in all music fields with a working knowledge of the professional art in which they will teach, perform, or create. The following are suggested as potential aids to the function of music theory:

(1) Increase of sight-reading (individual) training and drill in the ear training and dictation courses.

(2) Keyboard training which will prepare the music student to play the implied harmonic accompaniment to a melody as well as to realize a figured bass exercise at the keyboard.

(3) Combination or collaboration of orchestration with instrumental arranging classes for the music education major in the teaching of theory.

(4) In addition to the use of a freshman entrance test in music fundamentals for the purpose of class organization, sections of basic harmony and ear training courses could be divided as follows.

—Applied music and theory majors from music education majors.

—Students with previous training in piano from those without previous training.

(5) The cooperation of the applied music faculty in defining music terminology, formal patterns, music fundamentals, keyboard accompaniments to melody lines, etc., to the individual student.

(6) The Theory, Applied Music and Music Education departments should develop music graduates who will in turn send back to the colleges, universities, and music conservatories young potential musicians with a firm core of previous musical training.

In order to increase creative motivation for the college music student, the following items should be considered:

(1) The actual reproduction of harmony, counterpoint, and composition exercises in class with the proper medium.

(2) The use of media other than voice and piano for those exercises and creative works from the harmony, counterpoint, and composition classes.

(3) The inclusion of composition with the study of harmony, counterpoint, form and analysis, and orchestration.

(4) An annual or semi-annual student composition program for the public.

(5) The organization of student composition contests with the reward of public recognition and performance and/or cash awards.[2]

---

[1] From the report submitted by Gail de Stwolinski, Norman, Oklahoma, Southwestern Division Chairman, Music in American Education Committee on Music Literature, Composition, and Theory.

[2] Numbers (4) and (5) could apply to high school as well as college.

SECTION SIX

Curricular Resources

Audio-Visual Aids in Music Education
Chairman: Rose Marie Grentzer Spivacke, Washington, D. C.

Films, Slides and Film Strips
Delinda Roggensack, chairman, Mt. Vernon, Iowa

Television and Radio
Richard C. Berg, chairman, Springfield, Mass.

Recordings
William C. Hartshorn, chairman, Los Angeles, Calif.

Audio-Visual Equipment
Wolfgang Kuhn, chairman, Urbana, Ill.

✠

Contemporary Music for American Schools
Chairman: Elizabeth Meloy, Muncie, Ind.

✠

Opera in American Schools
Chairman: Clarke Maynard, Wilmington, Del.

CHAPTER XXIII

AUDIO-VISUAL AIDS IN MUSIC EDUCATION [1]

THE MANY RECENT developments in the field of audio-visual equipment, and to a lesser extent in audio-visual materials, have been remarkable. The interest of music educators has been most gratifying with requests for information revealing an understanding of its utility value in music teaching.

Caution should be used to guard against the use of any audio-visual tool because of its uniqueness, or interest being centered in the tool rather than the educational outcomes as a result of the use of the tool. It should be remembered that the primary work of a music teacher is to teach music to children and the use of any tool should be solely as an aid to improvement of instruction.

The following material deals with basic concepts and facts concerning the use of audio-visual materials and their relationships to the teaching of school music.

Films and Film Strips

The increasing number of fine music films which are being produced is very encouraging. It indicates that music educators are making use of existing films and that producers are cognizant of educational needs and are trying to meet them. The future is limitless for types of films produced or their effective utilization.

Unfortunately, music educators seem to expect even the shortest films to be all-inclusive. They forget that a film is only a "springboard." It is a jumping-off-place for the music teacher to do all the things he wishes the film had done.

Paul E. Long [2] was asked to share some of the questions which were most frequently asked by teachers after a first viewing of music films shown in the Audio-Visual Center at the 1952 MENC Convention, Philadelphia. He replied:

"After each film was shown one heard a variety of 'Why didn't they?' questions. 'Why didn't they show the care of the instrument in greater detail?' 'Why didn't they use another composition for demonstration?' Of course, the 'they' referred to were the film producers. Even though the majority of films shown were made only after thorough consultation with recognized authorities in the field of music, not a single film was used that did not invite vigorous comment and criticism. Perhaps there will never be a music film made that will receive universal approval. And, furthermore, if ten music instructors were asked to write the script for a prospective film, in all probability there would be ten different scripts and each one would possess some merit."

Therefore, the music teacher must be resourceful and always aware that the film is a tool and not an end in itself.

Most music educators have little knowledge about the operation and care of a motion picture projector. Distortion in sound usually is attributed to the sound track. However, the first thing to do is to check the equipment which in most cases needs attention. This is verified in an article by Mr. Long: [3]

---

[1] Material in this chapter, unless otherwise indicated, submitted by Rose Marie Grentzer Spivacke, National Chairman, Music in American Education Committee on Audio-Visual Aids in Music Education.
[2] Paul E. Long, Director, Audio-Visual Department, Philadelphia Public Schools.
[3] *Music Educators Journal*, January 1953, p. 37.

"Some of the films shown had been used in schools for several years. They were not recent productions. We soon became accustomed to the observation: 'I was quite surprised at the sound quality of a film I just saw. When I used it, it was terrible! Did the company send you an especially good copy?' We had to admit it was a print that had been used a good many times in our own school system, and to our knowledge we had not been selected to receive only the best of any producer's line. Projection manufacturers have done everything in their power to improve equipment, but the human factor still exists. If dirt gathers in the sound drum and is not removed, or if threading instructions are not followed carefully, even the most faithful reproduction will be 'terrible'."

Unfortunately, merely servicing equipment is not the complete solution to the problem of poor tonal reproduction. The projector must, in the first place, be adequate, which means that it should meet the minimum specifications.[1] If the buying is done by the audio-visual department the music teacher should survey his needs and make them known to the purchasing agent.

Music educators are still hoping that industry will further develop projectors which will give faithful reproduction of music, which means sound tracks that are true to pitch, free from "wow" and too great a percentage of distortion. There are mechanical problems in getting a good sound track on a 16mm film, but with increasing technical developments producers will find ways of improving the fidelity.

WHY USE FILMS

(1) If motion is essential to the concept to be taught, a good film can help the teacher. In a film, steps in a process may be followed easily. For example, films dealing with training the marching band for maneuvers, rhythmic activities, or making a violin.

(2) Through the use of animation, slow motion, and telescopic lens attachments, the film may depict scenes otherwise unobservable. For example, films dealing with acoustics of music (a phenomena presented through animation), technique of playing instruments (slow motion), vocal chords producing sounds (slow motion and use of telescopic lens in photography).

(3) A film can overcome difficulties of time and space limitations of student experiences (a) by giving the setting and mood of the past which is difficult to convey in any other way; (b) by bringing to the classroom musical performances by groups otherwise unavailable to school and community. For example, films dealing with history of music, biographies of composers, opera (music and drama), symphony orchestras (great conductors and well-known artists).

(4) The sound motion picture through dramatic incidents, stirring music, and wisely edited scenes can build attitudes toward outstanding problems. For example, such films as "The River" and "Colonial Williamsburg."

(5) The use of films lends variety and interest to teaching and makes teaching more effective. The use of films may aid in the following ways:

—Compel attention.

—Reach a mass audience.

—Build a common denominator of experiences.

—Convey aesthetic experiences to viewers by motivation, intensification, and verification through visual means certain experiences which otherwise are auditory.

---

[1] See page 232.

—Speed up the process of learning certain types of information by giving a better understanding of the relationship of procedures to outcomes.[1]

HOW TO EVALUATE FILMS [2]

(1) Does the film have a valid objective and does it fulfill this objective?

(2) Does it present the material clearly, concisely, and logically?

(3) Is the film accurate musically and historically or does it contain irrelevant facts?

(4) Do the instruments and voices sound authentic?

(5) Are the pictures of good quality (sharp and clear)?

(6) Is the material suitable for the age level, intelligence, and experience of the group for which it is designed? Is the film a suitable length for classroom use?

(7) Is the film sufficiently modern so that the pupils will not think it ludicrous?

(8) Are the performers natural?

(9) Does it possess good motivating qualities?

(10) Is the film worth the time, expense, and effort involved?

HOW TO USE FILMS

Music teachers know that the preparation and the activities related to the showing of a motion picture depend upon the subject that is being presented. The following basic and general suggestions may be helpful in the selection, preparation, and the presentation of a film.

Selection. To be effective teaching tools, films must be selected so that they are an integral part of the lesson. The teacher should be aware of the relation of the film (a) with the preceding learning experiences, (b) with the lesson or topic studied, and (c) between the learning outcomes and what follows so that a coherent learning atmosphere is maintained. The improvement of the students' taste and judgment is important along with increasing factual information.

Films may (a) furnish a historical background, (b) introduce new topics, ideas, or personalities, (c) present technical details, (d) set goals and standards for performance, (e) serve as a review or a summary, (f) introduce musical scores composed especially for the film, and (g) present technical details.

Preparation. In addition to being familiar with the teaching guide which usually accompanies films, the teacher should:

(1) Preview the film before using. If time permits the teacher may have a committee from the class help preview the film.

(2) Select content which is important and related to the lesson.

(3) Plan the type of discussion to be conducted after the viewing.

(4) Prepare leading questions. The students could help to formulate questions and perhaps lead the discussion in the class.

(5) Plan follow-up activities which will strengthen the concepts learned.

(6) Be familiar with the musical compositions used in the film. Recordings of the music heard in the film should be available for students to hear and study.

---

[1] William S. Hartley, *How to Use a Motion Picture* (Washington, D. C.: National Council for the Social Studies, 1951). The five main points are patterned after the "How To Do It Series."
[2] From the report submitted by C. E. McMeans, North Little Rock, Arkansas, Southwestern Division Chairman, Music in American Education Committee on Audio-Visual Aids in Music Education.

Presentation. The teacher should direct the attention and stimulate the interest of the class in the content of the film by listing on the board questions which the film should answer. After the showing, free discussion and critical thought should be encouraged to draw out impressions from the class.

Showings should be repeated in order to (a) clear up misconceptions, (b) stimulate thinking, (c) motivate creative activities, and (d) answer questions which arise from discussion. On repeated showings the sound might be shut off while pupils or teacher explain or discuss the action; the picture might be shut off to direct attention to the musical score; or the film might be shown in part.

HOW TO KEEP INFORMED ON FILM RELEASES

Announcements and reviews of films are to be found in the *Music Educators Journal* and in state music education periodicals. There are many magazines which list and review music films. The following are a few basic sources:

Rushes (published weekly). Film Council of America, 600 Davis Street, Evanston, Illinois. Lists all new films and filmstrips. Free.

The Educational Film Guide (issues monthly supplements). H. W. Wilson Company, 950 University Avenue, New York 52, N. Y.

Educational Screen (10 issues yearly). 64 East Lake Street, Chicago 1, Illinois.

Film Music (five issues yearly). 26 East 83rd Street, New York City, N. Y. Articles and news on film music.

WHERE TO GET FILMS[1]

Films may be purchased directly from the producer or rented for a small fee from local, regional and/or state audio-visual departments. For the most part producers of films do not rent films but sell directly to the consumer.

If there is no film library in your school and you want to rent a film:

—Consult your local library, state department of audio-visual instruction or state university.

—See *A Directory of 2,660 16mm Film Libraries*, Bulletin 1953, No. 7 (50¢), available from the Office of Education, Government Printing Office, Washington, D. C. This publication is revised frequently and lists resources and services of different libraries. Libraries are listed according to state, city and/or town with an indication of the kind of films distributed. Restrictions, if any, placed by the libraries on the distribution and use of these films are stated.

—Write to libraries in your area for catalogs of available films, together with the regulations, including rental rates governing the use of these films. Resources of various libraries may be investigated and those libraries selected which best meet your needs. Orders should be placed as far in advance as possible.

There are a number of fine films sponsored by private industry. These are available through the main or regional branches of the commercial concern.

RECOMMENDATIONS TO PRODUCERS

Film producers planning to supply the needs of music education should consider producing school films of high standards in the following classifications:

(1) *For General Music Techniques:* (a) Rhythm, including audience participation; and (b) choral and instrumental conducting, illustrating various styles for elementary and advanced.

(2) *For Choral Field:* (a) Teaching a rote song; (b) music reading; (c) choral techniques such as blending, dynamics, and diction; (d) changing voice; (e)

---

[1] *Handbook on 16 mm. Films for Music Education* (MENC), 1952. 72 pp. and cover. $1.50. Includes classified and annotated lists of films and helpful suggestions.

physiological aspects of vocal production; and (f) performances of excellent choral groups, large and small.

(3) *For Instrumental Field:* (a) First steps in playing all instruments— posture, position, diaphragmatic breathing, tonguing, correct embouchure, bowing of stringed instruments, and other details difficult to demonstrate correctly; (b) manufacturing of instruments, with consideration of physics of sound; (c) care and repair of instruments and making of reeds; (d) instrument class teaching techniques; (e) class piano teaching technique; and (f) aids in connection with printed textbook series.

(4) *For History and Appreciation:* (a) Condensed versions of operas, not more than forty-five minutes' duration; (b) films depicting native dancers, instruments, and folk singing; and (c) history of various instruments on one reel.

FILM STRIPS

Definition. A film strip is a short length of film, 10-100 frames, of a number of positives in black and white or color, each different but usually having some continuity. The pictures are placed in a logical sequence and joined together in a strip or a roll, often with proper captions. They are easily projected horizontally or vertically by means of a film strip projector. They may be with or without sound. Some projectors have record-playing equipment attached. Film strips may be shown simultaneously with sound on tapes or recordings.

Advantages of Using Film Strips. The equipment is inexpensive, easy to operate, and portable. The picture may be projected and studied as long as necessary. There is no limit to what may be photographed and so can be made to fit specific needs. Film strips can be made easily by schools but are available and inexpensive commercially.[1] The ease of carrying and storage is a great asset.

The following are selected useful film strips:

The Slide Film in Teaching—Young America Films.
Evaluation of Hand-made Violins—Scherl and Roth.
Group Instruction at the University of Illinois, (Class violin with tape recording)—Extension Division, University of Illinois.
How to Care for Your Drum (with script)—Leedy and Ludwig.
Fundamentals of Brass Instruments, Percussion and Woodwind Instruments, Stringed Instruments, Series I and Series II (with script)—University of Nebraska.
Music Stories, Firebird, Peter and the Wolf, The Nutcracker Suite, Hansel and Gretel, The Sorcerer's Apprentice, Peer Gynt—Jam Handy Organization.
Rhythm Magic (on rhythm reading)—Young America Films.
Young America Sings (with L.P. recordings), third, fourth and fifth grade units—Young America Films.

Television and Radio[2]

General Statement. Even though television is receiving considerable attention at present, due to its newness and seemingly all-encompassing power as a medium of mass communication, radio should not be discounted. It never has been fully explored as an educational tool, mainly because only a few educational institutions have seriously attempted to use it as a basic part of their instructional program.

---

[1] From an article by Wolfgang Kuhn. *Music Educators Journal*, September-October 1953, p. 35.
[2] From *A Guide to Teaching Music by Television and Radio*, edited by Richard C. Berg, Springfield, Massachusetts, National Chairman, Music in American Education Committee on Television and Radio. Available from Music Educators National Conference. 30¢.

This might very well be the ideal time to reconsider the unique values of radio as a source of enriching school music programs. Because television has released some of the pressures previously imposed on commercial radio stations, it could be that more free broadcast time will become available to schools. Radio must of necessity readjust and discover new fields of achievement as a means of recovering from the loss of areas preempted by television. Through the cooperation of broadcasters and educators, stations can regain status and listening audiences.

In the past, teaching music through radio was beyond the financial means of many school systems; today, with the increased facilities for educational programs, the permanent use of radio in education is insured. Therefore music educators should investigate the possibilities of gaining assistance from commercial broadcasters in their respective localities.

The first criterion governing the use of radio or television should be: Is *this* medium the most suitable for the achievement of specific objectives? Although radio is perhaps more readily available to most schools than television, such a consideration should be secondary. Since music is an aural art, there are teaching situations in which the addition of a visual dimension would detract or lessen the focus of attention upon the music itself.

Television excites the imagination tremendously. It may seem in moments of enthusiasm the answer to all we have sought for it combines in certain respects everything that radio, films, and recordings do separately. It offers a means of enrichment to already substantial music programs and a breath of life to musically impoverished sections of a city, county, or state. But not in all respects is it a total answer. As time goes on television will find its rightful place among the audio-visual devices, but it will not supplant the other types of aids. Television has the advantage over radio that the film has over a recording; it has an advantage whenever visual impressions are vital to the idea being presented. Like radio, on the other hand, it lacks the flexibility in use that films and recordings possess. Repeat broadcasts and telecasts are sometimes possible, but even this measure does not fit all the diversified schedules of many classes in many schools, nor does it permit repetition according to the needs of individual classes.

No music program is completely successful unless it influences the out-of-school activities of pupils. Therefore, discriminative tastes should be developed so that students will choose radio and television programs which offer worth-while music, produced in keeping with the aesthetic standards of the music.

School-produced Radio Programs. Organized weekly radio music lessons can be an efficient teaching method if prepared for and followed up by the room teacher. Radio can bring into a classroom musical experiences beyond the performing ability of the students and/or the teacher. Radio is an aid in supervision where services of a supervisor or special teacher are not available on a regular weekly basis. Testing programs can be administered by radio.

Certain types of radio music lessons require a producer to unify the entire program—balance, timing, etc. The scriptwriter must know music and music literature and keep in mind the interests, abilities, and vocabulary of the group for which he is writing. The broadcaster or narrator needs a pleasant, expressive voice. When a singer is used, the same requirements hold good together with excellent musical performance. The classroom teacher is more a vital part in leading activities impossible for the broadcaster because of the limitations of radio. Pupils, by the extent of their liking and learning, ultimately determine the desirability of continuing a series of radio lessons.

Children's interests and vocabularies change so rapidly that it is advisable to direct lessons to a limited age group—if possible, not more than two years dif-

221

ference. No lesson for elementary pupils should last more than thirty minutes; many educators believe that fifteen minutes is more satisfactory if the script is carefully prepared. Material used must be suitable for and interesting to the age level of the listeners. When broadcasting over commercial stations, music used must be checked with the station well in advance of the broadcast. Pupil participation in the classroom should be included in the broadcasts, especially at the primary level; participation is a satisfactory method of learning, and it is a means of concentrating on the lesson. Repetition is necessary to some degree where musical memory and accurate response are being developed. When directions are given only once, children quickly learn the habit of intent listening.

Probably the best method of telling whether or not a lesson does what is intended is to visit classrooms during reception of the lesson. Watch for alertness and accuracy of response, understanding, and enjoyment. Questionnaires to teachers will bring criticisms and suggestions as to materials, procedures, and vocabulary. Radio-administered tests can ascertain knowledge of material covered in certain radio lessons.

Planning and Producing Telecasts. Each teacher will find through experimentation what techniques are most applicable in his own work. The following suggestions are given with the hope that those about to set forth on initial TV adventures will be aided by the experiences of others.

IS TELEVISION THE BEST MEDIUM FOR THIS PROJECT?

Before embarking on an in-school project (a telecast to be viewed in classrooms) it is well to consider whether the presentation might be done as well or better by radio, film (is there a film on the subject, and if so, is it satisfactory for your specific purpose), workshop, or other means.

Then ask this question: Will participation be on a sufficiently wide basis to justify the use of a mass medium? If instruction could be given directly by classroom visits or by workshops for teachers, TV instruction would be no more than a novelty and unworthy of consideration.

Can the schedules of participating schools be so arranged that classes can tune in without conflict with other activities? Elementary schools are more readily scheduled for simultaneous instruction than secondary schools, a point worth bearing in mind when planning a TV instructional project.

Finally, there is the practical consideration: Are TV sets available for placement in classrooms?

HINTS ON TELEVISION PROGRAM PRODUCTION

If you plan to present a music group on TV, make arrangements for rehearsal with cameras if possible. If this is impossible, have a final dress rehearsal in the TV studio to check entrances and exits, standing positions in relation to cameras, and other details. Rehearsing in the studio will help to put students at ease.

Prepare a cue sheet for the program director. This can be brief—indicate numbers to be performed, names of performers, and any suggestions that will aid in getting good camera shots. As experience is gained, more elaborate camera instructions can be prepared. For the first few times, rely on the experience of the TV staff.

Time rehearsals carefully. Allow time for station announcements. Find out precisely the time allotment and cut or add until precision is achieved to prevent awkward or incomplete program endings.

Prepare a script, but have announcements memorized by on-the-air time. As a prompter during programs, cues may be placed on a blackboard or large cards *behind* the cameras.

For opening and closing the program a musical theme appropriate to the character and identity of your program and an identification card are necessary. The card size will be determined by station requirements, so check before painting a sign.

SELECTING A SUBJECT

As an entertainment medium or when used for certain types of demonstration and public relations programs, television can span a variety of background, interests, and age groups. In telecasting a musical program, for example, the viewing audience could range from elementary through high school age. A telecast which proposes to teach a specific skill, on the other hand, should be directed at a very specific age and grade group if it is to be successful. Specific skills can be taught best by in-school programming. This provides the valuable assistance of the classroom teacher as intermediary.

Even with in-school telecasts, the teaching subject needs to be selected carefully. If you decide to teach instruments, for example, there are important considerations to make. The tonette might be better for TV teaching than the clarinet. Here are several reasons why: (a) It is inexpensive, making it possible for all pupils of a selected grade to purchase instruments and participate in the lessons instead of a few; (b) it is simple to play and, therefore, simple to learn, making it adaptable to mass teaching techniques; and (c) tonettes are often taught by classroom teachers whereas clarinet instruction is usually given by special instrumental teachers. This makes the need for assistance greater in the one area since few classroom teachers can proceed without workshop or other in-service training.

Considerations of this type will vary from school system to school system; but the size of the potential audience, the adaptability of the subject to TV's idiosyncrasies, and the particular skills of the television teacher always should be taken into account.

VISUAL CONSIDERATIONS

Visual considerations range from unadorned, straightforward musical programs, with reliance upon the performers' actions for visual interest, to full-dress productions including sets and costumes. For TV demonstrations the equipment, action, or whatever is being demonstrated should hold the center of attention. Manner of presentation by the demonstrator is important; so is the camera work that reveals the important details of the demonstration. The TV director needs careful instructions (a written script and prebroadcast conferences) in order to get close-up shots when needed, and to follow the movement of the demonstration (from instructor to equipment, to participant, to blackboard—or whatever sequence of action the demonstration demands).

Motion pictures are somtimes used. If films are to be used in a telecast, check on two things: (a) Is the film you have in mind available for TV transmission? Remember that many are restricted from such use. (b) Will the station provide equipment and an operator for projecting the film? The transition from live demonstration to a film can increase the scope of your presentation. For smooth performance, edit the film sparingly to fit the script.

Photographs and slides, if used sparingly, sometimes will add just the right touch to a program or demonstration; for example, to illustrate an object that cannot be brought into the studio. Glossy prints reflect light into the camera; a flat, mat-finish paper is better. The photograph must adhere to the proportions of a TV screen, which are three-high by four wide, if all portions of the picture are to show.

When using charts or cards, avoid white paper because it produces a glare in the camera lenses; middle-grey with black letters is best.[1] The size of charts and the lettering on charts is important. It is safest to have a test run, if possible, to see how charts and other objects show up on a monitor screen.

AUDIO PROBLEMS OF TV MUSICAL PRODUCTION

To get a band, orchestra, or chorus to sound as well on tape as it does in the school auditorium is a challenge even for a professional sound engineer. A similar problem is encountered in telecasting.

Assuming that a group performs with reasonably good intonation, balance, and blend, the difference in the quality heard from a television receiver's speaker depends largely upon the use of microphones. In radio, where all emphasis is on the quality of sound, microphones are carefully placed. Unfortunately, in television the emphasis often is placed on video considerations (how the picture on the screen looks) to such a degree that audio (sound) requirements are completely neglected. When microphones are insufficient in number, poorly placed, or monitored by non-musicians, the result can be very different from what a group really sounds like.

All of this is of considerable importance to the director of a school music group slated to make a TV appearance. Rely on the TV director's experience to assist you with the visual presentation of a telecast, but check the program for sound and suggest modifications in group and soloist placement and action if any video arrangements cause unsatisfactory musical results. Fancy camera shots are fine but only when they do not sacrifice musical quality.

SCRIPT WRITING

The script is as vital to TV production as it is to radio, perhaps more so because it must include directions for cameras as well as microphones. It also gives stage directions and cues to participants.

The details of a script depend upon the nature of the program to be presented. For some musical programs it might be no more than a listing of the various soloists and ensembles in the order of their appearance. With such a sketchy outline of the program the complete responsibility can rest upon the TV producer for getting the best camera shots of each number played or sung. If the producer and camera crew are skilled they can sometimes do an effective job with such limited instructions, achieving a spontaneous, informal atmosphere. On the other hand, such haphazard methods are risks to smooth performance and limit themselves to only certain types of program.

PROGRAM OPENINGS AND CLOSINGS

Openings and closings can vary considerably in length and complexity. For in-school telecasting, where a program is intended to fit into the curriculum, beginnings and endings should be simple and short. For telecasts intended for public viewing, especially if the one aim is entertainment, pictures or even films of the school or of school life could be incorporated into a standard opening and closing format. To go with such pictures, a recorded version of the school alma mater by the chorus or band or orchestra could be standardized in the same way. This

---

[1] It is well to ask the technicians of the station about such matters.

would compare to the theme song used to identify many commercial programs. The purpose is to get a program on and off the air as smoothly as possible.

The opening should carry complete identification: What is the name of the school? Where is it located? Who is presenting the program? Does the program, or series of programs, have a title ("Say It With Music," etc.)? Part of this information can be written on a card displayed in the first moments on the air; part of it can be included in the script, to be announced simultaneously with the showing of a card, picture, or film. There are other possibilities, but one choice should give complete identification to the program.

INSURING MAXIMUM RESULTS

Public relations programs, broadcast for whoever may be tuned to the station at the time the school program is on the air, seek to attract as large an audience as possible for the purpose of demonstrating and interpreting the activities of the music department. The desired result would be public interest and support of the school music program. Another objective would be to provide cultural and educational enrichment to a given community or region.

Achievement of objectives is difficult to measure in specific terms as reliance has to be placed upon the receipt of voluntary written and oral comments. If opinions from persons well qualified to judge were solicited, at least a partial check could be secured on the strengths to be retained for use in future programming, and on weaknesses which could be corrected the next time preparation for a telecast was being made.

In-school telecasts, directed toward controlled (supervised) groups, can be utilized with maximum efficiency if three steps are taken in addition to ones already mentioned in connection with the actual planning and production of a program: (a) Give directions for classroom preparation for a telecast; (b) give directions for classroom follow-up of a telecast; (c) evaluate the results of instruction or demonstration in terms of what is actually learned in proportion to the knowledge and/or skills presented in the telecast or series of telecasts. The indispensable ally of the television teacher is the classroom teacher. She should be provided with clear, precise bulletins which give suggestions for ways in which pupils can best be readied for what is to be seen and heard on the receiving set in the room, and which insure maximum pupil participation during and following the telecast. If reading or practice of assigned lessons between weekly telecasts is essential, bulletins should be very specific in listing exactly what is required.

Evaluation can be accomplished by the use of questionnaires and other forms of written reports which indicate the opinions and suggestions of teachers engaged in the project. Visits to classrooms to observe at first hand the accomplishment of pupils is also important. The method of appraisal is unimportant, so long as it is objective and valid; but it is all important that some reliable means of measurement be used if television is to become recognized as a legitimate audio-visual aid. At this period in the development of television as a means of aiding the teaching of music, experimentation is necessary and desirable. Evaluation will help discover what significant contributions can be made to the field of music education.

Utilization of Commercial Programs. To hope that unsupervised student listening and viewing during the many hours spent away from the controls of the classroom will be spent in the enjoyment of only the finest which radio and television have to offer, is expecting a great deal.

Commercial radio and television are instruments of far-reaching influence which affect culture. Whether the organizations controlling what is transmitted over the air waves are to blame for the level at which commercial broadcasting operates in this country, or whether broadcasters are only attempting to give the public what it wants in the way of entertainment, is a question.

This issue is raised for positive reasons. It is felt that, regardless of the cause, music educators have both a vital responsibility and a great opportunity in connection with commercial programming. What students see and hear at home is reflected in their tastes and attitudes toward music which is sung, played, or listened to in the classroom; in turn, good teaching develops critical and discriminating listening habits which determine the kind of music that will be selected by students during their leisure hours.

Various efforts have been made to put pressure upon students to listen to and see the "right" things on radio and television. This seems a dubious approach, and not one calculated to develop long-lasting habits. External rewards, on the other hand, are desirable and helpful at certain ages and stages of development. To demand that a student turn in reports giving evidence that he has listened to certain prescribed programs on radio or television, with the threat that his grade will be affected if he fails to comply, seems incompatible with the desired objective, which is to get him to a point where he will turn to such programs of his own volition.

Teachers most successful in making serious music programs attractive have integrated in-school and out-of-school music activities. Local newspapers and television and radio guides list programs of special interest and value. Teachers can prepare students just as they would for films, recordings, or for attending a concert by familiarizing them with interesting information about the music to be heard, the artists participating, and other features which would appeal to the class age group. Bulletin boards have been used effectively to show pictures of performing artists and to list pertinent information about the date, time, and station on which recommended programs are to be carried.

Class discussion following programs heard or seen is important. Student evaluations arouse added interest in future programs and provide the opportunity for teachers to guide towards greater ability to discern what is good and what is unsatisfactory. Evaluation should concern itself with the worth of music heard as well as the manner in which it was performed, and when television is discussed the visual features should be appraised in terms of enhancement or detraction.

Radio and television clubs have been organized as extra-curricular activities. Since many excellent music programs are available only during evening hours or on week ends, groups of students in certain schools have on occasion met in the homes of class members. These activities are commendable and are endorsed as a means for providing additional opportunities for those students who desire to participate in extra sessions; the extracurricular type of listening should not, however, replace a classroom program which accounts for outside listening because it is important that every pupil be stimulated to increase his power of enjoying worth-while music.

Recordings in Music Education[1]

Since phonograph recordings first came into existence they have been an important aid to the teacher of music, and their contribution to music education has been of the utmost significance. Through the use of recordings, virtually the entire literature of music becomes accessible to the classroom.

---

[1] From the report submitted by William C. Hartshorn, Los Angeles, California, National Chairman, Music in American Education Committee on Recordings.

Developments. In recent years, three developments of major significance have had an important effect upon the use of recordings in the schools. The *first* of these was the introduction of the long-playing record and the subsequent replacement of the 78 rpm recordings. Problems of converting old equipment to the new speeds, of obtaining new equipment, and of learning how to use the new recordings (particularly in locating important themes on a long-playing record) have become familiar to the music educator.

The *second* significant development has been the rise of a considerable number of new recording companies. This has been advantageous to the music educator not only because it has tended to increase the scope of the repertoire available on records, but also because it has provided a greater number of options among the performers whose recordings of standard items are available in most catalogs.

The *third* development has been the cooperative action on the part of music pubishers and recording companies in making available to music educators recordings of song materials included in the various series of music textbooks. These recordings have great potential value for teachers in the elementary schools and involve the setting of a standard of correctness in such matters as pitch, tempo, tone quality, phrasing, and dynamics. They help teachers develop a concept of the expressive content and meaning of a song as a whole. Functions of this type are a very serious responsibility which has not been discharged with uniform success. It is important that the music educator exercise both discrimination and insight in the selection of such recordings for classroom use.

The values of these recordings for elementary children parallel those mentioned for the teacher, for through their use children have an opportunity to hear a song they may be studying in order to have some concept of its expressive quality and the way the song should sound.

Rural school teachers report the values of these recordings in relation to the singing program, especially in situations where teachers have not been privileged to have the kind of experiences that would prepare them adequately for the teaching of music.

Activities emphasizing music reading are aided by the use of recordings. The basic means of contact with music is through the ear. In the early stages of music reading, the visual symbols of notation seen by the eye reinforce and represent tonal concepts heard by the ear. The tonal meanings of musical notation easily become apparent as song recordings supply the tonal equivalents of the notation being observed, and this forms a solid foundation for subsequent growth leading to real skill in reading. In listening lessons involving instrumental music, similar values may be realized as the notation of themes is put on the blackboard or otherwise made available to students.

Listening for Appreciation. Listening lessons presented for purposes primarily appreciative in character depend largely upon recordings. Through the skillful presentation of listening lessons involving recordings, music can come into the lives of children in such a way that they will grow in both the scope and quality of their responsiveness to music, including both sheer enjoyment and a genuine understanding of its expressive meaning. There is music that is too difficult for children to perform, but there is none that is intrinsically too good for them to hear. Recordings provide the principal source of this type of experience.

Since the most basic response to music is to its quality of tone, it is important that music educators use only those recordings that can meet a high standard of tone quality; otherwise, the responsiveness of the listener may be negative and the over-all purpose of using the selection may be defeated. While good taste is difficult to define precisely, it can be said that one should avoid recordings in which effects are excessively exaggerated and which unquestionably violate the intent of the composer as indicated in his score. Teachers should exercise everything they know about what constitutes a good performance in selecting recordings for music listening.

Recordings make it possible for the resourceful teacher of listening lessons to prepare students for concerts they may attend and for music they may hear by means of radio or television. In addition, it becomes possible to capitalize in the classroom upon worth-while music which the young people may be hearing as a part of motion pictures currently being shown.

For Creative Rhythms. Activities of a creative nature may be stimulated by the use of recordings. Recordings aid in developing concepts of design in a tonal context which children may use in their own creative activities.

Recordings are essential to rhythmic activities, although with young children it is desirable to use them on a phonograph having variable speed in order to adapt tempo to the needs of a particular group. Recordings are virtually indispensable for development of interpretive and imaginative responses to music through bodily movement which contributes greatly to the early development of musical discrimination and insight.

For Instrumental Interest. Recordings may serve in arousing interest in instrumental music, in providing a standard of tone quality toward which students should grow, and, in certain instances, they may perform functions similar to those mentioned in connection with song recordings.

Secondary Schools. Since the principles basic to an effective program of music for children in the elementary schools apply equally to general music at the secondary level, the functions and values of recordings are parallel. Specialized instrumental and choral groups can learn much concerning quality of tone, phrasing, tempo, dynamics, and all other ingredients of a first-class performance by listening to such a performance on recordings. To hear a good recording of a selection a specialized student group is studying will pay dividends that are very great in proportion to the time spent.

Teachers of theory and harmony at the secondary level can find in recordings sources for examples of harmonic idioms and style both stimulating and instructive.

The learning of music history is virtually an abstract intellectual process without the use of recordings. The facts of music history take on meaning and relevance only when related to music itself, and an understanding of style and differences of the various periods of music history can be developed effectively through an extensive and resourceful use of recordings.

Music education is primarily "audio" and only secondarily "visual," and the most significant of all aids in this area is a fine recording played on a phonograph with good tone and used with skill and resourcefulness.

Sources of Information
Concerning Recordings Currently Available

American Record Guide, The, Department A, P. O. Building No. 11, Pelham 65, New York, N. Y.
Children's Reading Service, 1078 St. Johns Place, Brooklyn 13, N. Y.
Counterpoint, 700 Montgomery St., San Francisco 11, Calif.
Disc (Quarterly), City of Bristol Gramaphone Society, 47 Wellington Walk, Bristol, England.
Disques (Monthly), 59-61 Rue LaFayette, Paris 9e, France.
Gramaphone, The (Monthly), The Gramaphone Co., Ltd., 49 Ebrington Road, Kenton, Harow, Middlesex, England.
Hi-Fi Quarterly, Audio-Conn Inc., 264 Main St., Great Barrington, Mass.
High Fidelity. (Reviews by several critics), 2215 Publishing House, Great Barrington, Mass.
Liberty Record Review, New York, N. Y.
London Gramaphone Corporation, The, City and South Printing and Pub. Co., Ltd., London W/Cl, England.

Long Player Catalog, The, Sam Goody, 235 W. 49th St., New York 19, N. Y.
Music At Home, 215-A East 37th St., New York 16, N. Y.
Music Dealer, The, 114 E. 32nd St., New York 16, N. Y.
Musical America, 113 West 57th St., New York 19, N. Y.
Musical Courier, The (Semi-monthly), 119 West 57th St., New York 19, N. Y.
Musical Quarterly, The (Published by G. Schirmer, Inc.), 3 East 43rd St., New York 17, N. Y.
New Records, The, H. Royer Smith Co., 10th and Walnut Streets, Philadelphia 7, Pa.
New York Herald Tribune, The, 230 West 41st St., New York 18, N. Y.
New Yorker, The (Weekly), 25 East 43rd St., New York 18, N. Y.
Notes, Music Library Association, Library of Congress, Washington, D. C.
One Spot (Big catalog with monthly supplement), Tunnis Publishers, Oak Park, Ill.
Phonolog (Monthly supplement available), Phonolog Publishing Co., 458 South Spring St., Los Angeles, California.
Review of Recorded Music (Released by various community dealers), Gainsburg-Shack, Inc., New York, N. Y.
Saturday Review, The (Recordings reviewed by Irving Kolodin), 25 West 45th St., New York 36, N. Y.
Schwann Catalog of Long-Playing Records, 131 Clarendon St., Boston 16, Mass.
World's Encyclopedia of Recorded Music 1952

Use of Tape Recordings

General Uses. Tape recordings have been used successfully to record:

(1) Solo, ensemble, and group performances so that students may evaluate performance and check progress.

(2) Vocal and instrumental compositions (solo, ensemble, orchestra, band, chorus) of festival music or required works for compositions to set standards of performance.

(3) Artistically played piano accompaniments which soloists may use for rehearsal, or folk dance groups for performance.

(4) Programs for radio broadcast.

(5) Radio programs for future use in the classroom.

(6) Programs for exchange between grades and between schools.

(7) Classroom activities for playback at PTA meetings.

(8) Demonstration lessons for reference of classroom teachers.

(9) Rote songs, music for rhythmic activities for use by classroom teacher.

(10) Lessons taught by practice teachers.

(11) Concerts by visiting groups.

Vocal Program. In addition to the general suggestions, tape recordings may aid the vocal program by recording the following:

(1) Voices of out-of-tune singers for sake of record and to identify progress.

(2) Tone quality of voices; boys' changing voices, etc.

(3) One or two parts of part-songs as an aid to teaching part-singing.

(4) Rehearsal of music for mixed choirs when schedule will not permit combined rehearsals. Separate recordings are made of the girls' group and the boys' group. In rehearsal the missing parts are supplied by playback of the tape.

Instrumental Program. In addition to the general suggestions, tape recordings may aid the instrumental program by recording auditions for placement in orchestras, bands, choirs, and ensembles. The director may play auditions as often as necessary and in any order to evaluate performing ability. By giving each performer a code number, the tape may be played back to the entire group for them to evaluate the players.[1]

Tape Libraries. Throughout the country, state departments of education, state universities, and city systems are establishing tape libraries. Each library usually

---

[1] From an article by Merton S. Zahrt. *New York State School Music News*, October 1951.

has a catalog of available teaching materials. Music teachers may send tapes (in fiber shipping cases) to the library and indicate which program they wish recorded. The fee is approximately fifty cents for fifteen minutes, $1.00 for sixteen to thirty minutes of program material, plus return postage.

Criteria for Selecting Audio-Visual Aid Equipment

A major part of recent thinking about audio-visual aids and investigations of the field as it pertains to music education has been centered around the use of films, recordings, radio, and television. As more use is made in the classroom and special music room of audio-visual aids in teaching, and as a diversity of equipment is becoming available, there is an increasing need to select equipment of proper specifications and quality. Particularly is this true in the field of music, where "presence" of picture and sound, and fidelity of reproduction are paramount. In general, the adequate reproduction of music means that equipment used in the classroom should be as nearly as possible like that used in professional work.

Because good reproduction of music demands higher fidelity than for reproducing speech, it is essential that music educators be aware of the problems involved in the selection of proper equipment. The following material, as much as possible in the layman's language, is given as a reference guide to the selection of audio-visual equipment for appropriate use in the music room. These are minimum specifications.

GUIDE FOR SELECTING RECORDING AND REPRODUCING EQUIPMENT

I. Requirements for Tape Recorders[1]

Frequency Response: The amplifier of the recorder should have a frequency response of 40 to 15,000 cycles ± 2 db in order to reproduce music without loss of naturalism.

It is possible to get an amplifier that will reproduce frequencies from 10 to 40,000 but studies have shown that the best human ears scarcely ever can hear over 20,000 cycles and this top limit declines with age.

Non-Linear Distortion: The non-linear characteristics of the various elements of an amplifying system tend to introduce harmonic components not present in the original sound which tends to change the quality of the sound being reproduced. Any non-linear distortion of more than one or two percent is likely to be objectionable.

Tape Speed: The standard speed for recording music should be 7.5 inches per second. For professional use a speed of 15 inches per second may be employed. Speeds slower than 7.5 i.p.s. are generally not adequate to record music without distortion. At 7.5 i.p.s. the upper range of the frequencies which can be expected to be recorded is 8,000 cycles; at 15 i.p.s., it is 15,000 cycles.

Motor Speed Variations: Any variation in motor speed of the drive mechanism will cause "wow" or "flutter" in the recording which should not exceed 0.2% (peak to peak 0.4%).

Output Power: The output power of the amplifier for use in the average classroom should be from 10 to 15 watts. Even though this total output will not be needed, the use of a lower-power-rated amplifier may necessitate its use too close to its maximum output and cause distortion.

Ease of Operation: Threading for both recording and playback should be the same. Controls should be clearly marked and simple to operate. There should be a safety device to prevent recording or erasing a tape unintentionally.

Fast Forward Speed: A fast forward transport of the tape will facilitate the location of a particular spot within the tape. Valuable time is lost without this mechanism.

[1] "Quick Facts on Magnetic Tape Recorders," *Audio-Record* (New York: Audio Devices).

Portability: Portable equipment is essential for school use. Since most electronic equipment is heavy, there will be limitations to its portability. The equipment should be mounted in cases to afford suitable protection and ease of moving.

Availability of Servicing: It is desirable to select equipment that can be serviced adequately by local dealers or servicemen. Considerable time can be lost in shipping equipment to the manufacturer for minor repair or adjustment.

Speaker: Most tape recorders have small (3 to 5 inch) speakers for playback. Arrangements should be made for plugging in a large baffled speaker system that will give full frequency response.

II. Requirements for Microphones [1]

Impedance: Since the placement of the microphone for the most desirable pickup often necessitates the use of a long connecting cable between the microphone and the amplifier, it is advisable to purchase a *low* impedance microphone. This will allow for the use of a connecting cable as long as 75 feet.

Frequency Response: Since the frequency response requirement of the suggested recording equipment is ± 2 db 40 to 15,000 cycles, the frequency response of the microphone should be as good or better. This frequency response should be uniform over the angles included in its directivity characteristics.

Sensitivity: The sensitivity or output level of the microphone should be at least −70 to −80 db as compared to 0 db with 1 volt per dyne per om.

Directivity: A wide angle (120 degrees) uni-directional or "cardioid" pattern microphone is most desirable for picking up music. This uniforms pickup of the performing group and yet eliminates the pickup of echo or other background noise being produced in back of the microphone. A non-directional microphone will pick up sound from all directions including reflection from walls and other objects.

Number of Microphones: In most cases the most satisfactory pickup is obtained with the use of one microphone. It should be placed at a sufficient distance from the performing group so as to be located in the so-called "focal point" of sound, thus obtaining a good acoustical balance from the entire group. In the case of soloists appearing with the group, it might be advisable to use an additional directional microphone for the soloist. This microphone should be placed so that it will not pick up the larger group.

III. Requirements for Record Playing Equipment

Frequency Response: Same as for tape recorders.[2]

Non-Linear Distortion: Same as for tape recorders.[2]

Output Power: Same as tape recorders.[2]

Signal-to-Noise Ratio: The amplifier should have a signal-to-noise ratio of −60 to −70 db. This will reduce internal hum and tube noises to a level that will not be objectionable.

Turntable Speeds: The turntable should have all three speeds in common usage today: 33⅓, 45, and 78 R.P.M. ± 0.3%. Correct turntable speeds are essential in order to reproduce music accurately.

Tone Arm and Cartridge: The tone arm should have proper weight and stylus for playing both regular and microgroove recordings. The weight of the tone arm should not exceed 6 grams. There should be a separate stylus and cartridge for the playing of each type of recording. The use of the proper weight and stylus will reduce hiss, improve frequency response, and reduce wear on the recording. A hard sapphire or diamond stylus should be used. For the best frequency response a variable-reluctance or ceramic cartridge is recommended.

Speaker: A 12- to 14-inch speaker cone is necessary in order to obtain a satisfactory frequency response. Dual speakers having a "woofer" or large speaker cone for the low frequencies and a "tweeter" or small cone for the high frequencies provide excellent reproduction. For greatest efficiency and proper response the speakers should be mounted in baffles of suitable design. The vented or bass reflex

---

[1] "Making Good Recordings with a Single Microphone," an article by Eugene Carrington which appeared in *The Instrumentalist,* will be very helpful. Reprints are available from Allied Radio Corporation, 833 W. Jackson Blvd., Chicago, Ill.

[2] See "Requirements for Tape Recorders," p. 230.

type baffle and the acoustical labyrinth type baffle are both considered excellent for obtaining uniform frequency response.

Record Changer Mechanism: If the record player has an automatic record-changer mechanism there should also be a manual control. This is essential for classroom use if the teacher wishes to play only portions of the recording or wishes to spot certain themes.

Portability: Same as for tape recorders.[1]

Availability of Servicing: Same as for tape recorders.[1]

GUIDE FOR SELECTING PROJECTION EQUIPMENT

Opaque Projector. This machine makes possible the projection of printed, written, or other illustrative material. Advanced designing has made this projector so efficient that its use in the classroom has been broadened considerably. The *advantages* are: (a) It makes it possible for a large group to see an object at the same time, and in the same color as the original, (b) much material is available free or at low cost, and (c) inexpensive and simple to operate. The *disadvantages* are: (a) Older projectors have no fan, causing the visual material to curl and lose focus or burn, (b) bulkiness and weight of older models, (c) the room must be quite dark for good results, and (d) it is difficult to show fine detail.

To be adequate an opaque projector should have a scanning area at least large enough to accommodate an 8½ by 11 inch sheet of paper. The projected image should be bright enough to be seen clearly in a darkened classroom without losing its effectiveness if some stray light is present. The machine should have a mechanical blower-type cooling system to carry off excessive heat. The projector should have a lens of sufficient focal length to permit projection at the proper distance from the screen at which the projector needs to be used. A 5″ focal length is correct for use in a small classroom, but a 6″ or 7″ lens may be needed for projection in a large room. Lenses of different focal lengths should be interchangeable in the equipment.

Overhead Projector. This type of projector makes it possible for the teacher to face the class while projecting over her head to the screen behind her. The advantages are obvious and should be realized more fully by the music educator. The same general specifications given for the opaque projector apply to this machine.

Slide and Film Strip Projectors. The following general types fall into this category of projectors which utilize transparencies:

Standard Slide Projector. Handles 3¾″ by 4″ glass slides.

Miniature Slide Projector. Handles 2″ by 2″ transparencies, standard size of the 35 mm still camera.

Film Strip Projector. Handles 35 mm film strips from 12″ to 48″ in length, containing a dozen or more single frames in sequence. Machines that can project filmstrips both horizontally and vertically are recommended.

Combination Projectors. Many projectors combine the features of two or more of the types listed above, either through design or by special attachments. Among the newer designs are *Sound-Film Strip Projectors*, which allow synchronized slide or film strip projection with either tape or disk recordings.

To be adequate, slide and film strip projectors should be light, strong, and compact, for easy carrying from classroom to classroom. To obtain satisfactory results in a semi-darkened classroom with the window shades drawn, the projection bulb should be at least 500 to 1,000 watts.

In situations where several slides are to be shown in sequence, a mechanism should be provided which allows successive slides to be placed into position through a simple mechanical device. The focal length and need for cooling system are the same as given for the opaque projector.

Motion Picture Projectors—Silent and Sound. Safety 16mm films have become standard for school use. In analyzing the needs of your school situation many requirements and features should be taken into consideration. The following outline provides a guide for motion picture equipment.

In analyzing your needs in 16mm motion picture projection, the place where

---

[1] See "Requirements for Tape Recorders." p. 231.

the machine will be used, the number of machines, and operating personnel will need to be considered.

Type of Set-up Desired. If the showing of films is to be within the classroom, special attention must be given to portability of projector, speed of set-up and break-down of equipment, sound quality and room acoustics, picture brilliance and room darkness, emergency repair by the operator, blackout facilities, and the type of screen. If a special visual aids room is to be used, special attention can be given to picture quality, high fidelity of sound, silent and sound speeds, reverse, stop-frame, and other special features such as screen type adapted to the special room, and acoustical treatment.

Number of Projectors. If there is but a single projector, special attention should be given such features as having both sound and silent speeds in the one projector, reverse, stop-frame, dependability, PA and phonograph adaption, quality of sound in classroom and the auditorium, picture brillance, and speed of repair and service. For systems or building units with two or more projectors, the features indicated above become less important. Owning two or more different types of machines will permit adaptation to any special needs.

Operating Personnel. If student or teacher operators are used, special attention should be given to portability, simplicity of operation, ease in training students or teachers for operation, and minor maintenance. With an operator-specialist, simplicity and trainability are of less importance and other salient features may be stressed.

Features to consider in 16mm equipment are dependability, portability, simplicity of operation, picture and sound quality, and maintenance.

Dependability. Good service and repair history for a given make of projector in operation over a period of time; projector permanently mounted within a rugged carrying case; and ample protection of film against damage by scratching, tearing, etc., while projector is in operation.

Portability. This concerns a minimum of weight as well as compactness for projector and speaker.

Simplicity of Operation. For speed of set-up and break-down, the reel arms and belts should be attached and should not interfere with the table upon which the projector is mounted. For threading, the film gate and sprocket shoes should be handy to regulate; sufficient light source to aid in threading film in darkened room; a line indicator or other means to indicate film path; a regulator or line indicator for length of loops of film. A vernier elevation adjustment for projector case, a sensitive control for lens focus, and a frame line adjustment are necessary for correct focus and framing. All switches and controls should be readily accessible to the operator and easily read even in a darkened room. Adequate manual directions should be available and consulted.

Picture Quality and Brilliance. Maximum brilliance should be used. To permit operation under a wide variety of light conditions 1,000 watts is recommended. The field should be uniform and free from bright spots and shadows with sharp focus over entire area of picture. The SMPE [1] picture test reel provides ideal targets for testing. The picture should be steady.

Quality of Sound. The sound should be clear, intelligible, and free from distortion with an adequate power output of ten or more watts. Tone control should permit adjustments of balance between "highs" and "lows" for different rooms when control is at normal or high fidelity position. The amplifier output should be at least ten or more watts, to fill without distortion the largest auditorium in which the projector will be used. A large external speaker (12″ or more) should be provided.

Maintenance: Standardized replacement parts are easily secured. The ease of minor replacements will depend upon the accessibility of projection and exciter lamps, fuses, belts, etc. An emergency repair kit containing extra projection lamp, fuses, belts, small tools, oil, etc., and adequate service and checkup facilities for projector in your territory will be necessary.

Other Features. Older silent films (16 frames per second) can be shown on sound speed (24 frames per second), but the action is speeded up. For general use both speeds are desirable. On occasion reverse is desirable for certain films. The sound should be turned off during reversal. A stop-frame is of limited use for certain detailed study of a picture but the sound should be turned off for this feature. Different projection conditions demand lenses of different focal lengths

---

[1] Society of Motion Picture Engineers, Hotel Statler, New York, N. Y.

so it is wise to investigate the needs for average as well as for any special use for the projector. P.A. and phonograph use is sometimes advantageous and the special equipment—microphone and phonograph pickup—must be matched to the amplifier. Magnetic sound track equipment is now available utilizing a magnetic (rather than optical) sound track. This permits the teacher to record sound and edit it to fit special needs.

Other Mechanical and Electrical Equipment. In recent years, many electrical and mechanical devices have been developed which are useful in one or more phases of music education. Those items which have been discussd on audio-visual equipment, and those developments of most recent origin which give promise of future significance in music education merit inclusion.[1]

The Stroboscope. This electronic instrument (sometimes called the Stroboconn) provides an objective and accurate method of checking pitch by visual means. Many directors have found it to be an invaluable aid in developing optimum intonation possibilities of singers and of instrumentalists. This device is also useful in the tuning of pianos, organs, etc.

The Tachistoscope. This visual aid is a mechanized version of the "flash card" idea useful in the development of music reading. By control of exposure time and difficulty of a projected image, it is possible to develop speed and increase the span in reading music. The teacher can build a tachistoscope by adding a shutter arrangement to a regular slide or film strip projector.

Magnestrip Recording for Films. By means of this new process it is possible to provide your own tailor-made sound track on a motion picture film. The process is similar to tape recording, but provides permanent synchronization of sound and picture. For small groups a sound-treated studio is not required. Larger groups may use a stage, thus permitting some control of acoustics by closing, partly closing, or completely opening the regular stage curtains. In the absence of this special recording equipment a similar result can be produced by making a tape recording to accompany a silent motion picture film. The problem of synchronization is rather difficult.

Electronic Tuning Devices. The original device in this category appeared as a mechanized electronic substitute for the standard tuning bar. By means of this equipment, either an *A* or a *B flat* can be sounded continuously at either of two volume levels as a standard of comparison for members of instrumental music groups who desire to tune their instruments before rehearsals. The original device in this category was called the *Lecktro Tuner*. A more recent version of a similar item adds a so-called "magic eye" which provides a switch arrangement to allow visual corroboration when the correct pitch is matched by the student.

Screens. There are three common types of screens—beaded, flat, and silver. Each serves a somewhat different purpose. The beaded screen is best used in a small room. It picks up light and has a high reflective power, but the brightness falls off as the observer moves out from the center of the screen. The flat (matte) screen needs more illumination but it is better for large audience viewing, especially for spectators seated beyond the 30-degree angle. The silver screen is somewhere between the two in terms of intensity of illumination and even distribution of light to all seats, but it is less adequate for color reproduction.

Before selecting a screen it should be demonstrated in the auditorium or classroom under the conditions that it will be used. The portable roll screen is a practical answer for general classroom purposes. It is hoped that a permanent screen will become standard equipment for every classroom.

Slides[2]

Transparencies 2″ by 2″. The 2″by 2″ photographic slide may be in Kodachrome or black and white. For permanent use these slides should be mounted between glass.

This visual aid, which is in common use today, has innumerable uses such as for evaluation of progress by recording activities and events, to help the student

---

[1] Additional items are listed in *Music Education Source Book*, p. 158.
[2] From an article by Delinda Roggensack. *Music Educators Journal*, February-March 1953, p. 49.

see himself as others see him, to show good and bad embouchure, posture, to show marching band formations, to show instruments and combinations of instruments, for public relations—to show school activities in the community, and to show pictures of travel and historic places which can be correlated with music.

Lantern Slides 3¼″ by 4″. These slides are so simple to create that even the youngest students can make some kinds.[1] This type of slide has many uses and they are easy to project. With the use of a flash meter (tachistoscope) it can be a fine aid to the sight-reading program.

There are several varieties of slides, each of which serves a specific purpose:

(1) Silhouette or cutout slides perhaps best serve the earlier grades. The figure or cutout is mounted between two plain glass slides and taped together. Attractive ones may be made by using different colors of cellophane in place of opaque paper.

(2) With a gelatin coating (Knox's gelatin) or a thin coat of shellac (Eastman Kodak retouching fluid), very attractive slides can be made on plain glass with India ink, slide inks, or water color.

(3) The most common type and the most easily made is the etched glass slide. Pencil, or slide crayons, work very well and make beautiful slides. This slide magnifies many times, so unless color strokes are in the same direction the effect is not pleasing. If slides are to be a part of permanent equipment, etched glass should be covered with a plain glass and taped.

(4) Because glass slides are breakable, the plastic slide has an advantage. There are two kinds, clear and etched. One can accomplish the same effects as with glass slides. The tendency of plastic to curl necessitates the use of heavy paper or card frame.

(5) It is possible through the use of photographic solutions to transfer photographed materials to glass slides. Many of the commercial slides are so made.

(6) Typewritten materials may be used by utilizing a piece of cellophane cut to size with carbon paper folded over it so that the carbon side is against the cellophane on both front and back, or designs, charts, or symbols may be drawn. The cellophane thus prepared should be placed between glass slides to prevent smudging, wrinkling, or curling.

HIGH FIDELITY[2]

Within the last few years a class of people arose in this country known as the "audio-philes." They represent a cross section of America, united in one common interest—music, and the improved reproduction of music. The upsurge of musical interest in this country, as music educators well know, is simply astounding. The audio-phile is a part of the great movement for improved reproduction of music, and through his interest in high quality sound reproduction is making a significant contribution to American musical culture.

One of the most apparent aspects in dealing with high fidelity audio equipment is that there are a number of widely divergent opinions held by audio-philes. Therefore, in discussing "hi-fi" it is important to respect divergencies and to be concerned with some of the generally accepted basic principles.

Basically, there are only four units in any electronic phonograph system. These are the pickup, turntable, amplifier, and speaker. The pickup is classified as "input

---

[1] *How to make Hand-Made Lantern Slides* (Meadville, Pa.: Keystone View Co.). Booklet, 10¢.
[2] From the report submitted by Wolfgang Kuhn, Urbana, Illinois, National Chairman, Music in American Education Committee on Audio-Visual Equipment.

equipment," or units which feed into or drive the amplifier. In this classification are also **AM**, **FM**, and **TV** tuners, as well as tape, wire, and disc recorders, and microphones. The amplifier functions as its name implies. In turn the amplifier drives the speaker units which enable us to hear. This may be a very simple description, but it is the skeleton on which every electronic audio-system is built.

Given an understanding of the fundamental components of an audio system, one goes about getting acquainted with the varieties of equipment available. In the *first* place, there are excellent magazines,[1] which deal authoritatively in this field. *Secondly,* catalogues and other literature are available from some of the mail-order radio jobbers. Such catalogues will include much helpful information in this whole area.

Since the possible approaches to the problems of installing high-fidelity equipment are numerous, and since any budget provided for this purpose is necessarily limited in some respects, the following two general statements may be helpful. (a) The amplifier is the most important item of the system, and it is unwise to skimp on this component. (b) Approximately three times the cost of the amplifier can be spent on speaker systems and input equipment before the characteristics of these units will exceed those of the high fidelity amplifier. For example, suppose that $50 has been spent for an amplifier; then it would be in line to spend $150 for the pickup, turntable, or record changer, and speaker. If more than $150 is involved in the purchase of these items, it would be best to find a better amplifier in order to match the quality of the other components.

Before installing your first hi-fi set, it is suggested that you search out the nearest audio-phile. He will be delighted to demonstrate his equipment and by "hearing" his installation you will not only make a friend, but will gain undoubtedly some practical as well as theoretical help with your own audio problems.

BINAURAL OR STEREOPHONIC SOUND

The development called binaural or stereophonic sound may revolutionize mechanical and electronic reproduction of sound. Compared with customary, monaural sound (including high-fidelity reproduction), binaural sound approximates that which is heard with two ears, while all other recording methods are limited to a "one-eared" effect. Many authorities limit the term "binaural sound" to the use of listening through headphones which bring two separate sound sources. A magnetic tape recorder equipped for binaural sound uses two microphones and makes simultaneous dual recordings on separate tracks which, when played back simultaneously through dual speakers, give dimension and presence to sound.

While binaural or stereophonic reproduction is not available to the public on phonograph recordings as yet, it is in common use with three-dimensional motion pictures. It is being used experimentally on a few metropolitan radio and television broadcasts.

Equipment for binaural and stereophonic tape recording is now available from several sources. This new look in sound reproduction provides a new dimension that must be heard to be appreciated. It offers unlimited new possibilities for the development of realism in the re-creation of sound through broadcast and recording.

The possibilities for development in the field of music education through the use of new equipment for audio-visual stimulation at the hands of a resourceful teacher appear to be almost unlimited.

---

[1] See *High Fidelity Magazine* (Great Barrington, Mass.: Milton B. Sleeper).

236

FLAT MATERIALS [1]

Bulletin Board, Flash Cards, Posters. These visual aids should do the following: (a) help learning to be effective and at the same time pleasant; (b) boldly focus attention; (c) correct mistaken concepts or form new concepts; (d) short-cut the symbolizing process[2]; and (e) encourage initiative and creativity in students.

Wise use of color line to attract the eye to the center of interest, colorful mountings for pictures, sectioned areas for bulletin board, for cartoon and stick figures will add to the interest of the viewer.

Flannel-Board. These boards are available commercially in several different sizes but can be made easily by using stiff, light-weight material such as cardboard, wallboard, or plywood to form the support over which can be stretched rough felt or flannel. Cut-outs of the same kind of materials will adhere to the board with only a simple pressure of the hand. Models made of paper or other materials will adhere if they are backed by a small piece of sandpaper. Pressed or smooth felt is undesirable as the surface needs to be rough. The simplicity of the felt board makes it ideal for pupil participation as young children can illustrate songs or work out note combinations for many melodies. It is a fine device for teaching music symbols and reading skills.

THREE DIMENSIONAL MATERIALS

Models are essentially a recognizable imitation of the original, workable or not. In music, this could be a model of a symphony orchestra using pipe cleaners, shaped into stick figures for players and paper folded into chairs and podium.

Mock-Ups rearrange the essential elements of the original being studied and concentrates on certain central points. The mock-up is extremely flexible; for example, an organ constructed in such a way that pipes of the instrument are emphasized.

Diorama means, "to see through," and is defined as a three-dimensional representation composed of various symbolic and real materials (pictures and specimens) frequently utilizing both transmitted and reflected light to produce a natural scenic effect. This might be a stage setting of an operetta; scenes from operas with or without the figures; the living room of Mozart's home with furniture of the period and figures dressed in costumes of the day.

SELECTED BIBLIOGRAPHY—AUDIO-VISUAL AIDS

Barnette, G. C. *Learning Through Seeing with Tachistoscopic Teaching Techniques.* Dubuque, Iowa: W. C. Brown, 1951.
Bretz, R. *Techniques of Television Production.* New York: McGraw-Hill Book Company, Inc., 1953.
Callahan, J. W. *Television in School, College and Community.* New York: McGraw-Hill Book Company, Inc., 1953.
Chase, Gilbert. *Music in Radio Broadcasting, A Symposium.* New York: McGraw-Hill Book Company, Inc., 1946.
Cooley, H. *Vision in Television.* New York: Channel Press, 1952.
Crews, Albert. *Radio Production Writing.* New York: Houghton Mifflin Company, 1944.
Dale, E. *Audio-Visual Methods in Teaching.* New York: Dryden Press, 1954.
Denman, F. *Television, the Magic Window.* New York: The Macmillan Company, 1952.
Eady, W. C. *Television, the Eyes of Tomorrow.* New York: Prentice-Hall, Inc., 1945.
Folwell, A. *Introduction to Television.* New York: Anglobooks, 1953.
Gould, J. *All About Radio and TV.* New York: Random House, 1953.
Green, T. L. *Making and Using Filmstrips.* New York: Pitman Publishing Corp., 1950.
Haas, K. B. and Packer, H. Q. *Preparation and Use of Audio-Visual Aids.* New York: Prentice-Hall, Inc., 1950.
Hubbell, Richard W. *Television Programming and Production.* New York: Murray Hill Books, Inc., 1945.

---

[1] From an article by Delinda Roggensack. *Music Educators Journal*, February-March 1953, p. 49.

[2] Edgar Dale, *Audio-Visual Methods in Teaching* (New York: Dryden Press, 1946).

Jones, C. *Your Career in Motion Pictures.* New York: Sheridan, 1949.

Kaufman, W. *Your Career in TV.* New York: Merlin, 1950.

Kinder, J. S. *Audio-Visual Materials and Techniques.* New York: American Book Company, 1950.

La Parade, Ernest. *Broadcasting Music.* New York: Rinehart & Company, Inc., 1947.

Levenson, W. B. *Teaching Through Radio and TV.* New York: Rinehart & Company, Inc., 1952.

Marx, H. L. (ed.). *Television and Radio in American Life.* New York: The H. W. Wilson Company, 1953.

McGill, Earle. *Radio Directing.* New York: McGraw-Hill Book Company, Inc., 1945.

McKown, H. C. and Roberts, A. B. *Audio-Visual Aids to Instruction.* (2nd ed.). New York: McGraw-Hill Book Company, Inc., 1949.

Milner, C. D. *Making Lantern Slides and Filmstrips.* New York: Focal Press Ltd., 1953.

Phillips, D. C. et al. *Introduction to Radio and Television.* New York: The Ronald Press, 1954.

Siepmann, Charles A. *Radio's Second Chance.* Boston: Little, Brown & Company, 1946.

Sumner, W. L. *Visual Methods in Education.* London: Basil Blackwell and Mott, 1951.

White, M. R. *Beginning Television Production.* Minneapolis: Burgess Publishing Co., 1953.

Wittich, W. A. and Schuller, C. *Audio-Visual Materials.* New York: Harper and Brothers, 1953.

Woelfel, N. and Tyler, I. K. (ed.). *Radio and the School.* New York: World Book Co., 1945.

CHAPTER XXIV

CONTEMPORARY MUSIC FOR AMERICAN SCHOOLS[1]

THE TITLE INDICATES a shifting from general interest in the subject of contemporary music [2] to a specific concern for the part that it might play in a well-rounded experience with music in our schools. It was logical that the first efforts to awaken interest in the use of contemporary materials were made exclusively in the high school and college areas. Certainly it was at these levels that a considerable volume of materials was available.

Compilation of lists of contemporary music for bands, orchestras, and choral groups was made in 1944-46, supplemented in 1946-48, and subsequently revised. In 1952 these lists were merged, revised again, and brought up to date. This list is entitled *Contemporary Music for American Schools.*[3]

During the MENC Biennial Convention at Philadelphia in 1952 a need was sensed for extending the work of the committee to the elementary field. One of the three panel speakers told of experiences in using contemporary music in teaching children. A major portion of the program of the special session at Chicago in 1954 was devoted to the proposition that "contemporary music is for the elementary school too." A choir of forty-two children from the fourth, fifth, and sixth grades from Evanston, Illinois, sang nine songs, seven of which had been written especially for them. The two composers present testified it was their first experience in writing for children at this age level. They were excited by the singing of the children and found it a stimulating and rewarding experience. The director of the group, which was prepared entirely by rehearsals outside of school, commented that there were no discipline problems and that there was a great deal of enthusiasm for the project. It was felt that the music was too difficult for the typical grade teacher to present, which is an important consideration in a day when so much of the singing is directed by the regular room teacher.

The point of view of the publisher was expressed to be one of willingness to cooperate when the need for contemporary music became clear through demands of music educators. The fact that so many costly mistakes have been made in the past is apt to make the publisher somewhat cautious. The importance of the composer visiting the classroom to learn the limitations of performance was also stressed.

An attempt was made through an article in the *Music Educators Journal* to stimulate interest in the experimental use of contemporary music for children's songs, as well as for rhythmic and listening activities. Considerable interest was shown by the letters that came in from all parts of the United States asking for suggestions. There is obviously much work to be done before contemporary music is to be welcomed wholeheartedly at the elementary level.

Time and patience will be needed to convince teacher-training institutions that an experience with, and an understanding of, contemporary music is an essential part of the training of music teachers and general elementary teachers. For those already in the field, workshops which would fill in the gaps in previous train-

---

[1] From the report submitted by Elizabeth Meloy, Muncie, Indiana, National Chairman, Music in American Education Committee on Contemporary Music for American Schools.
[2] Defined by the committee as "music which departs from the conventional in tonality or rhythm, or both."
[3] MENC publication. 25¢.

ing by acquainting teachers with new songs and recordings of contemporary music could be of great help in giving teachers courage to attempt the use of less conventional materials. Some music textbook publishers have begun to include songs in their books for children by well-known composers who are recognized as being truly contemporary in spirit. Many of these songs are quite fresh in tonal and rhythmic feeling; others rather more conventional introduce unusual harmonies in the accompaniments, which provide children with enriched aural experiences.

An Examination of Present-Day Music prepared by Mary Elizabeth Whitner,[1] gives an excellent and quite comprehensive listing of early-grade piano material, books, and recordings. This should prove invaluable to the serious musician who wishes to keep up to date in his techniques and understanding of music.

Considerable work towards organizing a list of contemporary materials for small instrumental ensembles has been done. There is a possibility of merging this list with those of other agencies in MENC. A closer working relationship with various committees would seem to be a necessity to make contemporary music a vital force in American schools.

RECOMMENDATIONS

(1) Suggest the inclusion of more truly contemporary songs in basic music textbooks for children.

(2) Encourage a more experimental approach in teaching children through contemporary music. Observe the interest and ability of children to learn to sing in all idioms; note their reactions to listening experiences in the area of contemporary music, their ability to respond to unusual rhythms.

(3) Search out new contemporary materials suitable to all levels and bring these to the attention of music educators. This would imply periodic revision of existing lists, making deletions and additions.

(4) Urge choral and instrumental conductors to include some contemporary music on all programs prepared for national, divisional, state, or local meetings in order to insure well-rounded experiences for students and audiences. It is suggested that placing the contemporary numbers near the beginning of a program is more effective than at the end.

(5) Make recordings of contemporary songs available so that the singing experiences of children will not be unduly limited by the singing ability of the teacher.

(6) Promote a closer liaison between the composer and the schoolroom; between the committee on Contemporary Music for American Schools and all other MENC committees concerned with instruction and materials.

The Place of Contemporary Music in our Schools[2]

The following statement by Robert Iglehart,[3] chairman of the Department of Art Education, New York University, points out that the aesthetic of modern art is the basis for the best development in art education. Thus, his statement is of interest to the music teachers whose own program must be measured and justified by comparable criteria.

From the point of view of the academy the work of the child is meaningless and without value. The emphasis upon personal expression, spon-

---

[1] MENC. 30¢.

[2] Prepared by Mary Elizabeth Whitner, National Education Director, Carl Fischer, Inc., Los Angeles, California.

[3] Carolyn Howlett, editor, *Directions in Art Education* (Yearbook of the Illinois Art Association, 1952).

taneity, inner direction and self-justifying form are, specifically, concerns of modern art as they are of art education; and the art teacher who is hostile or apathetic to the work of her contemporaries is denying, by implication, the validity of her own activity.

The emphasis of modern education is upon the child and his world. Consequently, unless education wishes to deny its own avowed purpose, the child and the best contemporary thought and expression of his own time must meet in the classroom. Whether or not the introduction grows into the intimacy of understanding and acceptance depends largely upon the imaginative wisdom and vision of the teacher.

Advocating the development of a musical culture compatible with social progress and, at the same time, recognizing the importance of historical perspective, Lilla Belle Pitts[1] writes:

> Neither the expression nor yet the communication of human values through musical creativity can be realized by devoting our teaching mainly to acquainting children and the public with "the best that has been thought and said," musically speaking. . . . The retracting of steps of the past in contemplation and imagination should be for the sake of giving more strength and light for unobstructed forward movement, rather than for the comfort of escaping into a well-ordered world where the problems of living have already been met and solved.

The noted architect, Frank Lloyd Wright,[2] calls attention to the need for an indigenous culture and deplores the tendency to teach "the safe course of a good copy." He feels the great architecture of the world should be studied solely in regard to the spirit that found expression in the form.

> Buildings growing in response to actual needs, fitted into an environment by people who knew no better than to fit them to it with native feeling (buildings that grew as folk-lore and folk song grew), are better worth study than highly self-conscious academic attempts at the beautiful . . .

An indigenous culture can be achieved only through the creative consciousness of a people. The awareness of individual, independent thought, which is creative consciousness, must be stirred at the earliest possible moment so that each man turns from the safe anonymity of tradition to become a pioneer, relying upon his own courage, sense of values, and self-knowledge.

To the extent that both are concerned with a wise reconciliation of man with his environment, the aims of education and the arts are mutual. Through the use of the arts as a means of arousing and directing creative consciousness, education and, even more important, the needs of mankind are best served.

In its broadest sense, contemporary simply means "existing, living or occurring at the same time." Obviously, this all-inclusive interpretation, when applied to contemporary music, would cover all music existing or being created at the present time. We must therefore distinguish between what is merely contemporary in time and what is contemporary in spirit and thought—what is compatible with our present-day world. Putting aside such terms as music of our time, new music, twentieth-century music and present-day music, perhaps we should say that by contemporary music we simply mean modern music as partially defined, at least, by Igor Stravinsky.[1]

> What is modern is what is representative of its own time and what must be in keeping with and within the grasp of its own time. Sometimes

---

[1] Lilla Belle Pitts, *The Music Curriculum in a Changing World* (New York: Silver Burdett Company, 1944), pp. 102-103.
[2] Frank Lloyd Wright, *On Architecture, Selected Writings* 1894-1940 (New York: Duell, Sloan and Pearce, 1941), p. 63.
[1] Igor Stravinsky, *Poetics of Music* (Cambridge: Harvard University Press, 1947), p. 81.

artists are reproached for being too modern or not modern enough. One might just as well reproach the times with not being sufficiently modern or with being too modern.

The contemporary composer has unlimited technical and musical resources at his disposal. As stated by Aaron Copland,[1] "There is no such thing any longer as an inadmissable chord, or melody, or rhythm—given the proper context, of course." With such freedom, however, goes the responsibility of communication. Music as a language must be accessible and meaningful. Otherwise, the composer is defeated by what is variously referred to as "the convention of being unconventional," "the cult of the unintelligible," "the necessity of being absolutely modern"—all indicating a confusion of means with end, techniques with idea.

Implicit in modern education is its obligation to keep pace with contemporary thought. The modern music educator knows that he must present the *whole* of musical experience to those students under his guidance, including the music of their own time. Otherwise, he will find himself irrevocably reduced to "the safe course of a good copy." Modern art seems to have received more widespread recognition in the school program than has modern music, doubtless because changes and innovations in art may be more readily defined.

It is difficult, for example, to accomplish for music what is done for art by Rathbun and Hayes[2] in *Layman's Guide to Modern Art*. This book outlines in terms accessible to the layman the reasons for abstract forms in painting, comparisons of old and new techniques, and the influence of modern environment on the artist's use of abstract images. More thought should be given to comparably effective ways of presenting modern music so that the elements of tradition and innovation which exist side by side in our present-day music may be more easily grasped.

The child, being a creature of his own time, will accept the validity of modern artistic expression if he encounters it without self-consciousness and with the unprejudiced guidance of parent or teacher. Once his feet are planted firmly in traditional paths, he will have to be reconciled to contemporary thought and expression. In her remarkably helpful book, *Children and Music*, Beatrice Landeck[3] points out:

> The child who is familiar with the music of primitive cultures, who knows a wide variety of folk songs, and has himself spontaneously created music, will not be outraged—or even surprised—by the tonalities and rhythms of modern music.

Much remains to be done before modern music takes its place naturally and inevitably in the classroom experience. Not only must the sympathetic support of the teachers be enlisted, but also the composer must somehow become aware of the great need and opportunity offered in the educational field. The distance between the child and the composer is too great. Receptivity is one of the essential elements of communication, yet the composer loses his audience before he gains it.

"Each age—like each person—requires a new formulation of its expressive life, one that is in keeping with its own discovery of the world and the worth of life." Thus Lilla Belle Pitts[4] reminds us that what we most need in education, in the arts, and in our everyday experience is that creative consciousness which is a perpetual renewal of the spirit, a bright hope for tomorrow, without which no culture can long survive.

---

[1] Aaron Copland, *Music and Imagination* (Cambridge: Harvard University Press, 1952), p. 62.
[2] Mary Chalmers Rathbun and Bartlett H. Hayes, Jr., *Layman's Guide to Modern Art* (New York: Oxford University Press, 1949.)
[3] Beatrice Landeck, *Children and Music* (New York: William Sloane Associates, Inc., 1952), p. 225.
[4] Pitts, *op. cit.*, p. 99.

CHAPTER XXV

OPERA IN AMERICAN SCHOOLS[1]

THE OPERA IN AMERICAN SCHOOLS COMMITTEE concentrated on establishing in the minds of music educators:

——The adaptability of operatic material for the general music education of boys and girls.

——To make clear the type of material that was suitable for performance in chorus, orchestra, band, ensemble, and in operatic sources on all levels of music education. The basic concept was not centered in performance but rather in appreciation in the broadest application of the term.

Close affiliation with the Metropolitan Opera Guild and with its educational program was established, and the resources of the Guild were made available to the Conference committees. Division meetings of the MENC began by emphasizing the opera workshop on the college level, using cuttings from operatic material suitable for elementary schools, and puppet presentations of opera and creation of stage settings by boys and girls. Opera sings were held; groups of people sang excerpts and cuttings from opera in unison and simple arrangements; community opera relations were stressed and the scope of the project began to appear in perspective. The opera sing has become a popular feature of many division and conference programs. It was learned that much of the music in certain operas, especially from the older works, were good tunes and that boys and girls could sing and enjoy them. It was found that this music made enjoyable listening material.

Radio and the beginnings of television provided valuable resources for this total program with the emphasis on operatic materials. Syllabi, containing many sources of materials for vocal solos, instrumental solos, and ensembles of all kinds, were prepared through the cooperation of MENC and the Metropolitan Opera Guild.

The National Federation of Music Clubs in certain areas sponsored opera activity. This organization cooperated with our "Opera in Education" program and the forward movement began.

The Development. From 1947 to 1954, progress was steady as interest grew. The MENC sponsored the first American performance of "Let's Make An Opera," by Benjamin Britton. At St. Louis (1950), in addition to the Britton Opera, a very interesting opera-sing based on the "Marriage of Figaro" was presented featuring high school chorus, elementary chorus, and soloists.

At the Detroit Conference (1948), a concert version of "Tannhauser" suitable for boys and girls was given, and versions of "The Magic Flute" began to appear. Creative adaptations of existing works began to be offered by publishers and by individual teachers. The works of Sungaard and Wilder, including the "Lowland Sea" and "Cumberland Fair" were presented on conference programs. Symposiums and discussions of matters concerning the opera's place in music education were frequently held at In-and-About Clubs, at university centers, and on various national and division conference programs. Many persons participated in the process of developing and emphasizing opera as a part of school music.

One of the high lights of the Philadelphia MENC Convention (1952) was the Metropolitan Opera broadcast on a nationwide hookup presented as a feature of

---

[1] From the report submitted by Clarke Maynard, Wilmington, Delaware, National Chairman, Music in American Education Committee on Opera in American Schools.

the Conference program. At the Chicago convention of the MENC (1954), the opera workshop of the University of Michigan presented scenes from the "Masked Ball" by Verdi and "The Bartered Bride" by Smetana; in addition, a panel of experts discussed the various issues of operatic presentations and operetta material on all levels of instruction.

The whole history of this project has been one of emphasis rather than any attempt to indicate that operatic material was any new thought in general music education. Songbooks for years have included operatic excerpts and arias. Since the MENC programs have all emphasized this particular aspect of musical education, it is hoped that they will continue to do so.

The opera aims and objectives for the future should include the following:

(1) Continued emphasis of the educational approach to operatic material both from the past and contemporary repertoire as it operates from the appreciative standpoint in its broadest sense, as well as from the narrower aspect of performance of given works or excerpts.

(2) In dealing with the existing works, good taste must be exercised in order to present the plots and the musical difficulties suitably for students at given levels.

(3) The area should probably be expanded to encompass the *music drama* or *musical-dramatic performances*. Festivals which in organization are tied together and other pageant-like forms should be included so that the dramatic qualities of music which are wedded to a plot, a text, and a continuity get proper attention.

(4) Perhaps a contemporary work from a fine composer which will be adapted for young people of high school age could be commissioned, as well as the production of works which are of operatic nature for younger children. These should be expertly composed and tastefully wedded to a fine story.

(5) The appointment of an auxiliary committee of composers and other persons who can act as advisers is highly desirable. This would assure the on-going process of creation to meet the needs of boys and girls in the music-drama field.

(6) Affiliation in a broad way with such organizations as the Opera Guild, the National Federation of Music Clubs opera effort and other nationwide clubs for the promulgation of opera in the experiences of the people should be encouraged.

(7) Teachers of music in schools should be encouraged to make their own adaptations or "cuttings" and to try their hands in the creation of new materials. As the teaching profession becomes aware of ways to edit and adapt, its members will become more sensitive to good adaptations and editing on the part of others.

SELECTED BIBLIOGRAPHY

Cross, Milton. *Complete Stories of Four Great Operas.* New York: Doubleday & Company, Inc., 1947.
Davidson, G. *Stories from Gilbert and Sullivan.* Toronto: Smithers and Bonellie, 1952.
Goldovsky, Boris. *Accents on Opera.* New York: Farrar, Straus and Young, 1953.
Grabbe, Paul. *Story of a Hundred Operas.* New York: Grossett and Dunlap, Inc., 1940.
Graf, Herbert. *Opera for the People.* Minneapolis: University of Minnesota Press, 1951.
Grout, Donald J. *A Short History of Opera.* New York: Columbia University Press, 1947.
Kite, Helen. *Stories from the Great Metropolitan Operas.* New York: Random House, 1943.
Marek, George R. *Front Seat at the Opera.* New York: Allen, Towne and Heath, 1948.
Newman, Ernest. *Stories of Great Operas.* New York: Garden City Publishing Co., 1948.
————. *Opera Nights.* New York: G. P. Putnam's Sons, 1947.
O'Connell, Charles (ed.). *Victor Book of the Opera* (11th ed.). New York: Simon and Schuster, 1949.
Peltz, Mary Ellis. *Behind the Golden Curtain.* New York: Farrar, Straus and Young, 1950.
————. *Opera Lovers Companion.* New York: Biff-Davis, 1948.
Peltz, Mary E. and Lawrence, Robert. *Metropolitan Opera Guide.* New York: Random House, 1943.
Schwimmer, Franceska. *Great Musicians as Children* (set). New York: Doubleday & Company, Inc., 1940.
Smethurst, H. *Opera Production for Amateurs.* Toronto: Smithers and Bonellie, 1951.
Williams, S. *You and the Opera.* London: Macdonald and Evans, 1952.
Williams, S. *In the Opera House.* New York: McGraw-Hill Book Company, Inc., 1952.
Four Books of the Opera, "Aida," "Lohengrin," "Hansel and Gretel," "Ring of the Nibelung." New York: Grossett and Dunlap, Inc.
Folio of Opera Pictures. New York: Silver Burdett Company.

SECTION SEVEN

Study Projects

Credentials for Teaching Music in the Schools

Chairman: J. J. Weigand, Emporia, Kans.

✠

Music Education and Adult Education

Chairman: Jack M. Watson, Bloomington, Ind.

✠

Music Education for Exceptional Children

Chairman: Wilhelmina Harbert, Stockton, Calif.

Music Education in the Community

Chairman: Evelyn Waltman Becker, York, Pa.

✠

Music Education and the National Welfare

Chairman: Newell H. Long, Bloomington, Ind.

Cooperation with the Armed Services

Virginia Carty, chairman, Baltimore, Md.

CHAPTER XXVI

CREDENTIALS FOR TEACHING MUSIC
IN THE SCHOOLS[1]

THE CERTIFICATION of teachers in the United States has been a major problem of the profession in recent years. In investigating the area of music teacher certification it was found that the procedure for securing certificates varies in almost every state. Some guide books give specific credit hours of music and education and some suggest minimum hours; others give vague statements that allow teacher-training institutions to give either a bare minimum of music hours or an oversupply as happens in a few instances.

Some state music education associations have endeavored to make recommendations concerning certification to colleges and state departments of education during the last five years.

Those who are working in state music education associations should study continually the certification problems of music teachers within their state. An effort should be made to develop recommendations as to competencies deemed necessary for successful music teaching on both elementary and secondary levels. All schools within a state giving instruction leading to degrees in music education should be advised of recommendations presented to the state certification officers.

New materials concerning credentials from Tennessee, California, Georgia, and Oklahoma have come to attention recently. Other states are in the process of organizing material for presentation to state boards of education and local certification agencies.

California. In 1952 the Credentials Committee in California published a recommendation for distribution to certification agencies and schools for study in revising the current teaching certificate. The action included proposals from the association and a definite proposed curriculum.

Georgia. In May of 1953, the Committee on Teacher Education in Music of the Georgia Music Educators Association issued a publication entitled *Teacher Education in Music for Georgia*, which is being used by the State Teachers Education Council and the State Department of Education as a minimum guide in the certification of music teachers in Georgia. The preface states: "Along with the suggested degree program we have attempted to outline the job of a school music teacher. We have also made suggestions as to the type of background and training we feel it is necessary for a teacher to have who is to be entrusted with the training of teachers at the college level."

Oklahoma. The Oklahoma Music Educators Association published a booklet of recommendations to institutions of higher education approved for teacher training in education, and to local officials within the state.

Tennessee. Tennessee is now at work on a music teacher certification plan to fit the new Regulations for Certification of Teachers that went into effect in September, 1953.

---

[1] From the report submitted by J. J. Weigand, Emporia, Kansas, National Chairman, Music in American Education Committee on Credentials for Teaching Music in the Schools.

Organizations preparing to study the certification problem in local areas will find definite information in the following sources:

Armstrong, W. Earl and Stinnett, T. M. *A Manual on Certification Requirements for School Personnel in the United States*. Washington, D. C.: National Education Association, 1953. $2.00.

Hood, Marguerite V. *The Evaluation of Music Education* (Standards for the evaluation of the college curriculum for the training of school music teachers). Chicago: Music Educators National Conference, 1953. 20c.

Recommendations of the Oklahoma Music Educators Association. Norman, Okla.: University of Oklahoma, 1952.

Teacher Education in Music for Georgia. Athens, Ga.: University of Georgia, 1953.

Wolfe, Irving. *State Certification of Music Teachers*. Nashville, Tenn.: George Peabody College for Teachers, 1954. $1.25, paper bound; $2.00, cloth bound.

Results of Questionnaire Sent to Conservatories [1]

Of the various types of institutions sharing in the important task of preparing young people to teach music in the public schools, not all are affected equally by the problems of credentials and certification. To the music departments of, or the conservatories [2] affiliated with, colleges or universities, this matter is seldom of concern. For these college-connected institutions the path has been cleared by long-standing recognition of the specific academic programs of the colleges or universities of which they are a part. The independent nonaffiliated conservatories, however, moving entirely on their own, frequently have found obstacles on the road to recognition.

Recognizing the existence of this situation, the MENC Committee on Credentials for Teaching Music in the Schools undertook as one of its projects an investigation of how independent conservatories are faring with the problems of music education. A questionnaire was drawn up and, since almost all of the independent conservatories preparing school music teachers are or would probably eventually be members of the National Association of Schools of Music, accrediting agency in music at the college level, it was decided that the questionnaire should be sent to the independent member schools. (It should be noted here that the NASM membership also includes the music departments and affiliated music schools of very many leading colleges and universities.)

Of the twenty questionnaires sent, eighteen replies were received. Three replies from university affiliated schools were eliminated.

The questions and résumé of fifteen replies were as follows:

(1) *Is your institution accredited for certifying teachers in your state?* It was gratifying to receive a 100% affirmative answer. This would indicate that on the local scene, where the school is known, where the contacts can be made and the impact felt, there seems to be no special difficulty in securing recognition.

(2) *Does your state have a State Council or similar organization on Teacher Training, and are you represented thereon? Is there, in your state, a State Council or similar organization on Higher Education, and do you have representation thereon?* Ten replied that their states had such Councils, but only one stated that it was represented thereon. This would imply that although these institutions have the status of colleges, they are as yet almost completely ignored in the academic advisory and policy groups of the state—and this in spite of the growing recognition of music as a potent cultural and educational force.

(3) *Does your (or neighboring) state recognize the National Association of Schools of Music for purposes of accreditation or does it demand membership in such associations as the North Central Association only?* Ten declared that their

---

[1] Prepared by Samuel Berkman, Hartford, Connecticut, and Wiktor Labunski, Kansas City, Missouri. members of the National Committee on Credentials for Teaching Music in the Schools.

[2] The term "conservatory" is used here to apply to those music schools and colleges established for and limited primarily to offering courses in professional music.

states recognized NASM membership; five, that their states had no specific requirements for membership in any association; four, that the NASM was not recognized in some or all of their neighboring states; and one, that only Regional Academic Associations were recognized. It must be added to the above that in the experience of some of the member schools, there are a number of states which do not accept membership in the NASM for accreditation.

(4) *If the NASM is not recognized, does your state accept the endorsement of an approved college as implied through its willingness to accept the credentials of your students for advanced study?* Out of six replies three said "yes," one did not know, one said his state had no policy, and one that it was never required.

(5) *Do you have any difficulties in locating your education majors in public schools for practice teaching and observation?* All replied. There was only one affirmative answer, indicating good relations between the conservatory and its community.

(6) *Are you affiliated with a university, college, or teachers college?* One answered in the affirmative and the university with which it is affiliated actually awards the music education degree, so that there is no problem of recognition for that curriculum.

(7) *If you are not: (a) Are you facing problems concerning the offering of academic and educational subjects to your students? (b) What arrangements do you have with a university or teachers college in your city? (c) Do you accept credits earned by correspondence?* Three schools were found to have problems of transportation and scheduling, three were completely staffed, one was partially staffed and partially made arrangements with neighboring colleges, and five sent students to local colleges and universities for their academic work. On the question of the acceptance of credits earned by correspondence, six would accept a limited amount and four would accept none.

Summary. Although more research needs to be done before the picture can be entirely clear, this survey has brought to light valuable information. It is particularly gratifying to observe that the independent conservatories have been able to more than hold their own in the face of the difficulties they are known to have, especially with educators who do not quite understand how the professional music school fits into the educational scheme. It is evident that the private conservatory feels it must remain constant to its original purpose, which is to serve music as an art and to jealously safeguard professional and music standards.

CHAPTER XXVII

MUSIC AND ADULT EDUCATION[1]

MUSIC EDUCATORS cannot avoid being interested in, and concerned with, music in the lives of the adult members of our communities because of the very nature of music work. There are two aspects of this interest and concern.

(1) *The Current Status*, or *what is.* The present status of music for adults is an indication of the effectiveness of the work done in the public schools and colleges. If the aims of music education are viewed in more than "now-is-the-moment" terms (and this must be done if the needs of society are to be met), then there must be vital concern about the extent of carryover of musical activity from school life to adult life.

(2) *The Future Status*, or *what should be.* Ways of decreasing the gap between *what is* and *what should be* holds considerable challenge and deserves immediate attention.

As a source of insight into these two issues, three blocks of material are presented: An outline of a significant program which is now in operation in Denver, a concise statement of principles for organizing a community music program, and a summary of the proposals of Commission B of the International Conference on the Role of Music in the Education of Youth and Adults.

Some Principles for Organizing a Community Music Program [2]

General Objectives. The primary objective of a community music program should be to enrich the lives of as many people as possible through music. Musical responsiveness should be stimulated in many ways by means of many activities. Planning for a community program cannot, however, begin with activities. It must begin with the needs of the people who wish to be participants with orchestras, singing groups, etc., as a result. These organizations will be in answer to specific needs, will be adjusted to meet those needs, and will be augmented by many other activities scaled to the abilities and prior experiences of the members.

A second objective of a community music program should be to exploit the social values of music. Many serious social problems can be relieved in part by music activities. The necessity for recreation by the rapidly expanding aged population and the reduction of intergroup misunderstandings and tensions are two examples.

This type of music program can be an excellent laboratory in which the participants may learn not only music, but leadership and organizational skills as well.

Some Principles for Organizing a Program. Various basic principles are involved in the organization of a community music program which aims to serve the adult population of a given area. The following items should be considered in the light of local conditions and needs:

---

[1] From the report submitted by Jack M. Watson, Bloomington, Indiana, National Chairman, Music in American Education Committee on Music Education and Adult Education.
[2] Prepared by Mark Dolliver, Jr., Youngstown, Ohio.

(1) People who are to be affected by the program should take part in the planning; thus the participants would be more likely to identify themselves with the activity. They should be consulted continually through their representatives on a coordinating council. This would serve not only to get a consensus of opinion, but to keep before the participants the underlying motives of the program.

(2) Goals, both musical and social, immediate and far-reaching, should be kept in view by the leaders and the participants.

(3) Leaders and organizers who are music educators should be sure that the experiences in the various activities increase the participants' knowledge, understanding, and enjoyment of music.

(4) Activities should be correlated not only within the community music program, but with other educational and cultural activities within the city.

(5) Activities should have an informal, recreational quality.

(6) Participants should be made aware that modern music teaching methods are much more enjoyable than the lessons they may have experienced in their childhood.

(7) Planning too many or too few activities should be avoided.

(8) Participants should be helped sympathetically and intelligently even though their questions seem elementary or their tastes naive.

(9) Discouraging factors such as inaccessibility of facilities should be avoided as far as possible.

(10) Organizers should not try to imitate the programs of other cities. Although aiming for the same general goals and following the same underlying method, programs will differ in the particulars of organization and in the kinds and numbers of activities.

Upon these bases a program can be built. A community music council can be formed, activities organized, and leadership developed. The program can seek support from the city recreation department, the public school adult education program, the Community Chest, or whatever other agencies seem receptive. The final product should be a constantly expanding and improving education-recreational program rich in musical and social values.

The Municipal Music Program of the City and County of Denver [1]

Sponsorship. This municipal music program is sponsored by the Parks and Recreation Department of the City and County of Denver, under a coordinator of music, and had its beginning July, 1952.

Purpose. To provide opportunities for further participation in the fields of choral and instrumental music, by adults or postgraduates, for the purposes of recreation, relaxation, and education.

Objectives. (a) More and better music for more people through participation and through listening (audiences), and (b) to supplement, not supplant, existing musical opportunities in the city.

Organizations. The following organizations have been established since January 5, 1953, and comprise the Denver Municipal Musical Association: North Denver Chorus, South Denver Chorus, East Denver Chorus, Central Denver

---

[1] Prepared by Robert Smith, Coordinator of Music, City and County of Denver, and presented by John T. Roberts, Director of Music, Denver Public Schools, at the MENC Biennial Convention, Chicago, 1954.

Chorus, **Manual District Chorus**, "The Goldenaires" (a chorus for persons over 50 years of age), Denver Symphonic Band, Denver String Orchestra.

Each organization elects its own officers to assist the director and carry out the social affairs of the organization.

Membership. Open to all citizens of the City and County of Denver and surrounding communities. A membership fee of one dollar is set for all organizations for the year. This fee is a token payment and gives the participant the feeling of "belonging" to the organizations. It is the only expense incurred by the participants. The total 1954 paid-up membership was 486. Attendance at rehearsals averages between four and five hundred each week.

Staff. Directors and accompanists are engaged for each organization on a part-time basis and are selected from public school music teachers, University of Denver faculty, and local music teachers.

Directors are paid six dollars per hour and conduct one two-hour rehearsal each week. The requirements for directors are a master's degree or at least five years' experience in the choral or instrumental fields. Accompanists are paid four dollars per hour and must have a bachelor's degree, or be in the process of acquiring same. Directors and accompanists are paid for all concert appearances and administrative meetings called by the coordinator.

Rehearsal Facilities. Through the courtesy and cooperation of the director of music of the Denver Public Schools, who is also chairman of the Mayor's Music Committee, and the Board of Education, all the municipal musical organizations are permitted the use of the specially equipped music rooms of the Denver Public Schools at no charge. This is a most important factor in the success of the program. It also gives the taxpayer more value or spread for the tax dollar.

Performances. All organizations prepare for individual performances under their respective directors and massed performances under the coordinator. Individual performances in 1954 were scheduled at Thanksgiving, in February, and during Music Week. Massed performances were presented at Christmas and Easter. A twelve-week radio and television series is being arranged to feature all organizations.

Each group, with the director's approval, may appear at hospitals, music societies, church and civic organizations. Being a municipal organization, all groups have the use of the civic auditorium, arena, coliseum and Red Rocks amphitheatre at no rental cost.

Soloists for the massed performances have been selected by audition from the Rocky Mountain region and paid a professional fee. A fully professional orchestra is selected from local union musicians and teachers and the Denver Symphony, for the large choral works necessitating orchestral accompaniment. Local 20 of the A. F. of M. cooperates and assists from their transcription fund for such performances.

Music Library. The Denver Public Schools came to the assistance of the program in its initial stages by lending from their fine library. Gradually, a library will be established; more than three thousand dollars has been expended this past year for music. Each director selects his own music, which is screened by the coordinator before it is purchased.

Music in the choral field ranges from folk music arrangements to Bach, Brahms, Elgar, Delius, Holst, Vaughan Williams, Hindemith, Roy Harris, and Thompson. In the band field it extends from march selections to Bach, Leidzen, Cailliet, Grundman, Wood, Vaughan Williams, Curzan, and Grofe. The string

251

orchestra includes in its repertoire works by Bach, Frescobaldi, Gliere, Ferrabosco, Scarlatti, Samuel Barber, Bartok, Bridge, Copland, Thompson and Gillis.

Services. Parks and Recreation being a service unit to the public at large, many opportunities have been found to publicize the program, on request, through the medium of civic clubs, church groups, P.T.A., schools, colleges, trades and labor groups, radio and television. To date the coordinator has been privileged to appear before 479 groups, representing approximately 150,000 persons, and always as part of the program the audiences have participated in some form of community singing.

Expansion. From the public reaction to this program, which is only in its infancy, expansion will be controlled largely by the budget allowed by the City Council.

Music Committee. The director of music for the Denver Public Schools was appointed as chairman of the Mayor's Advisory Music Committee. This committee of local civic leaders, which is representative of all races, colors, and creeds in the City of Denver, has been most helpful to the coordinator and this program by its support, interest, suggestions, and counsel.

Budget. The budget allotted the coordinator for 1954 was $15,600. This includes (1) salary of coordinator, (2) salaries of directors and accompanists, (3) special performances ("Messiah" and "Elijah"), (4) purchase of music.

International Cooperation for Adult Music Education [1]

At the International Conference on the Role of Music in the Education of Youth and Adults in Brussels, Belgium, in 1953, Commission B, dealing with musical education of communities, arrived at the following conclusions, which are applicable to many of the problems of the Music Educators National Conference.

It was proposed:

(1) That national and international authorities should be urged to give financial support to projects for the improvement of music education in urban and rural centers, taking into account the sociological and psychological requirements, as well as the aesthetic needs, of each kind of community.

(2) That UNESCO should conduct an inquiry (a) into the various methods used in different countries to encourage the appreciation and performance of music as leisure-time activities in all centers of community life and through all organizations for youth and adult music education, and (b) into the methods employed and facilities provided for the specialized training of music leaders for such groups.

(3) To continue to facilitate and, as far as possible, extend through its exchange-of-persons program the means whereby people concerned with community music activities can study abroad, and notably to encourage and facilitate the exchange of visits between countries of nonprofessional, community music-performing groups.

(4) That UNESCO, in cooperation with other international, related groups, (a) facilitate exchange of recordings of nonschool groups in the various countries on a noncommercial basis, (b) initiate a cataloging of music available to the public (i.e. scores, parts, and records) for use by nonprofessional groups, (c) continue to encourage the commissioning and publishing of works by contemporary

---

[1] Submitted by Thomas E. Wilson, Conductor of the Lafayette (Indiana) Symphony and Opera Guild and Vice-President of the American Symphony Orchestra League.

composers, especially conceived for community groups, and (d) to maintain and prosecute its efforts toward removing barriers of currency restrictions, import limitations, and customs regulations on material for music educational purposes.

(5) In view of the technical developments of means for the mechanical reproduction and diffusion of music, and because of the influence which these can have upon the growth of the musical taste of young people and adults, the commission recommended that through the intermediary of UNESCO and its National Commissions strong representations be made to those public and private authorities responsible for the production and diffusion of these media of mass communication; and that (a) greater consideration be given to the choice and transmission of works of the highest quality, (b) programs and recordings be prepared in close consultation with music education specialists so as to assure the best interest of community music education, (c) in countries where music education is not yet highly developed, special programs of a simple nature but good in quality be devised so as gradually to lead to an improvement of musical appreciation, taste, and knowledge.

It is of paramount importance that a sound, vital program of adult music education be maintained in the United States if we, in turn, are to be more helpful on the international scene.

The problems of widespread adult musical participation and aesthetic appreciation, for the elevation of the human soul, are worthy of our utmost efforts for reaching the finest possible solutions throughout the world.

CHAPTER XXVIII

MUSIC EDUCATION IN THE COMMUNITY

Throughout the United States, in Canada, and in other countries, there is increased interest in community-planned music programs. The interest is, in part at least, an outgrowth of the program of music education in the schools. In fact, the community and the school music program are inseparable. Responsibility for the musical well-being of the community, therefore, must be shared by the school and community leaders.

What Is a Community Music Program? [1]

It is agreed that music reaches its fullest significance in a community when all of the people are active participants. They must participate not only as listeners to the performances of music played and sung by professionals, or by their neighbors, but by producing music themselves. No medium should be overlooked, however lowly it may seem to be, in comparison to the more formal ensembles.

A local music association or sponsoring group representing all of the interests of the community concerned with music is essential to such a development. Basically, such an association has an organizational purpose of closely knitting and integrating all local musical resources in an over-all program.

Such a local organization, if so planned, is a clearing house or coordinating office for all things musical in the community, serving as a civic and social agency in this respect. It also motivates the development of additional musical activities in which persons of all ages, races, creeds, and economic and social levels may have a neighborly part. The fullest functioning of such an organization involves cooperation of all musical organizations and also such institutions and groups as industries, mercantile establishments, lodges, schools, home service clubs, women's clubs, hospitals, etc.

It should be kept in mind that community music is not a *kind* of music; rather it is *all kinds* of music. The successful community music plan is designed primarily not to demonstrate what people do with music but *what music does to people*. Participation in the performance of music eliminates, or minimizes, the consciousness of differences in religious creed, political faith, economic status, social position, or age. From the social standpoint, music is an ideal common medium since boys, men, girls and women may, separately or in any combination, join in singing or playing.

A broad community music program may include not only those activities that provide for music participation, but also related activities. Community-wide programs should encourage and develop the fullest possible participation in all arts and crafts—of which music may be only one of the important factors. Through well-developed community music programs great festivals in the open-air stadium, formal events in the concert hall, and informal groups gathered in the church house, the lodge hall, or in one corner of the factory office or department store have been developed. Club programs, civic parades, informal home ensembles— all these and many others are important factors. In association with other arts,

[1] Adapted from *Music for Everybody*, an MENC publication by the Committee on School-Community Music Relations and Activities, Claude B. Smith, Evansville, Indiana, Chairman, 1946-1950.

music has its share in the production of drama, movies, light and grand operas, and community pageants and festivals, such as have been witnessed from coast to coast in connection with anniversary observances of cities and institutions. These musical contributions to other activities are present at all times.

Questions to be answered are: Do all of the people in the community know the full extent of the program of musical activities now in operation? Do all of the people who would like to have an opportunity to contribute to the program know that there is a place for them in the total community picture? *Are* there places for all of them? Is there a plan which recognizes every type of musical activity in the community as a factor in the total program? Are the rank and file of the citizens aware of the community's musical achievements, and proudly proprietary in their interest? Does the program provide maximum possible gratification and inspiration to the maximum number of people? The answers to these and other questions obviously determine whether or not the local people will feel that there is something more to be done in their community, through organization and the enlistment of leadership, to give meaning to the phrase "Music for Everybody."

What Is Meant by "School-Community Music Relations and Activities"?

A survey of musical activities in communities throughout the United States was made. One of the purposes of the survey was to help define just what is meant by "School-Community Music Relations and Activities" by means of a cross-country sampling which would depict some of the musical activities in which school children, their teachers, and other citizens actually participate. This sampling, although far from comprehensive, indicates that those influences which have contributed through music to the cultural life of the community have been far more potent than realized. Nevertheless, it is also evident that there is still much to be done if the work of the music educators in the schools is to attain anywhere near maximum fruitfulness through continuing musical experiences for our citizens after their school days are over.

The primary job of the school music teacher is to teach and guide, and to help make music an important living factor in the general program of education. However, music teachers have long recognized the community-wide ramifications of a good job of music teaching. Similarly, other subjects which are treated in the schools must specifically apply to the business, domestic, economic, political, spiritual, and cultural aspects of living.

Musical experiences in the school, if worth while for the values brought to the individual in school days, will become even more worth while through the contribution the individual makes to himself, his family, and to the life of his community after he takes up the responsibilities of adult citizenship. This does not mean that every music pupil in the school is expected to continue through his entire life as a player or singer. What he does with the skills he may have obtained, and the appreciation for music he may have developed, will depend altogether upon his own interest and aptitude—and the opportunities he himself helps create. He may be content to finish his life as a patron of music. If he has learned how to be an intelligent listener, he will not only receive continuing benefits from his school experiences with music, but he will be a leavening influence for the entire community, and should be one of those supporters who help maintain the kind of program of music activities with which this report is concerned.

Important among the issues are the items pertaining to continuing participation and interest on the part of the individual, and to the maintenance of media for such participation through local support of a broad program of musical activities of all kinds. Music teachers, in schools and in studios, should think in terms of preparing young people to become *active* influences for music in their communities. Under right guidance all music pupils are potential music missionaries because they want to share what they know, feel, and understand about music, as well as what they can do in the performance of music—but, most of all, because they themselves *enjoy* both listening and performing. To this end, there should be in every community a planned program which sets the stage and makes available the media through which the individual may make his contribution to the total life of the community; he will make this contribution if he can have the maximum opportunity for *his own enjoyment* of the musical resources he was helped to develop within himself by his experiences in school.

The fact that such opportunities are provided in so many communities, and that similar programs are being developed in many others, is a tribute to the vision and initiative of local leaders and supporting citizens. Experience has been gained and values established which should stimulate interest and action in other communities, as well as afford helpful patterns.

The task is too large and important to be undertaken by any one group alone. Music educators can and do help, but they can only share the responsibilities with other community leaders. Everywhere, there are workers and supporters ready to enlist if, through qualified leadership, the relatively simple plans and procedures are charted in an all-inclusive program which will permit all to do their parts in a most effective manner.

Community Relationships and
Professional and Amateur Music

For a number of years, many music educators have realized the problems caused by the diminishing line of demarcation between their function as classroom teachers and their function as community leaders and servants. In the very nature of things, it is possible for the school music teacher and his school music students to be in the position of providing entertainment for community affairs under the guise of community service.

Public performances of school music groups should always be regarded in the nature of demonstrations of the pupils' achievements in music study. When the *primary purpose* of any public performance of school groups is to furnish entertainment, all of the factors should be examined in order to determine whether or not such entertainment can be legitimately supplied by a school-maintained organization, or should be furnished by professional musicians who are paid for their services.

The development of the "Code of Ethics" more than ten years ago proved a most helpful means of establishing understanding and cooperation between the teachers and pupils of the public schools and the professional musicians, in such states as Ohio, Pennsylvania, and New York, where this Code was first applied on a state-wide basis. The same Code, with some extensions and minor alterations, was adopted jointly in 1947 on a national plane by the American Federation of Musicians, American Association of School Administrators, and the Music Educators National Conference. A copy of the Code should be in the hands of every person interested in school-community relationships and activities; [1] it offers an excellent guide, in addition to setting forth principles which concern the mutual interests and friendly relationships of professional musicians, music educators, and music students of all communities.

---

[1] See Appendix, p. 316.

This National Code of Ethics has demonstrated at the local and state levels its fairness and feasibility. If observed in spirit and practice, the Code will preclude misunderstandings which might arise from the pursuit of a community-wide music activities program. With such a guide at hand, it is not difficult to determine the dividing line between education, or community service, and professional entertainment. There should in no instance be conflicts of interest, but, rather, hearty cooperation between professional musicians and school and community music.

MUSIC EDUCATION IN THE COMMUNITY [1]

The over-all function of community music is to provide a variety of musical opportunities for all the people in a given community, using available talents to produce the best possible results through competent leadership.

Objectives of Music Education in the Community. The objectives can be stated briefly as follows: (a) To develop a consciousness on the part of the music educator of his responsibility for all community music activities, (b) to provide for continuous post school music participation, (c) to recognize and develop potential civic and community leadership, (d) to raise the standards of music appreciation in the community, and (e) to develop potential creative ability within the community.

Implementing the Program. The method of implementing a program of community music will vary among communities. The following are given as illustrations of successful projects.

CLEMSON, SOUTH CAROLINA

Aware of the value of music education in developing the cultural level of society, The A & M College at Clemson (enrol. 3,000, pop. 2,000) authorized the inauguration of a plan to activate interest in music on a college-community level. [2] A three-level plan was instituted in order to accommodate all participants. Active participation was made available on level one through amateur concerts and productions using local talent only; on level two through semi-professional productions and concerts giving the better local talent an opportunity to work with professional talent; and on level three participation was encouraged through attendance and instruction at a Concert Series already established. Provisions for participation in various phases of at least one major production per year, as well as choral and instrumental concerts with or without auditions, were made. Example: Community Chorus opened to all without auditions, Community Choir by auditions only.

At the end of the second year of the plan excellent results were apparent. Attendance at the annual Christmas Concert increased from a few hundred to several thousand. The caliber of the material performed had greatly increased and the number of participants had tripled.

Today Clemson has a large marching band, concert band, men's glee club, double male quartet, community choir, community chorus, as well as many small ensembles. The citizens of Clemson realize that competent leadership produces successful growth.

MADISON, WISCONSIN

The University of Wisconsin Extension Music Department, organized in 1950, has been working in the field of music for the community with the scope of the program broadly defined as "responsible for all off-campus music." This latitude

[1] From the report submitted by Evelyn Waltman Becker, York, Pennsylvania, National Chairman, Music in American Education Committee on Music Education in the Community.

[2] R. E. Lovett in charge.

has provided an opportunity to realize an organized program for developing music in the community on a state-wide basis.

The Wisconsin program of activity in extension music education at the present time consists of the following: Music Education through Correspondence Study, Music in the University Extension Centers, Music Clinics for Educators and Students, Industrial Music, Homemaker Choruses, Music for 4-H Club Programs, Music for Older Rural Youth, and Music Through Radio-Television Media.

It has become very evident that music education must be continuous and not terminal if education is to be for the individual's entire life. It is believed that the organization and opportunity in extension music education as demonstrated at Wisconsin is unique in being able to coordinate various programs into an over-all, state-wide program of continuous music education. By giving leadership and direction to this program it is hoped that music will play an integral part in the life of the citizens of the state.

Through working with the schools, it is hoped that music educators will see the value of contributing to the leadership in community music programs. By working with high school and college students to improve their level of development better musicians will be provided for adult music organizations. Through work with the rural segment of the state population, greater participation, understanding, and appreciation will result with that portion of the population often slighted in music.

Courses for Community Leadership. [1] Few public school and college music faculty members appreciate the real importance of good public relations in promoting community music activities. There seems to be an apparent lack of leadership training for community music. A college catalog survey revealed only a very few institutions of higher learning offering a course in preparation for community music leadership. Such a course could be included in the curriculums of colleges to good advantage. Suggested areas of instruction for a course in Community Music Leadership:

(1) The place of music in the community.
(2) Public relations; student, teacher, parent, community.
(3) Community problems: Customs; prejudices; relationship with other music groups such as choir directors, private teachers, Musicians Union.
(4) Music resources of the community.
(5) Music for the adult.
(6) Methods in conducting community choral and instrumental activities.
(7) Materials for community music activities.
(8) Music for special occasions.
(9) Recreational music.
(10) Industrial music.
(11) Community concert series.

Organizing the Local Music Forces for Community-Wide Music Planning [2]

Recognizing the trend in the direction of community-wide sharing in musical affairs, leaders have set up various means for cooperation at the planning and sponsoring level. In some instances, the cooperating group is—or was at first—concerned with a single major enterprise, such as a community-wide music festival. Sometimes one segment of the community's musical activities is involved. Church

[1] From the report submitted by B. M. Bakkegard, Austin, Texas, Southwestern Division Chairman, Music in American Education Committee on Music Education in the Community.
[2] Extracted from a bulletin published by the American Music Conference, 332 S. Michigan Ave., Chicago 4, Ill.

choir festivals and all-city school music events are among the most common of these. Another type of cooperation is in pre-season planning of the annual schedule by the sponsors of local concerts, recitals, festivals, and other principal music events. This helps preclude conflicting dates, and makes possible the publication of an annual calendar, with resulting benefits which are obvious.

Participating in these varied local community programs, and in others of similar purpose, are organizations and institutions whose combined resources constitute not only great strength, but a true cross section of the population and its educational, civic, and cultural resources. Besides school and college music departments, private music teacher groups, church choir leaders and members, organizations of professional musicians, music clubs, etc., there is a long list of organizations and institutions which have a part in the total local picture. Many communities maintain music committees or have their own musical groups, ranging from barbershop quartets to large choirs, bands, and orchestras, as well as plectrum clubs and dance ensembles. Others contribute through their support of musical activities.

In nearly every town there is a wealth of activity and interest in music. The opportunity to mobilize these resources for the benefit of the total community is a challenge to leadership. It is the acceptance of this challenge by sponsors of music activities who have taken the initiative in community-wide planning, or who wish to do so, that encouraged the development of the plan described in the paragraphs following.

Although originally prepared for a memorandum pertaining to a state-wide program, the suggestion included here may also be considered in connection with local or county-wide planning and organization projects.

COMMUNITY MUSIC CONFERENCES AND WORKSHOPS

Purpose and Scope: The purpose of the Community Music Workshops is to acquaint civic and music leaders with the techniques and objectives of developing Music Councils in their respective communities.

A Community Music Council serves as a coordinating medium for such purposes as (a) acting as a clearing house and cooperating medium for organizations, institutions, and groups sponsoring musical activities or otherwise interested in the musical life of the community; (b) developing opportunities for adults to participate in a variety of organized musical experiences; (c) mobilizing community support for the school music program.

Intercommunity cooperation could ultimately develop into large area music festivals or other programs or projects.

Organizational Procedure: A state-wide or regional program of Community Music Conferences (or workshops) may be organized under the auspices of such organizations as the State Music Educators Association, the State Department of Education, the State University Extension Divisions, Parent-Teacher Associations, County Rural Associations, Federation of Music Clubs, and the State Music Teachers Association. All of these organizations should be invited to send representatives to the workshops, regardless of the sponsoring group.

The president of the sponsoring organization and representatives of other cooperating groups should select four to six key workshop cities (more where necessary), preferably college cities, which should be chosen because of geographic location, populated areas, and other pertinent reasons.

A state committee should be set up to include the heads (or music chairmen) of all the organizations sponsoring the project, and the host city chairman referred to in the next paragraph.

A person with capacity for leadership should be selected as host city chairman in each of the workshop cities to direct the organizational mechanics of the workshop. The host city chairman should invite one or more civic and music leaders and a music supervisor, or teacher, from each community, large or small, within a radius of approximately seventy-five to one hundred miles (distance is determined at the state and workshop city level), to attend the one-day workshop. The school administrator should also be invited.

Because the school administrator or music supervisor in each community is usually familiar with local leadership, either or both persons should be consulted when selecting the civic and music leaders to be invited from a given community. At the completion of the conference, the persons thus selected may form the nucleus of a committee to develop their own Community Music Council.

THE AGENDA

The following paragraphs are therefore intended primarily to explain the nature and objectives of the conferences being held by and for leaders interested in community musical activities.

The entire group attending the conference should, so far as possible, participate in the discussions, and the sessions should be planned with a minimum of set speeches.

Since the main purpose of the conference is to stimulate interest in organizing community-wide cooperation in planning, developing, and supporting an overall program, the discussions and questions should be geared to the opportunities, problems, and procedures involved.

Written report, or reports, should be prepared by individuals or committees appointed for the purpose. Such reports should be of nutshell brevity and conciseness and should be presented at least in outline for acceptance by the group before adjournment.

If at all possible, the host city chairman and presiding chairman for all of the conferences planned in the state should be brought together at a central point for a preparatory conference, conducted in the manner planned for the succeeding regional conferences. Such a "preliminary" may well be made the first of the series of regional conferences, with sectional leaders present to participate.

Source people may include: A superintendent of schools and/or college administrator; a recreational director and/or community music specialist; a representative of the P.T.A.; a representative of the Federation of Music Clubs; a representative of the Church Choir group; a representative of the State Music Educators Association; a representative of the Chamber of Commerce and/or service club; a representative of the County Agricultural Agency.

Certain of the source people should be asked to be prepared to make brief statements on assigned topics, and should be informed that, in case the discussions or questions do not give opportunity to present the gist of the statement, the chairman will call upon them.

SUGGESTED TOPICS

(1) The purpose of the Conference.

(2) What does a well-balanced school-community program of music activities and enterprise include?

(3) How can the entire schedule of musical activities be made more effective from the standpoint of the community as a whole?

(4) What is your conception of a Civic Music Council or similar type of cooperative group that would best serve all interests and people in your community?

(5) What are the techniques for developing a Civic Music Council?

(6) Summarization.

The foregoing list contains suggestions based on successful practice in conferences of fifty or less persons. For a much larger group, a more formal technique may be required—but audience participation should be encouraged.

SUGGESTIONS FOR PROMOTING A COMMUNITY MUSIC COUNCIL [1]

Preplanning. Advance preparation is important. It should be clearly established that there is need and desire for community-wide music planning. The following points are suggested in the foundational work:

(1) First, have a small group of leaders meet informally and agree on objectives that will challenge the interest of a representative civic committee.

(2) Arrange to have a representative civic leader help organize a planning committee. Have this civic leader send invitations to heads of music and civic groups and others who are in positions of leadership in the community, and who are interested in the music and social affairs of the community.

(3) In issuing the call to the meeting, and in any publicity releases, be sure the purpose is clearly stated, and that the time for the meeting is cleared well in advance.

(4) Contact should be made with each person in advance by telephone or a personal interview to insure attendance.

Who may be invited? No arbitrary list can be made, but among others who would be considered for a part in the initial planning meeting would be officials of city and county governments, superintendents of schools, music supervisors of city or county, officers of civic clubs, 4-H Clubs, Boy Scouts, Girl Scouts, ministerial organizations, representatives of such organizations as YMCA, YWCA, CYO, Boys' Clubs, presidents and directors of major civic and school music groups, president or other officer of the Chamber of Commerce, representatives of newspapers and radio stations. It is important that careful survey be made in order to make sure that no important leader or major community group or activity is overlooked in issuing the invitations. Local school music leaders should work in the background, with civic leaders taking the initiative.

Promotion. Interest in the meeting and its purpose may be stimulated by judicious use of publicity media—the press, radio, talks at local club meetings.

First Objectives. It is important that there be a definite program set up and agreed upon at the first meeting. Among the outcomes of the first meeting there could be:

(1) Appointment or election of a small action committee to organize suggestions coming out of the meeting, and to prepare plans for a permanent organization.

(2) The initiation of plans for a survey of music interests in the community. As a result of this survey there could be issued a printed or mimeographed list of all the musical organizations and activities, and perhaps a calendar giving places, dates, and auspices of concerts and other musical activities.

(3) The initiation of plans for a community-wide event and events of sufficient scope to enlist the interest, participation, and support of the entire community and the leadership of all the groups represented at the meeting.

---

[1] Adapted from a memorandum issued by Edward H. Hamilton, Knoxville, Tennessee, Southern Division Chairman of the MENC Committee on School-Community Music Relations and Activities, 1946-1950.

Bibliography

BOOKS

Brightbill, Charles K. and Meyer, Harold D. *Recreation.* New York: Prentice-Hall, Inc., 1953.

Dahir, James. *Communities for Better Living.* New York: Harper and Brothers, 1950.

Fitzgerald, Gerald B. *Community Organization for Recreation.* New York: A. S. Barnes and Company, Inc., 1948.

Hutchinson, John L. *Principles of Recreation.* New York: A. S. Barnes and Company, Inc., 1951.

Leonhard, Charles. *Recreation Through Music.* New York: A. S. Barnes and Company, Inc., 1952.

ARTICLES

Bakkegard, B. M. "Music in the Junior College," *Junior College Journal,* October 1952, p. 87.

Barlow, H. "Practical Music," *Music Educators Journal,* January 1952, p. 23.

Barzin, L. "Music Should Serve the Community," *Etude,* April 1953, p. 11.

Lewis, J. A. "More Music for More People," *MTNA Proceedings,* 1949.

Morris, E. A. "Lost Chord," *The School Musician,* November 1953, p. 23.

Norton, W. W. "One Coordinating Agency for All Community Music Units," *MTNA Proceedings,* 1948.

Plank, D. T. "Putting Music to Work in the Community and Vice Versa," *Music Educators Journal,* April-May 1952, p. 54.

Schwejda, R. A. "School and Town," *Music Educators Journal,* January 1953, p. 42.

Swartz, J. "Civic Music Life and the Community College," *Junior College Journal,* April 1950.

—————. "Training Music Educators for Community Leadership," *Music Educators Journal,* April-May 1953, p. 10.

"The Flint Community Music Association," *Annual Reports,* I—XXVI, 1917-1953.

Watson, J. M. "Leadership and the Arts in the Community," *Education,* November 1952, p. 182.

Weddle, F. "Central Community Agency for the Arts," *Educational Music Magazine,* March 1953, p. 16.

"What is a Community Music Program?" *Music Educators Journal,* June-July 1950, p. 10.

"What Is Meant by School-Community Music Relations and Activities?" *Music Educators Journal,* June-July 1950, p. 12.

CHAPTER XXIX

MUSIC EDUCATION FOR EXCEPTIONAL CHILDREN[1]

P REVIOUS INVESTIGATION in the area of music education for exceptional children was confined quite largely to the functional aspects of music, particularly in relation to music in mental hospitals. Recently there has been an increasing emphasis on the development of a program of musical experience within public and special schools which would meet adequately the needs of the exceptional child. This has brought about the need for dissemination of material for teachers and supervisors to give a clearer understanding of the objectives of music in special education as well as some of the practical techniques which are currently being employed.

In almost every major city a special education program with provision for music to meet the needs of exceptional children is to be found. Therefore, it presents a challenge to the music educator who is able to look forward to the ever-widening horizons in this area, who is not limiting his efforts by considering that music is only for the masses, but who realizes that by meeting the needs of the individual exceptional child something which will bear some rich fruits in the future is produced.

Many music educators are devoted to the study of music education for the exceptional child as a whole child, particularly in relation to the music experience in the classroom, in special-purpose rooms, in related clinics for exceptional children, in private schools, and in residential institutions which are staffed by specially trained teachers.

If schools are to meet their responsibilities, they must provide educational opportunities for children, according to ability. Individual differences make it impossible to plan a single program to fit the needs of all. In addition to plans for the general music program, there are exceptional children for whom special provision should be made.

The following types of children can benefit greatly by the functional music experience which special education can promote:

—The blind and partially sighted.
—The deaf and hard of hearing.
—The child with speech limitations.
—The mentally retarded and slow learner.
—The brain-damaged child (cerebral palsied, etc.).
—The orthopedically limited.
—The emotionally disturbed child.
—The mentally superior or gifted child.

In developing concepts of a program which will meet the needs of the exceptional child, the following statement made by Dr. William M. Cruickshank, former president of the International Council for Exceptional Children, will be helpful:

The exceptional child is always to be considered as a child in need of certain specific adjustments, and the term "exceptional child" can include a wide variety of children. . . . Always accept the deviant child as a *child* —strip a child of all his aids and he is still a child. . . . In music, do not give him a separate program. If possible, bring him into the musical

---

[1] From the report submitted by Wilhelmina Harbert, Stockton, California, National Chairman, Music in American Education Committee on Music Education for Exceptional Children.

experiences of normal children, where the exceptional child can cease to be exceptional. . . . Emphasize similarities and not differences in children. . . . Use special-purpose rooms for exceptional children, but allow for integration into the group of so-called "normal" children. . . . . The exceptional child needs cultural experiences, creative art and music experiences—all in keeping, however, with his actual mental, physical, and emotional development. *Self-concept* is the key to adjustment for this child.

If the role which music plays in therapy for exceptional children is to be truly understood, the values of music for the so-called normal child and what music does to help achieve a satisfactory adjustment must be re-examined. There seems to be no reason why the same objectives and techniques cannot apply to the exceptional child as well as the so-called normal.

SOME SPECIFIC TECHNIQUES PRESENTLY IN USE

The Blind and Partially Sighted. In this grouping, music must be taught with the consideration of the vision of the individual children. Classes for those who are able to use their eyes under controlled conditions for reading print are called *sight-saving classes*. Those who have very serious eye conditions are referred to Braille classes and taught to read by use of their fingers. They need a greater variety of experience because nervousness due to eye conditions is easily aggravated by continuing one task too long. Blind children have a tendency to become ingrown and need stimulation of the imagination. Dramatization and impersonation add real interest to their experiences and aid in self-expression. If they cannot use books, songs are readily learned through hearing, a sense usually found to be very keen.

Rhythmic experience is very much needed. Frequently there is poor awareness and coordination; if this can be overlooked and attention not called to it, there will be noticeable growth. Eurythmics train these children to think and experience note values, pulses and phrases, and help to develop coordination, good posture, and grace—a real asset to the child without sight.

The sight-saving teacher should be consulted as to restrictions for eye conditions because any kind of vigorous exercise, such as jumping, bending over, straining, lifting, whirling, etc., should be avoided. These children may be adroitly chosen for slow movement. The picturing of a rhythmic notation on the board in large notes is helpful. Note values may be experienced in clapping, stepping, and other non-vigorous movements. Much can be done objectively in training the ear to recognize note values, rhythmic patterns, phrases, etc., and attention given to training the ear to recognize them.

In the field of instrumental music some children have enough vision to permit the use of notes. If the child shows potential talent and the oculist consents, he may study an instrument. The autoharp is adaptable and may lead to the study of fretted instruments such as the ukulele and guitar. Unless the eyesight is very poor he is able to play the piano, xylophone, or vibraharp by ear and even follow large legible numbers or pitch names. Violin and cello are possible for some; the flute is a good instrument because the act of blowing is quite gentle. The music teacher should confer with the special teacher about the use of a large staff with the songs in number, pitch names, or notes if this method is used for note reading.

The blind, in particular, with encouragement are capable of creating various musical activities. They are not easily distracted and usually retain what they hear. They may be counted on for ideas, because sitting quietly they may have gone far beyond the others.

Music is of inestimable value to the blind or visually limited child because it allows him to participate in group activity. If the child has more than a normal amount of musical ability, music is a way of keeping him socialized within the group of his sighted companions, and it gives him a feeling of being a necessary part of the whole. The normal, but visually limited child, desires to be treated as much like a normal child as possible.

It is regrettable that so little music has been published in large or sight-saving type. Many children with considerably impaired vision find the study of music notation difficult and discouraging because of this lack.

The rhythm band can be used with sight-saving classes, but the instruments that can be played with one hand are most desirable. The flutophone may be managed by most of these students. The sensitivity of the fingers and the hands, plus the ear, produces a fine combination for good tone quality. The set fingering pattern on the flutophone, song flute, tonette, or ocarina, and the small size of the instrument do not frighten the child and he is more willing to try. Some children learn by note and some learn to play by ear. In teaching a child to play an instrument, it must be remembered that a child with normal sight does much by imitation. A child with partial vision can usually profit by a demonstration by the teacher, but the teacher of the blind child must guide his hands in showing him how to manipulate and become familiar with the instrument. One of the greatest fallacies abroad today is that "all blind people are musical." Many children without sight begin their study of music with grave difficulties; however, they progress at various rates just as other children do.

Listening to recordings, the radio, and using tape recorders and other sound equipment, are vital experiences for the visually limited child since much of his comprehension depends upon listening. Music can train a child to live with his limitation through giving listening experiences to help strengthen his aural perception, thus making everyday living easier and more enjoyable because of the keenness of his ear.

The following suggestions are for the music teacher or supervisor of blind and partially sighted children:

(1) Consult your state department about aids which it might be able to recommend to meet these special musical needs.

(2) Seat the child where the light is best, where he can see the blackboard and the director with the least difficulty. Using him on a second or inner part will prove challenging, and give him a feeling of making a vital contribution to the general music program. Part singing may be attained by seating the blind or partially seeing child next to or in front of a strong leader. These children often have a natural gift for harmonization and may become leaders through this activity in the class.

(3) If, due to lack of vision, the child finds it necessary to learn his orchestra or chorus parts outside of school, he should be encouraged to do so. The parts may be tape recorded for this purpose.

(4) Clay modeling, soft chalk drawing, and finger painting to music provide an emotional release and stimulate a creative learning situation.

(5) In the music class, this child should be treated as much like the so-called normal child as possible. Special favoritism, unless it is entirely deserved, is not recommended.

The Deaf and Hard of Hearing. Present-day improvements in amplifying sound have made possible increased progress in this area. Adequate lighting is important, since children with hearing loss depend greatly upon visual instruction. Multiple group hearing aids, microphones, binaural earphones, sound mirrors, phonographs and recordings, much material for rhythm (such as piano, bells, drums, whistles, cymbals) and such visual aids as film strips, charts, art illustrations, etc., will aid greatly.

Classes for the hard of hearing should be limited to about fifteen children. Classes for the deaf should be limited to about eight. With proper seating and work adapted to their needs, practically all hard of hearing children can do regular work. Practically all of the pupils have at least some hearing ability, although it may be at only certain frequency ranges. The use of rhythms can be a great aid in dealing with certain speech problems found in hearing-deficient children.

The piano may be a great help by the teacher playing a selection in simple two-, three-, or four-meter, and allowing the children to feel the vibrations through their hands resting on the piano. Through this they discover the pattern of the rhythm, and may learn to identify simple songs. The songs may be placed on the blackboard and the children may repeat the words with the rhythm of the music. A sense of rhythm may be developed through touch, and activities such as the march, run, fly, skip, hop, and elephant walk, according to the age level, may be learned and named by feeling the vibrations through the piano.

The factors involved in instrumental music are selecting the proper instrument and providing conditions for a successful experience. Instrumental music is valuable therapeutically since there is a definite emotional response, combined with mild exercise, and a recreational diversional interest.

A good phonograph connected with multiple hearing aids and a suitable library of recordings will make possible listening and responding to music. A specially planned program of listening may be developed, using specially built hearing equipment which is very powerful, first by using the march rhythms which are already familiar, then dance rhythms, using both bands and orchestras. Pictures of instruments, such as drums, trumpets, trombones, and clarinets may be shown, and the children can learn to recognize them and imitate the way they are played. Deaf children and hard of hearing children can learn to distinguish whether the music is played by a band, orchestra, or some individual instrument. They can tell whether the piece is played fast or slowly. They learn to recognize a solo, a duet, and whether a man or woman is singing, or a group of men or women.

By visiting the class, the music teacher can help in the selection of listening material and in working with the special teacher so that the music program will be as meaningful as possible.

The constant work with speech and language creates a tension for the deaf, and through rhythmic experiences that tension can be lessened. Deaf children can learn many folk dances, from the first grade's "I See You" and "Shoemaker's Dance" to the older children's "Virginia Reel," "Rye Waltz" and square dances. Group participation should be encouraged. Deaf young people dance socially when they are in high school and later on in life. They feel the vibrations of the orchestra, and especially the rhythm of the bass and snare drums, through the floor and through the air.

A primary rhythm band is especially good to develop powers of attention, good rhythm, and poise. The autoharp serves as a means for the reception of vibrations for the deaf and hard of hearing, and provides a harmonic background for singing.

While music cannot be taken into the life of the deaf child with the same degree of achievement as is experienced by the hearing child, it can be a thrilling factor in fulfilling the inner needs. The sense of vibration first felt by the hands and body, the joy of dancing, the singing or speaking of songs, in rhythm, hearing for the first time on a recording someone singing or the song of a bird—all these can enrich the life of a deaf child and give him a fuller, richer life.

Children with Speech Limitations. Speech defects among children are common, and considerable emphasis is given in schools to correct them. They may or may not affect the individual's singing. Singing of the right type, in which emphasis is given to diction, correct pronunciation, and tone quality is a proven help. The speaking and singing voice of the teacher has a definite effect on the children in the class.

An effort should be made to discover the cause of the defects and proper corrective materials, such as singing games, dances, rhythms, choral speaking; and some of the attractive songs which have possibilities for dramatization and motor coordination should be used.

Stutterers and lispers need rhythm for relaxation. The child with a speech limitation can be taught phrases in reading when presented with a background of music that contains similar rhythmic phrase patterns. Having the child sway bodily aids in releasing tension of the vocal muscles. Participation in choirs and other singing groups under a skillful teacher helps greatly in speech correction.

To help children acquire receptive speech (understanding what others say), the teacher may use recordings which ask children to do things. Singing games help children to learn to listen and follow directions and help to achieve muscular relaxation for the entire body. For older pupils, square dancing should be encouraged.[1]

The Mentally Retarded and Slow Learner. The importance of music in the educational program of mentally retarded children is an accepted fact by those who work with them daily. Music furnishes a variety of interests and activities, and its material can be selected to appeal to many of these children. No other single educational area possesses the numerous possibilities as that of music, since music— by its very basic emotional and aesthetic nature and its potentiality for the inclusion of a variety of themes, lyrics and physical responses—is adaptable to almost any mental age, interest level, or degree of physical development. Like all activities included in a retardate's program, music can be either an extremely enjoyable or distasteful experience, depending upon the instructor, his approach, and his materials.

The musical experience can assist the teacher of the mentally retarded in the attainment of the following objectives which stress the value of music as a medium for individual growth rather than for artistic performance:

—Social maturation of the individual in relation to both himself and the group.
—Development of the child's ability for emotional and creative expression.
—Perpetuation and preservation of mental and physical health.
—Creation of an interest which may be transferred to leisure-time activity.
—Further growth in fundamental skills and an adequate self-concept.

In some cases simple responses to music or listening to others perform may be the only activities in which there can be participation for a long time. For all mentally retarded children music must remain a happy experience, free from pressure, with the teacher concentrating on evoking happy responses rather than on working for technical achievement. Through music the child is given more self-confidence as he finds freedom in expression. He joins in participation with a group and gains the feeling of belonging and of being an important part of his class.

The Slow Learner. In working with slow learners, emphasis must be on concrete situations with no expectancy of any specific amount of work or skills to be developed in a given time. Effective work will center around actual life situations which appeal, and provide experiences in which children can feel satisfaction

---

[1] *Sing Your Way to Better Speech,* by Walsh, is a book of familiar songs with words changed so as to give as much alliteration as possible.

in accomplishment. In many instances, children should go into regular classes where they can fit into the situation. They may be slow at books, but they often have ability in using their hands.

Some may have good voices, a good ear, and ability to play an instrument; or perhaps a good ear, a fine sense of rhythm but no special ability in singing, in which case a percussion instrument can be played with success. If they show mechanical ability, they can make many of their own instruments from materials easily available.

An adequate music program can assist the mentally retarded and slow-learning child in his perceptual, emotional, social, aesthetic, and physical growth in direct accordance with his needs, interests, and abilities. Music is an important phase of the retardate's educational curriculum and should be extended to all classes, trainable through advanced. The programs should include a variety of vocal, rhythmic, music listening, and creative experiences. Emphasis on simplicity in all musical activities will best serve to bring about desirable growth in this type of exceptional child.

Children With Brain Damage and Orthopedic Limitations. In considering the brain-damaged and orthopedically limited child, music educators should understand the nature of the limitation and how it may affect the child's ability to function in a classroom situation. Music for the cerebral palsied child should be primarily a source of joy, relaxation, and socialization. The average cerebral palsied child finds it difficult to function in group situations and often has speech involvements. Sometimes laughing to music serves as a significant outlet. Pantomime activities are accentuated by musical accompaniment and serve as an expressive interpretation to moods and feelings.

A music teacher in a school for the cerebral palsied must make allowances for physical therapy activities, coordinating and correlating the work of the physical therapist with musical activities. Calisthenics to music are indispensable in development of more controlled body movements.

The rhythmic program is necessarily limited, but of great value. Rhythm band is a delight to these children and is valuable in teaching them to coordinate physically. The teacher must be skillful in suiting the instrument to the child and ingenious in inventing devices which make some instruments easier to hold. It is a considerable achievement for some palsied children to learn to hold the drum sticks and strike a drum on the first beat of every measure. The piano can be played by some non-ambulatory children.

Songs involving finger play are beneficial to many children. For the older group the hula is a thrill. Many can learn the hand and arm motions though they cannot dance.

Children with cardiac involvement or lowered vitality due to illness naturally will be limited in any strenuous physical activity, such as games and folk dancing. Under the guidance of a physician, these children should participate in a limited program of singing and may also be taught to play certain instruments which do not require much exertion. A rich listening program is indicated, and related creative activities should be encouraged.

The Emotionally Disturbed Child. The emotionally disturbed child is faced with many adjustment problems which must be met through special understanding of the basic causes for deviant behavior patterns and through a therapeutic program designed to meet the needs of each individual child. An emphasis on individual progress or group progress, rather than on competition, is good mental hygiene for emotionally disturbed children and frequently stimulates better music production.

The child can use music as a means of self-expression which can help him achieve some control and mastery over his feelings. These children cannot always verbalize their attitudes or feelings, and music can often serve as an emotional release or catharsis. The emotionally disturbed child may not be accepted by the group because of poor performance or deviant behavior. He needs to be helped to change his behavior pattern, to follow directions, and to improve his playing or singing. He needs help in gaining insight into his behavior. Often the willingness to change study or behavior habits will be motivated by the group's refusal to accept him unless he does change. If the child is able to modify his behavior and adjust to the group, his integrative functioning and his normal ego development are both strengthened. His work in music improves, and the teacher-pupil relationship is established more satisfactorily. If the child is unable to modify his behavior, he needs the help of qualified persons who can go beyond the symptomatology to the basic cause for disturbance.

There are many combinations of factors of quite varied types which operate to produce emotional disturbances in children. Music can be used by the psychiatrist or psychologist in alleviating certain types of emotional distress. Composing music about fear often dissolves an inner fear or brings it out into the open so that insight may be gained. The same technique can be used to help solve conflicts, change escape mechanisms, alter negative attitudes, and redirect feelings of aggression and hostility.

The teacher's role in meeting the needs of the emotionally maladjusted child through music is to: Provide such experiences in the classroom as shall change patterns of behavior from negative to positive; emphasize music as a group and individual experience; provide adequate means of creative self-expression to aid in diagnosis of the maladjustment; and use music as a therapeutic aid and educational device to develop inner resources in the child.

Mentally Gifted Children.[1] Many music educators feel that gifted children are often neglected in an effort to raise the standards for the average and mentally retarded.

Opinion is divided as to whether gifted children should be taught in (a) a rapid advancement program in which children are accelerated and finish school at an earlier age; (b) an enrichment program in which there is not acceleration, but where, in each grade, they are offered an expanded program; or (c) a special class which provides for homogeneous grouping for instruction purposes only. While all three programs are suggested, (b) seems to be the one most generally accepted. Whatever plan is followed, care needs to be taken that there is no maladjustment or exploitation of the child. Gifted children should never be permitted mediocrity.

The musically gifted child will need careful direction in private instruction and well planned practice; experiences in performance as a soloist, accompanist, member of a special chamber music or other ensemble, and participation in interschool groups. Guidance into creative composition, extended readings, encouragement for research and experimentation beyond that of the regular class, will provide stimulation for greater musical insight and development.

The leadership of the future depends to a large degree upon the recognition and effective training of gifted children in our schools today. Early identification, training, and incentives for the development of capacities to the highest degree are most important. These children need direction in creative thinking and doing in an atmosphere which provides for exploration and development. Understanding and wise guidance through the cooperation of parents and teachers are necessary in providing a healthful environment for social living and learning.

---

[1] *Education of the Gifted* (Washington, D. C.: Educational Policies Commission).

There are certain basic principles underlying an educational program for gifted children. There is need:

—To make full use of human resources.

—To discover the gifted youths who have the ability to make contributions to potentially valuable kinds of human activity.

—To explore subcultural groups of these gifted youth.

—To determine the unique educational needs and interests of children who have superior intellectual capacity.

—To learn how to guide extreme deviates clear of dangers that threaten the consistency of their performance and personality development.

—To insist upon high standards of accomplishment and upon the necessity of working to maintain these high standards.

—To provide the gifted with many opportunities for independent thinking and creative work.

—To develop teachers and administrators who will be inventive, creative, and original, and who will be willing to break with tradition in meeting the unique learning needs of their gifted students.

Music educators should accept the challenge to relate music experience to the above basic principles in guiding musically gifted children into richer avenues of musical learning, creative self-expression, and cultural contribution.

The following "Credo" should be a part of the philosophy of all music educators dealing with exceptional children who are eager to improve the practices and techniques used in their everyday teaching:

(1) The exceptional child should be accepted as a whole child.

(2) Normal and deviant children should experience music together as much as possible.

(3) Music offers the exceptional child emotional release, personal satisfactions, feelings of success, social awareness, and an orderly sequence of educational experiences.

(4) Music experience for the exceptional child changes attitudes of behavior and helps to satisfy the desire for some type of musical achievement.

(5) Exceptional children are creative, and should be provided with opportunities for creativeness.

(6) Similarities should be emphasized and differences minimized in these children.

(7) Every means available should be used to help the exceptional child to his fullest self-concept, which is the key to adjustment for this child.

Selected Bibliography—Exceptional Children

Baker, H. J. *Introduction to Exceptional Children* (Rev. ed.). New York: The Macmillan Company, 1953.

Bender, L. *Dynamic Psychopathology of Childhood.* New York: Dodd, Mead & Company, 1954.

Burt, C. L. *Backward Child* (3rd ed.). London: University of London Press, 1952.

Collis, E. *Way of Life for the Handicapped Child.* London: Faber, Faber and Faber Ltd., 1947.

Cutts, N. E. and Moseley, N. *Bright Children.* New York: G. P. Putnam's Sons, 1953.

Dolch, E. *Helping Handicapped Children in School.* Champaign, Ill.; Garrard Press, 1948.

Ewing, I. R. and Ewing, A. W. *Handicap of Deafness.* Washington, D. C: Volta Bureau, 1948.

Fielder, M. F. *Deaf Children in a Hearing World.* New York: The Ronald Press, 1952.

Garrison, K. *Psychology of Exceptional Children.* (Rev. ed.) New York: The Ronald Press, 1950.

Heck, A. O. *Education of Exceptional Children.* New York: McGraw-Hill Book Company, Inc., 1953.

Ingram, C. P. *Education of the Slow-Learning Child* (2nd ed.) New York: The Ronald Press, 1953.

Kirk, S. A. and Johnson, G. O. *Educating the Retarded Child.* New York: Houghton Mifflin Company, 1951.

Lightfoot, G. F. *Personality Characteristics of Bright and Dull Children.* New York: Teachers College, Columbia University, 1951.

Scheifele, M. *Gifted Child in the Regular Classroom.* New York: Teachers College, Columbia University, 1953.

Segal, C. *Backward Children in the Making.* London: Fredrick Muller Ltd., 1950.

Smith, M. F. *Teaching the Slow Learning Child.* New York: Harper and Brothers, 1954.

Stinchfield, S. M. *Speech Therapy for Physically Handicapped.* Stanford University, Calif.: Stanford University Press, 1950.

Stone, E. B. and Deyton, J. *Corrective Therapy for the Handicapped Child.* New York: Prentice-Hall, Inc., 1951.

Wallin, J. *Personality Maladjustments and Mental Hygiene.* New York: McGraw-Hill Book Company, Inc., 1949.

Witty, Pane (Ed). *Gifted Children.* Boston: D. C. Heath Co., 1951.

271

CHAPTER XXX

MUSIC EDUCATION AND THE NATIONAL WELFARE

THERE IS A TRADITION of successful cooperation between music educators and various government agencies which has been built by many years of integrated activities which serve the common cause of national welfare.

While attention of the general public may be directed to this cooperation during times of stress, it is important to remember that these unified music activities are continuous.

Music for American Morale [1]

"There is something about the right kind of music that can raise the morale of an individual or of a whole people. Music can increase confidence and courage. In every great national crisis people express their hopes and aspirations through music peculiarly fitted to the times and circumstances." This statement by Dr. Alexander J. Stoddard, nationally known educator and superintendent of the Philadelphia public schools, is typical of expressions of the convictions of many eminent persons regarding the effectiveness of music as a force for maintaining national morale.

Edgard DeWitt Jones, clergyman and columnist, has said, "The place of music in steadying national morale in time of crisis is pivotal and powerful. There is something unific in the mass singing of the great old hymns, patriotic songs, and anthems. Home, church, school, and state, should be aware of the importance of music to inspire and unify in times of tension."

During World War II the late William Lyons Phelps proclaimed, "Music is the voice of civilization and we must not lose interest in the very things we are fighting to preserve. Instead of neglecting or slighting pure music, we should cultivate it more earnestly. To do this is to fulfill one of the highest aims of patriotism."

Experience as music educators confirms these statements and bolsters the belief that music can play a part in the development of patriotism and citizenship by strengthening for youth the spiritual foundations upon which an enduring love of country can be built. Faith, hope, devotion, respect, reverence, courage—these are the broad patriotic responses which music can arouse. Through these responses boys and girls will come to realize that they are benefactors, supporters, and defenders of their homeland. Music can contribute to a deeper and truer patriotism which is close to the thing called effective citizenship.

This type of citizenship involves a thoughtful weighing of one's duties to home town or to native land; citizenship includes unselfish action rationalized by consideration of what will be best for the ultimate good of the community and country; citizenship involves courageous action because the thinking patriot has weighed the sacrifices that lie ahead and recognized the need for patience and persistent effort. In most of us there is a fusion of the emotional, demonstrative patriotism with that which is rational and sacrificing. What vital and honest aid can musicians give to the development of patriotism and morale? The suggestions and warnings which follow may be helpful to school music teachers who wish to do their patriotic duty effectively and intelligently.

---

[1] From the report submitted by Newell H. Long, Bloomington, Indiana, National Chairman, Music in American Education Committee on Music Education and the National Welfare.

Specific Suggestions. The basic song repertory taught boys and girls should include those time-proven songs which have direct patriotic appeal and significance. The words and music of such songs as the "Star-Spangled Banner," "America," "America, the Beautiful," "God Bless America," "Battle Hymn of the Republic," "Dixie," and "Yankee Doodle" should certainly be learned by elementary school children and refreshed in the minds of secondary school pupils. Special effort should be made to have pupils memorize the third stanza of the "Star-Spangled Banner" [1] and the most significant verses of other patriotic songs.

Directors should be on the alert for opportunities to include one or more patriotic songs or selections in programs of public concerts and school assemblies. At the same time they should consider carefully whether each occasion is appropriate for this type of music.

Patriotic music should not be performed without adequate rehearsal. The performance of such music should not be permitted to become mere routine. The significance of patriotic songs to both performers and listeners is such that care and sincerity should characterize the preparation and presentation of this music. Texts of patriotic songs should be emphasized and understood.

The practice of including on public programs one or more well-known songs with morale implications in which the audience may participate is encouraged because it provides an excellent opportunity to remind people of their patriotic obligations, it enhances the pleasure derived from the concert by the auditors. Such group activity gives to its participants a sense of unification and belonging. Religious music has special value in giving youth a feeling for moral principles which are fundamental to the American way of life.

Since music festivals are examples of unity of purpose and action, it is particularly appropriate to include on festival programs music which stresses social unity, American loyalty, or other aims of enlightened citizenship. Marching band pageantry provides an excellent vehicle for effective and dramatic presentation of patriotic messages.

It should be remembered that the Salute to the Flag and the singing of the National Anthem and other patriotic songs must be presented with dignity and drama.

Holidays are particularly conducive to reflective thinking concerning national morale, for at these times people are drawn together to reaffirm their beliefs. It is a simple task to find music which will contribute to the mood and meaning of such occasions.

Music that contributes to patriotism is not confined to only those melodies which are labeled patriotic. Any music which leads toward peace of mind, toward greater loyalty to God, home and friends, toward deeper appreciation of eternal values, can be an aid in building for better citizenship on stronger foundations for free democracy.

During World War II the MENC, in conjunction with the MTNA, and the NASM, led a nation-wide movement to encourage the playing and singing of songs which embody the spirit and ideals of our United States. That program, which is even more applicable at the present time, suggested:

(1) The fervent and frequent singing of our national and patriotic songs, with full understanding of their meaning, both as to word content and as to their significance in relation to the history and future of our country.

(2) The maintenance and enhancement of respect for the rich heritage of music brought to America by various racial groups who are now Americans-all, and

---

[1] "The Code for the National Anthem of the United States of America" and the music for the Service Version of "The Star-Spangled Banner" will be found in the Appendix, p. 313.

whose cultural contributions have helped to make the United States a powerful and vital nation.

(3) A more extensive knowledge of and appreciation for, and more general use of America's folk and pioneer songs—a vast storehouse of strong, robust music which is inseparably linked with our national growth, but which is too little known by our teachers and too little used in our schools.

(4) More attention to the meritorious compositions by American composers, especially the music, both instrumental and vocal, which possesses unique American qualities or characteristics.

Basic Patriotic Song Repertory. A limited survey conducted by Peter W. Dykema in 1945 revealed that the following additional songs were considered desirable repertory for introduction to pupils in the grades as indicated:

Air Corps Songs—Grades 4, 5, 6
Anchors Aweigh—Grades 4, 5, 6
Artillery Song (Caisson Song)—Grades 4, 5, 6, 7
Battle Cry of Freedom—Grades 5, 6
Columbia, the Gem of the Ocean—Grades 5, 6
God of Our Fathers—Grades 5, 6
Grand Old Flag—Grades 4, 5, 6
Hail Columbia—Grades 5, 6, 7, 8
Marines Hymn—Grades 4, 5, 6
Maryland, My Maryland—Grades 4, 5, 6
Taps—Grades 4, 5, 6
Tenting Tonight—Grades 6, 7, 8
Tramp, Tramp, Tramp—Grades 6, 7, 8
When Johnny Comes Marching Home—Grades 4, 5, 6, 7, 8

National-International. The development of an international feeling should not detract from but rather enhance national loyalty and pride. One's appreciation and love for his own country is deepened by his acquaintance with and understanding of the customs and civilizations other than his own. Consequently, study of the folk music, art music and national airs of foreign countries may make the student more sensitive toward his own culture and heighten his determination to protect and preserve it.

Teachers should consider well whether a song or piece with a patriotic title is truly worthy of performance. Our country deserves the sincerest words and the noblest music that can be provided. The nation is not being well served if its musical taste is being cheapened.

Music teachers and pupils are willing to do their part in civic and patriotic activities, but music teachers have a responsibility to see that school music organizations are not unduly exploited in the name of patriotism.

Music Education and the National Welfare [1]

Does music education occupy a significant position in the total resources of the United States of America? Such a direct question calls for an equally direct answer. There are many reasons which might be offered to support an affirmative one. The following appear to be most important to our national welfare and most nearly incontrovertible:

(1) Participation in music gives a strong sense of identity with a group. This is true of all levels in our social structure—from the small home group, through

---

[1] By Harold W. Arberg, Soldier Music Adviser to the Adjutant General of the Army.

neighborhood, school, community, and state groups, to the level of the nation and, yes, the world. Whether we perform a song or a symphony, this essential feeling of belonging is enhanced through music. Schools and colleges have always given birth to pep songs, special songs with topical lyrics, and songs of alma mater, all of which serve to unite their student bodies in common purposes. Adult recreation, business, and social groups achieve solidarity through their music. Similarly, military groups, from the separate services down to individual units, have found music an incomparable tool for raising and maintaining "pride in outfit."

(2) The spiritual core of our culture, which exists in spite of all our outward emphasis on materialism, is nurtured and made manifest through the wide uses of sacred music. The "return to religion" which Toynbee advocates as the key to survival for our civilization can certainly be expedited through an even wider sharing of the spiritual values of music. (In this connection, music educators everywhere can help to kindle this awakening to the spiritual core of our National Anthem. How? By having their students learn and *sing* the *third* stanza of Francis Scott Key's "The Star-Spangled Banner," making particular note of his exhortation, "Blessed with vict'ry and peace, may the heav'n rescued land praise the Pow'r that hath made and preserved us a nation!") Cooperation between music educators and directors of church music in presenting their groups in joint performances of old and new works from the sacred repertory does much to strengthen our awareness of music as a source of spiritual strength.

(3) Music can and does serve industries not only by making working hours more pleasurable, and hence more productive, but also by providing through group performances those opportunities for individuals to continue in adult life the musical experiences begun during their school years. Here, too, music educators may serve as full- or part-time consultants or directors and thereby contribute to the strengthening of our industrial arm.

(4) Situations of national crisis or importance are made more bearable or memorable through music. Music as a spine-tingling adjunct to drives for the sale of government bonds or donors to blood banks is only one of many such uses which are important to our national welfare. At music and music education festivals and meetings throughout the world, performances of American music and information and materials pertaining to methods developed by American music educators can contribute to our international welfare, so to speak, by helping other nations to a truer understanding of our ways of living.

(5) Music still plays its traditionally vital role within our military establishment not only as an indispensable adjunct to training and ceremony, but also in the efforts of military commanders to provide, within the limits of reduced budgets and rigorous training schedules, facilities and opportunities which will permit young people to continue during their period of service the same development of their abilities and personalities which they enjoyed in their civilian, formative years.

It was against this background of need and challenge that work of the MENC Committee on Music Education and the Armed Forces was begun.

Music Education and the Armed Forces [1]

Because of the important role which the United States of America plays in the affairs of the world, its Armed Services must be maintained at considerable strength, and its youth with whom the educator is so closely associated carries this responsibility. Those charged with the fulfillment of the Armed Services basic mission, the security of this country and its people, stress the growth and development of the individual in home life and in military service, in so far as this concept

---

[1] From the report submitted by Virginia Carty, Baltimore, Maryland, National Chairman, Music in American Education Committee on Music Education and the Armed Forces.

is compatible with basic military aims. Music educators have worked faithfully and diligently for youth in the past and will continue to do so, sharing with the Armed Services the great responsibility for its growth and guidance through music.

While preserving the educational gains of the past generation in which music education has played a large part, the Armed Services are at the same time expanding the outlook of general education, including music education.

It is significant that the Armed Services have called upon music educators for special assistance in the development of their new concept. The use of volunteer civilian personnel in the recreational music programs of the services has been authorized by appropriate military directives. Music educators have been quick to see the great ultimate value of this new concept and to recognize the vital role which they must play.

Six principal areas of needed cooperation between music educators and the Armed Services have been found to exist: (a) curriculum activities, (b) listening activities, (c) participating activities, (d) equipment and facilities, (e) home hospitality, and (f) counseling.

These areas have been developed for the most part under three general classifications of opportunities for cooperation: (a) music activities of Armed Services personnel, (b) exchange of music opportunities between Armed Services personnel and near-by communities, and (c) music contributions from the community to Armed Services personnel. Local music educators can implement all three classifications.

The Music Educator. The value of active participation in musical activities is one with which all music educators are familiar. What has been said so often in so many ways about music as an essential in time of peace or war, significantly supported by leaders in curriculum development, is based upon the concept of music as a dynamic factor of human life and experience. It is the music educator's familiarity and understanding in this respect that so interests the Armed Services. The place of the music educator in the community and its cultural life should be such that it commands the attention and respect of the servicemen who find the music educator cooperating in the musical activities of their military organization.

While performing artists, experts in the fields of musicology and composition, and other professional fields, all willingly and gladly give of their special talents to assist the recreation programs of the Services, the music educator represents something more personal and important in the home and community experience of individual members of the Armed Services. It is the responsibility of all educators, and especially those in music, to carry on their daily jobs, serving youth in the community today, and at the same time assume added responsibilities for young people who are temporarily away from home in the service of their country.

There are many and varied professional or vocational areas in the musical life of the person in uniform which are of special interest to the music educator. As in elementary and secondary music education, music's most extensive sphere of influence in the Armed Service life is in the avocational and personal development of interests of its general personnel. Here music serves as a recreational and leisure time activity, providing educational and cultural challenges for the individual. Equally as important, however, music provides an important link between the serviceman and the community from which he comes and to which he has been assigned. In this respect special demands are made of the local music educator.

OPPORTUNITIES FOR MUSIC EDUCATORS

Music educators may contribute significantly to the participation and listening activities of Armed Services personnel by providing:

(1) Opportunities for servicemen to join community or civic orchestras, bands, choruses, church choirs, high school music groups, chamber music groups, and other organizations.

(2) Opportunities for service personnel to enroll in adult education courses, in music appreciation or theory courses, for private or class lessons in voice and/or instruments at local colleges and other schools.

(3) Opportunities for service personnel to hear and to borrow recordings, to enjoy radio, television and films at public libraries, recreation centers, schools and colleges, radio stations, USO, and in private homes.

(4) For the distribution of tickets for concert, theater, and museum attendance for performances by professional and nonprofessional organizations; at schools, colleges, churches, service clubs, fraternal groups, amateur groups, and civic recreation departments.

Music Educators may contribute to the exchange of opportunities between Armed Services personnel and the community by:

(1) Encouraging an exchange of invitations between military installation and community for band leaders, choral conductors, soloists, teachers, music consultants and advisers, adjudicators, arrangers and composers, and masters of ceremonies.

(2) Encouraging participation by community and military personnel in performances by bands, orchestras, choruses, glee clubs, chamber music groups, musical reviews, recitals, etc.

Music educators may develop opportunities for assistance from the community for on-base or off-base activities, such as:

(1) Contributions of recordings to library or service club collections.

(2) Assistance to military performing groups by lending equipment, supplies, etc.

(3) Performance on base or on post by school, church, community, and professional groups.

The Navy Music Career Program [1]

Naval history is marked by traditions which have been retold in countless fo'c'sle songs and sea chanteys. In olden days, sailors and mariners would gather together at evening and sing, as well as tell, their "sea stories" for many hours. Today the men of the United States Navy, ashore and afloat, are being entertained with some of the finest popular and classical music available, as performed by 65 Navy bands stationed throughout the world.

The U. S. Naval School of Music in Washington, D. C., is the central point around which revolves the entire musician branch of the Navy. More than 1,700 musicians make up the Navy Music Program, playing as bands and dance orchestras on the ships of the fleet and at Navy shore stations. The Naval School of Music, established in 1935 for the specific purpose of training Navy musicians for performances, offers a training program which is geared to handle musicians who wish to obtain a free music education in the Navy Music Career Program.

Now training 350 military musicians for performances in bands stationed at the world's focal points, the Naval School of Music is a major base of musical operations for the Armed Forces. Today the School of Music stands as a symbol of armed forces unification, with a curriculum of music courses set up for *Army* and *Marine Corps* as well as *Navy*. Sailor musicians now work and play side by

---

[1] Article from the *Music Educators Journal*, September-October 1954, by Donald M. Burns, Musician Second Class, a member of the U. S. Naval School of Music faculty, Washington, D. C.

side with soldier and marine musicians, and new instructors have been added from outstanding musicians in these services.

With sixty-five Navy unit bands now in operation, the Naval School of Music is furnishing the training, music, instruments, and all materials needed to maintain these bands and the men in them. Navy bands may be found in any part of the world, on a carrier deck in the Atlantic or in a concert hall in Europe, providing music for as many military and recreational activities as possible, and giving the men in uniform a more than well-deserved entertainment break.

THE TRAINING PROGRAM

Navy bandsmen, in the course of their duties, play for military ceremonies and honors, as well as for recreational functions of all types. Flexibility is a basic factor necessary to all military bandsmen, and this is an important part of the training program of the Navy music school. Students at the School of Music are called upon regularly to provide music for official activities in Washington, D. C., and the surrounding area. An excellent example of this phase of the Navy Music Program is the outstanding 120-piece marching band which participated in the last Inaugural Parade. In addition, the music school furnishes musicians for dances, concerts, and radio and television shows. The U. S. Naval School of Music is always ready with anything from a small dance combo to a 100-piece marching band. Diversity of program and organization activities are features of the School of Music.

While in training at the Navy music school, military bandsmen follow a schedule of musical studies similar to that offered by civilian music schools throughout the country. Each student musician is enrolled in music classes and scheduled concert and dance band rehearsals. During the day, each student has sectional warm-ups, two concert band rehearsals, one dance band rehearsal, a class in music harmony, and two study periods, or a combo rehearsal and one study period. In addition, the student bandsmen put in a certain amount of practice hours each week, under a supervised plan of practice, using the 40 sound-proofed rooms and areas of the Music School building.

Student bandsmen at the music school are organized into groups composed of four Navy concert bands and two Army concert bands, Marine Corps musicians are included with the Navy. These bands rehearse twice each day, reading all types of musical compositions written for the modern concert band. Dance bands, an integral part of the Navy music program, are organized from within the personnel of the concert bands, as well as combos and clinic bands.

Emphasis is placed upon instrumental proficiency in performance, because this is the first requirement of a good bandsman. Private lessons are given weekly to each student musician, and here problems that may arise in individual techniques and styles are discussed and clarified. Many instrumentalists at the Naval School of Music are required to develop good playing technique on a second instrument. For instance, all clarinet-players must "double" on saxophone, and vice-versa, and pianists must be able to double on a regular band instrument, usually percussion. Previous experience on a second instrument is not necessarily required, although it helps, because all instruction for these "major" and "minor" instrumentalists is provided by a staff of instructors from the armed services.

Student progress is measured after every third month of instruction by audition boards composed of departmental heads and instructors. These boards recommend aids and solutions for individual instrumental problems. Individual progress is also evaluated through weekly lessons, with all-around instrumental proficiency held foremost in mind.

FACILITIES

Musical facilities at the Naval School of Music, many of which are now irreplaceable, include (a) a well-equipped Recording Laboratory, (b) an ever-growing

Reference Library which now contains over 7,000 music texts, instrumental method books, music scores, and music magazines, as well as a collection of more than 2,000 LP recordings of symphonies, operas, military bands, and modern dance orchestras, and (c) the Band Music Library, which has over 10,000 compositions for all types of musical groups.

The use of recording facilities in the education program is one of the outstanding phases at the Naval School of Music. An extensive laboratory within the school is prepared to perform practically all of the operations of larger commercial recording laboratories. Records are cut of performances of concert bands, dance bands, instrumental ensembles, and soloists, and used in checking advancement. These records are also available for the students' own use.

The military bandsmen are supplied with all music materials, including equipment from the Navy's supply of brass, woodwind, and percussion instruments. All of the Navy school's horns and drums are kept in top condition by a staff of skilled repairmen who operate the instrument repair shops located in and near the school.

QUALIFICATIONS

Musicians at the Naval School of Music are selected from the enlisted ranks of the services, or by auditions while in civilian status prior to signing up as bluejacket bandsmen. All students at the School of Music are given an entrance audition to determine their musical ability and eligibility for the Navy Music Program. The Navy offers the civilian musician the opportunity of enlisting directly into the Navy Music Career Program by going to one of three Naval bases (at San Diego, Calif.; Great Lakes, Ill.; or at the School of Music in Washington, D. C.) at government expense for auditioning. In this pre-enlistment audition, the actual ability of the applicant to play his instrument and to read music written for that instrument is determined by a qualified audition board. Following their auditions, successful musicians are enlisted in the Navy. Unsuccessful applicants have the choice of returning to their homes or enlisting for general service in the U. S. Navy.

Immediately after signing up, the Musician Recruit is sent through regular "boot" training at one of the Naval Training Centers, where he will have the opportunity to play in a band composed of recruits like himself. Upon completion of his military training in boot camp, usually lasting from 12-14 weeks, the musician, now a Musician Seaman Apprentice, is transferred to the U. S. Naval School of Music in Washington, D. C., for the six-month course of musical study. This system of enlisting directly into the Navy Music Program eliminates the uncertainty of placement in military service, and duty as a musician in the Navy is assured.

Musicians who are considering applying for duty in the U. S. Navy and assignment to the U. S. Naval School of Music must meet the following general qualifications: (a) a working knowledge of major and minor scales, intervals, and key signatures most commonly encountered in band literature for their instrument, and fundamentals of music notation and terminology; (b) brass and woodwind players must have developed an embouchure which is basically correct and capable of producing a tone characteristic of the instrument played, throughout the practical range of that instrument; (c) they must be able to perform reasonably well at sight, the first chair parts of standard band literature of the grades medium-easy to medium, or the second and third parts of grades medium to difficult, with proper observance of phrasing, dynamics, breathing, and interpretation.

ACTIVITIES

Today, the Naval School of Music is giving more emphasis to musical activities of organizations other than their own, by bringing military and civilian musical units to the music school for program performances before the military bandsmen.

The U. S. Navy Band Orchestra also provides concerts for the student musicians from time to time.

A Band and Instrumental Music Clinic was conducted at the School of Music recently, under the sponsorship of the Maryland Music Educators Association. The Clinic was conducted by Lt. Comdr. John D. McDonald, Officer-in-Charge of musical and administrative processes of the Naval School of Music. The program included modern band material played by a military band, and performing panel clinics concerned with brass, woodwind, and percussion instruments.

With the many fine opportunities for furtherance of musical experience and education before them, musicians at the U. S. Naval School of Music are well situated in the music field. Upon graduation from the music school, the sailor musician is ready for assignment as a bandsman in one of the Navy's colorful musical units. It may be aboard a large aircraftcarrier or battleship at Naples, Italy. It may be with a Navy unit in Yokosuka, Japan, or it may be at one of the Naval bases in the United States or one of its possessions.

Wherever it is, the Navy unit band will be playing for all it is worth, providing music of which our Navy and our country may well be proud.[1]

Air Force Musical Careers [2]

"How can I continue my musical career, knowing that eventually I shall be drafted into the armed forces? If I enlist, which branch will offer me an opportunity for continued musical growth so that upon my return to civilian life I shall be a far better musician than when I enlisted?" These questions are on the lips of hundreds of young men, and they are serious questions which demand answers. As a music educator called to active duty with the United States Air Force, I believe I have found the answers to these questions in the *Air Force Music Career Program*.

Few people realize how much the typical Air Force Band of today differs from its counterpart of a decade ago. It is no longer a unit whose chief responsibilities are to play for reviews, marching formations, Base concerts, and other routine affairs. True, these duties still exist, but the program's scope has extended far beyond the concept held by both commanding officers and bandleaders of yesterday.

If one were to visit the training quarters of a modern Air Force band, he might find a glee club rehearsal in progress or perhaps a class deeply engrossed in ear-training, for the work of the band now includes such responsibilities. Development of a male glee club within the band, administration of an organized program of college-level theory courses, and active support of the Special Services program are within the scope of today's bandleader.

The majority of Air Force bandleaders are fully qualified music educators. Many of them, prior to entering the service, were teachers in our public schools. These men naturally enjoy and support the present-day Air Force policy, *"Every Air Force Band, a Music School."* As a music educator, the bandleader knows it is his responsibility to improve the musicianship of all of the members of his band through individual and class instruction. *"While the bandsman gives the Air Force his services, the Air Force, in turn, makes every possible effort to expand his music education so that upon the termination of his enlistment he may return either in civilian life a far better musician than when he enlisted or he can re-enlist and be well on the road to advancement in the music career program."*

---

[1] Further information concerning the Naval School of Music and a copy of the illustrated brochure, "A Musical Career in the United States Navy," may be obtained by writing to: Officer-in-Charge, U. S. Naval School of Music, U. S. Naval Receiving Station, Washington 25, D. C.

[2] Article from the *Music Educators Journal*, February-March 1954, by Benedict T. Hallgrimson, Warrant Officer Hallgrimson of the USAF Bandsman School at Bolling Air Force Base, Washington, D. C., was separated from active duty December 1952. During the summer months each year he returns to active duty with the Air Force.

Concurrent with civilian manpower demands brought about by the Korean war, thousands of young men were drawn into the service. Many of these men had actively participated in high school bands, some had completed one or two years of college, while others have earned music degrees. Should one of these men find his way to one of the Air Force indoctrination centers, he may be selected for assignment to Air Force bands only if he is musically qualified and can pass successfully the apprentice skill-level examination on a band instrument. He might be primarily a string player or a vocalist, but if he can pass an examination on a band instrument (a secondary instrument) he may enter the Air Force music program and know that in addition to his band duties, his training and talents will be further utilized in development of specialized music activities at his assigned air base. He might be assigned to one or more of the following activities: organizing glee clubs; assisting the Base chaplain in organizing church choirs, both Protestant and Catholic; teaching classes in music appreciation; establishing record clubs; or giving private instruction on various instruments to interested airmen.

Through these activities he helps to carry out a well-rounded music program which is limited only by individual foresight and initiative. In return he derives great benefit from these experiences that place him in the teaching field for which he has been specifically prepared during his college days. *"It makes him a more experienced educator so that upon his return to civilian life he is no longer a novice in the field of music education."* This program also acts as a real proving ground for Air Force bandleaders, should any one of these men desire to make a career of music in the service.

The pursuit of a music career in the Air Force has been made more attractive by the establishment of a proficiency examination program in addition to higher training standards for bandsmen. Under this program any bandsman who aspires to the grade of staff, technical or master sergeant is required to pass both theoretical and on-the-job type musical performance tests for each appropriate grade before being considered for promotion.

To further implement this program an Air Force Bandsman School was established at Bolling Air Force Base, Washington, D. C., in 1946. Headed by Lt. Harold Copenhaver, a graduate of American University, this school boasts a staff of highly qualified instructors possessing degrees from well-known schools of music. Bandsmen may apply for any one of the three-month class sessions offered each year, and enjoy a concentrated study of college-level music subjects in an endeavor to pass one of the grade level proficiency examinations. *"Promotions in the Air Force music field are made upon the basis of ability and ambition rather than length of time in the service."*

In order that this new philosophy of Air Force music may be developed to its fullest, a refresher course for bandleaders has been established at Bolling Air Force Base in connection with the official U. S. Air Force Band. Based on a plan of rotation, fifteen field bandleaders are temporarily relieved of duties at their home bases and brought to Washington, D. C., every three months for an intensive refresher period. Organized and directed by the writer, this program was designed for workshop activity. Each bandleader is encouraged to contribute to the program through his individual resources.

Every educator experienced in the field of music education realizes that the key to success for any music program exists in the proficiency of its teaching corps. This intrinsic factor, coupled with a disposition to think and act in the light of things as they are, forms the basis for the five-point program in the refresher course

(1) **Instrumental Techniques.** Knowledge in this subject matter is imparted through clinic demonstrations and lectures on all the woodwind and brass instru-

281

ments of the modern concert band. The instructors are chosen from the official U. S. Air Force Band and are of artist quality. (Prior to joining the AF Band most of these men were members of major symphony orchestras and engaged in studio teaching.) Emphasis is placed upon individual playing problems and their solutions. This is information every bandleader must have if he hopes to be successful in guiding the growth of musicians placed in his charge.

(2) **Advanced Conducting.** In this course it is assumed that each bandleader is experienced in the rudiments of baton movements. If detrimental peculiarities or deviations from accepted conducting form are evidenced, appropriate corrections are made. The principal objectives are to develop a desire for musical scholarship and successful rehearsal techniques. A quest for musical truth is the theme of this course. Score analyses are developed by each bandleader and presented before the class. Here the analyses must be defended, and the problems involved in rehearsal resolved. Finally, the class groups as a workshop band, which consummates the cycle of learning under actual playing conditions.

(3) **Percussion Techniques.** The percussion section is the least understood and the most neglected section of any average band. Fully realizing that this situation exists, special attention is given to it. Bandleaders share in a combination of class and private instruction in the twenty-six standard rudiments and the ten additional orchestral rudiments for snare drum. A study of tympani playing and the correct methods for playing miscellaneous traps are also included. Each bandleader must be able to pass a comprehensive playing examination on all percussion instruments, and at the conclusion of the course he is given a set of Air Force-produced recordings and mimeographed course materials. Not only as an audio-visual aid for field bandleaders but also for use in the training of field band drummers, all the rudiments and percussion exercises contained in the course have been meticulously recorded with an analysis of each rudiment and how to perfect it. Prepared thus with personal training and teaching aids, the bandleader can confidently guide his percussion section to equality with other sections of his band.

(4) **Advanced Ear Training and Sight Singing.** This course emphasizes the development of tonal acuity and tonal memory through melodic, harmonic and rhythmic dictation and sight singing. It is deemed essential that every bandleader must have a discriminating ear and that he must have the ability to accurately sing parts from the score while engaged in rehearsal. Much precious time can be lost in rehearsal in trying to explain how a certain part must be played when the quickest approach to the problem is for the director to sing it.

(5) **Vocal and Choral Techniques.** Every Air Force field band is busily engaged in the development of male glee clubs. Many young men entering the Air Force music program today have been previously trained as vocalists and choral directors, and are of invaluable assistance to the bandleader. However, to build a choral program on the premise that a trained enlistee might appear to provide leadership is plainly an absurd supposition. Therefore, every bandleader attending the refresher course receives individual voice lessons and in so doing develops an understanding of how to accurately classify voices, how to develop pleasing vocal tone, how to extend voice range, and how to develop an equalization of the voice registers. By participation in small choral ensembles and glee clubs the bandleader learns at first hand how to handle such principal aspects of choral conducting as balance and blend, purity of vowels, and the grouping of the consonants so that clarity of enunciation and diction will result. He becomes familiar with a wealth of worthwhile choral literature.

To round out this five-point program, miscellaneous lectures are included involving related subjects such as instrument repair, arranging, copyright laws, etc. *"The Air Force bandleader is no longer a forgotten man."*

This ambitious and far-reaching development of the Air Force music program has not happened just through the natural evolutionary progress of time. Behind the scenes lies the work of a highly competent organizer and administrator, a man with an extensive background as a music educator and professional musician, Colonel George Sallade Howard, Chief of Bands and Music, and conductor of the official United States Air Force Band and Symphony Orchestra.

Today's Air Force bandleader is fully indoctrinated and trained in the new philosophies of the Air Force music program, and a has a full realization of the mission to be accomplished by today's Air Force bandsmen.

APPENDIX

Resolutions

Outline of Program for Music Education

Recommendations of the North Central Association
of Colleges and Secondary Schools

The Child's Bill of Rights in Music

Music Buildings, Rooms and Equipment

Minimum Standards for String
Instruments in the Schools

The Code for the National Anthem of
The United States of America

Codes for Public Relations

Suggestions for a Cumulative Song List

Selected List of Books on Elementary
and Secondary Education

Facts About the Music Educators
National Conference

Music in American Life—Organization Plan

Calendar of Meetings

Constitutions and Bylaws

Music in American Education
Committee Personnel

RESOLUTIONS

Adopted by the Music Educators National Conference, Chicago, Illinois, 1954

[*In presenting these resolutions to the membership of the Music Educators National Conference at the biennial convention in Chicago, Fowler Smith, chairman, 1952-1954, of the Council of Past Presidents, which, by provision of the MENC constitution is charged with the responsibility of preparing the resolutions, said in part: "What do we music educators really believe in our hearts? Do we give lip service only to the ideals embodied in these resolutions which we are considering? Only to the extent to which each member of the Conference translates these ideals into action, will they be effective . . . . It is in this spirit that the Council of Past Presidents submits these resolutions to you. They reflect the thinking of our membership from every area of the country, and epitomize the resolutions adopted by all six Division Conferences submitted in 1953."*]

Music a Universal Need. The Music Educators National Conference reaffirms its conviction that music education is making a unique contribution to public education.

The American concept of public education demands that we provide, for all children, free educational opportunities that will develop their physical, intellectual, spiritual, moral, and social nature, contribute to their economic welfare and stimulate their sense of responsibility as good American citizens.

We, as members of the MENC, pledge our support to the total program of education. We declare our desire to study, to understand, and to aid in improving the school program. We will endeavor to interpret this program—its objectives and its needs—to the public it is designed to serve. We shall challenge and defend all attacks on our schools—whether born of malice or of misunderstanding.

We declare our deep conviction that every child has a right to the fuller self-realization provided through continuous, vital and inspiring musical experiences.

We believe that the highest values in music education reside in aesthetic experiences, in the elevation of spirit in response to beauty and in the symbolic expression of the inner life of feeling. A contribution so important to the well-rounded personality justifies a place of major importance for music in the total program of public education.

At the 1919 meeting of the Music Supervisors National Conference in St. Louis, Frances Elliott Clark made the following powerful statement which represents the best thinking of our Conference throughout the years: "The hour of *music as education* has struck. Not music for fun nor entertainment, nor as a pastime or accomplishment, nor yet as an art, standing alone—although at times it may be any or all of these—*but as one of the great vital forces of education.*"

Strength Through Unity. We reaffirm our faith in the Music Educators National Conference (its divisions and state organizations, and its affiliates) as a comprehensive and democratic organization capable of promoting the highest values of music education. We deplore any movement which tends to threaten its unity and weaken its influence. A unified and cooperative music education program to meet the needs of all children challenges the best in all of us.

Relationship with Professional Educational Organizations. (a) To the National Education Association, MENC expresses appreciation for constructive work which it is doing for all of education, and pledges its support to the Centennial Action Program, which we hope will come from every segment of the MENC.

(b) To the American Association of School Administrators, we express our appreciation of its broad, comprehensive educational outlook, and MENC welcomes the opportunity to work side by side with AASA and to actively participate in its forward looking programs.

Relationship with Closely Allied Organizations. The musical development of the youth is reflected and enhanced by the contribution made by agencies operating in specific areas outside of school jurisdiction. MENC and its members welcome the opportunity to support and actively cooperate with such organizations in promoting mutual understanding and working relationship. Mutual benefit is found in close cooperation with the Music Teachers National Association, the National Association of Schools of Music, the American Music Conference, the National Federation of Music Clubs, the American Association of Colleges of Teacher Education, the American Federation of Musicians, and other similar organizations on national, state and local levels.

International Society for Music Education. The formation of the International Society for Music Education in Brussels in July 1953 provides for the first time in history an opportunity for us to join with our colleagues in other countries in efforts to secure for children everywhere their right to music instruction as a part of general education. Both as an organization and as individuals we should support unfailingly this new world-wide organization. We accept the statement by Carlos Romulo in a speech to the United Nations Assembly: "The teachers' task now is to orient the mind of America's youth toward a wide appreciation of human affairs, that they may better grasp the unalterable fact of the oneness of man's destiny over and above the cultural differences of the various people that inhabit our planet."

Parent-Teacher Associations. The Conference expresses its high regard for the aims and achievements of the National Congress of Parents and Teachers, in both its national and local organizations, and bespeaks the continued support of the Congress in the promotion of a program of education which recognizes the importance of the fine arts, and gives to that segment of the curriculum appropriate and adequate emphasis.

Cost of Music Education. The cost of a well-equipped and well-administered program of music education is fully justified by the contribution it makes in the lives of our citizens. The Conference through its members is obligated to bring to the attention of administrators the information and recommendations of studies and surveys which set forth the needs of a well-functioning music program.

Schools should make provision for the following:

(a) Adequate housing including acoustically treated music rooms.

(b) Adequate equipment including pianos, record players, music libraries and other standard equipment.

(c) Adequate time allotment.

(d) Scheduling of classes to permit continuity of musical activity.

Music Curriculum to Provide for Basic Needs of All Children. The emphasis of general education toward an increased consideration for gifted children is supported by music educators, who regard the discovery and encouragement of talented students as one of their chief responsibilities. Such emphasis is not intended to minimize the operation of the thesis that music is the heritage of all children; and general music, designed for all students including those whose interest and abilities do not lead them into special performing groups, must be of major consideration in planning a program of music education.

Upgrading of Standards in Quality of Music Offerings in the Schools. We re-emphasize our conviction that only worthwhile music, well performed, has cumulative and permanent value. Excellent performance of music of ephemeral, or so-called popular music, falls short of the high purpose of music as a ministry in the realm of aesthetic and spiritual experience. We believe that social demands made of music can be met effectively without compromising high standards of quality of music to be performed.

Radio, Television, and Audio-Visual Aids. We extend grateful acknowledgment to the radio and television stations for the many fine musical programs which are being offered in increasing number, and for their cooperation in making available the facilities of their stations for broadcasting musical programs from the schools.

We commit our membership to the stimulation of listening audiences to programs of acceptable musical worth as a medium of developing discrimination and taste. At the same time, we recognize the need for encouragement of all students to participate in making music, individually and in groups, lest we become a nation of listeners only.

We encourage the increasing use of all audio-visual aids which will improve music instruction.

We especially commend those municipalities, states and educational institutions that are developing their own FM radio and television facilities designed solely for educational purposes.

Such a service is of particular value in the promotion of music in the rural and village schools.

Recruitment of Music Teachers. The advancement of the program of music education in the nation is faced with a crucial need of teachers prepared to teach music. It is important for music educators to assume a share of the responsibility for recruiting teachers of music. Today's music teacher has a wider task than that of adequately mastering the subject matter and performing skills in the field of music. Other important qualifications are: a desire to teach, respect and sympathy for learners of every kind as well as for people in general.

It, therefore, becomes the obligation of the music teacher to recognize these personal qualities, as well as musical capabilities, of students and acquaint them with the opportunities and personal satisfaction to be found in teaching, and guide them at an early age in the pursuit of musical study which will equip them for successful careers in teaching.

Acknowledgments. The Conference membership gratefully acknowledges the outstanding leadership of the central office and staff. We extend to Executive Secretary C. V. Buttelman, and Associate Executive Secretary Vanett Lawler, our deep appreciation for their devoted service and guidance in the continuity of an ever-broadening and expanding outlook, and in the increasing effectiveness of music education in the United States.

We commend President Ralph E. Rush, his executive committee, and his board of directors for efficiency and wisdom in administration of Conference affairs, and in building for this biennial meeting a program of great significance for the advancement of music education.

Democracy in action is exemplified in the splendid contributions made by the Music in American Education committees In division and national levels, which lift our sights to ever-expanding horizons.

The Conference further expresses appreciation for the hospitality and courtesy extended by the authorities and citizens of Chicago and the State of Illinois.

We express our thanks to the Chicago Board of Education, to Superintendent Benjamin C. Willis and his staff, and to the local committees who helped make this fourteenth biennial conference a success.

⊹

[*Members of the Council of Past Presidents as of April 1954: John W. Beattie, George Oscar Bowen, William Breach, Frances Elliott Clark, Louis W. Curtis, Charles M. Dennis, Will Earhart, Karl W. Gehrkens, Mabelle Glenn, Edgar B. Gordon, Marguerite V. Hood, John C. Kendel, Henrietta Baker Low, Joseph E. Maddy, W. Otto Miessner, Lilla Belle Pitts, Luther A. Richman, Herman F. Smith, and Fowler Smith. Ralph E. Rush, president 1952-1954, became a member of the Council upon the conclusion of his term, June 30, 1954.*]

Excerpts from Resolutions and Recommendations Adopted
at the 1953 Division Meetings of the MENC [1]

Musical Standards and Educational Values. "We recognize that over a period of years, music education has received widespread support from the public and educational leaders. We recognize further that a high degree of excellence has been obtained in relation to technical skill in performance, both vocal and instrumental. The ability of our young people in this regard has been recognized by musicians all over the world. We feel that we have reached the point in the development of music education where we should be greatly concerned over the quality of music being performed. The lasting values of music education can be realized only if we use materials of worth. As music educators, individually and as a group, we need seriously to resolve to raise the level of the music we use."

"We do not find quality (of music) and quantity (of music) incompatible. We consider that the ideal situation exists when highest musical standards are maintained by the maximum number of people. We do recognize, however, the subordination of musical to social values in music education and we deplore this trend."

"*Whereas*, we believe that the educational values of music are dependent upon the artistic merit of the music and also upon the excellence of its performance, *be it resolved* that we encourage the use of the most worthwhile materials appropriate to the situations in which they will be used, and that we encourage continued refinement of performance commensurate with the physical and mental development and capacities of the pupils who are performing."

Music in the Total Program of Education. "Inasmuch as . . . music education is at the present time increasingly becoming recognized as a functional part of the program of general education, and inasmuch as the music educator serves in the capacity both of musician and of educator, it is important to recognize and reaffirm our responsibilities to the total program of education and to support and actively participate as educators in programs initiated in behalf of public education as a unified whole."

"*Whereas*, we believe that music is an integral part of education, *be it resolved*, That the members of the . . . Conference recognize and assume their responsibilities to the total program of education and that they actively support their fellow teachers and their administrators in movements for the improvement of public education."

New Patterns of Music Education. "This board urges music educators on all levels of organization, State, Division or National, to re-evaluate present practices in all segments, elementary through teacher training, against the criterion of meeting the needs of rapidly growing school populations, to devise new patterns of music education where indicated and to revise present curricula and teacher procedures drastically in order to better serve the needs of all students in terms of a rapidly changing educational philosophy."

Music Curriculum Evaluations. "It is the conviction that music educators should from time to time evaluate the music education curriculum *in relation to the total curriculum,* and that such evaluations should be made *jointly* by music educators with administrators, superintendents, and principals in elementary and high schools, classroom teachers, teachers of other subject fields, etc. Based on this conviction, therefore, this board recommends that such an evaluation under such auspices can most advantageously stem from state departments of education and can at the same time be a part of and an outgrowth of the MENC Music in American Education Program."

The Gifted Child. "We support an apparent changing emphasis in general education toward increased consideration for the gifted child."

---

[1] Dates and places of 1953 MENC Division meetings, with names of the respective Division presidents are included in the Calendar of Meetings p. 332.

Attacks on Public Education. "Music educators should be well informed about attacks on public education which are becoming increasingly persistent and concerted and should do everything possible to assist administrators and boards of education to define and defend the position of public education."

Certification. "It is of the greatest importance that as soon as possible the MENC National Commission on Accreditation and Certification devise criteria and supply information which will be of assistance to the officers and members of the state music education associations in their work with state departments of education on this subject. Such assistance, which will supplement similar activities now under way in many of the states, will add solidarity and prestige to state-wide programs of music education, particularly in relation to state departments of education."

Recruitment of Teachers. "The problem of the recruitment of music educators, which involves guidance beginning at the elementary school level and extending to the secondary school level, as well as broader music education for all potential music educators at these levels, is one which needs to be seriously studied and discussed, not only by the Conference officers and leaders, but also needs to be better understood and evaluated and resolved in ways most consistent with all educational trends by the entire constituency."

Code of Ethics. "Another problem needing serious study and evaluation concerns the necessity of devising some criteria as guidance for music educators and music industry which will result in a higher degree of ethical practices.

"There is evidence of the need for a code of ethics on a national basis covering this problem, and its formulation should begin on a State and Division basis."

Studies, Projects, Discussion Groups. "It is the opinion of the board of directors that the MENC Music in American Education Committee organization plan should be encouraged and that the work of the respective committees should be activated with a view to improvement of instruction in music education as well as with a view to significant contributions which can be made to the forthcoming publication planned by the MENC as the successor to the current Source Book."

"In view of these considerations the board reviewed carefully the possibility of apportioning at future meetings a certain period of time for discussion group meetings. The amount of time for such group discussion was not recommended. Mention was made that perhaps one day of the four-day period might be considered for this purpose. Such a plan would also provide maximum participation of all members."

Interscholastic Activities Associations. "This board of directors is emphatic in its approval of the policy whereby state units work in closest possible cooperation with interscholastic activities associations. Where such close working relationships do not already exist, the board of directors urges that proper contacts be made, both by state units of music educators associations and state interscholastic activities associations, to effect such liaison."

Music Clinics and Workshops. "Responsible officials in state departments of education should be enlisted to cooperate actively with regularly established workshops and clinics under the auspices of the state music education associations."

Organizational Cooperation and Coordination. ". . . it is recommended that music educators foster a closer relationship on state and local levels with the American Association of School Administrators, the Department of Elementary School Principals of the National Education Association, the state units of the Association for Supervision and Curriculum Development, state units of the Department of Higher Education of the NEA, the state units of the Department of Classroom Teachers of the NEA, and the state units of other subject fields such as physical education, social studies, art, etc."

"It is of utmost importance for all music educators and their professional organizations to cooperate actively in all meetings of administrators on a state-wide basis. Such cooperation should include provision of music groups for programs and, *in addition*, arrangements for participation on programs of administrators, by music educators *as educators*."

"Recommended that an effort be made to bring about closer coordination between the state music educators associations and the state education associations, both in the matter of performing groups and in discussion and study sessions devoted to general education problems. This should be encouraged at both state levels and intra-state levels, as local conditions may demand."

Relationship with Closely Allied Organizations. "This board recommends that joint committees work cooperatively to clarify and reaffirm the relationship of the MENC on local, State and Division levels with such other professional groups as the Music Teachers National Association, the National Association of Teachers of Singing, The American Federation of Musicians, the American Guild of Organists, the Choral Directors Guild and any other such organizations."

Cooperation with Negro Educators. "The board of directors (of the Southern Division, MENC) reaffirms its position taken previously to work cooperatively with the Negro music educators and Negro educators and their professional organizations."

Performance Groups at Meetings. "Recommended that those charged with the responsibility of program building at the National and Division levels formulate plans to encourage maximum participation of the membership in consideration of the basic problems confronting music education today, and that, however important superior performing organizations are for inspirational purposes, they be carefully scheduled to prevent large groups from traveling long distances to appear before very small audiences."

". . . despite the insistence of committee chairmen that they have music programs for their meetings or the pressure from conductors beseeching 'just any spot' on a convention program, school music organizations should not travel long distances to appear before very limited audiences."

Pattern of Convention Programs. "This board urges that music educators charged with the responsibility of convention program building on any level of MENC avoid duplication of program content and sequence and build integrated programs to meet specific needs of the area and level for which the program is planned."

". . . the number and character of meetings and conventions at all levels need careful study."

". . . attendance at existing State, Division and National meetings constitutes a serious drain on time and resources of the members who attend all of them and that if a choice were to be made the first obligation is to the State."

". . . continued expansion of the programs at State conventions should be encouraged with limitations as to number or character of meetings being made at the Division and National levels."

". . . it is feasible and mutually profitable to hold Division board meetings and/or conferences in conjunction with conventions of the state associations in some of the states."

"Recommended . . . that the (National) Board of Directors and/or Executive Committee consider the desirability of initiating an investigation of ways in which the number of major Conference meetings might be reduced from thirteen each biennium (one National convention, six Division conventions and six planning conferences) to a smaller number which would make less heavy demands upon the membership, leadership, and staff of the MENC. It is further recommended that, in any revision of the periodic meetings and framework of our Conference meetings a determined effort be made to retain the inspirational festival features which have distinguished our conventions and which have played such an important role in the success of these meetings."

Resolutions Adopted by the Music Educators National Conference
Philadelphia, Pennsylvania, 1952[1]

SINCE IT IS BELIEVED that music education can contribute to every objective of general education, it is essential that music educators recognize their responsibility to serve these aims. Helping each student realize his full potential is implicit in all teaching. The true measure of the success of all types of education lies in the type of citizenship which results. Music educators should be determined to make the classroom experiences of their pupils an avenue to a democratic, honest, fair, cooperative, tolerant, and cultured community. The following are offered as statements representing some of the needs, opportunities and standards to which all members of the profession may conscientiously subscribe:

I

In the expanding curriculum, the Music Educators National Conference desires to stress the importance of the cultural arts and recommends that they be given full consideration when curricular changes are contemplated.

II

The Music Educators National Conference again places itself on record as insisting that the special teacher of music shall have had thorough preparation as a musician. The prospective music educator should also be taught to teach and administer, but we believe and assert that all other phases of his preparation for his work should be considered as invalid without fine musicianship.

III

Inasmuch as the teaching of music in the elementary grades is in most cases the responsibility of the classroom teachers, we strongly recommend that adequate preparation for such teaching be a consideration in the employment of elementary teachers, and that "in-service" training be provided for those presently employed who are not so prepared.

IV

Since instrumental music education in America is still out of proper balance, we urge all schools to provide equal opportunity and instruction in band and orchestral instruments, without undue emphasis on the utilitarian or public relations aspects of performing organizations, but with proper regard for equipping young people to meet the opportunities, responsibilities, and realities of civic adult life.

V

It is recognized that strong courses in vocal and instrumental music are provided in our schools, but we believe that more attention should be given to supplying courses, particularly in the secondary schools, which will appeal to those boys and girls not interested in performing music themselves, but who wish to have more knowledge and understanding of music.

VI

In the field of adult education, it is apparent that there is a need for encouraging musical activities in the welfare programs of many industrial groups throughout the nation. We would, therefore, recommend that music educators investigate the needs of their respective communities and lend assistance wherever possible in promoting an adequate program of musical activities for such groups.

VII

Because of the universal appeal of music, the Music Educators National Conference desires to reaffirm its belief in the importance of music education as a means of promoting mutual understanding and world friendship.

---

[1] Prepared by the MENC Council of Past Presidents, Herman F. Smith, chairman.

OUTLINE OF A PROGRAM FOR MUSIC EDUCATION

THE *Outline of a Program for Music Education* was prepared by the Music Education Research Council and adopted by the Music Educators National Conference at the 1940 biennial meeting. At the request of the Executive Committee of the MENC, the outline has been revised by a committee of the present Council.

It must be emphasized that the outline is intended to be a flexible guide to instruction which can be used with due consideration for the needs and capacities of children in small or large school systems. This is particularly true of the portion of the outline dealing with music in the elementary grades. It is our hope that this material will be considered as a suggested guide to the development of a program which will be educationally sound and assure the year-by-year musical development of the child.

East Lansing, Michigan, June, 1951

WILLIAM R. SUR, *Chairman 1948-1954*
Music Education Research Council

Preschool, Kindergarten, First Grade

Basic Music Activities
Minimum time, 20 minutes daily

1. *Singing*
   a. Learning songs by imitation.
   b. Matching tones.
   c. Playing singing games.
2. *Rhythmic*
   a. Making free rhythmic responses to music suitable for activities, such as walking, skipping, hopping, etc.
   b. Playing simple, directed folk dances and games.
3. *Listening*
   a. Distinguishing simple elements in music, such as mood, rhythm, instruments.
4. *Playing*
   a. Learning to use rhythm instruments —triangle, drum, and simple melody instruments, such as tone bells, marimba, etc.
5. *Creative*
   a. Giving opportunities for original responses in rhythms, songs, playing, listening.

Grades Two and Three

Basic Music Activities
Minimum time, 20 minutes daily

1. *Singing*
   a. Learning songs by imitation.
   b. Matching tones.
   c. Playing singing games.
   d. Attention to tonal and rhythmic characteristics of music, such as identifying high and low tones, like and unlike phrases, etc.

e. Singing of rounds and descants.
   f. Using song books to introduce the musical score in familiar songs and in new songs when the group is ready and interested.
2. *Rhythmic*
   a. Continuation of free rhythmic activity.
   b. Responding to note groups heard.
   c. Playing simple, directed folk dances and games.
3. *Listening*
   a. Distinguishing simple elements in music, such as mood, rhythm, instruments, themes.
   b. Recognizing the use of music by different groups and peoples such as Indians, Mexicans, etc.
4. *Playing*
   a. Continuing use of rhythm instruments, adding simple melody instruments such as melody bells, xylophone, psaltery, etc.
5. *Creative*
   a. Giving opportunities for original responses in rhythms, songs, playing, listening.

Grades Four and Five

Basic Music Activities
Minimum time, 25 to 30 minutes daily

1. *Singing*
   a. Learning songs by imitation.
   b. Continuing note reading songs.
   c. Continuing the use of song books and learning of the musical score in familiar and in new songs according to the skill and interests of the students, using both song and simple instrument activity.

294

d. Preparing for part singing by the use of rounds, descants, simple interval combinations and easy chording.

e. Singing two and three part songs when the group is ready and able to carry on such activities.

f. Large and small ensemble experience.

2. *Rhythmic*
   a. Playing directed folk and square dances.
   b. Playing rhythmic accompaniments to familiar songs using folk or standard rhythm instruments.

3. *Listening*
   a. Distinguishing simple elements in music, such as mood, rhythm, instruments, themes, form.
   b. Music of various peoples, operas of interest to children.

4. *Playing*
   a. Class instruction in piano.
   b. Rhythm instruments and simple melody instruments like marimba, song bells, and autoharp.
   c. Exploratory instruments, such as flutophone, tonette, song flute, and recorder.
   d. Class instruction on orchestral and band instruments.

5. *Creative*
   a. Continuing opportunities for original responses in rhythms, songs, playing, listening.
   b. Encouraging the composing of original melodies, rhythmic accompaniments to songs, simple harmonies to familiar songs.

Grade Six
Basic Music Activities
Minimum time, 25 to 30 minutes daily

1. *Singing*
   a. Learning songs by imitation.
   b. Continuing the reading program.
   c. Singing two and three part songs.
   d. Large and small ensemble experience.

2. *Rhythmic*
   a. Playing directed folk and square dances.
   b. Playing rhythmic accompaniments to familiar songs, using folk or standard rhythm instruments.

3. *Listening*
   a. Distinguishing simple elements in music, such as mood, rhythm, instruments, themes, form.

4. *Playing*
   a. Class instruction in piano.
   b. Rhythm instruments and simple melody instruments, like marimba, song bells, autoharp.
   c. Class instruction on orchestral and band instruments.
   d. Large and small ensemble experience.

5. *Creative*
   a. Continuing opportunities for original responses in rhythms, songs, playing, listening.
   b. Encouraging the composition of original melodies, rhythmic accompaniments to songs, simple harmonies to familiar songs.

Junior High School Grades
(VII, VIII, IX)

1. *General Music Course.* Open to all students regardless of previous musical experience. A course offering a variety of musical activities, such as playing, singing, listening, reading music, creative activity, etc.

2. *Vocal Music.* Boys' and girls' glee clubs, chorus or choir, small vocal ensembles, assembly singing for all students.

3. *Instrumental Music.* Orchestra, band, small instrumental ensembles; class instrumental instruction in wind, string and keyboard, for beginners and more advanced students; credit for private lessons available in Grade IX.

4. *Special Electives in Music.* In some junior high schools there is need for special elective classes in Music Appreciation and in Music Theory, especially in Grade IX.

5. *Relating and Coordinating Out-of-School Influences* (radio, television, motion picture, church and home) in all possible ways with those of the classroom.

Senior High School Grades

(X, XI, XII)

1. *Vocal Music.* Boys' and girls' glee clubs, chorus, choir, small vocal ensembles, voice classes, applied music credit for private lessons. Some of the large choral groups selective and others open for election by any interested student, unless the school is too small to allow for more than one group.

2. *General Music.* Open to all students, regardless of previous musical experience. A course similar to that described under Junior High School, but adjusted in its content to senior high school interests and needs.

3. *Instrumental Music.* Orchestra, band, small ensembles; class instrumental instruction in wind, string, percussion and keyboard for beginning and advanced students; dance band. Orchestra and band should be divided into beginning and advanced sections, or first and second groups if the enrollment warrants such division; applied music credit for private lessons.

4. *Elective Course Offerings.* Music Theory, Music Appreciation, Music History. Many high schools find it feasible to offer several years of instruction in each of these fields.

⊬

For All Students in Elementary and Secondary Grades

1. *Assembly Programs.* Music programs with singing by all the students, the appearance of school musical organizations, and appearance of outside artists and musical organizations.

2. *Recitals and Concerts by Student Performers.*

3. *Educational Concerts.*

4. *Music Clubs.* Clubs devoted to those interested in certain phases of music study or related areas: Record Collectors' Club, Conducting Club, Folk Dance Club, Recorder Club, etc.

5. *Musical Programs in the Community.*

RECOMMENDATIONS OF THE NORTH CENTRAL ASSOCIATION OF COLLEGES AND SECONDARY SCHOOLS

Report of the Contest Committee
1951

NOTE: At the 1951 meeting of the Commission on Secondary Schools of the North Central Association of Colleges and Secondary Schools, Chairman Lowell B. Fisher, on behalf of the NCA Contest Committee, presented a report embodying recommendations with respect to music and speech. This report was prepared, presented and accepted as a substitute for the much-discussed "contest" recommendation presented the previous year.[1] The North Central Association committee felt that the constructive, curriculum-wise approach represented by its 1951 report much better represents the purpose of the committee, the interests of the North Central Association schools, and the children they serve. It was for this reason that the committee enlisted the cooperation of the Music Educators National Conference, the Speech Association of America, and the National Art Education Association in the preparation of recommendations with respect to the subject fields represented by these three departments of the National Education Association. (The report with respect to art in the curriculum is to follow later.)

The accompanying introductory paragraphs from the committee's report and the section pertaining to music, are reprinted with permission.

It should be noted that in adopting the full report of the committee, the Commission on Secondary Schools also approved the section pertaining to speech as well as a number of other important recommendations, including a proposal that the name of the Contest Committee be changed to a title more appropriate to the scope of the committee's interests as developed through pursuit of its investigations and the curriculum studies resulting from its original assignment.

In its unanimous acceptance of the committee's report, the NCA Commission on Secondary Schools approved the content of the speech and music sections of the report as guides for interested principals and curriculum planners. The report, therefore, has the status of recommendation rather than regulation or criteria.

It should be noted that subsequent to the adoption of this report by the North Central Association of Colleges and Secondary Schools, and pursuant to the recommendation of the Contest Committee, the name of the committee was changed to "Activity Committee."—C.V.B.

*

CONTAINED in this report are copies of recommendations for complete programs in secondary schools for both music and speech. The recommendations with respect to music were prepared and authorized by the Music Educators National Conference of which Professor Marguerite V. Hood, University of Michigan, is president.[2] These recommendations are officially submitted by President Hood on behalf of the Music Educators National Conference. Contributions to these recommendations came from many persons and sources in the Conference and were compiled and written by officials of the Conference.

The recommendations with respect to the complete program of speech education in secondary schools, presented officially by the Speech Association of America, was prepared by a committee appointed by the Executive Council of the Speech Association.

The chairman of the Contest Committee[3] worked closely with both groups during the preparation of these recommendations. Excellent cooperation and a sincere desire to improve music and speech education was evident at all times by both the representatives of the Music Educators National Conference and the Speech Association of America.

RECOMMENDATIONS WITH RESPECT TO MUSIC AND SPEECH

It is recommended:

(1) That the recommendations prepared by the Music Educators National Conference and the Speech Association of America constitute the recommendations of the North Central Association with respect to suggested programs of music and speech education.

---

[1] Suggested references: "The Time to Call a Halt is Now," Paul Van Bodegraven, *Music Educators Journal* (September-October 1950); "Music and the North Central Association Contest Committee," Lowell B. Fisher, *Music Educators Journal* (January 1951).

[2] 1950-1952.

[3] See last paragraph of introductory note.

(2) That the Commission on Secondary Schools requests a sufficient appropriation to publish in brochure form these recommendations for nation-wide distribution at a nominal cost.

(3) That State Committees of the Association make a determined effort to encourage implementation for improving programs of music and speech in each of the member schools of the various states of the Association.

(4) That the Chairman of each State Committee contact in each state both the Director of Extension of the State University and the Superintendent of Public Instruction, or the Commissioner of Education, encouraging each to assist in the implementation of the proposed programs in music and speech.

(5) That the Contest Committee in general, and its Chairman in particular, do all possible to encourage school administrators and school boards to give serious consideration to the curricular needs of boys and girls with respect to music and speech.

(6) That each State Chairman contact the executive officer of the school board association in his state, encouraging a program of informing lay people of the needs for education in music and speech.

(7) That the contest element be handled in each member school in accordance with the general principles in the recommendations presented by the music and speech educators.

L. B. FISHER, *Chairman*
NCACSS Contest [Activities] Committee

Commission on Secondary Schools
North Central Association of Colleges
and Secondary Schools

⊹

PART ONE

The Child's Bill of Rights in Music[1]

Prelude

THE MEMORABLE Bill of Rights adopted by the General Assembly of the United Nations maintains that, "the recognition of the equal and inalienable rights of all members of the human family is the foundation of freedom, justice, and peace in the world."

Article XXVI asserts: "Everyone has the right to education which shall be directed to the full development of human personality and to the strengthening of respect for human rights and fundamental freedoms."

Article XXVII adds: "Everyone has the right freely to participate in the cultural life of the community, to enjoy the arts and to share in scientific advancement and its benefits."

It is evident that these and other sections of the preamble and thirty articles of the Declaration of Human Rights have important implications for educators throughout the world. The Music Educators National Conference submits some amplifications of certain aspects of the Bill of Rights as applied to the field of music education.[1]

---

[1] Resolutions adopted by the Music Educators National Conference at its biennial convention, St. Louis, Missouri, March 1950. Prepared by the MENC Council of Past Presidents (Official MENC Committee on Resolutions, Peter W. Dykema, chairman, 1948-1950. *The Child's Bill of Rights* was widely distributed throughout the world, through frequent reprinting in periodicals and other publications. Since the statement was incorporated as Part One in the report adopted in 1951 by the North Central Association of Colleges and Secondary Schools, it is given here and does not appear elsewhere in this volume. It is, however, published separately, and copies may be obtained from the MENC headquarters office.

The Child's Bill of Rights in Music

I

Every child has the right to full and free opportunity to explore and develop his capacities in the field of music in such ways as may bring him happiness and a sense of well-being; stimulate his imagination and stir his creative activities; and make him so responsive that he will cherish and seek to renew the fine feelings induced by music.

II

As his right, every child shall have the opportunity to experience music with other people so that his own enjoyment shall be heightened and he shall be led into greater appreciation of the feelings and aspirations of others.

III

As his right, every child shall have the opportunity to make music through being guided and instructed in singing, in playing at least one instrument both alone and with others, and, so far as his powers and interests permit, in composing music.

IV

As his right, every child shall have opportunity to grow in musical appreciation, knowledge, and skill, through instruction equal to that given in any other subject in all the free public educational programs that may be offered to children and youths.

V

As his right, every child shall be given the opportunity to have his interest and power in music explored and developed to the end that unusual talent may be utilized for the enrichment of the individual and society.

VI

Every child has the right to such teaching as will sensitize, refine, elevate, and enlarge not only his appreciation of music, but also his whole affective nature, to the end that the high part such developed feeling may play in raising the stature of mankind may be revealed to him.

Postlude

A philosophy of the arts is mainly concerned with a set of values different from the material ones that rightly have a large place in a philosophy of general education. Although current general educational concepts are often strongly materialistic, they are frequently given authority in moral and aesthetic fields in which they are inapplicable. Since moral, aesthetic, and material interests co-exist in life and are not mutually exclusive, those who would promote the arts, including music, should become acquainted with and should advocate a philosophy which affirms that *moral and aesthetic elements are part of the whole, equally with physical elements.*

Reality

The music teacher is, to a large extent, responsible for the implementation of the opportunities listed in our six articles. While the child must do his part in making use of them, his approach is greatly influenced by the teacher's attainments and attitudes. If the teacher is deeply and sensitively musical, follows high ideals in the practice of music, and views music as a ministration, the child is much more inclined to apply himself to the study of music, and thus come into his desired heritage. More and more the teacher must present musical material which, by its depth, intensity, and elevation, and its revelation of a buoyant spirit, shall produce significant effective reactions in our young people.

PART TWO

Music as Part of General Education (Music and the Common Learnings)

A. General Beliefs

As indicated in the preceding statement of beliefs, all students should have the opportunity for continuing experiences with music of a general nature, planned to meet their interests and needs. The so-called general music activities of singing, playing, and listening, together with many associated activities (rhythmic, creative, reading, etc.), are considered by most educators to be fundamental essentials in music for all children in the elementary schools. It is most important that *all* students have opportunity to continue these activities in keeping with their changing and developing interests and abilities in the junior and senior high school grades.

The opportunity to play an instrument, for example, is all too frequently reserved only for those secondary school students with previous instrumental experience or with the financial ability to pay for private instruction. Many young people reach the age of readiness (physically, mentally or in terms of interest) to begin to play a string, wind, percussion or keyboard instrument at the secondary school level. Such activity can be a source of tremendous individual and group satisfaction and understanding. It can be a force of great value in the life of the adolescent, developing stability and self-confidence, and giving him a worthy leisure-time activity which at the same time acts as a means of awakening cultural awareness.

B. Special Needs and Problems

(1) *Acquiring Use of the Singing Voice.* Most students can sing by the time they reach the secondary school level, but some will be found still unable to use their singing voices because of inadequate elementary school experiences or of a late development or readiness to learn to sing. Every secondary school should provide opportunity for the kind of remedial experiences such students need, and provide them in ways that will not embarrass the individual, but will rather allow for a development of a reasonable degree of self-confidence. Many talented students do not "find" their singing voices until after they reach junior or senior high school.

(2) *The Changing Voice.* The fact that voices are changing during this period adds to the importance of consistent fundamental singing activity for all students. A skillful, sympathetic teacher who carries on singing activities with them regularly while the voices are changing can develop in these students an intelligent interest in their voices and a confidence in their growing vocal skill. A school schedule which makes singing experiences intermittent only, with long periods when there is no opportunity for activity, is cheating its students of valuable guidance during a crucial period of growth.

The adolescent, particularly the boy, sometimes undergoes a mental and physical reaction to vocal and choral music which tends to destroy his interest in singing. Unless the student is kept in contact with vocal music during this trying period through the variety of activities afforded by general music classes, he is likely to terminate his contact with music at this point. The general music classes of the seventh and eighth grades, consisting of singing, playing simple instruments, etc., are recommended as a means of guiding students through this period when their judgment and attitude toward singing are, because of the physical and mental changes occurring, not too reliable.

(3) *Motor Control of Bodily Movement.* The rapid physical growth of adolescents, and the fact that this growth is frequently uneven throughout the body (some parts, such as hands and feet, growing to adult size before the rest of the body does), causes a problem of muscular control in many students. Simple rhythmic activities can do much to speed up development of a smooth control of body movement during this so-called

"awkward age." Such activities can include any type of marching experience (such as is offered by band, drum corps, and similar groups), folk games, dance activities, and the playing of instruments (band, orchestra, and keyboard instruments and also the various informal melody, harmony, and rhythm instruments).

(4) *Psychological Values.* Spontaneous, interested, well-directed musical activity is psychologically valuable to most adolescents. It can act as a stabilizing influence and as a force in the development of powers of attention and concentration. Also, a rapid development of emotional responses characterizes this period of a growing child's life. Many musical activities for the general student give opportunity for self-expression which act as a satisfying emotional outlet, and assist in developing sensitivity of feeling and understanding of other individuals and groups. Such activities include singing and playing an instrument (individually and in groups), listening to music, making rhythmic response to music by bodily movement, or by playing rhythm instrument accompaniments. The singing of folk, patriotic, and religious songs of our own people and other nations is an activity of particular importance at this time.

C. Kinds of Experience in Music for the General Student

All schools should develop the music curriculum with a view to serving every student. The practice of limiting the musical offerings to those requiring special interest, skill, and accomplishment is not in accord with the basic principles of American education, which demand that the school serve the needs of *all* children. Musical experience for the general student should be planned to meet the needs of:

(1) *The student who may have had no previous musical background* and needs at his own level of maturity of interest the most elementary of music activities from the point of view of skill required, to give him an immediate enjoyment of participation in music activities, to introduce him to possible participation in more advanced activities, and to develop in him an appreciation of the musical performance he hears.

(2) *The student with some interest and background in music,* who does not participate in the traditional, established musical performing groups such as band, orchestra or chorus, but who may become an active amateur in music (singing, playing, listening, etc.) in the community if given some school experience through informal, home-room and assembly singing, the general music classes, music club activities, etc.

(3) *The student whose chief interest in music is derived through listening to live recorded and broadcast music.* Many of these consumers of music are not at all interested in producing music. It is important that through music appreciation classes they be given an opportunity to develop an intelligent understanding of music, and the ability to enjoy the literature of great music which has become a permanent part of our cultural heritage.

D. Integration of Music and Other Subjects

In addition to classes and activities that are specifically musical in nature, the general student will profit greatly by the regular use of music in connection with other school subjects. Musical activities and experiences lend themselves easily and naturally to integration with many general education subject areas and cores. A school music program should include such integrative experiences so that the students begin to use music effectively and naturally in their daily living, outside of the special music class periods. Musical experiences of many different kinds have proved to be of value in such secondary school courses as those of literature, social studies, languages, physics, art, journalism, physical education and dance, dramatics, and home living. Successful planning of such integration requires the assistance of a teacher trained in music, sometimes only as an adviser, and sometimes as a participating teacher. This type of activity should not take the place of regularly scheduled musical activities, because music is an art of great interest and value in itself and requires for most uses certain skills which need time and experience to mature.

E. Recommendation for the Music Curriculum for the General Student

To provide the musical experiences outlined above for *all* students in the secondary schools, it is recommended that the instructional program in every school include specific *general music* and *music appreciation* course offerings open to every student regardless of previous experience. These courses will be in addition to the courses and performing groups designed for the students with special interest and previous training in music. School programs should also include specific attention to music experiences for everyone by means of the use of music in the teaching of other subjects, and by participation in music clubs and in regularly scheduled assembly music programs with assembly singing. (See outline for "The Instructional Program" on page 306.)

⌖

PART THREE

Special Education in Music

A. General Beliefs

The public school should provide additional opportunities for participation in musical activities beyond those planned for all students as a part of general education. A music curriculum designed with the sincere purpose of serving *all* students will recognize that *both the general students and those with special interests in music* must be served by curriculum offerings. These offerings should be designed to meet the special interests and aptitudes of students who desire continuing and broadening musical experiences.

The instruction given in the music courses and activities provided for this special interest group can be much more systematic and intensive than is possible in the general courses. The main purposes of such activities and courses are:

(1) *To give students the opportunity for growth in the practice of an art which provides activities whose interest and value continue beyond school hours during youth and in later life.* The fact that most of these musical activities are usable by individuals alone, and also in small groups or large groups playing or singing together, gives them great potential value in achieving desirable use of leisure time. This objective has increased significance in the light of the current military service requirements, and the needs of servicemen.

(2) *To give opportunity for students to make the acquaintance of great music* through studying about it, participating in its performance, and thus coming into direct touch with the cultural values inherent in it.

(3) *To provide opportunity for skillful performance* of music by students who will, through such performances and the intensive work required to prepare for them, be benefited in the growth of such characteristics as: ability to cooperate in group activity, self-confidence, ability to adjust to strict discipline, powers of concentration, stability of disposition, ability to follow orders, etc. Such performances are also of great value to a school student body and to a community through the entertainment and cultural growth they provide.

(4) *To give special music students individually and in groups the opportunity for musical growth and experience aside from the areas of performance*, through acquiring a good fundamental knowledge of elementary music theory, and an understanding of the use of music as a language for possible use in self-expression.

B. Basis for Organizing the Special Music Curriculum

Special music activities and classes should be designed to meet the needs of several groups of students:

(1) *Those whose enjoyment of previous participation in school music activities has made them desire further and more intensified participation in the secondary school.* Such students make up the SELECTIVE PERFORMING ORGANIZATIONS, and although most of them are satisfied to be musical amateurs, they set for themselves and for the groups to which they belong, a high standard of excellence in serious musical performance, and they enjoy the intensive work required to attain such excellence.

(2) *Those students whose enjoyment of previous participation in school music activities has made them desire to continue this participation but whose chief interest is in music as pleasant, entertaining, group activity, rather than a serious art.* Such students make up the NONSELECTIVE GROUPS which are open to all who wish to participate, and which usually require less intensive work of their members than do the selective groups.

(3) *Those who as secondary school students are just beginning to discover and develop a keen interest in music, and who, therefore, crave a more intensive activity program than is found in the general music classes.* These students are found in the BEGINNING CLASSES of all kinds (instrumental classes, and beginning bands, orchestras, and choruses, etc.), but their interests frequently move them ahead to qualify for participation with more advanced groups.

(4) *Those few students who will plan to continue in music as a profession.* A good music curriculum which is well-balanced to meet the needs of the general students as well as the one whose aim is amateur performance only, will meet most needs of these pre-professional students with an opportunity to elect courses in MUSIC APPRECIATION and HISTORY and THEORY, and continually to increase their performing skill through special study and through participation in school performing groups, large and small. Such students will be acquiring the solid musical foundation necessary for later specialization. At the same time they will acquire important social understanding through association with the other students in the performing groups. They will also, because of their special skills, make a substantial contribution to the activities of any school music group to which they belong.

C. Special Music Activities within the School Curriculum

(1) *Course Offerings.* Course offerings in music in the secondary school should include regularly scheduled vocal and instrumental groups, large and small; study groups like wind, string and keyboard instrumental classes, beginning choral groups, and beginning bands and orchestras; classes in music theory, appreciation and history; applied music (school credit for private lessons under a definite school plan. See under "The Instructional Program" on page 306). In planning and scheduling these course offerings, the importance of small vocal and instrumental groups should not be overlooked. Provision for such groups in the music program takes care of many problems of individual differences which would otherwise cause continuing difficulty in performing groups. These small groups are also very important in the carry-over of school music activities into out-of-school and adult life.

(2) *Credit for Music in the Secondary School.* It is customary to offer school credit for music courses beginning with Grade 9. The definite basis for giving such credits depends upon the situation in each individual school. Most schools offer regular academic course credit for classroom courses like music theory, music appreciation and history, and general music. Some schools consider performing groups like band, orchestra and choir as laboratory subjects, and give half the usual academic credit for participation in them. Some schools, however, have organized these performing group courses to include specific study of music theory and history and regularly scheduled outside individual practice, and then offer full academic credit for the work of the group.

Credit for small ensembles must depend entirely on the local situation and the amount of time devoted to them, as well as the progress made by the group. Many schools recognize that most students participate in small ensembles because of a love for the activity, and not for credit, and allow schedule time for them, but no credit. Many schools (and some states) have definitely worked out plans for allowing school credit for private lessons, which usually make specific arrangements for school records of the work done for credit, and also for the regular semester examination or jury which the student must take to receive the credit for work done with an outside teacher. Some schools give such credits only when the student concerned is a member of one of the school's musical organizations.

An increasing number of schools recognize music subjects as a major or a minor credit sequence in the high school. Very few students in any school care to take advantage of such a plan, but it is only reasonable to allow those students the same opportunity to do all possible study and receive credit for it, in a field which interests them to the extent of being a major or minor sequence. This allows them the same privilege as is extended to students in any other field of study in the high school, and without such a plan many students lose the opportunity for valuable pre-professional training because they must build up credit sequences in other fields. The fact that the entrance requirements of so many colleges and universities are being changed to meet these recent developments in high school credit requirements is evidence of the fact that the major or minor credit sequence in the high school is considered valuable for the student who will go on to advanced study.

D. Extra-Curricular Music Activities

CONTESTS, FESTIVALS, SPECIAL PROGRAMS

STATUS OF EXTRA-CURRICULAR ACTIVITIES IN MUSIC

Music is a subject which lends itself easily to a variety of extra-curricular uses. Part of the value of the in-school music activities is their ability to function by continuing on into after-school or out-of-school activities. These extra-curricular activities are sometimes the outcome of special clubs such as: Opera Club, Conducting Club, Record Collectors Club, Madrigal Ensemble, etc. At other times, extra-curricular music activities are a direct outcome or carry-over from in-school activities. In this class fall operettas, band performances at athletic contests, music contests and festivals, and other similar activities. All of these provide possible valuable outcomes; at the same time they also present difficult problems to be solved. There are three main points to be kept in mind in evaluating any activity or course:

(1) The most important factor to be considered in evaluating anything in connection with a school is its relation to the students. How valuable is it for the students concerned? Are the over-all results good enough to justify the amount of time required? The student and his needs must come first for consideration. If he is being exploited to satisfy the desires of community, school, parents or teacher, the activity is indefensible. If, however, he is gaining desirable experience which he needs at this time whether this experience be musical or in human relations, and if the activity is not harming him, certainly it is both acceptable and desirable.

(2) None of these extra-curricular activities in music can be substituted for a good, balanced music program in the school. They can be important and extremely valuable additions to the program, supplementing it, and greatly enriching the lives

of the students who participate. But no marching band or competition-festival program, or operetta, or any other such activity can fairly or feasibly be allowed to become the whole music program. Each has value only as a part of a program when used with due consideration for the needs of all the students, and not as means of exploiting or short-changing them. Thus the situation where the music teacher can get support or attention to music in the school only by putting on a big show, or preparing groups which win contests, is a reflection on the vision and integrity of the school administrator and level of understanding of the community. And, in the same way, the situation where the music teacher is interested only in producing top contest groups or flashy dramatic shows, without giving attention to a good program of music education throughout the school, reflects on the professional status of the teacher as a music educator. Sufficient teacher time has to be provided to meet the needs of music for both the general student and the one with special interest in music. And the music teacher and the administrator both must have the needs of the student uppermost in mind in working out a stimulating, balanced curriculum.

(3) It is not possible to make one blanket statement or decision on the specific values of any of these activities with relation to all schools in general. The needs of each school are unique and should be met in the way best to serve the students in that school. All of these activities—operetta, contest, band performance, etc.—depend for their ultimate values chiefly on the way they are used by individual teachers. An activity which brings forth undesirable results in one community may be, in other places, the spearhead for valuable growth in students to the delight of community, administration, teacher and student. Each school needs to evaluate its curriculum, both in-school and out-of-school, and decide for itself what is best for its students.

Public Performances[1]

In all public performances the emphasis should be on the truly artistic elements. Let the show elements be incidental. The idea that the public prefers the simple, obvious, or trite music is a fallacy.

(1) *Value of public performances:* (a) Presents vital goal toward which students may strive. (b) Provides opportunity for outstanding programming and achievement. (c) Promotes continued interest in music in school and in the community. (d) Spreads enthusiasm of students and instructor to entire school, the parents, and to the community. (e) Affords means for gaining public understanding of school music programs. (f) Provides excellent opportunities for raising standards of musical taste of students and of the public. (g) Students experience opportunities for creative and artistic expression as well as social broadening.

(2) *Types of performances:* (a) Concerts or presentations similar to those presented by professional organizations. (b) Interdepartment collaboration. (c) Programs wherein music supports a particular idea even though it is incidental. (d) Presentation of different musical groups of varying stages of training and ability. (e) Presentation of original music. (f) Music adapted to standard or original plays. (g) Pageants or festivals involving several schools or even the entire community. (h) Cooperation with civic events and organizations. Such participation should be more fundamental than a means of publicity or for providing mere entertainment. If little or no educational benefits can result from such collaboration the opportunity for participation should be tactfully declined by the musical director or by the school authorities.

---

[1] Material taken from Music Education Research Council Information Leaflet No. 206 (revised 1951).

PART FOUR

The Instructional Program in Music in the Secondary Schools

A. Areas of Instruction

JUNIOR HIGH SCHOOL

(1) *General Music Course* open to all students regardless of previous musical experience. A course offering a variety of musical activities such as playing, singing, listening, reading music, creative activity, etc.

(2) *Vocal Music.* Boys' and girls' glee clubs, chorus or choir, small vocal ensembles, assembly singing for all students.

(3) *Instrumental Music.* Orchestra, band, small instrumental ensembles, class instrumental instruction in wind, string and keyboard, for beginners and more advanced students, applied music study for credit available in Grade 9.

(4) *Special Electives in Music.* In some junior high schools there is need for special elective classes in Music Appreciation and in Music Theory, especially in Grade 9.

SENIOR HIGH SCHOOL

(1) *Vocal Music.* Boys' and girls' glee clubs, chorus, choir, small vocal ensembles, voice classes, applied music credit for private lessons. Some of the large choral groups selective and others open for election by any interested student, unless the school is too small to allow for more than one group.

(2) *General Music.* Open to all students, regardless of previous musical experience. A course similar to that described above under Junior High School, but adjusted in its content to senior high school interests and needs.

(3) *Instrumental Music.* Orchestra, band, small ensembles, class instrumental instruction, wind, string, percussion and keyboard for beginning and advanced students, dance band. Orchestra and band should be divided into beginning and advanced sections, or first and second groups, if the enrollment warrants such division.

(4) *Elective Course Offerings.* Music theory, music appreciation, music history. Many high schools find it feasible to offer several years of instruction in each of these fields.

FOR ALL STUDENTS IN JUNIOR AND SENIOR HIGH SCHOOL

(1) *Assembly Programs.* Music programs with singing by all the students, the appearance of school musical organizations, and the appearance of outside artists.

(2) *Recitals and Concerts* by student performers.

(3) *Educational Concerts.*

(4) *Music Clubs.* Clubs devoted to those interested in certain phases of music study or related areas: Record Collectors' Club, Conducting Club, Folk Dance Club, Recorder Club, etc.

B. Teacher Load

Many schools are demanding too much of their music teachers. This is perhaps more true of the smaller schools than of the larger units. It is recommended that a study of the teaching load of the music specialist be made with the view to adding more staff where necessary. Standards of instruction and the welfare of the teachers engaged in the profession are jeopardized when the administration fails to comprehend fully the physical strain involved in conducting musical activities. A balanced music program to serve all the children in the school will require that adequate teaching hours be available to do the work.

C. Scheduling

The tendency to reduce the number of periods in the school day has made it impossible for many principals to properly schedule music courses. Music can contribute sufficiently to the total school program to justify a serious consideration of the problems involved in scheduling it. Such a study must give due consideration to the scheduling needs of the performing instrumental and vocal organizations as well as to their training units.

306

MUSIC BUILDINGS, ROOMS
AND EQUIPMENT [1]

THE INSTRUCTION OF CHILDREN is the primary function of the schools. Although the school plant and equipment are usually classed in a noninstructional and therefore secondary category, it is imperative that the community provide the teacher with the proper physical surroundings and equipment to obtain maximum teaching and learning efficiency. The music activities should be housed in rooms which have been carefully planned for their specialized needs.

It is highly important that school music teachers and administrators be aware of some of the special factors that must be considered in planning the music rooms and facilities for teaching, practice, and performance. A few years ago this was a particularly difficult problem and was too frequently solved by processes of "trial and error." Guesswork was necessary; the information was not available. We are now beyond the experimental stages and can present sufficient information so that all factors can be studied and each school and community can make the decisions to suit their individual needs. School architects, acoustical experts and others have worked with the school administrators and music teachers in a large number of communities, and outstanding music rooms and music buildings are now available for inspection. Music teachers and school administrators are aware of the specialized needs of the music departments, so that the complex problem is no longer insurmountable.

Modern school-plant planning makes it imperative that the teachers take an active part in planning the rooms that they use for instructional purposes. Music teachers should have definite ideas as to the specialized needs in their department, so that they can contribute to the plant planning. As a rule the departmental needs will be taken care of if the suggestions are submitted early in the pre-planning stages. A careful study must be made of the present and future music offerings in the school and community before the building needs can be determined. Future expansion must be considered.

School music rooms are somewhat more expensive to construct than "ordinary" classrooms, and it is important that this fact be faced early in the planning. Before expenditures are made the school administrators and taxpayers want assurance that there is full utilization of space, and that present and future needs are realized. If the school music activities do not make full use of the music rooms during the day, provisions should be made for other music and nonmusic groups to use the facilities—especially at hours when there would be no interference with the school music program. A large music rehearsal room can be used for audio-visual needs, lectures, declamatory contests, debates, and other group meetings. Small practice rooms can be used for committee meetings, phonograph listening purposes, or as dressing and make-up rooms for the play-production staff—i.e., if located near the auditorium stage. It is also possible that some of the community educational, recreational, civic, social, and service organizations can make use of the music facilities. These are merely ideas to show full utilization of the space, so as to make it possible for the music department to get the specially constructed rooms—until such time that they can justify full use for their own needs.

Music Rooms and Equipment was the title of Music Education Research Council Bulletin No. 17, adopted by the MENC as an official publication at the biennial convention in Cleveland, Ohio, April 1932. Chairman of the Research Council's subcommittee which prepared the bulletin was Joseph E. Maddy.

A second edition embodying a number of minor revisions (1938) and subsequent reprintings were required by the constant and increasing demand for the bulletin, which was and still is the only publication giving exclusive attention to planning for special construction and equipment needed in the music education program in the schools.

---

[1] *Music Buildings, Rooms and Equipment* is the new title of the completely revised and much enlarged loose-leaf edition of Music Education Research Council Bulletin No. 17, published in 1955 by the Music Educators National Conference. This article is composed of paragraphs taken from the Preface and Introduction written by Elwyn Carter, Western Michigan College of Education, chairman of the Committee which prepared the revised edition.

In 1949 a completely revised and much enlarged edition of the Music Rooms and Equipment bulletin was prepared by the late Clarence J. Best in collaboration with William R. Sur, who was at that time chairman of the Research Council, with assistance from various persons—members of the MENC, and specialists in other fields. The new bulletin extended the success of its predecessor and became one of the most useful and widely called for publications issued by the MENC.

Because of the rapid developments which affect building techniques, materials, and equipment, and also because of the expanding needs of the school music program, another complete revision of the bulletin was indicated. The task of preparing such a revision was accepted by the MENC National Committee on Music Rooms and Equipment, and work began at the Philadelphia biennial convention of the MENC in 1952.

The table of contents of the book, printed here, provides a concise résumé of the eleven chapters. The illustrations—113 in number—include reproductions of interior and exterior photographs, floor plans and specifications. There is also an extensive bibliography.

The loose-leaf form in which this edition is printed provides for revisions or additions which are anticipated from time to time. These may include complete sections prepared to replace sections which become obsolete, or articles pertinent to a specific area published in the *Music Educators Journal*. Also there may be added from other sources material, suggestions or ideas which are important to the planning and maintenance of music facilities.

Contents of "Music Buildings Rooms and Equipment"

I. INTRODUCTION

II. PLANNING THE MUSIC FACILITIES
An analysis of basic principles. Suggestions to follow in planning a program of construction. Considerations of importance after initial planning.

III. LOCATION OF THE MUSIC ROOMS
Relationship to other classrooms in the school. Separate building or wing of main building. Advantages and disadvantages of specific locations such as auditorium stage, gymnasium, top floor, and classrooms.

IV. TYPES OF MUSIC ROOMS
Division of types. Large combined vocal-instrumental room. Comparative aspects of separate instrumental and choral rooms. Treatment of related smaller auxiliary rooms. Treatment of rooms used for other activities in addition to music.

V. THE SCHOOL AUDITORIUM
Cooperation and coordination needed between school administrators, music department heads, and architects. Size, importance, and function of fixed stage equipment. Construction features as related to the school stage. Orchestra pit factors affecting sound and personnel. Capacity and facilities of the auditorium proper. Auditorium sound reinforcement and acoustical problems.

VI. SHELLS
Evaluation and financing of the project. Design problems regarding acoustics. Effective and economical shell design.

VII. ACOUSTICS
The role of acoustics in music rooms and buildings. Providing realistic and effective acoustic environment for good hearing conditions. Acoustic criteria. Sound isolation, noise reduction, and structural sound transmission investigated graphically. The effect of room design and shape on sound distribution.

VIII. ILLUMINATION AND COLOR
Equalizing room lighting specifications with visual problems. Determining the value of colors to be used. Placement and selection of colors. Reflectance pattern. Provision for and choice of artificial luminaires.

IX. HEATING AND AIR CONDITIONING
Factors pertaining to the comfort and health of room occupants. Effect of air movement and temperature on the production of music. Problems of ventilation.

X. EQUIPMENT
Specialized requirements of the school music department. The construction and design of portable instrument and music cabinets. Specifications for school upright pianos. The storage and number of school-owned instruments. The importance and types of risers. Built-in storage facilities.

XI. AUDIO-VISUAL
Use and criteria of music room mechanical equipment. The sound reproducing media recommended for specialized subjects. Selection and engineering considerations relative to radio and television. Intercommunication, monitoring, and general sound distribution systems. Projection and other visual means used in class music instruction.

MINIMUM STANDARDS FOR STRING INSTRUMENTS IN THE SCHOOLS[1]

THE STRING INSTRUCTION COMMITTEE of the Music Educators National Conference, in collaboration with committee representation from the Music Teachers National Association, the National Association of Schools of Music and the American String Teachers Association, believe that by encouraging the purchase of string instruments and string instrument supplies which at least meet with the following minimum standards, string instruction and the development of orchestras in the schools can be materially advanced.

Because the "playability" of string instruments depends so much upon proper construction, correct adjustment and alignment, it is hoped these "Minimum Standards for String Instruments in the Schools" will be followed by consumers and teachers and complied with by merchants, irrespective of the price bracket in which the instruments happen to fall.

Measurements and Terminology of Sizes

Note: Measurements are given with a "plus or minus (+ or −) sign because instruments of different well-established makers (or even those of the same maker) will vary slightly. It is not the wish of the committee to rule out the many fine instruments that will vary slightly from the accepted "standards."

A. INSTRUMENT MEASUREMENTS

VIOLIN

Standard (full)	(4/4) body length 14"	+ or −	(35.56 cm. + or −)
Intermediate	(3/4)) body length 13¼"	+ or −	(33.65 cm. + or −)
Junior	(1/2) body length 12-7/16"	+ or −	(31.52 cm. + or −)

VIOLA

Standard	(4/4) (large) body length 16½" and up	(41.9 cm. and up)	
(full)	(4/4) body length 15¾" to 16½"	(40.9 cm. to 41.9)	
	(4/4) (small) body length 15" to 15¾"	(38.1 cm. to 40.9)	
Intermediate	body length 14"	+ or −	(35.56 cm. + or −)
Junior	body length 13¼"	+ or −	(33.65 cm. + or −)

CELLO

Standard (full)	(4/4) body length 29⅝"	+ or −	(75.3 cm. + or −)
Intermediate	(3/4) body length 27-5/16"	+ or −	(69.4 cm. + or −)
Junior	(1/2) body length 25½"	+ or −	(64.77 cm. + or −)

BASS

Standard	(3/4) body length 43¼" to 44½"	+ or −	(109.85 cm. to 113 + or −)
String length from fingerboard nut to bridge	41½" to 43½"	+ or −	(105.4 cm. to 109.85 + or −)
Intermediate	(1/2) body length 41¼"	+ or −	(104.8 cm. + or −)
String length from fingerboard nut to bridge	38¾"	+ or −	(98.45 cm. + or −)
Junior	(3/8) body length 36⅝"	+ or −	(93. cm. + or −)
String length from fingerboard nut to bridge	35"	+ or −	(88.9 cm. + or −)

---

[1] Developed by the Music in American Education Committee on String Instruction, Gilbert R. Waller, National Chairman; Frank W. Hill, Chairman of Subcommittee on Minimum Standards. Adopted March, 1952; revised, March, 1954.

B. BOW LENGTH (from tip to end of screw button)

Note: Bows for use with a particular instrument should be the same proportionate size as the instrument, as follows:

Violin (4/4)	29¼″	+ or −	(74.3 cm. + or −)
(3/4)	27″	+ or −	(68.6 cm. + or −)
(1/2)	24-9/16″	+ or −	(62.4 cm. + or −)
Viola Standard	29⅝″	+ or −	(75.2 cm. + or −)
Intermediate	29-3/16″	+ or −	(74.1 cm. + or −)
Junior	27¼″	+ or −	(69.2 cm. + or −)
Cello Standard	28⅛″	+ or −	(71.4 cm. + or −)
Hair length	23¾″	+ or −	(60.3 cm. + or −)
Intermediate	26-7/16″	+ or −	(67.1 cm. + or −)
Hair length	22-1/6″	+ or −	(56.2 cm. + or −)
Junior	24½″	+ or −	(61.6 cm. + or −)
Hair length	20⅜″	+ or −	(51.8 cm. + or −)
*Bass French Model	28-1/16″	+ or −	(71.5 cm. + or −)
Hair length	21-9/16″	+ or −	(57 cm. + or −)
German (Butler) Model	30⅜″	+ or −	(77.2 cm. + or −)
Hair length	22-1/16″	+ or −	(56 cm. + or −)

* Note: At the St. Louis MENC convention in 1950 and again at the Philadelphia meeting in 1952, the String Committee voted a strong preference for the French type bass bow.

Materials and Construction

A. INSTRUMENTS

1. Back, sides, scroll and top. Wood preferably seasoned seven years before use for instrument construction.
   a. Back sides and scroll—hard maple preferred. (carved).
   b. Top—spruce preferred (carved).
   c. Plywood approved for cellos and basses, thickness to be approved by committee.

2. Construction
   a. All joints glued tightly and reinforced with four full corner blocks and solid upper and lower blocks, full lining inside of top and back. Inlaid purfling preferred.
   b. All edges glued securely.
   c. All cracks, if any, properly repaired (reinforced and glued).
   d. Inlaid purfling strongly preferred over painted purfling.
   e. Bass bar should be of harder spruce than wood used for top itself. Bass bar must be glued in and not carved out from top wood.

3. Trimmings
   a. Pegs—ebony, rosewood, boxwood or cocobola.
   b. Fingerboard:
      (1) First choice—ebony.
      (2) Second choice—rosewood treated to resist absorption (bass and cello only).
   c. Nut and saddle—ebony preferred.
   d. Tailpiece (copper wire loop accepted for elementary school instruments):
      (1) First choice—ebony.
      (2) Second choice—boxwood.
      (3) Third choice—rosewood (cello and bass only).

e. Cello and Bass end pin:
   (1) Sturdy, metal adjustable, extra long.
   (2) Set screw, extra large "thumb—first finger" grip area.

4. Varnish
   a. Type—good quality of soft texture (oil type varnish preferred; thick hard glossy finish discouraged).
   b. The neck should not be coated with any finish which will prevent the hand from sliding smoothly.

   Recommended process: Wood surfaced with 00 sandpaper and 00 steel wool. Wood wiped with water-moistened cloth to cause loose fibers to "burr," then again rubbed with 00 steel wool; surfaced again with 00 steel wool and, after a second application of linseed oil, polished with a chamois or wool cloth. (Other processes producing this result acceptable.)

5. Attachments
   a. Chinrest—ebony, boxwood or plastic, suitable size, without sharp edges. Player to have choice to suit his own needs.
   b. Strings—should be good quality fresh strings, properly matched.

   Note: The following are recommended for the majority of instruments in most school situations. Climatic conditions and differences in instruments may suggest some deviation.

   (1) Gauges for gut strings (medium):
   Violin - E steel, with adjuster. (See Item 4 "Tuners" below.)
   single strand .010 (.25 mm.)
   aluminum wound on steel
   .011 (.27 mm.)

Violin Gut String Gauges (Con't.)
A .029 (.73 mm.) gut
D .034 (.85 mm.) aluminum on gut
G .032 (.80 mm.) silver on gut

Viola - A .029 (.73 mm.) gut
D .035 (.87 mm.) gut or aluminum on gut
G .033 (.82 mm.) silver on gut
C .045 (.112 mm.) silver on gut

Cello - A .044 (1.1 mm.) gut (metal smaller)
D .051 (1.126 mm.) gut (metal smaller)
.056 (1.35 mm.) aluminum on gut
G .054 (1.36 mm.) silverplated wire on gut
.053 (1.4 mm.) silver on gut
C .074 (1.75 mm.) silverplated wire on gut or silver on gut

Bass - G .088 (2.20 mm.) gut
D .114 (2.85 mm.) gut
A .110 (2.75 mm.) copper or silver (or plated copper) on gut
E .138 (3.45 mm.) copper or silver (or plated copper) on gut

Note: Standardization of large gear box in bass is hoped for.

(2) Metal strings are supplied by manufacturer in balanced sets.

(3) For general school use, metal strings with tuners (see Item 4 "Tuners" below) approved as follows:

Violin - E single strand .010 (.25 mm.)
E aluminum wound on steel .011 (.27 mm.)
A steel core with chromium or aluminum winding over silk or plastic underlay .017 (.43 mm.)

Viola - A (same as Violin A) .017 (.43 mm.)
D (same as Violin A) .024 (.60 mm.)

Cello - A (same as Violin A) .025 (.625 mm.)
D (same as Violin A) .036 (.90 mm.)

(4) Tuners (adjusters):
Violin-Viola—type which will not tilt tailpiece or mar top of instrument.
Cello—extra sturdy.

B. BOWS

1. Bow stick.
   a. First choice—Pernambuco, seasoned at least 10 years.
   b. Second choice—metal (aluminum).
   c. Third choice—brazilwood, seasoned at least 10 years.

2. Frogs and tip.
   a. Ebony frog preferred.

b. Ivory tip preferred; plastic tip acceptable (metal tip acceptable on bass bows.)

Note: Importers and dealers are urged to standardize eyelet threads on all bows.

3. The bow grip.

Sterling silver wire with thumb leather at lower end and leather ring at upper end preferred. The leather at both ends should be securely glued or shellacked to stick, and wire should be held together by two runs of solder or other appropriate adhesive. In wrapped bow grips, the winding should not be loose. Thumb leather should be of proper length and thickness at upper end.

C. CASES

1. Type—shaped or oblong type. Hard shell plywood with Keratol, leather or other durable covering preferred. Cases must fit the instrument as well as being of proportionate body area. Special attention should be given to viola cases since there are varied sizes within the 4/4 or standard group.

2. Interior.
   a. Lining soft and attractive (plush material preferred).
   b. Bottom and sides well padded.
   c. At least one accessory pocket and two bow holders.
   d. Zipper instrument cover highly desirable.

3. Zipper cover for case desirable, especially in colder climate.

4. Cello and Bass bags—zipper openings preferred. (Cloth or leather between zipper and bouts.)

Adjustments

A. PEGS

1. Must be properly fitted to give snug fit at both sides of peg box.

2. Must be lubricated with fresh yellow laundry soap, commercial peg soap, or ordinary chalk.

B. FINGERBOARD

1. Must be straight but slightly concave.

2. Must have medium curvature.

3. Distance from end of fingerboard to top of instrument should be as follows:
Violin (4/4): 19½—20½ mm.

Viola (4/4): 24—25 mm at a fingerboard length of 130½ mm.
(4/4 large instruments slightly more).
(4/4 small, intermediate (¾) and junior (½) sized instruments slightly less.

Cello (4/4): 62—65 mm at a fingerboard length of 58—60 cm.
(¾ and ½ sizes slightly less)

Bass Standard (¾): 9½—11 cm.
Intermediate (½): same
Junior (⅜): same

C. NUT

1. Height must be that to give small clearance below strings.

2. Over-all spacing of nut (full or standard size) center of string to string:

    Violin E to G 5/8″   (15.6 mm.)
    Viola   A to C 11/16″ (16.9 mm.)
    Cello   A to C 7/8″   (21.5 mm.)
    Bass   G to E 1-3/16″ (29.6 mm.)

D. BRIDGE

1. Curvature.
    a. Material—Hard maple preferred.
    b. The first requirement of bridge curvature is that it conform to the curvature of the fingerboard, assuming of course that the fingerboard curvature is correct. Although there are two distinct curvatures in existence, only the first (the French) is being recommended because it is more widely used and is considered by most teachers and performers to be the better.
    c. *French Curvature* possesses less curve (not as round) and is slightly lower at the A and D (violin) strings. It enables the player to perform more rapidly and to develop better and faster technic. Another advantage is the reduction of fatigue, since the actual distance between two strings is shorter, less motion of the bow arm is required. This curvature requires careful alignment of the fingerboard, lest the player touch two strings simultaneously. But this is also an advantage in that double stops and chords are more easily played.
    d. *Viennese Curvature* is slightly rounder and a trifle higher at the A and D (violin) strings. It is usually used when the fingerboard is not properly "dressed." The advantage is: more clearance for playing on each string; and the disadvantage is: wider travel of the bow and greater fatigue of the bow arm.

2. Grooves.
    a. Should be made just deep enough to hold the strings in place.
    b. Should be half round in shape and just large enough to accept the string which it is to accommodate.
    c. Ebony or equivalent inlay desirable under metal strings.

3. Height.
    a. Should be high enough to give the following clearance between strings and end of fingerboard (standard or full-sized instruments; smaller instruments slightly less):
    Violin - E 1/8″   (3.12 mm.)
    Violin - G 3/16″   (4.6 mm.)
    Viola - A 3/16″   (4.6 mm.)
    Viola - C 4/16″   (6.25 mm.)
    Cello - A 1/4″   (6.25 mm.)
    Cello - C 5/16″   (6.80 mm.)
    Bass   - G 7/16″   (10.9 mm.)
    Bass   - E 11/16″ (17.17 mm.)

4. Feet must be shaped to fit the instrument top, bridge tilted backward to form right angle between back side of bridge and top of instrument.

5. Unfitted bridge must be cut to medium thickness and tapered to the top thickness as listed below:
    Violin - 1/16″ (1.55 mm.)
    Viola - 1/16″ (1.55 mm.)
    Cello - 3/32″ (2.32 mm.)
    Bass   - 3/16″ (4.67 mm.)

6. Proper string spacing at bridge (center of string to center of string), full size (smaller instruments slightly less):
    Violin - 7/16″   (10.9 mm.)
    Viola - 1/2″   (12.5 mm.)
    Cello - 5/8″   (15.6 mm.)
    Bass   - 1-1/8″ (28.1 mm.)

7. Bridge should center on the inner F hole notches.

E. TAILPIECE

1. Gut should be just long enough so that the end of the tailpiece is even with the center of the saddle.

2. Saddle should be high enough so that the tailpiece and ends of tailpiece gut are well in the clear over the top plate. Violin, at least 1/16″ proportionately more for other instruments.

F. SOUND POST

1. Location immediately behind the right foot (1st string side) of the bridge. The distance between the back of the bridge and the front of the sound post should be approximately one-half the thickness of the post (a little more for some instruments).

2. Size:
    Violin - 1/4″   (6.1 mm.) diameter
    Viola - 1/4″   (6.1 mm.) diameter
    Cello - 7/16″ (10.9 mm.) diameter
    Bass   - 11/16″ (17.1 mm.) diameter

3. Fitting—must fit snugly (but never glued), ends beveled to fit flush with top and back.

G. BOW

1. When the frog is in full forward position, the hair should be relaxed (not loose) and the opposite test should also apply in tightening the bow screw.

2. The hair should be "sighted down" to make sure there are no crossed hairs.

3. The stick (tightened 1½ or 2 rounds for playing) should be "sighted down" to see that it is straight.

4. The frog should seat firmly on the bow, not rock from side to side.

5. The bow screw should work smoothly.

6. The bow grip should be properly attached. (See Item 3 under "Bow Materials").

Miscellaneous

(Direction sheet for Care of Instruments)

A. Keep bow and instrument in case when not in use.

B. Keep bow hair always under slight tension. To use, tighten bow screw only about two (+ or −) rounds.

C. Leave strings always tuned up to pitch.

D. Wipe rosin dust from instrument top and bow stick after playing.

E. Never leave an instrument near a radiator or in a cold room.

F. Do not allow anyone except your teacher to handle your instrument.

G. Have your teacher check frequently for cracks, bridge adjustment, buzzes, etc.

H. Keep case latched (but not locked with the key) when instrument is not in use.
(Excellent literature on the care of the instrument has been published by leading stringed instrument dealers.)

THE CODE FOR THE NATIONAL ANTHEM OF THE UNITED STATES OF AMERICA

THE STAR-SPANGLED BANNER should be sung or played only on programs and in ceremonies and other situations where its message can be projected effectively.

Since the message of the Anthem is carried largely in the text, it is essential that emphasis be placed upon the *singing* of The Star-Spangled Banner.

The leader should address himself to those assembled and invite their participation. If an announcement is necessary, it might be stated as follows: "We shall now sing our National Anthem," or "So-and-So will lead you in singing our National Anthem."

On all occasions the group singing the National Anthem should stand facing the flag or the leader, in an attitude of respectful attention. Outdoors, men should remove their hats.

It is suggested that, when it is not physically inconvenient to do so, the members of a band or orchestra stand while playing the National Anthem.

If only a single stanza of the National Anthem is sung, the first should be used.

Our National Anthem is customarily sung at the opening of a meeting or program, but special circumstances may warrant the placing of it elsewhere.

In publishing the National Anthem for general singing, the melody, harmony, and syllable divisions of the Service Version of 1918 should be used. In publishing for vocal groups, the voice parts of the Service Version should be adhered to. (The Service Version in A-flat is reproduced on the pages following.) For purposes of quick identification, the words "Service Version" should be printed under the title.

It is not good taste to make or use sophisticated concert versions of the National Anthem, as such. (This does not refer to incorporating the Anthem, or portions of it, in extended works for band, orchestra, or chorus.)

For general mass singing by adults, and for band, orchestra, or other instrumental performances, the key of A-flat is preferable. For treble voices, the key of B-flat may be used.

If an instrumental introduction is desired, it is suggested that the last two measures be used.

When the National Anthem is sung unaccompanied, care should be taken to establish the correct pitch.

The National Anthem should be sung at a moderate tempo. (The metronome indications in the Service Version are quarter note = 104 for the verse and quarter note = 96 for the chorus.)

The slighting of note values in the playing or singing of the National Anthem seriously impairs the beauty and effectiveness of both music and lyric. Conductors should rehearse painstakingly both instrumental and vocal groups in the meticulous observance of correct note values.

This Code for the National Anthem is intended to apply to every mode of civilian performance and to the publication of the music for such performance.

The Service Version of the National Anthem was prepared in 1918 by a joint committee of twelve, comprising John Alden Carpenter, Frederick S. Converse, Wallace Goodrich, and Walter R. Spalding, representing the War Department Commission on Training Camp Activities; Hollis E. Dann, Peter W. Dykema (Chairman), and Osbourne McConathy, representing the Music Educators National Conference (then known as Music Supervisors'

313

The Star-Spangled Banner

SERVICE VERSION

Francis Scott Key

Attributed to
John Stafford Smith

With spirit (♩=104)

1. O___ say! can you see,___ by the dawn's ear - ly
2. On the shore, dim - ly seen___ thro' the mists of the
3. O___ thus be it ev - er when___ free - men shall

light, What so proud - ly we hail'd at the twi - light's last
deep, Where the foe's haugh - ty host in dread si - lence re -
stand Be - tween their loved homes and the war's des - o -

gleam - ing? Whose broad stripes and bright stars, thro' the per - il - ous
pos - es, What is that which the breeze, o'er the tow - er - ing
la - tion! Blest with vic - t'ry and peace, may the heav'n - res - cued

fight, O'er the ram - parts we watch'd, were so gal - lant - ly
steep, As it fit - ful - ly blows, half con - ceals, half dis -
land Praise the Pow'r that hath made and pre - served us a

National Conference); Clarence C. Birchard, Carl Engel, William Arms Fisher, Arthur E. Johnstone, and E. W. Newton, representing the music publishers. See 1919 Yearbook of the MENC, p. 145, and *Music Supervisors' Journal* (*Music Educators Journal*) of November 1918, pp. 2-3.

The Service Version as reproduced on the pages following is the same as that prepared by the original joint committee, with the exception of the transposition to the key of A-flat, in order to make it more singable by audiences, and a few minor changes in punctuation and wording, in order to make the text more authentic.

The "Code" was adopted by the 1942 National Anthem Committee at the Milwaukee meeting of the Music Educators National Conference with the assistance of its two representatives from the War Department, Major

Howard C. Bronson, Music Officer in the Special Service Branch, and Major Harold W. Kent, Education Liaison Officer in the Radio Branch of the Bureau of Public Relations. Messrs. Dykema and McConathy represented the original committee on the 1942 committee, which included representatives of principal music and education organizations of the United States, among them: American Bandmasters' Association, Association for Education by Radio, Music Educators National Conference, Music Industries War Council, Music Teachers National Association, National Association of Band Instrument Manufacturers, National Association of Schools of Music, National Congress of Parents and Teachers, National Education Association, National Federation of Music Clubs, National School Band, Orchestra, and Vocal Association, Standard Music Publishers' Association of the United States.

315

CODES FOR PUBLIC RELATIONS

With the Professional Musicians

A Code of Ethics jointly agreed to and authorized by executive actions of the Music Educators National Conference, American Federation of Musicians, and American Association of School Administrators:

[First adopted jointly in 1947 and renewed in 1948 by the American Federation of Musicians, the American Association of School Administrators, and the Music Educators National Conference, this Code continues to serve as a basis and guide for maintaining good relations between schools and professional musicians in local situations throughout the United States. The Code is substantially the same as the agreements subscribed to prior to 1947 in Pennsylvania, Ohio, New York, and other states by the state organizations of music educators and professional musicians. The statement has been found to afford a fair representation in spirit and principle of the interests of all who are seriously concerned with the welfare of the professional musicians and the advancement of music education. The Code, which has had wide distribution, including printing in the official magazines of the AASA, AF of M, MENC, and various books and in other publications, has appeared numerous times in state and national periodicals. Copies of this reprint may be obtained from the MENC.]

———

THE competition of school bands and orchestras in the past years has been a matter of grave concern and, at times, even hardship to the professional musicians.

Music educators and professional musicians alike are committed to the general acceptance of music as a desirable factor in the social and cultural growth of our country. The music educators contribute to this end by fostering the study of music among the children, and by developing an interest in better music among the masses. The professional musicians strive to improve musical taste by providing increasingly artistic performances of worth-while musical works.

This unanimity of purpose is further exemplified by the fact that a great many professional musicians are music educators, and a great many music educators are, or have been, actively engaged in the field of professional performance.

The members of high school symphonic orchestras and bands look to the professional organizations for example and inspiration; they become active patrons of music in later life. They are not content to listen to a twelve-piece ensemble when an orchestra of symphonic proportions is necessary to give adequate performance. These former music students, through their influence on sponsors, employers, and program makers in demanding adequate musical performances, have a beneficial effect upon the prestige and economic status of the professional musicians.

Since it is in the interest of the music educator to attract public attention to his attainments for the purpose of enhancing his prestige and subsequently his income, and since it is in the interest of the professional musician to create more opportunities for employment at increased remuneration, it is only natural that upon certain occasions some incidents might occur in which the interests of the members of one or the other group might be infringed upon, either from lack of forethought or lack of ethical standards among individuals.

In order to establish a clear understanding as to the limitations of the fields of professional music and music education in the United States, the following statement of policy, adopted by the Music Educators National Conference and the American Federation of Musicians, and approved by the American Association of School Administrators, is recommended to those serving in their respective fields:

I. MUSIC EDUCATION

The field of music education, including the teaching of music and such demonstrations of music education as do not directly conflict with the interests of the professional musician, is the province of the music educator. It is the primary purpose of all the parties signatory hereto that the professional musician shall have the fullest protection in his efforts to earn his living from the rendition of music; to that end it is recognized and accepted that all music performances by school students under the "Code of Ethics" herein set forth shall be in connection with nonprofit, noncommercial enterprises. Under the heading of "Music Education" should be included the following:

(1) *School Functions* initiated by the schools as a part of a school program, whether in a school building or other building.

(2) *Community Functions* organized in the interest of the schools strictly for educational purposes, such as those that might be originated by the Parent-Teacher Association.

(3) *School Exhibits* prepared as a part of the school district's courtesies for educational organizations or educational conventions being entertained in the district.

(4) *Educational Broadcasts* which have the purpose of demonstrating or illustrating pupils' achievements in music study, or which represent the culmination of a period of study and rehearsal. Included in this category are local, state, regional, and national school music festivals and competitions held under the auspices of schools, colleges, and/or educational organizations on a nonprofit basis and broadcast to acquaint the public with the results of music instruction in the schools.

(5) *Civic Occasions* of local, state, or national patriotic interest, of sufficient breadth to enlist the sympathies and cooperation of all persons, such as those held by the GAR, American Legion, and Veterans of Foreign Wars in connection with their Memorial Day services in the cemeteries. It is understood that affairs of this kind may be participated in only when such participation does not in the least usurp the rights and privileges of local professional musicians.

(6) *Benefit Performances* for local charities, such as the Welfare Federations, Red Cross, hospitals, etc., when and where local professional musicians would likewise donate their services.

(7) *Educational or Civic Services* that might beforehand be mutually agreed upon by the school authorities and official representatives of the local professional musicians.

(8) *Audition Recordings* for study purposes made in the classroom or in connection with contest or festival performances by students, such recordings to be limited to exclusive use by the students and their teachers, and not offered for general sale or other public distribution. This definition pertains only to the purpose and utilization of audition recordings and not to matters concerned with copyright regulations. Compliance with copyright requirements applying to recording of compositions not in the public domain is the responsibility of the school, college, or educational organization under whose auspices the recordings are made.

II. ENTERTAINMENT

The field of entertainment is the province of the professional musician. Under this heading are the following:

(1) *Civic parades, ceremonies, expositions, community concerts, and community-center activities* (see I, paragraph 2 for further definition); *regattas, nonscholastic contests, festivals, athletic games, activities or celebrations, and the like; national, state, and county fairs* (See I, paragraph 5 for further definition).

(2) *Functions for the furtherance, directly or indirectly, of any public or private enterprise; functions by chambers of commerce, boards of trade, and commercial clubs or associations.*

(3) *Any occasion that is partisan or sectarian in character or purpose.*

(4) *Functions of clubs, societies, civic or fraternal organizations.*

Statements that funds are not available for the employment of professional musicians, or that if the talents of amateur musical organizations cannot be had, other musicians cannot or will not be employed, or that the amateur musicians are to play without remuneration of any kind, are all immaterial.

* * *

This Code shall remain in force for one year from September 22, 1947. At the end of one year the parties may come together for the purpose of making such revisions in this Code as they deem necessary and as shall be mutually agreed upon.*

JAMES C. PETRILLO
For American Federation of Musicians

LUTHER A. RICHMAN
For Music Educators National Conference

HEROLD C. HUNT
For American Association of School Administrators

Dated at Chicago, September 22, 1947.

---

* The Code was reviewed and renewed, as of September 22, 1948, by the Executive Committees of the subscribing organizations. It has continued in effect since that time to the advantage of all concerned. In 1954 and 1955 the MENC, AF of M, and AASA Executive Committees again reviewed the Code and each group voted reaffirmative without change.

✠

With the Music Merchants

A Code of Ethics between the Ohio Music Education Association and the Music Merchants Association of Ohio:

Whereas, both organizations are primarily interested in the music education of the school children of Ohio, and in furthering the interest of these young people in the art of music; and
Whereas, in this common effort, harmony and understanding should prevail;
Now the following Code of Ethics is adopted and approved:

First. The retail music merchant shall sell musical instruments and merchandise, of good quality at fair prices, to the public-school pupils of Ohio; and he shall, at all times, assist and help the community public-school music teacher in promoting an interest in the study of vocal and instrumental music.

Second. The public-school music teacher shall confine his activities to the teaching of music, as required by the laws of the State under Section 7718 G. C., and the regulations of the Educational Department, to the public-school pupils of Ohio; and he shall not sell musical instruments or merchandise directly or indirectly, to the pupils, or accept commissions of any kind, in any manner whatsoever, from any manufacturer, jobber, or music merchant for recommending any kind, brand, or make of musical merchandise.

Third. It shall be the prerogative of every public-school music teacher in Ohio, to examine and test the suitability of all musical instruments and merchandise purchased by pupils for use in school study, and, if found deficient, to communicate with the retail merchant selling the same, looking to the immediate adjustment of the difficulty, but the public-school music teacher in Ohio shall not recommend to his pupils or their parents any single make or brand of instrument exclusively.

Fourth. It shall be the duty of every retail music merchant in Ohio, readily and quickly to assist all public-school music teachers in his community, to see that pupils have proper and suitable instruments, by exchange or otherwise; to stock such musical instruments and merchandise for sale to pupils as the teachers may request or

---

NOTE: This code, adopted in Ohio in 1941, and the code following adopted at about the same time, are printed here by way of suggestion to organizations representing the music educators, music merchants, and private music teachers in states where such bases for cooperation and mutual understanding have not been established.]

recommend to the dealer; to arrange for the renting or loaning of instruments to talented pupils upon the recommendation of the teacher; and generally to cooperate with the public-school music teachers along these lines. In the event any local retail music merchant fails, neglects, or refuses so to cooperate with his public-school music teachers, then, and in that event, the teachers shall have the right and privilege, without violating this Code, to seek and find other retail sources for the musical instruments and merchandise necessary and required by the pupils in the proper study of music.

Approved by the undersigned committees at Cleveland, Ohio, May 18, 1941:

OHIO MUSIC EDUCATION ASSOCIATION COMMITTEE.

J. Leon Ruddick, Cleveland, Chairman; Arnold E. Hoffman, Struthers; Howard F. Brown, Lorain; Ralph E. Rush, Cleveland Heights, President (ex officio); Gerald M. Frank, Elyria, Executive Secretary (ex officio).

MUSIC MERCHANTS ASSOCIATION OF OHIO COMMITTEE.

Al S. Arnstan, Cincinnati, Chairman; George F. Schulte, Cleveland; Eugene Smart, Mansfield; Leslie L. Steward, Columbus, President (ex officio); Rexford C. Hyre, Cleveland, Executive Manager (ex officio).

⚜

With the Private Music Teachers

To promote cooperation in and understanding of the interrelating fields of music teaching the Ohio Music Teachers Association and the Ohio Music Education Association adopt the following statement of policy:

I. MUSIC EDUCATION

The school music teacher is a public employee and is obligated to serve the interests of the whole community. It shall be his privilege and responsibility to advise parents on questions pertaining to the private instruction of pupils under his jurisdiction. At all times the best interest of the pupil is of first importance. It shall be the obligation of the public-school music teacher to give to parents, upon request, the names of private teachers who are competent. In so doing, the school music teacher shall avoid recommending a single private teacher above all others, but shall suggest two or more, the final choice to be made by the parents. In communities where the choice is limited, it shall be incumbent upon the school music teacher to serve the interests of the student within the limitations of the resources available in the community.

II. MUSIC STUDIO INSTRUCTION

Music studio instruction is defined as lessons given for a consideration by individual music teachers or groups of teachers who are not employed by, or under the jurisdiction of, a public school or institution supported by public taxation.

As a citizen, the studio teacher shall cooperate in the support of public education, including music instruction at elementary music levels in the schools for the general good of the community.

III. AGREEMENT

It is mutually agreed, between the aforesaid organizations that it is unethical for any music teacher, whether teaching in school or in a private studio:

(a) To discuss with parents or pupils the work of another teacher in such manner as will injure the professional reputation of any teacher;

(b) To claim sole credit for the achievement of pupils under separate or cooperative instruction, when such claim shall reflect or imply discredit upon a preceding or cooperating teacher.

It is the common purpose of music teachers to cooperate:

(a) In raising standards of music instruction;

(b) In promoting interest in active participation in music performance;

(c) In developing wider appreciation of music;

(d) In establishing opportunities for elementary music instruction under the auspices of the school for exploratory purposes;

(e) In encouraging study with private teachers at the end of the period of exploratory instruction;

(f) In extending opportunities for music study to the underprivileged child through scholarships or extension of school instruction in individual instances;

(g) In encouraging regularity of attendance at both school and private lessons, rehearsals, recitals, and performances;

(h) In operating an organized plan for giving credit toward graduation study with recognized studio teachers;

(i) In alleviating the influence and practice of unethical methods of music instruction.

It is further agreed that each organization will maintain a permanent Code of Ethics Committee. These committees shall meet together during the month of May of each year.

(Signed) COMMITTEE FOR THE OMTA.

Frank Hruby, Chairman; George Hickman; John Samuel; Howard Swingle; Handel Wadsworth.

(Signed) COMMITTEE FOR THE OMEA.

J. Leon Ruddick, Chairman; Howard Brown; Gerald Frank; Arnold Hoffman; Ralph Rush.

SUGGESTIONS FOR A CUMULATIVE SONG LIST

For Classroom, Assembly, and Community Use

This classified list of songs, reprinted from the *Music Educators Journal*, September-October 1942, was compiled[1] with the cooperation of MENC members in various parts of the United States. It has been reissued numerous times by music educators and community leaders—in some instances just as given here, and often with variations of the categories, or with titles not in the original listing, or with other changes in keeping with the purpose to be served by the distribution of the list. The reprinting in the Second Source Book is for the same purpose that the list was originally prepared and made available, *i.e.*, to supply suggestions for the individual music educator or song leader to use as a basis for a "cumulative" list of titles compiled to meet his own specific needs.

I. *Songs that are physically stimulating and which arouse, therefore, a strong emotional response.*
   Anchors Aweigh
   Army Air Corps, The
   Battle Hymn of the Republic
   Caissons Go Rolling Along, The
   Marines' Hymn, The
   Over There
   Stout Hearted Men
   There's Something About a Soldier
   When Johnny Comes Marching Home

II. *Songs with the sense of fun and vigorous, salty humor characteristic of a young and vigorous people.*
   Billy Boy
   Camptown Races
   Cindy
   Glendy Burke, The
   Jingle Bells
   Oh! Susanna
   Old Dan Tucker
   She'll Be Comin' 'round the Mountain
   Turkey in the Straw
   Yankee Doodle
   *Yankee Doodle Dandy

III. *Simple, heartwarming songs of love and longing—emotions which are shared by young and old, high and low, regardless of race, color, or creed.*
   Carry Me Back to Old Virginny
   Deep River
   Home on the Range
   Home Road, The (Carpenter)
   Home, Sweet Home
   Keep the Home Fires Burning
   Long, Long Trail, The
   My Old Kentucky Home
   Old Folks at Home

IV. *Songs of loyalty to our country, tributes testifying to our confidence and devotion.*
   America
   America (Bloch)
   America, the Beautiful
   American Hymn (Speed Our Republic)
   *America, My Own (Cain)
   Columbia, the Gem of the Ocean
   God Bless America
   Hail Columbia

V. *Songs asserting courage upheld by the strength of united purpose.*
   God of Our Fathers
   *Hail, Land of Freedom (Turner)
   *Land of Our Birth (Lowell Mason—Kipling)
   Onward Christian Soldiers
   Song of Freedom
   Star-Spangled Banner, The
   *This Is My Country

VI. *Songs attesting man's persistent faith in the ideals of human worth and the right to freedom.*
   Chester (Early American, by Billings)
   Faith of Our Fathers
   Go Down Moses (Negro spiritual)
   Netherlands Hymn
   On, Thou Soul (Slavic)
   Song of Hope (Hebrew)

VII. *Songs expressing the serenity and peace that come from confident faith in things of the spirit.*
   *Brother James' Air (The Lord Is My Shepherd)
   Faith of Our Fathers
   *Lord's Prayer, The (Malotte)
   Mighty Fortress, A
   Now Thank We All Our God
   Now the Day Is Over
   O God, Beneath Thy Guiding Hand
   O God, Our Help in Ages Past

VIII. *Songs that convey the stability and sense of belonging that derive from the sheltering, protective quality of family affections.*
   All Through the Night
   At the Gates of Heaven
   Golden Slumbers
   Lullaby (Brahms)
   Sleep and Rest (Mozart)
   Sweet and Low

IX. *Songs that promote friendliness among a group of people through their sharing the delight of singing beautiful melodies together.*
   A Cuba (Cuban)
   Beautiful Dreamer (U. S.)
   Carmela (Mexican)
   Drink to Me Only (English)
   La Golondrina (Mexican)
   I Dream of Jeanie (U. S.)
   Londonderry Air (Irish)
   La paloma azul or Cielito linda (Mexican)
   Rose of Tralee, The (Irish)
   Santa Lucia (Italian)
   Scarlet Sarafan (Russian)

X. *Popular songs, i.e., songs of the people, because of common acceptance.*
   Bicycle Built for Two
   East Side, West Side
   Irish Eyes Are Smiling
   I Want a Girl
   Let Me Call You Sweetheart
   (and *appropriate* current favorites)

* Songs marked with an asterisk (*), unlike the others listed, will not be found in the usual community song collections. These are in octavo form and are suggested as typical of the kind of material to use where special choral and instrumental groups collaborate with general or community group singing.

[1] By Lilla Belle Pitts, President of the MENC, 1942-1944.

SELECTED LIST OF BOOKS ON ELEMENTARY AND SECONDARY EDUCATION[1]

ADULT EDUCATION

Sheats, Paul H.; Jayne, Clarence D.; and Spence, Ralph B. *Adult Education.* New York: Dryden Press, Inc., 1953. 530 pp. Presents a comprehensive survey of adult education—past, present, and future.

AUDIO-VISUAL EDUCATION

Dale, Edgar. *Audio-Visual Methods in Teaching.* Revised edition. New York: Dryden Press, Inc., 1954. 534 pp. Gives insights into the methods and materials which can be employed by the classroom teacher to create vicarious experiences for children.

Wittich, Walter A., and Schuller, Charles F. *Audio-Visual Materials—Their Nature and Use.* New York: Harper and Brothers, 1953. 564 pp. Describes the nature of audio-visual materials and contains many suggestions for using them.

CITIZENSHIP

American Association of School Administrators. *Educating for American Citizenship.* Thirty-Second Yearbook. Washington, D. C.: The Association, a department of the National Education Association, 1954. 615 pp. $5. Discusses education for citizenship as a part of the total life of the school.

National Council for the Social Studies. *Education for Democratic Citizenship.* Twenty-Second Yearbook. Washington D. C.: The Council, a department of the National Education Association, 1951. 161 pp. Cloth, $3.50; paper, $3. Presents a broad definition of citizenship for all school personnel and citizens concerned with the fundamentals of democratic living.

Pflieger, Elmer F., and Weston, Grace L. *Emotional Adjustment: A Key to Good Citizenship.* A report of the Citizenship Education Study. Detroit: Wayne University Press, 1953. 152 pp. Discusses the practices employed in elementary, junior and senior high schools in Detroit in an attempt to improve citizenship of boys and girls.

COMMUNITY

Association for Supervision and Curriculum Development. *Forces Affecting American Education.* 1953 Yearbook. Washington, D. C.: The Association, a department of the National Education Association, 1953. 208 pp. $3.50. Analyzes the cultural forces affecting American education. Defines good modern schools in terms of what they actually do towards meeting the needs of youth, and emphasizes the importance of good school-community relations.

National Education Association, Department of Rural Education. *The Community School and the Intermediate Unit.* Yearbook 1954. Washington, D. C.: The Association, 1954. 259 pp. Cloth, $3; paper $2.50. Describes ways of getting adequate service and instructional opportunities for schools in small communities.

National Society for the Study of Education. *The Community School.* Fifty-Second Yearbook, Part II. Chicago: University of Chicago Press, 1953. 292 pp. Presents an overview of the development and present status of education with special emphasis on demonstration and research.

Olsen, Edward G., editor. *The Modern Community School.* New York: Appleton-Century-Crofts, 1953. 246 pp. Discusses the development of community education programs.

CURRENT CONTENTIONS OF EDUCATION AND SCHOOLS

Scott, C. Winfield, and Hill, Clyde M. *Public Education Under Criticism.* New York: Prentice-Hall, Inc., 1954. 414 pp. An anthology of articles concerning the public school which appeared in periodicals during 1951.

ELEMENTARY SCHOOL—METHODS AND CURRICULUM

Association for Supervision and Curriculum Development. *The Three R's in the Elementary School.* Washington, D. C.: The Association, a department of the National Education Association, 1952. 152 pp. $1.50. Discusses and clarifies issues related to the teaching of the "Three R's."

Beck, Robert H.; Cook, Walter W.; and Kearney, Nolan C. *Curriculum in the Modern Elementary School.* New York: Prentice-Hall, Inc., 1953. 584 pp. Considers the basic principles of psychology, the development of the learning process, types of curriculums, and effective treatment of subject areas.

Cantor, Nathaniel. *The Teaching-Learning Process.* New York: Dryden Press, Inc., 1953. 350 pp. Explores and reports on class participation.

Gans, Roma; Stendler, Celia B.; and Almy, Millie. *Teaching Young Children.* New York: World Book Co., 1952. 454 pp. Written in nontechnical language; a book for anyone who has an interest in young children, including the preschool age group. Contains many helpful suggestions.

Kearney, Nolan C. *Elementary School Objectives.* New York: Russell Sage Foundation, 1953. 189 pp. The report, prepared for the Mid-Century Committee on Elementary Education, analyzes the objectives of the elementary school.

---

[1] Compiled by the NEA Research Division with the advice of staff members of various NEA Departments for the Music Educators National Conference, December, 1954.

Lee, J. Murray, and Lee, Doris M. *The Child and His Curriculum.* Second edition. New York: Appleton-Century-Crofts, 1950. 710 pp. Treats the whole teaching-learning process.

Ragan, William B. *Modern Elementary Curriculum.* New York: Dryden Press, Inc., 1953. 570 pp. Considering all the experiences of children for which the school accepts responsibility, the author gives consistent attention to the problems involved.

EXCEPTIONAL CHILDREN

National Association of Secondary-School Principals. *Handicapped and Gifted Pupils in Secondary Schools.* Bulletin No. 207. Washington, D. C.: The Association, a department of the National Education Association, January 1955. 240 pp. $1.50. Consists of selected articles on how high schools can more adequately serve handicapped and gifted teenagers.

National Society for the Study of Education. *The Education of Exceptional Children.* Forty-Ninth Yearbook, Part II. Chicago: University of Chicago Press, 1950. 356 pp. Describes the appropriate procedures for the various areas of special education.

Witty, Paul, editor. *The Gifted Child.* New York: D. C. Heath and Co., 1951. 338 pp. Presents practical suggestions for handling the problems of the gifted child.

GROWTH AND DEVELOPMENT

Garrison, Karl. *Psychology of Adolescence.* Fourth edition. New York: Prentice-Hall, Inc., 1951. 510 pp. Gives a view of adolescents and their transition from childhood to adulthood.

Martin, William E., and Stendler, Celia B. *Readings in Child Development.* New York: Harcourt, Brace and Co., 1954. 513 pp. Selections in this book concern child development, society, and culture.

Millard, Cecil V. *School and Child.* East Lansing, Mich.: Michigan State College Press, 1954. 221 pp. A study of the growth and development of elementary school children.

HEALTH SERVICES

Cassidy, Rosalind. *Curriculum Development in Physical Education.* New York: Harper and Brothers, 1954. 399 pp. A guide for the study and improvement of the physical education program of any school.

National Education Association and American Medical Association, Joint Committee on Health Problems in Education. *Health Education.* Fourth edition. Washington, D. C.: National Education Association, 1948. 413 pp. $3. A comprehensive guide for school health services with specific recommendations and practical illustrations.

National Education Association and American Medical Association. *School Health Services.* Washington, D. C.: National Education Association, 1953. 486 pp. $5. A comprehensive guide for health procedures in small or large school systems.

HIGH SCHOOL—METHODS AND CURRICULUM

Alberty, Harold. *Reorganizing the High-School Curriculum.* Revised edition. New York: The Macmillan Company, 1953. 560 pp. Presents a broad view of the high school, past and present, and clarifies educational purposes and their implication for the curriculum.

National Association of Secondary-School Principals. *Planning for American Youth.* Washington, D. C.: The Association, a department of the National Education Association, 1951. 63 pp. 50¢. An aid to teachers, parents, and administrators in planning the types of school experiences which will educate all youth.

INTERNATIONAL UNDERSTANDING

Hall, Robert King; Hans, N.; and Lauwerys, J. A., editors. *Status and Position of Teachers.* Yearbook of Education. New York: World Book Co., 1953. 587 pp. Gives an insight into the status and position of teachers throughout the world.

National Council for the Social Studies. *Approaches to an Understanding of World Affairs.* Twenty-Fifth Yearbook. Washington, D. C.: The Council, a department of the National Education Association, 1954. 478 pp. Cloth, $4; paper, $3.50. Selections concerning the cultural patterns of other peoples and how students may learn to understand themselves and others better.

JUNIOR HIGH SCHOOL—METHODS AND CURRICULUM

Noar, Gertrude. *Junior High School—Today and Tomorrow.* New York: Prentice-Hall, Inc., 1953. 373 pp. Discusses the philosophy, objectives, functions, and practices of the modern junior high school and the responsibilities involved.

Wisconsin Cooperative Educational Planning Program. *Guides to Curriculum Building.* Illinois Secondary School Curriculum Program, Bulletin No. 8. Springfield: Illinois Department of Public Instruction, 1950. 181 pp. A handbook containing suggestions for building a curriculum to meet the needs of the junior high school age group.

LEARNING THEORY

Cronbach, Lee J. *Educational Psychology.* New York: Harcourt, Brace and Co., 1954. 628 pp. Sets forth in operational terms at the classroom level, the implications of some of our basic learning theory in elementary and high schools.

MEASUREMENT AND GUIDANCE

National Education Association, Department of Elementary School Principals. *Guidance for Today's Children.* Thirty-Third Yearbook. Washington, D. C.: The Department, 1954. 278 pp. $3.50. Discusses the problems and responsibilities in the administration of a good guidance program.

Ross, Clay C., and Stanley, Julian. *Measurement in Today's Schools.* Third edition. New York: Prentice-Hall, Inc., 1954. 485 pp. Presents in an interesting readable style the history, use, and value of testing devices.

Traxler, Arthur E., and others. *Introduction to Testing and the Use of Test Results in Public Schools.* New York: Harper and Brothers, 1953. 113 pp. A practical, nontechnical book for teachers and counselors in public schools.

MENTAL HEALTH

Association for Supervision and Curriculum Development. *Fostering Mental Health in the Classroom.* 1950 Yearbook. Washington, D. C.: The Association, a department of the National Education Association, 1950. 320 pp. $3. Reviews techniques for diagnosing the well-being of individuals. Refers particularly to the ways of improving mental health among school children through teaching and guidance.

PUBLIC RELATIONS

American Association of School Administrators. *Public Relations for America's Schools.* Twenty-Eighth Yearbook. Washington, D. C.: The Association, a department of the National Education Association, 1950. 497 pp. $4. Discusses the purposes, principles, relationships, and values in school public relations programs.

National School Public Relations Association. *It Starts in the Classroom.* Washington, D. C.: The Association, a department of the National Education Association, June, 1951. 64 pp. $1. A discussion of good public relations methods for the classroom teacher.

SCHOOL ADMINISTRATION

Douglass, Harl R. *Modern Administration of Secondary Schools.* New York: Ginn and Company, 1954. 601 pp. A detailed practical guide for high school administrators.

Edmonson, J. B.; Roemer, Joseph; and Bacon, Francis L. *The Administration of the Modern Secondary School.* Fourth edition. New York: The Macmillan Company, 1953. 614 pp. A history of the growth and development of the secondary school, present-day functions, objectives, and problems, with guiding principles for the administrator of the modern public secondary school.

Elsbree, Willard, and Reutter, E. Edmund, Jr. *Staff Personnel in the Public Schools.* New York: Prentice-Hall, Inc., 1954. 438 pp. Analyses of the problems relating to public school professional staff members.

Grieder, Calvin, and Rosenstengel, William E. *Public School Administration.* New York: The Ronald Press, 1954. 622 pp. A comprehensive text and reference book for all those interested in or actively engaged in school administration.

Lawson, Douglas E. *School Administration.* New York: Odyssey Press, 1953. 405 pp. A practical source book of major policies, principles, and procedures involved in functional administrative practice.

Otto, Henry J. *Elementary-School Organization and Administration.* Third edition. New York: Appleton-Century-Crofts, 1954. 719 pp. Analyses of the basic problems of organization and administration which face the administrator of elementary education.

Reavis, William C., and others. *Administering the Elementary School.* New York: Prentice-Hall, Inc., 1953. 631 pp. Discusses a practical philosophy of cooperation among school principals, teachers, and parents in the task of creating realistic living and learning situations for elementary school children.

Reader, Ward G. *School Boards and Superintendents.* Revised edition. New York: The Macmillan Company, 1954. 254 pp. A carefully organized and readable manual on the powers and duties of school boards and the characteristics of an efficient school public relations program.

SUPERVISION

Reeder, Edwin H. *Supervision in the Elementary School.* Boston: Houghton Mifflin Company, 1953. 386 pp. Discusses the theory of supervision to meet changing methods in education.

Spears, Harold. *Improving the Supervision of Instruction.* New York: Prentice-Hall, Inc., 1953. 478 pp. Gives insights into current philosophy and practices of supervision in the public elementary and secondary schools.

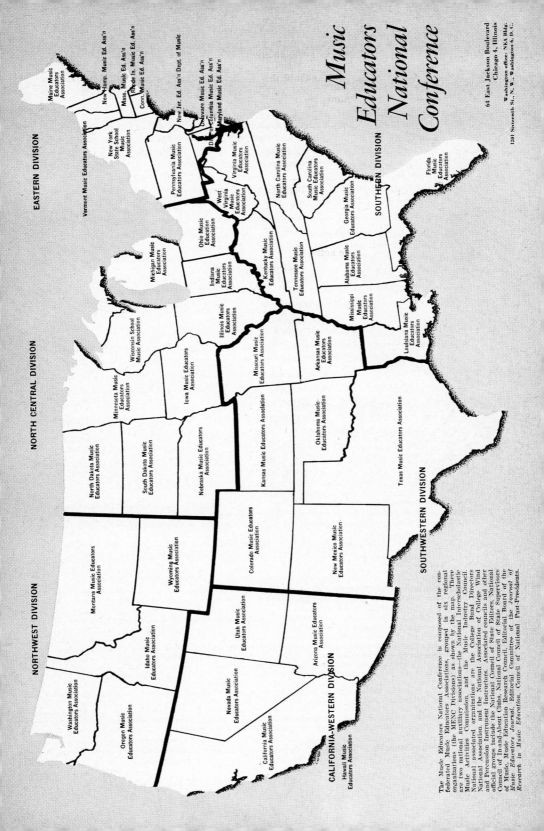

Music
Educators
National
Conference

64 East Jackson Boulevard
Chicago 4, Illinois

Washington office: NEA Bldg.
1201 Sixteenth St., N. W., Washington 6, D. C.

EASTERN DIVISION

Maine Music Educators Association
New Hamp. Music Ed. Ass'n
Mass. Music Ed. Ass'n
Rhode Is. Music Ed. Ass'n
Conn. Music Ed. Ass'n
New Jer. Ed. Ass'n's Dept. of Music
Delaware Music Ed. Ass'n
Dist. of Columbia Music Ed. Ass'n
Maryland Music Ed. Ass'n
Vermont Music Educators Association
New York State School Music Association
Pennsylvania Music Educators Association
West Virginia Music Educators Association
Virginia Music Educators Association

SOUTHERN DIVISION

North Carolina Music Educators Association
South Carolina Music Educators Association
Georgia Music Educators Association
Florida Music Educators Association
Kentucky Music Educators Association
Tennessee Music Educators Association
Alabama Music Educators Association
Mississippi Music Educators Association
Louisiana Music Educators Association

NORTH CENTRAL DIVISION

Ohio Music Education Association
Michigan Music Educators Association
Indiana Music Educators Association
Illinois Music Educators Association
Wisconsin School Music Association
Minnesota Music Educators Association
Iowa Music Educators Association
Missouri Music Educators Association
Arkansas Music Educators Association
North Dakota Music Educators Association
South Dakota Music Educators Association
Nebraska Music Educators Association
Kansas Music Educators Association

NORTHWEST DIVISION

Washington Music Educators Association
Montana Music Educators Association
Oregon Music Educators Association
Idaho Music Educators Association
Wyoming Music Educators Association

SOUTHWESTERN DIVISION

Colorado Music Educators Association
New Mexico Music Educators Association
Oklahoma Music Educators Association
Texas Music Educators Association

CALIFORNIA-WESTERN DIVISION

Utah Music Educators Association
Nevada Music Educators Association
Arizona Music Educators Association
California Music Educators Association
Hawaii Music Educators Association

The Music Educators National Conference is composed of the con-
federated Music Educators Associations, grouped in six regional
organizations (the MENC Divisions) as shown by the map. There
are two national auxiliary organizations—the National Interscholastic
Music Activities Commission, and the Music Industry Council.
National associated organizations are the College Band Directors
National Association, and the National Association of College Wind
and Percussion Instrument Instructors. Associated councils and other
official groups include the National Council of State Editors, National
Council of In-and-About Clubs, National Council of State Supervisors
of Music, Music Education Research Council, Editorial Board of the
Music Educators Journal, Editorial Committee of the Journal of
Research in Music Education, Council of National Past-Presidents.

FACTS ABOUT THE MUSIC EDUCATORS
NATIONAL CONFERENCE

The Organization

What Is the MENC? The Music Educators National Conference is the Department of Music of the National Education Association. It is the recognized spokesman for music education in the United States. Its activities and publications have been chiefly responsible for the establishment of music education as a profession, and for the promotion and guidance of music instruction in the schools as an integral part of general education. Since its inception in 1907, the growth of the MENC in strength and service has been paralleled by the growth in scope and effectiveness of the music education program.

How Is It Organized? On a voluntary member-service cooperative basis. The organization structure integrates geographical units—substate, state, division, and national—at all education levels, pre-school through college and university, encompassing all areas of music education—vocal and instrumental instruction, general music classes, listening programs, adult education, community services, and related activities.[1]

Purpose. The Constitution of the MENC states that "its object shall be the advancement of music education." For furtherance of this end, the planned program of the MENC is to:

—Insure a useful and broad program of music education in the schools.

—Serve music educators through a permanent organization with professional, publication, and business headquarters offices.

—Correlate and provide a clearinghouse for all school music activities and interests.

—Give prestige and influence to the music education profession as an important segment of the general education profession.

—Serve as the official public relations medium for the music education profession.

—Correlate school music activities of the United States and in other parts of the world.

---

[1] The Music Educators National Conference is composed of the federated state music educators associations, and the auxiliary and associated organizations as set up under the provisions of the constitution. The state associations are grouped in six divisions. The states and territories included in the respective divisions are as follows:

California-Western Division: Arizona, California, Hawaii, Nevada, Utah.

Eastern Division: Connecticut, Delaware, District of Columbia, Maine, Maryland, Massachusetts, New Hampshire, New Jersey, New York, Pennsylvania, Rhode Island, Vermont.

North Central Division: Illinois, Indiana, Iowa, Michigan, Minnesota, Nebraska, North Dakota, Ohio, South Dakota, Wisconsin.

Northwest Division: Alaska, Idaho, Montana, Oregon, Washington, Wyoming.

Southern Division: Alabama, Florida, Georgia, Kentucky, Louisiana, Mississippi, North Carolina, South Carolina, Tennessee, Virginia, West Virginia.

Southwestern Division: Arkansas, Colorado, Kansas, Missouri, New Mexico, Oklahoma, Texas.

Provision is made in the Bylaws (Article I, Section 4) for redistricting or consolidating divisions if and when any such course is deemed to be in the best interests of the National Conference, the division, and the state units involved.

The State Affiliation Plan covered in the Constitution and Bylaws had its inception in 1933 and 1934. By 1935 there were several state affiliates, including Ohio, New Jersey, Louisiana, and Delaware. The first to function under the state unit plan of relationship to the National Conference was Ohio, which was followed closely by Louisiana. These affiliations were on a "voluntary" basis, so far as the state associations were concerned, as there was at that time no coverage of the state unit affiliation in the MENC constitution. Other states followed, until in 1940—when the state unit plan was recognized and provided for in a revision of the MENC constitution—there were functioning state units in twelve states, as follows: Colorado, Georgia, Idaho, Iowa, Louisiana, Missouri, Montana, New York, Ohio, Pennsylvania, West Virginia, Wyoming.

As of February, 1955, there are thirty-seven additional units, as follows (total of forty-nine, including Hawaii and District of Columbia): Alabama, Arizona, California, Connecticut, Delaware, District of Columbia, Florida, Hawaii, Illinois, Indiana, Kansas, Kentucky, Maine, Maryland, Massachusetts, Michigan, Minnesota, Mississippi, Nebraska, Nevada, New Hampshire, New Jersey, New Mexico, North Carolina, North Dakota, Oklahoma, Oregon, Rhode Island, South Carolina, South Dakota, Tennessee, Texas, Utah, Vermont, Virginia, Washington, Wisconsin.

The Dominion of Canada: Steps have been taken by music educators in various parts of Canada with a view to establishing closer relationship with the MENC through participation in the affiliation plan. Pending such develop-

The Professional Program of the MENC

Professional Meetings

For Music Educators. Professional meetings are regularly planned at all organization levels, state, division, and national.

For Non-Music Specialists. Provisions are made at official MENC meetings, state, division, and national, for special sessions and workshops for the general classroom teachers in the elementary schools who have responsibilities in the instructional program of music.

For School Administrators. The MENC cooperates in program plans of the American Association of School Administrators, the National Association of Secondary-School Principals, the Association for Supervision and Curriculum Development, the Departments of Elementary School Principals, Rural Education, and Exceptional Children of the NEA, by providing performing groups, music education workshops, and other program contributions.

Publications

The *Music Educators Journal* is the principal publication of the MENC. Subscription (six issues a year) is covered by membership dues.

The *Journal of Research in Music Education* is one of the important MENC publications begun in the last few years.

The *Music Education Source Book* and *Music in American Education* (Source Book No. II) comprise a compendium of official reports on professional aspects of the music education field. [Only four principal MENC publications are mentioned here. A detailed list may be secured from the headquarters office.]

Public Relations

Maintenance of cooperative relationships with professional, educational, and lay groups is an important part of MENC activities, and a determining factor in the constantly developing position of authority and influence of the MENC. Groups with which the MENC maintains cooperative programs include the National Education Association and its departments, Music Teachers National Association, National Association of Schools of Music, American Symphony Orchestra League, Association of Junior Leagues of America, National Congress of Parents and Teachers, American Council on Education, Joint Committee on Educational Television, United States Office of Education, Junior Red Cross, Society for the Preservation and Encouragement of Barbershop Quartet Singing, American Music Conference, Music Publishers' Association of the United States, American Federation of Musicians, American Association of Colleges for Teacher Education, National Commission on Accrediting, National Council for the Accreditation of Teacher Education.

International Aspects

As the spokesman for music education in the United States, MENC through its professional program literally reaches around the world. Three important factors in the area of international cooperation are: (1) Official contact with the Music Committee of the United States National Commission of UNESCO. (2) Close working relationship with the headquarters staff of UNESCO and with the staff of the International Music Council, both of whose headquarters are at Avenue Kleber 19, Paris. (3) Official liaison with the Inter-

---

ments, all active members, student members, and cooperating organizations in Canada continue to have the same relationship to the Conference as do those in an unaffiliated state or territory of the United States. The respective jurisdictions of the Eastern, North Central, and Northwest Divisions include portions of Canada, as follows:

Eastern: The western boundary line of the division extends into the Dominion of Canada to include Eastern Ontario, Quebec, New Brunswick, Nova Scotia, and Prince Edward Island.

North Central: The eastern boundary line of the division extends into the Dominion of Canada to include that part of the Province of Ontario lying west of a line running in a northerly direction with the Niagara River, all of Manitoba, and a portion of Eastern Saskatchewan.

Northwest: The eastern boundary line extends into the Dominion of Canada to include the major portion of Saskatchewan, Alberta, and British Columbia.

national Society of Music Education which was established in Brussels in 1953. The headquarters of ISME are in the MENC office at 1201 Sixteenth St., N. W., Washington 6, D. C.

Committee Activities

Membership participation in committee activities has been a basic factor in the co-operative services and achievements of the organization, and in the professional growth of the many music educators who have shared the work.

"Music in American Life" is the theme of the current MENC committee organization plan, which is described in detail in the next following article.

The Business Side

How Is the MENC Financed? The MENC is financed, for the most part, from operating revenues. (This of course is also true of the financing of the state units.) The principal sources of MENC revenue at the national level are:

—Membership dues.

—Subscriptions to the *Music Educators Journal*.

—Advertising in the *Music Educators Journal*.

—Exhibit fees at national and division conventions.

—Sale of publications.

—Donations.

Approximately 20% of the total revenue above described is derived from membership dues, 22% from subscriptions to the *Music Educators Journal*, 37% from advertising in the *Music Educators Journal*, 16% from exhibit fees at national and division meetings. The balance of MENC revenue is derived from other sources which vary in origin and amount from year to year.

What Is the Revenue Used For? The following items comprise the principal categories of MENC expenditures:

—Printing and mailing the *Music Educators Journal*.

—Printing and mailing the *Journal of Research in Music Education*.

—Business management, production supervision of *Music Educators Journal*, and other publications.

—Editorial and technical work for MENC periodical publications, and all other publications.

—Printing of books, bulletins, information leaflets, and other publications; printing, or reproducing in various processes, committee reports, membership forms, other necessary materials.

—Professional assistance and business management for biennial national meetings, division leadership and planning conferences, biennial division conventions, and assistance in connection with many state unit meetings.

—Membership record service—state, division, national.

—Services to MENC Student Member Chapters.

—Services to MENC auxiliary organizations: the National Interscholastic Music Activities Commission and the Music Industry Council.

—Services to MENC associated organizations.

—Accounting services of all MENC funds.

Membership

Benefits. The success of any voluntary professional organization stems from benefits and responsibilities shared by members. Among those most often cited as values received and/or given are: Personal and professional growth through participation in activities, local, state, regional, and national; practical aids afforded by official publications; opportunities afforded to keep abreast of current trends and new thought; the privilege of sharing the work and the costs of the professional program of the organization; the opportunity to help build a united profession, to help choose representative leadership at all levels, to join forces with colleagues in helping create and maintain at maximum strength the voice, influence, and service of our branch of the teaching profession.

Enrollment. The unified membership plan of the Music Educators National Conference provides for payment which includes dues at state, division, and national levels. The active membership fee covers all privileges of membership at these levels, the official publication of the state unit, and subscription to the *Music Educators Journal.* (Names of the state units are listed elsewhere in the appendix.)

Student Membership

This membership classification is for students in colleges and universities in training for the profession of music education. For information write to MENC, 64 East Jackson Blvd., Chicago.

This material is taken from an information folder, where it appears under the heading, "What Music Educators Should Know About Their Professional Organization." Copies of the folder may be secured without charge from the MENC headquarters office.

✠

MUSIC IN AMERICAN LIFE

THE PROFESSIONAL PROGRAM of the Music Educators National Conference has been carried on since the beginning of the organization in 1907 chiefly through committee work. In 1942 a nation-wide committee plan was inaugurated on an integrated and comprehensive basis at state, division, and national levels. From 1942 through the 1952-54 biennium (twelve years) there have been three major periods of such committee activity, respectively, "Widening Horizons for Music Education," "Music Education Advancement," and "Music in American Education." Important among the outcomes of these committee enterprises have been various publications, chief among them the *Music Education Source Book* and this volume *Music in American Education* (Source Book No. II). The theme of the current MENC committee organization plan, "Music in American Life," epitomizes the philosophy inherent in the aspects of the MENC program emphasized by the themes of the three preceding periods of organized committee study and activity.

It is felt that the Music in American Life plan[1] represents another step forward in its conception and in the opportunity it affords for integrated participation of all music educators, with the fullest possible utilization of the organization machinery of the Music Educators National Conference. Basic in the operation of the plan is the establishment of ten commissions. Incorporated within the operating framework of certain of these com-

---

[1] This plan was formulated by Robert A. Choate, President of MENC, 1954-56, in cooperation with the Executive Committee. The project was launched at once, and the selection of chairmen and members of the Commissions and Committees was largely completed by midyear, 1955.

missions are committees assigned to phases, aspects, or activities of the respective areas. Following are the areas covered by the commissions:

Basic Concepts in Music Education.
Standards of Music Literature and Performance.
Music in General School Administration.
Music in Preschool, Kindergarten, Elementary School.
Music in Junior High School.
Music in Senior High School.
Music in Higher Education.
Music in the Community.
Music in Media of Mass Communication.
Accreditation and Certification.

In addition to the ten Commissions, and the correlated committees set up for Commissions II through IX inclusive,[1] there are provided for at present four Standing Committees assigned to specific areas, as follows: Music for Exceptional Children, Music in International Relations, Organ Instruction in the Schools, Piano Instruction in the Schools.

Also basic in the plan are joint committees with other organizations to be established as needs may indicate. Such committees are to be set up in cooperation with groups in related and associated fields of music and education which contribute to the activities and services of the MENC through publications, studies, public relations programs, and other media. Such joint committees will be established with other organizations for the purposes described and for the development of mutually helpful relations in the areas of the Music in American Life program in which there is common interest.

The Music in American Life plan is set up to provide for participation of music educators on an organization-wide basis. The MENC state, division, and national pattern provides for Commission and Committee organization at the national level, with participation at the state level on a strictly voluntary basis, depending on the needs and wishes of the state leadership. Division coordinators are appointed for each Commission area and for each Standing Committee to assist in joint planning by state Commission and Committee chairmen in connection with Division biennial programs.

Cooperating in the development and implementation of the Music in American Life program are the officers and members of the MENC, its six Divisions, and the federated State Music Educators Associations; the national auxiliary organizations—the National Interscholastic Music Activities Commission and the Music Industry Council; the associated organizations—the College Band Directors National Association and the National Association of College Wind and Percussion Instrument Instructors. Various other groups and councils within the MENC are also participating, and members of the Music Education Research Council serve *ex officio* on the various commissions.

✠

The nation-wide and organization-wide educational activities program described here, states MENC President Robert A. Choate, continues and intensifies the state-division-national membership participation plan which has distinguished the work of the MENC for more than a decade. The "Music in American Life" Commissions and Committees constitute a framework of organization within which studies, appraisals, evaluations, public relations, and various other activities of the MENC can be carried on . . . .

President Choate emphasizes the fact that the Music in American Life plan is not to be regarded as a new departure but rather as the basis for a period of renewed activity and productivity in the continuing pursuit of the MENC purpose—the advancement of music education.

From the *Music Educators Journal*, November-December, 1954

---

[1] See charts.

MUSIC IN AMERICAN LIFE–Organization Plan

NATIONAL	DIVISION	STATE
Commissions on Music Education *Purpose* (1) To provide appraisal, evaluation and study in broad areas which are of continuing, substantial and enduring concern to the music education profession. (2) To recommend publications and to be responsible for content when publications are indicated. (3) To be responsible for meetings at MENC biennial programs. (4) To establish contacts directly with Committees in similar areas in state units and directly with Commission Coordinators of MENC Divisions for purpose of mutual resource function.	**Coordination of State Unit Commissions** *Purpose* Coordinators are appointed for each Commission area for the purpose of assisting in the joint planning undertaken by State Commission chairmen for Division biennial programs. (At the Division level, the Plan parallels the current pattern of Division structure wherein State presidents and Division officers comprise the Division Boards.)	**Commissions on Music Education** *Purpose* (1) To be appointed for purpose of meeting specific needs of state units. It is recommended that the following Commissions be appointed by MENC state units: Music in Preschool, Kindergarten and Elementary School; Music in Junior High School; Music in Senior High School; Music in Higher Education. (Commissions paralleling the National Commissions are not appointed in any state *unless* there is indicated a direct need for such Commission (a) within the state in connection with the state program of activities, or (b) as a Commission resource at the division and/or national levels.) (2) To serve as core Commissions with Divisional Coordination in planning for Division biennial programs. (3) To serve as resource leaders in discussion groups planned for National biennial program.
Commission I **Basic Concepts in Music Education** (interdisciplinary, to include aesthetics, psychology, sociology). Commission Members: Total of five.	**Commission I** **Basic Concepts in Music Education** (interdisciplinary, to include aesthetics, psychology, sociology). Division Coordinator.	**Commission I** **Basic Concepts in Music Education** (interdisciplinary, to include aesthetics, psychology, sociology). Commission appointed if desired.
Commission II **Standards of Music Literature and Performance.** Commission Members—General Chairman and Chairmen of following Committees: (1) Music for Elementary Schools—Choral and Instrumental. (2) Literature and Interpretation of Music for Choral Organizations. (3) Literature and Interpretation of Music for Band. (4) Literature and interpretation of Music for Orchestra and String Orchestra. (5) Literature and Interpretation of Music for Vocal Ensembles. (6) Literature and Interpretation of Music for Instrumental Ensembles. (7) Music for the Opera Workshop.	**Commission II** **Standards of Music Literature and Performance.** Division Coordinator.	**Commission II** **Standards of Music Literature and Performance.** State Committees appointed as needed.
Commission III **Music in General School Administration.** Commission Members—General Chairman and Chairmen of following Committees: (1) Administration and Supervision of Music Education. (2) Ethics in Public Relations. (3) Interscholastic Music Activities. (4) Music Curriculum and Schedules. (5) Budget and Finance.	**Commission III** **Music in General School Administration.** Division Coordinator.	**Commission III** **Music in General School Administration.** State Committees appointed as needed.
Commission IV **Music in Preschool, Kindergarten and Elementary School.** Commission Members—General Chairman and Chairmen of following Committees: (1) Preschool and Kindergarten. (2) Vocal Instruction. (3) Instrumental Instruction. (4) Related Programs—Rhythmic, Listening, Creative. (5) Integrated Activities.	**Commission IV** **Music in Preschool, Kindergarten and Elementary School.** Division Coordinator.	**Commission IV** **Music in Preschool, Kindergarten and Elementary School.** Appointment of State Unit Commission recommended.
Commission V **Music in Junior High School.** Commission Members—General Chairman and Chairmen of following Committees: (1) General Music, Singing, Listening, Creative, and Correlated Activities. (2) Vocal Instruction. (3) Instrumental Instruction. (4) Related Programs—Assemblies, Extra-curricular Activities. (5) Functional Theory and Music Literature.	**Commission V** **Music in Junior High School.** Division Coordinator.	**Commission V** **Music in Junior High School.** Appointment of State Unit Commission recommended.

NATIONAL	DIVISION	STATE
Commission VI **Music in Senior High School.** Commission Members—General Chairman and Chairmen of following Committees: (1) General Music. (2) Vocal Instruction and Ensembles. (3) Band, Wind, Percussion Instruction and Ensembles. (4) Orchestra and String Instruction and Ensembles. (5) Music Literature, Composition and Theory. (6) Related Programs—Assemblies, Music Production, Correlated and Extra-curricular Activities.	**Commission VI** **Music in Senior High School.** Division Coordinator.	**Commission VI** **Music in Senior High School.** Appointment of State Unit Commission recommended.
Commission VII **Music in Higher Education.** Commission Members—General Chairman and Chairmen of following Committees: (1) Junior College. (2) Education of the Music Teacher. (3) Training of General Elementary Teacher. (4) Music Literature, Composition, and Theory. (5) Graduate Studies. (6) Choral and Ensemble Activities. (7) Orchestra and Ensemble Activities. (8) Band and Ensemble Activities.	**Commission VII** **Music in Higher Education.** Division Coordinator.	**Commission VII** **Music in Higher Education.** Appointment of State Unit Commission recommended.
Commission VIII **Music in the Community.** Commission Members—General Chairman and Chairmen of following Committees: (1) Music in Adult Education. (2) Music in Churches. (3) Music and Community Agencies. (4) Music in General Industry.	**Commission VIII** **Music in the Community.** Division Coordinator.	**Commission VIII** **Music in the Community.** State Committees appointed as needed.
Commission IX **Music in Media of Mass Communications.** Commission Members—General Chairman and Chairmen of following Committees: (1) Radio-Television. (2) Records. (3) Films, Filmstrips, Slides. (4) Press. (5) Recording Equipment.	**Commission IX** **Music in Media of Mass Communications.** Division Coordinator.	**Commission IX** **Music in Media of Mass Communications.** State Committees appointed as needed.
Commission X **Commission on Accreditation and Certification.** Commission Members: Six.	**Commission X** **Commission on Accreditation and Certification.** Division Coordinator.	**Commission X** **Commission on Accreditation and Certification.** Commission appointed if needed.

NATIONAL	DIVISION	STATE
Standing Committees in Music Education *Purpose* (1) To address themselves to specific functions resulting in independent studies or studies undertaken in cooperation with or as a part of studies of the Commissions. (2) Sponsorship of meetings at MENC biennial programs. I. Music for Exceptional Children II. Music in International Relations. III. Organ Instruction in the Schools. IV. Piano Instruction in the Schools.	**Coordination of State Unit Standing Committees** *Purpose* Coordinators are appointed for each Standing Committee for the purpose of assisting in the joint planning undertaken by State Standing Committee Chairmen for Division biennial programs. I. Music for Exceptional Children. II. Music in International Relations. III. Organ Instruction in the Schools. IV. Piano Instruction in the Schools.	**Standing Committees in Music Education** *Purpose* To be appointed for purpose of meeting specific needs of state units (Standing Committees are not appointed in states paralleling the National Standing Committees *unless* there is indicated a direct need for such a Standing Committee within the state unit first of all, or that the appointment of such a Committee will constitute a direct resource at a Division or National level.) I. Music for Exceptional Children. II. Music in International Relations. III. Organ Instruction in the Schools. IV. Piano Instruction in the Schools.

Joint Committees with Other Organizations

It is also planned to have Joint Committees with other organizations for the purpose of (a) providing resource areas in related and associated fields of music education, and (b) enhancement of public relations program of the music education profession.

CALENDAR OF MEETINGS

Music Educators National Conference

Date	Place	President	Secretary
1907	Keokuk, Iowa (Organized)	Frances Elliott Clark	P. C. Hayden
1909	Indianapolis, Indiana	P. C. Hayden	Stella R. Root
1910	Cincinnati, Ohio	E. L. Coburn	Stella R. Root
1911	Detroit, Michigan	E. B. Birge	Clyde E. Foster
1912	St. Louis, Missouri	Charles A. Fullerton	M. Ethel Hudson
1913	Rochester, New York	Henrietta G. Baker Low	Helen Cook
1914	Minneapolis, Minnesota	Elizabeth Casterton	May E. Kimberly
1915	Pittsburgh, Pennsylvania	Arthur W. Mason	Charles H. Miller
1916	Lincoln, Nebraska	Will Earhart	Agnes Benson
1917	Grand Rapids, Michigan	Peter W. Dykema	Julia E. Crane
1918	Evansville, Indiana	C. H. Miller	Ella M. Brownell
1919	St. Louis, Missouri	Osbourne McConathy	Mabelle Glenn
1920	Philadelphia, Pennsylvania	Hollis Dann	Elizabeth Pratt
1921	St. Joseph, Missouri	John W. Beattie	E. Jane Wisenall
1922	Nashville, Tennessee	Frank A. Beach	Ada Bicking
1923	Cleveland, Ohio	Karl W. Gehrkens	Alice E. Jones
1924	Cincinnati, Ohio	W. Otto Miessner	Winifred V. Smith
1925	Kansas City, Missouri	William Breach	Grace V. Wilson
1926	Detroit, Michigan	Edgar B. Gordon	Elizabeth Carmichael
1927	Worcester, Massachusetts (Eastern)	Victor L. F. Rebmann	Grace E. Pierce
	Springfield, Illinois (North Central)	Anton H. Embs	Alice E. Jones
	Richmond, Virginia (Southern)	Louis L. Stookey	Irma Lee Batey
	Tulsa, Oklahoma (Southwestern)	Mabelle Glenn	Frank A. Beach
1928	Chicago, Illinois (First Biennial)	George Oscar Bowen	Marian Cotton
1929	Philadelphia, Pennsylvania (Eastern)	E. S. Pitcher	Grace E. Pierce
	Milwaukee, Wisconsin (North Central)	Ada Bicking	Fanny C. Amidon
	Spokane, Washington (Northwest)	Letha L. McClure	Edna McKee
	Asheville, North Carolina (Southern)	William Breach	Ella M. Hayes
	Wichita, Kansas (Southwestern)	John C. Kendel	Mary M. Conway
1930	Chicago, Illinois (Second Biennial)	Mabelle Glenn	Sadie Rafferty
1931	Los Angeles, California (Calif.-Western)	Herman Trutner, Jr.	S. Grace Gantt
	Syracuse, New York (Eastern)	M. Claude Rosenberry	Marion Knightly Wilson
	Des Moines, Iowa (North Central)	Herman F. Smith	Edith M. Keller
	Spokane, Washington (Northwest)	Frances Dickey	Helen Coy Boucher
	Memphis, Tennessee (Southern)	Grace P. Woodman	Minnie D. Stensland
	Colorado Springs, Colorado (Southwestern)	Grace V. Wilson	Sarah K. White
1932	Cleveland, Ohio (Third Biennial)	Russell V. Morgan	C. V. Buttelman
1933	Oakland, California (Calif.-Western)	Gertrude B. Parsons	Edna O. Douthit
	Providence, Rhode Island (Eastern)	Ralph G. Winslow	Elisabeth Gleason
	Grand Rapids, Michigan (North Central)	Wm. W. Norton	Carol M. Pitts
	Seattle, Washington (Northwest)	Anne Landsbury Beck	Margaret Lee Maaske
1934	Chicago, Illinois (Fourth Biennial)	Walter H. Butterfield	C. V. Buttelman
1935	Pasadena, California (Calif.-Western)	Arthur G. Wahlberg	Helen M. Garvin
	Pittsburgh, Pennsylvania (Eastern)	Laura Bryant	Anna Louise McInerney
	Indianapolis, Indiana (North Central)	Fowler Smith	Florence Flanagan
	Boise, Idaho (Northwest)	Charles R. Cutts	Berenice Barnard
	New Orleans, Louisiana (Southern)	J. Henry Francis	Jennie Belle Smith
	Springfield, Missouri (Southwestern)	Frances Smith Catron	Lena Milam
1936	New York, New York (Fifth Biennial)	Herman F. Smith	C. V. Buttelman
1937	San Francisco, California (Calif.-Western)	Mary E. Ireland	Sylvia Garrison
	Buffalo, New York (Eastern)	George L. Lindsay	Elizabeth V. Beach
	Minneapolis, Minnesota (North Central)	Carol M. Pitts	Ann Dixon
	Portland, Oregon (Northwest)	Ethel M. Henson	Andrew Loney, Jr.
	Columbia, South Carolina (Southern)	Grace Van Dyke More	Georgia B. Wagner
	Tulsa, Oklahoma (Southwestern)	John C. Kendel	T. Frank Coulter
1938	St. Louis, Missouri (Sixth Biennial)	Joseph E. Maddy	C. V. Buttelman

Date	Place	President	*Secretary
1939	Long Beach, California (Calif.-Western)	S. Earle Blakeslee	L. Alice Sturdy
	Boston, Massachusetts (Eastern)	F. Colwell Conklin	Mary C. Donovan
	Detroit, Michigan (North Central)	Charles B. Righter	Ruth B. Hill
	Tacoma, Washington (Northwest)	Louis G. Wersen	Esther C. Leake
	Louisville, Kentucky (Southern)	Edwin N. C. Barnes	Veronica Davis
	San Antonio, Texas (Southwestern)	Catharine E. Strouse	Gratia Boyle
1940	Los Angeles, California (Seventh Biennial)	Louis W. Curtis	C. V. Buttelman
1941	San Jose, California (Calif.-Western)	Glenn H. Woods	Clarence Heagy
	Atlantic City, New Jersey (Eastern)	Glenn Gildersleeve	John H. Jaquish
	Des Moines, Iowa (North Central)	Edith M. Keller	Harold E. Winslow
	Spokane, Washington (Northwest)	Andrew G. Loney, Jr.	Raymond Howell
	Charlotte, North Carolina (Southern)	Mildred Lewis	Lloyd V. Funchess
	Wichita, Kansas (Southwestern)	James L. Waller	Ruth Klepper Settle
1942	Milwaukee, Wisconsin (Eighth Biennial)	Fowler Smith	C. V. Buttelman
1943	Santa Barbara, California (Calif.-Western)	Helen C. Dill	Virginia Short
	Rochester, New York (Eastern)	John H. Jaquish	Wilbert Hitchner
	Cincinnati, Ohio (North Central)	J. Leon Ruddick	Lytton S. Davis
	Eugene, Oregon (Northwest)	Walter C. Welke	John Stehn
	Atlanta, Georgia (Southern)	Luther A. Richman	Max S. Noah
	Oklahoma City, Oklahoma (Southwestern)	Dean E. Douglass	Gratia Boyle
1944	St. Louis, Missouri (Ninth Biennial)	Lilla Belle Pitts	C. V. Buttelman
1945	Fresno, California (Calif.-Western)	Vincent A. Hiden	Elsa Brenneman
	New York, New York (Eastern)	Alfred Spouse	Arthur Ward
	Chicago, Illinois (North Central)	Hazel B. Nohavec	Delinda Roggensack
	Spokane, Washington (Northwest)	Wayne S. Hertz	Alvah A. Beecher
	Birmingham, Alabama (Southern)	Max S. Noah	Anne Grace O'Callaghan
	Wichita, Kansas (Southwestern)	Gratia Boyle	Ann Brittson
1946	Cleveland, Ohio (Tenth Biennial)	John C. Kendel	C. V. Buttelman
1947	Salt Lake City, Utah (Calif.-Western)	Lorin Wheelwright	Charles S. Hayward
	Scranton, Pennsylvania (Eastern)	Helen Hosmer	Wilbert Hitchner
	Indianapolis, Indiana (North Central)	Marguerite V. Hood	Erwin A. Hertz
	Seattle, Washington (Northwest)	Stanley M. Teel	Leslie Armstrong
	Birmingham, Alabama (Southern)	Lloyd V. Funchess	Paul W. Mathews
	Tulsa, Oklahoma (Southwestern)	Hugh E. McMillen	Paul R. Utt
1948	Detroit, Michigan (Eleventh Biennial)	Luther A. Richman	C. V. Buttelman
1949	Sacramento, California (Calif.-Western)	Amy Grau Miller	J. Chandler Henderson
	Baltimore, Maryland (Eastern)	Hummel Fishburn	Bertha W. Bailey
	Davenport, Iowa (North Central)	William B. McBride	Newell H. Long
	Portland, Oregon (Northwest)	Wallace H. Hannah	Rodney K. Berg
	Tampa, Florida (Southern)	Paul W. Mathews	Polly Gibbs
	Colorado Springs, Colorado (Southwestern)	Archie N. Jones	David Robertson
1950	St. Louis, Missouri (Twelfth Biennial)	Charles M. Dennis	C. V. Buttelman
1951	San Diego, California (Calif.-Western)	William E. Knuth	Lyllis D. Lundkvist
	Atlantic City, New Jersey (Eastern)	Bertha W. Bailey	John D. Raymond
	Missoula, Montana (Northwest)	Karl D. Ernst	Howard F. Miller
	Fort Wayne, Indiana (North Central)	Newell H. Long	F. E. Mortiboy
	Richmond, Virginia (Southern)	Anne Grace O'Callaghan	Otto J. Kraushaar
	Oklahoma City, Oklahoma (Southwestern)	Gillian Buchanan	Walter Duerksen
1952	Philadelphia, Pa. (Thirteenth Biennial)	Marguerite V. Hood	C. V. Buttelman
1953	Tucson, Arizona (Calif.-Western)	Ralph Hess	George F. Barr
	Buffalo, New York (Eastern)	Arthur E. Ward	Miriam L. Hoffman
	Milwaukee, Wisconsin (North Central)	Joseph E. Skornicka	Harriet Nordholm
	Bellingham, Washington (Northwest)	Leslie H. Armstrong	A. Bert Christianson
	Chattanooga, Tennessee (Southern)	Edward H. Hamilton	Earluth Epting
	Springfield, Missouri (Southwestern)	Gerald Whitney	E. E. Mohr
1954	Chicago, Illinois (Fourteenth Biennial)	Ralph E. Rush	C. V. Buttelman
1955	Berkeley, California (Calif.-Western)	George F. Barr	Joseph W. Landon
	Boston, Massachusetts (Eastern)	Mary M. Hunter	Elvin L. Freeman
	Cleveland, Ohio (North Central)	Harriet Nordholm	Clayton C. Hathaway
	Eugene, Oregon (Northwest)	A. Bert Christianson	Ferd Haruda
	New Orleans, Louisiana (Southern)	Wiley L. Housewright	Gene Morlan
	Hutchinson, Kansas (Southwestern)	E. E. Mohr	Robert Milton
1956	St. Louis, Missouri (Fifteenth Biennial)	Robert A. Choate	C. V. Buttelman

* The revision of the MENC Constitution adopted at the 1940 National convention eliminated the office of Division Secretary and made provision that the Division Second Vice-President "shall assist the Executive Secretary in the collection of official records and material, and shall serve as recording secretary of the Division Board of Directors" (Bylaws, Article I, Section 3). Therefore, beginning with 1941 the names of the Second Vice-Presidents of the respective Divisions are listed in this column.

THE CONSTITUTION AND BYLAWS OF THE MUSIC EDUCATORS NATIONAL CONFERENCE

ALTHOUGH THE ORGANIZATION came into being at a meeting held in Keokuk, Iowa in 1907, the date of the adoption of the first Constitution and Bylaws by the Music Supervisors National Conference was May 6, 1910. This was on the occasion of the meeting held in Cincinnati, Ohio in the third year of the Conference. The first revision of the Constitution and Bylaws was voted at the eleventh annual meeting held in Evansville, Indiana in 1918. Among the important provisions of the 1918 revision was the addition of the office of Second Vice-President, the incumbent of which was designated as chairman of the standing committee on publicity, and subsequently editor of the *Music Supervisors Journal*. Minor amendments were made from time to time during the following years, but the next important change in the Constitution and Bylaws (1926 at Kansas City, Missouri) made provision for biennial national conventions paralleled by biennial administrative terms. This action was the foundation for the development which led to the integration of the regional, or sectional, conferences, now operating as the six divisions of the National Conference. In 1930 another vital change in the Constitution and Bylaws provided a plan of business administration, with headquarters and publication offices to serve the entire organization. In 1934 an amendment was adopted changing the name of the organization to Music Educators National Conference. Ten years after the 1930 revision, at the biennial convention held in 1940 at Los Angeles, California, another revision of the Constitution and Bylaws was presented and unanimously adopted. This document provided for the recognition of the affiliated state music educators associations as geographical and organizational units of the Music Educators National Conference. Provision was also made for the affiliation of the Conference and the entire MENC confederation of affiliates and auxiliaries with the National Education Association as its Department of Music. The ensuing decade was one of remarkable growth in the professional stature and achievements of the official organization of music education. To meet the organizational and professional requirements of these developments, and to make preparation for further growth, a rewriting of the Constitution and Bylaws was again required. The following is the revision as adopted at the biennial meeting held in St. Louis, Missouri in 1950, and amended in Chicago in 1954 at the thirty-third (fourteenth biennial) meeting of the Music Educators National Conference.

CONSTITUTION

ARTICLE I—NAME

This organization shall be known as the Music Educators National Conference, a Department of the National Education Association.

ARTICLE II—OBJECT

Its object shall be the advancement of music education.

ARTICLE III—MEMBERSHIP AND DUES

Section 1. Active Membership. Active membership shall be open to all persons engaged in music teaching or other music educational work and shall provide the privileges of participation in the activities of the organization, including the right to vote and hold office, and admission to meetings upon the member's compliance with registration requirements. Annual dues shall be $4.00 to which shall be added the amount of active membership dues of the affiliated state association to which the member belongs; $1.50 of the dues collected shall be for annual subscription to the national official magazine, the MUSIC EDUCATORS JOURNAL.

Sec. 2. Partial Membership. Partial membership shall be available to members of affiliated state music educators associations whose constitutions provide for such membership in accordance with the stipulations of Article IX of this Constitution. Annual partial dues shall be $2.00 (in addition to the amount of state active dues), of which $1.50 shall be for annual subscription to the official magazine of the Music Educators National Conference. Partial members may not participate in the privileges of the Music Educators National Conference as stipulated for active members in Section 1 above, but, if qualified, may transfer from partial to full active membership status by payment of the required additional amount of dues ($2.00) at any time during the membership year, and thereby shall be entitled to all privileges of full active membership in the Music Educators National Conference.

Sec. 3. Associate Membership. Associate membership shall be open to residents of areas where Conference meetings are being held who are not professionally engaged in music education, and to others who wish to support the program of the Conference. Annual dues shall be $3.00 and shall provide for admission to meetings of the Conference, but shall not include a subscription to the official magazine or provide for the right to vote and hold office.

Sec. 4. Student Chapter Membership. Student chapter membership shall be open to students of music education at the college level who are not employed as teachers. Annual dues shall be $1.00 in addition to the amount of the annual dues collected for the affiliated state association in whose territory is located the institution sponsoring the chapter in which the student member is enrolled. The said annual dues of $1.00 shall be applied in full as payment for the student member's annual group subscription to the national official magazine, the MUSIC EDUCATORS JOURNAL. Student members shall be admitted to state, division, and national meetings upon compliance with registration requirements, and shall receive all privileges of active membership except the right to vote and hold office.

Sec. 5. Contributing Membership. Contributing membership shall be open to individuals who wish to contribute $15.00 or more annually to the support of the Conference. Contributing members who are eligible for active membership shall have the rights and privileges of such membership.

Sec. 6. Sustaining Membership. Sustaining membership shall be open to organizations, institutions, or business firms who wish to contribute $25.00 or more to the Conference. Sustaining membership may include an individual membership assigned to the person designated by the sustaining member firm, organization, or institution. Such individual membership shall convey, to the person to whom it is so assigned, full rights and privileges of active membership provided such person is qualified for such membership as stipulated in Section 1, Article III, of this Constitution.

Sec. 7. Life Membership. Life membership shall be open to individuals who are eligible for active membership, and who wish to contribute $150.00 to an endowment fund for the Conference. Life members shall have all the privileges of active membership, as stipulated in Section 1, Article III, of this Constitution, without further payment of annual dues.

Sec. 8. Patron Membership. Patron membership shall be open to individuals, organizations, institutions, or business firms wishing to contribute $500.00 or more for endowment, research, or a specified activity. Patron membership may include an individual membership assigned to the person designated by the patron member firm, organization, or institution. Such individual membership shall convey to the person to whom it is so assigned full rights and privileges of active membership for the year, provided such person is qualified for such membership as stipulated in Section 1, Article III, of this Constitution.

Sec. 9. Honorary Life Membership. Honorary life membership shall be conferred by vote of the Conference in recognition of distinguished service to music education. Nominations for honorary membership must be approved by the Board of Directors before being presented at a business meeting. Honorary life members who qualify for active membership shall have all rights and privileges of active membership without further payment of annual dues.

Sec. 10. Remittance of Dues. Dues shall be paid to the Conference business office, to an officially designated representative of that office, or to the treasurer of the affiliated state association to which the member belongs.

ARTICLE IV—GOVERNMENT

Section 1. National Officers. The officers of the Music Educators National Conference shall be a President, a First Vice-President who shall be the immediate past-president, and a Second Vice-President. The President and the Second Vice-President shall be elected at the National Biennial Convention, or by mail as provided in the Bylaws.

Sec. 2. National Board of Directors. The National Board of Directors shall be composed of the National President, National First Vice-President, National Second Vice-President, Presidents of the six Divisions, Presidents of the auxiliary organizations, and six members-at-large, three of whom shall be elected for a four-year term at each biennial National Convention. The National Board of Directors shall have power to increase the size of its membership when such seems for the best interests of the Conference.

Sec. 3. National Executive Committee. The National Executive Committee shall be composed of the three National officers, and five additional members elected by the National Board of Directors from their own membership. The terms of office for members of the National Executive Committee shall be for two years, concurrent with the terms of the National officers.

Sec. 4. National Cabinet. The National President and the Presidents of the six Divisions shall function as a National Cabinet in matters pertaining to their individual and joint responsibilities in the administration of the affairs of the Conference. The National President shall serve as chairman of the National Cabinet.

Sec. 5. Officers of the Divisions. The officers of each Division shall be a President, a First Vice-President who shall be the immediate past-president, and a Second Vice-President. The President and Second Vice-President for each Division shall be elected at the biennial Division Convention, or by mail as provided in the Bylaws.

Sec. 6. Division Board of Directors. The Board of each Division shall be composed of the Division officers, the Presidents of the affiliated state organizations in the Division area, one representative from each state in the area not having an affiliated state association.

Sec. 7. State Presidents National Assembly. The Presidents of the affiliated State Music Educators Associations shall constitute an advisory board to the National Board of Directors. Biennial meetings of this body, which shall be known as the State Presidents National Assembly, shall be held at the time of the biennial National Convention. The incumbent First Vice-President of the National Conference shall act as chairman and be the presiding officer. The National officers of the Conference and the Division Presidents shall be ex-officio members of the Assembly.

Sec. 8. Council of Past Presidents. The past presidents of the National Conference shall serve as an advisory body to the National Board of Directors, to the Music Education Research Council, and to the Editorial Board. They shall act as the Resolutions Committee for the Music Educators National Conference, shall have the right to recommend educational policies, and shall assume such other duties as may be assigned by the National Board of Directors. At each National biennial meeting they shall elect, from their membership, a chairman and a secretary for the ensuing biennium.

334

ARTICLE V—ELECTIONS

On or before the day of the official opening of each biennial National Convention and each biennial Division Convention the Board of Directors (National or Division, as the case may be) shall select a Nominating Committee of seven, one of whom shall be designated as chairman. The National Nominating Committee shall consist of one member from each of the six Divisions and one member-at-large who shall be named as chairman. On or before the day of the National biennial business meeting the Nominating Committee shall present for election the names of two candidates each for President and Second Vice-President, and for each member-at-large to be elected. On or before the day of the Division biennial business meeting the Nominating Committee shall present for election the names of two candidates each for President and Second Vice-President. The election shall be held on the day of this business meeting and shall be by ballot, or the election may be conducted by mail if authorized by action of the National Board of Directors as provided in the Bylaws. A majority of votes cast shall be required to elect.

ARTICLE VI—MEETINGS

Section 1. Conventions. National meetings of the Conference shall be held bienially in the even-numbered years between the dates of February 15 and July 15, or at such other time as may be determined by the National Board of Directors. Division meetings shall be held in the odd-numbered years. A business session shall be held not later than the day preceding the closing day of each biennial National or Division Convention. Five per cent of the active members registered at the convention shall constitute a quorum.

Sec. 2. Departmental Meeting of the National Education Association. The Music Educators National Conference, in its function as a Department of the National Education Association, as prescribed in Article IX of this Constitution, shall hold one or more sessions at the time and place of the annual meeting of the National Education Association.

Sec. 3. Board of Directors Meeting. The Board of Directors (National or Division) shall meet at the call of its President, or upon the joint request of not less than five members of that Board. A quorum of not less than fifty per cent of the members of such National or Division Board shall be required for the transaction of business. Authority for emergency action by the National Board or by a Division Board may be secured by mail, and action thus taken shall be effective until confirmed or reconsidered at the next official meeting of the Board concerned.

Sec. 4. National Executive Committee. The National Executive Committee shall meet at the call of the President, or upon the joint request of not fewer than three members of the Executive Committee. A quorum of five members of the Executive Committee shall be required for the transaction of business. Authority for emergency action may be secured by mail, and action thus taken shall be effective until confirmed or reconsidered at the next official meeting of the Executive Committee or Board of Directors.

Sec. 5. National Cabinet. The National Cabinet shall meet upon call of the National President.

ARTICLE VII—MUSIC EDUCATION RESEARCH COUNCIL

Section 1. Personnel, Purpose, and Authority. The Music Education Research Council shall consist of eighteen members elected as stipulated in Section 2 below. The Council shall, by means of its own membership and of such Conference Committees and other members as it may call into cooperation, conduct studies and investigations of such phases of music education as shall be referred to it by the Conference, or as shall originate within itself, and, on the basis of its findings, shall make reports and interpret educational tendencies. It shall serve in an advisory capacity to the Editorial Board. In no case shall the Council assume administrative, executive, or publicity functions. The Research Council shall convene at the time and place of the National Biennial Convention, and at such other times and places as may be arranged by the Chairman to meet needs and convenience.

Sec. 2. Members of Research Council. At each National biennial business meeting the National Board of Directors, after consultation with the Music Education Research Council, shall present to the members of the Conference for confirmation the names of six active members of the Conference to serve on the Research Council for the ensuing six-year term, said six members to take office immediately. The Research Council shall, at each biennial convention of the Conference, elect from its membership a Chairman and a Secretary to serve for the ensuing two-year period.

ARTICLE VIII—AFFILIATED AND AUXILIARY ORGANIZATIONS

The National Board of Directors may, at its discretion, accept from an established organized group an application for auxiliary or affiliate relationship with the Conference, provided the activities of the applicant organization do not duplicate or conflict with the program of any similar organization previously recognized by the Conference. The constitutions of organizations accepted for such affiliate or auxiliary relationships shall not conflict with any provision of the Constitution of the Music Educators National Conference.

ARTICLE IX—AFFILIATION WITH THE NATIONAL EDUCATION ASSOCIATION

The Music Educators National Conference shall be affiliated with the National Education Association, and shall function as the Department of Music of that organization. Such affiliation shall not restrict or alter the provisions of this Constitution and the accompanying Bylaws; nor shall such affiliation alter the status of the Music Educators National Conference in its relationship to its auxiliary and affiliate organizations, nor the operation and activities thereof, nor the rights and privileges of individual members as herein set forth.

ARTICLE X—AMENDMENTS

This Constitution may be altered or amended by an approving vote of two-thirds of the members voting at a biennial National election; or the Constitution may be altered, or amended, by an approving vote of two-thirds of the active membership balloting by mail in accordance with the stipulations of the Bylaws, provided, however, that in any case sixty days' notice of such contemplated amendment or alteration shall be given by mail or otherwise, to all active members of record.

Amendments to this Constitution may be initiated by the Executive Committee, the Board of Directors, or by a petition signed by five per cent (5%) of the membership in each of fifteen affiliated state organizations, after approval of the National Board of Directors.

335

BYLAWS

ARTICLE I—DUTIES OF NATIONAL OFFICERS

Section 1. National President. The National President shall preside at National meetings of the Conference, of the National Board of Directors, of the National Executive Committee, and of the National Cabinet. He shall have the power to appoint committees not otherwise provided for in the Constitution and Bylaws. He shall plan the programs for the National meetings of the Conference, and shall perform all other duties pertaining to his office.

Sec. 2. National First Vice-President. The First Vice-President shall serve as adviser to the President, shall serve as permanent chairman and presiding officer of the State Presidents National Assembly, and shall have such other duties as may be assigned to him by the President and the Board of Directors.

Sec. 3. National Second Vice-President. The Second Vice-President shall assume all duties of the National President in case of the disability or absence of the President, and shall have such other duties as may be assigned to him.

Sec. 4. National Board of Directors. The National Board shall: (1) administer the business and educational affairs of the National Conference, and have responsibility for its general policies and program of activities; (2) fill vacancies in National offices by temporary appointments pending regular elections; (3) have jurisdiction in all matters pertaining to the geographical divisions of the National Conference, and, with the concurrence of the Boards of the Divisions affected, have power to authorize the combining, dividing, or redistricting of Divisions for the purpose of holding Division meetings, or for other reasons deemed to be in the interest of the Divisions affected and the Conference as a whole; (4) nominate the members of the Music Education Research Council, select the members of the National Nominating Committee, and elect the members of the Executive Committee.

Sec. 5. National Executive Committee. The National Executive Committee shall: (1) be responsible for the business management and operation of the organization, and for the management and control of the funds thereof; (2) fix the time and place of the National biennial meetings and cooperate with the President in planning the details of such meetings; (3) represent, and act for, the National Board of Directors in the intervals between the meetings of that body; (4) appoint an Executive Secretary, prescribe his duties and compensation, and have full supervision and control of his acts as Executive Secretary; (5) provide annually for a complete auditing of the accounts of the Conference by a duly qualified accountant; (6) appoint an editor, or editors, or an editorial board, for Conference publications, and have full supervision and control of the acts of such person, or persons, in the performance of editorial duties; (7) supervise and direct the publication of yearbooks, proceedings, bulletins, Research Council reports, committee reports, and all other official publications.

Sec. 6. Eligibility for Holding National Office. All persons serving in any of the offices listed in the Bylaws, Article I, Sections 1, 2, 3, 4, and 5, shall concurrently be employed in an administrative or teaching capacity in the field of music education.

ARTICLE II—DUTIES OF DIVISION OFFICERS

Section 1. Division President. The Division President shall preside at all meetings of his Division and at all meetings of the Division Board of Directors. He shall have the power to appoint committees not otherwise provided for in the Constitution and Bylaws. He shall, in consultation with the Division Board, prepare a program for the biennial meeting of his Division, and shall perform all duties pertaining to his office. He shall be responsible for implementing the over-all program of the Conference within his Division. He shall serve as chief coordinating officer for the affiliated state associations in the Division. He shall be a member of the National Cabinet.

Sec. 2. Division First Vice-President. The First Vice-President of the Division shall serve as adviser to the Division President, and shall have such other duties as may be assigned to him by the Division President and the Division Board of Directors.

Sec. 3. Division Second Vice-President. The Second Vice-President of the Division shall assume the duties of the Division President in case of the disability or absence of the Division President. He shall assist the Executive Secretary in the collection of official records and material, and shall serve as recording secretary of the Division Board of Directors.

Sec. 4. Division Board of Directors. The Division Board of Directors shall: (1) have general jurisdiction over and responsibility for the functions of the Division as a geographical and organizational segment of the Conference, such as the biennial Division meetings and similar activities; (2) serve as the coordinating medium for the affiliated state associations comprising the Division; (3) assist the President in an advisory capacity in the appointment of committees; (4) fill unexpired terms in the case of vacancies in the said Board.

Sec. 5. Eligibility for Holding Division Offices. All persons serving in any of the offices listed in the Bylaws, Article II, Sections 1, 2, 3, and 4, shall concurrently be employed in an administrative or teaching capacity in the field of music education.

ARTICLE III—STATE PRESIDENTS NATIONAL ASSEMBLY

The State Presidents National Assembly, besides serving as a clearing house and advisory body in matters pertaining to policies, organizational functions, activities, and interrelationships of affiliated state associations (state units of the MENC), may recommend to the National Board of Directors educational programs or activities which can be implemented or aided through the activities programs or organizational facilities of the state associations. The assembly may also make recommendations to the Council of Past Presidents and the Music Education Research Council for study and consideration in connection with the respective responsibilities of these bodies.

ARTICLE IV—EDITORIAL BOARD

The Executive Committee shall appoint an Editorial Board of not less than ten members, one of whom shall be designated as Chairman. It shall be the duty of this group to supervise the publication of the MUSIC EDUCATORS JOURNAL, and to act as an evaluation committee for all articles submitted for publication. The Editorial Board shall also act as an advisory committee on all other publications of the Conference. It shall report to the Executive Committee on the value to music education of all books, brochures, or pamphlets being considered for publication by the Music Educators National Conference. The Executive Secretary shall be a member of the Editorial Board.

Section 1. Auxiliary Organizations. An auxiliary organization shall be construed as an association performing special functions within the field and organizational framework of the National Conference. It shall be responsible for such activities as shall be assigned to it by the National Board of Directors.

Sec. 2. Expenses for Maintenance of Auxiliary. Expenses for maintenance and operation of such auxiliary organization shall be paid from funds secured directly by the auxiliary, but the facilities and services of the Music Educators National Conference headquarters office and its staff may be utilized by the auxiliary. The auxiliary organization shall pay all direct expenses for special services, printing and postage, travel, etc., incurred by the headquarters office and staff members in behalf of the auxiliary organization. The official magazine of the Music Educators National Conference, and none other, shall be the national official magazine of each such auxiliary organization.

Sec. 3. President of Auxiliary. The President of an auxiliary shall be a member of the National Board of Directors of the Music Educators National Conference (Section 2, Article IV, of the Constitution).

Sec. 4. State Affiliation. State affiliation may be effected when approved by the National Board of Directors by a provision in the Constitution of the state organization applying for affiliate relationship whereby active membership dues in the state association shall include $2.00 for MENC partial membership of which $1.50 shall be for annual subscription to the national official magazine, the MUSIC EDUCATORS JOURNAL. Facilities and services of the headquarters office pertaining to membership promotion and processing, record-keeping, and mailing lists shall be available to affiliate organizations. Other special services may be provided under the terms stipulated in Section 1 of this Article for Auxiliary Organizations. To be considered for affiliation the applicant organization must be an established statewide music educators association, recognized within its state as fully representative of all school music education interests of the state.

The President of a state affiliate shall be a member of the Board of Directors of the Division of the MENC of which the affiliate is a state unit. The State President shall also represent his association in the State Presidents National Assembly. (Article IV, Sections 6 and 7, of the Constitution.)

Sec. 5. Maintenance of Affiliate or Auxiliary Relationship. To maintain its status as a state affiliate or auxiliary of the Music Educators National Conference there must be at least one meeting each year of such state affiliate or auxiliary, or of its central governing board. Failure to hold such a meeting during a period of two years shall automatically give cause for suspension of such affiliate or auxiliary. Failure to hold any such meeting for a period of three years shall give cause for cancellation of the affiliate or auxiliary relationship to the Music Educators National Conference.

Before either suspension or cancellation of affiliate or auxiliary relationship shall take effect, thirty days' notice by registered mail shall be given by the MENC Executive Committee to the officers and/or members of the executive body of the delinquent organization last registered in the records of the MENC headquarters office. The MENC Executive Committee may, at its discretion, instruct the headquarters office to withhold transfer of the state's share of dues collected from members in any state where the affiliated state association has become inactive. Such dues shall be held for the account of the state association, subject to the instructions of authorized and qualified officers of the state association. The Music Educators National Conference shall not collect the state's portion of dues from members in a state wherein the state affiliate relationship with MENC has been suspended under the regulations of this Section.

ARTICLE VI—ASSOCIATED ORGANIZATIONS

Section 1. An organization established and functioning within the field of music education, whose members are qualified for active membership in the Music Educators National Conference, may, upon application, be recognized by the MENC Board of Directors as an associated organization. To qualify for such recognition, the purpose and the Constitution and Bylaws of the applicant organization must be in accord with the over-all objectives and with the provisions of the Constitution and Bylaws of the Music Educators National Conference.

Sec. 2. Facilities and services of the Music Educators National Conference headquarters office may, by order of the MENC Board of Directors, be made available to associated organizations in accordance with the stipulated provisions for Auxiliary Organizations, Article V, Section 2, of these Bylaws.

ARTICLE VII—PERSONNEL OF THE NATIONAL BOARD, NATIONAL EXECUTIVE COMMITTEE, DIVISION BOARDS, AND MUSIC EDUCATION RESEARCH COUNCIL

Section 1. Personnel of the National Board of Directors. The National Board of Directors shall consist of the three National officers, the Presidents of the six Divisions, six members-at-large, and the Presidents of the auxiliary organizations. The terms of office of the members of the National Board shall be as prescribed in the Constitution and Bylaws. The Board, with the cooperation of the Boards of the auxiliaries and Divisions, shall have the power to fill vacancies in the Board caused by death or resignation, or other emergency, for the unexpired term of the vacancy.

In the event that the term of a member of the Board of Directors, who has been elected to serve on the Executive Committee, shall expire prior to the end of the biennial period for which he was elected to the Executive Committee, he shall continue to serve on the Executive Committee and shall be ex officio on the Board of Directors until the end of the biennial term for which he was elected to the Executive Committee.

Sec. 2. Personnel and Election of the National Executive Committee. The National Executive Committee shall consist of the National President, National First Vice-President, National Second Vice-President, and five other members elected from the National Board of Directors. The five elected members shall be chosen as follows: A nominating ballot shall be taken by the Board, each member nominating three Division Presidents for election to the Executive Committee; the four names receiving the largest number of votes shall be considered nominated, and a second ballot shall be taken; the three receiving the highest number of votes shall be declared elected. A similar nominating ballot shall be taken with each Board member nominating two persons from the members of the Board, other than the Division Presidents. The three names receiving the largest number of votes shall be considered nominated, and a second ballot shall be taken; the two receiving the highest number of votes shall be declared elected.

Sec. 3.   Personnel of the Division Boards.   The Division Boards shall, respectively, be comprised of the Division President, First Vice-President, Second Vice-President, the Presidents of the affiliated state associations within the Division, and the elected state representatives of states not having affiliated state units.   The Division Board shall have the authority to fill vacancies or unexpired terms caused by the resignation or death of a member-at-large or of a state representative from an unaffiliated state.

The President and Second Vice-President shall serve for the biennial period for which they are elected.   The First Vice-President shall serve for the biennial period following his term of office as President.   State Presidents shall serve as members of the Board during the term for which they have been elected to serve as State Presidents.   The members-at-large of Division Boards shall serve for four years, with the exception that, at the time of the first election following the adoption of these Bylaws, two members-at-large shall be elected for the ensuing term of two years, and two members-at-large for the ensuing term of four years; thereafter, two members-at-large shall be elected for a four-year term at each biennial Division meeting.

In the event that the President of an affiliated state association shall be retired from office by the election of his successor within the twelve-months period prior to the close of the administrative term of the Division, such retiring State President shall continue to serve as a member of the Division Board for the balance of the administrative term of the Division, together with the succeeding President of the said affiliated state association.

Sec. 4.   Personnel of the Research Council.   Any person holding active membership status in the Music Educators National Conference is eligible for membership in the Research Council, if duly elected.   Six months prior to each national biennial business meeting of the National Board of Directors, the Chairman of the Music Education Research Council shall submit to the President of the Conference the names of those Conference members the Council wishes to have considered by the Board for membership.   The Board of Directors shall also select names for consideration.   Any active member of the Conference may make similar recommendations.   At each national biennial business meeting the Board of Directors, after consultation with the Music Education Research Council, shall present to the members of the Conference, for confirmation, the names of six active members of the Conference to serve on its Research Council for the ensuing six-year term.   Any member of the Council, who, for good cause, desires to retire from the Council, shall be replaced by the National Board of Directors immediately upon his resignation.   Any member of the Council who is inactive may be automatically replaced in the same manner, upon recommendation of the Chairman and seven members of the Council.

ARTICLE VIII—LIMITATION OF RESPONSIBILITY OF THE OFFICERS

The authority and responsibility for the management and for the maintenance of the good will and credit of the Conference is vested in the Executive Committee, but it is expressly understood that neither the Executive Committee, nor any member thereof, nor any salaried officer, nor any member of the Conference shall be required to accept personal financial responsibility for duly authorized bills or obligations, or for suits or litigation which may develop from authorized activities of the organization carried on in good faith and in pursuit of the objectives, purposes, and achievements outlined in this Constitution.

ARTICLE IX—DISPOSITION OF ASSETS IN CASE OF DISBANDMENT

In the event of the disbandment or dissolution of the organization and the liquidation of its physical and financial assets, all funds remaining after the payment of the legitimate bills, and all accrued legal costs and financial obligations, including salaries of employees and expense allowances of officers, shall be transferred to the National Education Association, unless other disposition of such funds or assets shall be directed by legal action of the membership, upon recommendation of the Executive Committee.   It is expressly stipulated that, in the event of liquidation, funds of the Music Educators National Conference remaining in the treasury after all financial obligations have been taken care of, shall be utilized only for the purpose of furtherance of education in the United States, or some similar related objective which shall be in keeping with the purposes of the organization and of its parent organization, the National Education Association.

ARTICLE X—TERMS OF OFFICE

Section 1.   National and Division Officers.   Terms of office for the National and Division Presidents, First Vice-Presidents, and Second Vice-Presidents, shall be for two years beginning with the opening of the fiscal and administrative year following their election.

Sec. 2.   Members-at-large of the National Board.   Members-at-large of the National Board shall serve for four years, their terms of office beginning at the opening of the fiscal and administrative year following their election.

Sec. 3.   Other Members of the National Board.   Presidents of the Division Conferences shall serve as members of the National Board for the biennial period of their incumbency as Division Presidents, beginning at the opening of the fiscal year next following their election.   Presidents of the auxiliaries recognized and accepted in such auxiliary status at the time of the adoption of this Constitution shall serve as members of the National Board during their respective terms of office.   Additional members of the National Board of Directors may be elected by the Board to serve for the biennial period beginning at the opening of the fiscal year next following their election.

Sec. 4.   Music Education Research Council.   The term of members of the Research Council shall be for six years beginning immediately at the time of the election.   Vacancies in the membership of the Council, caused by death or resignation or other reason, shall be filled by the Board of Directors for the period of the unexpired term of the vacancy.

ARTICLE XI—REELECTION OF OFFICERS

National and Division officers and members of the Research Council may not be reelected to succeed themselves, but may be returned to the same office after a period of one or more terms has elapsed.

ARTICLE XII—LIFE MEMBERSHIP FUND

Section 1.   During the life of a life member, there shall be apportioned annually to the general fund, from the income from the life membership fund, the amount required for annual active national and state dues for such life member. Any surplus accruing from the income of the life membership fund, after such payment of the life member's annual dues, shall automatically revert to the general operating fund.

Sec. 2. Upon the demise of a life member the principal of his life membership fee shall remain in the endowment fund. It is expressly stipulated, however, that, in the event the total amount of annual national and state active dues for such life member paid from, or charged against, the life membership fund during the tenure of his life membership shall be in excess of the interest earned by the principal of his life membership fee, then a sufficient amount to cover the excess of the total amount paid for annual dues over the total income earned by his invested life membership fee shall be withdrawn from the endowment fund and credited to the general operating fund.

Sec. 3. The National Board is empowered to make loans from the life membership fund to the general fund to meet temporary emergencies or to finance special activities such as publications and other projects, provided that at the time of making any such loan provision is made to set up a reserve for the reimbursement thereof from the general fund.

ARTICLE XIII—PATRON MEMBERSHIP CONTRIBUTIONS

The principal and income received from patron membership contributions shall be utilized under the authority of the Executive Committee for such purposes as designated by the patron life members. In the absence of specific instructions from a patron life member, his patron contribution shall be placed in the life membership fund or utilized otherwise as in the discretion of the Executive Committee seems desirable and in the interest of the organization.

ARTICLE XIV—COMMITTEES

Special committees shall serve during the term of the administration in which they are appointed, or for such period as may be determined by the responsible administrative officers. Committees dealing with specific educational projects shall base their general plan of action on policies adopted by the Conference, or approved by the National Board of Directors.

ARTICLE XV—EXECUTIVE OFFICERS

Section 1. Executive Secretary. The Executive Secretary shall keep a complete and accurate record of all National and Division business meetings of the Conference, all meetings of the National Board of Directors and Executive Committee, and all meetings of the Division Boards. He shall conduct the business of the Conference in accordance with the Constitution and Bylaws, and in all matters shall be under the direction of the Executive Committee. In the absence of instruction from the Executive Committee, he shall be under the direction of the National President. He shall receive all moneys due the Conference, and shall countersign all bills. He shall be custodian of all property of the Conference and shall serve as Secretary of the National Board of Directors, the National Executive Committee, and the Division Boards. He shall have the proper records available at all official meetings. He shall give such bond as may be required by the Executive Committee. He shall act as business manager of the official Conference publications, and shall send monthly statements of the Conference to the Board of Directors. He shall submit an annual report to the Executive Committee. At the expiration of his term of office, he shall turn over to his successor all money, books, and other property of the Conference.

Sec. 2. Assistants to the Executive Secretary. The Executive Secretary may engage an assistant, or assistants, to whom he may delegate authority, with the approval of the National Executive Committee.

ARTICLE XVI—FISCAL AND ADMINISTRATIVE YEAR

The fiscal and administrative year shall be from July 1 to June 30, or such other period as may be determined by the National Board of Directors.

ARTICLE XVII—MEMBERSHIP YEAR

The annual period for which payment of membership dues shall be applied shall be the calendar year, January 1 to December 31.

ARTICLE XVIII—STATE AND NATIONAL ACTIVE MEMBERSHIP DUES

Section 1. It is expressly stipulated that active membership dues for the Music Educators National Conference shall include, in addition to the amount specified in Section 1, Article III, of the Constitution, the required amount of active dues for the affiliated state association in whose territory the member resides. Whether such active dues are remitted to the state association office, to the MENC headquarters office, or to an authorized agent, the state share of such dues shall accrue to the treasury of the state association, and the national share to the treasury of the National Conference.

Sec. 2. Active membership dues accruing from contributing, sustaining, life, and patron memberships, as described in Article III, Sections 5, 6, 7, and 8, respectively, of the Constitution, shall include the state (and national) share of active membership dues as stipulated by the national Constitution and the Constitution of the state association in the territory of which resides the member paying such dues, in accordance with the provisions of said Sections 5, 6, 7, and 8, Article III, of the Constitution. Such active dues shall be credited and disbursed as provided in Section 1 above, and in accordance with the provisions of Sections 1, 5, 6, 7, and 8, Article III, of the Constitution.

ARTICLE XIX—VOTING BY MAIL

The Board of Directors may authorize voting by mail for the purpose of conducting a biennial National or Division election, or for any other purpose or purposes for which a vote of the membership of the Conference shall be required. Mail voting shall be conducted in accordance with the instructions of the Board of Directors, and shall make provision for all members of record to receive ballots and necessary supporting information in ample time to return their ballots before the date of the close of the voting. Such closing date shall be designated by the Board of Directors, and printed on all ballots and other material issued to the members preliminary to the vote by mail.

This Bylaw also applies to the authorization by the National Board of Directors for any such voting by mail. It is expressly stipulated that voting by mail, when duly authorized, shall be conducted instead of voting at the time and place of a meeting at which said voting would normally take place, or during the interim between regular meetings; there shall be no combination of the two voting procedures for an election, or for any other purpose for which balloting by the membership may be required.

Article XX—Rules of Order

Robert's Rules of Order Revised shall govern in all business meetings of the Conference.

Article XXI—Amendments

The Bylaws may be altered or amended in the same manner as that provided in Article X of the Constitution

✠

NATIONAL INTERSCHOLASTIC MUSIC ACTIVITIES COMMISSION

BYLAWS

Article I—Function and Purpose

The National Interscholastic Music Activities Commission (formerly the National School Band, Orchestra and Vocal Association) shall function within the organizational framework of the Music Educators National Conference in accordance with the provisions of the Constitution of the Conference pertaining to auxiliary organizations. The purpose of the NIMAC shall be to cooperate with the sponsors of interscholastic music activities in the development and maintenance of high standards in teaching, performance, adjudication, management and other matters related to the conduct and educational values of such activities. It shall also accept responsibility for such assignments as may be designated by the National Board of Directors of the Music Educators National Conference or by the MENC State Presidents National Assembly.

Article II—Organization

The National Interscholastic Music Activities Commission shall be organized on the state-division-national pattern of the MENC.

Article III—Direction and Operation

Section 1. The functions of the National Interscholastic Music Activities Commission shall be under the direction of an Executive Council composed of seven members, five of whom shall be elected by the National Board of Control of the Commission, and the other two of whom shall be the MENC National President and the MENC Executive Secretary, as provided in Article VI.

Sec. 2. The National Board of Control shall be the legislative body of the National Interscholastic Music Activities Commission. Each of the six MENC Divisions shall be represented on the National Board of Control by four delegates, three of whom shall be elected by the NIMAC Board of the Division. The fourth delegate from each Division shall be the chairman of the NIMAC Division Board, or his duly authorized representative. The national president and the executive secretary of the MENC, and the presidents of the MENC Divisions shall be ex officio members of the National Board of Control.

Sec. 3. The Division Boards shall be composed, respectively, of four delegates from each state in the Division. Three of the delegates from each state shall be designated by the affiliated state music educators association of said state (state unit of the MENC) and shall be members of the committee or group of the affiliated state unit to which is assigned responsibility by the said state unit for conducting or supervising the official state interscholastic music activities. In the case of a state wherein such activities are sponsored by an organization or institution other than the MENC state unit, the three delegates shall be members of the committee or group currently representing the MENC state unit, in advisory or other capacity, in connection with the management or policy-making and/or educational aspects of the officially approved interscholastic music activities in the said state.

The fourth member of each delegation on the Division Board shall be the president of the affiliated state association.

Alternates for the three elected delegates may be named and included in the state's delegation as such. One delegate, if so authorized by the state unit, may represent either or both of the other appointed or elected three delegates from a given state.

Sec. 4. Each NIMAC Division Board shall, at its biennial meeting, elect a chairman from its own number for the ensuing biennium.

Section 1. The NIMAC Division Board shall serve as a coordinating medium and clearing house for the officially approved interscholastic music activities of the states in the Division and/or the sponsors of such activities. The NIMAC Division Board shall perform such services as may be assigned by the MENC Division president in connection with the Division conventions and/or general educational program.

Sec. 2. Each NIMAC Division Board shall from its own personnel choose three delegates to the National Board of Control, of which delegation the chairman of the NIMAC Division Board shall automatically be the fourth member. The NIMAC Division Board shall instruct its delegation to the National Board of Control to present to the National Board any matters which the Division Board recommends for consideration and/or action by the National Board. The Division delegation may be instructed to refer to the National Board of Control for consideration and/or recommendation matters which have been presented to the Division Board by a state unit, or by a recognized sponsor of state interscholastic music activities.

ARTICLE V—DUTIES AND PRIVILEGES OF THE STATE DELEGATES TO THE DIVISION BOARDS

Section 1. Beside their official responsibilities and functions at the state level, for which they are accountable to their respective state associations, the members of each state delegation shall serve, through the medium of the NIMAC Division Board, and directly when necessary, as liaison between the National Commission and the sponsors of the officially recognized interscholastic music activities of their respective states.

Sec. 2. Through the president of the affiliated MENC state unit (who is automatically a member of the state delegation) the state delegation has the privilege of presenting matters deemed for the good of the order, educationally or otherwise, directly to the Executive Council of the Commission, and may request action by the Council under the provisions of Article VI, Sections 7, 8 and 9.

ARTICLE VI—DUTIES AND AUTHORITY OF THE NATIONAL BOARD OF CONTROL, ITS OFFICERS, AND THE EXECUTIVE COUNCIL

Section 1. The National Board of Control shall elect from its own membership a president, vice-president, and three members-at-large who, with the MENC national president and the MENC executive secretary, shall comprise the Executive Council of the Commission.

Sec. 2. The president shall preside at all meetings of the National Board of Control. He shall serve as chairman of the Executive Council, and have the responsibilities and authority customarily assigned to the chief administrative officer.

Sec. 3. The vice-president shall assume the duties of the president in case the latter is unable to perform said duties. If the office of president is vacated, the vice-president shall succeed to the presidency for the balance of the biennial term for which the president was elected. The vice-president shall serve as vice-chairman of the Executive Council.

Sec. 4. The MENC executive secretary shall serve as secretary of the Executive Council and of the National Board of Control. Under his responsibility as a bonded officer of the MENC the executive office of the MENC shall have the responsibility for the functions of treasurer.

Sec. 5. The Executive Council shall be responsible for carrying out the program of activities and services of the National Interscholastic Music Activities Commission in accordance with the directions of the NIMAC National Board of Control.

Sec. 6. The Executive Council shall have full authority to act on behalf of the Commission in the interims between meetings of the National Board of Control.

Sec. 7. The Executive Council may, at its discretion, take action in regard to matters of emergency nature, or when requests are made by state authorities because of an imminent need or problem.

Sec. 8. The Council may present, by mail or otherwise, to the National Board of Control, and/or to the MENC Executive Committee, and/or the State Presidents National Assembly, any matters which it deems of sufficient importance or urgency to warrant such action.

Sec. 9. Matters presented directly to the Executive Council by a state unit of the MENC or a sponsor of state interscholastic music activities may be referred by the Council to the NIMAC Division Board having jurisdiction. In the instance of an appeal or proposal presented immediately prior to a stated meeting of the National Board of Control, the Executive Council may, at its discretion, place the item in the agenda for the session of the National Board of Control.

ARTICLE VII—TERMS OF OFFICE—ADMINISTRATIVE AND FISCAL PERIODS

Section 1. The chairmen of the Division Boards and the Division delegates to the National Board of Control shall be elected for a two-year term paralleling the biennium of the MENC Divisions.

Sec. 2. The members of the state delegations shall serve as members of their respective Division Boards for such periods as conform to their tenure of office in the respective state associations. (This is to assure participation of state delegates who are currently in service in connection with their responsibilities to the state association. See Article III, Section 2.)

Sec. 3. The administrative and fiscal year of the Commission shall parallel the MENC administrative and fiscal year: July 1 through June 30.

Sec. 4. The president of the National Board of Control (who automatically serves as chairman of the Executive Council), the vice-president (who automatically serves as vice-chairman of the Executive Council), and the three members-at-large of the Executive Council shall be elected for a two-year period paralleling the MENC national biennium. They shall take office July 1, which is the first day of the national biennium and the first day of the fiscal and administrative year as prescribed by the Bylaws of the MENC. The Division chairmen shall take office on July 1 immediately following the time of their election, which is the first day of the Division biennium and the first day of the fiscal and administrative year of the MENC.

341

Article VIII—Meetings and Elections

Section 1. The meetings and elections of the Division Boards shall be held at the times and places of the respective MENC Division biennial conventions. Meetings of the National Board of Control shall be held at the time and place of the MENC national biennial convention.

Sec. 2. Special meetings of the National Interscholastic Activities Commission Board of Control and/or of the Executive Council, between the stated biennial meetings of the National Board of Control, may be called by the president with the approval of the members of the Executive Council.

Sec. 3. Special meetings of any NIMAC Division Board may be called by the Division chairman with the approval of the Executive Council.

Article IX—Vacancies

Section 1. In the event that for any reason the office of national president is vacated, the vice-president shall assume the duties of president.

Sec. 2. In the event that the vice-president assumes the duties of president, or if for any other reason the office of vice-president is vacated, the remaining members of the Executive Council shall elect one of their number to serve as vice-president until the next biennial election.

Sec. 3. A vacancy or vacancies occurring among the members-at-large of the Executive Council may be filled, for the unexpired term, by appointment by the president with the confirmation of the remaining members of the Executive Council.

Sec. 4. In the event that the position of chairman of a Division Board is vacated for any reason, the presidents of the state associations of the Division shall choose from the members of the encumbent state delegations a chairman, whose name shall be presented to the Executive Council for confirmation.

Sec. 5. Action by mail for filling of vacancies shall be legal.

Article XII—Quorums

A majority of states duly represented by delegates, who are duly authorized as prescribed by these Bylaws, shall constitute a quorum of a Division Board.

A duly authorized representation of four Divisions is required for a quorum of the National Board of Control.

Five members of the Executive Council, including the chairman, or the vice-chairman in case the chairman is unable to be present, shall constitute a quorum.

Article XIII—Voting

On any action pertaining to the policies, program, or activities of the Commission, voting in the National Board of Control shall be by states—one vote for each state.

Article XIV—Headquarters Office

Section 1. The Executive Office of the MENC shall be the headquarters and publication office of the NIMAC, in accordance with the provisions of the MENC Constitution.

Sec. 2. The general fund of the MENC shall be reimbursed at least annually for overhead and operation expenses incurred by the Executive Office in carrying on the various services required for the NIMAC—its publication production, shipping, bookkeeping and other essential activities. The annual amount of such reimbursement shall be determined by the MENC Budget Committee, with the approval of the NIMAC Executive Council and the MENC Executive Committee.

Article XV—Official Magazine

The official magazine of the NIMAC shall be the *Music Educators Journal.*

Article XVI—Conformity with the MENC Constitution

These Bylaws are appended to and subject to the provisions of the MENC Constitution. No article or section of these Bylaws shall be construed as in conflict with any provision or any organizational, business, or educational policy of the MENC as set forth in the MENC Constitution and Bylaws.

Article XVII—Amendments

These Bylaws may be amended in any biennial meeting of the National Board of Control or at a special meeting thereof duly called by the president with the approval of the Executive Council.

MUSIC INDUSTRY COUNCIL

AT THE BIENNIAL meeting of the Music Educators National Conference in Chicago in 1953, the Music Education Exhibitors Association approved a new constitution and bylaws changing its name to the Music Industry Council, and shifting the emphasis of the organization from matters of exhibits to the policies, practices, and growth of the entire musical industry as it affects the parent organization, the Music Educators National Conference.

The Music Industry Council, an auxiliary of the Music Educators National Conference, describes its purpose as (a) to promote a frank exchange of ideas on music problems among all interested groups; (b) to maintain friendly contacts with fellow-members of the Council; (c) to encourage and cooperate with music associations and music and educational journals in the dissemination of useful and practical information; (d) to improve and enlarge the facilities for a better acquaintance by music educators with the personnel and products of the Council members.

The Music Industry Council has two types of membership: (a) regular voting members who participate in the entire program of the Council, and (b) nonvoting associate members who limit their activities to exhibits only.

The regular meetings of the Council are held only at the time and place of the Music Educators National Conference or, in the odd years, at a divisional conference of the Conference, the particular one to be designated by the Executive Board.

With the ever-growing number of services provided by commercial firms to music educators and education, the Music Industry Council has a responsibility to the Music Educators National Conference to cooperate in business and professional matters, in developing a proper code of ethics for the industry, and in maintaining the highest level of business procedures at conventions in advertising, and in all relations with the public.

The business of education through music, direct or incidental, is the concern of all— teachers, supervisors, specialists, administrators, editors, salesmen, businessmen. The particular responsibility of the Music Industry Council is to encourage the production, manufacture, distribution, and proper use of musical materials, instruments, equipment. It is the purpose of the Music Industry Council to provide a strong and exceedingly valuable and reliable arm of the Music Educators National Conference.

Prepared by George L. White, Silver Burdett Co., President of MIC, 1954-1956

⊹

CONSTITUTION

ARTICLE I—NAME

The name of this organization shall be the Music Industry Council.

ARTICLE II

The Music Industry Council shall be an auxiliary of Music Educators National Conference, which is the Department of Music of the National Education Association of the United States.

ARTICLE III—PURPOSE

The purpose of the Music Industry Council shall be to effect a non-profit organization through which closer contacts may be maintained between the professional and commercial interests in the music education field; to promote a frank exchange of ideas involving mutual interests; to maintain friendly contacts with fellow-members of this Council; to encourage and cooperate with music associations and music and educational journals in the dissemination of useful and practical knowledge to our mutual benefit; to improve and enlarge the facilities for a better acquaintance by music educators with the personnel and products of the Council members.

ARTICLE IV—MEMBERSHIP

Any individual, firm or corporation that subscribes in letter and spirit to the Constitution and Bylaws of this Council is eligible for election to membership.

Article V—Officers

The officers shall be President, Vice-President, Secretary-Treasurer.

Article VI—Executive Board

The Executive Board shall consist of President, Vice-President, Secretary-Treasurer and four additional members, chosen at large from the membership.

Article VII—Government

The government and management of the Council shall be vested in the Executive Board, which shall meet upon the call of the President whenever the business of the Council requires it or at the written request of three members of the Executive Board.

Article VIII—Duties of Officers

The President, or in his absence the Vice-President, shall preside at all meetings of the Council and of the Executive Board and shall serve as the representative on the MENC Board of Directors. The Secretary-Treasurer by and with the approval of the Executive Board, shall conduct the correspondence of the Council, issue all notices to members, keep minutes at meetings, collect all monies due the Council and disburse same.

Article IX—Meetings

The regular meetings of the Council shall be held annually at the time and place of the Music Educators National Conference or at Sectional Conferences of the Music Educators National Conference to be designated by the Executive Board. Special meetings shall be called at any time by the President or by a majority of the Executive Board or upon request in writing of 10 (ten) members. Two weeks' notice of such special meetings must be sent by the Secretary to all members.

Article X—Committees

Auditing. The President shall appoint an Auditing Committee of three members of the Council, not more than one of whom may be a member of the Executive Board, thirty days before the termination of his term of office. It shall be the duty of this Committee to audit the Secretary-Treasurer's books and accounts, and to make a full and complete report which shall be mailed to the membership within thirty days of the Committee's appointment.

Membership. The membership committee, appointed by the President, shall consist of five whose duty it shall be to receive applications for membership in the Council and make recommendations thereon to the Executive Board.

Exhibits. There shall be an Exhibit Committee consisting of five members, appointed by the President, at least three of whom shall be members of the Executive Board, whose duty it shall be to cooperate with the proper officers and officials of the various education associations with which the Council may have official relations.

Article XI—Amendments

Either the Constitution or the Bylaws may be altered or amended by a two-thirds vote of the members present at any regular meeting of the Council, provided the alterations of amendments shall have been proposed in writing at least sixty days prior to the meeting at which action is taken and due announcements of the proposed action shall have been sent to all members of the Council.

BYLAWS

Article I—Election of Officers

The election of the President, the Secretary-Treasurer, and members of the Executive Board shall take place at the biennial meeting which coincides with the Music Educators National Conference. The retiring President shall automatically become Vice-President. The term of office for all officers shall be two years of until their successors are elected, but at the first election two of the four members of the Executive Board shall be elected for two years and two of the members of the Executive Board shall be elected for four years. Members of the Executive Board shall not be eligible for election to succeed themselves.

Article II—Procedure for Election

Section 1. The President shall appoint, at least two weeks before the biennial meeting, a Nominating Committee of five members, two of whom shall be members of the Executive Board, whose duty it shall be to submit to the Secretary-Treasurer two days before the biennial meeting the names of two candidates for each of the officers and Executive Board to be elected. The candidates for President and Secretary-Treasurer shall be offered as joint nominations and voted for as a unit. Further, the two candidates of each unit shall be selected from the same section of the country. The directors, however, may be chosen from any part of the country. The Secretary-Treasurer shall be required to see that each member of the Council in good standing in attendance at the Biennial Meeting receives a copy of these nominations at least twenty-four hours before the meeting takes place.

Sec. 2. The Chairman of the Nominating Committee shall offer the names of the candidates selected by his committee for election. Any member present in good standing may make nominations from the floor. When all nominations are made the election shall be held and the candidates receiving a majority of the votes of the members present and voting shall be declared elected.

344

Article III—Vote and Quorum

Each member, whether an individual, firm, or corporation, shall be entitled to one vote, and ten members shall constitute a quorum for the transaction of business. No individual, firm, or corporation shall be entitled to more than one membership in the Council.

Article IV—Membership

Section 1. Effective as of the date of this amendment all present members of the Music Education Exhibitors Association will automatically be continued as members of the Music Industry Council by their own written request. As provided in the Constitution the Membership Committee shall refer with its recommendations to the Executive Board all future applications for membership. It shall be the duty of the Executive Board to accept or reject such applications. In considering applications for membership the Executive Board shall keep constantly in mind the ideals of our Council; truth and honesty and the fulfillment of every promise in our relations with schools and educators, pride in the confidence our organization enjoys, absence of questionable or unfair competitive methods among our membership, maintenance of highest degree of business ethics in our relations with those we serve, and to strive to foster and improve the cordial and friendly relationship that exists among our membership and between our Council and the education association with which we work.

Sec. 2. Non-voting associate membership shall be open to exhibitors who do not desire to become members or who in the opinion of the Executive Committee are not eligible for membership.

Article V—Dues

Section 1. The regular dues for membership in the Music Industry Council shall be $20.00 annually, payable July first for the ensuing fiscal year. These dues include one individual firm membership in the Music Educators National Conference.

Sec. 2. Dues for associate membership shall be $10.00 payable upon acceptance. The dues do not include membership in the Music Educators National Conference.

Article VI—Order of Business

The official order of business at all meetings of the Council unless waived by a majority of those present, shall be as follows:—

Roll-call
Reading of the Secretary's minutes of the preceding meeting
Report of standing committees
Report of special committees

Old business
New business
Treasurer's report
Election of officers.

PERSONNEL OF THE
MUSIC IN AMERICAN EDUCATION COMMITTEE
ORGANIZATION

THIS ALPHABETICAL LISTING includes the names of MENC members and advisors who served on or cooperated with the Music in American Education State-Division-National Committee Organization during the period (1951-1954) devoted to the studies and investigations from which were derived the major portion of the contents of this volume. In addition to the Chairmen and members of the State, Division and National Committees and the participating State, Division and National officers, the list also includes names of officers and members of the Music Education Research Council, MENC Editorial Board, the Editorial Committee of the Journal of Research in Music, Education, National Interscholastic Music Activities Commission, Music Industry Council, MENC Council of State Supervisors of Music, MENC Council of Past Presidents, MENC Council of State Editors, College Band Directors National Association, National Association of College Wind and Percussion Instructors, American String Teachers Association, and other groups represented by the contributions herein.

Aas, Selma, Ottumwa, Iowa
Abel, Paul, Missoula, Mont.
Achelpohl, LaVera, Gunnison, Colo.
Adair, Dorothy Love, Huntsville, Ala.
Adcock, Donald B., Deming, N. Mex.
Ahearn, Mrs. Ella Mason, Westfield, N. J.
Ainsworth, Mrs. J. V., Moss Point, Miss.
Aker, Charles L., Arlington, Va.
Albertson, Marjorie, Portland, Ore.
Alexander, Caryl, Lander, Wyo.
Alexander, Mrs. James A., Florence, Ala.
Allen, Florence, Salt Lake City, Utah
Allen, Frances, Louisville, Ky.
Allen, Frank, Phoenix, Ariz.
Allen, Lillian M., Washington, D. C.
Allen, Lydia, West Hartford, Conn.
Allen, Mary Emma, Martinsburg, W. Va.
Allen, Warren D., Tallahassee, Fla.
Alviani, Doric, Amherst, Mass.
Anderson, Maynard, Watertown, S. Dak.
Anderson, Paul, Milwaukee, Wis.
Anderson, Raymond, Birmingham, Ala.
Anderson, Russel, Wayne, Nebr.
Anderson, Virgil, Bucklin, Mo.
Andrew, Mildred, Norman, Okla.
Andrews, Frances, State College, Pa.
Andrews, Miriam, Gorham, Maine
Anifantis, Eleanor, Arlington, Mass.
Annett, Thomas, LaCrosse, Wis.
Ardrey, Eldon A., Flagstaff, Ariz.
Arentsen, Harold W., Oshkosh, Wis.
Armstrong, Donald D., Grand Rapids, Mich.
Armstrong, Leslie H., Olympia, Wash.
Arner, David M., Greensboro, N. C.
Arnold, Mrs. Gladys H., Slippery Rock, Pa.
Asch, Moses, New York, N. Y.
Atherton, Lilla, Oakland, Maine
Atkinson, Ralph, Stuttgart, Ark.
Aupperle, Donald K., Idaho Falls, Idaho
Austin, Lorena, West Orange, N. J.
Austin, Stanley, Westwood, N. J.

Baal, Mrs. Genevieve, Des Moines, Iowa
Bach, Vincent, New York, N. Y.
Bachman, Harold, Gainesville, Fla.
Bachmann, Gertrude, Rapid City, S. Dak.
Bacon, Madi, Berkeley, Calif.

Bailey, Blanche C., Sunapee, N. H.
Bailey, Mildred, New Bedford, Mass.
Bailey, Nina, Gorham, Maine
Bainbridge, John L., Staten Island, N. Y.
Baird, Forrest J., San Jose, Calif.
Baker, Dwight B., Slippery Rock, Pa.
Bakewell, Ruth, Billings, Mont.
Bakkegard, B. M., Austin, Texas
Baldwin, Harriet, Milwaukie, Ore.
Baldwin, Lillian, Cleveland, Ohio
Ball, Sarah Lee, Jackson, Miss.
Ballinger, J. Stanley, Hays, Kans.
Bane, Mildred, Alexandria, Va.
Bannan, Mary Francis, East Lansing, Mich.
Banner, Bob, New York, N. Y.
Barbour, Richard E., Bethel, Maine
Barnard, Berenice, Ventura, Calif.
Barnard, Floyd, Minneapolis, Minn.
Barnes, James W., Terre Haute, Ind.
Barnett, Helen, Santa Barbara, Calif.
Barnum, Walter, Seattle, Wash.
Barr, E. Lawrence, Kalamazoo, Mich.
Barr, George F., Sacramento, Calif.
Barr, Robert, Royal Oak, Mich.
Barr, Robert M., Columbus, Ga.
Barrett, James H., Hutchinson, Kans.
Barth, George, Lafayette, La.
Bartholomew, Orin, Eunice, N. Mex.
Bartlett, Katherine, Portland, Maine
Barton, H. E., Clovis, N. Mex.
Baum, Claire, Kensington, Md.
Baumann, Victor H., Phoenix, Ariz.
Baumgarner, Alice A. D., Concord, N. H.
Baumle, Dorothy, Arlington, Va.
Beach, Earl E., Athens, Ga.
Beach, Joseph M., Lexington, Ky.
Bean, Bryant, South Paris, Maine
Beattie, John W., Evanston, Ill.
Beck, Chester L., Santa Rosa, Calif.
Becker, Evelyn Waltman, York, Pa.
Becker, Lawrence, Okmulgee, Okla.
Becker, Robert, Laramie, Wyo.
Beckmeyer, W. H., Mt. Vernon, Ill.
Beddoe, Lucy, Bedford, Ind.
Beebee, C. Scripps, East Orange, N. J.
Behrens, F. W. R., Medina, Ohio
Beiser, M. J., Eaton Rapids, Mich.

Bell, Jane Tweed, Penasco, N. Mex.
Bellis, Warren, Moscow, Idaho
Bellman, Mrs. Helen M., College Park, Md.
Belsheim, George N., Minneapolis, Minn.
Belsheim, O. T., Dickinson, N. Dak.
Benn, Oleta, Pittsburgh, Pa.
Bennett, Elizabeth C., Milford, Del.
Berdahl, Arthur, Fresno, Calif.
Berentz, George, Leavenworth, Kans.
Berg, Richard C., Springfield, Mass.
Berg, Sidney, Norfolk, Va.
Bergan, Hal, Lansing, Mich.
Bergan, Paul E., Galveston, Texas
Berger, Arthur W., Trenton, N. J.
Bergethon, Bjornar, Urbana, Ill.
Berggren, Thorsteen, Billings, Mont.
Bergh, Frances Hovey, Coral Gables, Fla.
Berkman, Samuel, Hartford, Conn.
Berquist, H. O., Fargo, N. Dak.
Berryman, Joe, New Orleans, La.
Bigbee, Jane, Severna Park, Md.
Bird, K. J., American Fork, Utah
Bishop, Dorothy, Los Angeles, Calif.
Bishop, James R., Moss Point, Miss.
Bishop, Lynn, La Grande, Ore.
Bishop, Meredith, Phoenix, Ariz.
Blaine, Ruby, Farmington, Maine
Blair, Livingston, Washington, D. C.
Blakely, Lloyd G., Bolivar, Mo.
Bleckschmidt, Alfred W., Jefferson City, Mo.
Blodgett, Ellen F., Gardiner, Maine
Blossom, Charles, Helena, Mont.
Blough, William M., Sharon, Pa.
Bohlke, Boyd, Sioux Falls, S. Dak.
Bohm, Earl W., St. Louis Park, Minn.
Bolles, Robert S., Gainesville, Fla.
Bondurant, Dorothy, Waterloo, Iowa
Bonell, Hannah, Falls Church, Va.
Bonnin, Reginald, Skowhegan, Maine
Booker, Florence, Arlington, Va.
Boone, Paul, Shawnee, Okla.
Borin, Betty, Miami, Fla.
Borlag, Leonard, Watford City, N. Dak.
Bornoff, Walter, Newton Centre, Mass.
Borup, Edgar, Chicago, Ill.
Boswell, George, Clarksville, Tenn.
Boswell, Helen, Louisville, Ky.
Bowen, George Oscar, Tulsa, Okla.
Bowlsbey, Mrs. Blanche F., Baltimore, Md.
Bowman, Lorraine, Salt Lake City, Utah
Bowmar, Florence, Unionville, Conn.
Boyer, George F., Vermillion, S. Dak.
Boyle, Gratia, Wichita, Kans.
Bozearth, Elizabeth, Woodstown, N. J.
Brady, Stanley J., Provo, Utah
Brandenburg, Arthur, Elizabeth, N. J.
Brandon, J. Raymond, Little Rock, Ark.
Branigan, Duane A., Urbana, Ill.
Brant, Roger, Lordsburg, N. Mex.
Bratton, Edith M., Lewistown, Pa.
Bratton, Karl H., Durham, N. H.
Bray, Bruce, Albany, Ore.
Bray, Mabel E., Trenton, N. J.
Breach, William, Buffalo, N. Y.
Bredenberg, Ralph, Chowchilla, Calif.
Brennan, Maurice, Salem, Ore.
Bricker, Ainslee, Washington, D. C.
Briggs, Robert, Tallahassee, Fla.
Briggs, Willard, Scarsdale, N. Y.
Brigham, Forrest, Spokane, Wash.
Brimhall, Keith, Murtaugh, Idaho
Brinegar, Warren, Santa Fe, N. Mex.
Brite, George, Pawhuska, Okla.
Britton, Allen P., Ann Arbor, Mich.
Brooks, Edna, Beaumont, Texas
Brooks, Elizabeth, Newington, Conn.
Brooks, Harvey, Caldwell, Idaho
Brooks, Marjorie, Mansfield, Pa.
Broucek, Jack W., Collegeboro, Ga.
Brousseau, Mrs. Lillian, Washington, D. C.
Brown, Billy Joe, Belton, Texas
Brown, C. F., Eudora, Ark.
Brown, Clifford W., Morgantown, W. Va.
Brown, George, Lafayette, La.
Brown, Harold A., Weehawken, N. J.
Brown, Howard, Nashville, Tenn.
Brown, Louis, Washington, D. C.
Brown, ReMona, Waukesha, Wis.
Brown, Ruby White, East Point, Ga.
Brubeck, Howard, San Diego, Calif.

Bruggemann, Frederic, Baker, Mont.
Brumberg, Lewis M., Selbyville, Del.
Brush, Nell, Dallas, Texas
Bryan, Charles, Helena, Ala.
Bryan, Charles F., Nashville, Tenn.
Bryant, Laura, Ithaca, N. Y.
Bryant, Marshall, Portland, Maine
Brye, Joseph C., Corvallis, Ore.
Bryon, Arthur, Fresno, Calif.
Bryson, Roy G., Longview, Wash.
Buchanan, Gillian, Portales, N. Mex.
Buchanan, Mary, San Marcos, Texas
Bucher, Lester S., Richmond, Va.
Buchholz, Fay, Butte, Mont.
Buckborough, James A., Huntington Woods, Mich.
Buckhauser, Andrew W., Tucson, Ariz.
Budd, Vera, Washington, D. C.
Budleski, Frances, Yalesville, Conn.
Buerky, Bessie R., St. Louis, Mo.
Buggert, Robert, Wichita, Kans.
Buhaults, John F., Hobbs, N. Mex.
Bulber, F. G., Lake Charles, La.
Bunnell, John H., Milford, Del.
Buntley, H. H., Sioux City, Iowa
Burau, Gertrude, Harrisonburg, Va.
Burbank, Albert, Fairview, Mont.
Burch, Frank M., Basehor, Kans.
Burchuk, David, Silver Spring, Md.
Burg, Clarence, Oklahoma City, Okla.
Burges, Tom, Tucson, Ariz.
Burmeister, C. A., Evanston, Ill.
Burns, Claudeane, Chicago, Ill.
Burns, Rev. Martin J., Newark, N. J.
Burns, S. T., Madison, Wis.
Buskirk, Everette C., Williamsburg, Va.
Butchart, Maro, Kalispell, Mont.
Butler, Bernard J., Kelso, Wash.
Buttelman, C. V., Chicago, Ill.
Buzzell, Dale, Buffalo, Wyo.
Byler, Mrs. Leland, Jackson, Miss.

Cady, Loren, Bay City, Mich.
Cagle, Herbert, Eldorado, Ark.
Cahn, Meyer M., San Francisco, Calif.
Caldwell, Ivan C., Holdrege, Nebr.
Caldwell, Lee, Tooele, Utah
Callan, Edward, Wichita, Kans.
Cambern, Carroll G., Los Angeles, Calif.
Campbell, Dan, Brainerd, Minn.
Campbell, Esther, Edinboro, Pa.
Campbell, Gabriella, Pittsburg, Kans.
Campbell, W. Paul, Hershey, Pa.
Canavan, M. Elizabeth, Augusta, Maine
Caniff, Flo, Princeton, Ind.
Canine, Margaret, Crawfordsville, Ind.
Cannan, E. B., Conroe, Texas
Carey, Margaretta A., Carbondale, Ill.
Carey, Milburn, Enid, Okla.
Carl, Raymond A., Salem, Ore.
Carlson, Clifford, Havre, Mont.
Carlyon, Genevieve, Watsonville, Calif.
Carney, William, Utica, N. Y.
Carpenter, Flora, Kezer Falls, Maine
Carpenter, Kenneth, Osage, Iowa
Carpenter, Maureen, Aberdeen, S. Dak.
Carpenter, R. Lillian, Louisville, Ky.
Carr, Raymond N., Glen Ellyn. Ill.
Carrell, H. Franklin, Dover, Del.
Carson, Paul E., West Chester, Pa.
Carter, Cecil, Dover, N. H.
Carter, Elwyn F., Kalamazoo, Mich.
Carter, Lucille, Bartlesville, Okla.
Carter, Malcolm, Aberdeen, Miss.
Carter, Robert L., Greenville, N. C.
Carty, Virginia, Baltimore, Md.
Caruso, James V., Pittsburgh, Pa.
Caswell, Arnold, Minneapolis. Minn.
Catir, H. Frank, Pasadena, Calif.
Cawthon, Mildred G., Santa Fe, N. Mex.
Cayting, A. Stanley, Bangor, Maine
Chaffee, Carleton A., Vermillion, S. Dak.
Champlin, Doris, Essex, Conn.
Champlin, Helene, Bakersfield, Calif.
Chance, Varner M., Berea, Ohio
Chang, Wallace, Honolulu, Hawaii
Charlton, Harriet, Seattle, Wash.
Chartier, R. C., Albuquerque, N. Mex.
Chase, C. D., Oklahoma City, Okla.
Chatlas, Andrew J., Centre Hall, Pa.

Checketts, Wendell, Gooding, Idaho
Cheney, Gertrude, Oakland, Calif.
Cheyette, Irving, Syracuse, N. Y.
Chidester, L. W., Kingsville, Texas
Chiuminotto, Anthony, St. Paul, Minn.
Choate, Robert A., Boston, Mass.
Christ, Lorna, Chatham, N. J.
Christiansen, J. D., Payson, Utah
Christiansen, N. W., Logan, Utah
Christianson, A. Bert, Ellensburg, Wash.
Christman, Russell B., Harrisburg, Pa.
Christopher, George A., Port Washington, N. Y.
Christy, Van A., Santa Barbara, Calif.
Church, Norval L., Hastings-on-Hudson, N. Y.
Cisneros, Viola R., Santa Fe, N. Mex.
Civis, Mrs. Frances Jackman, Baltimore, Md.
Clair, Arnold V., Kingston, R. I.
Clark, Emily, Farmville, Va.
Clark, Frances Elliott, Salt Lake City, Utah
Clark, Mrs. L. E., Louisville, Miss.
Clark, Opal, Ft. Smith, Ark.
Clark, William B., Reno, Nev.
Clauser, Barbara, Eden, Idaho
Cleino, Edward, University, Ala.
Clem, Thomas R., Anderson, Ind.
Clement, Robert, Moorhead, Miss.
Clifford, Timothy, Salem, Mass.
Cline, Sarah Y., Cincinnati, Ohio
Clinesmith, Carl B., Fort Scott, Kans.
Clippenger, Glenn, Detroit, Mich.
Cobb, Janice, Ann Arbor, Mich.
Cockrell, Richard, East Lansing, Mich.
Coddington, E. C., Ipswich, S. Dak.
Coffey, Merle, Presque Isle, Maine
Coffman, Ashley, Conway, Ark.
Cole, James H., Missoula, Mont.
Cole, Starr, Wilmington, Del.
Collins, Keith, Sikeston, Mo.
Collins, Mahlin, Corning, Iowa
Collins, Robert, Willamina, Ore.
Collins, T. C., Miami, Fla.
Collins, Wilbur L., Victoria, Texas
Collyer, Esther Ritz, Fort Wayne, Ind.
Colombo, Franco, New York, N. Y.
Comstock, W. B. Hillard, Philadelphia, Pa.
Connelly, Brother John, Philadelphia, Pa.
Constable, Marion E., Bergenfield, N. J.
Contino, Joseph, Amherst, Mass.
Cook, James, Rochester, N. H.
Cook, Lawrence, Adel, Iowa
Cook, Ronald W., Fresno, Calif.
Coolidge, Arlan R., Providence, R. I.
Coombs, Cecile C., East St. Louis, Ill.
Cooney, Bryan N., Freeport, Texas
Cooper, Irvin, Tallahassee, Fla.
Coplin, Walter L., Morgantown, W. Va.
Corley, Robert, Westbrook, Maine
Cornelius, Merl, Oklahoma City, Okla.
Cory, Philip B., Grand Forks, N. Dak.
Cotey, Alexander, Lewiston, Maine
Cotton, Edith M., Ruston, La.
Coulter, Charles, Phoenix, Ariz.
Covington, Weldon, Austin, Texas
Cowling, Elizabeth, Greensboro, N. C.
Cox, Mary Alice, Lafayette, La.
Crabb, Rebecca V., Victoria, Texas
Cramer, Carl L., Albuquerque, N. Mex.
Cramer, William, Las Cruces, N. Mex.
Cravener, Mrs. Helen G., Grant Park, Ill.
Cravens, Ray, Ft. Smith, Ark.
Crawford, Loren, Garden City, Kans.
Crawford, Marguerite, Croswell, Mich.
Crawford, Wilford, Midland, Mich.
Creekmore, Ida, Tulsa, Okla.
Creitz, Dale P., Iola, Kans.
Crews, Katherine, Maryville, Tenn.
Critchley, Mrs. Darline, Ft. Wayne, Ind.
Crockett, Frank, University, Miss.
Crook, Elizabeth, Newark, Del.
Crooks, Clements B., Portales, N. Mex.
Cross, Florence, Newark, N. J.
Cross, Loren, Las Vegas, Nev.
Cross, Mary, Silver Spring, Md.
Crumb, Frederick W., Potsdam, N. Y.
Cunning, Charles, Ponca City, Okla.
Cunningham, Robert, Eugene, Ore.
Curnutt, Leah, Greencastle, Ind.
Curry, Pat, Snowflake, Ariz.
Curtis, Gertrude, Yakima, Wash.
Curtis, Louis Woodson, Hollywood, Calif.

Cushing, Deveda, Littleton, N. H.
Cuthbert, Kenneth W., Greenville, N. C.
Cutts, Charles R., Billings, Mont.

Dabczynski, Mrs. Henry, Towaco, N. J.
Dagort, Vincent A., Los Angeles, Calif.
Daigle, Brad, Lake Charles, La.
Dalby, Phil, Logan, Utah
D'Andrea, Frank L., Bellingham, Wash.
Danfelser, Byrdis, Albuquerque, N. Mex.
Daniel, Gerald, Long Beach, Calif.
Daniels, LeRoy Willard, Milwaukee, Wis.
Darnes, Robert, Garden City, Kans.
Davidson, R. C., Plainview, Texas
Davies, Ruth Davis, Scranton, Pa.
*Davis, Ennis, New York, N. Y. (1953)
Davis, F. Edna, Philadelphia, Pa.
Davis, Jesse, Naugatuck, Conn.
Davis, Joseph L., New Hartford, N. Y.
Davis, Lytton S., Omaha, Nebr.
Day, Carolyn, Bay Minette, Ala.
Dean, Bill, Haskell, Texas
Deen, Frances, Miami, Fla.
Dellinger, Hal D., Joliet, Ill.
Dengler, Clyde R., Upper Darby, Pa.
Dennis, Charles M., San Francisco, Calif.
Dennis, Perry, Greenwood, Miss.
Dennis, Roger, Oshkosh, Wis.
Dennis, William, Platteville, Wis.
Denton, Ben, Chandler, Ariz.
Denzl, Arlys, St. Paul, Minn.
de Stwolinski, Gail, Norman, Okla.
deVermond, Mary F., Silver Spring, Md.
DeVillafranca, Mrs. Ruth, Danbury, Conn.
Dexter, Scott, Huron, S. Dak.
Dick, Corrine V., Coffeyville, Kans.
Dickerson, Chester, Middleburg, N. Y.
Dickinson, Mrs. Marjorie, Las Vegas, Nev.
Dieffenbach, Ruth, New London, Conn.
Diers, Francis, Fredonia, N. Y.
Dill, Helen C., Beverly Hills, Calif.
Dillard, James A., Winston-Salem, N. C.
Dilliard, John, Carrollton, Ga.
Dillon, Robert, Bethany, Okla.
Dilsner, Laurence, Long Branch, N. J.
Dinehart, Jane K., Elkhart, Ind.
Disbrow, Loren, Rockford, Mich.
Disler, Alma, Washington, D. C.
Ditsler, Gladys, Miami, Fla.
DiVilbiss, Raymond, Winterset, Iowa
Doerhoff, Ray, St. Elizabeth, Mo.
Doll, G. Lewis, San Antonio, Texas
Dolliver, Mark, Jr., Youngstown, Ohio
Donaldson, Robert, Centerville, Iowa
Doolittle, Theodosia, Cincinnati, Ohio
Dorward, Marion, Machias, Maine
Doty, E. W., Austin, Texas
Doty, Frances, Washington, D. C.
Doverspike, George, Antigo, Wis.
Downey, Marvin, Salina, Kans.
Dresskell, Miles, Tempe, Ariz.
Dressler, Robert E., Jamestown, N. Dak.
Dries, Eleanor M., Ellicott City, Md.
Driscoll, Martina McDonald, Boston, Mass.
Drumwright, Pearl, Baton Rouge, La.
DuBois, Charlotte, Austin, Texas
duBois, E., Williamsburg, Ky.
Duerksen, Walter, Wichita, Kans.
Duffield, Paul, Philadelphia, Pa.
Duguid, Helen, Hartford, Conn.
Dulfer, Ary, Brunswick, Maine
Dulfer, Rebecca, Brunswick, Maine
Duncan, Esther, Springfield, Ill.
Dungan, Earl W., Greeley, Colo.
Dunham, Franklin, Washington, D. C.
Dunlop, James W., State College, Pa.
Durham, Lowell, Salt Lake City, Utah
Duvall, Clyde Jr., Norfolk, Va.
Dvorak, Leo J., Charleston, Ill.
Dvorak, Raymond, Madison, Wis.
Dyer, Mrs. Frances, Reno, Nev.

Eagler, Granville Kean, Salisbury, Md.
Earhart, Will, Portland, Ore.
Earl, Boyd, Paul, Idaho
Eberly, Lawrence, Terre Haute, Ind.
Echols, L. W., Elkhart, Ind.
Edes, Nancy, Minneapolis, Minn.

Edgar, Alvin R., Ames, Iowa
Edgeley, Farris, Pocatello, Idaho
Edlund, Gordon, Aberdeen, Wash.
Edmundson, Warren, Fredonia, Kans.
Edwards, William, Durant, Okla.
Ehlert, J. K., Indianapolis, Ind.
Eitel, Butler, Edina, Minn.
Ela, Katherine, North Anson, Maine
Eldred, Reginald H., Center Line, Mich.
Ellefson, Floyd T., Springfield, Ore.
Elliott, Harrison W., Inman, S. C.
Elliott, Virginia Ward, McMinnville, Ore.
Ellis, Merrill, Joplin, Mo.
Ellison, Charlotte, Beresford, S. Dak.
Elwell, John S., Ypsilanti, Mich.
Engwicht, Curt, Chapman, Kans.
Enlow, Cece, Oakland, Calif.
Enrico, Margaret Souders, Red Lodge, Mont.
Enright, Josephine, Pittsfield, Mass.
Ensinger, Harold, Flint, Mich.
Epperley, Glenn, Stillwater, Okla.
Epperson, Emery, Salt Lake City, Utah
Epting, Earluth, Atlanta, Ga.
Erdman, Harvard, Wautoma, Wis.
Erickson, Anthony, Milwaukee, Wis.
Ernst, Karl D., San Jose, Calif.
Ersfeld, Ernest J., Nutley, N. J.
Essers, Hendrik, Washington, D. C.
Estes, Joseph E., Lewistown, Mont.
Euren, William, Fargo, N. Dak.
Evans, Betty, Muskogee, Okla.
Evans, George, Meridian, Miss.
Evans, Polly Smith, Atlanta, Ga.
Evans, T. R., Lakewood, Ohio
Evanson, Jacob, Pittsburgh, Pa.
Evenson, Pattee, San Diego, Calif.
Everett, Mrs. W. W., Sartartia, Miss.
Everman, Katherine, Anderson, Ind.
Evingson, Ethel, Fargo, N. Dak.
Exum, Glenn, Kellogg, Idaho

Fackert, Dorothy M., Jersey City, N. J.
Fandrich, Walter, Madison, Wis.
Farley, Belmont, Washington, D. C.
Farnum, Stephen E., Riverside, R. I.
Feese, Maurice, Hampton, Iowa
Fehr, Carl, Williamsburg, Va.
Feighner, Bruce, Royal Oak, Mich.
Feist, Leonard, New York, N. Y.
Fennell, Frederick, Rochester, N. Y.
Fennema, Marvin R., Newark, Del.
Fenton, Esther, Newark, Del.
Fenton, Winifred G., Grosse Pointe, Mich.
Ferrell, Ernestine, Vicksburg, Miss.
Field, Elizabeth Staton, Willimantic, Conn.
Fielder, Robert E., Abilene, Texas
Finch, Dallas W., Grandview, Wash.
Fink, Donald D., Grand Rapids, Mich.
Finley, Mary Lou, Okmulgee, Okla.
Fischer, Alberta, New London, N. H.
Fishburn, Hummel, State College, Pa.
Fisher, Paul J., Martinsburg, Pa.
Fisher, William R., Lowell, Mass.
Fick, R. G., Decatur, Miss.
Fite, Elwin, Tahlequah, Okla.
Fitzgerald, Lynn, Phoenix, Ariz.
Fitzpatrick, Angela DeMino, Waterford, N. Y.
Flagg, Marion, Dallas, Texas
Flanagan, Florence, Milwaukee, Wis.
Fleming, Jessie L., Salisbury, Md.
Flye, Richard, San Diego, Calif.
Folland, Helen, Salt Lake City, Utah
Foltz, David, Lincoln, Nebr.
Forbes, A. Irving, Kittery Point, Maine
Forbes, Duane, Jerome, Idaho
Forbes, Vernon, Scottsbluff, Nebr.
Forney, Martha, Moscow, Idaho
Forsling, Mildred, Yakima, Wash.
Forster, Frances A., Inglewood, Calif.
Fortenberry, John, Jonesboro, Ark.
Foss, Ardeen, Sioux Falls, S. Dak.
Fosso, Paul, Spokane, Wash.
Foster, Alton, Great Bend, Kans.
Foster, Estill, Bishop, Texas
Foster, Jess, Portland, Ore.
Foster, Marion, Exeter, N. H.
Foster, Viola, Wethersfield, Conn.
Foth, Henry, Oklahoma City, Okla.
Foust, Kenneth E., Fairbury, Nebr.

Fowler, Edwina, Pittsburg, Kans.
Fowler, Katharine, Washington, D. C.
Fox, Fordyce, Mayville, N. Y.
Fox, Frederick, New York, N. Y.
Fox, Mark, Washington, D. C.
Foy, Clarence A., Bryn Mawr, Pa.
Fraleigh, Alton, Norwalk, Conn.
Frank, Laura Mae, Joplin, Mo.
Franseen, Maybelle, Kaukauna, Wis.
Fransham, Robert W., Bozeman, Mont.
Franz, Mrs. Margaret, Madison, Wis.
Frazer, Dorothy, Tucson, Ariz.
Fredrickson, Darwin, Powell, Wyo.
Freeburg, Roy E., San Francisco, Calif.
Freeman, Elvin L., Pulaski, N. Y.
French, Richard F., New York, N. Y.
Frieswyck, Sieboldt, Newark, N. J.
Frisch, Fay Templeton, New Rochelle, N. Y.
Fry, James, Bedford, Ohio
Frye, Herbert, Ypsilanti, Mich.
Fuller, Helen, Takoma Park, Md.
Fuller, W. S., Eldorado, Ark.
Fultz, A. Flagler, Boston, Mass.
Funchess, Gladys, Baton Rouge, La.
Funchess, Lloyd V., Baton Rouge, La.
Funk, Floyd, Nashville, Tenn.

Gable, Paul D., Silver Spring, Md.
Gaiser, Norma, Waterloo, Iowa
Gardner, Don, New York, N. Y.
Garnett, Maude, Denton, Texas
Garrison, Cecil, Mesilla Park, N. Mex.
Garster, Charles H., Leipsic, Ohio
Garton, Daisy H., Bloomington, Ind.
Gary, Charles L., Clarksville, Tenn.
Gaston, E. Thayer, Lawrence, Kans.
Gatlin, F. Nathaniel, Petersburg, Va.
Gaughf, Turner, Macon, Ga.
Gause, Wallace, Clearwater, Fla.
Gay, Donald, Auburn, Maine
Gee, Edith White, Cleveland Heights, Ohio
Gee, Russell, Cleveland Heights, Ohio
Gehrkens, Karl W., Elk Rapids, Mich.
George, C. Richard, Wilmington, Del.
George, Harold E., Merriam, Kans.
Georigian, Nector, Pawtucket, R. I.
Geringer, Ted, Lamar, Colo.
Gerke, Madge Cathcart, Indianapolis, Ind.
Gerkowski, Raymond D., Flint, Mich.
Gerlach, Marian, Northbrook, Ill.
Gerren, Nicholas L., Houston, Texas
Gibbons, Hugh F., St. Paul, Minn.
Gibbs, Polly, Baton Rouge, La.
Gibson, Marjorie, Shreveport, La.
Gidmark, Laurence A., Moorhead, Minn.
Gilbert, Arline, Rutherford, N. J.
Gilday, Edward, Framingham, Mass.
Gildersleeve, Glenn, Harrisonburg, Va.
Giles, Ruth, Laurel, Miss.
Gill, Mary Ellen, Newberg, Ore.
Gillam, Russell C., Lock Haven, Pa.
Gillespie, Mary E., Annville, Pa.
Gillette, Elizabeth, Orange, N. J.
Gilliland, Esther Goetz, Chicago, Ill.
Gillman, Ralph, Akron, Ohio
Gilson, Melvin, Newberg, Ore.
Glarum, Stanley, Portland, Ore.
Glass, Phyllis W., New Brunswick, N. J.
Glenn, Mabelle, Kansas City, Mo.
Glenn, Neal, Athens, Ohio
Godfrey, James H., Pulaski, Va.
Goerk, Jettie D., New York, N. Y.
Goff, Forrest, Denver, Colo.
Goodman, Harold A., Flagstaff, Ariz.
Goodsell, Evelyn, Cheney, Wash.
Goodsell, Slocum, Albuquerque, N. Mex.
Goranson, R. F., Pocatello, Idaho
Gordon, Edgar B., Madison, Wis.
Gordon, Philip, Orange, N. J.
Gordon, Roderick D., Denton, Texas
Gordown, Agnes, Phillipsburg, N. J.
Gorton, Thomas, Lawrence, Kans.
Gove, Veronica Davis, Deland, Fla.
Gowdy, William L., Elkhart, Ind.
Gracie, Jack, Anthony, N. Mex.
Graffam, Clinton W., Portland, Maine
Graham, Ben G., Richmond, Ind.
Graham, Marion B., Bethlehem, Pa.
Graichen, Fred H., Los Angeles, Calif.

Grammer, Lois, Sioux City, Iowa
Grange, Hollis, Kaysville, Utah
Grasso, Benjamin V., New York, N. Y.
Graves, Ruth, Denver, Colo.
Gray, George, Stamford, Conn.
Gray, J. Justin, Missoula, Mont.
Grayson, Norman, Hackettstown, N. J.
Green, John E., Iowa City, Iowa
Green, Merwyn A., Mayville, N. Dak.
Green, Myron B., San Diego, Calif.
Green, Ray, New York, N. Y.
Green, Sherman, Norfolk, Va.
Green, Willard E., W. Hartford, Conn.
Greene, Maurice M., West Hartford, Conn.
Greer, Charles W., New York, N. Y.
Gregor, Boyd, Mandan, N. Dak.
Gregory, Joseph, Arlington, Vt.
Gregory, Ronald D., Salt Lake City, Utah
Greim, Helen, Morehead, Ky.
Griest, R. Byron, Massillon, Ohio
Griffey, Robert M., Roanoke, Va.
Griffin, Sammy A., Shreveport, La.
Griffith, Charles E., New York, N. Y.
Grill, K. R. N., Wausau, Wis.
Grimler, Janet M., Westfield, N. J.
Grimm, Walter, Winona, Minn.
Groesbeck, Lue S., Salt Lake City, Utah
Groff, Frank H., West Hartford, Conn.
Grove, Eugene, Mt. Pleasant, Mich.
Guenther, L. W., Midland, Mich.
Gulson, J. Arthur, Trent, S. Dak.
Gunderson, Hugh, Bowling Green, Ky.

Haan, Trena, Grand Rapids, Mich.
Hackett, Mabel T., Long Island City, N. Y.
Hackney, C. R., Huntsville, Texas
Hackney, Lois, Huntley Project, Mont.
Hagan, N. Taylor, Nashville, Tenn.
Hahn, Lawrence M., Minot, N. Dak.
Haines, Clark J., Dayton, Ohio
Haines, Maude, Portland, Maine
Haldiman, Geraldine, Eldon, Mo.
Hales, Bernell, Salt Lake City, Utah
Hall, Helen, Seattle, Wash.
Hallgrimson, Benedict T., Cheney, Wash.
Halliday, John, Provo, Utah
Halliday, Nina, Salt Lake City, Utah
Halme, Viljo, West Allis, Wis.
Halvorson, Henry M., Boston, Mass.
Hamaker, Harold W., Mitchell, S. Dak.
Hamilton, Edward H., Knoxville, Tenn.
Hamilton, Gene, Aztec, N. Mex.
Hammack, S. Edith, Albert Lea, Minn.
Hammond, Chester, Gardiner, Maine
Hammond, Francis, Shaker Heights, Ohio
Hammond, Vernon, Philadelphia, Pa.
Hamper, H. E., Salmon, Idaho
Hand, Bessie, Louisville, Ky.
Hannaford, Harry, Summit, N. J.
Hannah, W. H., Vancouver, Wash.
Hannen, Helen, Cleveland, Ohio
Hannon, Alleta, Washington, D. C.
Hanson, Curtis, Brainerd, Minn.
Hanson, Gene, Scottsdale, Ariz.
Hanson, Howard, Rochester, N. Y.
Harbert, Wilhelmina, Stockton, Calif.
Harding, Austin A., Urbana, Ill.
Harding, John Y., Hot Springs, Ark.
Hardt, Victor, Menomonie, Wis.
Harley, Alexander M., Park Ridge, Ill.
Harmon, Homer, Kingfisher, Okla.
Harrell, Arthur G., Wichita, Kans.
Harriman, J. Kimball, Greensboro, N. C.
Harrington, Dean L., Hornell, N. Y.
Harrington, Ross D., Fortuna, Calif.
Harris, Arthur, Monticello, Ark.
Harris, Ernest E., New York, N. Y.
Harris, Richard L., Grove City, Ohio
Harrison, Mary, Eugene, Ore.
Harrison, Russell, Eugene, Ore.
Harstad, Duff, Bozeman, Mont.
Hart, Floyd T., Dover, Del.
Hartley, C. A., Magnolia, Ark.
Hartman, Ruth, Manhattan, Kans.
Hartse, Ralph, Miles City, Mont.
Hartsell, O. M., Helena, Mont.
Hartshorn, Alma, Los Angeles, Calif.
Hartshorn, William C., Los Angeles, Calif.
Hartwig, A. L., Havre, Mont.

Haruda, Ferd, Emmett, Idaho
Harvey, Abbie, Westbrook, Maine
Harvey, Dorothy, Silver Creek, N. Y.
Haseltine, Edna, Richmond, Mo.
Haskell, Duane H., State College, Ark.
Haslanger, Jane, Baraboo, Wis.
Hatch, Harmon R., Springville, Utah
Hatchett, Hilliary R., Richmond, Va.
Hatchett, W. Edward, San Benito, Texas
Hathaway, Clayton C., Fort Dodge, Iowa
Haupt, David D. M., Upper Darby, Pa.
Hauser, Arthur A., Bryn Mawr, Pa.
Hawkins, Robert, Gunnison, Colo.
Hawkins, Wendell F., South Glastonbury, Conn.
Hawkinson, Janice Bryan, Los Angeles, Calif.
Hay, Millicent Garland, Butler, Pa.
Hayes, Don R., Littlefield, Texas
Hayes, Dorothy, Reuben, Idaho
Hayes, Mary F., Springfield, Mass.
Haynes, Barbara Lee, McGill, Nev.
Haynie, William S., Jackson, Miss.
Hazelman, Herbert, Greensboro, N. C.
Healy, Geraldine Smith, Los Angeles, Calif.
Heaton, Thelma J., Great Falls, Mont.
Heaton, Wallace, Philadelphia, Pa.
Heck, Mathilda, St. Paul, Minn.
Heck, William, Winchester, N. H.
Heel, Helen, South Windham, Maine
Heid, Della Ericson, Dickinson, N. Dak.
Helms, Julian W., Charlotte, N. C.
Helstrom, Einar, Portsmouth, Ohio
Heltman, Rollie V., Los Alamos, N. Mex.
Heltne, Paul O., Austin, Minn.
Hemmle, Gene L., Lubbock, Texas
Henderson, Eva, Washington, D. C.
Henderson, J. Chandler, Reedley, Calif.
Hendricks, Everett, Kansas City, Mo.
Hennessey, Grace L., Reno, Nev.
Henson, Ethel M., Seattle, Wash.
Herbst, William T., Yakima, Wash.
Hermann, Edward J., Shreveport, La.
Hertz, Erwin, St. Cloud, Minn.
Hertz, Wayne S., Ellensburg, Wash.
Hesch, C. J., Richmond, Va.
Heskin, Orland, Bismarck, N. Dak.
Hess, Ralph, Phoenix, Ariz.
Hessler, Katherine, Hibbing, Minn.
Heth, Edward L., Hampton, Va.
Hickman, Felton, Reno, Nev.
Hickok, Dorothy Jane, Oswego, N. Y.
Hicks, George Raymond, Harrisonburg, Va.
Hilgendorff, John G., Provo, Utah
Hill, Arthur D., Jr., Elkhart, Ind.
Hill, Double E., Nampa, Idaho
Hill, Frank W., Cedar Falls, Iowa
Hilton, Winston, Baton Rouge, La.
Hinchcliff, Lester, Ogden, Utah
Hinshaw, Jay, Chicago, Ill.
Hintz, Elmer M., Hartford, Conn.
Hipwell, Marie, Claymont, Del.
Hjelmervik, Kenneth, Baltimore, Md.
Hodges, Wendell, Anthony, Kans.
Hodson, E. L., Chicago, Ill.
Hoersch, Isabelle H., Detroit, Mich.
Hoffman, Daniel, Stillwater, Okla.
Hoffman, Frances, Dickinson, N. Dak.
Hoffman, Lilburne, Valley Center, Kans.
Hoffman, Mark, Oxford, Miss.
Hoffman, Miriam, Hagerstown, Md.
Hoffmann, Arnold E., Raleigh, N. C.
Hogan, Mai, Waverly, Iowa
Hoggard, Lara, Hemet, Calif.
Holbrook, Genevieve Hargiss, Missoula, Mont.
Hollenshead, Margaret, Chanute, Kans.
Holloway, Birdie, Greensboro, N. C.
Holmbeck, Alice, Coos Bay, Ore.
Holmberg, Harry E., Chadron, Nebr.
Holmes, Markwood, Pittsburg, Kans.
Holmgren, Hazel, Valley City, N. Dak.
Holsinger, Clyde W., North Manchester, Ind.
Hood, Jane, Orlando, Fla.
Hood, Marguerite V., Ann Arbor, Mich.
Hooker, Ione, Hanford, Calif.
Hoover, Harold, Sioux Falls, S. Dak.
Hoover, John G., Livingston, Ala.
Hoppe, William A., Cleveland, Miss.
Hornig, Roger O., Wisconsin Rapids, Wis.
Hosmer, Helen, Potsdam, N. Y.
Housewright, Wiley L., Tallahassee, Fla.
Houts, Jack, Athens, Tenn.

Hovey, Howard, Riverhead, N. Y.
Hovey, Nilo W., Indianapolis, Ind.
Howard, John E., Grand Forks, N. Dak.
Howden, Bruce, Jr., Northfield, Minn.
Howe, Helen, Chicago, Ill.
Howe, Walter, Bethesda, Md.
Howerton, George, Evanston, Ill.
Hoyt, Hatcher, Little Rock, Ark.
Huckba, Louise, Portland, Ore.
Huckriede, Irma, Louisville, Ky.
Huffaker, Analee, Chattanooga, Tenn.
Huffines, Katharine, Greensboro, N. C.
Hughes, Mrs. R. W., Henryetta, Okla.
Hugoboom, R. Wayne, Huntington, W. Va.
Huls, Helen, St. Cloud, Minn.
Hulshizer, Stanford, Des Moines, Iowa
Hulsman, Allen F., Dayton, Ohio
Humphreys, Alfred W., Knoxville, Tenn.
Humphreys, Arthur F., Tarkio, Mo.
Humphreys, Hilda, Detroit, Mich.
Humpstone, Carol, Grand Forks, N. Dak.
Hunkins, Eusebia, Athens, Ohio
Hunn, Hiram, Des Moines, Iowa
Hunt, C. B., Nashville, Tenn.
Hunter, Edna Martz, Raleigh, N. C.
Hunter, Mary M., Baltimore, Md.
Hurd, Lyman, Burlington, Vt.
Hurst, H. Deverl, Salt Lake City, Utah
Hurt, William J., Clarksville, Tenn.
Hutcherson, Rita J., Greeley, Colo.
Hutchins, John, Cedar Rapids, Iowa
Hutchinson, Florence, Monmouth, Ore.
Hyde, Bess, Ypsilanti, Mich.

Ihrke, Walter R., Storrs, Conn.
Imig, Warner, Boulder, Colo.
Ingalls, K. Elizabeth, Jersey City, N. J.
Ingelfield, Paul D., Meadville, Pa.
Ivory, Paul S., Minneapolis, Minn.

Jackson, Donald, Ashland, Wis.
Jackson, Franklin, Washington, D. C.
Jackson, Katherine, New York, N. Y.
Jackson, Sumner, Beloit, Wis.
Jacobi, Roger E., Ann Arbor, Mich.
Jacobs, Carl, State College, N. Mex.
Jacobs, Marion L., Grand Junction, Colo.
Jadinak, Nicholas, River Falls, Wis.
Jakey, Howard R., Seattle, Wash.
Jansky, Nelson M., Boston, Mass.
Jaquish, John H., Atlantic City, N. J.
Jarvis, Maxwell, Passaic, N. J.
Jeans, Harold, Portland, Ore.
Jenkins, Maggie, Milledgeville, Ga.
Jensen, Lloyd S., Sterling, Colo.
Jepson, J. Ellwood, Salt Lake City, Utah
Jerles, Elizabeth, Wickenburg, Ariz.
John, Robert W., Durham, N. C.
Johnson, Alfred H., Washington, D. C.
Johnson, Arthur, Oklahoma City, Okla.
Johnson, Ben S., Lexington, Mo.
Johnson, Clair W., Ogden, Utah
Johnson, Duane L., Rapid City, S. Dak.
Johnson, J. Wayne, Brigham City, Utah
Johnson, Lorraine, Boise, Idaho
Johnson, M. O., Independence, Mo.
Johnson, Marguerite A., Fairhaven, Mass.
Johnson, Merry Lynn, Rochester, Mich.
Johnson, Orland, Harlingen, Texas
Johnson, Orville, Independence, Mo.
Johnson, Robert, Fairfield, Mont.
Johnson, Robert, Waupun, Wis.
Johnson, Rolf C., Laurel, Mont.
Johnson, Violet, Elizabeth, N. J.
Johnston, Norman, Duluth, Minn.
Joio, Norman Della, Westport, Conn.
Jonas, Rodney, Brunswick, Ga.
Jones, Archie N., Austin, Texas
Jones, Dan K., Sisseton, S. Dak.
Jones, Dorothy C., Amherst, Ohio
Jones, Edna Marie, Abilene, Texas
Jones, Nathen, Des Moines, Iowa
Jones, Oscar, Findlay, Ohio
Jones, Sara Ellen, Manitowoc, Wis.
Jones, William, Manitowoc, Wis.
Jordalen, Marion, Sacramento, Calif.
Jordan, William H., Sumter, S. C.
Jorgensen, Elin, Lawrence, Kans.

Jorgensen, Gene, Tremonton, Utah
Jorgensen, Hans, Plymouth, N. H.
Joy, Margaret, Wichita, Kans.
Judkins, Joseph, Milford, Ind.
Jurgenson, James, Wharton, Texas
Just, Amanda, Pullman, Wash.

Kaplan, David, Worcester, Mass.
Karel, Leon, Kirksville, Mo.
Kaulili, Alvina, Honolulu, Hawaii
Kautzman, Daniel, Summit, N. J.
Keegan, Arthur J., Jersey City, N. J.
Keeney, Melvin, Fairview, Okla.
Kehn, Edward A., Arvada, Colo.
Keil, Carrie Drummond, Helena, Mont.
Keller, Anna M., Clarion, Pa.
Keller, Dorothy Young, Algonquin, Ill.
Keller, Edith M., Columbus, Ohio
Keller, Esther, Cleveland, Ohio
Keller, Kenneth, Columbus, Ohio
Keller, Marjorie, Dallas, Texas
Kelley, Dorothy G., Bloomington, Ind.
Kemble, Mrs. Mary A., College Park, Md.
Kemmerer, Mildred, Allentown, Pa.
Kendall, Raymond, Los Angeles, Calif.
Kendel, John C., Chicago, Ill.
Keniston, Dorothy, Portsmouth, N. H.
Kennedy, Arthur, Boston, Mass.
Kennedy, V. J., Austin, Texas
Kent, Earle L., Elkhart, Ind.
Kent, Richard, Fitchburg, Mass.
Keyworth, R. W., Chicago, Ill.
Kilduff, Helen, New Britain, Conn.
Kincaid, James H., Hobbs, N. Mex.
Kincheloe, Kenneth V., Peoria, Ill.
King, Harry, Fredonia, N. Y.
King, J. R., Newark, Del.
King, Wilson, Hampton, Va.
Kinscella, Hazel Gertrude, Seattle, Wash.
Kintzer, Frederick C., Centralia, Wash.
Kircher, Winfield, Jerome, Idaho
Kissel, Erle, Sparks, Nev.
Kizer, George, Pauls Valley, Okla.
Klaiman, Frieda, Newark, N. J.
Klammer, E. W., St. Louis, Mo.
Kleckner, Garth, Lock Haven, Pa.
Klein, Arthur F., Nashville, Tenn.
Klein, M. William, New York, N. Y.
Klepinger, Glenn, Detroit, Mich.
Klier, Josephine, Lake Arthur, N. Mex.
Knaak, Gordon, Bismarck, N. Dak.
Knepper, Noah A., Topeka, Kans.
Knudson, Emma R., Normal, Ill.
Knuth, William E., San Francisco, Calif.
Koch, Frances Ernestine, Mishawaka, Ind.
Kohlenstein, Elsie, Ferndale, Mich.
Koski, George, Birmingham, Ala.
Kozinski, Amelie, Wilmington, Del.
Kozinski, David B., Wilmington, Del.
Kramer, A. Walter, New York, N. Y.
Krasser, Paul, University City, Mo.
Kratt, Theodore, Eugene, Ore.
Kraushaar, Otto, Miami, Fla.
Krauss, John, Flemington, N. J.
Krenz, Edward, Puyallup, Wash.
Kriete, Alma, Louisville, Ky.
Krone, Max T., Los Angeles, Calif.
Krueger, Arnold C., Owatonna, Minn.
Krumweide, Luroy C., Saltville, Va.
Kruth, Edwin C., San Francisco, Calif.
Kuhn, Wolfgang, Urbana, Ill.
Kushious, David, Portsmouth, N. H.
Kyme, George H., Oakland, Calif.

Labunski, Wiktor, Kansas City, Mo.
Lackey, Mary McFie, Santa Fe, N. Mex.
LaGassey, Homer C., Detroit, Mich.
Lagen, Peggy, Rochester, N. Y.
Lake, Walter, Fort Dodge, Iowa
LaMaster, Robert, Fullerton, Calif.
Lancaster, A. J., Portsmouth, Va.
Landon, Joseph W., San Bernardino, Calif.
Laney, Maurice, Louisville, Ky.
Lang, Phillip J., Freeport, N. Y.
Langenus, Alan G., New York, N. Y.
Langley, J. Edward, Daytona Beach, Fla.
Lanning, Charles, Danbury, Conn.
Lape, A. F., Little Rock, Ark.

Lapham, G. Frank, Syracuse, N. Y.
LaPine, Virginia McManus, Albuquerque, N. Mex.
Larsen, A. B., Cedar City, Utah
Larson, Arnold, Mandan, N. Dak.
Larson, Clarion, Bismarck, N. Dak.
Larson, William S., Rochester, N. Y.
Lawler, Vanett, Washington, D. C.
Lawless, Clarence, Sand Springs, Okla.
Lawrence, Ruth, Fargo, N. Dak.
Lawrence, Thomas R., Towson, Md.
Lawson, Warner W., Washington, D. C.
Laxson, C. Robert, Chico, Calif.
Leavengood, Luther, Manhattan, Kans.
Ledgerwood, Dora Jane, Hot Springs, Ark.
Ledue, William, Weirsdale, Fla.
Lee, Ardith, St. Louis Park, Minn.
Lee, Hans, Zeeland, N. Dak.
Lee, Ira D., Eugene, Ore.
Lee, Jane F., Canton, Ohio
Lee, Mary C., Silver Spring, Md.
Leeder, Joseph A., Columbus, Ohio
Lee Master, Vernon J., Salt Lake City, Utah
LeFevre, Jane, Abilene, Texas
Lehman, Charles F., Ft. Worth, Texas
Leist, Fred, Oshkosh, Wis.
Lekvold, A. D., Oxford, Ohio
Lemert, Harry, Monroe, La.
Lenox, Robert, Stratford, Conn.
Lenz, Doris, Detroit, Mich.
Leonhard, Charles, Urbana, Ill.
Leppert, Otto, Chicago, Ill.
Lewis, Aden, Cumberland, Md.
Lewis, George, Helena, Mont.
Lewis, John, Stockton, Calif.
Lewis, Lew J., High Point, N. C.
Lewis, Mary Louise, Elkins, W. Va.
Lidral, Frank W., Warrensburg, Mo.
Lidstrom, H. L., Rochester, Minn.
Light, Raymond E., Whitewater, Wis.
Lindgren, Frank, Reedley, Calif.
Lindsay, Mae L., Milton, Mass.
Linger, Robert, Martinsburg, W. Va.
Linger, Roderick B., Martinsburg, W. Va.
Lingo, J. Collins, Youngstown, Ohio
Linton, Stanley, Oshkosh, Wis.
Lobbato, Joseph F., Corvallis, Ore.
Lobben, Gertie A., North Fargo, N. Dak.
Lockard, Gladys, Washington, D. C.
Locke, Russell F., Brunswick, Maine
Locklear, Anson, Columbus, Ga.
Lockwood, Richard, Austin, Minn.
Lodgen, Dorothy, Hartford, Conn.
Loney, Andrew, Jr., Klamath Falls, Ore.
Long, A. H., Ponca City, Okla.
Long, Grayce E., Hartford, Conn.
Long, Newell H., Bloomington, Ind.
Long, William J., Woodville, Ohio
Lopatin, Arnold M., Grand Rapids, Mich.
Lorenz, Ellen Jane, Dayton, Ohio
Lotspeich, S. K., Madison, S. Dak.
Loudis, Anthony J., Newark, Del.
Low, George H., Rutland, Vt.
Low, Henrietta G. Baker, Baltimore, Md.
Lowe, Frederick C., Jr., Sunbury, Pa.
Loy, Arthur E., Albuquerque, N. Mex.
Lucke, Katheryn, Baltimore, Md.
Luckenbill, Donald, Oyster Bay, L. I., N. Y.
Lundkvist, Lyllis D., Fresno, Calif.
Lunsford, Floyd, Anacortes, Wash.
Lutton, Charles A., Chicago, Ill.
Lyman, Roy, Hettinger, N. Dak.
Lyon, Ernest E., Louisville, Ky.

MacDonald, John, Riverhead, N. Y.
Mackenzie, Mrs. Clemewell, Seattle, Wash.
Macklin, Hall, Moscow, Idaho
Maddox, Robert L., Odessa, Texas
Maddy, Joseph E., Ann Arbor, Mich.
Madison, Thurber H., Bloomington, Ind.
Madsen, Farrell D., Provo, Utah
Magnell, Elmer P., Tallahassee, Fla.
Maier, Harvey E., Yakima, Wash.
Malin, Donald F., Boston, Mass.
Malone, Marjorie, Baton Rouge, La.
Manor, Harold, Jonesboro, Ark.
Manring, Ernest, Cleveland, Ohio
Manry, Jack, El Campo, Texas
March, Donald, West Newton, Mass.

Marek, George R., New York, N. Y.
Marsh, Frank, Jr., Hattiesburg, Miss.
Marsh, Lillian, Manitowoc, Wis.
Marshall, Ted, Hermiston, Ore.
Marshall, Val, Logansport, La.
Martin, Helen, El Reno, Okla.
Martin, Helen, New Castle, Ind.
Martin, Helen E., Philadelphia, Pa.
Martin, Lureata R., Huntington, W. Va.
Martinson, Reuben, Birmingham, Ala.
Marty, E. J., Fayetteville, Ark.
Marvel, Lorene, St. Cloud, Minn.
Masailo, Michael, Meriden, Conn.
Mason, Bernard, Washington, D. C.
Mason, Chester W., San Jose, Calif.
Mason, LeRoy F., Jackson, Mo.
Mason, Loraine, Fairmont, W. Va.
Mason, Walter, Jacksonville, Ala.
Mason, Wilton, Chapel Hill, N. C.
Masson, Mrs. Lucille, Baltimore, Md.
Matheny, Louise, Norfolk, Va.
Matson, Dorothea, Los Angeles, Calif.
Matson, Seigfried, Columbus, Miss.
Mattern, David, Ann Arbor, Mich.
Matteson, Maurice, Frostburg, Md.
Mathews, James, Lawton, Okla.
Mathews, Paul W., Columbia, Mo.
Matthews, Glenn, Ashland, Ore.
Matthews, Grant, Caldwell, Idaho
Matthews, Walter E., Briarcliff Manor, N. Y.
Mattingly, Pauline, Washington, D. C.
Matz, Mrs. Eugenia A., Wilmington, Del.
Mauk, Mary Vic, Troy, Ala.
Mauritzen, Vernon P., Sunburst, Mont.
May, Elizabeth, Los Angeles, Calif.
May, Rodney F., Brockton, Mass.
Maybee, Harper C., Dearborn, Mich.
Mayerson, Paul, Conway, N. H.
Maynard, Clarke, Wilmington, Del.
Mayo, Curtis, Houston, Texas
McAdow, Maurice, Denton, Texas
McAllister, Forrest L., Joliet, Ill.
McAllister, Ray, Grants Pass, Ore.
McArthur, Grace, Aberdeen, S. Dak.
McBride, Helen J., Louisville, Ky.
McBride, William B., Columbus, Ohio
McBrier, Vivian F., Washington, D. C.
McCall, Mrs. Adeline, Chapel Hill, N. C.
McCalla, Carolyn, Memphis, Tenn.
McCann, Lorell, Salinas, Calif.
McCarty, Nellie, Chicago, Ill.
McClure, Ann, Miami Beach, Fla.
McCollister, Edith, Redlands, Calif.
McComb, Harry F., Ft. Lauderda'e, Fla.
McConnell, Jean Marie, Lexington, Ky.
McCord, Willet, Harrisburg, Pa.
McCorkle, T. Smith, Fort Worth, Texas
McDermott, Gertrude, University, Miss.
McDonald, Elizabeth C., Medina, N .Y.
McEachern, Edna, Montclair, N. J.
McEwen, M. C., Bowling Green, Ohio
McGarrity, Anna W., Pawtucket, R. I.
McGee, John, Freeport, Texas
McGhee, C. Bernard, LaCrosse, Wis.
McGonaghy, Patricia, Elkhorn, Wis.
McGuire, Eleanor, Columbus, Ohio
McGunigle, Gertrude, Providence, R. I.
McHugh, Catherine, Fayetteville, Ark.
McInerney, Anna L., Auburn, R. I.
McKee, C. J., Topeka, Kans.
McKeever, Earle, Nampa, Idaho
McKinney, Mrs. George, Tulsa, Okla.
McKinney, Howard D., New Brunswick, N. J.
McKissack, E. D., State College, Miss.
McLain, James, Washington, D. C.
McLean, Gordon, Muscatine, Iowa
McLellan, Beth, Riverside, Calif.
McManus, John, McMinnville, Ore.
McMeans, C. E., North Little Rock, Ark.
McMillan, Eileen, Bellingham, Wash.
McMillen, Hugh E., Boulder, Colo.
McMullan, Andrew, Storrs, Conn.
McNiel, L. Brier, Redwood Valley, Calif.
McVeigh, Josephine K., Orangesburg, N. Y.
Meloy, Elizabeth, Muncie, Ind.
Merrill, John A., Ann Arbor, Mich.
Merritt, Wesley, Newtonville, Mass.
Mesrobian, Peter, Port Washington, N. Y.
Messerschmitt, Joanna, Trenton, N. J.
Messick, George, Milford, Del.

Messner, Adah, Battle Creek, Mich.
Metcalf, Roy D., Kent, Ohio
Meyer, Gertrude, Terre Haute, Ind.
Meyer, Henry, Georgetown, Texas
Meyers, Owen, Evanston, Ill.
Middleton, James W., Fostoria, Ohio
Middleton, S. Powell, West Chester, Pa.
Miessner, W. Otto, Winter Park, Fla.
Milam, Lena, Beaumont, Texas
Miland, Emil Q., Alameda, Calif.
Miles, Harold, Minneapolis, Minn.
Miles, Mabel, East Lansing, Mich.
Miles, Mildred, Dayton, Ohio
Milkey, Ted, New York, N. Y.
Miller, Amy Grau, Pasadena, Calif.
Miller, Byron L., Eugene, Ore.
Miller, Edith, Washington, D. C.
Miller, Emerson, Missoula, Mont.
Miller, Frank, South Euclid, Ohio
Miller, Frank D., Cleveland, Ohio
Miller, Howard, Artesia, N. Mex.
Miller, Howard F., Salem, Ore.
Miller, Hugh, Albuquerque, N. Mex.
Miller, Kurt, Prescott, Ariz.
Miller, Malloy, Pueblo, Colo.
Miller, Rhea E., Saginaw, Mich.
Miller, Robert, Olympia, Wash.
Miller, Ruth M., Maryville, Mo.
Milton, Robert W., Kansas City, Mo.
Minelli, Charles, Athens, Ohio
Mininberg, Ian, New Haven, Conn.
Minkler, Raymond, Excelsior, Minn.
Minniear, Walter C., Shreveport, La.
Miraglia, John, Brewer, Maine
Mirliani, Fred, Auburn, Mass.
Mitchell, Harlan C., Oil City, Pa.
Mitchell, John W., Cedar Falls, Iowa
Mitchell, Josephine, Artesia, Calif.
Mitchell, Lloyd C., West Chester, Pa.
Mitchell, Lucille, Arlington, Va.
Mitchell, Max A., Stillwater, Okla.
Mitchell, Walter, Wilmington, Del.
Moe, Edna S., Dillon, Mont.
Moffat, Dana, Temple City, Calif.
Mohr, Donald F., Milwaukee, Wis.
Mohr, E. E., Greeley, Colo.
Monlux, Zelma, Waukesha, Wis.
Monogoven, Muriel, Mitchell, S. Dak.
Monroe, Mary E., Georgetown, Del.
Monroe, Thomas, Rutherford, N. J.
Monsour, Sally, Ann Arbor, Mich.
Montgomery, Merle, New York, N. Y.
Moody, Leo, Pueblo, Colo.
Moore, Donald I., Waco, Texas
Moore, Earl V., Ann Arbor, Mich.
Moore, Eleanor, Gloucester, Mass.
Moore, Laurleen, Duncan, Okla.
Mordy, Lloyd, Independence, Kans.
Morel, Bernard, Skowhegan, Maine
Morgan, Gertrude, Davenport, Iowa
Morgan, Haydn, Ypsilanti, Mich.
Morgan, Hazel B., Evanston, Ill.
Mori, Virgillio, Barre, Vt.
Morlan, Betty, Nashville, Tenn.
Morlan, Gene, Nashville, Tenn.
Morris, Charles, Stone Mountain, Ga.
Mortiboy, F. E., Davenport, Iowa
Moseley, J. O. B., Baltimore, Md.
Mulford, Florence, Bridgeton, N. J.
Mullaney, Katherine, Providence, R. I.
Muller, J. Frederick, Cleveland, Ohio
Mumaw, Otis, Pittsburg, Kans.
Mumma, Fred, Merrill, Wis.
Mundy, Millard C., Honolulu, Hawaii
Munk, Cecil W., Berea, Ohio
Murphy, George, Salem, Mass.
Murphy, Howard, New York, N. Y.

Murray, Alva Retta, Honolulu, Hawaii
Murray, Catherine, Washington, D. C.
Murray, Joseph E., West Hartford, Conn.
Mursell, James E., New York, N. Y.
Musser, Willard, Scotia, N. Y.
Myers, Robert, Albert Lea, Minn.

Napier, N. V., Salina, Kans.
Nash, Gordon, Boone, N. C.
Nee, Thomas, St. Paul, Minn.
Neff, Charlotte, New Brunswick, N. J.
Neilson, James, Oklahoma City, Okla.
Nelsen, Marian, Kansas City, Mo.
Nelson, Cecelia R., Eugene, Ore.
Nelson, Everett, Oxford, Ohio
Nelson, Fred, Plymouth, Mich.
Nelson, Geneva C., Ann Arbor, Mich.
Nelson, Henry, Superior, Wis.
Nelson, Mary Jarman, Winter Park, Fla.
Nervig, Adolph, Minneapolis, Minn.
Nettleton, Howard, Belmont, Mass.
Neumeyer, Carl M., Bloomington, Ill.
Nevin, Lewis, Orono, Maine
Newton, Margaret, Moorhead, Minn.
Niblack, Stephen L., Missoula, Mont.
Nichols, Mary, Georgetown, Del.
Nickerson, James F., Bozeman, Mont.
Nicodemus, Harmon, Takoma Park, Md.
Niemi, Allen L., Marquette, Mich.
Niles, Ben L., Greensburg, Ind.
Niven, Lewis, Orono, Maine
Nix, Frances, Point Arena, Calif.
Nixon, Melbern W., El Reno, Okla.
Noah, Max, Milledgeville, Ga.
Noble, Robert F., Torrington, Wyo.
Nordholm, Harriet, East Lansing, Mich.
Normann, Theodore F., Seattle, Wash.
Norton, William Wellington, Stockton, Calif.
Norwood, Stanley, Worcester, Mass.
Noyes, Nobert, Pittsfield, Maine
Nye, Robert E., Eugene, Ore.

Oakland, Lloyd C., Missoula, Mont.
Oberg, Paul, Minneapolis, Minn.
O'Callaghan, Anne Grace, Atlanta, Ga.
O'Connell, Howard, Manchester, Conn.
O'Connor, John A., Corvallis, Ore.
O'Connor, Katherine, Paterson, N. J.
O'Day, Marguerite, Denver, Colo.
Odell, Harold D., Enfield, N. H.
O'Donnell, Vance, Alliance, Ohio
Oglesby, Marguerite, Tulsa, Okla.
O'Hara, Marvel, Detroit, Mich.
Ohlendorf, Fred, Long Beach, Calif.
Ohlsen, Donald F., Chicago, Ill.
O'Leary, Marcella, Racine, Wis.
Olenchek, Frank R., Galax, Va.
Oliver, Marie, Carmel, Calif.
Olsen, Richard, Chicago, Ill.
Olson, Inez Eidbo, Valley City, N. Dak.
O'Malley, Sara, Chicago, Ill.
O'Neil, William J., Thompsonville, Conn.
Opp, Lester E., Bozeman, Mont.
Opsata, Mrs. Helen, Kensington, Md.
Orendorff, Harold, Glenville, W. Va.
Osborne, Kenneth, Fayetteville, Ark.
O'Steen, Alton, University, Ala.
Ostrow, Sylvia, San Antonio, Texas
Ostwald, Ernest, Staten Island, N. Y.
Oszuscik, Josef, Jacksonville, Fla.
Otteson, Florence, Highland Park, Ill.
Otto, Richard A., Wallingford, Conn.
Overgard, Graham T., Detroit, Mich.

Painter, Paul, Urbana, Ill.
Painter, Viola, Vinton, Va.

Palmason, Victor B., Salem, Ore.
Palmer, Harold, Hays, Kans.
Palmer, Mary Ruth, Anderson, Ind.
Pankratz, Elbert, Ardmore, Okla.
Papagalos, Gabriel, Phoenix, Ariz.
Parfrey, Fred, Beaver Dam, Wis.
Parisi, Antonio, Meriden, Conn.
Parker, Josephine, Carlsbad, N. Mex.
Pascal, Edward R., Bridgeport, Conn.
Patterson, E. H., Conroe, Texas
Patterson, Mildred, Knoxville, Tenn.
Patton, Glenn, Libby, Mont.
Paul, John B., Washington, D. C.
Paul, Ouida Fay, Gainesville, Fla.
Paxton, J. Russell, Madison, Wis.
Pearson, G. Albert, Manchester, Conn.
Peck, Samuel, Belleville, N. J.
Pecker, Max, New Brunswick, N. J.
Pence, Don P., Bend, Ore.
Penick, Cochrane, Columbus, Miss.
Perazzi, Madeline, South Portland, Maine
Perkins, L. N., Stillwater, Okla.
Perrotta, Isabella, Springfield, Vt.
Perrotti, Abramo, Silver City, N. Mex.
Perry, Helen, Forsyth, Mont.
Perry, Jessie, Salt Lake City, Utah
Perry, Margaret, Boulder, Colo.
Perry, Ruth, Longmeadow, Mass.
Peterson, Alma, New Orleans, La.
Peterson, Carl J., Erie, Pa.
Peterson, Carl J., Keyser, W. Va.
Peterson, Ralph J., Los Angeles, Calif.
Petranek, Chester, Silver Spring, Md.
Petrasso, David, Estacada, Ore.
Petzold, Robert, Madison, Wis.
Pfaltzgraff, Robert, Spencer, Iowa
Phelps, Norman, Columbus, Ohio
Phillippi, Ken, Durango, Colo.
Phillips, Norman, Flushing, N. Y.
Phillips, Theodore D., Institute, W. Va.
Piccolo, Salvatore, South Harwich, Mass.
Pichierri, Louis, Concord, N. H.
Pickard, Paul, Morgantown, W. Va.
Pierce, Anne E., Iowa City, Iowa
Piersol, Frank A., Ames, Iowa
Pike, Caroline, Bolivar, Mo.
Pitcher, Gladys, Boston, Mass.
Pitts, Lilla Belle, New York, N. Y.
Pixley, Ralph, Des Moines, Iowa
Platt, Jack, Cumberland, Md.
Plummer, Stanley R., Walla Walla, Wash.
Poindexter, Anna Grace, San Diego, Calif.
Post, Theodore, Reno, Nev.
Pottag, Max P., Chicago, Ill.
Potter, Floy Young, Sacramento, Calif.
Potter, Robert, Salt Lake City, Utah
Prescott, Gerald, Minneapolis, Minn.
Preston, Daniel, Forest Grove, Ore.
Preston, Valentine, Mitchell, S. Dak.
Prigge, Olga, Cincinnati, Ohio
Pritchard, James D., Sumter, S. C.
Pritchett, Mrs. Roxa, Whitewater, Wis.
Procasky, Charles, St. Louis, Mo.
Pugh, Mrs. Stanlie, San Diego, Calif.
Pyle, F. J., Des Moines, Iowa

Quigley, Rev. Thomas, Pittsburgh, Pa.
Quinn, Villa H., Augusta, Maine
Quinto, Lenard, Washington, D. C.

Radmer, Donald, Sheboygan, Wis.
Rafferty, Sadie M., Evanston, Ill.
Ramirez, David, Las Vegas, N. Mex.
Ramsey, Roberta, Silver City, N. Mex.
Ramsey, Wayne, Columbus, Ohio
Randall, Arne W., Washington, D. C.

Randall, Gregg, Las Cruces, N. Mex.
Randall, Harlan, College Park, Md.
Randall, John P., Albuquerque, N. Mex.
Ratcliffe, Janet A., New Bedford, Mass.
Raymond, John D., Easton, Pa.
Rayner, Doris, East Hartford, Conn.
Redding, Edwyl, Gunnison, Colo.
Redfield, Helen, Arlington, Va.
Reed, Alice, Miami, Fla.
Reed, Frank, Elkhart, Ind.
Reese, Gustave, New York, N. Y.
Rehfeldt, Herbert, Stevens Point, Wis.
Reid, Eugene, Ogden, Utah
Reilly, Patricia, Stevens Point, Wis.
Reisinger, A. Leon, Harrisburg, Pa.
Remley, James, Newtonville, Mass.
Rennick, J. H., Greenville, Miss.
Retzloff, Lillian, Phoenix, Ariz.
Reynolds, Carl T., East Chicago, Ind.
Rhea, Raymond, Corpus Christi, Texas
Rhoads, William, Alamogordo, N. Mex.
Rhodes, J. Clark, Knoxville, Tenn.
Rich, Mrs. Alma H., Washington, D. C.
Richards, Elsie, Wilmington, Del.
Richards, Stanley, Billings, Mont.
Richardson, Arlie H., Oakland, Calif.
Richardson, Helen, Algonquin, Ill.
Richardson, Thomas S., Urbana, Ill.
Richeson, Mary Carter, Portsmouth, Va.
Richman, Luther A., Missoula, Mont.
Richter, Alexander, New York, N. Y.
Rieckhoff, Gustav J., West Branch, Iowa
Riggs, Will C., Waltham, Mass.
Rimer, Robert H., Cleveland, Ohio
Ringling, Mrs. G. W., Durant, Okla.
Ringo, Lucille P., University City, Mo.
Risinger, Max, Portland, Ore.
Ritscher, Richard C., Dickinson, N. Dak.
Roach, Antrinette, Bethel, Conn.
Roach, J. Tatian, New York, N. Y.
Roark, Basil, Atchison, Kans.
Robb, J. D., Albuquerque, N. Mex.
Robbins, Paul, Charlestown, N. H.
Roberts, Carl, Starke, Fla.
Roberts, John T., Denver, Colo.
Roberts, Thomas, Corvallis, Ore.
Roberts, William O., Forty Fort, Pa.
Robertson, Irene, Los Angeles, Calif.
Robertson, Leroy, Salt Lake City, Utah
Robinson, Alton, Southwest Harbor, Maine
Robinson, Donald, Ann Arbor, Mich.
Robinson, Eugenia, Dallas, Texas
Robinson, Ferne, Detroit, Mich.
Robinson, Frank C., Bartlesville, Okla.
Robison, Charles, Weatherford, Okla.
Rockhill, Randy, Renton, Wash.
Rogers, Laura, Newark, N. J.
Roggensack, Delinda, Mt. Vernon, Iowa
Rohulich, Nick, Jonesboro, Ark.
Romaine, Westervelt, College Park, Md.
Ronfeldt, Lewis, Pomona, Calif.
Root, Catherine, Seattle, Wash.
Rorke, Genevieve, Los Angeles, Calif.
Rose, Claude E., Bowling Green, Ky.
Rosenberry, M. Claude, Harrisburg, Pa.
Rosenthal, Herman J., Troy, N. Y.
Ross, Harold W., Chester, Pa.
Ross, Laura E., Philadelphia, Pa.
Ross, Richard, Baltimore, Md.
Ross, Russell, Ellensburg, Wash.
Roundy, Arthur F., Fairfield, Maine
Routch, W. Valgene, Lock Haven, Pa.
Rowe, Clarence H., South Portland, Maine
Rowland, H. C., Grand Forks, N. Dak.
Rowles, William Lloyd, Cheney, Wash.
Royce, Letha, Lake Worth, Fla.
Rozehnal, B. J., River Falls, Wis.

Rumbaugh, Lester H., Cedar Falls, Iowa
Rumble, Douglas, Atlanta, Ga.
Rundell, Glenna, Sioux Falls, S. Dak.
Runge, Robert L., El Segundo, Calif.
Runkle, Thomas, Sturgeon Bay, Wis.
Rusch, Milton, Milwaukee, Wis.
Rush, Ralph E., Los Angeles, Calif.
Rushworth, E. D., Chattanooga, Tenn.
Russell, Catherine, Bridgeport, Conn.
Russell, Myron, Cedar Falls, Iowa
Rutledge, William, Houlton, Maine

Sacher, Ray, Camden, N. J.
Saetre, Gilbert T., Hattiesburg, Miss.
Saetveit, Joseph G., Albany, N. Y.
Salazar, Joe, Pojoaque, N. Mex.
Salzman, Edwin, Pearl River, N. Y.
Samp, Eldon B., Flandreau, S. Dak.
Sams, Lynn L., San Francisco, Calif.
Samuelson, A. L., Casper, Wyo.
Sandberg, Mabel R., Minneapolis, Minn.
Sanders, Mrs. Gladys, Washington, D. C.
Sanderson, E. S., Newton, Kans.
Sanderson, Wendell, Richmond, Va.
Sarig, Emmett R., Madison, Wis.
Satz, Ralph, New York, N. Y.
Saunders, R. Leslie, Lebanon, Pa.
Saunders, Russell, Des Moines, Iowa
Savage, Howard S., Plainfield, N. J.
Sawhill, Clarence E., Los Angeles, Calif.
Sawyer, Ruth, Concord, N. H.
Scanlon, Marie, Newark, N. J.
Scarbrough, Gilbert L., Oak Ridge, Tenn.
Scarchard, Mrs. William, Cambridge, Mass.
Schaer, Dorothy, Sherwood, Ore.
Schatz, Elizabeth L., East Lansing, Mich.
Schermerhorn, Marlo K., Lancaster, N. Y.
Schilde, Ed, Cushing, Okla.
Schill, Edmund, Verona, N. J.
Schilling, Richard, Oxford, Ohio
Schliestett, Patty, Pasadena, Calif.
Schmidt, Doris T., Gainesville, Fla.
Schmidt, Elizabeth, Minot, N. Dak.
Schmitt, Willard, Kansas City, Mo.
Schmucker, Martha, Auburn, N. Y.
Schmutz, Stan, St. George, Utah
Schneider, Erwin H., Knoxville, Tenn.
Schneider, Frederick, Chicago, Ill.
Schneider, Melvin, Cedar Falls, Iowa
Schoepfle, Irene, Santa Ana, Calif.
Schoonmaker, Ralph I., Medford, Mass.
Schowalter, Wilbur H., Redlands, Calif.
Schreiner, Alexander, Salt Lake City, Utah
Schrepel, H. Arthur, Pawnee City, Nebr.
Schultz, E. J., Norman, Okla.
Schultz, G. Lloyd, Madison, Wis.
Schultz, Henry, Tupelo, Miss.
Schwartz, Elwyn, Moscow, Idaho
Schwin, Helen L., Chicago, Ill.
Scilingo, Armando G., Harrison, N. Y.
Scott, Donald C., La Grande, Ore.
Scott, J. L., Philadelphia, Pa.
Seaboldt, A. B., Randolph, Nebr.
Seale, John, Jamestown, N. Dak.
Searight, Roland, Cedar Falls, Iowa
Seaver, Cedric L., Houston, Texas
Sedivy, E. P., Bozeman, Mont.
Seeger, Charles, Santa Barbara, Calif.
*Seeger, Ruth Crawford, Chevy Chase, Md. (1953)
Sellers, Marjorie T., Phoenix, Ariz.
Seltenrich, Charles, Laramie, Wyo.
Serposs, Emile H., Baltimore, Md.
Settle, Frances B., Cambridge, Mass.
Settle, Ruth Klepper, Little Rock, Ark.
Sexton, Haskell, Urbana, Ill.
Shacklette, Bennett, Santa Fe, N. Mex.
Shackson, Lee, Westerville, Ohio
Shadley, Maurice, Bloomington, Ind.
Shambaugh, Robert, Fort Wayne, Ind.
Shaughnessy, Robert, Putnam, Conn.
Shaul, Verrolton C., Champaign, Ill.
Shaw, Francis, Bangor, Maine
Shaw, Helen, Bethesda, Md.
Shaw, Philip, Phoenix, Ariz.
Sheldon, Robert, Columbia, Mo.
Shelley, Ardith, Phoenix, Ariz.
Shelley, Del, Phoenix, Ariz.
Shelton, Travis, Dallas, Texas
Shepard, Volney, Richmond, Va.

Sheppard, Joe G., Ruston, La.
Sherman, J. R., Haynesville, La.
Shetler, Donald, Ann Arbor, Mich.
Shiffert, Beatrice Harlor, Wilmington, Del.
Shive, Herbert, Bloomington, Ind.
Short, Dorothy Jean, Los Angeles, Calif.
Short, Virginia, Stockton, Calif.
Shouse, Mary, Long Beach, Calif.
Shufelt, Clayton F., Windsor, Conn.
Shultz, Robert J., Indianapolis, Ind.
Shuttlesworth, Russell E., Harrisburg, Pa.
Siebenthal, Stanley, Carlsbad, N. Mex.
Siekmann, Frank, Smyrna, Del.
Silfies, Rollin, Oakland, Calif.
Silverman, Herbert H., Malden, Mass.
Silvey, Clel T., Indiana, Pa.
Simmonds, K. Gene, Hollywood, Calif.
Simmons, Carolyn W., Bethel, Vt.
Simmons, Mildred, Bristol, Conn.
Simmons, Wilber D., Peoria, Ill.
Simons, Ruth L., Spearfish, S. Dak.
Sines, Thelma, Logansport, Ind.
Singer, Gerhard, Los Angeles, Calif.
Sister M. Augusta, Clinton, Iowa
Sister M. Dolores Purcell, Toledo, Ohio
Sister Sabina Mary Henderson, Davenport, Iowa
Sistrunk, Sara Dunn, Wichita Falls, Texas
Sites, Donald P., Corvallis, Ore.
Skilbred, Lawrence, Fond du Lac, Wis.
Skinner, Eunice, Berkeley, Calif.
Skoog, Vernon, Birmingham, Ala.
Skornicka, Joseph E., Milwaukee, Wis.
Skyrm, Richard, Caldwell, Idaho
Sliger, Kathryn J., Baltimore, Md.
Slind, Lloyd H., Tallahassee, Fla.
Smith, Cecil, New York, N. Y.
Smith, Charlotte M., Coloma, Mich.
Smith, Claude B., Evansville, Ind.
Smith, David, Durham, N. H.
Smith, Dorothy A., Collins, Miss.
Smith, Elna, Oklahoma City, Okla.
Smith, Ford, Weiser, Idaho
Smith, Fowler, Detroit, Mich.
Smith, Frances, Casper, Wyo.
Smith, Herman F., Milwaukee, Wis.
Smith, Leonora, Chattanooga, Tenn.
Smith, Margaret C., Baton Rouge, La.
Smith, Marlowe G., Rochester, N. Y.
Smith, Maxine, Fort Lauderdale, Fla.
Smith, Norman, Terrebonne, La.
Smith, Rachel, Bridgeport, Conn.
Smith, Richard, Lewistown, Pa.
Smith, Richard, Twin Falls, Ore.
Smith, Walter, Klamath Falls, Ore.
Smith, Wesley E., Boulder, Colo.
Smoots, Isabel D., Spearfish, S. Dak.
Smyers, Myllan, Montgomery, W. Va.
Snider, Jack R., Lincoln, Neb.
Snodgrass, Jack, Ellensburg, Wash.
Snow, Ira Jean, Lawton, Okla.
Snyder, Alice, San Francisco, Calif.
Snyder, Edith Roach, Pontiac, Mich.
Snyder, Hartley D., Tucson, Ariz.
Soifer, Joseph H., Hartford, Conn.
Soltys, Henry A., Allentown, Pa.
Somerville, Leslie, Albuquerque, N. Mex.
Sonnenburg, Eldon, Sherman, Texas
Sorenson, Alice, Seattle, Wash.
Sorlien, L. C., Fargo, N. Dak.
Southern, Orrin Clayton, Oxford, Pa.
Southwick, Richard E., Salisbury, N. C.
Sower, Burke, Kendrick, Idaho
Spaulding, Vernon E., Crawfordsville, Ind.
Spicer, Randall, Pullman, Wash.
Spivacke, Harold, Washington, D. C.
Spivacke, Rose M. Grentzer, Washington, D. C.
Spouse, Alfred, Rochester, N. Y.
Spurbeck, Samuel, Potsdam, N. Y.
Squire, Russel, Los Angeles, Calif.
Stacey, Jack, Salt Lake City, Utah
Stafford, Mrs. Elizabeth, Wilmington, Del.
Stanley, Burton E., Cortland, N. Y.
Starks, Thomas I., Watsonville, Calif.
Steadman, Gwendolyn, Hattiesburg, Miss.
Steele, Charles, Cottage Grove, Ore.
Steele, Joan, Seaford, Del.
Stehn, John H., Portland, Ore.
Stein, Edwin E., Lexington, Ky.
Stein, Gertrude, Springfield, Ohio
Steiner, Edward, Claymont, Del.

Stenson, Orvis, Choteau, Mont.
Stephens, Lala, Memphis, Tenn.
Stephenson, Jack R., Albuquerque, N. Mex.
Stepner, Bernard, Janesville, Wis.
Stevenson, Alina, Hebron, N. Dak.
Stevenson, Charlotte F., Bellflower, Calif.
Stewart, Albert R., Lafayette, Ind.
Stinebaugh, Galen, Bridgewater, Va.
Stineman, Chester, Jr., Lansford, Pa.
Stocker, Richard J., Springfield, Ohio
Stocking, R. Milton, Sacramento, Calif.
Stocks, Ned, Rupert, Idaho
Stone, Bernard B., Jackson, Mich.
Stone, David, Philadelphia, Pa.
Stone, George, Cleveland, Ohio
Stoney, William, St. Cloud, Minn.
Stookey, C. M., Portales, N. Mex.
Storey, Margaret S., Dover, Del.
Stoughton, Paul W., Northfield, Minn.
Stout, Barrett, Baton Rouge, La.
Stout, George, Houston, Texas
Stout, Kemble, Pullman, Wash.
Strain, Theresa, Norman, Okla.
Stratemeyer, Theodosia, New York, N. Y.
Street, Norman N., Portland, Ore.
Streim, Francis J., Vermillion, S. Dak.
Strohm, John, Minot, N. Dak.
Stull, Charles C. T., Frederick, Md.
Stumpf, Florence R., Tampa, Fla.
Stumpf, Louis, Beaumont, Texas
Sturdevant, Keith, St. Joseph, Mich.
Sturgis, V. D., Sarasota, Fla.
Suddendorf, Sidney, Rochester, Minn.
Sunderman, Lloyd F., Toledo, Ohio
Sur, William R., East Lansing, Mich.
Sutcliffe, Richard, Leominster, Mass.
Sutton, Robert, Missoula, Mont.
Swain, Margaret, Atlanta, Ga.
Swanson, Betty, Visalia, Calif.
Swarm, Paul, Decatur, Ill.
Swartley, Lloyd, Duluth, Minn.
Swartz, Jack, Flagstaff, Ariz.
Swift, Frederic Fay, Oneonta, N. Y.
Switzer, Russell W., Chicago, Ill.
Swope, M. Clair, Slippery Rock, Pa.

Taipale, Helmi, Minneapolis, Minn.
Tammi, Paul, Battle Creek, Mich.
Tampke, R. A., San Marcos, Texas
Taylor, Aaron, Baltimore, Md.
Taylor, Corwin, Baltimore, Md.
Taylor, Dorothea, Albuquerque, N. Mex.
Taylor, Maurice D., Montrose, Pa.
Taylor, Renwick, Tacoma, Wash.
Taylor, Robert C., Washington, Md.
Teare, Ronald C., Greensville, Pa.
Tebow, Kenneth, Chanute, Kans.
*Teel, Stanley M., Missoula, Mont. (1954)
Teeter, Marguerite, Joplin, Mo.
Tellaisha, John V., Reno, Nevada
Tellingheusen, A. E., Greenville, Miss.
Tennant, Donald, Richmond, Va.
Tepping, Mrs. Ruth C., Washington, D. C.
Terry, Elvis, Salt Lake City, Utah
Terry, J. L., Morgan, Utah
Tersyak, Anthony, Waterville, Maine
Terwilliger, Wichita, Kans.
Thayer, Audrey, Elmwood, Conn.
Thelan, Carl, Salem, Ore.
Theodore, Peter C., Hyattsville, Md.
Thomas, Howard M., Bedford, Ind.
Thomas, J. Harrison, Tallahassee, Fla.
Thompson, Carl, Bemidji, Minn.
Thompson, E. L., Washington, D. C.
Thompson, Floren, Portales, N. Mex.
Thompson, Luther F., Darien, Conn.
Thorson, T. W., Crookston, Minn.
Thune, Anna, Valley City, N. Dak.
Timm, Everett, Baton Rouge, La.
Tinkham, Glenn, Marshfield, Wis.
Tipton, Gladys, New York, N. Y.
Tirey, Ruth Hill, Terre Haute, Ind.
Tjaden, Dallas, Ames, Iowa
Tkach, Peter D., Minneapolis, Minn.
Tolbert, Mary, Columbus, Ohio
Tonks, S. Ethel, Ridgewood, N. J.
Triplett, Lamar, Bessemer, Ala.
Trongone, Joseph, West Roxbury, Mass.
Trudgen, S. Erle, Lansing, Mich.

Trusler, Ivan, Emporia, Kans.
Trusler, Milton, Conway, Ark.
Tsika, Angelo, Millinockett, Maine
Tueller, Arch, Salt Lake City, Utah
Turner, Louise, Commerce, Texas
Turrentine, Logan, Coral Gables, Fla.
Tuttle, Donald C., Rapid City, S. Dak.
Tyrone, Champ, Las Vegas, N. Mex.

Uhlinger, Ray, Marquette, Mich.
Underwood, Lucas, Stockton, Calif.
Underwood, Rex, Portland, Ore.
Utgaard, Merton, Muncie, Ind.

Van Bodegraven, Paul, New York, N. Y.
Van Buren, Frank N., Kingston, R. I.
Van Cleave, Emerson S., Montgomery, Ala.
Vander Hart, Margaret, Alma, Mich.
Van Doren, Robert L., Columbia, S. C.
Van Heuvelen, Harold, Bismarck, N. Dak.
Van Peursem, James E., Richmond, Ky.
Van Sickle, Wallace, Texarkana, Ark.
Van Velson, A. A., Riverton, Wyo.
Van Vlissingen, Ernst, Fargo, N. Dak.
Varnedoe, Mrs. S. M., Jacksonville, Fla.
Veidt, Lorraine, Medford, Ore.
Verrall, John, Seattle, Wash.
Vinal, Dean L., Hamilton, Mont.
Vincent, John, Los Angeles, Calif.
Vincent, Mitchell C., Irvington-on-Hudson, N. Y.
Von Charlton, Rudolph, Prairie View, Texas
Von der Heide, Henry, Boise, Idaho
Voxman, Himie, Iowa City, Iowa

Wadley, Marvin L., Las Cruces, N. Mex.
Wainwright, Dorothy D., Petersburg, Va.
Walden, Eleanor, Norfolk, Va.
Walker, B. H., Gaffney, S. C.
Walker, James, Putnam City, Okla.
Walker, Kermit A., New York, N. Y.
Waller, Gilbert R., Urbana, Ill.
Walls, Robert B., Corvallis, Ore.
Waln, George, Oberlin, Ohio
Walstrum, Theodore, Laramie, Wyo.
Walter, Arnold, Toronto, Ontario, Canada
Walter, Don C., Bellingham, Wash.
Walter, F. Austin, New Brunswick, N. J.
Walters, W. Gibson, San Jose, Calif.
Walton, Bernard, Washington, D. C.
Ward, Arthur E., Montclair, N. J.
Ward, Dolly Connally, Norman, Okla.
Wardwell, Ethel, Lisbon Falls, Maine
Warren, Catherine, Nashville, Tenn.
Wassell, Albert, Trenton, N. J.
Wassum, Sally, Evanston, Ill.
Waterman, C. R., Laramie, Wyo.
Watrous, Aleen, Wichita, Kans.
Watson, Jack M., Bloomington, Ind.
Watson, R. B., Pine Bluff, Ark.
Watters, Lorrain, Des Moines, Iowa
Watts, Ruth Emmert, Johnson City, Tenn.
Waugh, Harvey R., St. Cloud, Minn.
Wayne, Elsbeth, Sheffield, Mass.
Wayne, Margaret, Darien, Conn.
Weaver, Minnie D., Deming, N. Mex.
Webb, Fredrick N., Provo, Utah
Weegand, Ruth, Atlanta, Ga.
Weegar, Carlton E., Gouverneur, N. Y.
Wegner, H. C., Madison, Wis.
Weichselfelder, Louis, Eureka, Calif.
Weigand, J. J., Emporia, Kans.
Weigel, Eugene, Columbus, Ohio
Weight, Ormon, Salt Lake City, Utah
Weiner, Benjamin, Turners Falls, Mass.
Weixel, Angela, Upper Marlboro, Md.
Welch, Dorothy Hope, Mechanicville, N. Y.
Welke, Walter C., Seattle, Wash.
Welliver, H. B., Minot, N. Dak.
Wells, Charles H., Bowling Green, Mo.
Wells, L. Jeannette, Washington, D. C.
Wendelin, Andrew, Fort Wayne, Ind.
Wenner, Gladys O., Staunton, Va.
Werder, Richard H., Washington, D. C.
Wersen, Louis G., Philadelphia, Pa.
West, Edward, Des Moines, Iowa
West, Mrs. George, Oklahoma City, Okla.
West, Sally, Washington, D. C.
West, Thomas E., State College, Miss.

Westafer, Walter, Demorest, Ga.
Westbrook, Arthur E., Lincoln, Nebr.
Westman, Sheldon C., Blue Island, Ill.
Westphal, Frederick W., Sacramento, Calif.
Wheeler, Joan R., North Providence, R. I.
Wheeler, Rufus A., Schenectady, N. Y.
Wheeler, W. R., Levelland, Texas
Wheelwright, D. Sterling, San Francisco, Calif.
Wheelwright, Lorin F., Salt Lake City, Utah
White, Adolph, Northfield, Minn.
White, George L., New York, N. Y.
White, Jerry R., Roanoke, Va.
White, Robert, Portland, Ore.
White, Ruth S., Los Angeles, Calif.
Whitlock, Jean, New York, N. Y.
Whitmore, Rogers, Columbia, Mo.
Whitney, Gerald, Tulsa, Okla.
Whitney, Leta F., Boston, Mass.
Whitney, Maurice C., Glens Falls, N. Y.
Whitney, Norman, Prineville, Ore.
Whitsey, Edna A., Cleveland, Ohio
Wickstrom, Muriel, St. Paul, Minn.
Widder, Roger, Fayetteville, Ark.
Wigent, John, Washington, D. C.
Wikstrom, Thomas, Lincoln, Nebr.
Wiley, D. O., Lubbock, Texas
Wiley, Russell, Lawrence, Kans.
Wilhousky, Peter, Brooklyn, N. Y.
Wilkins, Cecil, Norfolk, Va.
Will, Reba, Washington, D. C.
Williams, Annie Lou, South Hill, Va.
Williams, Arthur L., Oberlin, Ohio
Williams, Bernard E., Laconia, N. H.
Williams, Clifton, Austin, Texas
Williams, Dale, Blackwell, Okla.
Williams, E. Russell, Wilmington, Del.
Williams, Hugh, Warrensburg, Mo.
Williams, Ross, Winfield, Kans.
Williams, Russell, Norfolk, Va.
Williamson, E. E., Grant Falls, Mont.
Willing, Donald, San Antonio, Texas
Willison, Dorothy, Cumberland, Md.
Willman, Allan, Laramie, Wyo.
Wilmot, David L., Jacksonville, Fla.
Wilson, A. Verne, Portland, Ore.
Wilson, Charles, Nampa, Idaho
Wilson, Clarence H., St. Louis, Mo.
Wilson, Dorris, Bozeman, Mont.
Wilson, Richard O., Des Moines, Iowa
Wilson, Thomas E., West Lafayette, Ind.
Wilson, Velma K., Urbana, Ill.

Wilson, Warren H., Boise, Idaho
Winter, Ruth, Waukesha, Wis.
Witherspoon, Gene, Russellville, Ark.
Witherspoon, Mrs. Herbert, New York, N. Y.
Witte, Arthur F. A., Yonkers, N. Y.
Wolcott, Ruth, West Hartford, Conn.
Wold, Milo, McMinnville, Ore.
Wolfe, Irving W., Nashville, Tenn.
Wolfer, Marjorie, Detroit, Mich.
Wolff, Juanita, Portland, Ore.
Wood, Alfred F., Westerby, R. I.
Wood, Elizabeth, Roselle Park, N. J.
Wood, Ellis P., Longview, Texas
Wood, Roy V., Winter Haven, Fla.
Wood, Sena B., Norfolk, Va.
Woodlen, Mrs. Etta, Wilmington, Del.
Woodruff, Jane, Newman, Ga.
Woods, J. Ross, Lewiston, Idaho
Woolf, Ruby, Winston-Salem, N. C.
Work, John, Nashville, Tenn.
Work, Robert W., Oxford, Miss.
Wright, Al G., West LaFayette, Ind.
Wright, Mary Ellen, Clarksdale, Miss.
Wright, Ralph W., Indianapolis, Ind.
Wunderlich, Mrs. Helen, Missoula, Mont.
Wynd, Doris, Chandler, Okla.

Yanetovich, Stephen, Clearwater, Fla.
Yates, Annetta, Cumberland, Md.
Yerger, Ray D., Havertown, Pa.
Yingling, Robert, Storrs, Conn.
Yocum, Rex, Lusk, Wyo.
Yost, Mrs. Dixie, Phoenix, Ariz.
Young, Dow, Salt Lake City, Utah
Young, Marvin, Salt Lake City, Utah
Youngberg, Harold, Oakland, Calif.

Zahradka, Paul, Gunnison, Colo.
Zahrt, Merton S., Chicago, Ill.
Zander, Beulah I., Springfield, Ill.
Zanzig, Augustus, Brookline, Mass.
Zaugg, Philip, Toledo, Ohio
Zech, Norman F., Reedley, Calif.
Zerkle, Zaner B., Lexington, Ky.
Zesiger, William, Devils Lake, N. Dak.
Zimmer, Albert A., Monongahela, Pa.
Zimmerman, Alex H., San Diego, Calif.
Zimmerman, Henry P., Roselle Park, N. J.
Zohn, Roberta H., Las Vegas, N. Mex.

INDEX

INDEX

362

Recordings: appreciation, 227; bibliography, 228; blind and partially sighted, 265; collectors clubs, 296; development, 227; listening, 227; rural school, 227; secondary school, 228; sources, 228; use of, 226
Records: student, 24
Recruitment: music teacher, 289, 291
Relations: civic, 26; commercial trade, 26; other departments, 27; public, 25, 39; school-community, 39
Relationships: interadministrational, 27
Repair: instruments, 25
Repertory: patriotic, 274
Required music: junior high school, 105
Requisitions: 19
Research: departmental, 23; instruments of, 156; Journal of Music Education, 119
Research council: 18; MENC, 37
Resolutions: MENC, 287, 290, 293; MENC child's bill of rights in music, 298
Resource person: supervision, 35
Resources: community, 65; strings, 167
Responsibilities: professional, 8
Rhythm band: blind and partially sighted, 265; exceptional children, 266
Rhythmic: experiences, 72
Rhythmic activities: elementary, 76
Rhythms: elementary, 63; intermediate grades, 295; instruments, 63; primary grades, 294
Risers: 25
Rural school: bibliography, 87; bulletin, 84; one room, 84; practical experiences, 85; recordings, 227; supervision, 84; survey, 83; teacher requirements, 84; two room, 84; Wisconsin, 82

Salaries: instructional, 24
Schedule: music class, 306
School of Music: Navy, 277
Schools: organ instruction, 196
Schools of Education: 49
Schools of Music: 49
Scholarship: advanced degree, 153
Screens: types of, 234
Script writing: radio, 224; television, 224
Seating: string class, 174
Second grade: basic music activities, 294
Secondary school: appreciation, 228; assemblies, 103; bibliography, 320, 321; credit for music, 303; curriculum, 97; democratic teaching, 10; general music class, 160; instructional program, 102; instructional program in music, 306; music for 96; overview, 101; recitals, 103; recordings, 228; selected book list, 321; supervision, 33
Selected reference book list: NEA, 320
Self-expression: 3
Senior high school music: See Chapter XII, 111
Senior high school references: activities, 111; assembly singing, 112, 205; bibliography, 114; choral music, 205; electives, 103, 296; general music, 103, 111, 296, 306; individual lessons, 113; instrumental music, 103, 296, 306; minimum activities, 114; music appreciation, 113; music electives, 306; music history, 113; organization, 22; outline program, 296; performing groups, 112; piano class, 192; theory, 211; theory and harmony, 113; vocal music, 102, 296, 306. See also under secondary school
Servicing: audio-visual equipment, 232
Shells: music, 308
Singing: acquiring use of voice, 300; assembly, 206; elementary, 63; elementary grades, 75; elementary school, 202; experiences, 62, 72; intermediate grades, 295; junior high school, 107; primary grades, 294; sight, 208
Singers: uncertain, 203
Sixth grade: basic music activities, 295
Slides: lantern, 235; projectors, 232
Slow learner: music for, 267
Small ensemble: vocal, 209
Social values: 55; strings, 170; instrumental music, 164
Society: 17; American, 12; American Musicological, 120; International Music Education, 120
Song list: bibliography, 319; cumulative, 319
Songs and rhythms: bibliography, 74, 92
Sound: binaural, 236; stereophonic, 236
Sound post: string instrument, 312
Special education in music: beliefs, 302
Specialist: music, 1
Specifications: microphones, 231; pianos, 25; record players, 231; tape recorders, 230
Spiritual values: 5
Standards: brasses, 186; percussion, 186; string instruments, 309; upgrading, 288
Storage: instruments, 25

String bass: measurements, 309
String class: basic principles, 174; seating, 174
String instruments: bridges, 312; cases, 311; construction, 310; fingerboards, 311; minimum standards, 309; pegs, 311; sound post, 312
String specialist: curriculum, 173
Strings: cultural values, 170; films, 220; use of fingers, 178; hobby, 171; importance, 166; parallelism, 180; posture, 175; recommendations, 172; resources, 167; rote playing, 177; shifting, 181; social values, 170; teacher training, 172; technique, 178; tone production, 180
Stroboscope: 234
Student: preferences, 78; recitals, 296; records, 24
Student membership: MENC, 327
Student officers: choral groups, 206
Superintendent: role of, 67
Supervision: bibliography, 40, 322; consultant, 35; function, 34; general, 29; intermediate grades, 31; need for, 30; philosophy, 33; primary grades, 30; resource person, 35, 37; rural, 84; secondary school, 33; selected book list, 322
Supervision of music education: See Chapter III, 29
Supervisor: elementary music, 30, 68; instructional, 68
Supervisors: piano ability, 193
Supplies: general, 24
Survey: composition, 213; conservatories, 247; general college student, 132; junior college music, 124; junior college trends, 122; junior high school, 108; organ, 198; rural school music, 83
Symphony: professional, 171

Tachistoscope: 234
Tape: libraries, 229
Tape recorder: instrument, 25; specifications, 230
Tape recordings: instrumental program, 229; use of, 229; vocal program, 229
Taste: discriminating, 162
Teacher: attributes, 135; childhood, 57; class organ, 196; conference, 38; elementary, 63; general college music, 133; in-service training, 38; musical performance, 139; private music, 50; rural school, 82; special music, 293; training, 168; virtuoso, 118
Teacher education: insights, 144; certification, 246
Teacher load: 20, 306
Teacher training: junior high school, 106; music, 137; strings, 172; theory, 142
Teachers college: curriculum, 147
Teachers meetings: 21
Technique: air force music, 281, 282; bow, 176; strings, 178, 179; vibrato, 179
Techniques: choral, 208; educational, 144; exceptional children, 264; films, 219
Telecasts: producing, 222
Television: 220, 288; clubs, 226; commercial programs, 225; musical problems, 224; piano instruction, 194; script writing, 224; use, 32; visual consideration, 223
Terminal courses: junior college, 125
Textbook adoption: 35
Texts: general college music, 133
Theory: 210; college, 211; doctors degree, 155; elementary school, 211; function, 214; junior high school, 211; senior high school, 113; teacher competency, 142
Therapy: national association, 120
Third grade: basic music activities, 294
Three dimensional: diorama, 237; mock-ups, 237; models, 237
Tone production: choral, 208; clarinet, 184; flute, 185; strings, 180
Training: in-service, 90; string teacher, 172
Transparencies: 234
Trends: junior college, 122; music education, 47; new, 48
Tuning: electronic, 234
Two room: rural school, 84

Understanding: growth, 90
UNESCO: 46, 252, 253, 325
United Nations: bibliography, 51
United States: Department of State, 43; information centers, 42
United States: Department of State, 43
Unity: strength, 287
Universal language: 8
Universal need: public education, 287
University: music, 118
Upgrading: standards, 288

Values: disciplinary, 7; general music, 160; intellectual, 55; intercultural, 55; moral and spiritual, 5; psychological, 301; social, 55